A Time to Speak

AMERICAN IDEALS AND INSTITUTIONS SERIES

Robert P. George, series editor

Published in partnership with the James Madison Program in American Ideals and Institutions at Princeton University, this series is dedicated to the exploration of enduring questions of political thought and constitutional law; to the promotion of the canon of the Western intellectual tradition as it nourishes and informs contemporary politics; and to the application of foundational Western principles to modern social problems.

OTHER BOOKS BY ROBERT H. BORK

The Antitrust Paradox: A Policy at War With Itself
The Tempting of America: The Political Seduction of the Law
Slouching Towards Gomorrah: Modern Liberalism and American Decline
Coercing Virtue: The Worldwide Rule of Judges
"A Country I Do Not Recognize": The Legal Assault on American Values
     (editor and author)

A TIME TO SPEAK

Selected Writings and Arguments

ROBERT H. BORK

WILMINGTON, DELAWARE

This book is the inaugural title in the ISI Regnery Legacy Project, which is being conducted in honor of the pioneering publisher of important and enduring conservative titles, Henry Regnery.

Bork, Robert H.

    A time to speak : selected writings and arguments / Robert H. Bork. —1st ed.—Wilmington, Del. : ISI Books, c2008.

    p. ; cm.
    (American ideals and institutions series)
    ISBN: 978-1-933859-68-2

       1. Constitutional law—United States. 2. Antitrust law—United States. 3. International law. 4. Political questions and judicial power—United States. 5. Sociological jurisprudence. I. Title. II. Series.

KF4550 .B67 2009   2008934870
342.73—dc22   0811

ISI Books
Intercollegiate Studies Institute
Post Office Box 4431
Wilmington, DE 19807-0431
www.isibooks.org

For Mary Ellen

"To every thing there is a season, and a time to every purpose under the heaven . . . a time to speak."

—*Ecclesiastes 3:1–7*

CONTENTS

Foreword   xi

II. Antitrust Law
Articles

Opinions

III. International Law

IV. Politics and Public Policy

V. Personal Appreciations

VI. Frivolities

The author would like to thank the following publishers and copyright holders for permission to reprint their material: *American Economic Review*, the *American Enterprise Institute*, *American Journal of International Law*, *Antitrust Law Journal*, the *American Bar Association*, *Commentary*, *First Things*, *Indiana Law Journal*, the *Intercollegiate Review*, *San Diego Law Review*, the *Wall Street Journal*, and the *Yale Law Journal*. Every effort was made to obtain permission to reprint all articles and court cases. There are a number of articles reprinted in this book that originally appeared in *National Review*, the *New Criterion*, and the *New York Times*, that are the possession of Robert H. Bork.

FOREWORD

A word about the structure of this book: The shorter works gathered here include articles, both popular and academic, briefs filed in courts, transcripts of oral arguments before the Supreme Court, judicial opinions, and even letters to editors. When the Intercollegiate Studies Institute asked me to undertake this project, I realized that I had expressed my opinions in a variety of forms and contexts. The briefs and oral arguments selected, for example, are as much expressions of my views as the academic works and journalistic essays reprinted here. Taken as a whole, this body of shorter works both augments and extends discussions in my books.

The book is organized by subject matter. The result, taking constitutional law as an example, is a mix of all the forms of expression just mentioned. That mix does not seem problematic since it is possible and desirable that both academic and judicial arguments be readily understandable by the lay reader. Conversely, it is possible to set forth the major ideas of law and politics in the language of popular journalism. Where it has seemed useful, additional commentary on some topics is set out in italics to distinguish it from the original text.

My thanks are due to the following organizations whose grants have made this and other work possible: The Lynde and Harry Bradley Foundation; the National Review Institute; the William E. Simon Foundation; and the Intercollegiate Studies Institute.

I wish also to express my gratitude to Matthew Glover and Darren Beattie, two extraordinarily capable young men, who, as Research Associates, provided indispensable assistance on this and other books in progress.

I.

Constitutional Law

A. Briefs and Oral Arguments

This subsection consists of two briefs and three oral arguments. The first brief and the accompanying oral argument in Gregg v. Georgia were addressed to the Supreme Court and succeeded in restoring the constitutionality of the death penalty. The brief and argument have continuing relevance as the Supreme Court, in defiance of both the Constitution and the explicit commands of elected representatives, continues to restrict the death penalty's use.

The second brief, filed in a district court, took up the question whether a president or a vice president of the United States may be prosecuted for crimes while still in office. We concluded that an incumbent vice president may be prosecuted but that an incumbent president may not. The issue was not resolved in that case and the subject of criminal prosecution was debated during the terms in office of Richard Nixon and William Jefferson Clinton. If we are fortunate, the topic will not arise in the future, but of course we may not be fortunate.

I claim no more than co-authorship of these briefs. In both I worked with brilliant lawyers in the Office of the Solicitor General: in Gregg with A. Raymond Randolph and Frank H. Easterbrook, both of whom went on to become federal appeals court judges; in Agnew's case with Keith A. Jones and Edmund W. Kitch.

The question of indicting Vice President Spiro Agnew was extremely delicate and complex and we had only one week to put the brief together (along with another opposing Agnew's motion to shut down the grand jury because of alleged leaks), filing it on Saturday evening, which left me only Sunday to prepare my first ever argument in the Supreme Court on Monday morning.

Gregg v. Georgia
Amicus Brief for the United States

In the Supreme Court of the United States

October Term, 1975
No. 74–6257
Troy Leon Gregg, petitioner
v.
State of Georgia

No. 75–5394
Jerry Lane Jurek, petitioner
v.
State of Texas

No. 75–5491
James Tyrone Woodson and Luby Waxton, petitioners
v.
State of North Carolina

No. 75–5706
Charles William Proffitt, petitioner
v.
State of Florida

No. 75–5844
Stanislaus Roberts, petitioner
v.
State of Louisiana

On writs of certiorari to the Supreme Court of Georgia, the Court of Criminal Appeals of Texas, and the Supreme Courts of North Carolina, Florida, and Louisiana

Brief for the United States as Amicus Curiae

This brief is filed in response to the Court's invitation of January 22, 1976.

Question Presented

The United States will address the question whether the death penalty is always or inevitably cruel and unusual punishment within the meaning of the Eighth Amendment.

Interest of the United States

Petitioners argue that the death penalty is unconstitutional because it is excessively cruel and because it is invariably applied arbitrarily. Acceptance of either argument will affect, if not decide, the validity of any death penalty statute, whatever the crime and however the statute is framed.

The United States believes that imposition of the death penalty may sometimes be a necessary and appropriate measure to achieve the traditional goals of criminal justice. At the time this Court decided *Furman v. Georgia,* 408 U.S. 238, no fewer than 13 federal statutes provided for capital punishment, at the discretion of the jury, for certain crimes.[1] The validity of all these statutes was called into question by *Furman.* Congress then enacted a statute providing the death penalty for aircraft piracy that results in death. 49 U.S.C. (Supp. IV) 1472 and 1473, 88 Stat. 410–13. This statute places substantial constraints upon the discretion of the jury. The court must impose death if the jury finds that at least one of a specified group of aggravating factors exists and that none of a specified group of mitigating factors exists.

---

1. See 10 U.S.C. 856 (punishment upon conviction by court-martial); 18 U.S.C. 34 (destruction of aircraft or motor vehicle when death results); 18 U.S.C. 351 (assassination of a member of Congress); 18 U.S.C. 794 (espionage); 18 U.S.C. 1111 (murder within the special maritime and territorial jurisdiction of the United States); 18 U.S.C. (1970 ed.) 1201 (kidnapping that results in death); 18 U.S.C. 1716 (mailing prohibited articles when death results); 18 U.S.C. 1751 (assassination of the President); 18 U.S.C. 1992 (wrecking a train when death results); 18 U.S.C. 2031 (rape within the special maritime and territorial jurisdiction of the United States); 18 U.S.C. 2113(e) (bank robbery that leads to death or kidnapping); 18 U.S.C. 2381 (treason); 49 U.S.C. (1970 ed.) 1472 (aircraft piracy). We previously have argued that, because of the important differences between the civilian and the military justice systems, 10 U.S.C. 856 was not invalidated by *Furman.* See Brief for the respondent in *Schick v. Reed,* No. 73–5677, October Term, 1974.

Under any other circumstances the court must impose life imprisonment. The government bears the burden of proving the existence of an aggravating factor. This statute is similar to the Florida statute now before the Court.[2]

Congress has under consideration other bills that would authorize the death penalty in different circumstances. See, *e.g.,* S. 1, 94th Cong., 1st Sess. (1975), the proposed revision and recodification of the federal criminal code, which is pending in the Senate Judiciary Committee. Sections 2401 and 2402 of S. 1, which provide for capital punishment, are supported by the President and are reprinted as Appendix D to this brief.

Although we do not specifically address the approach of the Antihijacking Act of 1974, S. 1, or any particular alternative approach, the United States has an important interest in this case because the Court's decision could affect the validity of every alternative approach and, if petitioners' arguments are accepted, render the death penalty per se unconstitutional.

Summary of Argument

The death penalty is a traditional sanction for those offenses society considers the most dangerous. Whether that penalty is necessary, or even appropriate, in a particular case is a judgment properly left to the representatives of the people and to the judges and juries who must decide whether to impose society's ultimate sanction. We submit that it is inappropriate for this Court to substitute its judgment about the propriety of the death penalty for that of the legislatures both more properly charged with the duty of making that judgment and more advantageously situated to collect and assess the relevant information.

We will not recount the positions taken by all nine members of this Court in *Furman* v. *Georgia,* 408 U.S. 238. Our argument is limited to those

---

2. The Florida statute allows a jury to "balance" certain listed aggravating and mitigating factors. It also allows the trial judge to discard the jury's findings. Because 49 U.S.C. (Supp. IV) 1473 provides that the presence of any mitigating factor precludes the imposition of a death sentence, outcomes are more certain than are those under the Florida statute. See also pages 93–99, *infra.* The Texas and Georgia statutes, although structuring and confining the exercise of the jury's discretion, are dissimilar to the federal statute and to each other. Texas law provides that the death penalty will be imposed (for authorized crimes) if and only if the defendant's acts deliberately created an excessive risk of death, the defendant is likely to commit additional crimes unless incapacitated, and the crime for which he was convicted was unprovoked. Georgia law provides that the death penalty will be imposed (for authorized crimes) only if the jury finds that at least one aggravating circumstance was present and only if the jury does not recommend mercy. For a typology of these and other post-*Furman* statutes see Note, *Discretion and the Constitutionality of the New Death Penalty Statutes,* 87 Harv. L. Rev. 1690, 1699–1712 (1974).

aspects of the capital punishment controversy that concern the propriety of this Court's exercise of power to nullify the considered judgments of the legislatures in thirty-five states, and of Congress, that capital punishment is a legitimate response to certain crimes. We do not discuss the constitutionality or the propriety of any particular laws; instead we argue that neither the harshness of the penalty, nor the procedures necessarily used to administer it, render capital punishment unconstitutional per se. Judicially ascertainable changing standards of decency and the discretion built into our criminal justice system do not operate to make all death penalties cruel and unusual punishment.

I.

The Constitution mentions capital punishment in four places, demonstrating that the framers intended to permit its use. At the time the Eighth Amendment was approved by the states capital punishment was a common sanction for serious crimes. The first Congress provided for use of the death penalty. If the meaning of that amendment were fixed by the practices in use at the time of its adoption, the outcome of this case would not be in doubt. But even if the cruel and unusual punishments clause must also be considered in light of the evolving standards of decency that mark a maturing society, the history of the amendment provides guidance to the understanding of how contemporary standards are to be evaluated, and how they are to be weighed against competing social goals.

The cruel and unusual punishments clause first appeared in the Bill of Rights of 1689, a reaction by Parliament to the excesses of the Stuart courts, and particularly to Lord Chief Justice Jeffreys, who invented new combinations of punishments, not authorized by Parliament, and applied them in unusual fashions against the King's enemies. At the time the cruel and unusual punishments clause first appeared, drawing and quartering, and burning alive, were the usual methods of execution in England, and apparently were unaffected by the new clause. The clause appears to have been one chapter among many in the long struggle between King and Parliament to allocate the right to govern—cruel punishments were to be forbidden unless authorized by Parliament. The clause did not, however, restrict the power of Parliament to invent or prescribe punishments appropriate to an offense.

The clause was adopted in the United States with little debate, and we therefore cannot know whether the framers intended to adopt the clause with its English meaning. There is some evidence in the debates that it was directed against "barbarous" punishment that would amount to "torture."

Others who originally had called for such a clause were concerned about the potentially unbridled punishing power of Congress. We can conclude from these debates that the American cruel and unusual punishments clause, unlike the English, binds legislators as well as judges. But nothing in the debates supports an inference that the framers thought that capital punishment, accepted as legitimate elsewhere in the Constitution, would be prohibited.

II.

This Court's Eighth Amendment decisions have established the principle that the cruel and unusual punishments clause prohibits punishments that lie outside the bounds of tolerable social behavior. But all of the cases that have held punishments unconstitutional under the clause have dealt either with a strange form of punishment not used in American law (see, *e.g., Weems* v. *United States,* 217 U.S. 349) or punishment applied to a "status" to which no penalty, however light, could attach (*Robinson* v. *California,* 370 U.S. 660). In each case involving the former category, it has been necessary to ascertain the limits established by the social consensus, and then to determine whether they have been transgressed. It also has been helpful to determine the reason why society had not rid itself of the apparently aberrant punishment without the need for judicial intervention.

When a penalty is enacted by a legislature and imposed only by a unanimous jury, the sanction is very unlikely to be outside the bounds of social tolerance. In our form of democracy the will of the people is expressed through their representatives. Since this Court's decision in *Furman* v. *Georgia* at least thirty-five states and the United States have enacted new statutes providing for the death penalty. We submit that it is utterly implausible that so many legislatures can, time and again, fail to reflect the will of the people concerning capital punishment. Were this Court to hold the death penalty unconstitutional, it would have to conclude that it—whose justices are not elected and have been given life tenure in order to insulate them from popular and political opinion—is more conscious of and more responsive to the will of the people than are the representatives directly elected by and responsible to those people. Petitioners seek a referendum among judges as a proxy for the "true" will of the people. But if the people are to give their verdict of what is cruel and unusual, the people—through their elected representatives and through juries—must sit in judgment.

To the extent the constitutionality of capital punishment depends not only on the limits of current social tolerance, but also on the nature of the purposes served by the sanction, we submit that capital punishment serves important and legitimate purposes. Because capital punishment is society's "ultimate" sanction, it is likely to have a stronger effect as a deterrent than do alternative sanctions. Two recent studies of the deterrent efficacy of the death penalty support this intuitive conclusion. Other studies of the death penalty are infected by serious analytical flaws, and so do not provide support for a contrary conclusion. But quite aside from empirical studies, the legislature is entitled to credit the logical argument that capital punishment deters crime because it is society's most severe sanction. This alone is sufficient to satisfy any constitutional requirement that the death penalty serve important social purposes.

Capital punishment of course has other purposes as well. The death penalty serves a vital function as society's expression of moral outrage, and marks off some crimes as so repulsive that they are to be avoided by those individuals with even a trace of social responsibility. Some crimes, too, are so vicious, so offensive to society's standards of decency, that they call out for an ultimate sanction in order to reinforce the social feeling of revulsion to acts of that character. This response—retribution perhaps, although without vindictiveness—has been endorsed by respected commentators and seems an essential ingredient of a healthy society.

Finally, capital punishment incapacitates some individuals who, if allowed to remain alive, would be so immune to normal forms of social control that they would continue to commit murders even if sentenced to life imprisonment without possibility of parole. The federal prison system now confines at least one man who, since his incarceration for murder, has committed and been convicted of murders within prison on three separate occasions. This man, and others like him, will find opportunities to kill again, regardless of the care taken to guard them, and we submit that the Eighth Amendment does not compel society to grant them those opportunities.

Although there may be legitimate differences of opinion regarding capital punishment's propriety and utility in modern society, its value as a deterrent, and society's need for it to reinforce social values and incapacitate dangerous offenders, those differences of opinion are to be resolved by the legislature. The legislative judgment on these matters should be accepted by the judicial arm. Once the Court has satisfied itself that there is support for the legislature's decision, its role has been exhausted. An omniscient observer might conclude that all legislatures were mistaken in believing that capital punishment is ever appropriate, but the data such an observer would use, and the standards he would apply when weighing the moral values implicated in the death penalty, are beyond the ken of courts and perhaps beyond the ken of mankind. The judgment of a legislature that capital punishment is necessary and appropriate is based on its evaluation of unsettled empirical and moral questions, and its resolution of those questions should not be cast aside.

Several of the Justices who concurred in *Furman* advanced empirical arguments that led them to a different conclusion. But the validity of these arguments is now open to question. The response of state legislatures, and of Congress, to *Furman* has demonstrated that the legislative will is frustrated unless the death penalty is imposed upon some individuals. The same legislative response has established that capital punishment is "necessary" in our society to achieve articulable and rational goals. And some legislatures have been willing to impose capital punishment with considerable frequency.

III.

Beyond these considerations, it is important to note that no pattern of racial discrimination in the imposition of the death penalty for murder has been shown, and apparently none can be shown. Although blacks are sentenced to death at an apparently high rate, they also commit a disproportionate share of the capital crimes. Nearly 60 percent of those arrested for willful homicide are black, a proportion very close to the ratio of blacks to whites among those sentenced to death. Much of the argument here asks the Court simply to assume the existence of racial discrimination. But no such assumption is justified by the available data, and the most recent study indicates the absence of discrimination.

IV.

We agree with petitioners that the process by which the criminal justice system operates, involving charging discretion, plea bargaining, the jury's ability to acquit, and executive clemency, involves discretion that will be with us so long as we have a system of criminal *justice*. But the inevitable presence of such discretion cannot render the death penalty unconstitutional—indeed, it is an odd argument to make, because it requires the Court to conclude, although the Eighth Amendment does not of its own force bar death as a form of punishment, that the death penalty can never be imposed under the criminal justice system established by our Constitution. To the extent it is a challenge against discretion in the criminal justice system, the argument assails that discretion as applied to all crimes, whether or not a death penalty results. Every argument petitioners make is equally applicable to life imprisonment.

Petitioners' argument also is odd because it is cast in Eighth Amendment rather than in Fifth Amendment terms. We would suppose that if a court were concerned with the procedures by which capital punishment is imposed, the appropriate avenue of inquiry would be the Fifth Amendment's command that no person may be "deprived of life . . . without due process of law." That, of course, was the argument in *McGautha* v. *California,* 402 U.S. 183, with respect to jury discretion, and the Court rejected it. The argument should be cast in that form here as well. Some of petitioners' contentions—such as the claim that laws providing for capital punishment often are too vague to enable the jury to decide when such a crime has been committed, or that plea bargaining offers opportunities for discrimination—are particularly appropriate candidates for such narrow presentation. The vagueness doctrine is well defined, and excessively vague statutes may be set aside without calling into question the ability of the legislature to provide for capital punishment. Similarly, racial or other invidious discrimination occurring in plea bargaining, or at other stages of the criminal justice system, is unconstitutional and may be challenged directly. But this is not an argument against the imposition of the death penalty by a criminal justice system that does not so discriminate. No one would argue that because juries might unlawfully discriminate, juries should be abolished. Similarly, if, as we argue, the death penalty is not a forbidden type of punishment, it cannot be abolished on the basis that some individuals might seek to impose it for invalid reasons. The same can be said for any punishment.

As for the remaining avenues of discretion, each is either required or encouraged by the Constitution itself. The prosecutor's unfettered discretion to decline to prosecute is largely a product of the separation of powers in our constitutional system. It is a discretion necessary to enable the prosecutor to fulfill his duty under the Due Process Clause not to prosecute an individual unless there is a reasonable prospect of conviction.

Plea bargaining has been approved by this Court, which has stated that it is to be "encouraged." *Santobello* v. *New York,* 404 U.S. 257, 260. Moreover, plea bargaining, like the other sources of discretion assailed by petitioners, operates in favor of an accused, and (unlike some other sources of discretion) only at his behest. An individual need not engage in such bargaining unless he believes it will be advantageous.

The power of a jury to acquit despite evidence justifying conviction derives from and is protected by the Sixth Amendment right to trial by jury, and the same provision creates the jury's right to convict of lesser included offenses (again at the behest of the accused) if it finds facts that make such a conviction appropriate.

The power of the judge and jury, acting under statutory guidelines, to select between sentences of death or life imprisonment involves far less discretion than the standardless discretion upheld against constitutional challenge in *McGautha, supra.* In any event, most of petitioners' challenge to this discretion is in reality an argument that the statutory criteria are unconstitutionally vague. That argument has nothing to do with the constitutionality of capital punishment, for vague statutes can be construed or appropriately amended.

Finally, the power of the executive to grant clemency is established by the Constitution, and as this Court recently held (*Schick* v. *Reed,* 419 U.S. 256) it is an unfettered power because the essence of mercy is discretion.

In the last analysis, petitioners seek to convince this Court that procedures required or encouraged by one part of the Constitution inevitably produce a result forbidden by the Eighth Amendment. But the Eighth Amendment requires no such result, and, to the extent there is any leeway in construction, the Amendment should be read in a manner that makes it harmonious with, rather than antagonistic to, the remainder of the Constitution. The Court should not rule that although the process and procedures used imposing the death penalty are constitutionally permissible, indeed in many instances compelled, the death penalty is nevertheless unconstitutional under the Eighth Amendment *because* of those very processes and procedures. Yet that, we submit, is the essence of petitioners' argument in this regard.

Argument[3]

I. The Origins of the Eighth Amendment Show That a Legislature May Constitutionally Provide for Capital Punishment

A. The Text of The Constitution Demonstrates That the Framers Intended to Allow Capital Punishment

The Fifth Amendment, adopted at the same time as the Eighth, shows that the framers of the Constitution contemplated the continued use of capital punishment. That sanction is addressed three times in the Fifth Amend-

---

3. This brief augments the arguments we made in our brief amicus curiae in *Fowler* v. *North Carolina*, No. 73–7031. Further reference to our Fowler brief consequently is unnecessary.

ment's requirement of a presentment or indictment by a grand jury in capital cases, its prohibition of double jeopardy of life, and its requirement that there be due process of law in deprivation of life. It is, of course, impossible that the framers intended the Eighth Amendment to ban a punishment while simultaneously specifying the procedural safeguards for the infliction of that punishment. The Fourteenth Amendment, adopted just over three quarters of a century later, also contemplates the validity of the capital sanction, providing that no state shall deprive any person of "life, liberty, or property" without due process of law.[4]

The clear lesson of the text concerning the framers' intention is supported by history. At the time the Eighth Amendment was ratified by the states, capital punishment was a common sanction in every state for serious crimes. There is nothing in the debates accompanying its adoption to indicate any anticipation that the Eighth Amendment would, either immediately or in the future, prohibit the imposition of capital punishment. Indeed, the First Congress of the United States enacted legislation providing death as the penalty for a variety of offenses. 1 Stat. 112.

B. For Nearly Two Centuries The Eighth Amendment Was Understood To Allow Capital Punishment

For nearly two centuries this nation justifiably assumed that the death penalty was a permissible sanction, to be imposed according to statute—a sanction legislatures could choose as the necessary and appropriate response to certain criminal activity. This consensus was so complete that the constitutionality of the death penalty never directly came before this Court. Because no Justice believed that the penalty itself was improper, it was unnecessary even to discuss the proposition. Cases turned simply on the manner of its imposition. *See Wilkerson v. Utah,* 99 U.S. 130 (death by public shooting not cruel and unusual); *in re Kemmler,* 136 U.S. 436 (death by electrocution not cruel and unusual); *Louisiana ex rel. Francis v. Resweber,* 329 U.S. 459 (death by repeated electrocutions not cruel and unusual); *Trop v. Dulles,* 356 U.S. 86, 99 (dictum). Cf. *Weems v. United States,* 217 U.S. 349, 382, 409 (White, J., joined by Holmes, J., dissenting); *McGautha v. California,* 402 U.S. 183, 226 (opinion of Black, J.). See also *Storti v. Commonwealth,* 178 Mass. 549 (Holmes, C.J.).

If the meaning of the Eighth Amendment were fixed by the intentions

---

4. Indeed, the cruel and unusual punishments clause of the Eighth Amendment applies to the states only through the due process clause of the Fourteenth Amendment. It would be anomalous if the clause specifying the means by which a state can deprive a person of "life" should now be held to forbid such a deprivation entirely. Cf. *Richardson* v. *Ramirez,* 418 U.S. 24.

and practices of its framers, the outcome of this case would not be in question. However, this Court has concluded that the legality of a penalty under the Eight Amendment must also be considered in light of the changing standards of decency that mark an evolving society. *Weems* v. *United States, supra; Trop* v. *Dulles, supra* (plurality opinion). If the cruelty and the unusualness of a penalty is to depend in part on the changing standards of decency in society, so that the amendment is, to that degree, a barometer of contemporary "social conscience" as well as a reflection of historical traditions, it is necessary to know how contemporary standards are to be evaluated, and once evaluated, how this data is to be weighed. Nevertheless, one thing is certain: the historical background of the Eighth Amendment must be consulted in order to determine the meaning of "cruel and unusual punishments." History may not completely fix the meaning of the Constitution, but it sets limits, and the words used by the framers acquire scope and function from the events they summarize. See generally *United States* v. *Watson,* No. 74–538, decided January 26, 1976; *Ex parte Grossman,* 267 U.S. 87, 108–109; *United States* v. *Wong Kim Ark,* 169 U.S. 649, 655–656.

C. The English Experience

Until the late 1600's England had developed no general prohibition against cruel, barbarous, or illegal punishments. The Magna Carta forbade excessive punishments, but "excessive" meant death for a trifling offense. Holt, *Magna Carta* 323 (1965); cf. Barrington, *The Magna Charta and other Great Charters of England* 181, 199 (1900). The criminal law was severe and unyielding; even though some charters reserved great punishments for "great" crimes, most thefts were felonies, and felonies were capital offenses. 1 Stephen, *History of the Criminal Law in England* 457–492 (1883). The slogan, often accepted even in the seventeenth century, that "the punishment should fit the crime" (see Perry, *Sources of Our Liberties* 236 (1959)) simply meant that, however much greater the punishment than the harm inflicted by the crime, some measure of proportionality was necessary, and a comparison to other authorized punishments appropriate.

The phrase "cruel and unusual punishments" was first used in the Bill of Rights of 1689, drawn up by Parliament as part of the accession of William and Mary. Perry, *supra,* at 247. Most historians have attributed this clause to Parliamentary reaction to the "Bloody Assize" of 1685, a series of treason trials held after the abortive uprising by the Duke of Monmouth. See generally Granucci, *"Nor Cruel and Unusual Punishments Inflicted": The Original Meaning,* 57 Calif. L. Rev. 839. 852–860 (1969) (which questions this attribution).

Monmouth's rebellion was an attempt to overthrow King James II. Monmouth was defeated and the king appointed Chief Justice Jeffreys of the King's Bench to a special assize to try the captured rebels. Because of the number of treasonous prisoners a series of trials would have been lengthy and complicated; Jeffreys undertook to simplify his task by engaging in plea bargaining. Those who pleaded guilty were promised that their lives would be spared; many did so, but James II and Jeffreys reneged on the bargain and executed many of the prisoners the next winter. After James II had fled, Parliament reacted to the Bloody Assize of the previous year with proposals to secure the people against the "illegal and cruel" punishments inflicted by such special (and unauthorized) tribunals. See Somers, *A Vindication of the Late Parliament of England* 3 (1690).[5]

Granucci, on the other hand, attributes the cruel and unusual punishments clause of 1689 to the history of Titus Oates and the "Popish Plot" of 1678–79. Granucci, *supra,* at 856–860. The "Popish Plot" was a ruse by Oates to convince his countrymen that Catholic agents would assassinate Charles II and place the Catholic James II on the throne. Oates swore to the fictitious "plot" and in the ensuing commotion fifteen Catholics were tried and executed.

Oates's perjury was exposed after the succession of James II, and Oates himself was tried and convicted by the King's Bench, Chief Justice Jeffreys presiding, and sentenced to a fine, life imprisonment, whippings, defrocking, and to pillorying four times yearly. The House of Lords upheld the judgment, but the Commons intervened on behalf of Oates, on the basis that this punishment was inhumane and illegal because not authorized by Parliament. The objection again was that the combination of pains and penalties had never been authorized as a response to the crime of perjury, and that the court was without jurisdiction to impose it, even though life imprisonment, whippings and pilloryings were common sanctions both singly and in combination, and could not, in the seventeenth century, have been thought "excessive" for a crime that had sent 15 innocent people to their deaths.

The English history of the prohibition of cruel and unusual punishments, therefore, supports at most a prohibition against punishments unauthorized

---

5. The methods of punishment used by the Bloody Assize were not "cruel" within the English experience. The rebels were hanged, cut down and disemboweled while alive, drawn and quartered. Females were burned while alive. But the punishments were imposed by a royal tribunal, free of Parlimentary control or authorization. To that extent they were unauthorized. And, of course, because many of the executions were in violation of the original pleas and judgments, they were "illegal."

for the crime, and against egregiously disproportionate punishments for nonfelony offenses. The prohibition did not restrict the punishing power, nor did it limit punishments to those minimally "necessary" in light of the crime. Parliament was attempting to bridle the King's courts;[6] there is no hint that Parliament was attempting to inhibit its own judgments or was authorizing the courts to do so.[7] The Bill of Rights of 1689 did not secure the liberties of the people. It was simply another tool in the extended struggle between Parliament and King to allocate the power to govern.

D. The United States' Derivation of the Clause

The debates at the time of the adoption of the Eighth Amendment reveal little about the framers' understanding of its origins or meaning. The Senate debates on the amendments were closed entirely (Goebel, *History of The Supreme Court of the United States, Vol. I: Antecedents and Beginnings to 1801* 444 (1971)) and little was said about the clause in the recorded debates.

The materials available from colonial times are not sufficiently comprehensive to enable historians to ascertain the source of most of the amendments that comprise the bill of rights. Professor Goebel has speculated that the proposed amendments were compiled in a grab-bag fashion from lists of rights that were known to the colonies from treatises on English law and had, in one fashion or another, become part of the law of one or more of the colonies. See also Levy, *The Origins of the Fifth Amendment* 411 (1968). The cruel and unusual punishments clause of the Eighth Amendment was taken verbatim from the English Bill of Rights of 1689, although several of the colonial constitutions had similar provisions.

Its insertion may well have been prompted by complaints in the state ratifying conventions that the Constitution contained no limits on the methods of federal punishment. For example, in the Massachusetts convention of January 1788, an objection was made that

---

6. The preamble to the Bill of Rights of 1689 stated that James II and his courts were arbitrarily "assuming and exercising the power of dispensing with and suspending of laws and the execution of laws, without consent of parliament." The King had claimed such power. See Kenyon, *The Stuart Constitution 1603–1688*, 420–26 (1966).

7. Cf. *Martin v. United States*, 317 F.2d 753, 755 (C.A. 9): "[I]t is well settled that a sentence that falls within the terms of a valid statute cannot amount to a cruel and unusual punishment. . . ." Even in 1769 Blackstone believed that cruel and excessive punishments were controlled only by the "tacit consent" of the people, 4 Blackstone, *Commentaries on the Laws of England* 369–73 (1769), and that the Bill of Rights of 1689 did not constrain Parliament.

> [Congress will] have to ascertain . . . and determine, what kinds of punishments shall be inflicted on persons convicted of crimes. They are nowhere restrained from inventing the most cruel and unheard-of punishments and annexing them to crimes; and there is no constitutional check of them, but that *racks* and *gibbets* may be amongst the most mild instruments of their discipline. [2 Elliot, *The Debates in the Several State Conventions on the Adoption of the Federal Constitution* 111 (2d ed. 1836).]

See also *Furman, supra,* 408 U.S. at 320–321 (Marshall, J., concurring). In the Virginia debates Patrick Henry objected to the possibility of uncontrolled use of "tortures" and "barbarous" punishments, and George Mason explained that such punishments were prohibited in Virginia by the Virginia constitution's cruel and unusual punishments clause, which would forbid all "torture." 3 Elliott, *supra,* at 447, 452.

These expressions may indicate that the framers desired a clause that would bind legislators as well as judges; there is no contrary indication in the sparse debates in the House of Representatives. But the emphasis by those who objected to a lack of a cruel and unusual punishments clause was the need for a prohibition of "torture" or other barbarous forms of punishment, thus showing that legislatures were to continue to have considerable leeway in determining the scale of punishments to be used.

During the debates on the floor of the House only two representatives spoke to the cruel and unusual punishments clause. Mr. Smith of South Carolina believed that the clause was too "indefinite" and Mr. Livermore thought it unnecessary. Mr. Livermore went on to argue that some punishments (such as hanging, whipping, and cutting off of ears) were "cruel" but necessary. 1 Annals of Congress 753–54 (1789).

It is difficult to interpret the vote in favor of the clause immediately after this objection. Because hanging was an accepted penalty for crime at the time, and because the first Congress itself provided for capital punishment, it can be inferred that these early congressmen thought Livermore's interpretation of the clause not well taken; even though a punishment might be "cruel" in a general sense, it was not necessarily "cruel" in the constitutional sense and so not inevitably to be prohibited by the clause. In affixing individual responsibility, Congress would be permitted to use its judgment, weighing the inevitable cruelty of *any* punishment against the social need for it.

The amendment fell into desuetude after its adoption; cases rarely discussed it, and no penalty was held forbidden under it until *Weems* was decided in 1909. This was probably the proper fate for the amendment in light of its history, for the history discloses, to the extent it discloses anything, that the amendment was an attempt to guarantee against the new national government, concerning which many persons were apprehensive, a then-prevalent social consensus that some punishments were simply beyond the pale of civility. The apprehensions were not well-founded, and the guarantee, given our form of government, was largely (though, as we will show, not completely) unnecessary. Any such punishment would almost invariably be extinguished by the legislature before it could be tested in the courts. Were a punishment intolerable, it would be rejected by the people themselves—and that rejection would come not only by legislative repeal or alteration but also by the refusal of juries to convict of crimes carrying the intolerable punishment. In this light, the amendment states a standard below which communities and their legislatures may not fall; it provides a safeguard against the aberrational case, in which the punishment imposed is profoundly and demonstrably contrary to prevailing standards of decency.

E. Judicial Construction

If the Eighth Amendment enforces the evolving standards of decency that mark a civilized society, the first task is to ascertain whether there is a particular social consensus concerning the practical and ethical values that pertain to punishment, and whether a particular punishment transgresses the limits established by that consensus. This Court's Eighth Amendment decisions have attempted to undertake such an inquiry, and have facilitated that investigation with an additional inquiry into the reasons why society failed to prevent the "intolerable" punishment without judicial intervention. If such a reason explaining the apparently deviant assessment of punishment is present there will be additional support for the judicial inference that those who have imposed the punishment—rather than those who sit in ultimate judgment—have misapprehended the social standards of decency.

In *Weems v. United States, supra,* this Court dealt with *cadena temporal,* a Philippine traditional punishment (for even petty offenses) that imposed fifteen years' "hard and painful labor," the constant wearing of chains, loss of all civil rights, and perpetual surveillance. The punishment failed the "consensus" test because it was not native to this country and never had been an accepted punishment for crimes here. The penalty, by all American standards, was patently harsh and disproportionate to the offense. Nor was it difficult to see why the consensus had failed to make itself felt without judicial intervention: the penalty had been invented by a foreign legislature and was imposed by a foreign judicial system unaccustomed to our sensibilities.

In *Trop* v. *Dulles, supra,* a plurality of this Court concluded that denationalization was cruel and unusual punishment. The power to denationalize a deserting soldier had been placed in the hands of military officials, and they had used it to strip citizenship from Trop, who had "deserted" for a single day and voluntarily surrendered. There, too, the consensus had failed. Denationalization was not a traditional American punishment for crime; it was (of course) not used by any state. The plurality concluded that citizenship is not subject to the general powers of Congress; Congress therefore could not authorize this admittedly unusual punishment whether or not it was appropriate—an issue the plurality thought irrelevant. Mr. Justice Brennan, concurring (356 U.S. at 105), agreed. Moreover, the Court highlighted the mechanism through which the social consensus had been avoided: the decision to denationalize had been removed from a jury, which could refuse to impose socially unacceptable punishments, and had been placed in the hands of military authorities (a general court-martial convicts by less than unanimous vote and therefore is, for example, less likely to reject unacceptable punishments, and courts-martial are not designed to produce a cross-section of the civilian community). See the opinion of Mr. Justice Black, concurring, 356 U.S. at 104–105.

The use of the Eighth Amendment in *Robinson* v. *California,* 370 U.S. 660, varies somewhat from this pattern but is not inconsistent with it. In *Robinson* the Court did not hold that some particular penalty was cruel and unusual, but that *any* penalty for narcotic addiction would be cruel and unusual because a status, as distinguished from an act, could not be a crime. That is a decision different in kind from the decision to be made in these cases. *Robinson* decided that some things could not be made crimes, not that the legislature was forbidden to apply a particular penalty to a particular crime.

In other cases in which this Court has upheld specific penalties it has decided that the penalty itself did not overstep the tolerance of the social conscience. For example, in *Howard* v. *Fleming,* 191 U.S. 126, the Court rejected a claim that ten years' incarceration for conspiracy to defraud was cruel and unusual; the Court concluded that such a course had not been rejected by the people as barbarous or depraved, was accepted by many legislatures, and was not egregiously disproportional to the provocation. See also *Badders* v. *United States,* 240 U.S. 391; *United States ex rel. Milwaukee Social Democratic Publishing Co.* v. *Burleson,* 255 U.S. 407.

The lower courts have, in the main, followed a similar course. They have approved legislatively prescribed penalties unless there was evidence that other jurisdictions rejected those penalties and, in addition, the penalties appeared to be so excessive that they are repulsive and unnecessary. See, e.g., *United States* v. *Beverely*, 416 F.2d 263 (C.A. 9) (upholding the twenty-five-year minimum sentence for aggravated mail robbery).[8]

Considerably less deference has been shown to punishments decreed or augmented by administrative officials; in such cases there are greater opportunities for individuals to impose punishments for which the representatives of the people would not vote and which society would not tolerate were the punishments known. The smaller the decision-making body, the more likely it is to err in its reading of the demands of the social mores and the less likely the penalty will be brought to public attention for correction. Moreover, to the extent punishment is imposed or augmented by administrative officials without specific sanction from the legislature, the responsibility for punishment has been removed from a body ultimately responsible to the people. There has, therefore, been a greater willingness to examine the potentially barbaric conditions created by isolated prison officials (see, e.g., *Holt* v. *Sarver*, 442 F.2d 304 (C.A. 8); *Finney* v. *Arkansas Board of Correction*, 505 F.2d 194 (C.A. 8)) or even by individuals within a prison system who act to deprive an inmate of medical care or protection from other aggressive inmates (see, e.g., *Newman* v. *Alabama*, 503 F.2d 1320, 1330–1332 (C.A. 5)).

Because even at its broadest interpretation the cruel and unusual punishments clause protects against only those punishments utterly outside the bounds of social tolerance, it is not surprising that great deference should be shown to penalties selected by a legislature and enforced by the unanimous decision of a jury. In a representative democracy the legislature speaks for the people that elected it. Once enacted, the penalty cannot be imposed unless the people themselves, acting as a jury of the peers of the accused, agree to its imposition. And the jury, with its prerogative to "nullify" laws and penalties repellent to its sensibilities, is an effective ultimate check against legislative aberrations.

Thus, if a penalty can pass the dual test of enactment by the people's representatives, and application by the people themselves sitting as a jury, it is almost certainly not so cruel, disproportionate, or repulsive to the sensi-

---

8. Following the same analysis, but reaching a different result, is *Hart* v. *Coiner*, 483 F.2d 136 (C.A. 4), certiorari denied, 415 U.S. 983, which holds that life imprisonment for petty recidivism is cruel and unusual because it has been rejected by almost all states. See also *Downey* v. *Parini*, 518 F.2d 1288 (C.A. 6), vacated and remanded for reconsideration, December 2, 1975, No. 75–219, which holds that 60 years' imprisonment for possession and sale of marijuana is cruel and unusual on a similar theory. Cf. Note, 44 Fordham L. Rev. 637 (1975) (collecting cases).

bilities of modern society that it is forbidden by the cruel and unusual punishments clause. Those who would paint it so must make their case by clear and convincing evidence. They cannot call on this Court to sit as a "super-legislature" (*Burns Baking Co.* v. *Bryan,* 264 U.S. 504, 534 (Brandeis and Holmes, JJ., dissenting)) and assess merely whether the legislature's decision was wise.[9]

II. This Court Should Uphold a Penalty Enacted by a Legislature, Serving Legitimate Purposes, and Accepted by Contemporary Society

If our analysis of the cruel and unusual punishments clause is correct, that clause forbids only penalties similar in nature to those the framers wished to forbid (a category certainly not involved here) or penalties that fall so far beyond the pale of social acceptability that they appear as aberrations. The clause is appropriately directed to such aberrations, in which, through a combination of circumstances (whether uninformed, accidental, or malign), a punishment utterly unacceptable to society has been decreed or imposed. A solitary individual, whether he be legislator, prison administrator, judge, or juror, could assess a penalty or create conditions offensive to contemporary standards of decency. But it is difficult to see how such a mistake, such a gross misunderstanding, can be made time and again by legislatures of the several states and the Congress, and by the juries that assess guilt with the knowledge of the potential penalties. There are too many participants in the process, too many individuals (including, as well, the prosecutor, grand jury, and governor or other clemency authority) *each* of whom would have to be ignorant of or flaunt society's demands, for it to be true that a legislatively enacted and judicially enforced penalty could constitute cruel and unusual punishment.

We do not claim that even this process can never err. It is conceivable that aberrant laws can be passed and aberrant juries found. But the challenge raised by petitioners is not a challenge to unusual or freakish events; most states provide for capital punishment, and in 1974 alone 151 individuals were sentenced to death. At the end of 1974 at least 254 individuals had been sentenced to death since *Furman* and were awaiting execution.[10]

---

9. See also *Ferguson* v. *Skrupa*, 372 U.S. 726, 731.

10. Law Enforcement Assistance Administration, *Capital Punishment* 1974, 1 and Table 7, 26 (1975). As petitioner Jurek concedes, this is a "not inconsiderable" number. *Jurek* Br. 67–69, n.108. Cf. id. at 83–84, n.147 (discussing data collected by the NAACP, which shows 454 death

How then can it be declared by this Court, by any court, that the death penalty contravenes evolving standards of decency or contemporary notions of human dignity or society's currently-held moral values? The framers of the Constitution "might have made the judge the mouthpiece of the common will, finding it out by his contacts with people generally; but he would then have been ruler, like the Judges of Israel."[11] The question cannot be avoided: if this Court were to hold that the death penalty violates evolving standards of decency, would not one then be required to conclude that thirty-five state legislatures and the Congress of the United States are unenlightened, that they are out of step with contemporary moral standards and the will and spirit of the people who elected them? Courts announce their view of society's standards of decency and, by doing so, encourage public acceptance of what can at best be only a prediction. But with respect to the death penalty the Court has previously spoken,[12] and it has seen the response.

This is not to say that a position espoused by an enlightened few is to be ignored. It is not. In all societies, in all ages, the ideas of those in a minority have influenced and inspired those in the majority. But this describes the legislative process, not the judicial. Only when a minority opinion has gradually made its way to acceptance by the society can we be sure that it was and is the enlightened view and not merely an unpopular and unpersuasive opinion. If judges anticipate the moral verdict of society, they will frequently anticipate incorrectly and fasten their own views upon the nation in the name of enlightenment. Such a theory of judicial power resembles too closely Rousseau's concept of the general will, which is entitled to govern even when possessed only by a minority, and is antithetical to the tenets of representative democracies. If, as the Eighth Amendment contemplates, the people are to give their verdict of what is cruel and unusual, the people—through their elected representatives—must sit in judgment.

A. Capital Punishment Serves Legitimate Purposes

In enacting death penalty statutes, the legislatures throughout the country have not acted irrationally. Capital punishment serves several important social purposes, among which are deterring crimes and expressing society's moral outrage in a manner that shapes and reinforces the community's standards.

---

sentences through February 25, 1976).

11. Learned Hand, "How Far is a Judge Free in Rendering a Decision?" (1935), in *The Spirit of Liberty* 109 (Dilliard ed. 1960).

12. *Furman v. Georgia, supra.*

1. Capital Punishment Deters Crime.

There is an inherent logic to the belief that the death penalty deters at least some people from committing crimes. "Belief in the deterrent efficacy of penal sanctions is as old as the criminal law itself." Zimring & Hawkins, *Deterrence* 1 (1973). Just as some penalty deters a prospective offender by making the prospect of crime less attractive, so does a more severe penalty make crime still less attractive, and so less likely to occur.[13] Because death is perceived by most potential law breakers as the maximum feasible penalty, it is probably the most effective deterrent force. "*Prima facie* the penalty of death is likely to have a stronger effect as a deterrent to normal human beings than any other form of punishment. . . ." Royal Commission on Capital Punishment, *1949–1953 Report,* ¶ 61 (1953). It is not unreasonable or insupportable for a legislature to credit an argument with such strong plausibility.

The primary arguments against the deterrent force of capital punishment are that criminals (by definition) are not "normal" people, and so do not respond in "normal" ways, and that many murders or other capital crimes are crimes of passion and hence not deterrable. Neither argument supports a conclusion that capital punishment does not have a deterrent effect. The only surface evidence that criminals are not "normal" is their failure to conform to some social "norms"; that evidence alone is not proof (or even support) for the proposition that "criminals" do not respond to incentives, to the prospect of pain or pleasure.[14]

We can conclude, perhaps, that those who do not obey the laws have little respect for the law per se, and in that sense lack a "normal" trait. But we cannot conclude that all criminals are completely insensitive to deterrence merely because they commit crimes; we can validly conclude only that they have evaluated the prospects of success (and the "cost" to them of apprehension) differently from those who have the propensity to offend but do not. See Packer, *The Limits of the Criminal Sanction* 40–45 (1968). Indeed, the efforts of most criminals to avoid detection, and to escape after being

---

13. There is strong empirical evidence that the threat of imprisonment deters crime (including murder) and that longer sentences are a more effective deterrent. See Ehrlich, *Participation in Illegitimate Activities: A Theoretical and Empirical Investigation*, 81 J. Pol. Econ. 521 (1973); Block and Lind, *An Economic Analysis of Crimes Punishable by Imprisonment*, 4 J. Legal Studies 479 (1975); Ehrlich, *The Deterrent Effect of Criminal Law Enforcement*, 1 J. Legal Studies 259 (1972); Gibbs, *Crime, Punishment, and Deterrence*, 48 Sw. Soc. Sci. Q. 515 (1968). Other studies are collected in van den Haag, *Punishing Criminals* 130–42 (1975).

14. Cf. Holmes, *The Path of the Law*, 10 Harv. L. Rev. 457, 458–59 (1897) (it is the "bad man" whom the law regards as "normal," for only when a man is "bad" must the law depend on its threats of pain to change his behavior).

caught, show very clearly that they are sensitive to a calculus of pains and pleasures.

Similarly, although there are many crimes committed in such intense passion that the offender may altogether neglect to consider the prospect of punishment in the future, the existence of such people and such crimes of passion does not indicate that there are no deterrable crimes. Some murders are committed for money, some after lengthy contemplation. Treason, espionage, sabotage, aircraft piracy, and deliberate wrecking of trains (all of them federal capital offenses) are prime examples of entire categories of offense committed after calculation and in pursuit of ulterior goals. The people who commit such crimes are rational (albeit misguided or evil) individuals, and there is no reason to believe they will not attend their own self-interest and consider the potential severity of the penalty that might be meted out in response. These crimes (at least) are sufficiently narrow and clearly defined, and sufficiently open to discussion by deterrence, that capital punishment is permissible for them regardless of its deterrent value as applied to other crimes.[15] The death penalty could realistically be made a fully predictable response to these crimes, and those contemplating such criminal activity could be required to take into account a very great probability of execution if caught.

Moreover, although an individual may use a weapon in a fit of passion, the decision to carry a weapon at all is made with a cool head and (often) considerable forethought. The prospect that he will find himself unable or unwilling to control the use of that weapon may cause many people not to possess or carry it, and consequently decrease the number of "passionate" killings. Legislators may also legitimately conclude that many crimes committed in passion are deterrable even if some are not, and that the death penalty is appropriately applied to the entire category to save as many innocent lives as possible. The choice of crimes for which capital punishment is to be authorized is, unless indisputably aberrant and grossly disproportionate, a legislative choice.

Legislators are not alone in believing that the death penalty is a more effective deterrent than is life imprisonment. A recent study has tentatively

---

15. The Supreme Judicial Court of Massachusetts recently struck down under the Massachusetts Constitution a pre-*Furman* death penalty statute. *Commonwealth* v. *O'Neal*, 339 N.E.2d 676. The Justices divided four to three on the constitutional question. Two of the four Justices in the majority expressly noted that capital punishment might well be constitutional for carefully described categories of clearly deterrable crimes. See 339 N.E.2d at 694 (Hennessey, J., concurring); *id.* at 695 (Wilkins, J., concurring).

concluded that when capital punishment was *actually used* a significant number of lives were saved: over the period studied, and after controlling for the effects of other variables, using the death penalty instead of imprisonment may have deterred approximately eight murders for each execution actually carried out. See Ehrlich, *The Deterrent Effect of Capital Punishment,* 65 Am. Econ. Rev. 397 (1975).[16] Two statisticians, although critical of some of Professor Ehrlich's technical methods, have duplicated his results; using data other than those used by Ehrlich, these investigators produced "results . . . similar to Ehrlich's." Bowers and Pierce, *The Illusion of Deterrence in Isaac Ehrlich's Research on Capital Punishment,* 85 Yale L. J. 187, 196 (1975) (footnote omitted). Moreover, another recent study, using methodology significantly different from Ehrlich's, has concluded that Ehrlich actually underestimated the deterrent force of capital punishment by a factor of five "and that the evidence is better consistent with the view that one execution will deter at least 50 homicides." Yunker, *The Deterrent Effect of Capital Punishment: Comment* (unpublished manuscript).[17] See also Schuessler, *The Deterrent Influence of the Death Penalty,* 284 Annals 54, 60 (1952) ("The correlation between these two indices [the number of executions per 1,000 homicides and the homicide rate in 41 death penalty states] was -.26, indicating a slight tendency for the homicide rate to diminish as the probability of execution increases."). These studies provide important empirical support for the *a priori* logical belief that the use of the death penalty decreases the number of murders.[18]

Other studies of the deterrent value of the death penalty (see, *e.g.,* Sellin, *The Death Penalty* (1959)) have not concluded that there is proof that capital punishment deters crime. But neither have they supplied proof that it fails to deter. Zimring & Hawkins, *supra,* at 254–55, 257–58. All of the earlier studies that have found no measurable deterrent effect from the death penalty have shared certain investigatory flaws. For example, these studies have relied not upon the actual *use* of the death penalty, but upon its statutory authorization, as the independent variable against which the murder rate was

---

16. This paper is a revised and shortened version of Ehrlich, *The Deterrent Effect of Capital Punishment: A Question of Life and Death,* 18 National Bureau of Economic Research Working Papers (November 1973), which we lodged with the Court in connection with *Fowler* v. *North Carolina,* No. 73–7031.

17. We are lodging 10 copies of the Yunker manuscript with the Clerk for distribution to the Court and have furnished a copy of the manuscript to counsel for the parties.

18. Several commentators have criticized Professor Ehrlich's work. For the reasons we discuss at pages 43–45, *infra,* we believe that this criticism is irrelevant because legislators, not courts, must resolve such debates. However that may be, we discuss in Appendix B, *infra,* the debate between Ehrlich and his critics.

compared.[19] The effects of mere statutory authorization of capital punishment tell us nothing about the effects of its use, as Sellin himself admitted. Sellin, *supra,* at 20. All of the studies have evaluated the effect of the death penalty on the overall murder rate, rather than on the rate of capital murders, and so the studies cannot exclude the possibility that the death penalty deters the commission of those murders to which it applies.[20] None of the studies has attempted to isolate the effect of the death penalty on special and highly deterrable capital crimes, such as murder for hire. And, perhaps most importantly, all of the earlier studies failed to hold constant factors other than the death penalty that might influence the rate of murders. Only if the death penalty is the sole determinant of the murder rate, or if other determinants are identical in states having different execution rates, would it be proper to infer from these studies that the death penalty has no deterrent effect.[21]

But states—even the contiguous states studies by Sellin—have important differences. Indeed, these very differences may explain why one state chooses to use the death penalty and another does not, and still other differences might have an independent effect directly on the rate of violent crime. Or suppose that a state that had abolished capital punishment also had a high arrest and conviction rate for murder, so that although a murderer would be punished less severely, his expectation of net punishment would be greater in this state than in a state with capital punishment but a low arrest and conviction rate. Unless factors such as this are held constant—as the most recent studies have done—no valid conclusions may be drawn. As one opponent of capital punishment has remarked about the previous studies:

---

19. In fact, of the nine pairs of contiguous states studies by Bowers, eight pairs included a "death penalty state" that was *de facto* abolitionist. Bowers, *Executions in America* 137–63 (1974).

20. Commentators frequently have explained why the statistical material on the death penalty's deterrent value has until now been inconclusive. See, *e.g.*, S. Rep. No. 93–721, 93d Cong., 1st Sess. 8–11 (1974); Royal Commission on Capital Punishment, *supra*, at ¶¶ 62–67; 2 *Working Papers of the National Commission on Reform of the Federal Criminal Laws* 1354 (1970); Gibbs, *Crime, Punishment, and Deterrence*, 48 Sw. Soc. Sci. Q. 515 (1968): Hart, *Murder and the Principles of Punishment: England and the United States*, 52 Nw. U. L. Rev. 433, 457 (1957).

21. In any event, we do not think that the meaning of the Eighth Amendment should turn on the results of the latest social science research. Neither should it turn on the secular trend in the murder rate, although it could be argued that, if the Court declared the death penalty unconstitutional and the murder rate increased, the increase would be evidence that a deterrent had been removed, and hence that the death penalty would again be constitutional. The alternative, that society would have to accept a higher murder rate because of a mistaken empirical estimate by the judiciary, seems unacceptable.

> The inescapable flaw is, of course, that social conditions in any state are
> not constant through time, and that social conditions are not the same in
> any two states. If an effect [from the presence or absence of capital punish-
> ment] were observed (and the observed effects, one way or another, are
> not large) then one could not at all tell whether any of this effect is attrib-
> utable to the presence or absence of capital punishment. A "scientific"—
> that is to say, a soundly based—conclusion is simply impossible. [Black,
> *Capital Punishment: The Inevitability of Caprice and Mistake* 25–26 (1974).]

Professor Passell, upon whom petitioners rely (*Jurek* Pet. Br. App. 2, Sub-
app. E), agrees. He has written: "It cannot be proven that executions do
not serve as a deterrent to murder. Proof is simply beyond the capacities of
empirical social science." Passell, *The Deterrent Effect of the Death Penalty: A
Statistical Test,* 28 Stan. L. Rev. 61, 79 (1975). And, he writes (*id.* at 62–63),
"even were one to accept without qualification the validity of the [pre-Eh-
rlich] research designs and the accuracy of the data employed, their evidence
against deterrence could not be considered conclusive."

The older studies suggesting that capital punishment has no observable
deterrent effect are deficient in yet another respect. Their results may have
been produced by an entirely practical problem: the real deterrent value of
capital punishment may be sufficiently small in relation to the number of
murders committed each year that it is difficult to detect, given the deficiencies in data gathering (many crimes are not reported, and changes in the
reporting rate are impossible to detect; in some cases it is difficult to determine whether a particular death is a "murder") and the very bulk of the raw
data. In recent years there have been more than 15,000 murders per year,[22]
so that even if one execution deterred 10 murders, the effect on the murder
rate might become lost in the statistical "noise."

We submit that the states are entitled to make use of the death penalty
even if the effects are "small" in comparison to the gross murder rate. We
do not imply by this argument that the deterrent value of capital punishment is "small" in human terms; every murder is supremely important to
the victim and to his or her family and acquaintances. Indeed, it is supremely
important to society, its morale, its sense of community, its sense of the security not only of lives but of values. Suppose that a state finds it necessary
to impose the death penalty only a few (two, three, or four) times yearly on

---

22. Approximately 20,600 murders were committed in 1974. Uniform Crime Reports of the
Federal Bureau of Investigation, *Crime in the United States* 1974, 15–19 (1975). Of course, not all
of these murders were defined as capital crimes. There is no accurate data indicating the number
of capital crimes committed each year.

the worst offenders. In all probability the resultant difference in the capital murder rate will be difficult to detect by even the most powerful statistical techniques. Yet the deterrent effect may be real—and the state is entitled to take the measures necessary to save the several lives that would be lost in the absence of the death penalty. A "small" saving in human life is not so insignificant or immaterial that it can be brushed aside as a permissible basis for legislative judgment.

In sum, although the evidence supporting the logical position that the death penalty deters capital crimes more effectively than life imprisonment is not yet conclusive, the evidence that there is no deterrent value will never be, and indeed cannot ever be, conclusive. The debate will persist unless and until the evidence of deterrence becomes conclusive, a possibility not to be ruled out. And so long as rational men can debate whether the death penalty deters crime, legislatures should be allowed to resolve that question for themselves and to act upon their decision free from interference by a judicial body that is neither well situated to collect and sift facts nor charged by the Constitution with that task. "[I]n passing on the validity of [legislation], it is not the province of a court to hear and examine evidence for the purpose of deciding again a question which the legislature has already decided. Its function is only to determine whether it is possible to say that the legislative decision is without rational basis. . . . [W]here, as here, the evidence . . . shows that it is at least a debatable question . . . , decision is for the legislature and not the courts." *Clark* v. *Paul Gray, Inc.,* 306 U.S. 583, 594. Congress and thirty-five states have resolved the debate in favor of capital punishment. "It was for Congress, as the branch that made this judgment, to assess and weigh the various conflicting considerations. . . . It is not for us to review the congressional resolution of these factors. It is enough that we be able to perceive a basis upon which the Congress might resolve the conflict as it did." *Katzenbach* v. *Morgan,* 384 U.S. 641, 653.[23]

2. Capital Punishment Reinforces Important Social Values.
a. Expression of Moral Outrage.

Just as the legislature legitimately may conclude that capital punishment deters crime, so it may conclude that capital punishment serves a vital social function as society's expression of moral outrage. Although sometimes capital punishment is authorized for a crime because society views that crime as serious, the use of capital punishment itself also has an effect on society's

---

23. See also *Munn* v. *Illinois,* 94 U.S. 113, 132; *Powell* v. *Pennsylvania,* 127 U.S. 678, 685. See generally Cox, *The Role of Congress in Constitutional Determinations,* 40 U. Cin. L. Rev. 199 (1971).

view of the crime. Capital punishment marks some crimes as particularly outrageous and offensive, and therefore to be avoided by those individuals with even a trace of social responsibility.[24]

> There is a heavy symbolic significance in the operation of the criminal sanction; for the process of ascribing guilt, responsibility, and punishment goes on day after day against the background of all human history. . . . It is not simply the threat of punishment or its actual imposition that contributes to the total deterrent effect but the entire criminal process, standing as a paradigm of good and evil, in which we are reminded by devices far more subtle than literal threats that the wicked do not flourish. These public rituals, it is plausible to suppose, strengthen the identification of the majority with a value-system that places a premium on law-abiding behavior. [Packer, *The Limits of the Criminal Sanction* 43–44 (1968).]

Moreover, this venting of outrage at the violation of society's most important rules—"retribution" perhaps, although stripped of its vindictiveness—is itself an important, perhaps a necessary, social function, and has been approved by the most respected commentators (see, *e.g.,* Packer, *supra,* at 36–37; Royal Commission on Capital Punishment, *supra,* at ¶53; Cohen, *Reason and Law* 50 (1950); Hart, *The Aims of the Criminal Law,* 23 L. & Contemp. Prob. 401 (1958)); and by this Court. It is difficult to imagine any social goal other than "retribution" served by the execution of Nazi leaders for war crimes and genocide (cf. *In re Yamashita,* 327 U.S. 1). A criminal justice theory that rested entirely upon deterrence would have been unable to support any punishment whatever for Adolf Hitler, had he been captured, and his chief lieutenants. That example alone should warn against the denigration of "retribution" as a completely legitimate social response to truly heinous crimes.

Although the social cohesiveness function served by "retribution" is not the entire end of criminal punishment, it is not a forbidden end, or inconsistent with our respect for ourselves or the dignity of others. See, *e.g., Williams* v. *New York,* 337 U.S. 241, 248; *Powell* v. *Texas,* 392 U.S. 514, 530–531 (opinion of Marshall, J.). Sometimes nothing less is required to reinforce our respect for ourselves or the dignity of others.[25]

---

24. This effect should be distinguished from deterrence; it achieves obedience to the law's commands not because of the anticipation of punishment but because some individuals will shrink from committing "serious" crimes that strike at the heart of the social order, regardless of the punishment anticipated.

25. Or as Lord Justice Denning stated to the Royal Commission on Capital Punishment, *supra,*

> [W]ithout a sense of retribution we may lose our sense of wrong. Retribution in punishment is an expression of the community's disapproval of crime, and if this retribution is not given recognition then the disapproval may also disappear. A community which is too ready to forgive the wrongdoer may end by condoning the crime. [Goodhart, *English Law and the Moral Law* 93 (1953).]

Perhaps the mixture of reprobation and expiation known as "retribution" is disapproved by some humanitarian and behavioral theorists, but that theoretical disapproval is utterly inadequate to support a constitutional rejection of a carefully considered and rationally supported legislative judgment.

b. Death is Not Excessive in Relation to All Crimes.

It has been argued by some that although punishment in general appropriately may be used to deter crimes and express the society's moral outrage over certain crimes, death is always an excessive device even when applied to these legitimate ends. We submit, however, that capital punishment is not excessive in comparison to all provocations and social needs. The "uniqueness" and finality of the death penalty cut two ways: although death becomes an especial object of moral concern, it also becomes uniquely appropriate as society's ultimate sanction, all the more appropriate to the perpetrators of "ultimate" crimes because death alone can be the "ultimate" penalty.

To say that death is inevitably excessive because it affronts human dignity, or imposes suffering, is to beg the question. All punishments offend human dignity and impose suffering to some degree; although capital punishment may be harsh, or even repellent to some, it does not follow that it is "excessive."

> [T]here are a number of things we do not wish to think about that are disgusting and perhaps revolting but that we also acknowledge as necessary. Enemas, the vivisection of monkeys, cleaning up outhouses, all are disgusting or abhorrent, but they may also be necessary. Imprisonment is

---

at ¶ 53:

> The punishment inflicted for grave crimes should adequately reflect the revulsion felt by the great majority of citizens for them. It is a mistake to consider the objects of punishment as being deterrent or reformative or preventive and nothing else. . . . The ultimate justification of any punishment is not that it is a deterrent, but that it is the emphatic denunciation by the community of a crime: and from this point of view, there are some murders which, in the present state of public opinion, demand the most emphatic denunciation of all, namely the death penalty.

> abhorrent—people would find it so if they knew more about it—but it is
> hardly, in itself, cruel and unusual punishment. [Polsby, *The Death of Capi-
> tal Punishment?* Furman v. Georgia, 1972 Sup. Ct. Rev. 1, 24.]

We do not contend that death is an appropriate response to any crime
the legislature might, in an academic hypothetical, be imagined to select, or
that it is never excessive in relation to the crime and to alternative methods
of punishment. But there are at least some crimes so serious, so qualitatively
different from other crimes, that a qualitatively different penalty is called
for out of our understanding of the seriousness of the offense. The Eighth
Amendment does not bar such a penalty.

> There is one crime for which neither fines nor incarceration may provide
> an adequate remedy: murder. The cost to the victim is very high, and may
> indeed approach infinity. . . . Even prolonged incarceration may not im-
> pose on the murderer costs equal to those of the victim. [Posner, *Economic
> Analysis of Law* 364 (1973).]

At least in relation to murder death is manifestly "proportional" and hence
not excessive. And, of course, it is arguably even more appropriate in relation to certain aggravated forms of murder; there are some crimes so heinous
that death seems the only appropriate social reply consistent with our beliefs
about the seriousness of the offense. Any more "moderate" reply denigrates
the seriousness of the crime and the loss to the victims.

3. Capital Punishment Incapacitates Dangerous Offenders.

It is, perhaps, almost too obvious to dwell upon that those who have been
executed cannot commit additional capital crimes. Their execution incapacitates them and saves the lives of those whom they would have killed if
they had been allowed to remain alive.

It has been argued in response that the recidivism rate for murder is low,
and that incapacitation therefore is not an adequate justification for capital
punishment. Although the premise is correct, the conclusion does not follow. There are some sociopathic individuals who, although not insane by any
definition, are so immune to normal forms of social control that they are
quite apt to commit additional murders even if sentenced to life imprisonment without possibility of parole. These individuals can be detected, and,
once detected, it should be constitutionally permissible to execute them.

For example, the defendant in *State* v. *Jarrette,* 284 N.C. 625, petition
for a writ of certiorari pending, No. 73–6877, was sentenced to a term of

imprisonment for two separate murders. While serving that term he escaped and, within two days of his escape, kidnapped and raped a 16-year-old girl and robbed and murdered a 16-year-old boy. We submit that this defendant has sufficiently indicated a proclivity repeatedly to commit heinous offenses so that execution would be justified solely by the need to incapacitate him. Petitioner Jurek also may be within this category. Within the federal prison system there are a number of individuals who have been placed into administrative segregation on a continuous basis because, even in the carefully structured prison existence, they are essentially uncontrollable and likely to commit additional violent offenses that might result in death.[26]

We would scarcely argue that the need to incapacitate certain offenders is a good ground for the execution of all offenders. But offenders may by their actions become open to capital punishment under this rationale, perhaps after committing a second murder.[27] In any event, this justification for capital punishment, like the other justifications, does not stand alone. It is cumulative with the others; together, even if not separately, they indicate that legislatures rationally could decide that capital punishment is an appropriate response to some crimes. The Constitution requires no more.

B. Capital Punishment Is Accepted by Modern American Society

The best available evidence that the public has not rejected capital punishment lies in the actions of the representatives of that public. Since the decision less than four years ago in *Furman* v. *Georgia, supra,* at least thirty-five states (*Fowler* Pet. Br. App. A; *Jurek* Pet. Br. App. 2, Sub-app. A and App. 4) and the United States (App. C, *infra*) have enacted statutes providing for the death penalty for at least some crimes, and other states are considering whether to take similar action. Such statutes could not have been enacted in so many states in such a short period of time if our society rejected capital punishment.

This blunt fact cannot be avoided with the contention that elected legislators and chief executives do not necessarily reflect the moral belief of

---

26. The Bureau of Prisons holds one individual who has been convicted of killing three people while in prison. No action other than execution (or, perhaps, constant and heavy sedation) can surely prevent him from killing again. The Bureau holds 20 other individuals who, while serving sentences of 25 years or more for various crimes, have been convicted of murdering a fellow inmate or a member of the prison staff. The prospect of an additional sentence of imprisonment is unlikely to dissuade these individuals from their pattern of aggressive behavior.

27. See 49 U.S.C. (Supp. IV) 1473 (c) (7) (B) (i), reprinted in App. C, *infra*, pages 22a–23a; Section 2401 (a) (2) (B) of the proposed revision to the federal criminal code, reprinted in App. D, *infra*, page 25a.

the communities they represent. They certainly reflect it more accurately than does the judiciary, which was made independent precisely in order to insulate judges from majority sentiment. The assumption underlying representative democracy is that the legislative process reflects the will of the people, and that if legislators interpret this will inaccurately new legislators, more sensitive to the public's desires, will be elected and unacceptable laws repealed. Petitioners dispute that assumption and seek an anomalous referendum among judges as a proxy for the "true" will of the electorate. That is not the function of judicial review in our constitutional system.

The attempt to attack capital punishment by distinguishing between the people and their elected representatives fails on other grounds as well. If the distinction were to be made, the salient difference that appears is that the representatives are better informed than the electorate. The former have had to debate the issue of capital punishment, to listen to the arguments for and against, and to confront and make the moral and prudential choices.

Petitioners' object of distinguishing between the society and its representatives, however, is not to prove that the generality of voters are better informed or more "enlightened" morally than their representatives but to suggest, in fact to speculate, that the sentiment of the public, contrary to that of the representatives, may be against capital punishment. That speculation may not properly be entertained by a court reviewing a legislative determination. A court's constitutional function does not encompass guessing what a referendum might show.

If such speculation were relevant, however, what direct evidence there is suggests that the people themselves support the death penalty; there is no social consensus that the ultimate punishment is barbaric, or even that it is offensive. Far from it. For example, after the Supreme Court of California struck down the death penalty under that state's constitution, the people of California promptly amended their constitution by initiative. The vote in favor of the initiative was overwhelming. California Constitution Art. I, §27. A referendum in 1968 in Massachusetts showed that the citizens of that state also support capital punishment.[28] Evidence from public opinion polls also indicates that popular support for the death penalty has been increasing in recent years and that supporters of capital punishment outnumber opponents by a ratio of two to one. See S. Rep. No. 93–721, 93d Cong., 1st Sess. 13–14 (1974) (reprinting polls). Cf. Vidmar & Ellsworth, *Public Opinion and the Death Penalty,* 26 Stan. L. Rev. 1245, 1249 (1974). We do not introduce

---

28. The results are reproduced in *Commonwealth* v. *O'Neal, supra,* 339 N.E.2d at 708 (Reardon, J., dissenting).

the results of these polls as a suggestion that the constitutionality of a particular penalty depends on today's straw polls. The interpretation of survey research may be a legislative function; it is not a judicial function. We cite it merely to demonstrate that, even if one proceeded on an incorrect view of the judicial function, the evidence necessary to a judgment against the death penalty is not only absent but contradicted. The polls offer no evidence that the public rejects or is revolted by the idea of capital punishment; instead, the public supports the penalty.

There is other and more persuasive evidence of the feelings of the people in general. No defendant may be sent to his death unless he first is convicted by a jury of his peers, and that conviction requires the unanimous vote of twelve.[29] If there were overwhelming rejection of the death penalty in the community, juries (which may not be death-qualified, *Witherspoon* v. *Illinois,* 391 U.S. 510) would fail to reach verdicts condemning men to death. But the fact that there have been more than 150 such convictions and death sentences in 1974 alone demonstrates that this is not so. Some juries may fail to convict; many do convict, unanimously.

The only remaining indicia from which it might be concluded that the death penalty actually has been rejected by society at large is the fact that death in recent years has been imposed on only a small number of those who have committed capital crimes. The argument proceeds to the false conclusion that this demonstrates that public acceptance of the idea of capital punishment is a mirage—that capital punishment is accepted in theory but rejected in fact.

To a great extent the decline in the use of capital punishment in recent years is the effect of judicial activity—of stays forbidding the death penalty pending completion of additional litigation and collateral attacks; of judicial willingness to find in a capital case error that would be unnoticed or "harmless" in another case; of an expanded arsenal of procedural claims available for collateral attack; of the *Furman* decision itself and the litigation that preceded it. Such inactivity as has resulted from these causes shows no rejection of the death penalty itself; it shows at most that the criminal justice system is increasingly willing to examine the propriety of a particular death penalty. To the extent executions have been stayed by the federal judiciary, the "trend" against capital punishment has been produced by individuals not accountable to the will of the people. Federal judges were afforded life tenure

---

29. No state provides for capital juries of less than twelve, and none allows conviction of such an offense by other than unanimous vote. See *Johnson* v. *Louisiana,* 406 U.S. 356; *Apodaca* v. *Oregon,* 406 U.S. 404; *Williams* v. *Florida,* 399 U.S. 78, 89, 103.

in order to provide insulation from such influences, and it would therefore be inaccurate to interpret judicial queasiness over capital punishment as an expression of the popular will.

To the extent that the decrease in the number of deaths by execution in recent years has been the result of legislative or executive activity, it is consistent with explanations other than "rejection" of the use of death as an instrument of social policy:

> To be sure, the penalty of death is infrequently imposed. An entirely valid inference from this bare fact would be, not that the society has repudiated the penalty, but that it wishes to preserve its use to a small number of cases. A reluctance to impose a penalty is not necessarily the same as its repudiation. Reluctance may spring from moral revulsion; but it may just as commonly proceed from a humane and heart-felt sorrow. [Polsby, *supra*, at 20.]

A reverence for the importance of human life may explain a thoroughly considered (and entirely acceptable) social policy to limit to a minimum the number who must be put to death, while reserving that extreme penalty to a few extreme cases. Perhaps, alternatively, reserving the sanction to a few "exemplary" cases, sparing others who might be "eligible" to die but whose deaths would add little to whatever social goals can be served by some lesser number of executions. The Constitution ought not to be read to compel the state to engage in mass executions in order to preserve the power to execute anyone at all.

C. Differences of Opinion Concerning the Propriety of the Death Penalty Must Be Resolved in Favor of the Legislative Judgment

We have suggested that the cruel and unusual punishments clause of the Eighth Amendment, understood in its historical context, properly is interpreted as a device for enforcing the overwhelming social consensus of the times, and properly may be used to curb aberrations occurring when isolated individuals (or legislatures), through ignorance or malice, flaunt those standards and create or impose punishments utterly unacceptable to society and degrading to society's dignity. This statement of the scope of the amendment carries with it a statement about the limits of judicial review. A punishment is not "cruel and unusual" unless utterly outside the bounds of social tolerance.

The bases of support for capital punishment that we have discussed above suggest that, wherever the bounds of social tolerance may be, they are not exceeded by capital punishment. It is approved by many legislatures and imposed by numerous unanimous juries. It is supported by substantial majorities in opinion polls. It is not excessive when compared to crimes such as murder. There is room for legislative debate and honest difference of opinion concerning whether it deters others and expresses legitimate social approbation of heinous deeds.

The careful balance of considerations supporting the death penalty against the moral or humane concerns of those who oppose death perhaps accounts for the great debate capital punishment has generated throughout the history of this country.[30] It has been a subject of debate since the founding of the republic (see, *e.g.,* Bradford, *An Enquiry How Far the Punishment of Death is Necessary in Pennsylvania* (1793)), and the debate bids well to continue. It has been a subject of intense debate precisely because there is much to be said on each side, and because neither proponent nor opponent has any argument that must convince all rational people of that side's validity.

Even if the cruel and unusual punishments clause were not limited to enforcing a social consensus that has broken down in an individual case, the propriety of the death penalty would nevertheless be apparent. The death penalty is rationally supported and rationally supportable: reasonable men can and do disagree about the merits of capital punishment, but reasonable men cannot say that no reasonable man would support the death penalty. Because the evidence and the moral concerns are so balanced, the Court cannot conclude that the legislatures and juries have made such a "clear mistake" (cf. Thayer, *The Origin and Scope of the American Doctrine of Constitutional Law,* 7 Harv. L. Rev. 129 (1893)), that their considered deliberations must be disregarded and the law set aside. Or, as Judge Learned Hand put the matter, when dealing with an amendment that grew out of the seventeenth century procedural victories of Parliament over the Crown:

> [I]n such cases I cannot see why courts should intervene, unless it appears
> that the statutes are not honest choices between values and sacrifices honestly appraised. [Hand, *The Bill of Rights* 66 (1958).]

There are in this area no clear mistakes by the legislature. A given legislature may be "mistaken" in applying capital punishment to a given crime or

---

30. What better evidence of the equipoise of the debate, and consequently of the validity of legislative choice, than this concession (*Fowler* Pet. Br. 118–19): "The opposition to capital punishment . . . has been vigorously asserted on the basis of 'fundamental moral and societal values in our civilization and in our society.' Proponents of the death penalty have responded with equal moral fervor. Surely no other criminal sanction has evoked such passionate, ceaseless philosophical argument" (footnotes omitted).

another legislature may be equally "mistaken" in failing to apply it. Indeed, there seems to be no way to exclude the possibility that an omniscient observer would conclude that all legislatures were mistaken in believing that capital punishment is ever appropriate or, to the contrary, that capital punishment is appropriate to many more instances of crime than legislatures and juries now believe. But the data such an omniscient observer would use, and the standards he would apply when weighing the moral values implicated in the death penalty, are beyond the ken of courts and perhaps beyond the ken of mankind. There are no neutral principles by which the death penalty may be condemned; there is nothing more than a belief that the legislature, after consideration of weighty policy considerations on both sides, may have chosen the "unwise" course. That is not enough. Courts

> are not representative bodies. They are not designed to be a good reflex of a democratic society. Their judgment is best informed, and therefore most dependable, within narrow limits. Their essential quality is detachment, founded on independence. History teaches us that the independence of the judiciary is jeopardized when courts become embroiled in the passions of the day and assume primary responsibility in choosing between competing political, economic, and social pressures.
>
> Primary responsibility for adjusting the interests which compete in the situation before us of necessity belongs to the Congress. The nature of the power to be exercised by this Court has been delineated in decisions not charged with the emotional appeal of situations such as those now before us. We are to set aside the judgment of those whose duty it is to legislate only if there is no reasonable basis for it. . . . Beyond these powers we must not go; we must scrupulously observe the narrow limits of judicial authority even though self-restraint is alone set over us. [*Dennis* v. *United States,* 341 U.S. 494, 525–26 (Frankfurter, J., concurring).]

The core of petitioners' argument is that Congress and thirty-five state legislatures have lost their moral compass and can no longer be trusted to legislate in the interest of the entire people. Petitioners ask this Court to assume the tasks of those legislatures that do not share their moral values. That, of course, is not the constitutional function assigned the federal judiciary.

D. Several of the Empirical Observations by the Justices Who Concurred in Furman Require Reassessment in Light of Subsequent Evidence

The Justices who comprised the majority in *Furman* advanced several rationales for their decisions. Some of the arguments have their roots in the history of the cruel and unusual punishments clause. We have addressed these arguments at pages 16–34, *supra*. Other of the arguments are more factual in nature and were facilitated by a number of essentially empirical observations about the nature and utility of capital punishment. We believe that the force of many of these arguments has been eroded by post-*Furman* developments, and that others are factual arguments properly within the legislative sphere.

1. At least two of the Justices who concurred in *Furman* relied upon the belief that the "legislative will is not frustrated if the [death] penalty is never imposed" (408 U.S. at 311 (White, J., concurring); *id.* at 309 (Stewart, J., concurring)). That is an empirical observation. At the time *Furman* was decided, the validity of that statement could have been disputed. But we submit that the evidence is now in, and that there is no longer room for doubt. Congress and the state legislatures have responded to *Furman* by enacting statutes that disclose their will. Indeed, several states enacted mandatory death penalty statutes; given by this Court's decision in *Furman* what they believed to be a choice between sentencing all of those convicted of first degree murder to death, and sentencing all to life imprisonment, these states selected death. Some legislatures have responded to *Furman* not by extending mercy to all, but by removing mercy that previously had been extended to some. It is now clear that the legislative will *is* frustrated unless the death penalty is imposed upon some individuals.

2. At least three Justices expressed the view in *Furman* that capital punishment is cruel because it "goes beyond what is necessary not only in degree, but in kind." See 408 U.S. at 287–90, 301–302 (Brennan, J., concurring); *id.* at 306, 309 (Stewart, J., concurring); *id.* at 347–54 (Marshall, J., concurring). This proposition, too, is empirical. Its validity depends upon the meaning of the word "necessary." If that word refers to the perceptions of legislatures, any doubts that may have existed now have been resolved, for legislature after legislature has responded to *Furman* by enacting (or reenacting) capital punishment statutes, demonstrating that the legislature believes that capital punishment is "necessary."

The proposition might alternatively be an objective observation of either of two sorts. The first—the "strong" sense of "necessary"—is that capital punishment is not necessary because modern society can survive without it. But this would be a test without any support in the Constitution. No legislation is required to stand or fall on the question whether that particular law is essential, is a *sine qua non,* for the preservation of our way of life. The death penalty obviously is not necessary in this strong sense, nor need it be.

The weaker sense of "necessary" is used in constitutional adjudication: a statute passes constitutional muster if it serves ascertainable legislative purposes.[31] The argument then would be that the death penalty is not "necessary" because it serves no useful purpose. We have discussed at pages 34–51, *supra,* of this brief the purposes served by capital punishment. Although there may be debate concerning the effectiveness of capital punishment in achieving these ends, we do not see how it is possible to contend that it would be arbitrary or irrational for a legislature to resolve such disputes in favor of the effectiveness (and hence "necessity") of capital punishment. The empirical nature of the dispute suggests that legislative resolution is appropriate.

3. Mr. Justice White argued (408 U.S. at 312) that "a major goal of the criminal law—to deter others by punishing the convicted criminal—would not be substantially served where the penalty is so seldom invoked that it ceases to be the credible threat essential to influence the conduct of others. . . . [C]ommon sense and experience tell us that seldom-enforced laws become ineffective measures for controlling human conduct and that the death penalty, unless imposed with sufficient frequency, will make little contribution to deterring those crimes for which it may be exacted." See also *id.* at 309 (Stewart, J., concurring).

It is now clear that some states, of which North Carolina is one example, are willing to impose the death penalty with substantial frequency. The concern of Mr. Justice White would not apply to these states. But even as to other states that elect to make less use of the death penalty, this argument is empirical, and we do not believe that it is accurate. Some states simply have made the legislative judgment that their ends can be achieved without the need to execute large numbers of people, that such harshness would be unnecessary. What judicially ascertainable facts would enable the Court to impeach this judgment? If the legislature is entitled to conclude that 100 executions would deter 500 murders, by what standard could a court conclude that five executions would deter none?[32] A legislature entitled to conclude that 100 executions would deter 500 murders also is entitled to conclude, based on the available evidence, that five executions would deter 25 murders. It equally properly could conclude that five executions would deter 50 murders, for there may be diminishing returns to executions, just as there

---

31. See, *e.g., Marshall* v. *United States*, 414 U.S. 417, which uses this standard to adjudicate a challenge to the rationality of a statute imprisoning some criminals while allowing others to receive treatment.

32. Cf. *Buckley* v. *Valco*, No. 75–436, decided January 30, 1976, Mr. Justice White, concurring and dissenting, slip op. 5–11.

are diminishing returns to many of our other activities. A few executions in a state each year might well generate as much publicity as many executions, and if potential criminals desire to avoid the *risk* of execution as well as the actuality of it many would hesitate—and some would desist—from committing murder.

But the core of the matter is simply that it is for the legislatures to choose the goals that will be pursued. There is no constitutional requirement that the legislature must select the goal of deterring a substantial number of murders yearly. As we have said before, a "small" saving in human life achieved by a "small" deterrent effect is not so insignificant that it can be denigrated as a permissible basis for legislative choice. See pages 42–43, *supra*.

III. Capital Punishment Is Not Imposed on the Basis of Race

The selection of those to be executed might be open to serious question if it were influenced by the race of the defendant. We submit that the data do not show that race is a factor.[33] We have included in Appendix A to this brief an analysis of the findings of the studies relied upon by petitioners and others. These studies contradict each other, and the most recent (and sophisticated) study, the Stanford Note (*A Study of the California Penalty Jury in First-Degree-Murder Cases: Standardless Sentencing*, 21 Stan. L. Rev. 1297 (1969)), found no evidence whatever of racial discrimination in capital punishment for murder. We are aware of no properly-conducted study that supports a contrary conclusion.

The only studies that even inferentially suggest a possibility of racial discrimination were conducted in the South during a time when blacks were often excluded from grand and petit juries. They do not demonstrate that discrimination persists now that blacks sit in judgment on other blacks. It is true that both the National Prisoner Statistics (Law Enforcement Assistance Administration, *Capital Punishment 1974*, Table 16 (1975)) and information compiled by the NAACP (*Jurek* Pet. Br. 83–84, n.147) indicate that approximately 50 to 60 percent of all those sentenced to death are black. This is only the beginning of the inquiry, however. In order to determine whether this indicates discrimination, we would need to know what proportion of all capital crimes are committed by blacks.[34] Although there is no direct

---

33. See also *Furman v. Georgia, supra*, 408 U.S. at 389–90, n.12 (Burger, C.J., dissenting); *id.* at 310, n.14 (Stewart, J., concurring); *id.* at 447 (Powell, J., dissenting).

34. "These statistics alone, of course, do not reveal elements of judicial bias in the administration

measure of that proportion, the number of arrests for willful felonious homicide may be the closest approximation. The Uniform Crime Reports of the Federal Bureau of Investigation (*Crime in the United States 1974,* 191 (1975)) indicate that 57.1 percent of those arrested for willful felonious homicides are black. There is, therefore, little or no discernable discrimination against blacks from the time of arrest through the pronouncement of a sentence of death; blacks are not a higher proportion of those sentenced to die than they are of those arrested for the most serious types of murder.[35] Nor is there any evidence that blacks are arrested for their crimes more often than are whites. The evidence concerning arrest is consistent with the evidence concerning the race of the victim. Exactly half of all murder victims are black. *Crime in the United States 1974,* 15 (1975). If capital punishment deters murders (as legislatures are entitled to conclude), it would follow that abolition of capital punishment would work to the detriment of the poor and the blacks, who are disproportionately the victims of murder.

If it is proper to assume that some individuals in the criminal justice system discriminate on account of race or other impermissible factors, the existence or extent of this discrimination will vary from time to time, place to place, and state to state. Proof of discrimination by the prosecutor and juries of one county in one state would not prove that petitioners in these five cases are the objects of discrimination. It is unlikely that discrimination can account for the sentences imposed upon petitioners Gregg, Jurek, and Proffitt, who are white. The argument that blacks may be treated harshly when they have committed crimes against whites is not an argument against the penalty imposed upon a black who murders another black, as was the case in *Fowler.*

In short, the possibility of racial discrimination in the selection or imposition of a particular punishment depends strictly upon the facts and circumstances of the case. It is not an argument against all capital punishment for all time. Indeed, the argument has nothing whatever to do with capital punishment. *Any* punishment selected or augmented on racial grounds is im-

---

of criminal law. It is also well recognized that blacks in American society . . . have a criminal homicide rate that is between four and ten times greater than that of whites." Wolfgang and Riedel, *Race, Judicial Discretion, and the Death Penalty,* 407 Annals 119, 123 (1973). See also White, *The Role of the Social Sciences in Determining the Constitutionality of Capital Punishment,* 13 Duq. L. Rev. 279, 281–85 (1974).

35. Many murders or other capital crimes grow out of other violent felonies. The Uniform Crime Reports indicate that blacks are arrested for these crimes, too, in disproportionate numbers. Of those arrested for robbery 62.3 percent are black; of those arrested for aggravated assault 41.2 percent are black. *Crime in the United States 1974,* 191 (1975).

permissible. No petitioner has contended that he was discriminated against on account of his race. Accordingly, the possibility that racial discrimination exists upon occasion in the criminal justice system is not an argument against the penalty imposed upon petitioners.

IV. Capital Punishment May Be Imposed Under the Criminal Justice System's Present Procedures. Each Procedure Is Either Required or Permitted by the Constitution Itself

Petitioners devote much of their briefs (see also *Fowler* Pet. Br. 42–101, upon which several petitioners rely) to the argument that the procedures for processing capital cases are arbitrary and capricious. Petitioners object to the discretion involved in the prosecutor's decision to charge, in plea bargaining, in the jury's determination of guilt and punishments, and in executive clemency. This "elaborate argument . . . does not need an elaborate answer."[36] Petitioners obviously do not contend for a system in which the prosecutor must charge a capital offense whenever there has been a killing, in which the defendant could not plead to a lesser offense, in which the jury must convict, in which clemency could not be exercised. We would then have the rule of the Tyrant which ancient Greece replaced with the rule of law millenia ago. The generalization that the death penalty always violates the Eighth Amendment can be made *only* because the discretion petitioners find objectionable will be inevitable so long as we have a constitutional system of criminal justice.[37]

Indeed, it is strange that petitioners even frame this procedural argument in terms of the Eighth Amendment. One would have supposed that if the evil is in the process, the remedy is in the command that no person may be "deprived of life . . . without due process of law." That of course was the argument in *McGautha* v. *California,* 402 U.S. 183, 207, with respect to jury discretion, and the Court rejected it. To cast the same argument differently

---

36. Mr. Justice Holmes, in *United States* v. *Wurzbach*, 280 U.S. 396, 399.

37. In regard to prosecutorial discretion, the brief in *Fowler*, upon which several petitioners rely, points out that it is "*necessarily and unavoidably arbitrary*" (Br. 53) (emphasis changed).

In regard to plea bargaining, the brief notes that the acceptance of pleas to lesser offenses "is doubtless inevitable" (*id*. at 61).

In regard to the exercise of discretion by the jury, the brief does not impugn the jurors' integrity but only "acknowledge[s] that they are human" (*id*. at 75) and that there is an "inevitable propensity" for juries to alleviate the harshest of penalties (*id*. at 91–92).

In regard to executive clemency, the brief appears to recognize that the very concept encompasses discretion (*id*. at 95–96). See *Schick* v. *Reed*, 419 U.S. 256.

and say that the Eighth Amendment proscribes some unattained and unattainable system for processing capital cases is to contend that this constitutional provision contains its own refutation. The Eighth Amendment cannot mean that, although the death penalty is a permissible type of punishment, it can never be imposed under our criminal justice system because the system cannot, should not, be altered to meet petitioners' objections to it. Yet (unless we misapprehended their position) that is what petitioners would have this Court rule.

Petitioners state that they are not suggesting that the selective discretion present at any of the separate stages of the criminal process would be constitutionally objectionable in a non-capital case. With all respect, we submit that they are suggesting just that. There is not a single argument petitioners put forward in this regard that could not equally be made in regard, for example, to the penalty of life imprisonment for first-degree murder. Petitioners argue that the "procedure for processing capital cases involves a series of uncontrolled discretionary judgments that operate to spare the lives of some defendants while others in similar circumstances are sentenced to die."[38] If the Court accepts that proposition as the basis for striking down the death penalty, how can the Court hold unobjectionable the "procedure for processing criminal cases which involves a series of 'uncontrolled' discretionary judgments that operate to spare the liberty of some defendants while others in similar circumstances are sentenced to imprisonment?"[39]

Petitioners' analysis begs the question whether the difference in penalty is a constitutional difference. If a state properly can prescribe the death penalty for at least some crimes, as we have argued above, then it is impossible to turn to the Eighth Amendment as a source of a constitutionally-supported principle that this difference in the penalty imposed requires a difference in the process used. Perhaps one could argue that for due process purposes death is different because more serious, and that the process that is "due" for crimes with less severe sanctions is insufficient for more serious ones. But petitioners have eschewed the due process argument and, as we noted above, a similar due process argument failed to persuade the Court in *McGautha*.

Since a conclusion by this Court that the procedures of the criminal justice system are too discretionary will inevitably impugn those procedures in regard to penalties other than death, claims of that nature properly should

---

38. See *Fowler* Pet. Br. 15.

39. Appellate review is part of what petitioners call the "procedure for processing capital cases," yet it cannot be that the death penalty is unconstitutional because, for example, this Court has discretion to deny petitions for writs of certiorari in capital cases.

be consigned to particular allegations against particular areas of discretion, rather than to an overall, and therefore less-well-focused, inquiry. Thus, for example, petitioners contend that capital crimes are so vaguely defined that a jury sometimes will have difficulty ascertaining when one has been committed. But, of course, this is not always so. There is no difficulty in the definition of murder by lying in wait, or by poison; there is little difficulty in the definition of murder for hire or in the course of a kidnapping. The definitional difficulties in other forms of murder are more considerable: premeditation and malice aforethought invite consideration of a sometimes elusive element of intent.

But if there is to be a vagueness-type challenge to a particular definition, it is a challenge potentially available to one whose conduct is within the zone of uncertainty, not one whose conduct is clearly prohibited. *Parker* v. *Levy,* 417 U.S. 733; *United States* v. *Harriss,* 347 U.S. 612, 618. The assertion that some capital statutes are vague as applied to some crimes committed by other individuals is an inadequate foundation for petitioners' contention that capital punishment itself inevitably is arbitrarily or capriciously imposed.[40]

For the foregoing reasons, we believe petitioners' procedural contention must be rejected. We are, however, somewhat hesitant to conclude our discussion of the matter at this point. The discretion inherent in our system of criminal justice may need no defense, but it serves such important goals that further elaboration is, we believe, appropriate.

A. Discretion in the Criminal Justice System Serves Important Social Functions

The need for some discretion in a system of criminal justice arises because the varieties of human endeavor are endless and unpredictable. The variety of the circumstances of offense and offender is so great that it cannot usefully be anticipated in a single criminal statute. Nor, for that matter, is our language sufficiently precise to enable legislation to account for these differences, even if all could be anticipated. Perhaps it approaches the limit of human abilities to specify some reasonably clear criteria that mark off those

---

40. It would be more appropriate to tender more narrow challenges to other sources of discretion in the criminal justice process as well. Many of the points of choice discussed by petitioners could be altered to produce more predictable and uniform decisions in response to particularized complaint. See, *e.g.*, Ark. Stat. Ann. 41–4714 (1973 Cum. Supp.) (governor must give reasons for commuting death sentence); Ill. Rev. Stat. ch. 38, Section 1005–8-1A (1974 Cum. Supp.) (prosecutor must seek death when aggravating circumstances appear); N.Y. ch. 367, Section 10 (1974 Legis. Assembly, May 6, 1974) (defendant may not plead guilty to a capital crime).

whose crimes are sufficiently serious that capital punishment is "authorized," and to provide that for at least some of those for whom it is authorized, it is also appropriate.

In the formative years of this country most statutes providing for the death penalty were "mandatory"; all convicted under them were sentenced to death. For the reasons discussed in this Court's decision in *McGautha, supra,* 402 U.S. at 196–208, this procedure was unsatisfactory because these statutes selected some men who did not merit the ultimate penalty—depending on the reaction of the jury, such individuals unjustly might be sent to death, or they might be acquitted entirely as the jury, acting as the conscience of the community, refused *despite* the evidence to convict a man whom they believe should not be executed. The conscious decision to extend to the jury the ability to do openly what it had been forced to do covertly was one of the major advances of American criminal justice:

> Those who have come to grips with the hard task of actually attempting to draft means of channeling capital sentencing discretion have confirmed the lesson taught by the history recounted above. To identify before the fact those characteristics of criminal homicides and their perpetrators which call for the death penalty, and to express these characteristics in language which can be fairly understood and applied by the sentencing authority, appear to be tasks which are beyond present human ability. [*McGautha, supra,* 402 U.S. at 204.]

Nevertheless, in response to this Court's decision in *Furman,* those states that have reenacted death penalty statutes have attempted to structure and confine the discretion available to the sentencing authority. One course, adopted by North Carolina and Louisiana, eliminates sentencing discretion entirely. Another course, adopted by the United States (see App. C, *infra*), Georgia, Texas, and Florida, enumerates those aggravating characteristics without which no crime is "capital."[41] This, in turn (petitioners assert) simply transfers the exercise of discretion to other locations in the criminal justice system. Even if we were to agree with this premise, the conclusion that the death penalty is unconstitutional does not follow, for we believe that *McGautha* correctly concluded that some discretion is permissibly a part of the process of determining who is to be executed. Cf. *Winston* v. *United States,* 172 U.S. 303 (attempt to limit jury discretion in capital case impermissible).

---

41. See Note, "Discretion and the Constitutionality of the New Death Penalty Statutes", 87 *Harv. L. Rev.* 1690, 1699–1712 (1974), for a more complete typology of the post-*Furman* statutes.

One objective of modern criminal justice is to tailor the punishment, at least to some extent, to the offender as well as to the offense. We assume that petitioners would not embrace a rule that legitimated capital punishment only when it followed automatically and without variation from the mere fact of an offense described in the broadest possible terms; that alternative has been rejected (without the need for constitutional compulsion) by the states. Still less can be said that the Constitution *requires* that all offenders equally receive terms of life imprisonment (although we do not deny the legislatures' power to make that choice, too). Despite the superficial uniformity of such a course, there is real inequality in treating identically individuals who are different in essential characteristics and who have committed crimes factually dissimilar, even though language and human forethought are inadequate to commit all relevant differences to expression in the form of "rules." And, if the Constitution admits of any discretion in this fashion, the discretion currently present in the criminal justice system is not so excessive or unprincipled that its mere presence as a means of administering mercy precludes the imposition of any capital punishment whatsoever.

B. The Discretion in the Criminal Justice System Does Not Result in "Freakish" Imposition of Capital Punishment

Four Justices in the *Furman* majority asserted that capital punishment is unconstitutionally "unusual" because it is infrequently used. See 408 U.S. at 256–257 (Douglas, J., concurring); *id.* at 291–292 (Brennan, J., concurring); *id.* at 309 (Stewart, J., concurring); *id.* at 312–313 (White, J., concurring).

This is a proposition that deserves further analysis. It is not immediately clear why a particular individual should be able to block his own execution (if it is otherwise justified) on the ground that not enough individuals are being executed with him. But, pretermitting that difficulty, we believe that the problem with the argument is that frequency is a relative phenomenon. Capital punishment can be "infrequent" only in relation to something else. The implicit assumption may be that frequency should be assessed in relation to the number of convictions for crimes for which the death penalty is authorized.[42]

---

42. Several Justices also intimated that capital punishment is unusual because it is imposed for a diminishing number of crimes. We do not believe that this is an argument against the death penalty; legislatures should not be taken to task for reevaluating the need for this extreme sanction and confining its use to those crimes for which it is both most appropriate (in the sense that the punishment is proportional to the offense) and most needed (in the sense that society must deter the commission of the offense and express its disapprobation). In any event, the absolute

Assuming that this is the proper standard of comparison, the available evidence indicates that when capital punishment is authorized for a serious crime it is prescribed relatively often. For example, in California, during the period studied by Note, *A Study of the California Penalty Jury in First-Degree-Murder Cases: Standardless Sentencing,* 21 Stan. L. Rev. 1297, 1299 (1969), the jury set the death penalty for 103 of 238 individuals convicted of first degree murder. In North Carolina a death sentence now is imposed upon every individual convicted of first degree murder, and there have been more than 115 such convictions in the last three years (*Woodson* Pet. Br. App. A; *Fowler* Pet. Br. App. B).

We do not believe, however, that this is the relevant comparison for constitutional purposes. It would be more appropriate to compare the number of executions carried out with the perceived need for the death penalty. Sentences of life imprisonment, too, are "infrequent" compared with sentences of five years or less. Sentences of life imprisonment are rarely carried out, for the individual subject to such a sentence often is released on parole. But this hardly establishes that life imprisonment is unconstitutionally unusual, for the constitutional concept must include an element of proportionality to the perceived social need to impose the punishment in question. The paucity of actual executions in recent years—to the extent it is attributable to explanations other than the decisions of this Court and other courts—suggests that our society has decided to confine the use of its extreme sanction within fairly narrow bounds, that although a large absolute number of executions is not thought necessary, some smaller number is appropriate. See pages 42–43, 56–57, *supra.* The death penalty should not be held to be unconstitutionally unusual unless it is very infrequent in relation to the perceived need for it, and there is no reason to believe that it is infrequent under this standard.

For many of the same reasons, we respectfully suggest that the death penalty, when actually imposed, is not imposed "capriciously," "wantonly," or "freakishly" (see 408 U.S. at 309 (Stewart, J., concurring); *id.* at 295 (Brennan, J., concurring). Petitioners embellish this argument, which, as we have argued at pages 69–76, *supra,* is a Due Process attack in disguise. For that reason, if accepted, it would imperil the validity of any conceivable

frequency of capital punishment is still quite high. *Furman* spared approximately 600 individuals; in less than four years since *Furman,* and despite the damping effect that decision produces on the use of the death penalty, more than 400 individuals have been placed under sentence of death, 151 of them in 1974 alone. Petitioner Jurek concedes that this is a "not inconsiderable" number. *Jurek* Pet. Br. 67, n.108. In large measure the "infrequency" of capital punishment is due to judicial decisions, and so cannot be assigned as an argument against the constitutionality of a legislative decision that some capital punishment is necessary.

penalty. Is it "freakish" when an individual is sentenced to five years' imprisonment rather than three, when the statutory maximum is life imprisonment?[43] To argue that capital punishment makes a difference in this regard is
to beg the question—if it can be explained *why* capital punishment makes the
difference, then the constitutionality of the death penalty can be resolved in
Eighth Amendment terms, *based on the nature of that difference,* without regard
to the process by which it is imposed. And if the nature of that difference
cannot be drawn from the Eighth Amendment, the fact that the imposition
of capital punishment is no more arbitrary than the imposition of any other
particular punishment under our constitutional system of criminal justice
disposes of the argument based on "arbitrariness."

To the extent the argument based upon "arbitrariness" has any content,
it must be directed to the nature of the process by which the sentence has
been prescribed. "[C]an there be any reason to accuse a state of arbitrariness in passing out sentences of death if the process cannot be shown to have
been operated unfairly in producing this result?" Polsby, *The Death of Capital
Punishment?* Furman v. Georgia, 1972 Sup. Ct. Rev. 1, 14. And, at this point,
the argument collapses, for, as we discuss at pages 82–100, *infra,* each of the
steps by which the death penalty is imposed is either required or permitted
by the Constitution itself. If there is no unfairness in the process, the result
of that process cannot be unfair.

It would make more sense to say that the result of the process by which
death is prescribed as punishment for crime is "freakish" if some random or
invidious factor were introduced that aggravated the potential punishment
for specific individuals. But that is not what happens. The discretion inherent
in the criminal justice system is weighted heavily in favor of mercy. The ability of the prosecutor to charge lesser crimes and to accept a plea bargain; the
power of the jury to acquit altogether or to convict of lesser included offenses; the power of the executive to grant clemency; these and other instances
of discretion serve to mitigate the harshness of a penalty, not to increase its
harshness. As Professor Polsby put the matter (1972 Sup. Ct. Rev. at 20):

> Consider arbitrariness. Does it follow "inescapably" that a punishment is
> being inflicted arbitrarily (and therefore impermissibly) when it is "in-
> flicted in a trivial number of the cases in which it is legally available"?
> It seems to me inherently plausible that juries, judges, and governors of
> states conduct themselves with deliberation and caution so as to err on

---

43. Cf. *Griffin* v. *Warden*, 517 F.2d 756 (C.A. 4), holding that the Due Process Clause allows a
state to give a prosecutor unbridled discretion to seek life imprisonment.

the side of mercy, reserving their ultimate punishment for those whose transgressions are most clearly established and seem to them most revolting. This explanation if it is accurate (and no one knows whether it is) is not arbitrariness but the antithesis of arbitrariness.

As the criminal justice system now stands, it is utterly impossible for one person or several persons, acting out of prejudice, malice, or stupidity, to inflict the death penalty. But at every stage it is possible for one person or a small group of people to prevent its infliction. The multiplication of occasions for mercy is the system's great safeguard. It cannot simultaneously be the source of its unconstitutionality.

If the explanation from mercy is incorrect, the burden of establishing its inaccuracy should fall upon those who seek to upset the judgment of the legislature. Petitioners have not discharged (or even shouldered) that burden.[44]

C. Each of the Particular Sources of Discretion in the Criminal Justice System Is Either Permitted or Compelled by the Constitution Itself

Petitioners attack the discretion now possessed by prosecutors (in conjunction with the grand jury) to decide whom to charge and with what crime; the discretion of prosecutors (in conjunction with the court) to accept a plea to a lesser and non-capital offense; the power of a jury to avoid a conviction that sends a defendant to his death either by acquitting in spite of the evidence or by convicting of a lesser included (and non-capital) offense; the power of the judge and jury to weigh aggravating and mitigating circumstances; and the power of the executive to grant clemency. We submit that the discretion

---

44. Moreover, even if (contrary to the fact) capital punishment were imposed upon a group selected at random, it is far from clear that this would be a constitutional defect. The governmental purpose often can be achieved by imposing a detriment on less than all of those who are "eligible" for it. When this can be done, random selection is the most fair device. There is no need to burden the entire population when the governmental purpose can be achieved by less onerous means. For example, people have been selected by lot for conscription into the military, while others, identically situated, have been excused. School assignments for elementary and secondary schools are often made by lot, where some pupils must be transported over a distance while others can be allowed to attend nearby schools. There are many other examples. So long as the criteria used for selection are not invidious, there can be no reasonable argument that such selection is constitutionally infirm.

For the reasons we have discussed above and at pages 42–43, 56–57, *supra*, there are sound reasons, grounded in mercy and humane compassion, for desiring to hold to a minimum the number who must be executed. If society could accomplish that aim by holding a lottery among all those convicted of first degree murder, how could it be unconstitutional to accomplish the same aim by a discretionary system of selection weighted in favor of mercy and considering the needs of the individual and the nature of his crime?

possessed by each of these actors serves important goals of criminal justice, and for that reason has been upheld by this Court as consistent with the Constitution. Moreover, several of the sources of discretion are the result of specific constitutional commands, and any attempts to confine or eliminate the discretion would be unconstitutional. Because each of these sources of discretion is either permitted or encouraged by provisions in the Constitution other than the Eighth Amendment, the product (the sentence) of this fully acceptable process cannot itself violate the Constitution.

1. The Charging Decision.

A federal prosecutor has an unfettered power to decline to bring charges against any individual. The prosecutor need not seek an indictment, and under Fed. R. Crim. P. 7(c) the United States Attorney may, by declining to sign an indictment, prevent prosecution of a case in which the grand jury has concluded that there is good ground to prosecute. See *United States* v. *Cox,* 342 F.2d 167 (C.A. 5), certiorari denied *sub. nom. Cox* v. *Hauberg,* 381 U.S. 935; *In re Grand Jury January, 1969,* 315 F. Supp. 662 (D. MD.). But this prosecutorial power is to a large extent created by the Constitution itself; it inheres in the separation of the executive function from the judicial function. Both the executive and judicial branches have independent power, not subject to control by the other, over the course of such proceedings. *Buckley* v. *Valeo,* No. 75–436, decided January 30, 1976, slip op. 132–135; *The Confiscation Cases,* 7 Wall. 454; *Georgia* v. *Mitchell,* 450 F.2d 1317 (C.A.D.C.); *Powell* v. *Katzenbach,* 359 F.2d 234 (C.A.D.C.), certiorari denied, 384 U.S. 906 (collecting cases). Cf. *Linda R.S.* v. *Richard D.,* 410 U.S. 614.

　　The federal prosecutor's discretion not to commence criminal prosecution is thus part of our constitutionally-created system of government. It is, of course, conceivable that in particular circumstances prosecutorial discretion will be abused and slanted along racial lines (see, *e.g., Yick Wo* v. *Hopkins,* 118 U.S. 356; *Littleton* v. *Berbling,* 468 F.2d 389 (C.A. 7), vacated on other grounds *sub nom. Spomer* v. *Littleton,* 414 U.S. 514) or over impermissible grounds. When that happens independent remedies are available. However, the prosecutorial discretion, which is a product of the Constitution itself, does not produce unconstitutional results merely because the prosecutor has no precise set of rules that control his prosecutorial decisions. "[T]he conscious exercise of some selectivity in enforcement is not in itself a federal constitutional violation." *Oyler* v. *Boles,* 368 U.S. 448, 456.

　　The prosecution is under a duty—indeed, a constitutional duty—not to charge and prosecute an individual unless the prosecutor legitimately believes that the individual can be convicted. The evaluation of that probability of conviction is a difficult one, involving an assessment of the evidence available, the predilections of witnesses, and the possibility that the jury (the composition of which is unknown) will agree with the prosecutor's evaluation. All of these factual inferences must then be analyzed against the available categories of crime that may be comprehended in a single criminal transaction, and a decision made about which prosecution would be most likely to succeed and would be most advantageous to the public welfare if successful. Finally, the prosecutor must evaluate the resources of his own office; because manpower is limited in relation to the number of crimes that have been committed, decisions sometimes must be made to forego particular prosecutions, even though there is a reasonable chance of conviction, in order to concentrate prosecutorial efforts where they may be more urgently needed.

In many civil law countries prosecutors are under a duty to prosecute all major crimes known to them. See Langbein, *Controlling Prosecutorial Discretion in Germany,* 41 U. Chi. L. Rev. 439 (1974); Herrmann, *The Rule of Compulsory Prosecution and the Scope of Prosecutorial Discretion in Germany,* 41 U. Chi. L. Rev. 468 (1974). Even within these compulsory prosecution systems the prosecutor remains free to evaluate the evidence; prosecution is commenced only when there is "a sufficient factual basis."[45] Moreover, the logic of compulsory prosecution is more compelling in an inquisitorial (rather than adversarial) system of criminal justice. In the inquisitorial system the court itself has substantial factfinding and prosecutorial functions; the "prosecutor" is simply an instrument to commence the process, placing further proceedings in the hands of the investigating magistrate. Restriction of prosecutorial discretion is a necessary facet of a system structured around an inquisitorial magistrate, and is simply an allocation of discretion to the magistrate rather than the prosecutor. It certainly is not, at all events, a discretion-free system. Herrmann, *supra,* at 474–503.

2. Plea Bargaining.

Although (unlike federal charging discretion) plea bargaining has not been established by the Constitution itself, it is nevertheless an essential part of our system of criminal justice and has received the approval and encouragement of this Court.[46] *Brady* v. *United States,* 397 U.S. 742, 752–753; *Santo-*

---

45. Federal Republic of Germany, Code of Criminal Procedure 152(2).

46. Sometimes, as is apparently the case in *Woodson,* a plea bargain with some defendants is absolutely essential to produce the evidence necessary to convict other participants in the crime.

bello v. *New York,* 404 U.S. 257, 260. Like the other forms of discretion present in the criminal justice system and assailed by petitioners, plea bargaining reduces the potential punishment a defendant may suffer; it never operates to increase the maximum punishment. Moreover, unlike other forms of discretion, plea bargaining operates only with the acquiescence (and usually at the behest) of the accused and works to the accused's advantage. Were it otherwise, the accused would not enter into the plea arrangement. It is difficult to understand how this procedure, operating with the permission of the accused and for his benefit, can cause the penalty received by those who do not enter into such bargains to be unconstitutional.

The most difficult question raised by plea bargaining is, petitioners assert, the failure of the prosecutor to enter into such bargains with some defendants, thereby depriving those defendants of an opportunity to escape the death penalty.[47] Perhaps a prosecutor might make such a decision for improper motives; in all probability, if such motives could be shown, the procedure would be vulnerable. Cf. *Littleton* v. *Berbling, supra.* But petitioners have not even alleged (let alone adduced proof) that such a practice exists in their states. If a prosecutor were bending his actions in a forbidden manner, it would at most impugn the acts of the prosecutor, and not be an argument against the constitutionality of all death penalties everywhere. Cf. *United States* v. *Bell,* 506 F.2d 207, 221–222 (C.A.D.C.). And, of course, the failure of a prosecutor to accept a plea arrangement suggested by an accused does no more than cause the accused to stand trial—it is simply a failure to relieve a defendant of the burden properly placed on him by the indictment charging a capital offense. Once a prosecution has begun, its continuation is within the control of the court, and discretion in plea bargaining may then to a limited extent be controlled judicially. See, *e.g., United States* v. *Cowan,* 524 F.2d 504 (C.A. 5); *United States* v. *Ammidown,* 497 F.2d 615 (C.A.D.C.); Fed. R. Crim. P. 11(e). If plea arrangement procedures are so seriously defective the proper cure is their improvement, rather than the invalidation of the death penalty for those who do not enter into such arrangements.

See *State* v. *Woodson,* 215 S.E.2d 607, 616–18. Rational selectivity of this sort cannot operate to invalidate the penalty ultimately imposed.

47. Only one of petitioners has claimed that he offered to plead guilty to a lesser charge and that this request was refused. Petitioner Waxton offered to plead guilty to armed robbery and to being an accessory after the fact to murder. This offer, coming after all of the evidence at trial had been taken, was apparently declined because the evidence showed overwhelmingly that Waxton had committed the murders personally. See *Woodson* Pet. Br. 11–13.

3. Jury Nullification.

The power of the jury to acquit despite evidence justifying conviction is a power created and protected by the Constitution itself. The Sixth Amendment confers an unquestioned right to a jury trial (*Duncan* v. *Louisiana,* 391 U.S. 145) and that right, together with the Double Jeopardy Clause of the Fifth Amendment, secures to a jury the power to acquit even those whom some all-knowing observer would say were guilty beyond a reasonable doubt. The jury's function as the "conscience of the community" (*Witherspoon* v. *Illinois, supra,* 391 U.S. at 519) is best served when it considers all of the important facets of the crime, including the culpability of the defendant as well as the fact of his legal guilt. See Scheflin, *Jury Nullification: The Right to Say No,* 45 S. Calif. L. Rev. 168 (1972).

On the other hand, the power of a jury to acquit despite the evidence (or to convict of a lesser included offense although the evidence supports the greater offense) is not an exercise of standardless discretion as was the jury's power to recommend, after conviction, whether a defendant shall be sent to death. The jury's power to nullify is a power, but not an authorization. It is a power because society uses no sanctions to deter it. It is a power because the Constitution allows juries to convict or acquit, and establishes no external standards by which an acquittal may be called "improper"; the fact-finding power is lodged in the jury and when it acquits, what it finds to be "true" *is* true within the boundaries of the legal system. But the power of juries to do these things is not unbounded. There are standards to guide the exercise of that power. The judge carefully instructs the jury on the law, and informs jurors how they should respond to the facts they have found. The jury is told that if they have a particular view of the facts, they should take a specific action. They are not told that if they have found (for example) that the accused committed a killing for hire they may convict of first degree murder, second degree murder, or acquit; they are told, instead, that they should convict of first degree murder. There are multiple standards to guide the jury's decisions; the jury has "discretion" only in the sense that it has the power to disregard these directions.[48]

The potential vice of jury nullification, even though its availability is created by the Constitution, is that the jury may acquit in an irrational or prejudicial manner. However, the constitutional guarantee of a jury trial

---

48. If the instructions given to the jury are vague or defective, the proper recourse is either a claim that the statutes defining the crimes are unconstitutionally vague (see pages 72–73, *supra*) or a claim of simple error in framing the charge.

rests on the assumption that the jury is not animated by bias, and that the jury is capable responsibly of discharging its duties. If the jury is given to caprice, it would undermine convictions for any crime no less than convictions for capital crimes. But this Court has always assumed that, at least when screened from prejudicial pressures and from legally inadmissible but "powerfully incriminating extrajudicial statements" (*Bruton* v. *United States,* 391 U.S. 123, 135), the jury can be trusted to decide the controversy reasonably, conscientiously, and intelligently. See *McGautha, supra.* Cf. *Duncan* v. *Louisiana, supra,* 391 U.S. at 157.

The argument that juries will act unfairly and arbitrarily assumes that, on this most serious decision, twelve jurors who have been carefully screened by defense counsel will silently cast their votes for private reasons without reference to the commands of the law. The available evidence is to the contrary. Professors Harry Kalven, Jr. and Hans Zeisel, in preparing their massive study *The American Jury* (1966), analyzed in depth the workings of more than 3,500 jury trials, and concluded that in the great majority of cases in which the jury declined to convict (whether or not of a capital offense) when the evidence apparently was persuasive, the jury was making a reasoned and reasonable response to the excessiveness of a penalty in light of the nature of the crime and the circumstances of the defendant. The authors uncovered no evidence that the jury was behaving capriciously in these instances of "nullification" (*id.* at 306–312).

We submit that there is simply no evidence that the jury, when deciding whether to convict in capital cases, acts in a wanton or freakish or discriminatory manner. The jury is fulfilling a function given to it by the Constitution itself; more is needed than petitioners' groundless speculation that the jury might act irrationally to demonstrate that the Constitution's guarantee of trial by jury is a bar to the imposition of capital punishment.

4. Lesser Included Offenses.

Most of the arguments we have made above with respect to juries also apply to the function of juries as they consider conviction for lesser included offenses. There is no evidence that juries act in a freakish manner; petitioners' assertion of the potential for such action does not establish that such arbitrary behavior occurs.

Moreover, the Sixth Amendment's right to trial by jury includes within it a constitutional right to have the jury consider any lesser included offenses to the major charge. When the defendant controverts any element of the charge (and defendant's assertion, if correct, would entitle him to conviction on a lesser charge) he is entitled to have that charge put to the jury so that it can exercise its constitutional fact-finding function. *Berra* v. *United States,* 351 U.S. 131, 134; *Stevenson* v. *United States,* 162 U.S. 313. This does not mean, of course, that a defendant is required to accept such a charge; he or she is entitled to submit the case to the jury on the counts of the indictment in the expectation (or hope) of a complete acquittal. And, under federal law, a defendant is not entitled to a lesser included offense instruction unless there is some evidence that would support conviction of that charge.[49] *United States* v. *Bishop,* 412 U.S. 346, 361; *Sansone* v. *United States,* 380 U.S. 343, 350.

There is thus no evidence that juries use their ability to convict of a lesser included offense in a capricious manner. Their ability to convict of a lesser included offense is in any event created by the Sixth Amendment itself. Petitioners' claim regarding the opportunity for discretion does not make capital punishment invariably cruel and unusual.

5. *Jury Discretion at the Punishment Phase.*

Petitioners Gregg, Jurek, and Proffitt were sentenced to death under statutes allowing the judge and jury to exercise some controlled discretion in selecting the punishment appropriate for those convicted of capital crimes. The Antihijacking Act of 1974 (App. C, *infra*) also allows the jury to exercise some discretion. The Antihijacking Act provides that if death results from a hijacking, and if the defendant is convicted of the crime, the factfinder then must consider the penalty to be imposed. Capital punishment is permissible only if the prosecution can prove by a preponderance of the evidence that one of five aggravating factors is present. These factors include: that the defendant previously had been convicted of any crime for which a sentence of life imprisonment or death was imposable, that the defendant previously had been convicted of two felonies involving the infliction of serious bodily injury, that the defendant knowingly created a grave risk of death to at least one person in addition to the person who died, or that the defendant committed the crime in "an especially heinous, cruel, or depraved manner." If the factfinder explicitly determines that one of the aggravating circumstances existed, the defendant must be sentenced to death unless the factfinder also determines that a mitigating circumstance exists. The five

---

49. Some petitioners contend that in their states a lesser included offense instruction may be given even though there is no evidence to support the lesser offense. However, we do not consider this further because it does not apply to the federal system and is not, in any event, an avenue of inherent or inescapable discretion. If it is excessively standardless, it may be assailed directly in an appropriate case.

enumerated mitigating circumstances are: that the defendant was under the age of 18 when he committed the crime, that the defendant's capacity to appreciate the wrongfulness of his conduct was substantially impaired, that the defendant was under substantial duress, that the defendant's participation in a crime primarily committed by another was relatively minor, or that the defendant could not reasonably have foreseen that his conduct would create a grave risk of causing the death of the victim. If the factfinder explicitly determines that one of these mitigating circumstances existed, the defendant must be sentenced to life imprisonment.[50]

There is nothing in the idea of discretion concerning the penalty to be imposed that renders capital punishment unconstitutional. This Court already has upheld, as consistent with the Constitution, state statutes that vest absolute discretion in the jury. It wrote: "In light of history, experience, and the present limitations of human knowledge, we find it quite impossible to say that committing to the untrammeled discretion of the jury the power to pronounce life or death in capital cases is offensive to anything in the Constitution." *McGautha* v. *California, supra,* 402 U.S. at 207 (footnote omitted). If absolute discretion is permissible under the Constitution, *a fortiori* discretion that has been structured and confined by statutory standards is consistent with the Constitution.

There is no reason to believe that judges and juries will exercise the discretion thus conferred upon them in arbitrary or freakish ways. Kalven and Zeisel studied the experience under laws committing the decision to the complete discretion of the jury and concluded that when either the judge or the jury had available both a capital disposition and a noncapital disposition[51] they agreed in a remarkable number of cases—81 percent. This indicates that standards are at work behind the decisions. In those cases in which there was disagreement Professors Kalven and Zeisel could find a rational basis for

50. The discretion conferred upon the factfinder by the Antihijacking Act is significantly less than that conferred by the three state statutes before the Court. The Florida statute, which is perhaps most similar to the Antihijacking Act, allows a jury to "balance" aggravating and mitigating factors and allows it to recommend a sentence of death even when it finds a mitigating factor. It does not require explicit findings on the presence of absence of each factor. The judge is free to rebalance the factors and to disregard the jury's recommendation. The Georgia statute allows the death penalty to be imposed only if the jury finds at least one aggravating factor, but it grants the jury complete discretion to recommend mercy, and so to prevent execution. The Texas statute permits the imposition of the death penalty only if three very broadly-worded conditions are satisfied; a jury would have substantial discretion to determine the existence of these conditions.

51. Whether because the jury could determine the sentence or because a jury could convict of a noncapital lesser included offense.

that disagreement in all but two cases. Kalven & Zeisel, *The American Jury* 445 (1966). Perhaps most significantly, a clear pattern of aggravation of the worst sort marked those cases in which judge and jury agreed that the death penalty was appropriate.

> The cases in which jury and judge agree that the defendant should pay for his crime with his life are marked for the most part by peculiar heinousness. In many, a clear pattern emerges; there is an aspect of almost gratuitous violence. [*Id.* at 437.]

The other major study of the workings of the modern jury system was conducted by the *Stanford Law Review*. See Note, "A Study of the California Penalty Jury in First-Degree-Murder Cases: Standardless Sentencing", 21 *Stan. L. Rev.* 1297 (1969). That study, which confined its attention to the penalty phase of sentencing by juries that had convicted the defendant, establishes that the jury makes rational and consistent penalty decisions even in the absence of standards. The authors of the study analyzed 178 separate variables that might have entered into the penalty decision in each of the 238 cases studied. The results, apparently to the surprise of the student editors, showed that there are "definite patterns of jury decisionmaking, precluding the possibility that juries make their decisions wholly at random" (*id.* at 1419). The editors concluded that even without standards presented by the judge, the California juries reached conclusions astonishingly similar to those that would have been produced by an "objective" observer applying the aggravating mitigating criteria proposed by the Model Penal Code (*id.* at 1429). This study, like the work of Kalven and Zeisel, demonstrates the propriety of this Court's conclusion in *McGautha* v. *California, supra,* 402 U.S. at 207–208, that "[t]he States are entitled to assume that jurors confronted with the truly awesome responsibility of decreeing death for a fellow human will act with due regard for the consequences of their decision" and that, with or without formal standards, juries consider the appropriate criteria.

Although we therefore believe that the standardless discretion approved by this Court in *McGautha* satisfies all constitutional requirements, it also should be clear that the standards contained in the Antihijacking Act and the state statutes under review provide substantial uniformity in decisionmaking and alleviate any remaining concerns about arbitrariness. Petitioners argue that the standards contained in these statutes are meaningless and that the results their application produces are "freakish." But the entire corpus of the criminal law and administrative law is based upon the premise that rules and standards do make a difference, indeed a vital difference, in many cases. See generally K.C. Davis, *Discretionary Justice: A Preliminary Inquiry* (1969). Standards may not eliminate discretion, but they "canalize [it] within banks that keep it from overflowing." *A.L.A. Schechter Poultry Corp.* v. *United States,* 295 U.S. 495, 551 (Cardozo, J., concurring). The varieties of human experience allow no more, and the Constitution requires no more.

It follows that it makes little constitutional difference whether the factors articulated for the jury's consideration are quite specific (as they are in the federal Antihijacking Act) or are more general (as they are under the Texas statute). But to the extent the degree of generality of the standards is important, the importance relates to the requirements of the Due Process Clause, not to the Eighth Amendment. Petitioners Gregg, Jurek, and Proffitt are in effect contending that the standards used in their cases are unconstitutionally vague. But vagueness can be cured by judicial construction or by legislative amendment of defective statutes. Excessively vague statutes can be invalidated without impugning the legislative prerogative to prescribe capital punishment under suitably clear statutes.[52]

Moreover, even if a vagueness challenge to the Georgia, Texas, and Florida statutes can be maintained, it "is well established that [such] challenges to statutes which do not involve First Amendment freedoms must be examined in the light of the facts of the case at hand." *United States* v. *Mazurie,* 419 U.S. 544, 550. A statute is not unconstitutional merely because it may be uncertain in some applications or because it deals with matters of degree. "[T]he law is full of instances where a man's fate depends on his estimating rightly, that is, as the jury subsequently estimates it, some matter of degree." *Nash* v. *United States,* 229 U.S. 373, 377. The statute can be unconstitutional only if its words describe "no comprehensible course of conduct at all." *United States* v. *Powell,* No. 74–884, decided December 2, 1975, slip op. 5. That is hardly the case here, for such descriptions of human conduct as "deliberately and with the reasonable expectation that the death of the deceased or another would result" and "whether the conduct . . . was unreasonable in response to the provocation,"[53] of which petitioner Jurek complains, and similar phrases in the other state statutes, are the staples of the criminal law. They are no less precise than the statutes upheld in *Powell, Mazurie, Nash,* and innumerable other decisions by this Court.[54]

---

52. That is the course followed by the Supreme Court of Illinois, which struck down a post-*Furnam* statute on the grounds that it was too vague and that it had created a "new court" in violation of the Illinois constitution. *People ex rel. Rice* v. *Cunningham,* 336 N.E.2d 1.

53. Vernon's Texas Code of Crim. Pro., Art. 37.071 (b) (1974).

54. See, *e.g., United States* v. *National Dairy Products Corp.,* 372 U.S. 29 ("unreasonably low pric-

6. Clemency.

We return here to a now familiar theme. At least in the federal system the President's ability to pardon or grant clemency on such terms as he thinks fit is established by the Constitution itself, and thus shielded from legislative or judicial constraint. *Ex parte Garland,* 4 Wall. 333, 380; *Schick* v. *Reed,* 419 U.S. 256. As Hamilton explained in the 74th *Federalist:*

> Humanity and good policy conspire to dictate, that the benign prerogative of pardoning should be as little as possible fettered or embarrassed. The criminal code of every country partakes so much of necessary severity, that without an easy access to exceptions in favor of unfortunate guilt, justice would wear a countenance too sanguinary and cruel. [473 (Wright ed. 1961).]

In *Schick* this Court concluded that the pardoning power of the President flows from the Constitution alone and therefore may be exercised by him at his will without regard to a need for consistency of decision. "The very essence of the pardoning power is to treat each case individually" (419 U.S. at 265). "Individual acts of clemency inherently call for discriminating choices because no two cases are the same" (*id.* at 268). Because the executive power to grant clemency is unfettered and unfetterable, it cannot logically follow that it is unconstitutional to treat in accordance with a court's judgment *those whom the executive declines to pardon.*

D. All Discretion Taken Together Does Not Prevent the Death Sentence From Being Validly Imposed

The net effect of the instances of discretion in the criminal justice system is no greater than the sum of its parts. Petitioners' argument is that the Constitution affirmatively provides (or at least permits) so many avenues of escape from death, so many rights the defendant can invoke, and so many op-

---

es"); *United States* v. *Korpan,* 354 U.S. 271, 273, n.2 ("coin operated amusement or gaming device"); *Boyce Motor Lines* v. *United States,* 342 U.S. 337 ("so far as practicable, . . . driving into or through congested thoroughfares"); *Robinson* v. *United States,* 324 U.S. 282 ("liberated unharmed" in kidnapping statute); *United States* v. *Gaskin,* 320 U.S. 527 ("condition of peonage"); *United States* v. *Ragen,* 314 U.S. 513, 517 ("reasonable allowance for salaries"); *Sproles* v. *Binford,* 286 U.S. 374 ("shortest practicable route"); *United States* v. *Alford,* 274 U.S. 264 ("in or near any forest, timber, or other inflammable material"); *Miller* v. *Oregon,* 273 U.S. 657 (explained at 274 U.S. 464–65) (drive a vehicle in "a careful and prudent manner"); *Omacchevarria* v. *Idaho,* 246 U.S. 343, 345, n.3 (any range "usually occupied by any cattle grower").

portunities for mercy, each designed expressly to shield an accused from unjust conviction or punishment, that only an arbitrarily or freakishly selected few of those who "really deserve" death escape the net of safeguards against injustice. Then, the argument concludes, it must be unjust to punish those remaining who have not been spared, even though they deserve their fate.

The Constitution does not impose this incredible result on the criminal justice system. Those whose execution is not averted by one of the avenues of discretionary mercy or constitutional safeguard have been sent to their death because none of a large number of actors thought they deserved to be spared. Such a procedure is the opposite of arbitrariness. It is instead a decision by consensus—only by unanimous agreement of the grand jury, the prosecutor, the judge, the jury (itself unanimous), and the clemency authority may death be imposed.[55] There is nothing in the Eighth Amendment (or in the Due Process Clause) that precludes such action by consensus. And there is no justification for reaching a conclusion that the combination of provisions, each of constitutional origin, granting discretion to a number of actors, inevitably renders the criminal justice system incapable of producing a constitutional sentence.

In the last analysis petitioners are seeking to convince this Court that the Eighth Amendment cannot coexist with the Fifth and Sixth Amendments, because procedures either compelled or permitted by those amendments, and by other provisions of the Constitution, invariably produce a result intolerable under the Eighth Amendment. But the Constitution is not an instrument so inconsistent within itself that the commands of one amendment nullify the commands of others.

When each step in the process is constitutionally permitted, indeed in many instances compelled, when all that the Constitution required to be done was done, when nevertheless the resulting penalty, although not of a type forbidden, is then claimed to be unconstitutional *because* of the process

---

55. In the Due Process Clause the framers ensured that the risk of the execution of an innocent man would be held to a minimum. Because the framers themselves authorized capital punishment (1 Stat. 112) and because, as we have argued, the Eighth Amendment does not forbid that type of punishment for crime, the framers expressed their belief that the benefits of capital punishment—including protecting the lives of innocent people by deterring murders—outweigh whatever very slight risk there may be of an unwarranted execution. This Court has scrutinized capital cases carefully in order further to minimize that risk. The safeguards and avenues of discretionary mercy we have discussed in this part of the brief stand as a bulwark against the possibility of error that could produce an unjustified execution and, because of the evolution of stronger safeguards in the criminal justice system, it is much less likely today than it was at the time of the framers that such errors will be made.

followed in imposing it—in short, when the foundation of petitioners' argument is exposed, the conclusion built upon it must fall. The course chosen by at least thirty-five states and the United States since *Furman* should not be nullified by this Court.

Conclusion

The United States submits that capital punishment is not per se unconstitutional.

Respectfully submitted.

Robert H. Bork, Solicitor General.
A. Raymond Randolph, Jr., Deputy Solicitor General.
Frank H. Easterbrook, Assistant to the Solicitor General.
March 1976

MR. BORK: Mr. Chief Justice, and may it please the Court:

The United States appears as amicus curiae in these cases because the Congress has enacted and various Presidents have signed into law statutes that permit capital punishment for various serious crimes.

The constitutional argument made by petitioners' counsel in challenging capital punishment generally I think is rather diffused, in fact I think part of its persuasiveness arises from its diffusion, and I will try to sort out these various propositions that are being urged and attempt to show their inadequacy either singly or collectively to outlaw capital punishment.

To begin with, we know as a fact that the men who framed the Eighth Amendment did not mean—did not intend as an original matter to outlaw capital punishment because, as has been mentioned, they prescribed the procedures that must be used in inflicting it in the Fifth Amendment. We know that the men who framed and ratified the Fourteenth Amendment did not intend to outlaw capital punishment, because they also discussed and framed the procedures that must be followed in inflicting it.

So we know in an original matter, as a matter of original intention, it is quite certain that the Eighth Amendment was not intended to bar the death penalty, and the Constitution contemplates its infliction.

Now, petitioners respond to this in their brief by pointing out that the Fifth Amendment also refers to the infliction of being put twice in jeopardy of life or limb, and they say obviously the Eighth Amendment would bar disfigurement today. Of course it would, but I don't think that avoids the argument from the constitutional text, because punishments for disfigurement are today regarded as cruel and unusual, precisely because the American people came to that conclusion and legislatures stopped enacting such punishments. So that today I think the Court, if some legislature in an aberration tried to direct such a punishment would find it cruel and unusual.

But the point is it was not judicial movement that made that change, it was an evolution in the standards of decency in American society.

Now, the Eighth Amendment, like some other provisions of the Constitution, does have in it a principle of evolution. The intention of the framers, it seems to me, is entitled to enormous respect, but one cannot exclude the possibility that cruel or unusual punishment means something different today than it meant then. But the principle is one of controlled evolution. The amendment is not an uncontrolled delegation of power to the judiciary to judge punishments. There are criteria by which the judiciary judges punishments. And I will try to demonstrate that the principle of evolution is applicable here, which controls the case here, not only does not outlaw the death penalty, but in fact affirmatively supports it.

Having done that, I will urge three other propositions that are raised in an Eighth Amendment context by counsel, but I don't think belong there and hence have no proper place in this case, but I will nevertheless discuss them.

I will suggest first that capital punishment is rationally related to legitimate legislative goals of the deterrence of crime and the expression of moral outrage among them; secondly, that capital punishment has not been shown to be inflicted on the basis of race, and that in any event that question is irrelevant to the issue of the type of punishment; and, thirdly, I will argue that capital punishment is not outlawed because the criminal justice system, which is mandated and permitted by the Constitution, has elements of discretion in it which are intended to be a safeguard of the system.

The principle of evolution that controls the meaning of the cruel and unusual punishments clause is that punishments may not be used which fall far outside the mainstream of our jurisprudence and which are rejected by the current moral consensus. That is consistent with the history of the clause and the cases this Court has decided under the clause.

Apparently, the cruel and unusual punishments clause of the Eighth Amendment, like the rest of the Bill of Rights, was adopted because the anti-federalists who, objected to the ratification of the Constitution, posed a series of terrible imaginings about the coming tyranny that the federal government would impose upon the citizens and the states. And one part of the rhetoric employed was the suggestion that the federal government would use torture, the screw, and the rack, in enforcing its laws.

The Eighth Amendment promised that that would not happen. And since the federal government, of course, had no such intention and did no such thing, the Eighth Amendment became dormant from its adoption, which strongly indicates an understanding at the time that the clause was not to alter existing practices, but was to prevent intolerable innovations or reversions. Punishments native to our jurisprudence and still in use were simply not touched by the clause.

Now, I think the cases reflect that. We have discussed them at some length in our brief, but it was not until 1909, in *Weems* v. *United States*, that this Court struck down a punishment, and that punishment was cruel and unusual in every sense. It was a very cruel Spanish punishment, of incredible severity, imposed there for false entries in official accounts. And this Court said in that case, such penalties for such offenses amaze those who have formed their conception of the relation of a state to even its offending citizens from the practice of American commonwealths, and believe that as a precept of justice that punishment for crime should be graduated and proportioned to offense, and I think that is the test of the cruel and unusual punishments clause.

Q: You do accept that principle under the Eighth Amendment, that punishments that are disproportionate or sufficiently disproportionate are impermissible in—

MR. BORK: I do, Mr. Justice White, I think that is quite correct. And I think this case, *Weems*, tells us what those words mean, cruel and unusual. Unusual means amazing in the light of the practice of the American commonwealths, well outside the mainstream of our jurisprudence, as I was putting it before.

Q: That is a little different from—

MR. BORK: Beg pardon?

Q: That is a little different from just disproportionality.

MR. BORK: No, no, that is unusual. I think cruel is where disproportionality comes in, Mr. Justice White.

Q: What you are saying, I take it, is that the frequency or infrequency has nothing to do with the term unusual as used in the Eighth Amendment?

MR. BORK: I think that is right, Mr. Chief Justice. I think it is the infrequency of the type of punishment, that is, in *Weems* we had cadena temporal, an extraordinary Spanish punishment, unknown to our jurisprudence, and that is why it was unusual, and not because it was only rarely inflicted.

Q: How frequently was it inflicted in the Philippines, do you know?

MR. BORK: I do not know, Mr. Justice Stewart. But the Court didn't make a point of that. The Court made a point of the type of punishment it was.

Now, I think cruel, as the Court suggested in *Weems*, means a punishment which is amazing in its lack of proportion to the offense. I don't think the Court defines calibration, whether there is an exact propotion. I think it has to be so wildly out of proportion that it becomes cruel.

Q: It means that, perhaps, but it doesn't mean only that. I mean, in other words, you would concede, I would suppose, that if a state imposed and inflicted capital punishment for jaywalking, it would be cruel and unusual punishment, even though, as you submitted to us, capital punishment per se is not cruel and unusual? But it means—and that is your point now—but also what if a state said for the most heinous kind of first degree murders, we are going to inflict breaking a man on the wheel and then disemboweling him while he is still alive, and then burning him up, what would you say to that?

MR. BORK: I would say that that practice is so out of step with modern morality and modern jurisprudence that the state cannot return to it. That kind of torture was precisely what the framers thought they were outlawing when they wrote the cruel and unusual punishment clause.

Q: So it is not just disproportionality, is it?

MR. BORK: No, no. It is also that it is foreign to our jurisprudence, but that has become for some time and completely out of step with our morality, which that has become, so the state could not revert to those kinds of punishments.

Q: So you also accept judging the cruelty in the light of contemporary morality?

MR. BORK: I do indeed, Mr. Justice White. I accept that or I think however that once we have thirty-five legislators in the Congress of the United States adopting a penalty, it is impossible to say that it is in conflict with current morality, because I think there is no other source of current morality to which a court may properly look, that is it may not look to the writings of the more enlightened professors.

Q: And do you say the same as to the question of proportionality or do courts have some independent input into that question?

MR. BORK: I think the proportionality would have to be judged on objective standards as well, that is not a—for example, proportionality would be judged by the frequency with which legislatures choose. If one jurisdiction only suddenly imposed death for jaywalking or flogging for jaywalking, I think, looking across the spectrum of the American commonwealths and seeing that that was wildly out of proportion with every other jurisdiction, would be one way of judging proportionality.

Q: So if enough legislatures pass a law, you would say the courts have no basis to say that the penalty is disproportionate?

MR. BORK: I doubt very much, Mr. Justice White, whether a court could—disproportionateness depends in great part upon the moral understanding of the community. If the moral understanding of the community in a very widespread way views the punishment as proportionate, I don't know what independent source a court would have to look to.

Q: I take it you are advancing this not as an original argument but simply in response to the suggestion of the petitioners in these cases and in the prior cases that capital punishment is indeed out of step with present day thinking?

MR. BORK: I am indeed, Mr. Chief Justice.

Q: You don't need to defend it affirmatively or no state needs to defend it affirmatively on that concept, does it?

MR. BORK: No, no, Mr. Chief Justice, that is precisely my point. I think once it is seen that it is within the moral standards of the community as shown by the legislatures of America, including the Congress, and once it is recognized that it is a traditional penalty in our jurisprudence, I think the Eighth Amendment inquiry is at an end. In fact, I think this case is at an end.

Q: Do you think we should overturn *Furman* then, on the basis—

MR. BORK: I was preparing to suggest that later in my argument, Mr. Justice White.

Q: I thought so. But do you think it is required by your argument?

MR. BORK: No, I don't think what I have said yet requires it, nor do I think that sustaining the validity of the statutes now before this Court requires it, but I think other reasons make it desirable, and I would like to develop those when I discuss discretion.

Q: That is consistent with the position of the United States in prior years.

MR. BORK: How, I think the things I have just said, it may have been possible, it was possible to think differently about the moral standards of the American community, when *Furman* v. *Georgia* was decided. I don't think it is any longer possible to think differently.

There were factual estimates, empirical judgments made in various concurring opinions in *Furman* v. *Georgia* which were fairly made but which subsequent events have shown to be incorrect, and those propositions in *Furman* are now I think no longer available as premises for constitutional judgment, and I would like to mention them briefly.

First, it was said because the statutes in *Furman* provided for discretion, whether or not to impose capital punishment in that particular case, the legislative will is not frustrated if capital punishment is never imposed. We know now, I think, that that was not the meaning to be drawn from the existence of discretion in the statutes. By reenacting death penalty statutes, many of them mandatory under certain circumstances, Congress and thirty-five states have shown that the legislative will is frustrated if the death penalty is never imposed.

Discretion was built into the prior statutes to distinguish between types of killings and types of killers. Congress and the legislatures of the states have shown that if *Furman* presses them to the choice, they prefer a mandatory death penalty to none.

Secondly, it was said in *Furman* that capital punishment is cruel because it goes beyond what is necessary not only in degree but in kind. We now know that legislature after legislature thinks that capital punishment is necessary in degree and in kind. Though I think that this Court cannot really look behind that legislative determination, in a moment I will try to show that the legislatures had every reason to think it was necessary. They made an eminently rational judgment.

Third, it was said in *Furman* again that the penalty is unusual because it is infrequently imposed. As I have just said in response to the Chief Justice, that seems to me not the constitutional meaning of unusual. That unusual refers to the type of penalty, rare in our jurisprudence, like cadena temporal in *Weems*, or like denationalization in *Trop* v. *Dulles*.

Indeed, I don't think the death penalty is unusual in any relevant sense. It is imposed in a number of cases each year. It is true that legislators and juries and judges restrict it to the most outrageous crimes, but I don't see how it can become unconstitutional because it is used carefully and sparingly, rather than across the board.

The petitioners' argument it seems to me suggests that very broad categories of crimes for which the death penalty was mandatory would make it somehow more constitutional. I think that is a very odd conclusion.

Now, we submit therefore that the death penalty is clearly not a cruel and unusual punishment under the meaning of the Eighth Amendment. And I submit that the Eighth Amendment is not a warrant for requiring the states or the Congress to come here and justify affirmatively the punishments they wish to use; once it has been seen that the punishment is traditional, the—

Q: Mr. Attorney General, what is your understanding of the meaning of disproportionality? You say that is one of the principles under the Eighth Amendment. Could you spell out what your understanding is of that rule? Disproportionate to what? What difference does it make?

MR. BORK: Well, I think it is shown by *Weems*, in which this Court said that here a man is given fifteen years cadena temporal, which involves painful labor, not hard labor, involves wearing a chain on his wrist and ankle, he is not allowed to sit with counsel, he is deprived of all rights of his family, and for the rest of his life he has to live where the government tells him to, even after he is out, under surveillance, and the Court said to punish, to inflict that punishment for a false entry in official records, which can be done even if it is not shown to harm anyone, is just so out of proportion with what American jurisprudence shows. American commonwealths just don't punish that way.

Q: Is that what it means or—

MR. BORK: Pardon me? Is that a question—

Q: Is that what it means, or does it mean disproportionate to the offense? These two are quite different things.

MR. BORK: I'm sorry, Mr. Justice Stewart, I meant disproportionate to the offense as shown by the proportions to offenses that the American commonwealths use. We look—the Court says that we look at what the American commonwealths do, and they have nothing as severe for this kind of an offense, maybe two years in prison.

Q: Apparently the state or the government would get out of imposing that offense, it would get out of it whatever you get out of imposing punishments, and you think it is disproportionate is that you don't get out of it the injury inflicted is disproportionate to what return the state can be expected to get? I mean, deterring false entries just isn't worth imposing that kind of punishment?

MR. BORK: It is regarded as immoral, but those are things the Court determined in *Weems*, not because it had some internal scale of what is worth what, but because the Court looked to the practice of American governments and said American governments, state and national, do not impose penalties anything like that severe for that kind of an offense, and this is just way out of proportion, it is aberrational.

Q: That may have been the evidence they looked to to determine whether what they got out of it was worth it, but that nevertheless, determining whether it was worth it was part of it, I take it?

MR. BORK: Maybe part of. What I am suggesting is that the Court looked to objective external standards, rather than to any subjective feeling about whether it is worth it.

Q: Do you think it would be possible that the Court might have come to that same conclusion in *Weems* if there had been a more severe crime, that is, bank robbery, as distinguished from manipulating figures?

MR. BORK: I do not know, Mr. Chief Justice, because obviously—well, it might have come to that conclusion in any event, because there simply was no American punishment like that for any crime. The wearing of chains and being sentenced to painful labor and being deprived of the right of even to sit in the family councils, being deprived of all civil rights forever, being required to live where the government told you, forever under their perpetual surveillance—these are just punishments that we don't inflict of any sort.

Q: Well, don't you think really that the Supreme Court in the *Weems* case at that time would have said that about a bank robbery, if that punishment had been inflicted for bank robbery?

MR. BORK: You mean it was cruel and unusual?

Q: Yes.

MR. BORK: That is what I am suggesting, Mr. Chief Justice, by saying that—

Q: That is cruel, I don't know about the disproportionate.

MR. BORK: Well, it is unusual, certainly.

Q: Sure. Well, it might have been unusual, but not in—what about murder?

MR. BORK: Well, I have been suggesting, Mr. Justice White, that these judgments are made by two factors, is it a traditional punishment in our jurisprudence, so that it is not unusual—and the answer to that is no, that is an unusual punishment in our jurisprudence for any crime—and, secondly, is it disproportionate, and the disproportionate question is also judged by the practice of the American states and the American national government, and it is disproportionate by those practices, even for murder. It is just a terribly unusual crime.

But I don't think I have to argue that *Weems* would have gone the same way had murder been involved.

Q: Am I correct in my understanding that even in *Weems* the Court was not unanimous?

MR. BORK: There was a dissent by Justice White and Justice Holmes, I believe.

Q: So Holmes joined the dissent?

MR. BORK: Yes, he did.

I said I would, having said I think that—what I have said so far I think disposes of the case, because I think there is no Eighth Amendment inconsistency here. And to go on to the other arguments I think is to step into arguments that come from different parts of the Constitution and are not properly before this Court.

Q: Well, the Fourteenth Amendment is embraced in the question, isn't it?

MR. BORK: I thought it was merely the cruel and unusual punishments clause that we were judging, but perhaps I am wrong. In any event, I will go on to the others.

I would like to discuss the element of discretion, because that seems to me to be the crucial part of petitioners' counsel's argument. And the argument appears to be that the fact that at various states in the criminal justice system, people are entitled to make judgments renders the death penalty unconstitutional. I don't think there is any logic to that claim, and I don't think it is a constitutional proposition.

There are a number of difficulties with it. One is the utter implausibility of the idea. The framers wrote a Constitution that both recognized the death penalty and mandated a criminal justice system with discretion in it. I don't think it can be that they wrote a Constitution in which one part makes another part unconstitutional. The mind boggles at the thought that the Constitution is unconstitutional.

When two features have values which compete, they have to be resolved. One does not obliterate the other, yet that is exactly what we are being told happens here. Every element of discretion that petitioners' counsel complains of is either permitted or compelled by the Constitution. That is true of the charging decision, it is true of the plea bargaining, it is true of the power of the jury to acquit despite the evidence—

Q: Mr. Solicitor General, if I may just interrupt with one question, it would be helpful to me if in discussing the subject of discretion you would differentiate between meeting the argument that Mr. Amsterdam has advanced and meeting the holding of *Furman*, if one can identify it, if there is a difference between them. Certainly discretion was significant in that holding, and I wonder if you are attacking the decision or merely meeting an argument, or to what extent are you doing one rather than the other?

MR. BORK: Well, I think I am doing both, Mr. Justice Stevens. I am going to suggest that *McGautha* was correctly decided and that it really is not quite possible for *McGautha* and *Furman* to live together. And though it is not necessary for the decision of these cases, that we would be much better to overrule *Furman* and adhere to *McGautha*.

The states have been put to a choice by *Furman* that I think they ought not to have been put to. They have been put in the position of choosing their second preference in modes of imposing capital punishment, and some of them have moved to mandatory statutes. I think that is unfortunate, and I think they ought to be allowed to go back to a position in which they choose the form of statute that they think is just and efficient, so long as it meets due process requirements.

Mr. Amsterdam said yesterday that he thought *McGautha* and *Furman* could live together, and I take it that the argument that was made was that *McGautha* holds that jury discretion meets the requirements of due process. But *Furman* holds that while that may be true, the results of the process are intolerable.

Now, I don't understand how a process which produces intolerable results can be due process. So it seems to me that there is a necessary contradiction between those two cases.

Q: Well, they did involve, as you pointed out just a moment ago, two different provisions of the Constitution.

MR. BORK: That is quite true, Mr. Justice Stewart, but that gets us back into the position where the Constitution mandates discretion in a criminal justice system, and that discretion mandated by the Constitution renders illegal a punishment which the Constitution recognizes as legally allowable.

Q: Well, it certainly isn't an unusual situation. It has something that is perfectly permissible under one provision of the Constitution and violates another provision of the Constitution. There is nothing unusual about that.

MR. BORK: I think this is unique, Mr. Justice Stewart. The Fifth Amendment and the Fourteenth Amendment say use due process of law when you impose the death penalty. To then say that the procedure by which you use due process of law makes it cruel and unusual punishment under the Eighth Amendment, so that all along there was no death penalty, seems to me to be a logical impossibility.

Q: Mr. Solicitor General, let me put another question on the table, and you comment as you see fit as you go along on this matter of discretion. I ask pretty much the same question of Mr. Amsterdam. To what extent do you think *Furman* properly understood rests on the universe of crimes which merit the capital punishment? Is that relevant to trying to identify the precise holding of *Furman*? Do you understand my question?

MR. BORK: I am not entirely sure that I do, Mr. Justice Stevens. If you mean—

Q: Well, let me rephrase it a little bit. Is the legal question precisely the same if you have one narrowly defined capital offense in which there are the elements of discretion in the process in the particular case, at the prosecutorial stage, the clemency stage, the jury stage, is that the same legal issue as a case in which the crime for which the defendant is being charged is one of several crimes which bear a capital offense, all the way, ranging from rape through the various offenses before the court—that have been before the court from time to time? Is the discretion issue the same in the two different hypothetical cases?

MR. BORK: I would think that it was, Mr. Justice Stevens, at least at the moment I don't perceive any distinction.

Q: If the states single out one crime and said that the killing of a police officer in the line of duty and in the context of the commission of a crime by the killer, that that and only that would be subject to mandatory death penalty, that there is the same breadth of discretion, the same kind of an approach that were suggested in some of the opinions in Furman would apply?

MR. BORK: No, I don't think it would, Mr. Chief Justice, but I take it I was being asked whether the narrowness of the definition of the crime or the number of crimes made any difference in the existence of discretion, and I did not think so. I think the type of statute that you refer to, of course, does avoid the objection that was made in *Furman*. That is why I say that these cases don't require an overruling of *Furman*, but—

Q: Let me be sure I understand. Your point is that for your argument, it makes no difference? You understand that it makes a difference in interpreting the affect of *Furman* on what we have to do with these cases?

MR. BORK: I'm sorry, Mr. Justice Stevens, I—

Q: Do you think *Furman* rests at all on the wide variety of crimes which bore the death penalty?

MR. BORK: I didn't think so. I thought it rested upon the number—in part, as well as upon discretion, in part upon the empirical judgments I discussed about what the legislative will was, and that is why I tried to say that those empirical judgments, while they were plausible or arguable at the time, and since been disproved, so I think that part of *Furman* is undermined.

Q: Then could you tell me one thing before you finish: If it is not necessary to overrule *Furman* to decide these cases, as the government contends they should be decided, why not? Why is not *Furman* controlling?

MR. BORK: Because I think *Furman* refers to standardless jury discretion, that is all it really applies to. I think the statutes that have been enacted in response to *Furman* now put standards into the process and therefore is not necessary to overrule *Furman*.

But I think counsel made it plain that he objects to every element of discretion in the system, not just jury discretion. He objects to them collectively and, if I understood him correctly yesterday, he objects—he would object to them singly. The power of an executive to exercise clemency alone would render—if that were the only element of discretion—would render the death penalty unconstitutional.

There is apparently no way, according to this argument, that anybody could devise a system of justice in which anybody used any judgment about the thing which could then inflict the death penalty. The system—the only system that would meet counsel's objections would be one that was so rigid and automatic and insensitive that it would be morally reprehensible, and then apparently it would meet the moral standards of the Constitution.

The instance of discretion that *McGautha* recognized, that are built into our system, were built in progressively to make the system safer, and progress in criminal justice has occurred precisely by multiplying the instances and the stages at which discretion can be exercised.

As the system now stands, it is utterly impossible for one person or for several persons, acting freakishly or capriciously, out of malice or prejudice or stupidity, to inflict the death penalty. At every stage, it is possible for a small group and sometimes for one person to prevent imposition of the penalty.

Counsel's real complaint is not that anybody is freakishly convicted and executed but, rather, that some murderers are freakishly spared and given life imprisonment. In other words, the fault in the system which makes it unconstitutional to inflict the death penalty is that it errs, if it errs at all, on the side of mercy and the side of safety, and that is what we are told makes it unconstitutional.

The more counsel explains that argument, the less I understand it. Yesterday he said that it was true that all these careful procedures that were worked out by the states and by the federal government help some defendants, but, he said, that means by ineluctable logic that the procedures disadvantage others. I have seldom heard logic more eluctable.

It is impossible to see how these procedures disadvantage anybody, because the persons who are not spared are not made worse off. They were certainly not disadvantaged by the existence of a chance to escape the death penalty. The argument I think is specious. But there are other defects in it.

These arguments that are made against the death penalty could be made against any other form of punishment. There is not one of them that does not apply to life imprisonment.

Now, the sole answer that counsel gives to this is that capital punishment is unique, it is different. Of course, it is different. Life imprisonment is different from a year imprisonment. Life imprisonment is different from a fine.

Q: But it is different in kind from any term of imprisonment, is it not, in two or three different respects? At least it is wholly retrievable, for one thing—

MR. BORK: Well, I suppose—

Q:—by contrast to any term of imprisonment?
MR. BORK: Mr. Justice Stewart, I don't know how a life spent in prison is—

Q: Well, if you made a mistake, you can cancel it—

MR. BORK: Oh, I see.

Q:—and undo it.

MR. BORK: You can undo it to the extent you set him free when you discover the mistake, but the years are gone.

Q: That's right. And it wholly discards any notion of rehabilitation, of course. It is different in that respect.

MR. BORK: It does that.

Q: And it is different in other respects, is it not, not in degree but in kind, it is, and—

MR. BORK: Well, I would suggest as to that, Mr. Justice Stewart, there is only one respect in which it is not different, and that is in contemplation of the Constitution, because the Constitution provides for it, with imprisonment. It draws no line between them. A legislative line can be drawn between them, but I don't think a constitutional line can be drawn between them.

Capital punishment is also different in one other respect, which I would like to come to, if I have time. It is different in that it deters more than any other punishment. There are some categories of criminals who cannot be deterred any other way. For example, the man serving life imprisonment, and he knows it is a real life term, has no incentive not to kill, and some of them have done so. A man who has committed an offense which carries life imprisonment, but who has not yet been apprehended, has no incentive not to kill to escape and to commit other crimes, except the prospect of a death penalty.

So that, as the ultimate sanction, capital punishment is unique, it is different in the sense that it deters more and thereby saves more innocent lives, and it is unique in that it upholds the basic values of our society symbolically and internalizes them for us more than any other punishment.

So its uniqueness I think is something that has to be weighed in favor of the punishment as well. But I return to my point that I don't think it is unique in the constitutional sense. In fact, the argument for its uniqueness was made yesterday, was that we recognize it is unique because we surround it by precautions, procedural safenets other punishments don't have.

Well, I think that is true although I don't see why the very existence of precautions makes it unconstitutional, what we were told. Presumably the same thing would happen if we began to add the same precautions to life imprisonment, it would become unconstitutional, because we recognize its uniqueness.

Q: A good many of these precautions, as you have described them, were generated by the opinion of the Court in the *Furman* case, the five cases now before us.

MR. BORK: That is entirely true, Mr. Chief Justice. I think that the *Furman* case did take a step, and the attempt of the legislatures to comply with that case is now what is said to make their efforts unconstitutional. Apparently we are told that the only way they could have had a chance is to come back with a sweeping mandatory death statute for all kinds of crimes, which would make it not unique, which seems to me a very strange position.

But I want to say something about the—I think what I have said so far is sufficient to dispose of this argument of discretion and what makes the statute unconstitutional. I want to say something else. We have been assuming, and petitioners' counsel have been assuming that discretion means arbitrariness and capriciousness. In using those as synonyms, they are not.

There is really no reason to assume—certainly *McGautha* didn't assume it, and certainly our criminal jurisprudence doesn't assume it—there is no reason to assume that the men and women, lawyers and judges who man our criminal justice system, and the ordinary people who man the grand juries and the petit juries, do not take their responsibilities in capital cases seriously, and that they do not share and reflect a general social understanding of when a crime is serious or heinous.

Petitioners' counsel's argument really requires him to convince this court that the more serious the issue, the more capricious will be the jury, and that the more standards that are given to a jury, the less they will heed any standards. I think that is a reverse argument.

As I said, our system of justice rests upon the thought that people do take their obligations seriously in the system. *McGautha* specifically rested upon that point. And the evidence suggest that the framers were right to require a jury as a way of eliminating caprice and arbitrariness.

We cited the *Stanford Law Review* note in our brief, which discusses jury behavior in capital cases, it finds a rational and consistent pattern. We have discussed the book by Messrs. Kalven and Zaisel, "The American Jury."

Now, to support his argument that there is caprice and freakishness and arbitrariness throughout the system at any time a judgment is to be made, petitioners' counsel really ought to have more than assertion in adverse. He ought to come in here with a study for the entire Nation comparable in seriousness and scope and depth to what Stanford did for California. He ought to come in here with studies not only for the juries but for every stage in the discretionary process, if we are to be told to believe that there is no sense to this process.

The evidence is that there is sense to the process. The assumption of our system is that there is sense to the process, and we have nothing to indicate that there is not.

Q: Mr. Solicitor General, did not the Stanford study show a bias against the blue collar worker as opposed to the white collar worker?

MR. BORK: Well, they thought so. Professor Kalven, who wrote the introduction to that study, noted that he thought that their judgment on that issue was corrupted somewhat by their desire to find a constitutional argument against capital punishment, and he thought that that was not really an accurate conclusion to draw and that there were other explanations for it.

In any event, I don't think that that—you see, if we found a bias of any kind in the system, I don't know what we would do. It wouldn't be an argument for this case, and this goes to racial bias as well as to any other, because if it is true that capital punishment is inflicted disproportionately by sex or by race or by social economic group, because of bias, not because of other reasons, then—and that hasn't been shown around here—then it must also be true that all other punishments are inflicted with equal bias, because it is the same prosecutors, the same jurors, the same people drawn from the same community, the same judges, the same governor, and I doubt that if we saw a skewing of the system according to some bias that any court would outlaw all punishments for all crimes. We would attack the bias institutionally and in other ways to try to eliminate its effects on the system. But it is an irrelevant question to the question of what punishment you use.

And indeed in our brief—I doubt that I will have time to reach the point, but we do discuss, and petitioners' counsel comes back with an attack upon our discussion, which I still think is correct. The evidence of racial bias I think is not here. There is some in some studies in the past in the deep South at a time when blacks were systematically excluded from grand and petit juries. I don't think there is enough here anyway to carry the bias argument.

But in any event—and I would point out that the Ehrlich study on deterrance, which we are told is so worthless that it may be utterly disregarded, a point with which I disagree, we are told worthless. That study is a masterpiece of sophistication, compared to these rather trivial studies of racial discrimination we are asked to rely upon. But I don't want to get onto that point, because I wish to conclude the point about discretion.

I have examined the discretion point and I have suggested that I think the states should be free to make their first choice about how the death penalty should be decided upon, and I have suggested that I don't think *Furman* and *McGautha* can pull it together, and that although it is not necessary, that *Furman* should be overruled.

The odd thing about this case is that petitioners' counsel argues that the criminal justice system is too imperfect to permit the death penalty at precisely that moment in our history when the sytem has more procedural safeguards than at any other time in the history of Anglo American Law. Indeed, that is his complaint about it, too many safeguards.

The better our system becomes, the angrier its opponents become. The real claim here is that the criminal justice system cannot inflict the death penalty so long as human beings are running the system and making any judgments. Whatever that may be, that is not a constitutional argument.

Ultimately, these five cases are cases about democratic government, the right of various legislatures of the United States to choose or reject, according to their own judgment, according to their own moral sense and that of their people, the death penalty, in accordance with the Constitution, this Court, speaking through Mr. Justice Black, once before I think gave the correct answer to that question in *Robinson* v. *United States*. The Court said it is for Congress and not for us to decide whether it is wise public policy to inflict the death penalty at all. We do not know what provision of law, constitutional or statutory, gives us power holding to nullify the clearly expressed purpose of Congress to authorize the death penalty. Because of a doubt as to the precise congressional purpose in regard to hypothetical cases, that may never arise.

That statement of the Court, we submit, was true throughout our history, and it is as true today as it was when *Robinson* was decided. The large majority of American states and the Congress of the United States have reaffirmed their judgment that capital punishment is both moral and necessary, and all that is said here by petitioners' counsel is that these legislatures and the people they represent have behaved immorally and unwisely. That is not the test of the Eighth Amendment.

This case is merely the latest in a continuing series seeking to obtain from this Court a political judgment that the opponents of capital punishment have been unable to obtain from the political branches of government. The United States asks that the constitutionality of the death penalty to be upheld.

Q: Mr. Solicitor General, you haven't had an opportunity to address in your oral argument the issue of deterrence. I recognize, of course, that the statistical data can be construed in various ways, and I would agree that it is perhaps not controlling or conclusive. Yet I would invite your attention to some figures and then ask you a question. I have before me the 1973 report of the Federal Bureau of Investigation. It states that in 1968, 15,720 people were murdered in this country; in 1973, the latest year reported in this report, 19,510 people were murdered—that is an increase of 42 percent; in gross numbers, that is an increase of 5,790 people. I do not have the more recent figures. I think I have read in the press that they show some slight down-trend.

It is perfectly obvious from these figures that we need some way to deter the slaughter of Americans. I use the word "slaughter" because that word was used in connection with the disaster in Vietnam, in which 55,000 Americans were killed over a six or seven-year period. If the FBI figures are correct, there were more Americans killed in this country, murdered, than there were on the battlefields of Vietnam. Would you care to comment, elaborate, or state your views with respect to the deterrent effect, if any, of the death sentences?

MR. BORK: Mr. Justice Powell, it seems to me that it cannot rationally be questioned that the death penalty has a deterrent effect. Mankind has always thought that throughout its history. We know, as a matter of common sense and common observation, we know that all other aspects of human behavior, as you raise the cost and the risk, the amount of the activity goes down. I don't know why murder should be any different.

I wouldn't have thought that anybody would have doubted that or listened to a couple of academicians who doubted it. And we introduce the Ehrlich study and the Yunker study only to show that there is respectable academic evidence on the side of deterrence. But I would have thought that it is common sense, and I would have thought that in fact the judgment of the legislatures of this country, that they think it deters, is enough—it is a rational judgment—we think it is enough for this Court.

And I must say, at a time when international and domestic terrorism is going up, at a time when brutal murders are going up, it is an awesome responsibility to take from the states what they think is a necessary deterrent and save a few hundred guilty people and thereby probably condemn to death thousands of innocent people. That is truly an awesome responsibility.

Q: Granting all of that, Mr. Solicitor General, not that it matters in this case, but the death penalty for drugs hasn't done much good, has it? You would just put that as an exception to the rule, wouldn't you?

MR. BORK: Oh, no, no. Mr. Justice Marshall, many things affect—

Q: I mean it didn't deter the drug people at all, did it?

MR. BORK: I don't know how one could say that it did not. You can't deter perhaps an existing addict, which may be the reason for *Robinson* v. *California*, but it is not at all clear that you can't deter people from becoming addicts, from taking the first step.

Brief Against Vice President Spiro Agnew

Agnew, while governor of Maryland, had taken bribes in connection with the letting of contracts and was still receiving payments while Vice President of the United States. The evidence was being presented to a federal grand jury when Agnew's attorneys filed a motion seeking immunity on the theory that a vice president, like the president, could not be indicted and tried until he resigned or was removed from office through impeachment by the House of Representatives and conviction in the Senate. Agnew approached the Speaker of the House, Carl Albert, claiming that the Department of Justice was usurping the impeachment authority of the House. Albert sent a letter to that effect to Attorney General Elliot Richardson. Our brief dealt with the Speaker's concerns. Although the Solicitor General typically appears only in the Supreme Court, Nixon and Richardson decided that in this instance, because the Vice President was the defendant, the briefing and argument should be handled by the highest legal officer of the government. Hence the brief reproduced here.

United States District Court
District of Maryland
In Re Proceedings of The Grand Jury Impaneled December 5, 1972:
Application of Spiro T. Agnew
Vice President of the United States
Case Number Civil 73–965
Memorandum for the United States
Concerning the Vice President's
Claim of Constitutional Immunity

The motion by the Vice President poses a grave and unresolved constitutional issue: whether the Vice President of the United States is subject to federal grand jury investigation and possible indictment and trial while still in office.

Due to the historic independence and vital function of the grand jury, motions to interfere with or restrict its investigations have traditionally met with disfavor. See, *e.g., United States* v. *Dionisio,* 410 U.S. 1 (1973); *Branzburg* v. *Hayes,* 408 U.S. 665 (1972); *United States* v. *Ryan,* 402 U.S. 530 (1971). Thus in ordinary circumstances we would oppose litigious interference with grand jury proceedings without regard to the underlying merits of any asserted claim of immunity. But in the special circumstances of this case, which involve a constitutional issue of utmost importance, we believe it appropriate, in the interest of both the Vice President and the nation, that the Court resolve the issue at this stage of the proceedings.

Counsel for the Vice President have ably advanced arguments that the Constitution prohibits the investigation and indictment of an incumbent Vice President. We acknowledge the weight of their contentions. In order that judicial resolution of the issues may be fully informed, however, we wish to submit considerations that suggest a different conclusion: that the Congress and the judiciary possess concurrent jurisdiction over allegations made concerning a Vice President.

This makes it appropriate that the Department of Justice state now its intended procedure should the Court conclude that an incumbent Vice President is amenable to federal jurisdiction prior to removal from office. The United States Attorney will, in that event, complete the presentation of evidence to the grand jury and await that body's determination of whether to return an indictment. Should the grand jury return an indictment, the Department will hold the proceedings in abeyance for a reasonable time, if the Vice President consents to a delay, in order to offer the House of Representatives an opportunity to consider the desirability of impeachment proceedings.[1]

The Department believes that this deference to the House of Representatives at the post-indictment stage, though not constitutionally required, is an appropriate accommodation of the respective interests involved. It reflects a proper comity between the different branches of government, especially in view of the significance of this matter for the nation. We also appreciate the fact that the Vice President has expressed a desire to have this matter considered in the forum provided by the Congress. The issuance of an indictment, if any, would in the meantime toll the statute of limitations and preserve the matter for subsequent judicial resolution.

---

1. We note that the Speaker of the House, Representative Carl Albert though declining to take action at this stage, has not foreclosed the possibility that he might recommend House action at a subsequent stage.

We will first state the posture of this matter and then offer to the Court considerations based upon the Constitution's text, history, and rationale which indicate that all civil officers of the United States other than the president are amenable to the federal criminal process either before or after the conclusion of impeachment proceedings.

Statement

A grand jury in this District, impaneled December 5, 1972, is currently conducting an investigation of possible violations by Spiro T. Agnew, Vice President of the United States, and others of certain provisions of the United States Criminal Code, including 18 U.S.C. 1951, 1952 and 371, and certain criminal provisions of the Internal Revenue Code of 1954. This investigation is now well advanced and the grand jury is in the process of receiving evidence.

The Vice President has moved to enjoin "the Grand Jury from conducting any investigation looking to his possible indictment . . . and from issuing any indictment, presentment, or other charge or statement pertaining to [him]" (Motion, 1). The Vice President has further moved "to enjoin the Attorney General of the United States, the United States Attorney for the District of Maryland and all officials of the United States Department of Justice from presenting to the Grand Jury any testimony, documents, or other materials looking to possible indictment of [him] and from discussing with or disclosing to any person any such testimony, document, or materials" (Motion, 1–2).

The Vice President's motion is based on two contentions: (1) that "[t]he Constitution forbids that the Vice President be indicted or tried in any criminal court," and (2) that "officials of the prosecutorial arm have engaged in a steady campaign of statements to the press which could have no purpose and effect other than to prejudice any grand or petit jury hearing evidence relating to the Vice President . . . " (Motion, 2).

On September 28, 1973, this court directed that the Department of Justice submit its brief on the constitutional issue on October 5 and its brief on the remaining issue on October 8, that the Vice President's counsel file a reply brief on October 11, and that oral argument be had on October 12. This Memorandum is submitted on behalf of the United States, the grand jury, and the individual respondents named in the motion, in opposition to the claim that the grand jury should be enjoined because the Vice President cannot "be indicted or tried in any criminal court" (Motion, 1).

I. The Text of the Constitution and Historic Practice Under It Do Not Support a Broad Immunity of Civil Officers Prior to Removal.

Analysis of the Constitution's text indicates that no general immunity from the criminal process exists for civil officers who are subject to impeachment.

A. The Only Explicit Immunity in the Constitution is the Limited Immunity Granted Congressmen.

The Constitution provides no explicit immunity from criminal sanctions for any civil officer. The only express immunity in the entire document is found in Article I, Section 6, which provides:

> The Senators and Representatives . . . shall in all Cases except Treason, Felony, and Breach of the Peace, be privileged from Arrest during their Attendance at the Session of their respective Houses, and in going to and returning from the same. . . .

Since the Framers knew how to, and did, spell out an immunity, the natural inference is that no immunity exists where none is mentioned. Indeed, any other reading would turn the constitutional text on its head: the construction advanced by counsel for the Vice President requires that the explicit grant of immunity to legislators be read as in fact a partial withdrawal of a complete immunity legislators would otherwise have possessed in common with other government officers. The intent of the Framers was to the contrary. Cf. *United States* v. *Johnson,* 383 U.S. 169, 177–185 (1966).

In the face of this strong textual showing it would require a compelling constitutional argument to erect such an immunity for a Vice President. Counsel for the Vice President contend that such an argument is provided by Article I, Section 3, Clause 7, by Article II, Section 4, and by the Twelfth Amendment. We will examine each of these contentions in turn.

B. The Meaning of Article I, Section 3, Clause 7.

Article I, Section 3, Clause 7 provides:

> Judgment in Cases of Impeachment shall not extend further than to removal from Office, and disqualification to hold and enjoy any Office of Honor, Trust, or Profit under the United States: but the Party convicted shall nevertheless be liable and subject to Indictment, Trial, Judgment, and Punishment, according to law.

Counsel for the Vice President argue that this clause means impeachment must precede indictment. The records of the debates of the constitutional convention, however, show that the Framers contemplated that this sequence should be mandatory only as to the President.

During most of the debate over the impeachment clause, the Framers' attention was directed specifically to the Office of the Presidency, and their remarks strongly suggest an understanding that the President, as Chief Executive, would not be subject to the ordinary criminal process. See 2 Farrand, *Records of the Federal Convention* 64–69, 626 (New Haven, 1911). For example, as the memorandum submitted on behalf of the Vice President points out (Memo., 9), Gouveneur Morris observed that the Supreme Court would "try the President after the trial of impeachment." 2 Farrand, *supra,* at 500. It is, of course, significant that such remarks referred only to the President, not to the Vice President and other civil officers.

However, the Framers did not debate the question whether impeachment generally must precede indictment. Their assumption that the President would not be subject to criminal process was based upon the crucial nature of his executive powers. Moreover, the debates concerning the impeachment clause itself related almost exclusively to the Presidency.[2] The impeachment clause was expanded to cover the Vice President and other civil officers only toward the very end of the convention. Berger, *Impeachment: The Constitutional Problems* 146–47 (Cambridge, MA, 1973). Indeed creation of the Office of the Vice Presidency itself "came in the closing days of the Constitutional Convention." S. Rep. No. 66, 89th Cong., 1st Sess., 9 (1965). Thus none of the general impeachment debates addressed or considered the particular nature of the powers of the Vice President or other civil officers. Certainly nothing in the debates suggests that the immunity contemplated for the President would extend to any lesser officer.

As it applies to civil officers other than the President, the principal operative effect of Article I, Section 3, Clause 7, is solely the preclusion of pleas of double jeopardy in criminal prosecutions following convictions upon impeachments. The President's immunity rests not only upon the matters just

---

2. As a recent commentator has observed:

> One thing is clear: in the impeachment debate the Convention was almost exclusively concerned with the President. The extent to which the President occupied center stage can be gathered from the fact that the addition to the impeachment clause of the "Vice President and all civil officers" only took place on September 8, shortly before the Convention adjourned. [Berger, *Impeachment: The Constitutional Problems* 100 (Cambridge, MA, 1973)]

discussed but also upon his unique constitutional position and powers. See *infra*, 17–20. There are substantial reasons, embedded not only in the constitutional framework but in the exigencies of government, for distinguishing in this regard between the President and all lesser officers including the Vice President.

Notwithstanding the paucity of debate or contemporaneous commentary on the issue, it is clear that the Framers and their contemporaries understood that lesser impeachable officers are subject to criminal process. The first Congress, many of whose members had been delegates to the Constitutional Convention, promptly enacted Section 21 of the Act of April 30, 1790, 1 Stat. 117, recognizing that sitting federal judges were criminally punishable for bribery and providing for their disqualification from office upon conviction. And in 1796, Attorney General Lee informed Congress that a judge of a territorial court, a civil officer subject to impeachment, was indictable for criminal offenses while in office. 3 Hinds, *Precedents of the House of Representatives* 982–83 (Washington, 1907). These considerations, together with those rooted in the constitutional text and practicalities of government that we discuss below, have led subsequent commentators to conclude, with virtual unanimity, that the Framers did not intend civil officers generally to be immune from criminal process. See, *e.g.*, Rawle, *A View on the Constitution of the United States of America* 169, 215 (Philadelphia, 1829); Simpson, *supra*, 52–53; Feerick, *Impeaching Federal Judges: A Study of the Constitutional Provisions*, 39 Fordham L. Rev. 1, 55 (1970).

The sole purpose of the caveat in Article I, Section 3, that the party convicted upon impeachment may nevertheless be punished criminally, is to preclude the argument that the doctrine of double jeopardy saves the offender from the second trial. This was the interpretation of the clause offered by Luther Martin, a member of the Constitutional Convention and Judge Chase's counsel, during Chase's impeachment. 14 Annals of Congress, 8th Cong., 2d Sess., 423. In truth, impeachment and the criminal process serve different ends so that the outcome of one has no legal effect upon the outcome of the other. James Wilson, an important participant in the Constitutional Convention,[3] put the matter succinctly:

---

3. "James Wilson was the strongest member of this [the Pennsylvania] delegation and Washington considerd him to be one of the strongest men in the convention. . . . He had served several times in Congress, and had been one of the signers of the Declaration of Independence. At forty-five he was regarded as one of the ablest lawyers in America." Farrand, *The Framing of the Constitution* 21 (New Haven, CT, 1913).

Impeachments . . . come not . . . within the sphere of ordinary jurisprudence. They are founded on different principles; are governed by different
maxims, and are directed to different objects; for this reason, the trial
and punishment of an offense in the impeachment, is no bar to a trial of
the same offense at common law. [I Wilson, *Works* 324 (Cambridge, MA,
1967).]

Because the two processes have different objects, the considerations relevant to one may not be relevant to the other. For that reason, neither conviction nor acquittal in one trial, though it may be persuasive, need automatically determine the result in the other trial. To take an obvious example, a
civil officer found not guilty by reason of insanity in a criminal trial could
certainly be impeached nonetheless.

The argument advanced by counsel for the Vice President, which insists
that only a party actually convicted upon impeachment may be tried criminally, would tie the two processes together in a manner not contemplated by
the Constitution. Impeachment trials, as that of President Andrew Johnson
reminds us, may sometimes be influenced by political passions and interests
that would be rigorously excluded from a criminal trial. Or somewhat more
than one-third of the Senate might conclude that a particular offense, though
properly punishable in the courts, did not warrant conviction on impeachment. Hence, if Article I, Section 3, Clause 7, were read to mean that no one
not convicted upon impeachment could be tried criminally, the failure of
the House to vote an impeachment, or the failure of the impeachment in the
Senate, would confer upon the civil officer accused complete and—were the
statute of limitations permitted to run—permanent immunity from criminal prosecution however plain his guilt.[4] There is no such requirement in
the Constitution or in reason. To adopt that view would give Congress the
power to pardon by acquittal or even by mere inaction, since the officer
would never be a "Party convicted" upon impeachment, even though the

---

4. The Congress could only avoid this result by attending to complaints of criminal conduct
against all civil officers so protected. Since the Office of the Vice President appears indistinguishable in this respect from that of other civil officers, the construction of the Constitution
offered by counsel for the Vice President would place a significant burden on the Congress. As
the result of historic experience, the Congress has chosen to make sparing use of its impeachment power. The House is not structured to act with any frequency as a prosecutor nor the
Senate as a jury. A construction of the Constitution that forces the Congress to choose between
impeachment or immunization would deprive Congress of the discretion of how and to what
extent it wishes to exercise its impeachment jurisdiction. It might also frequently immobilize
the Congress, preventing it from dealing with pressing national affairs, to the harm of both
Congress and the country.

Constitution lodges the power to grant clemency exclusively in the President. The Framers certainly never supposed that failure to obtain conviction upon impeachment conferred permanent criminal immunity.

The conclusion seems required, therefore, that the Constitution provides that the "Party convicted" is nonetheless subject to criminal punishment, not to establish the sequence of the two processes, but solely to establish that conviction upon impeachment does not raise a double jeopardy defense in a criminal trial.[5] A similar conclusion has been reached under state constitutions containing provisions modeled upon Article I, Section 3, Clause 7. These state constitutional provisions have been held not to bar prosecution of impeachable state officers while in office. See, *e.g., Commonwealth* v. *Rowe,* 112 Ky. 482, 66 S.W. 29 (1902); *State* v. *Jefferson,* 90 N.J.L. 507, 101 A. 569 (E. & A., 1917). Indeed, indictment, trial, and conviction of state officers while in office has been common. See generally, *Anno: Officer—Conviction of Crime,* 71 A.L.R. 2d 593 (1960).

C. The Meaning of Article II, Section 4.

Article II, Section 4 provides:

> The President, Vice President, and all civil Officers of the United States, shall be removed from Office on Impeachment for, and Conviction of, Treason, Bribery, or other high crimes and Misdemeanors.

The Vice President's contention that he is immune from criminal process while in office rests heavily on the assumption that even initiation of the process of indictment, trial, and punishment upon conviction, would effect his practical removal from office in a manner violative of the exclusivity of the impeachment power (See, *e.g.,* Memo., 2, 5–6). This assumption is without foundation in history or logic.

We agree that conviction upon impeachment is the exclusive means for removing a Vice President from office. Although non-elective civil officers

---

5. Just as an individual may be both criminally prosecuted and deported for the same offense (see *Fong Yue Ting* v. *United States,* 149 U.S. 698 (1893)), a civil officer could be both impeached and criminally punished even absent the Article I, Section 3 proviso. Moreover, the civil nature of an impeachment under the Constitution renders the English precedent—involving an impeachment process that was both criminal and political—inapposite. Whereas conviction of impeachment under our Constitution has no criminal consequences, impeachment in England was designed to accomplish punishment as well as removal, for peers of the realm were not subject to ordinary criminal process. As a consequence, the relationship between the impeachment power and the criminal process in the two countries is wholly different. See generally, Berger, *supra,* 78–85.

in the executive branch may be dismissed from office by the President, and Senators and Representatives may be expelled by their respective Houses, historically the President, Vice President, and federal judges have been removable from office only by impeachment.[6] But it is clear from history that a criminal indictment, or even trial and conviction, does not, standing alone, effect the removal of an impeachable federal officer.

As counsel for the Vice President point out (Memo., 14–15), one of his predecessors, Aaron Burr, was subject to simultaneous indictment in two states while in office, yet he continued to exercise his constitutional responsibilities until the expiration of his term.[7] Judge John Warren Davis of the United States Court of Appeals for the Third Circuit and Judge Albert W. Johnson of the United States District Court for the Middle District of Pennsylvania, were both indicted and tried while in office; neither was convicted, and each continued to hold office during trial. See Borkin, *The Corrupt Judge* 95–186 (New York, 1962). Judge Kerner of the Seventh Circuit, whose conviction is currently pending on appeal, has not yet been removed from office. Similarly, the criminal conviction of Congressmen does not act to remove them from office: "the final judgment of conviction [does] not operate, *ipso facto*, to vacate the seat of the convicted Senator, nor compel the Senate to expel him or to regard him as expelled by force alone of the judgment." *Burton v. United States,* 202 U.S. 344, 369.

This is not to say that trial and punishment would not interfere in some degree with an officer's exercise of his public duties, although, as the case of Aaron Burr illustrates, mere indictment standing alone apparently does not seriously hinder full exercise of the powers of the vice presidency. But the relationship between trial and punishment, on the one hand, and actual removal from office, on the other, is far from automatic. As perhaps the

---

6. We do not here address the question of whether 18 U.S.C. §201 (e) constitutionally operates to remove a civil officer without impeachment. We only note that the federal statutes contain no general provision, as do the statutes of many states, providing that a vacancy exists in any civil office whenever the incumbent is convicted of a serious crime. These statutes have been upheld as operating to remove the officer without impeachment. See State v. Sullivan, 188 P.2d 592 (Ariz. 1948). See generally. *Anno: Officer—Conviction of Crime*, 71 A.L.R. 2d 593 (1960). If such a statute were passed by the Congress, its application to judges, who serve during "good behavior" (Article III, §1) might be different than its application to the Vice President, who has a term of office of four years (Article II, §1).

7. Apparently neither Burr nor his contemporaries considered him constitutionally immune from indictment. Although counsel for the Vice President assert that Burr's indictments were "allowed to die" (Memo., 15), that was merely because "Burr thought it best not to visit either New York or New Jersey." Parmet & Hecht, *Aaron Burr: Portrait of an Ambitious Man*, 231 (New York, 1967).

leading American commentator on impeachment has observed (Simpson, *A Treatise on Federal Impeachment* 52 (Philadelphia, 1916)):

> A public officer may be criminally convicted of trespass, though acting under a claim of right, or for excessively speeding his automobile, yet neither would justify impeachment. If, however, the conviction was followed by imprisonment, impeachment might be well maintained, for the office would be brought into contempt if a convict were allowed to administer it. It may be said that, in that event, impeachment would depend on the severity or lenity of a trial judge, and this would be so, but for the office's sake, a man may be said to be guilty of a "high misdemeanor" if he so acts as to be imprisoned.

Whether conviction of and imprisonment for minor offenses must lead to removal on conviction of impeachment therefore depends, in any given case, on the sound judgment of the Congress and the President's exercise of his pardoning power. Certainly it is clear that criminal indictment, trial, and even conviction of a Vice President would not, *ipso facto,* cause his removal; subjection of a Vice President to the criminal process therefore does not violate the exclusivity of the impeachment power as the means of his removal from office.

D. The Twelfth Amendment

Counsel for the Vice President suggest (Memo., 7–8, 18) that adoption of the Twelfth Amendment, providing for separate elections of the President and Vice President, in some way supports immunity for a Vice President. In fact, the implication of the Amendment is the contrary.

The original constitutional plan was that each elector should vote for two persons for President. The man receiving the greatest vote was to be President and the runner-up was to be Vice President. The Vice President was thus the next most powerful contender for the presidency. The Framers, however, did not foresee the development of political parties which ran "tickets," one man standing for President and the other for Vice President. An elector would then cast one ballot for each of these candidates which had the embarrassing result that Thomas Jefferson and Aaron Burr, though regarded by their party as candidates for, respectively, President and Vice President, received an equal number of votes. There being no constitutionally elected President, the election was thrown into the House of Representatives.

The Twelfth Amendment, adopted in response, provided separate elections so that a man wanted only as Vice President should not thus block the election of the man wanted as President. The adoption of the Twelfth Amendment, therefore, was recognition that the Vice President, under a party system, is not the second most desired man for President but rather an understudy chosen by the presidential candidate. That recognition does not magnify the constitutional position of a Vice President.[8]

II. The Structure of the Constitution and the Workings of the Constitutional System Do Not Imply an Immunity for a Vice President

The Constitution is an intensely practical document and judicial derivation of powers and immunities is necessarily based upon consideration of the document's structure and of the practical results of alternative interpretations. *McCulloch* v. *Maryland,* 4 Wheat. 316 (1819); *Stuart* v. *Laird,* 1 Cranch 299, 308 (1803); *Field* v. *Clark,* 143 U.S. 649, 691 (1892); *United States* v. *Midwest Oil Co.,* 236 U.S. 459, 472–73 (1915); *United States* v. *Curtis-Wright Corp.,* 299 U.S. 304, 328–29 (1936). We turn, therefore, to a structural and functional analysis of the Constitution in relation to the immunity claimed for Vice Presidents.

> *A. Immunity Should be Implied for an Officer Only if Subjecting Him to the Criminal Process Would Substantially Impair the Functioning of a Branch of Government.*

The real question underlying the issue of whether indictment of any particular civil officer can precede conviction upon impeachment—and it is constitutional in every sense because it goes to the heart of the operation of government—is whether a governmental function would be seriously impaired if a particular civil officer were liable to indictment before being tried on impeachment. The answer to that question must necessarily vary with the nature and functions of the office involved.

---

8. Counsel for the Vice President additionally argue that since the Framers could not have intended the President, through his Attorney General, to harass political rivals, therefore the Vice President must be immune from criminal process (see Memo., 18). This argument appears unsound. Once he accepts the secondary office, the Vice President is rarely, if ever, an important political rival of the incumbent President. Moreover, the logical implication of the argument is that all major politicians—Senators, Governors, and many persons not even holding office—must be freed of responsibility for criminal acts.

1. We may begin with a category of civil officers subject to impeachment whom we think may clearly be tried and convicted prior to removal from office through the impeachment process: federal judges.[9] A judge may be hampered in the performance of his duty when he is on trial for a felony but his personal incapacity in no way threatens the ability of the judicial branch to continue to function effectively. There have been frequent occasions where death, illness, or disqualification has removed all of the available judges from a district or a circuit and even this extreme circumstances has been met effectively by the assignment of judges from other districts and circuits.

Similar considerations apply to Congressmen, and these practical judgments are reflected in the Constitution. As already noted, Article I, Section 6 provides a very limited immunity for Senators and Representatives but explicitly permits them to be tried for felonies and breaches of the peace. This limited grant of immunity demonstrates a recognition that, although the functions of the legislature are not lightly to be interfered with, the public interest in the expeditious and even-handed administration of the criminal law outweighs the cost imposed by the incapacity of a single legislator. Such incapacity does not seriously impair the functioning of Congress.

2. Almost all legal commentators agree, on the other hand, that an incumbent President must be removed from office through conviction upon an impeachment before being subject to the criminal process. Indeed, counsel for the Vice President takes this position (Memo, 5–8), so it is not in dispute. It will be instructive to examine the basis for that immunity in order to see whether its rationale also fits an incumbent Vice President, for that is the crux of the question before the Court.

As we have noted, page 6, *supra,* the Framers' discussions assumed that impeachment would precede criminal trial because their attention was focused upon the presidency. See also, 2 Farrand, *Records of the Federal Convention, supra,* 500, and Hamilton, *The Federalist,* Nos. 65 and 69. They assumed that the nation's Chief Executive, responsible as no other single officer is for the affairs of the United States, would not be taken from duties that only he can perform unless and until it is determined that he is to be shorn of those duties by the Senate.

---

9. The Department of Justice is now contending that a United States court of appeals judge is subject to indictment, conviction, and sentencing prior to removal through the impeachment process. See *United States* v. *Kerner,* now pending in the Court of Appeals for the Seventh Circuit. This, of course, is the historic position of the Department. See page 12, *supra.* It seems too clear for argument that other civil officers, such as heads of executive departments, are fully subject to criminal sanctions whether or not first removed from office.

The scope of the powers lodged in the single man occupying the presidency is shown by the briefest review of Article II of the Constitution. The whole "executive Power" is vested in him and that includes the powers of the "Commander in Chief of the Army and the Navy," the power to command the executive departments, the power shared with the Senate to make treaties and to appoint ambassadors, the power shared with the Senate to appoint Justices of the Supreme Court and other civil officers, the power and responsibility to execute the laws, and the power to grant reprieves and pardons. The constitutional outline of the powers and duties of the Presidency, though more complete than noted here, does not flesh out the full importance of the office, but this is so universally recognized that we do not pause to emphasize it.

The singular importance of the Presidency, in comparison with all other offices, is further demonstrated by the Twenty-Fifth Amendment, Sections 3 and 4. The problem, as we have noted, is one of the functioning of a branch of government, and it is noteworthy that the President is the only officer of government for whose temporary disability the Constitution provides procedures to qualify a replacement. This is recognition that the President is the only officer whose temporary disability while in office incapacitates an entire branch of government. The Constitution makes no provision, because none is needed, for such disability of a Vice President, a judge, a legislator, or any subordinate executive branch officer.

3. Without in any way denigrating the constitutional functions of a Vice President—or those of any individual Supreme Court Justice or Senator, for that matter—they are clearly less crucial to the operations of the executive branch of government than are the functions of a President. Although the office of the Vice Presidency is of course a high one, it is not indispensable to the orderly operation of government. There have been many occasions in our history when the nation lacked a Vice President, and yet suffered no ill consequences. And, as has been discussed above (page 12, *supra*), at least one Vice President successfully fulfilled the responsibilities of his office while under indictment in two states. There is in fact no comparison between the importance of the Presidency and the Vice Presidency.

A Vice President has only three constitutional functions: (1) to replace the President in the event of the President's removal from office, or his death, resignation, or inability to discharge the powers and duties of his office (Twenty-Fifth Amendment, Sections 1, 3, and 4); (2) to make, together with a majority of either the principal officers of the executive departments or such other body as Congress may by law provide, a written declaration of the President's inability (Twenty-Fifth Amendment, Section 3); and, (3) to preside over the Senate, which Vice Presidents rarely do, and cast the deciding vote in case of a tie (Article I, Section 3).[10]

None of a Vice President's constitutional functions are substantially impaired by his liability to the criminal process.[11] The only problem that might arise would be the death of a President at the time a Vice President was the defendant in a criminal trial.[12] That would pose no practical difficulty, however. The criminal proceedings could be suspended or terminated and the impeachment process begun. This would leave the nation in the same practical situation as would the institution of impeachment proceedings against an incumbent President, the sole legal difference being that the successor to office would be the Speaker of the House of Representatives rather than the Vice President.

> *B. The Function of the President are not only Indispensable to the Operation of Government, They are Inconsistent with His Subjection to the Criminal Process; There is no Similar Inconsistency in the Case of a Vice President.*

The inference that only the President is immune from indictment and trial prior to removal from office also arises from an examination of other structural features of the Constitution. The Framers could not have contemplated prosecution of an incumbent President because they vested in him complete power over the execution of the laws, which includes, of course, the power to control prosecutions (Article I, Section 3). And they gave him "Power to grant Reprieves and Pardons for Offenses against the United States, except in Cases of Impeachment" (Article I, Section 2, Clause 1), a power that is consistent only with the conclusion that the President must be removed by impeachment, and so deprived of the power to pardon, before criminal process can be instituted against him. A Vice President, of course, has no power either to control prosecutions or to grant pardons. The functions of the Vice

---

10. The Framers assumed that Vice Presidents would not regularly preside over the Senate, for they expressly provided in Article I, Section 3, Clause 5 for the election of a President *pro tempore* to act in the Vice President's absence.

11. Counsel for the Vice President stresses the importance of the Vice President's role, under the Twenty-Fifth Amendment, with respect to a declaration of Presidential inability. But that responsibility is not an active, continuous executive function. It is, to the contrary, a responsibility—never yet exercised—that entails only a single act, one that could be performed by a Vice President who was, for example, under indictment. Moreover, it is a responsibility that is shared with a majority of the Cabinet members, who are themselves subject to the criminal process.

12. We assume, for reasons stated above (13, *supra*), that conviction and imprisonment of a Vice President, or any civil officer, would lead to prompt removal through impeachment.

Presidency are thus not at all inconsistent with the conclusion that an incumbent may be prosecuted and convicted while still in office.

C. *Basic Considerations of Law Enforcement Militate Against Extension of Immunity to Officers other than the President.*

Thus we conclude that considerations derived from the structure of the Constitution itself indicate that only a President possesses immunity from the criminal process prior to impeachment. The position of a Vice President would appear to be similar to that of judges, congressmen, and other civil officers. There are also, however, practical considerations that point in the same direction. Such considerations are entitled to weight in the absence of compelling constitutional reasons for an immunity of the sort we have shown exist only for the Presidency. In many cases, for instance, problems will be posed by the presence of co-conspirators and the running of the statute of limitations.

An official may have co-conspirators and even if the officer were immune, his co-conspirators would not be. The result would be that the grand and petit juries would receive evidence about the illegal transactions and that evidence would inevitably name the officer. The trial might end in the conviction of the co-conspirators for their dealings with the officer, yet the officer would not be on trial, would not have the opportunity to cross-examine and present testimony on his own behalf. The man and his office would be slandered and demeaned without a trial in which he was heard. The individual might prefer that to the risk of punishment, but the courts should not adopt a rule that opens the office to such a damaging procedure.

This practical problem is raised by the motion here which asks this Court to prohibit "the Grand Jury from conducting any investigation looking to the [Vice President's] possible indictment" and to enjoin the prosecutors from presenting any evidence to the grand jury "looking to [his] possible indictment" (Motion, 1).

The criminal investigation being conducted by the grand jury is wide-ranging, and the Vice President is not its sole subject. The evidence being presented, while it touches on the Vice President, involves others also. It would be virtually impossible to exclude all evidence relating to the Vice President and at the same time present meaningful evidence relating to possible co-conspirators. Thus, enjoining the investigation and presentation of evidence "looking to the possible indictment of [the Vice President]" would require the investigations of other persons also to be suspended. The relief therefore would plainly "frustrate the public's interest in the fair and expeditious administration of the criminal laws" (*United States* v. *Dionisio, supra,* 410 U.S. at 17).

The statute of limitations with respect to some of the possible illegal activities being investigated will run as early as October 26, 1973. A suspension of the grand jury's investigation of the Vice President and others could therefore jeopardize the possibility of a timely indictment. Should this Court suspend the grand jury investigation the result would likely be to accord the Vice President and other persons permanent immunity from prosecution through the running of the statute of limitations even though it is unlikely he is entitled even to the temporary immunity, pending conviction upon impeachment, that his counsel claim for him.

Conclusion

Nothing we have said is intended to deprecate in any way the high office of the Vice Presidency or its importance in the Constitutional scheme. We acknowledge that the issue raised by counsel for the Vice President is a momentous and difficult one for any court. However, in order to assist the Court in resolving this troublesome question, we have set forth arguments that counter those advanced by counsel for the Vice President.

For the reasons stated, applicant's motions should be denied.

Respectfully submitted,

Robert H. Bork, *Solicitor General.*
Keith A. Jones, Edmund W. Kitch, *Assistants to the Solicitor General.*
October 5, 1973

I did not present an oral argument to the district court because, after the briefing was completed, Agnew chose to plea bargain, trading his resignation for an agreement by the Department of Justice not to seek a prison sentence. Richardson later wrote that he thought Agnew's decision not to go forward was probably influenced by the strength of our brief. Richardson decided, correctly in my opinion, that the Agnew deal was in the country's best interest. Richard Nixon's impeachment looked increasing likely. It would, Richardson thought, be a shattering blow to the nation's morale, the effectiveness of the government, and to America's prestige and credibility abroad if the President was on trial in the Senate on articles of impeachment while, simultaneously, the Vice President was in the dock on criminal charges. Nobody had any confidence in the Speaker of the House, who was next in the line of succession. So it was that Representative Gerald Ford was nominated and confirmed as vice president in accordance with the Twenty-Fifth Amendment and ultimately succeeded to the presidency upon President Nixon's resignation.

The remaining two items in this subsection are oral arguments about the application of the speech clause of the First Amendment in military contexts. The federal judiciary, displaying a tendency since grown stronger, had shown a willingness to interfere with the traditional rules and operations of the military, a tendency I thought extremely unwise and worth opposing in the Supreme Court. In these cases, the authority of the military was upheld.

Secretary of the Navy v. Avrech

In the Supreme Court of the United States
Secretary of the Navy
Appellant
v.
Mark Avrech
No. 72–1713
Washington, D.C.
Wednesday, February 20, 1974

Oral Argument of Robert H. Bork,
Solicitor General of the United States
On Behalf of the Appellant

MR. BORK: Mr. Chief Justice and may it please the Court, this case turns on the constitutionality of Article 134 of the Uniform Code of Military Justice. That article punishes, among other things, all disorders and neglects to the prejudice of good order and discipline in the Armed Forces and all conduct of a nature to bring discredit upon the Armed Forces.

The Article entered our military jurisprudence when it was enacted by the Continental Congress in 1775 and has been reenacted repeatedly since then by Congress, the first reenactment occurring in 1806.

Apparently the men who wrote the Constitution had no doubt of its compatibility with this Article.

It has been in effect as an organic part of our military law now for just under 200 years and in our history, millions and tens of millions of service men and women have served under this Article.

It is as settled a piece of our jurisprudence, I suppose, as there is.

At stake in the constitutionality of this Article, of course, are several fundamental values of our society. Appellee, here, urges the values of fair warning and due process and free speech.

I will attempt to show that Article 134 is fully compatible with those values and does not threaten them. What must also be recognized, however, is that the judicial destruction of Article 134 would jeopardize two other important values in our society. The first, of course, is the effectiveness of the American Armed Forces upon which the safety of the nation rests.

The second, however, is a value which I think is not sufficiently recognized and that is the importance of Article 134 in confining the role of the military in our national political processes and decisions.

Should speech of the sort involved in this case and in Captain Levy's case, which we argue next, come to be permitted in the military, there would be real danger that our military would become so unreliable as to frustrate civilian policy and to be unable to carry out civilian policy. But worse than that, it seems to me that there might be a danger of a politicized military establishment with all the dangers that prospect poses for the principle of civilian control of the military.

This is speech in these cases in opposition to war aims and if it is permissible for a Pfc. and a captain to make these publications or attempt these publications and make these speeches under these circumstances, then I do not see why it would not be permissible, equally, for general officers and admirals to address their troops about their political views and about their disagreements with the President of the United States and about their disagreements with war aims.

We are not dealing with small issues in this case. The Appellee, Mark Avrech, brought this action in the District Court for the District of Columbia to expunge his courtmartial conviction which was under Article 80, which punishes attempts and the attempt was to violate Article 134 of the Uniform Code of Military Justice.

The District Court dismissed his suit, but the Court of Appeals reversed, holding that Article 134 was unconstitutionally vague.

The conduct underlying the courtmartial conviction occurred at the Marble Mountain Air Facility in Danang in Vietnam, where Pfc. Avrech was on active duty with the Marine Corps in a combat zone.

While on night duty, in the group supply offices at his base, Avrech typed up a stencil of a statement entitled, "The Truth," and marked Volume I, No. 1." He intended to circulate it, he said, only to eight or ten of his friends in the Marine Corps.

The statement is a denunciation of the United States' military role in Vietnam and it contains such sentences as these: "Why should we go out and fight their battles while they sit home and complain about communist agression? What are we, cannon fodder or human beings?"

Going on, "The United States has no business over here. Are your opinions worth risking a court-martial? We must strive for peace and if not peace, then a complete U.S. withdrawal. We have been sitting ducks for too long."

The statement is more extensive than that and it is, in tone and, in substance, a denunciation, as I say, of United States' war aims.

I think that there is no doubt that had Pfc. Avrech succeeded in publishing that statement, the document would tend to create disaffection among the troops and it would certainly create lowered morale among troops in a combat zone.

Q: Well, I suppose it might be reasonably said that it would stimulate some debate on the subject and you'd have one group of soldiers one way—or Marines—on one side and another group on another side.

MR. BORK: It certainly would stimulate debate. I think that is certainly fair, Mr. Chief Justice. In addition to that, apparently, although he was not charged with it, the record in the case, the summary of the record in the case—the original record of the transcript has been destroyed—indicates that Pfc. Avrech constantly stimulated debate among his fellows about the wrongness of United States' war aims.

Having typed up, on a stencil, his denunciation of the war aims of the United States for circulation to the troops—and it was entitled, "Volume I, Part I" because Pfc. Avrech testified that he had intended to publish other such statements as his thinking developed along these lines—having typed up this first statement, Avrech attempted to gain access to the supply office mimeograph machine in order to run the statement off and in the process, he showed it to a corporal who controlled the machine.

The corporal took the statement, gave it to a superior and, as a result, Avrech was tried before a special court-martial on charges of violating Articles 134 and 80.

The court-martial acquitted him on the Article 134 charge but convicted him under Article 80 which, as I say, punishes attempts to commit offenses and here the specification of the charge under Article 80 charged an attempt to commit an offense under Article 134, namely, an attempt to publish to members of the Armed Forces with design to promote disloyalty and disaffection among the troops, a statement disloyal to the United States.

The Appellee challenges this conviction under one Fifth Amendment doctrine, void for vagueness and two aspects of the First Amendment doctrine, overbreadth and the claim that the statement he attempted to issue was protected speech.

I think none of these contentions can withstand examination and I would like to examine the vagueness point first.

Now, I think it is essential to realize that there is no doubt that a parallel statute applied to the civilian population would be unconstitutionally vague. Nobody would know, in a free and permissive society, what was conceivably meant by something like disorders and neglect to the prejudice of social order.

The difference, of course, is that a civilian society is basically a free society. It is not—and, furthermore, it has no single mission, unlike the military. The military society is an ordered society. It has a mission. It has a structure and for that reason, one knows what tends to detract from that mission, what tends to break down discipline and good order.

Now, counsel for the Appellee argue this case as if it did involve a statute applied to the civilian population and they refuse, I think, to face the only issue, the real issue, which is the military context in which this Article exists, indeed, of which this Article has been an organic part for 200 years and that is what makes all the difference in this case.

That context and the limiting constructions given by the United States Court of Military Appeals give Article 134 the definiteness it requires.

Q: What did the Court of Appeals say about that argument of yours?

MR. BORK: The Court of Appeals thought that the military context did not give it sufficient definiteness, Mr. Justice Douglas, but I think I can demonstrate that it does.

One, it seems to me, extremely telling point in this case is that Counsel for the Appellee argued this case by a series of hypotheticals. Although this Article has been in use for 200 years, they do not cite a single case of injustice done by the military under this Article. They do not cite a single case in which convicted servicemen could not—in which a convicted serviceman could have entertained any doubt that what he did was prejudicial to good order and discipline and that what he did was wrong and illegal so far as a military society was concerned.

Whatever superficial plausibility Appellee's challenge has is gained only by ignoring the meaning given by military function and context by ignoring the actual operation of the military system and arguing, instead, from wholly imaginary cases.

The Court of Military Appeals repeatedly said of this Article that it reaches only misconduct and disorders which are directly and probably prejudicial to good order and discipline so that the construction placed upon it by the Court of Military Appeals and followed by the courts-martial is that the tendency to injure good order and discipline must be direct and it must be obvious for a reasonable man.

In addition to that, of course, the Manual for Courts Martial, which is in the Appendix to our brief, discusses, at page 7, this Article and the specific charge of disloyal speech.

Now, knowledge of what conduct directly—

Q: Listen, the average enlisted man is not familiar with the Manual at all, is he?

MR. BORK: Mr. Justice Marshall, I think that is quite true. The average enlisted man is not, although more enlisted men than one might think, are, particularly enlisted men who recognize themselves as coming into brush, possibly, with disciplinary authority.

Q: Well, I wonder how many Manuals of Court Martial they had in Vietnam altogether?

MR. BORK: I do not know that. I do know, though, Mr. Justice Marshall, that the Articles of War—the Articles appeared—

Q: I am just wondering if you need that.

MR. BORK: Pardon me?

Q: I am just wondering if you need that.

MR. BORK: Well, I don't need it, but I think I'd like to use it if I may. The Articles are explained to the troops as part of their basic training.

Q: I see.

MR. BORK: The Manual is available and I would suggest that the Manual is really as available to an enlisted man in the Marine Corps as is a criminal code of Illinois, say, to the man who gets into a brush—

Q: The whole problem is if the Manual is explained to him.

MR. BORK: The Manual was explained—

Q: He may not have the Manual itself.

MR. BORK: That is correct.

But aside from history and tradition, it seems to me that the most important and obvious fact about this case is that the military does comprise a specialized community. It has a well-understood and a specialized function which is something a civilian community does not have and the need for order and discipline in that specialized community is known throughout our culture and it is obvious to everyone.

[Q: How many Manuals did you ever read?]

MR. BORK: It is also obvious what kinds of behavior tend to break that down.

Now, at this point, I would like to say that the military use of this kind of penal statute is by no means unique in our law. This is not confined to military law by any means.

Courts frequently apply standards of sort when they are given content by an understood function and although, on the face of the words, they may seem vague, when they are in context, they are not vague and I think this is true in a variety of areas and I'd like to mention a few:

In the first place, and most obviously, the Sherman Act's vague criminal prescriptions against things like combinations in restraint of trade were upheld in *Nash against the United States* largely because—Justice Holmes said because of the antecedent common law among other things. The antecedent common law really was not a great deal of help but in the—he explained further in *International Harvester against Kentucky* that criminal law is not unconstitutional merely because it throws upon men the risk of rightly estimating a matter of degree and here, the matter of degree is what is an undue restraint of trade.

Because between the obviously illegal and the plainly lawful, there is a gradual approach and that the complexity of life makes it impossible to draw a line in advance without an artificial simplification that would be unjust, the conditions are as permanent as anything human and the conditions there, of course, were the conditions of trade and economics.

Here, the conditions are the mission and the understood function of the military and the great body of precedents on the civil side, coupled with familiar practice, make it comparatively easy for common sense to keep to what is safe.

That passage, I think, with any superficial alterations, could have been written in defense of Article 134 and Article 134, if I may say so, is, if anything, clearer than the Sherman Act was before it received construction.

Q: Mr. Solicitor General, you said a little earlier that your brothers have not pointed to any case where—I don't know just how you put it—I think where there has been any great injustice or, I think you said, where there wasn't fair notice, more or less. But, I, in looking at these examples in the Appendix of the Appellee's brief see—some of them seem to me to be arguably, while they are all, of course, conduct falling below what we like to think of as ideal, some of them really have nothing to do with the good order and discipline of the Armed Forces, do they? I mean, obtaining telephone services from a telephone company with intent to defraud, for example, or negligent failure to maintain sufficient bank funds?

MR. BORK: May I speak to those?

Q: Or even mistreatment of the members of your family, for instance, or refusing to testify at a coroner's inquest?

MR. BORK: I think that list in the Appendix, Mr. Justice Stewart, requires use with a great deal of caution. If you will look at those cases, and I am sorry to say that I seem to have mislaid my analysis of them. A number of them, for example, are cases in which it was held that the behavior cited there was not a violation of Article 134. Those are merely cases where somebody was charged.

Q: Well—

MR. BORK: And, in addition to that, for example, the—

Q: You can argue that both ways, Mr. Solicitor General, as to the validity of this.

MR. BORK: Well, I think not, Mr. Justice Stewart, because if one looked at civilian jurisprudence and said, look at the number of cases in which people have been charged with murder and look how many of them were acquitted, one would not say—

Q: No, but we know what murder is. It does involve killing another human being.

MR. BORK: Well, one of my examples here is manslaughter, which is, I suppose, a negligent killing under the circumstances.

Q: Umn hmn.

MR. BORK: Is a quite vague criminal proscription. But I wish to say about this, for example, not only are some of these examples in the Appendix held not to be violations of Article 134, in addition, some of them are not described fully enough: For example, cheating at bingo.

Q: Yes.

MR. BORK: That was the gentleman who was calling out wrong numbers to rig the game with servicemen and then splitting the proceeds.

Q: Well, I assumed it was something like that. That is the reason I didn't ask you about that one.

MR. BORK: Jumping off a ship, which sounds a little bit carefree, as a matter of fact, was a man who had made a large wager that he could do a backflip off an aircraft carrier in motion and cause the Navy to send a destroyer out to rescue him.

Q: Umn hmn.

MR. BORK: These are cases, when you look at the full case, I don't think there is any case here in which it is not—in which a man was convicted—in which it is not clear that he should have known that the conduct was to the prejudice of good order and discipline or that it would serve as discrediting in the eyes of the civilian population with which he was dealing.

Q: Of course, any deviation from an ideal conduct by a man in uniform tends to bring discredit upon the uniform that he wears and the military organization to which he belongs. Isn't that correct?

MR. BORK: That certainly is correct, your Honor, but any deviation from ideal conduct is not charged under this Article. It has to be a serious, direct, obvious impact upon—prejudicial impact upon good order and discipline. Anyone who has lived among troops knows that if deviations from ideal conduct were prosecuted, that we would have nothing but courts-martial.

That is not the way this Article is used and I think some attention has to be given to the way this Article is used, and the way it is controlled by the Court of Military Appeals and, indeed, by the reviewing legal staffs that go over every one of these convictions.

But I have mentioned the vagueness of the Sherman Act, which was saved by its context and by our knowledge of economics—the criminal offense of manslaughter, we rely upon common understanding of man as to what is dangerously negligent behavior in a vast multiplicity of examples that would be beyond the skill of a legislative draftsman to reach.

Now, if I turn to examples involving speech, I might mention that courts often permit indefinite wordings if the context gives the wording meaning and a parallel example, it seems to me, is *Grayned against City of Rockford* and this Court there upheld a conviction under an anti-noise ordinance that published, "The wilful making of noise or diversion that disturbs or tends to disturb the peace or good order of schools," interpreting with the reply the actual or imminent interference with peace or good order and relying upon the school context as giving meaning to the disturbance's impact upon the normal activities of the school.

The context there gave fair notice and I think the context in the military gives fair notice to a statute—to an Article which is written very much like the anti-noise ordinance was in *Grayned against the City of Rockford*.

I might also suggest that courts regularly apply penalties for contempt of court. That would seem to be a fairly vague standard and it does inhibit speech quite directly but it is made sufficiently definite by the common understanding of the function of a court room, the function of the legal system, and what that function requires in the way of good order and discipline by the part of attorneys who take place—argue in the court room.

And, finally, I would like to cite as very close to this case the clear and present danger test. That is a test that is read into criminal statutes on speech about overthrow of the government or violence, advocacy of violence and, hence, it becomes a warning—the clear and present danger test is a warning that must be intelligible to those the law threatens and in *Dennis against the United States,* this Court explained those words as follows:

It said that Chief Judge Learned Hand, writing for the majority below, interpreted the phrase as follows: "In each case, courts must ask whether the gravity of the evil, discounted by its improbability, justifies such invasion of free speech as is necessary to avoid the danger."

Then this Court said, "We adopt this statement of the rule. As articulated by Chief Judge Hand, it is as succinct and inclusive as any other we might devise at this time. It takes into consideration those factors which we deem relevant and relates their significances. More, we cannot expect from words."

It seems to me that Article 134 is certainly no vaguer than that standard. I agree that "More, we cannot expect from words" in the context in which 134 is applied.

I think it does an equally good job of relating the factors and their significance.

And there is one other parallel I'd like to draw, that between Article 134 and the Hatch Act. This Court upheld the Hatch Act last term in *Civil Service Commission against National Association of Letter Carriers* and at this point, I am discussing not so much vagueness as overbreadth and the legitimate interest of Government.

This Court held, in a civilian context, that the legitimate interest of Government, in good government and in a fair political process, was enough to uphold the Hatch Act's restrictions upon government employees' political activities against First Amendment claims.

So, here, I think, the legitimate interest in an effective military and in a military that does not " . . . dictate civilian policy, either by becoming ineffective so that it cannot carry out policy or by becoming so politicized that it refuses to carry out the policy made by civilians," justifies Article 134's very limited inhibitions on speech, just as the Hatch Act was justified for parallel reasons.

In this case, I think it is obvious that the publication Avrech would have published would have tended to spread disaffection among troops in the combat zone and that cannot be tolerated by any effective military organization.

There may have been armies that tolerated that kind of behavior, but they were armies on the verge of dissolution and not armies that win wars and, aside from the tendency to disaffect others, statements such as these, even if they convince no one, have a deleterious effect upon morale, because they signal to others that at least one man in the unit is not to be relied upon, he is already disaffected, and he may be unreliable in dangerous or difficult situations, which I think is surely a factor the military are entitled to take into account.

It is apparent, I think, that the Article, as applied in this case, was not unduly vague, nor does it violate Avrech's First Amendment rights, since those rights must vary according to the time, place, and circumstances and speech of this sort in a combat zone can hardly be protected.

It might be different in other military circumstances. It might be different if he were in the States in civilian uniform talking to men off base.

In a combat zone, it cannot be protected speech, I would not think.

Q: Doesn't the Court of Military Appeals apply the standards that this Court has applied in civil procedures, as respects vagueness?

MR. BORK: I think it does, Mr. Justice Douglas, but it recognizes that each of these standards has a slightly different application depending upon the context and the circumstances in which it must be applied.

Q: Well, that would be true in the civilian branch of the law, too.

MR. BORK: That is true. That is true.

Q: And the Court of Military Appeals has explicitly upheld the validity of Article 134, has it now?

MR. BORK: They have, indeed.

Q: How recently?

MR. BORK: I think it has upheld it, Mr. Justice Stewart, within the last year or two. I can get the citation for you, it's—

Q: It's quite recently, in any event.

MR. BORK: Quite recently.

Q: Is that the *France* case?

MR. BORK: I believe it was the *France* case.

Q: Well, I have it here. I can give it to Justice Stewart.

MR. BORK: All right.

Q: I take it that the major argument of yours is that because the Article has been construed so often and it has been held to include so many things that, at the very least, it should not be invalidated on its face.

MR. BORK: Well, I think that is an argument that I make and I think it should not be invalidated on its face, again, for two other reasons, not just because it has been construed so often.

One is because this article has its primary impingement upon conduct which is not speech.

Q: And you say it should not be declared invalid on its face in connection with any crime; it should be tested for vagueness as applied?

MR. BORK: That is correct. I think, as I say, for one thing, in the military so many aspects of human conduct are necessarily regulated that are left completely unregulated in civilian life, it would be, I think, impossible to write a specific and definite code that covered all of the things that might prejudice good order and discipline, from speech to nonspeech.

That being the case, to strike down a statute like this on its face, I think makes no particular sense. You'd have to strike down whatever replaced it, on its face because one would always be left with the need of some form of general article.

Q: Oh, wherever it has been construed and applied and the conviction upheld, to that extent, meaning has been given to the Article.

MR. BORK: That is correct.

Q: And any identical crime, any person committing an identical crime, would know in advance.

MR. BORK: That is correct, Mr. Justice White, but I would like to say that there are, in addition, areas that have not yet been applied in which it is still valid.

Q: I understand.

MR. BORK: Like this one.

Q: Why would you always be left with a need of some general article? I understand, from reading these briefs, which was over the weekend—I don't have it in mind, I think it was a former highranking military officer of the legal department who has written an article or given us a speech saying to the effect that we don't, the military doesn't need these.

MR. BORK: He did give that speech, Mr. Justice Stewart. I understand that—I am informed that in the heated debate which followed his publication of that article, he recanted slightly.

Q: Was he prosecuted under 134? [Laughter.]

MR. BORK: That had not occurred to me, but it could be considered.

Q: But in all seriousness, why do you say the military needs this?

MR. BORK: They need it, Mr. Justice—

Q: I mean, we don't need it in civilian society.

MR. BORK: That is because civilian society—

Q: Because you say it is diverse and permissive and free and the military is an authoritarian organization with a specific mission. I understand this, but why does that lead to the conclusion that you need a catchall thing like this?

What is wrong with spelling out what you don't want soldiers and sailors to do?

MR. BORK: Let me say this, Mr. Justice Stewart, addressing merely the speech area, I think that the numbers of ways in which servicemen can find to prejudice discipline in nonspeech ways are limitless, but let's address just the speech area, which is only a minor part of this article.

One ranges from the serviceman speaking or discussing with two friends off base over a drink in somebody's livingroom out of uniform, the aims of the war in a discursive fashion, all the way through the wide variety of circumstances to the serviceman in a combat zone, perhaps in action, denouncing what they are doing and urging others to pull out of the action.

There are so many gradations and variations and alterations and circumstances between there, that I cannot imagine that one could draft specific articles that did not look like the code, the Internal Revenue Code and even then we know that the Internal Revenue Code has its areas of vagueness.

Q: Well, Mr. Solicitor, on this one where, the urging them not to fight, wouldn't he be violating conduct in the presence of the enemy, which is a specific one?

MR. BORK: It certainly would, Mr. Justice Marshall.

Q: And on all of those you have mentioned, specific ones that could be covered by a specific article.

MR. BORK: Well, I think there are too many. I think there are too many variations in circumstances.

Q: In this particular case, if the commanding officer said, "Private, do not distribute that," and he distributed it, he would be charged with what?

MR. BORK: Distribution—

Q: Disobeying an order.

MR. BORK: Article 90, that is quite true.

Q: So he wouldn't have to go to this indefinite one here.

MR. BORK: No, that is quite correct, but this man—

Q: In the first place, he could have said, "Don't use that mimeograph machine," that would be the end of it.

MR. BORK: Well, I hardly think it is practical, Mr. Justice Marshall, for the commanding officer to go about catching people, investigating people, to see what they were likely to publish and then issue an order not to do so.

Q: I understood that was given to the commanding officer, this piece of paper.

MR. BORK: That is correct.

Q: At that stage, the commanding officer could have said one of two things: "This can be mimeographed. It can't be distributed," or he could have ordered him not to distribute it and that would have been the end of it.

MR. BORK: That is correct.

Q: But instead of that, you bring him in on this charge.

MR. BORK: But it would have to be——

Q: And that is why it seems to me the availability of this is, if you don't want to go to the other one, well, we always got this one.

MR. BORK: Well——

Q: Doesn't it look to you like it is the one where if I can't get you on anything else, I got you on this one?

MR. BORK: No, sir, Mr. Justice Marshall, it does not look to me like that. It looks to me like a necessarily general statement because it is impossible, in any length short of a tax code, which would not give notice to anybody in the enlisted level, to convey all of the instances in which the military may object to behavior as being obviously prejudicial to good order and discipline.

The argument you make, that the commander could have issued a direct order, is quite true, but that would be an argument that says, you may never punish for any attempt to do anything because when the attempt is discovered, the commanding officer may always issue an order not to do it and then if it is done, you may be punished for direct disobedience of a lawful order of a superior commissioned officer but so long as the attempt article, Article 80, has any validity—and I don't think it is questioned for this, it is valid, then an attempt may be punished although the commander could have overlooked it and just issued an order.

Parker v. Levy *is a companion case argued the same day. Levy urged troops to refuse deployment to Vietnam. The convictions of both Levy and Avrech were upheld on essentially the same grounds. See* Parker v. Levy 417 U.S. 733 (1974).

GREER V. SPOCK

In the Supreme Court of the United States
Thomas U. Greer, Commander, Fort Dix Military Reservation, et. al.,
Petitioners,
v.
Benjamin Spock, et. al.,
Respondents.
No. 74–848
Washington, D.C.
Wednesday, November 5, 1975.

Oral Argument of Robert H. Bork, Esq.,
On Behalf of the Petitioners

MR. BORK: Mr. Chief Justice, may it please the Court:

We're here on writ of certiorari to the Court of Appeals for the Third Circuit. The Court held that the petitioners, one of whom is the Commander of Fort Dix in New Jersey, is required by the First Amendment to the Constitution to permit political campaign speeches by respondent, and the distribution of literature in areas of Fort Dix that are open to the civilian public.

Respondents Spock and Hobson have been denied permission to hold a political rally on the base under Fort Dix Regulation 210–26, which I will describe in a moment.

And the other four respondents were barred from the base for the unauthorized distribution of literature, under Fort Dix Regulation 210–27.

The content of the particular literature is not in issue. Respondents were barred because they refused to seek prior written approval.

I think it will facilitate discussion if I take up the two issues separately. And I would like to begin with the issue of political speech and campaign rallies on a military base.

The regulation at issue states simply that "Demonstrations, picketing, sit-ins, protest marches, political speeches, and similar activities are prohibited and will not be conducted on the Fort Dix Military Reservation."

Now, the only part of that regulation that's really at issue here is the part that applies to and prohibits political speech. Not political speech in the informal sense, but a formal political speech.

Now, respondents, I think, in their brief and in their argument and, indeed, I think the Court of Appeals for the Third Circuit discussed that regulation as if it were subject to the same analysis as the ordinance of a city council, applying to civilians within that city. And I have no trouble in agreeing that if that were the case, if this were not a special context, indeed, the ordinance, such an ordinance would be unconstitutional under the First Amendment.

But we're dealing here with a military base, devoted to the training of soldiers, and it's never been held, I think,—or it's never been suggested, I don't believe—that the First Amendment converts a military base into a Hyde Park for the convenience of those who wish to make campaign speeches.

The fact that Fort Dix has, as it does have, some streets and parking lots, I don't think makes it a wide open forum for partisan political rallies. And I should note here that the difference from the civilian context is marked by the fact—and I think it's undoubted—that the Commander of Fort Dix has the lawful power to exclude all civilians from the base.

I take it that that's true from *Cafeteria Workers* v. *McElroy,* I take it that that's true from 18 U.S.C. 1382, and, indeed, I take that to be true because I think it's conceded in this case.

Q: Well, it was true in *Flower,* too, wasn't it?

MR. BORK: It's true in *Flower,* also. I think *Flower* is a different case, in a variety of reasons I'm going to come to. One, I think—one reason, one point of difference, it seems to me, is that that street was indistinguishable from any other civilian street, indeed continued straight through from the city, in a way that is not true at Fort Dix.

But I think that there are other reasons that *Flower* does not govern this case.

Q: If I recall correctly, *Flower* put emphasis on the fact that this was a public street, in fact, going through that base,—

MR. BORK: That's true.

Q:—as a part of the base.

MR. BORK: That's true. I think that street was indistinguishable from any other public street, with shops and civilians on it, and so forth.

Q: It merely meant that the base there was divided into two parts by a public highway that went through some major portion.

MR. BORK: That is true, and I think the Court said there that the military had abandoned control over that street. I think that definitely in Fort Dix that is not true.

Q: Well, but civilians can certainly come onto Fort Dix without being stopped at a guard's gate or anything like that.

MR. BORK: They can. The Commander, I think, retains the lawful power to change that at any time.

Q: Well, but didn't he retain that power in Fort Sam Houston in *Flower,* too?

MR. BORK: Mr. Justice Rehnquist, if I thought that *Flower* had announced a principle so broad as to say that if the Commander lets civilians on the base, then he must let them on the base for all purposes; that is, that any access means all access, then I would, without hesitation, ask this Court to modify or overrule *Flower.*

I don't think it should be read that broadly. One reason, I think, is that this Court thought that street had been abandoned, I don't think there's any abandonment here, for reasons I'll go into; secondly, ten days after *Flower,* in the *Lloyd Corporation* v. *Tanner* case, this Court discussed the fact that a shopping center, which allowed civilians or shoppers or people to enter freely, nevertheless did not extend a full invitation for all purposes.

Now, I would take it that if a shopping center is capable of limiting the scope of the invitation, so as to exclude the exercise of First Amendment leafletting, then, *a fortiori,* a military base has at least the same powers.

Q: Well, can't you argue just the opposite, though, that since the shopping center is, in many respects, private, it may be able to limit an invitation in a way that the government, which is not private in any respect, can't?

MR. BORK: If, Your Honor, you're referring to the State action difference, I don't think—I think there may be that difference. On the other hand, in *Logan Valley Plaza* State action was seen, and in that section of *Lloyd Corporation* v. *Tanner,* which discusses the ability of the shopping center to extend an invitation which is limited in scope, they are not dealing with the State action problem. So that I think that aspect of that opinion is fully applicable here.

But, in any event, I take it as a premise that it's undenied that the Commander of the base could exclude all civilians. I take it, also, as a premise that some deference is due to the judgment of the military commander, indeed, that deference is expressed in 18 U.S.C. 1382, as to what activities harm the function of the military.

The fact that there are open spaces here and streets, I think in no way conforms this case to cases involving the civilian context, as *Hague* v. *C.I.O.* speaks of the streets from time immemorial being used as places for discussion in the exchange of political ideas. And it's that tradition, that use, that makes them a public forum in some sense.

In *Lehman* v. *Shaker Heights,* this Court quoted the words of Lord Dunedin, who said—and I think it's perfectly applicable here—"the truth is that open spaces and public places differ very much in their character, and before you could say whether a certain thing could be done in a certain place you would have to know the history of the particular place."

The history of military bases in this country has been uniform. Campaign speeches have not been given on them. That has been something that has never been allowed. So far as I know, Dr. Spock is the first candidate for a national public office, or indeed for any public office, who has attempted to give a political speech on a base.

Q: What about, say, a charter amendment in a city or some initiative or referendum matter?

MR. BORK: I—the—

Q: A speech in support or in opposition to—

MR. BORK: You mean as opposed to a candidate? An issue speech.

Mr. Justice White, the regulation at Fort Dix, I take it, would cover that, because it would be a political speech, I take it. I'm not sure that they mean partisan political speech by that. I think they might mean issue political speech as well.

But that, of course, is not what's before us, in this particular case.

Q: But you are positing—but you are justifying the regulation on the grounds that particular kinds of speech just don't fit in the military?

MR. BORK: Yes.

Q: Unh-hunh.

MR. BORK: Yes, I am.

And I would have thought that that was clear from the tradition of this country, and that the law was clear to that effect. And, indeed, it seems to me there are only really two arguments advanced by the Court of Appeals and by the respondents against it.

Q: But you would, I suppose—but you're saying the regulations prohibit all political speech, it's just not some?

MR. BORK: That is true.

Q: And you wouldn't be here, I suppose, if it just prohibited some kinds of political speech?

MR. BORK: If it were discriminatory, you mean, Mr. Justice White?

Q: Yes.

MR. BORK: No, I would not be here. This is a non-discriminatory regulation, designed for very good purposes.

Q: You'd let that case be argued by the general counsel of the Army, then?

MR. BORK: I would authorize—I might, at the outset, authorize the filing of a brief, Mr. Justice Rehnquist.

But the Court of Appeals' argument rests upon two propositions, both of which I think are demonstrably false.

The first is, and I quote, "if the reservation is open to all the rest of the public, there is no basis for holding that it may be closed selectively to political candidates or to distributors of unapproved literature."

Now, since it's conceded that the base commander could seal the base to all civilians, that argument merely asserts that if the commander allows any access by civilians, he is constitutionally required to allow all access.

Q: Well, wouldn't you concede that if he does in certain areas of the base allow access to the public, he has to allow access to every member of the public who isn't misbehaving or showing some—

MR. BORK: Well, I think he has to allow access to every—

Q: I mean, he has to allow access to Dr. Spock.

MR. BORK: Allow access to—Dr. Spock has complete access to the base, any base, Mr. Justice Stewart. I'm talking about Dr. Spock for the purpose of making a political campaign speech—

Q: But the way you put it was not quite the way you intended it, perhaps.

MR. BORK: Access for all purposes, perhaps, would be better. If he allows access for any purposes, the Court seems to be saying he must allow access for all purposes.

Q: Yes, that's a different—

MR. BORK: Now, that proposition, I think, if it were true, would force every commander to choose between sealing his base tight or allowing it to become Hyde Park, a forum for political discussion.

And, indeed, if that proposition were true, I take it this Court would face much the same choice, because this Court has limited access, political banners and campaign speeches may not be made in this building or on these premises, although access is allowed to the public. So I take it that if that proposition were generally true, this Court would be put to the same choice of excluding the public or allowing political speech when it didn't interfere with a particular session of the Court.

Any of those choices would be quite wrong, and they would be quite wrong, I think, for reasons that parallel the reasons of forcing such a choice upon the military would be quite wrong.

And, as I've mentioned, also, the Court of Appeals' proposition, that access for any purpose is access for all purposes, seems to me, also, to be contradicted by the later opinion in *Lloyd Corporation* v. *Tanner*.

It is a simple non sequitur, and I think there must be some other policy reasons one would have to search for.

Now, the only other argument worth mentioning, made by the Court of Appeals, is that a wide range of newspapers and magazines are permitted on the base, and the troops are allowed to listen to radio and television without restriction in their off-duty hours. And the Court notes that sometimes minor-party candidates don't get as much media coverage, and they don't have as much money to buy media coverage as more popular or better-known candidates do, and therefore must make do with face-to-face campaigning.

Now, the Court concludes from that that the minor-party candidate is harmed because he needs to get on the base to have face-to-face campaigning, although there's the rest of the nation to engage in it, whereas major-party candidates are reported in the New York Times or any of the magazines or on television. And the Court concludes this remarkable analysis by referring to the Fort Dix policy, therefore, as, quote, "a feigned neutrality that serves no discernible military purpose."

And I would like to raise several objections to that, although there are more than several that could be made. And, in the first place, I would like to raise the objection, or like to point out that the statement that there is no discernible military policy is simply wrong. In fact, there is a crucial military policy, and that policy is the traditional safeguard in this nation of the separation of the military establishment from our political processes.

It's not a question of will these people passing out leaflets or making speeches interfere with the training exercise, of course that can be prevented. And it's not a question of will political opinion reach the soldiers, they reach it all kinds of ways. Soldiers are citizens and they get opinions through the media, from each other, from civilians outside, in a variety of ways.

Q: Mr. Solicitor, I have a problem, a little problem, with just one point. You could mail these leaflets, and that's okay?

MR. BORK: That is true. Well, if the leaflets—

Q: If they were mailed, there's no restriction against that. If they were mailed to each soldier on the base.

MR. BORK: There's no restriction in the sense that the mail isn't covered.

Q: Right.

MR. BORK: But I think, Mr. Justice Marshall,—

Q: But you can't hand them out. Now,—

MR. BORK: Well, you can hand them out if you get prior approval, and prior approval, the regulation says, will be granted.

Q: But you don't get prior approval of the mailing.

MR. BORK: Well, no, but that's, it seems to me, not a good objection to this policy, to say that the military hasn't expanded the policy to cover censorship of the mails. The military has been quite reasonable about these policies, and it has not attempted to censor or cut things out. It has tried to impose minimal regulations.

Q: Well, if they do, I imagine that would be litigated, too.

MR. BORK: I imagine it might be, Mr. Justice Marshall.
　　But I think the fact that they have not tried to censor the mails is not a reason to object to their attempts to make sure that leaflets are not distributed, which pose a clear danger, as they say, to discipline, morale, and—

Q: Well, do you think—could the base forbid soldiers stationed there from attending political meetings off base?

MR. BORK: No. They do not, Mr. Justice White.

Q: Well, could they?

MR. BORK: Could they? I do not believe so. They do have a regulation that says if they attend political—partisan political meetings off base, they shouldn't—they must not attend in uniform.

Q: That's right.

MR. BORK: Which points out the clear symbolic line that the military is trying to draw between military activity and political activity.

Q: So it isn't that—it's the way—their worry is how the military would look to the public, rather than any danger to the soldier?

MR. BORK: Oh, no, I think not. I think not. I think the American soldier—

Q: Well, they're going to let him go off the base and attend any political meeting he wants to attend.

MR. BORK: That's right. That's quite true, Mr. Justice White, and this is not an attempt to prevent him from hearing any ideas.

Q: And they let him listen to the radio all he wants to or read all the magazines and—

MR. BORK: I must say, the fact that the military allows all of these things—

Q: Yes.

MR. BORK:—and is so wide open, it seems to me not an argument against that narrow—

Q: Well, what is the reason, then, for the regulation?

MR. BORK: Well, I think it's simply this: It has always been understood that there is this separation between the military and the political process. It's understood that you are also a citizen. But when you come on the base, at that point you leave organized, partisan political activity behind you, it's not part of your military life. And I think that is largely a symbolic difference, but it's a crucial symbolic difference. It separates it in the minds of the soldier. He knows when he's in his unit he's not a political animal. He may have an opinion, but right now he's being a military man.

That has been a tradition in American politics and in American military life throughout most of the history of this Republic, and I think it's a crucial tradition. It's crucial for two reasons, crucial in two aspects.

Q: Yes, but while they are sitting there on the base, and they listen to—they're free to listen to political speeches on the radio or on television—

MR. BORK: That, it seems to me,—

Q:—they are free to sit around in their uniform and read the magazines, read the speeches.

MR. BORK: That is true. That is true. I think we are dealing, as we must in this area, with differences of degree which, at some point, become so large that they become differences in kind. And it seems to me that the soldier listening to the radio, reading a speech, talking in the barracks, going to a rally elsewhere—well, eliminate the last. The first three examples is reached as an individual and that is quite a different thing from rallying soldiers on a base, where they perceive themselves as soldiers, and subjecting them to political exhortation, that, I think, encourages a blurring of the distinction between the military and the civilian—and the regular political process. And that's a distinction I think we would be in very bad shape if we blurred.

And, of course, it requires drawing lines. The military here has drawn the line as far back as they can and allowed as much as they can, which I think ought not to be turned against them. I think it's commendable that they have drawn the line and the regulation as narrowly as they have.

If we once blur this distinction, so that troops are subjected to political speeches on base, gathered in crowds on base, we then begin to teach them that political ideas properly mix with military enclaves, military functions. That, it seems to me, is a very bad idea. It may affect ultimately their performance of their military duties, it may affect their attitude toward their superiors or towards their juniors.

There will be times in this country again, I'm sure, of enormous unrest and great dissent, of civil disobedience. One thing we ought to preserve is the idea that the military doesn't take part in that as military. So that we don't get military disobedience in the name of political ideas.

The other thing about that that one ought to mention—we live in quiet times now, but if political speeches and campaign rallies can be held on the base by civilians, I don't see how troops can be kept from holding their own political rallies and campaign speeches on a base. There may be times and conditions in this country in which there will be a military viewpoint, or at least you encourage the formation of a military viewpoint, if you allow that kind of thing. And I think that would be very bad for American politics, if there were a military political viewpoint.

What this regulation is designed to implement, narrowly and carefully, is a tradition that prevents a politicized military and a tradition that prevents militarized politics.

And that's what I think is at stake here.

And I think the fact that so many other sources of information are open to the troops is not a reason to question this policy.

Now, the statement that the neutrality is feigned I think—I mean, I hope I have shown that there is a discernible, indeed a crucial, military policy that is served by these regulations.

But I should like to address—

Q: You've been addressing yourself up to now primarily to Regulation 210–26 2a, haven't you?

MR. BORK: I had been, Mr. Justice Stewart, but got drawn into this—

Q: I know you did.

MR. BORK:—to the leafletting as well.

Q: I know you did, but it was your purpose to separate the two and discuss them separately.

MR. BORK: At the outset, that was my purpose.

Q: Yes.

MR. BORK: And I have been addressing this, although I think the leafletting regulation is close to it.

But I wanted to say one other thing about this statement that this is a feigned neutrality.

It is a real neutrality, and if there is a disadvantage in getting media, proportional media coverage by these candidates, financially disadvantaged candidates have no greater First Amendment rights than other candidates.

The Constitution does not require the commander at Fort Dix to make his troops available, as compensation for a candidate's inability to buy ads or to attract the New York Times or the attention of NBC.

If, indeed, that were the Constitution, which the Third Circuit appears to think it is, I would suppose it would be true that if the commander could close his base to all civilians except minor-party candidates—because he'd be required to use his base as a reservoir to compensate disadvantaged candidates.

Now, there are more objections to it, but I trust that I have shown at least that the policy is real, and that the neutrality is not feigned, but real.

Now, the leafletting regulation is really here on its face, in effect, because we have no example of the leaflets, they are not in evidence because they weren't submitted for approval. But I should say that the way this operates is the leaflets are—or any matter that would be passed out, is presented to the base commander. He is directed by the regulations that he is to allow distribution, unless he makes a finding—unless he makes a finding—supported by evidence that he can state that there would be a clear danger to morale and discipline on his base.

Q: Have there in fact been instances where he has done that, Mr. Solicitor General? Where he has made those findings?

MR. BORK: I believe so at Fort Dix. I believe so, but if I'm wrong, I'll correct myself later.

If he makes such a finding, he must forward it, by telephonic communication, to a higher echelon, indeed to Army Headquarters, so that they can decide and impose a uniform national policy on this. So that we don't have base commanders doing aberrational things. And he is specifically instructed that whether he likes the literature or not has nothing to do with it, he is specifically instructed that it doesn't matter if the literature is critical of U.S. policies or officials, and it doesn't matter even if it's unfairly critical.

All he may judge is whether it poses a clear danger to the discipline and good order and morale of the troops.

Q: Mr. Solicitor General, maybe it takes us out of order back to the historical aspect, but isn't there some history that during the Civil War commanders who favored Lincoln gave special treatment to campaigners who came on the bases and out into Army camps, even in the field, at the time they were setting up arrangements for the balloting of soldiers?

MR. BORK: Indeed there have been violations of this tradition throughout history, and I think those were examples of it, Mr. Chief Justice.

However, to say that a tradition has been violated, I don't think means that it is not important, not crucial, and not worth trying to preserve. Indeed, Congress, in a number of statutes, I think, has attempted to—page 36 of our brief. We list some statutes in which Congress has tried to shore-up this tradition. And it may be precisely because of knowledge that in the past some violations and breaches of that tradition have occurred.

I was—my attention was called just yesterday to a letter by President Lincoln to General Hooker, when he appointed him in his command, in which he said: "I'm appointing you, there are some things about you I like and some things about you I don't like," he said, "but you do keep"—it was a very straightforward President, and he said, "but you do keep your military duties and politics separate, and that I like."

So I think that this has been a tradition and a safeguard that we have tried to insist upon, that has been violated from time to time, but I think that is only all the more reason to try to insist upon it now and to continue to insist upon it.

I should like to reserve the remainder of my time.

Rebuttal Argument of Robert H. Bork, Esq., On Behalf of the Petitioners

There are just a few matters I would like to clear up.

There has been repeated reference to the Army Times, which appears in the second part of the Exhibit, Plaintiff's Exhibit 7, on E-3, and a censorship by the base, or something of that sort.

I think it should be made perfectly clear that the *Army Times* is a civilian publication, it is not published by the Army, the Army has no control over it. That ad could appear in the New York Times and come on the base, as well.

As to the other points I wish to touch upon, there's reference to the fact that the candidates can't get at these soldiers because they are confined to the base. The truth is only the trainees are confined to the base for the first four weeks of their training, which means that there are three weekends, total, denied to respondents in their efforts to reach these gentlemen off the base.

Mr. Justice White mentioned the fact that coming onto the base was an attempt to appeal to soldiers as soldiers, and I think that's crucial.

I would refer the Court to the first volume of the Appendix, in several places, but particularly at page 178, where Mr. Hardy testifies to the reason he wants to get back onto leafletting. He says:

"There are troops in both Thailand and the Gulf of Tonkin which could be easily re-introduced into some active role there, so anti-war activity among G.I.'s is still, in my opinion, and in the opinion of Resistance, an important aspect of our work in something we need to continue."

There is no doubt that this leafletting and this speech was aimed at these people, not because they were an enclave of citizens they could not reach, but because they were soldiers whom they wished to influence in their attitudes toward the war.

Now, I suppose I should say something about *Flower,* since it's been discussed repeatedly. The picture, E-2, which we have been asked to look at, is entirely different from the picture I recall seeing of New Braunfels Avenue. You can see an obvious line where the town stops. There is an ordinary civilian community, with cleaners and laundries and pizza houses and so forth there, and suddenly all of that community activity stops and you're clearly on a military base.

So it's not indistinguishable from the community, there's a clear line.

Here, Mr. Kairys says, quite correctly, that there was no abandonment in this case. Military jurisdiction over even traffic violations is complete, and any case goes to a U. S. magistrate or, if necessary, to a U. S. court.

Q: Mr. Solicitor General, what difference would it make if the topography and color of the highway pavement and the quality of the sidewalks and the kinds of house were exactly the same before you got on the base and after you got there? What's the difference—

MR. BORK: I don't think it would make—

Q: Just the difference that soldiers exclusively occupy the base.

MR. BORK: I don't think it would make any difference, Mr. Chief Justice, because all of the policy reasons would apply, and that's why I don't believe in this expanded reading that we're getting of the *Flower* case.

Because if that's what *Flower* really meant, then it really is a trivial point, and I can't believe that it is. It becomes a trivial point in that all the military need do is spend the additional money to put a sentry at the post and say, "Show me your pass" or "Get a pass." What that has to do with political campaign rallies on the base, I don't know. I don't see the nexus between spending the money to close the base in that sense and the First Amendment question and the separation of military and—

Q: Indeed, some bases do have a sentry box there, and they have a fence around them. But I take it from the arguments made that the same arguments would be advanced if there was a ten-foot wall and two sentries at the gate.

MR. BORK: I take it so, because if the point is that the base commander must use his troops to compensate Dr. Spock or other minor-party candidates for an inability to get a good Nielsen rating, then I think it wouldn't matter whether there's a wall or whether the base is open.

And I would point once more to *Lloyd Corporation* v. *Tanner* and, indeed, to *Grayned* v. *City of Rockford,* which said that even a public sidewalk could be denied its use for some purposes, because of the interest in running schools. I think the interest here, in the separation of the military and the political, is clearly of that caliber; and, furthermore, it is not a public sidewalk, it is a military base, which, by tradition in this country, has been closed to this kind of activity.

B. OPINIONS

The three items in this subsection are opinions I wrote as a judge on the United States Court of Appeals for the District of Columbia Circuit. Dronenburg *rejected a claim that a petty officer could not constitutionally be discharged from the Navy for homosexual conduct in a barracks. The main argument here is unaffected by the Supreme Court's decision in* Lawrence v. Texas *(2003) making homosexual conduct a constitutional right in the civilian context.* Ollman *turned down, on First Amendment grounds, a libel action against the columnists Evans and Novak.* Lebron *upheld the petitioner's First Amendment right to put up in subway stations posters harshly critical of President Ronald Reagan.*

Dronenburg v. Zech

James L. Dronenburg,
Appellant
v.
Vice Admiral Lando Zech,
Chief of Naval Personnel, et. al.,
No. 82–2304

741 F.2d 1388

United States Court of Appeals for the District of Columbia Circuit

Argued Sept. 29, 1983
Decided Aug. 17, 1984

Before Bork and Scalia, Circuit Judges, and Williams, Senior District Judge, United States District Court for the Central District of California.

Opinion for the Court filed by Circuit Judge Bork.

Bork, Circuit Judge:

James L Dronenburg appeals from a district court decision upholding the United States Navy's action administratively discharging him for homosexual conduct. Appellant contends that the Navy's policy of mandatory discharge for homosexual conduct violates his constitutional rights to privacy and equal protection of the laws. The district court granted summary judgment for the Navy, holding that private, consensual, homosexual conduct is not constitutionally protected. We affirm.

I.

On April 21, 1981, the United States Navy discharged James L. Dronenburg for homosexual conduct. For the previous nine years he had served in the Navy as a Korean linguist and cryptographer with a top-security clearance. During that time he maintained an unblemished service record and earned many citations praising his job performance. At the time of his discharge Dronenburg, then a 27-year-old petty officer, was enrolled as a student in the Defense Language Institute in Monterey, California.

The Navy's investigation of Dronenburg began eight months prior to the discharge, in August, 1980, when a 19-year-old seaman recruit and student of the Language Institute made sworn statements implicating Dronenburg in repeated homosexual acts. The appellant, after initially denying these allegations, subsequently admitted that he was a homosexual and that he had repeatedly engaged in homosexual conduct in a barracks on the Navy base. On September 18, 1980, the Navy gave Dronenburg formal notice that it was considering administratively discharging him for misconduct due to homosexual acts, a violation of SEC/NAV Instruction 1900.9C (Jan. 20, 1978); Joint Appendix ("J.A.") at 216, which provided in pertinent part, that

> [a]ny member [of the Navy] who solicits, attempts or engages in homosexual acts shall normally be separated from the naval service. The presence of such a member in a military environment seriously impairs combat readiness, efficiency, security, and morale.[1]

---

1. Discharge for homosexual conduct was not invariably mandatory. Instruction 1900.9C 6b (Jan. 20, 1978) provides that:

> A member who has solicited, attempted, or engaged in a homosexual act on a single occasion and who does not profess or demonstrate proclivity to repeat such an act may be considered for retention in the light of all relevant circumstances. Retention is to be permitted only if the aforesaid conduct is not likely to present any adverse impact either upon the member's continued performance of military duties or upon the readiness, efficiency, or morale of the unit to which the member is assigned either at the time of the conduct or at the time of processing according to the alternatives set forth herein.

J.A. at 218. Moreover, the Secretary of the Navy retained the power to keep a person in service despite homosexual conduct on an ad hoc basis for reasons of military necessity.

These regulations have since been replaced by SEC/NAV Instruction 1900.9D (Mar. 12, 1981) which implements a Department of Defense Directive. J.A. at 219. The policy of 1900.9C, under which appellant was discharged, is continued in effect by 1900.9D.

On January 20 and 22, 1981, at a hearing before a Navy Administrative Discharge Board ("Board") Dronenburg testified at length in his own behalf, with counsel representing him. He again acknowledged engaging in homosexual acts in a Navy barracks.

The Board voted unanimously to recommend Dronenburg's discharge for misconduct due to homosexual acts. Two members of the Board voted that the discharge be characterized as a general one, while the third member voted that the discharge be an honorable one. The Secretary of the Navy, reviewing this case at appellant's request, affirmed the discharge but ordered that it be characterized as honorable. On April 20, 1981, the appellant filed suit in district court challenging the Navy's policy mandating discharge of all homosexuals. The district court granted summary judgment for the Navy.

II.

[1] As a threshold matter, we must dispose of appellees' contention that the district court lacked subject matter jurisdiction over this action. According to appellees, the doctrine of sovereign immunity precludes the bringing of this action except insofar as the Tucker Act permits damage suits in the Claims Court. Brief for Federal Appellees at 11–16. Appellees reason that the appellant's action is essentially one for damages; specifically, back pay against the government. The Claims Court, appellees allege, has exclusive jurisdiction over such actions where, as here, the amount is in excess of $10,000. In the alternative, appellees claim, appellant may waive the damages to the extent they exceed $10,000 and bring the suit in the district where Dronenburg resides, the Northern District of California. Brief for Federal Appellees at 15.

This circuit has held in a case remarkably similar to this one that the federal courts have jurisdiction to determine the legality and constitutionality of a military discharge. *Matlovich v. Secretary of the Air Force*, 591 F.2d 852, 859 (D.C.Cir.1978). Matlovich, like the appellant here, challenged the Air Force's decision to discharge him based upon his homosexual activities. In vacating and remanding the determination to the district court, this court relied upon the "power and the duty [of the federal courts] to inquire whether a military discharge was properly issued under the Constitution, statutes, and regulations." 591 F.2d at 859, citing *Harmon v. Brucker*, 355 U.S. 579, 78 S.Ct. 433, 2 L.Ed.2d 503 (1958); *Van Bourg v. Nitze*, 388 F.2d 557, 563 (D.C.Cir.1967); *Hodges v. Callaway*, 499 F.2d 417, 423 (5th Cir.1974). We are bound by that prior determination and therefore are not free to refuse to hear this case on jurisdictional grounds.

We are further bound by another decision of this court holding that "the United States and its officers are [not] insulated from suit for injunctive relief by the doctrine of sovereign immunity." *Schnapper* v. *Foley,* 667 F.2d 102, 107 (D.C.Cir. 1981), cert. denied, 455 U.S. 948, 102 S.Ct. 1448, 71 L.Ed.2d 661 (1982). See also *Sea-Land Service, Inc.* v. *Alaska R.R.,* 659 F.2d 243, 244 (D.C.Cir.1981). In *Schnapper,* the complainants alleged that certain officials of the Administrative Office of the United States Courts and the Register of Copyrights violated, among other things, various provisions of the Constitution, the old Copyright ARIA 17 U.S.C. § 105 (1976) and 17 U.S.C. § 8 (1970), and portions of the Communications and Public Broadcasting Acts. 667 F.2d at 106. The complaint sought injunctive and declaratory relief, as does the complaint here.[2] In finding that the District Court for the District of Columbia did in fact have jurisdiction, the court held that 5 U.S.C. § 702 was intended to waive the sovereign immunity of the United States in suits for injunctive relief. That section provides, in part, that

> [a]n action in a court of the United States seeking relief other that [sic] money damages and stating a claim that an agency or an employee thereof acted or failed to act in an official capacity or under color of legal authority shall not be dismissed nor relief thereon denied on the ground that it is against the United States. . . .

5 U.S.C. § 702 (1982). In discussing the legislative history of this section, the court said:

> The legislative history of this provision could not be more lucid. It states that this language was intended "to eliminate the defense of sovereign immunity with respect to any action in a court of the United States seeking relief other than money damages and based on the assertion of unlawful official action by a federal official. . . ." S.Rep. No. 996, 94th Cong., 2d Sess. at 2 (1976).

Schnapper, 667 F.2d at 108. The court also noted that the Senate Report had expressly stated that "the time [has] now come to eliminate the sovereign immunity defense in all equitable actions for specific relief against a Federal agency or officer acting in an official capacity." *Id.,* quoting S.Rep. No, 996, 94th Cong., 2d Sess. 7–8 (1976). The *Schnapper* court concluded by stating its belief that "section 702 retains the defense of sovereign immunity only

---

2. In his amended complaint, appellant eliminated any damages claim. Reply Brief of Appellant at 6 n. 6. Specifically, appellant seeks to have this court enjoin the Navy from discharging him and order his reinstatement. Complaint at 12; J.A. at 12.

when another statute expressly or implicitly forecloses injunctive relief." *Id.* Because no such statute has been pointed to by the appellees here, we are bound to take jurisdiction over this case.[3]

III.

Appellant advances two constitutional arguments, a right of privacy and a right to equal protection of the laws. Resolution of the second argument is to some extent dependent upon that of the first. Whether the appellant's asserted constitutional right to privacy is based upon fundamental human rights, substantive due process, the ninth amendment or emanations from the Bill of Rights, if no such right exists, then appellant's right to equal protection is not infringed unless the Navy's policy is not rationally related to a permissible end. *Kelley* v. *Johnson*, 426 U.S. 238, 247–49, 96 S.Ct. 1440, 1445–47, 47 L.Ed.2d 708 (1976). We think neither right has been violated by the Navy.

A.

According to appellant, *Griswold* v. *Connecticut*, 381 U.S. 479, 86 S.Ct. 1678, 14 L.Ed.2d 510 (1965), and the cases that came after it, such as *Loving* v. *Virginia*, 388 U.S. 1, 87 S.Ct. 1817, 18 L.Ed.2d 1010 (1967); *Eisenstadt* v. *Baird*, 405 U.S. 438, 92 S.Ct. 1029, 31 L.Ed.2d 349 (1972); *Roe* v. *Wade*, 410 U.S. 113, 93 S.Ct. 705, 35 L.Ed.2d 147 (1973); and *Carey* v. *Population Services International*, 431 U.S. 678, 97 S.Ct. 2010, 52 L.Ed.2d 675 (1977), have "de-

---

3. We note that there has been some disagreement on the question whether 5 U.S.C. § 702 (1982) does in fact waive sovereign immunity in suits under 28 U.S.C. § 1331 (1982). The Second Circuit first held, as an alternative ground for a correct decision, that the 1976 amendments to § 702 "did not remove the defense of sovereign immunity in actions under [28 U.S.C.] § 1331." *Estate of Watson* v. *Blumenthal*, 586 F.2d 925, 932 (2d Cir.1978). Later, however, another of that circuit's panels, one which included within it the author of the opinion in *Watson*, disagreed with that determination, *B.K. Instrument, Inc.* v. *United States*, 715 F.2d 713, 724 (2d Cir.1983), as have the Third, Fifth, Sixth and Ninth Circuits. *Jaffee* v. *United States*, 592 F.2d 712, 718–19 (3d Cir.), *cert. denied*, 441 U.S. 961, 99 S.Ct. 2406, 60 L.Ed.2d 1066 (1979); *Sheehan* v. *Army & Air Force Exchange Service*, 619 F.2d 1132, 1139 (5th Cir.1980), *rev'd on other grounds*, 456 U.S. 728, 102 S.Ct. 2118, 72 L.Ed.2d 520 (1982); *Warin* v. *Director, Dept of Treasury*, 672 F.2d 590, 591–92 (6th Cir.1982) (per curiam); *Beller* v. *Middendorf*, 632 F.2d 788, 796–97 (9th Cir.), *cert. denied*, 452 U.S. 905, 101 S.Ct. 3030, 69 L.Ed.2d 405 (1980). See P. Bator, P. Mishkin, D. Shapiro & H. Wechsler, *Hart & Wechsler's The Federal Courts and the Federal System* 346 (2d ed. Supp.1981) ("Since the Administrative Procedure Act does not itself confer jurisdiction, [the determination in *Watson*] would mean, would it not, that the amendments had no affect on immunity at all?").

veloped a right of privacy of constitutional dimension." Appellant's opening Brief on Appeal at 14–15. Appellant finds in these cases "a thread of principle: that the government should not interfere with an individual's freedom to control intimate personal decisions regarding his or her own body" except by the least restrictive means available and in the presence of a compelling state interest *Id.* at 15. Given this principle, he urges, private consensual homosexual activity must be held to fall within the zone of constitutionally protected privacy. *Id.*

[2,3] Whatever thread of principle may be discerned in the right-of-privacy cases, we do not think it is the one discerned by appellant. Certainly the Supreme Court has never defined the right so broadly as to encompass homosexual conduct. Various opinions have expressly disclaimed any such sweep, see, e.g., *Poe* v. *Ullman,* 367 U.S. 497, 553, 81 S.Ct. 1752, 1782, 6 L.Ed.2d 989 (1961) (Harlan, J., dissenting from a decision that the controversy was not yet justiciable and expressing views on the merits later substantially adopted in *Griswold*). More to the point, the Court in *Doe* v. *Commonwealth's Attorney for Richmond,* 425 U.S. 901, 96 S.Ct. 1489, 47 L.Ed.2d 751 (1976), summarily affirmed a district court judgment, 403 F.Supp. 1199 (E.D.Va.1975), upholding a Virginia statute making it a criminal offense to engage in private consensual homosexual conduct. The district court in *Doe* had found that the right to privacy did not extend to private homosexual conduct because the latter bears no relation to marriage, procreation, or family life, 403 F Supp. at 1200. The Supreme Court's summary disposition of a case constitutes a vote on the merits; as such, it is binding on lower federal courts. See *Hicks* v. *Miranda,* 422 U.S, 332, 343–45, 95 S.Ct. 2281, 2288–90, 45 L.Ed.2d 223 (1975); *Ohio ex rel. Eaton* v. *Price,* 360 246, 247, 79 S Ct. 978, 978, 3 L.Ed.2d 1200 (1959). *Cf. Port Authority Bondholders Protective Committee* v. *Port of New York Authority,* 387 F.2d 259, 263 n. 3 (2d Cir.1967). If a statute proscribing homosexual conduct in a civilian context is sustainable, then such a regulation is certainly sustainable in a military context. That the military has needs for discipline and good order justifying restrictions that go beyond the needs of civilian society has repeatedly been made clear by the Supreme Court. See, e.g., *Greer* v. *Spock,* 424 U.S. 828, 96 S.Ct. 1211, 47 L.Ed.2d 505 (1976); *Parker* v. *Levy,* 417 U.S. 733, 94 S.Ct. 2547, 41 L.Ed.2d 43e (1974).

It is urged upon us, however, that *Doe* v. *Commonwealth's Attorney* cannot be taken as an authoritative decision by the Supreme Court. The case should be viewed, it is said, as an affirmance based not on the constitutionality of the statute but rather upon plaintiffs' lack of standing. Plaintiffs were homosexuals who had not been threatened with prosecution under the statute. Indeed, those plaintiffs may have lacked standing, but the majority of the three-judge district court placed its decision squarely on the constitutionality of the statute, and the Supreme Court's summary affirmance gives no indication that the Court proceeded upon any other rationale. It would have been easy enough to affirm summarily giving a lack of standing as the reason. Under these circumstances, we doubt that a court of appeals ought to distinguish a Supreme Court precedent on the speculation that the Court might possibly have had something else in mind.

But even should we agree that *Doe* v. *Commonwealth's* Attorney is somewhat ambiguous precedent, we would not extend the right of privacy created by the Supreme Court to cover appellant's conduct here. An examination of the cases cited by appellant shows that they contain little guidance for lower courts. The right of privacy first achieved constitutional stature in *Griswold* v. *Connecticut*, 881 U,S, 479, 85 S.Ct. 1678, 14 L.Ec1.24 510 (1965), The *Griswold* Court began by noting that "specific guarantees in the Bill of Rights have penumbras, formed by emanations from those guarantees that help give them life and substance," 381 U.S, at 484, 86 S.Ct. at 1681. The cases cited in support of that unexceptional proposition demonstrated, for example, that a state could not force disclosure of the NAACP's membership lists because of the chilling effect upon the members' first amendment rights of assembly and political advocacy. The "penumbra" was no more than a perception that it is sometimes necessary to protect actions or associations not guaranteed by the Constitution in order to protect an activity that is. The penumbral right has no life of its own as a right independent of its relationship to a first amendment freedom. Where that relationship does not exist, the penumbral right evaporates. The Court referred to the first amendment's penumbra as a protection of "privacy," noted that other amendments created "zones of privacy," and concluded that there was a general right of privacy that lay outside the "zones" or "penumbras" of particular amendments. *Id.* It was not explained how areas not lying within any "penumbra" or "zone of privacy" became part of a more general "right of privacy," but clearly that is what the Court intended. The right of a husband and wife to use contraceptives, which the challenged Connecticut statute prohibited, was held to be guaranteed by this general right, though not by any individual amendment, penumbra, or zone. The *Griswold* opinion stressed the sanctity of marriage. It did not indicate what other activities might be protected by the new right of privacy and did not provide any guidance for reasoning about future claims laid under that right.

Loving v. *Virginia*, 388 U.S. 1, 87 S.Ct. 1817, 18 L.Ed.2d 1010 (1967), struck down a state antimiscegenation statute because it constituted an invidious racial classification violative of the equal protection clause of the Fourteenth Amendment and because it deprived appellants of liberty without due process of law in violation of the same amendment. The equal protection ruling followed from prior cases and the historical purpose of the clause. It is not entirely clear whether the due process analysis broke new ground. The Court spoke of a right of marriage but emphasized heavily the racial discrimination worked by this statute, a point central to the equal protection holding. In its brief analysis of the due process holding, the Court said only:

> The freedom to marry has long been recognized as one of the vital personal rights essential to the orderly pursuit of happiness by free men.
>
> Marriage is one of the "basic civil rights of man," fundamental to our very existence and survival. *Skinner* v. *Oklahoma*, 316 U.S. 535, 541 [62 S.Ct. 1110, 1113, 86 L.Ed. 1655] (1942). See also *Maynard* v. *Hill*, 125 U.S. 190 [8 S.Ct. 723, 31 L.Ed. 654] (1888). To deny this fundamental freedom on so unsupportable a basis as the racial classifications embodied in these statutes, classifications so directly subversive to the principle of equality at the heart of the Fourteenth Amendment, is surely to deprive all the State's citizens of liberty without due process of law. The Fourteenth Amendment requires that the freedom of choice to marry not be restricted by invidious racial discriminations. Under our Constitution, the freedom to marry, or not marry, a person of another race resides with the individual and cannot be infringed by the State.

388 U.S. at 11–12, 87 S.Ct. at 1824. There is in this passage no mode of analysis that suggests an answer to the present case, certainly none that favors appellant.

Eisenstadt v. *Baird,* 405 U.S. 438, 92 S.Ct. 1029, 81 L.Ed.2d 349 (1972), invalidated under the equal protection clause of the Fourteenth Amendment a Massachusetts law prohibiting the distribution of contraceptives. The law in question provided that married persons could obtain contraceptives to prevent pregnancy on prescription only, single persons could not obtain contraceptives at all in order to prevent pregnancy, and married and single persons could obtain contraceptives from anyone to prevent the spread of disease. *Id.* at 442, 92 S.Ct. at 1032. The Court reasoned that there was no "ground of difference that rationally explains the different treatment accorded married and unmarried persons" under the statute. *Id.* at 447, 92 S.Ct. at 1035. The

Court demonstrated that the purpose of the statute could not rationally be to deter fornication or to safeguard health. The opinion then came to the aspect presumably of most interest here: could the statute be sustained simply as a prohibition on contraception? The Court explicitly declined to decide whether such a law would conflict with "fundamental human rights" and offered instead this line of reasoning:

> If under *Griswold* the distribution of contraceptives to married persons cannot be prohibited, a ban on distribution to unmarried persons would be equally impermissible. It is true that in *Griswold* the right of privacy in question inhered in the marital relationship. Yet the marital couple is not an independent entity with a mind and heart of its own, but an association, of two individuals each with a separate intellectual and emotional make-up. If the right of privacy means anything, it is the right of the *individual*, married or single, to be free from unwarranted governmental intrusion into matters so fundamentally affecting a person as the decision whether to bear or beget a child.

Id. at 453, 92 S.Ct. at 1038 (emphasis in original). In order to apply *Eisenstadt* to a future case not involving the same personal decision, a court would have to know whether the challenged governmental regulation was "unwarranted" and whether the regulation was of a matter "so fundamentally affecting a person as the decision whether to "bear or beget a child." *Eisenstadt* itself does not provide any criteria by which either of those decisions can be made.

Roe v. Wade, 410 U.S. 113, 93 S.Ct. 705, 35 L.Ed.2d 147 (1973), severely limited the states' power to regulate abortions in the name of the right of privacy. The pivotal legal discussion was as follows:

> The Constitution does not explicitly mention any right of privacy. In a line of decisions, however, going back perhaps as far as *Union Pacific R. Co. v. Botsford*, 141 U.S. 250, 251 [11 S.Ct. 1000, 1001, 35 L.Ed. 734] (1891), the Court has recognized that a right of personal privacy, or a guarantee of certain areas or zones of privacy, does exist under the Constitution. In varying contexts, the Court or individual Justices have, indeed, found at least the roots of that right in the First Amendment, *Stanley* v. *Georgia*, 394 U.S. 557, 564 [89 S.Ct. 1243, 1247, 22 L.Ed.2d 542] (1969); in the Fourth and Fifth Amendments, *Terry* v. *Ohio*, 392 U.S. 1, 8–9 [88 S.Ct. 1868, 1872–1873, 20 L.Ed.2d 889] (1968), *Katz* v. *United States*, 389 U.S. 347, 350 [88 S.Ct. 507, 510, 19 L.Ed.2d 576] (1967), *Boyd* v. *United States*, 116 U.S. 616 [6 S.Ct. 524, 29 L.Ed. 746] (1886), see *Olmstead* v.

United States, 277 U.S. 438, 478 [48 S.Ct. 564, 572, 72 L.Ed. 944] (1928) (Brandeis, J., dissenting); in the penumbras of the Bill of Rights, *Griswold* v. *Connecticut*, 381 U.S. at 484–85 [85 S.Ct. at 1681–1682]; in the Ninth Amendment, *Id.* at 486 [85 S.Ct. at 1682] (Goldberg J., concurring); or in the concept of liberty guaranteed by the first section of the Fourteenth Amendment, see *Meyer* v. *Nebraska*, 262 U.S. 390, 399 [43 S.Ct. 625, 626, 67 L.Ed. 1042] (1923). These decisions make it clear that only personal rights that can be deemed "fundamental" or "implicit in the concept of ordered liberty," *Palko* v. *Connecticut*, 302 U.S. 319, 325 [58 S.Ct. 149, 152, 82 L.Ed. 288] (1937), are included in this guarantee of personal privacy. They also make it clear that the right has some extension to activities relating to marriage, *Loving* v. *Virginia,* 388 U.S. 1, 12 [87 S.Ct. 1817, 1823, 18 L.Ed.2d 1010] (1967); procreation, *Skinner* v. *Oklahoma*, 316 US. 535, 541–542 [62 8.Ct. 1110, 1113–1114, 86 L.Ed. 1655] (1942); contraception, *Eisenstadt* v. *Baird*, 405 U.S., at 453–54 [92 S.Ct. at 1038–1039]; *id.* at 460, 463–65 [92 S.Ct. at 1041, 1043–1044] (White, J., concurring in result); family relationships, *Prince* v. *Massachusetts*, 321 U.S. 158, 166 [64 S.Ct. 438, 442, 88 L.Ed. 645] (1944); and child rearing and education, *Pierce* v. *Society of Sisters*, 268 U.S. 510, 535 [45 S.Ct. 571, 573, 69 L.Ed. 1070] (1925), *Meyer* v. *Nebraska, supra.*

This right of privacy, whether it be founded in the Fourteenth Amendment's concept of personal liberty and restrictions upon state action, as we feel it is, or, as the District Court determined, in the Ninth Amendment's reservation of rights to the people, is broad enough to encompass a woman's decision whether or not to terminate her pregnancy. The detriment that the State would impose upon the pregnant woman by denying this choice altogether is apparent. Specific and direct harm medically diagnosable even in early pregnancy may be involved. Maternity, or additional offspring, may force upon the woman a distressful life and future. Psychological harm may be imminent. Mental and physical health may be taxed by child care. There is also the distress, for all concerned, associated with the unwanted child, and there is the problem of bringing a child into a family already unable, psychologically and otherwise, to care for it. In other cases, as in this one, the additional difficulties and continuing stigma of unwed motherhood may be involved. All these are factors the woman and her responsible physician necessarily will consider in consultation.

410 U.S. at 152–53, 93 S.Ct. at 726–27. The Court nevertheless refused to accept the argument that the right to abort is absolute.

The Court's decisions recognizing a right of privacy also acknowledge that some state regulation in areas protected by that right is appropriate. As noted above, a State may properly assert important interests in safeguarding health, in maintaining medical standards, and in protecting potential life. At some point in pregnancy, these respective interests become sufficiently compelling to sustain regulation of the factors that govern the abortion decision. The privacy right involved, therefore, cannot be said to be absolute. In fact, it is not clear to us that the claim asserted by some amici that one has an unlimited right to do with one's body as one pleases bears a close relationship to the right of privacy previously articulated in the Court's decisions. The Court has refused to recognize an unlimited right of this kind in the past. *Jacobson* v. *Massachusetts*, 197 U.S. 11 [25 S.Ct. 358, 49 L.Ed. 643] (1905) (vaccination); *Buck* v. *Bell*, 274 U.S. 200 [47 S.Ct. 584, 71 L.Ed. 1000] (1927) (sterilization).

Id. at 153–54, 93 S.Ct. at 727 (emphasis added). Thus, though the Court gave an illustrative list of privacy rights, it also denied that the right was as broad as the right to do as one pleases with one's body. Aside from listing prior holdings, the Court provided no explanatory principle that informs a lower court how to reason about what is and what is not encompassed by the right of privacy.

Carey v. *Population Services International,* 431 U.S. 678, 97 S.Ct. 2010, 62 L.Ed.2d 675 (1977), held unconstitutional yet another regulation of access to contraceptives on grounds of privacy. The New York statute required that distribution of contraceptives to persons over sixteen be only by a licensed pharmacist. That provision was held unconstitutional because no compelling state interest was perceived that could overcome "the teaching of *Griswold* . . . that the Constitution protects individual decisions in matters of childbearing from unjustified intrusion by the State." *Id.* at 687, 97 S.Ct. at 2017. A compelling state interest was required not because there is an independent fundamental 'right of access to contraceptives,' but because such access is essential to exercise of the constitutionally protected right of decision in matters of childbearing that is the underlying foundation of the holdings in *Griswold, Eisenstadt* v. *Baird*, and *Roe* v. *Wade.*" *Id.* at 688–89, 97 S.Ct. at 2018. Limiting distribution to licensed pharmacists significantly burdened that right. *Id.* at 689, 97 S.Ct. at 2018.[4]

---

4. The Court also struck down a provision of the law forbidding distribution of contraceptives to those less than 16 years old, but there was no majority rationale for this result and it would not advance our inquiry to discuss the various opinions offered.

These cases, and the suggestion that we apply them to protect homosexual conduct in the Navy, pose a peculiar jurisprudential problem. When the Supreme Court decides cases under a specific provision or amendment to the Constitution it explicates the meaning and suggests the contours of a value already stated in the document or implied by the Constitution's structure and history. The lower court judge finds in the Supreme Court's reasoning about those legal materials, as well as in the materials themselves, guidance for applying the provision or amendment to a new situation. But when the Court creates new rights, as some Justices who have engaged in the process state that they have done, see, e.g., *Doe* v. *Bolton*, 410 U.S. 179, 221–22, 93 S.Ct. 739, 762–63, 36 L.Ed.2d 201 (1973) (White, J., dissenting); *Roe* v. *Wade*, 410 U.S. 113, 167–68, 93 S.Ct. 705, 733–34, 35 L.Ed.2d 147 (1973) (Stewart, J., concurring), lower courts have none of these materials available and can look only to what the Supreme Court has stated to be the principle involved.

In this group of cases, and in those cited in the quoted language from the Court's opinions, we do not find any principle articulated even approaching in breadth that which appellant seeks to have us adopt. The Court has listed as illustrative of the right of privacy such matters as activities relating to marriage, procreation, contraception, family relationships, and child rearing and education. It need hardly be said that none of these covers a right to homosexual conduct.

The question then becomes whether there is a more general principle that explains these cases and is capable of extrapolation to new claims not previously decided by the Supreme Court. It is true that the principle appellant advances would explain all of these cases, but then so would many other, less sweeping principles. The most the Court has said on that topic is that only rights that are "fundamental" or "implicit in the concept of ordered liberty" are included in the right of privacy. These formulations are not particularly helpful to us, however, because they are less prescriptions of a mode of reasoning than they are conclusions about particular rights enunciated. We would find it impossible to conclude that a right to homosexual conduct is "fundamental" or "implicit in the concept of ordered liberty" unless any and all private sexual behavior falls within those categories, a conclusion we are unwilling to draw.

In dealing with a topic like this, in which we are asked to protect from regulation a form of behavior never before protected, and indeed traditionally condemned, we do well to bear in mind the concerns expressed by Justice White, dissenting in *Moore* v. *City of East Cleveland*, 431 U.S. 494, 544, 97 S.Ct. 1932, 1958–59, 52 LEd.2d 531 (1977):

That the Court has ample precedent for the creation of new constitutional rights should not lead it to repeat the process at will. The Judiciary, including this Court, is the most vulnerable and comes nearest to illegitimacy when it deals with judge-made constitutional law having little or no cognizable roots in the language or even the design of the Constitution. Realizing that the present construction of the Due Process Clause represents a major judicial gloss on its terms, as well as on the anticipation of the Framers, and that much of the underpinning for the broad, substantive application of the Clause disappeared in the conflict between the Executive and the Judiciary in the 1930's and 1940's, the Court should be extremely reluctant to breathe still further substantive content into the Due Process Clause so as to strike down legislation adopted by a State or city to promote its welfare. Whenever the Judiciary does so, it unavoidably pre-empts for itself another part of the governance of the country without express constitutional authority.

Whatever its application to the Supreme Court, we think this admonition should be taken very seriously by inferior federal courts. No doubt there is "ample precedent for the creation of new constitutional rights," but, as Justice White said, the creation of such rights "comes nearest to illegitimacy" when judges make "law having little or no cognizable roots in the language or even the design of the Constitution." If it is in any degree doubtful that the Supreme Court should freely create new constitutional rights,[5] we think it certain that lower courts should not do so. We have no guidance from the Constitution or, as we have shown with respect to the case at hand, from articulated Supreme Court principle. If courts of appeals should, in such circumstances, begin to create new rights freely, the volume of decisions would mean that many would grow up, and we would have "preempt[ed]

---

5. It may be only candid to say at this point that the author of this opinion, when in academic life, expressed the view that no court should create new constitutional rights; that is, rights must be fairly derived by standard modes of legal interpretation from the text, structure, and history of the Constitution. Or, as it has been aptly put, "the work of the political branches is to be invalidated only in accord with an inference whose starting point, whose underlying premise, is fairly discoverable in the Constitution. That the complete inference will not be found there—because the situation is not likely to have been foreseen—is generally common ground." J. Ely, *Democracy and Distrust* 2 (1980). These views are, however, completely irrelevant to the function of a circuit judge. The Supreme Court has decided that it may create new constitutional rights and, as judges of constitutionally inferior courts, we are bound absolutely by that determination. The only questions open for us are whether the Supreme Court has created a right which, fairly defined, covers the case before us or whether the Supreme Court has specified a mode of analysis, a methodology, which, honestly applied, reaches the case we must now decide.

for [ourselves] another part of the governance of the country without express constitutional authority." If the revolution in sexual mores that appellant proclaims is in fact ever to arrive, we think it must arrive through the moral choices of the people and their elected representatives, not through the ukase of this court.

Turning from the decided cases, which we do not think provide even an ambiguous warrant for the constitutional right he seeks, appellant offers arguments based upon a constitutional theory. Though that theory is obviously untenable, it is so often heard that it is worth stating briefly why we reject it.

Appellant denies that morality can ever be the basis for legislation or, more specifically, for a naval regulation, and asserts two reasons why that is so. The first argument is: "if the military can defend its blanket exclusion of homosexuals on the ground that they are offensive to the majority or to the military's view of what is socially acceptable, then no rights are safe from encroachment and no minority is protected against discrimination." Appellant's Opening Brief on Appeal at 11–12. Passing the inaccurate characterization of the Navy's position here, it deserves to be said that this argument is completely frivolous. The Constitution has provisions that create specific rights. These protect, among others, racial, ethnic, and religious minorities. If a court refuses to create a new constitutional right to protect homosexual conduct, the court does not thereby destroy established constitutional rights that are solidly based in constitutional text and history.

Appellant goes further, however, and contends that the existence of moral disapproval for certain types of behavior is the very fact that disables government from regulating it. He says that as a matter of general constitutional principle, "it is difficult to understand how an adult's selection of a partner to share sexual intimacy is not immune from the burden by the state as an element of constitutionally protected privacy. That the particular choice of partner may be repugnant to the majority argues for its vigilant protection—not its vulnerability to sanction." Appellant's Opening Brief on Appeal at 13. This theory that majority morality and majority choice is always made presumptively invalid by the Constitution attacks the very predicate of democratic government. When the Constitution does not speak to the contrary, the choices of those put in authority by the electoral process, or those who are accountable to such persons, come before us not as suspect because majoritarian but as conclusively valid for that very reason. We stress, because the possibility of being misunderstood is so great, that this deference to democratic choice does not apply where the Constitution removes the choice from majorities. Appellant's theory would, in fact, destroy the basis for much of the most valued legislation our society has. It would, for example, render legislation about civil rights, worker safety, the preservation of the environment, and much more, unconstitutional. In each of these areas, legislative majorities have made moral choices contrary to the desires of minorities. It is to be doubted that very many laws exist whose ultimate justification does not rest upon the society's morality.[6] For these reasons, appellant's argument will not withstand examination.

[4] We conclude, therefore, that we can find no constitutional right to engage in homosexual conduct and that, as judges, we have no warrant to create one. We need ask, therefore, only whether the Navy's policy is rationally related to a permissible end. See *Kelley* v. *Johnson*, 425 U.S. 238, 247–49, 96 S.Ct. 1440, 1445–47, 47 LEd2d 708 (1976). We have said that legislation may implement morality. So viewed, this regulation bears a rational relationship to a permissible end. It may be argued, however, that a naval regulation, unlike the act of a legislature, must be rationally related not to morality for its own sake but to some further end which the Navy is entitled to pursue because of the Navy's assigned function. We need not decide that question because, if such a connection is required, this regulation is plainly a rational means of advancing a legitimate, indeed a crucial, interest common to all our armed forces. To ask the question is to answer it. The effects of homosexual conduct within a naval or military unit are almost certain to be harmful to morale and discipline. The Navy is not required to produce social science data or the results of controlled experiments to prove what common sense and common experience demonstrate. This very case illustrates dangers of the sort the Navy is entitled to consider. A 27-year-old petty officer had repeated sexual relations with a 19-year-old seaman recruit. The latter then chose to break off the relationship. Episodes of this sort are certain to be deleterious to morale and discipline, to call into question the even-handedness of superiors' dealings with lower ranks, to make personal dealings uncomfortable where the relationship is sexually ambiguous, to generate dislike and disapproval among many who find homosexuality morally offensive, and, it must be said, given the powers of military superiors over their inferiors, to enhance the possibility of homosexual seduction.

---

6. At oral argument, appellant's counsel was pressed by the court concerning his proposition that the naval regulations may not permissibly be founded in moral judgments. Asked whether moral abhorrence could ever be a basis for a regulation, counsel replied that it could not. Asked then about the propriety of prohibiting bestiality, counsel replied that that could be prohibited but on the ground of cruelty to animals. The objection to cruelty to animals is, of course, the objection on grounds of morality.

The Navy's policy requiring discharge of those who engage in homosexual conduct serves legitimate state interests which include the maintenance of "discipline, good order and morale[,] . . . mutual trust and confidence among service members, . . . insur[ing] the integrity of the system of rank and command, . . . recruit[ing] and retain[ing] members of the naval service and . . . prevent[ing] breaches of security." SEC/NAV 1940.91) (ar. 12, 1981); J.A. at 219. We believe that the policy requiring discharge for homosexual conduct is rational means of achieving these legitimate interests. See *Beller* v. *Middendorf*, 632 F.2d 788, 812 (9th Cir,), cert. denied, 452 U.S. 905, 101 S.Ct. 3030, 69 L.Ed.2d 405 (1 980). The unique needs of the military, "a specialized society separate from civilian society," *Parker* v. *Levy*, 417 U.S. 733, 743, 94 S.Ct. 2547, 2556, 41 L.Ed.2d 439 (1974), justify the Navy's determination that homosexual conduct impairs its capacity to carry out its mission.

Affirmed.

OLLMAN V. EVANS & NOVAK

Bertell Ollman,
Appellant
v.
Rowland Evans, Robert Novak
No. 79–2265
750 f.2d 970

United States Court of Appeals,
District of Columbia Circuit.

Reargued *En Banc* March 6, 1984
Decided Dec. 6, 1984
As Amended Dec. 6, 1984

Before Robinson, Chief Judge Wright, Tamm, Wilkey, Wald, Edwards, Ginsburg, Bork, Scalia, and Starr, Circuit Judges, and MacKinnon, Senior Circuit Judge.

Opinion for the Court filed by Circuit Judge Starr.

Concurring opinion filed by Circuit Judge Bork, with whom Circuit Judges Wilkey, Ginsburg, and Senior Circuit Judge MacKinnon join.

Concurring opinion filed by Senior Circuit Judge MacKinnon.

Opinion dissenting in part, filed by Chief Judge Spottswood W. Robinson, III, with whom Circuit Judge J. Skelly Wright joins.

Opinion dissenting in part filed by Circuit Judge Wald, with whom Circuit Judges Harry T. Edwards and Scalia join.

Statement concurring in part and dissenting in part filed by Circuit Judge Harry T. Edwards.

Opinion dissenting in part file by Circuit Judge Scalia, with whom Circuit Judges Wald and Harry T. Edwards join.

BORK, Circuit Judge, with whom Wilkey and Ginsburg, Circuit Judges, and MacKinnon, Senior Circuit Judge, join, concurring:

While I concur in the judgment of the court and in much of Judge Starr's scholarly exposition, I write separately because I do not think he has adequately demonstrated that all of the allegedly libelous statements at issue here can be immunized as expressions of opinion. The dissents, on the-other-hand, while acknowledging the importance of additional factors, seem actually premised on the idea that the law makes a clear distinction between opinions, which are not actionable as libel, and facts, which are. In my view, the law as enunciated by the Supreme Court imposes no such sharp dichotomy. Some lower courts have assumed, as do some members of this court, not only that this opinion vs. fact formula is controlling but that it is governed at least primarily by grammatical analysis. I think that incorrect. Any such rigid doctrinal framework is inadequate to resolve the sometimes contradictory claims of the libel laws and the freedom of the press.

This case illustrates that point. It arouses concern that a freshening stream of libel actions, which often seem as much designed to punish writers and publications as to recover damages for real injuries, may threaten the public and constitutional interest in free, and frequently rough, discussion. Those who step into areas of public dispute, who choose the pleasures and distractions of controversy, must be willing to bear criticism, disparagement, and even wounding assessments. Perhaps it would be better if disputation were conducted in measured phrases and calibrated assessments, and with strict avoidance of the ad hominem; better, that is, if the opinion and editorial pages of the public press were modeled on *The Federalist Papers*. But that is not the world in which we live, ever have lived, or are ever likely to know, and the law of the first amendment must not try to make public dispute safe and comfortable for all the participants. That would only stifle the debate. In our world, the kind of commentary that the columnists Rowland Evans and Robert Novak have engaged in here is the coin in which controversialists are commonly paid.

These reflections lead me to conclude that Professor Ollman cannot press a libel action. But I do not find it easy to reach that result through a blunt distinction between opinion and fact, which while sometimes useful in just that crude dichotomy, is not adequate to the task here.

This inadequacy is most apparent in dealing with what Judge Starr calls "the most troublesome statement in the column," that concerning Ollman's reputation. It will be well to place the statement more completely in its context. Toward the end of their column, Evans and Novak say this:

> Ollman's principal scholarly work, "Alienation: Marx's Conception of Man in Capitalist Society," is a ponderous tome in adoration of the master (Marxism "is like a magnificently rich tapestry"). Published in 1971, it does not abandon hope for the revolution forecast by Karl Marx in 1848. "The present youth rebellion," he writes, by "helping to change the workers of tomorrow" will, along with other factors, make possible "a socialist revolution."
>
> Such pamphleteering is hooted at by one political scientist in a major eastern university, whose scholarship and reputation as a liberal are well known. "Ollman has no status within the profession, but is a pure and simple activist," he said. Would he say that publicly? "No chance of it. Our academic culture does not permit the raising of such questions."

Judge Starr's opinion for the majority contends that, in the circumstances of this case and in the context of the column as a whole, the quoted statement that "Ollman has no status within the profession, but is a pure and simple activist" qualifies as an opinion and so is constitutionally protected. The dissents, on the other hand, suggest that an assertion about one's general reputation is an assertion of fact. If common usage were the test, and if we looked at the sentence standing alone, the dissent's characterization would certainly be correct. The challenged language is a statement that others hold a particular opinion. Whether or not they do is a question of fact, though, as I will try to show, it is a "fact" of a peculiar nature in the context of first amendment litigation. If placing the bare assertion in question into one of two compartments labeled "opinion" and "fact" were the only issue we were allowed to consider, I would join the dissent. But I do not think these simple categories, semantically defined, with their flat and barren descriptive nature, their utter lack of subtlety and resonance, are nearly sufficient to encompass the rich variety of factors that should go into analysis when there is a sense, which I certainly have here, that values meant to be protected by the first amendment are threatened.

The temptation to adhere to sharply-defined categories is understandable. Judges generalize, they articulate concepts, they enunciate such things as four-factor frame works, three-pronged tests, and two-tiered analyses in an effort, laudable by and large, to bring order to a universe of unruly happenings and to give guidance for the future to themselves and to others. But it is certain that life will bring up cases whose facts simply cannot be handled by purely verbal formulas, or at least not handled with any sophistication and feeling for the underlying values at stake. When such a case appears and a court attempts nevertheless to force the old construct upon the new situation, the result is mechanical jurisprudence. Here we face such a case, and it seems to me better to revert to first principles than to employ categories which, in these circumstances, inadequately enforce the First Amendment's design.

Viewed from that perspective, the statement challenged in this lawsuit, in terms of the policies of the First Amendment, is functionally, more like an "opinion" than a "fact" and should not be actionable. It thus falls within the category the Supreme Court calls "rhetorical hyperbole." *See* pages 975–79, infra. I will try to set out the factors in this case that justify application of that concept.

Because Evans and Novak wrote that an anonymous political science professor said he had "no status" among political scientists, Ollman wants to ask a jury to award him $1,000,000 in compensatory damages and an additional $5,400,000 in punitive damages. In the field of journalism, these are enormous sums. They are quite capable of silencing political commentators forever. Unless the defamation was heinous and devastating, the amounts sought are entirely disproportionate. No one would think it appropriate for a state to levy such amounts as fines upon writers for statements of the sort made here. But, under current doctrine, lower courts have no way of saying that such sums may not be sought in libel actions, *Gertz v. Robert Welch, Inc.,* 418 U.S. 323, 94 S.Ct. 2997, 41 L.Ed.2d 789 (1974), or, indeed, of saying that damages may not be awarded as punishment or that such components of compensation as psychological anguish are inconsistent with the First Amendment when the libel occurs in a public, political dispute. *Time, Inc. v. Firestone,* 424 U.S. 448, 460, 96 S.Ct. 958, 968, 47 L.Ed.2d 154 (1976). Instead, unless we continue to develop doctrine to fit first amendment concerns, we are remitted to old categories which, applied woodenly, do not address modern problems.

The American press is extraordinarily free and vigorous, as it should be. It should be, not because it is free of inaccuracy, oversimplification, and bias, but because the alternative to that freedom is worse than those failings. Yet the area in which legal doctrine is currently least adequate to preserve press freedom is the area of defamation law, the area in which this action lies. We are said to have in the first amendment "a profound national commitment to the principle that debate on public issues should be uninhibited, robust, and wide-open." *New York Times Co.* v. *Sullivan,* 376 U.S. 254, 270, 84 S.Ct. 710, 721, 11 L.Ed.2d 686 (1964). That principle has resulted in the almost total abolition of prior restraints on publication; *New York Times Co.* v. *United States,* 403 U.S. 718, 91 S.Ct. 2140, 29 L.Ed.2d 822 (1971); *Nebraska Press Association* v. *Stuart,* 427 U.S. 539, 96 S.Ct, 2791, 49 L.Ed.2d 683 (1976); the curtailment of the possibility of criminal sanctions; *Garrison* v. *Louisiana,* 379 U.S. 64, 85 S.Ct. 209, 13 L.Ed.2d 125 (1964); and, in *Sullivan* itself, the construction of serious obstacles to private defamation actions by government officials. The cases that came afterward deployed similar obstacles to defamation actions by "public figures," *Curtis Publishing Co,* v. *Butts,* 388 U.S. 130, 87 S.Ct. 1975, 18 L.Ed.2d 1094 (1967); *Rosenbloom* v. *Metromedia, Inc.,* 403 U.S. 29, 91 S.Ct. 1811, 29 L.Ed.2d 296 (1971); *Gertz,* 418 U.S. at 345, 94 S.Ct. at 3009. Thus, we have a judicial tradition of a continuing evolution of doctrine to serve the central purpose of the first amendment.

Judge Scalia's dissent implies that the idea of evolving constitutional doctrine should be anathema to judges who adhere to a philosophy of judicial restraint. But most doctrine is merely the judge-made superstructure that implements basic constitutional principles. There is not at issue here the question of creating new constitutional rights or principles, a question which would divide members of this court along other lines than that of the division in this case. When there is a known principle to be explicated the evolution of doctrine is inevitable. Judges given stewardship of a constitutional provision—such as the First Amendment—whose core is known but whose outer reach and contours are ill-defined, face the never-ending task of discerning the meaning of the provision from one case to the next. There would be little need for judges—and certainly no office for a philosophy of judging—if the boundaries of every constitutional provision were self-evident. They are not. In a case like this, it is the task of the judge in this generation to discern how the framers' values, defined in the context of the world they knew, apply to the world we know. The world changes in which unchanging values find their application. The Fourth Amendment was framed by men who did not foresee electronic surveillance. But that does not make it wrong for judges to apply the central value of that amendment to electronic invasions of personal privacy. The commerce power was established by men who did not foresee the scope and intricate interdependence of today's economic activities. But that does not make it wrong for judges to forbid states the power to impose burdensome regulations on the interstate movement of trailer trucks. The first amendment's guarantee of freedom of the press was written by men who had not the remotest idea of modern forms of communication. But that does not make it wrong for a judge to find the values of the first amendment relevant to radio and television broadcasting.

So it is with defamation actions. We know very little of the precise intentions of the framers and ratifiers of the speech and press clauses of the First Amendment. But we do know that they gave into our keeping the value of preserving free expression and, in particular, the preservation of political expression, which is commonly conceded to be the value at the core of those clauses. Perhaps the framers did not envision libel actions as a major threat to that freedom. I may grant that, for the sake of the point to be made. But if, over time, the libel action becomes a threat to the central meaning of the first amendment, why should not judges adapt their doctrines? Why is it different to refine and evolve doctrine here, so long as one is faithful to the basic meaning of the amendment, than it is to adapt the Fourth Amendment to take account of electronic surveillance, the commerce clause to adjust to interstate motor carriage, or the first amendment to encompass the electronic media? I do not believe there is a difference. To say that such matters must be left to the legislature is to say that changes in circumstances must be permitted to render constitutional guarantees meaningless. It is to say that not merely the particular rules but the entire enterprise of the Supreme Court in *New York Times* v. *Sullivan* was illegitimate.

We must never hesitate to apply old values to new circumstances, whether those circumstances are changes in technology or changes in the impact of traditional common law actions, *Sullivan* was an instance of the Supreme Court doing precisely this as *Brown* v. *Board of Education,* 347 U.S. 483, 492–95, 74 S,Ct. 686, 690–92, 98 L.Ed. 843 (1954), was more generally an example of the Court applying an old principle according to a new understanding of a social situation. The important thing, the ultimate consideration, is the constitutional freedom that is given into our keeping. A judge who refuses to see new threats to an established constitutional value, and hence provides a crabbed interpretation that robs a provision of its full, fair, and reasonable meaning, fails in his judicial duty. That duty, I repeat, is to ensure that the powers and freedoms the framers specified are made effective in today's circumstances. The evolution of doctrine to accomplish that end contravenes no postulate of judicial restraint. The evolution I suggest does not constitute a major change in doctrine but is, as will be shown, entirely consistent with the implications of Supreme Court precedents.

We now face a need similar to that which courts have met in the past. *Sullivan,* for reasons that need not detain us here, seems not to have provided in full measure the protection for the marketplace of ideas that it was designed to do. Instead, in the past few years a remarkable upsurge in libel actions, accompanied by a startling inflation of damage awards, has threatened to impose a self-censorship on the press which can as effectively inhibit debate and criticism as would overt governmental regulation that the first amendment most certainly would not permit. *See* Lewis, *New York Times* v. *Sullivan Reconsidered: Time to Return to "The Central Meaning of the First Amendment,"* 83 Colum. L. Rev. 603 (1983).[1] It is not merely the size of damage awards but an entire shift in the application of libel laws that raises problems for press freedom. *See* Smolla, *Let the Author Beware: The Rejuvenation of the American Law of Libel,* 132 U.Pa.L.Rev. 1 (1983).[2] Taking such matters into account is not,

1. Lewis makes clear that, unlike some journalists, he is not given to reflexive perceptions of approaching tyranny in every decision that goes against the press; nevertheless he writes:

> This is an appropriate time to think again about that great case [*New York Times* v. *Sullivan*]. It is a time of growing libel litigation, of enormous judgments and enormous costs. The press and its lawyers are deeply worried; the protection that they thought was won for free expression in *New York Times* v. *Sullivan* seems to them to be crumbling. Some would say that libel actions are a more serious threat than ever. Now the American press is addicted to self-pity. Although it is the freest in the world, and freer now than it ever has been, it often cries that doom is at hand. But this time even someone as skeptical of press claims as I am must admit that there is something to the concern. *Id.* at 603 (footnote omitted).

2. Smolla refers to "a dramatic proliferation of highly publicized libel actions brought by well-known figures who seek, and often receive, staggering sums of money." *Id.* at 1. He suggests some interesting reasons why libel litigation has so suddenly been reinvigorated:

> I contend that there are four contributing causes to the recent rejuvenation of American libel law. . . . The first factor is a new legal and cultural seriousness about the inner self. Tort law has undergone a relaxation of rules that formerly prohibited recovery for purely emotional or psychic injury, a doctrinal evolution that parallels the growth of the "me-generation." A second factor is the infiltration into the law of defamation of many of the attitudes that have produced a trend in tort law over the past twenty years favoring compensation and risk-spreading goals over fault principles in the selection of liability rules. A third cause of the new era in libel is the increasing difficulty in distinguishing between the informing and entertaining functions of the media. The blurring of this line between entertainment and information has affected the method and substance of communications in important ways and highlights the inadequacies of the current legal standards governing defamation

as one dissent suggests, to engage in sociological jurisprudence, at least not in any improper sense. Doing what I suggest here does not require courts to take account of social conditions or practical considerations to any greater extent than the Supreme Court has routinely done in such cases as *Sullivan.* Nor does analysis here even approach the degree to which the Supreme Court quite properly took such matters into account in *Brown,* 347 U.S. at 492–95, 74 S.Ct. at 690–92. Matters such as the relaxation of legal rules about permissible recovery, the changes in tort law to favor compensation, and the existence of doctrinal confusion, *see* Smolla, *supra,* are matters that courts know well. Indeed, courts are responsible for these developments.

The only solution to the problem libel actions pose would appear to be close judicial scrutiny to ensure that cases about types of speech and writing essential to a vigorous first amendment do not reach the jury.[3] *See Bose Corp.* v. *Consumers Union of United States, Inc.,*— U.S.—, 104 S.Ct. 1949, 1965, 80 1 . . . Ed.2d 502 (1984). This requires a consideration of the totality of the circumstances that provide the context in which the statement occurs and which determine both its meaning and the extent to which making it actionable would burden freedom of speech or press. That, it must be confessed, is a balancing test and risks admitting into the law an element of judicial subjectivity. To that objection there are various answers. A balancing test is better than no protection at all. Given the appellate process, moreover, the subjective judgment of no single judge will be controlling. Over time, as reasons are given, the element of subjectivity will be reduced. There is, in any event, at this stage of the law's evolution, no satisfactory alternative. Hard categories and sharply-defined principles are admirable, if they are available, but usually, in the world in which we live, they share the problem of absolutes, of which they are a subgenre: they do not stand up when put to the test of hard cases. In the process of "balancing," I will state my reasons fully so that it may be judged whether they are rooted adequately in central first amendment concerns and so that guidance may be given as to how I think cases should be decided in the future.

---

actions. The final factor is doctrinal confusion, caused in large part by a pervasive failure to accommodate constitutional and common law values in a coherent set of standards that is responsive to the realities of modern communications. That doctrinal confusion is particularly telling in an environment where cultural trends, such as a heightened concern for the inner self, and legal trends, such as the trend in tort law in favor of strict liability, both work against the ideals of free expression. *Id.* at 11.

3. Since most libel plaintiffs demand a jury, as Ollman did, I discuss the problem in the context of jury trials. I doubt the problem would be greatly mitigated if the factfinder were a judge.

Two general considerations lead me to conclude that Professor Ollman should not be allowed to try his case to a jury. First, the state of doctrine in this area, if not precisely embryonic, is certainly still developing. Nothing in case law that is binding upon this court requires us to ignore context and the purposes of the first amendment and, instead, to apply a rigid opinion-fact dichotomy and to define the compartments of that dichotomy by semantic analysis. Indeed, the Supreme Court has indicated that we are not to do that. *See* 975–79, *infra.* We are required, therefore, to continue the evolution of the law in accordance with the deepest rationale of the first amendment. Second, the central concerns of the first amendment are implicated in this case so that a damage award would have a heavily inhibiting effect upon the journalism of opinion. On the other hand, the statement challenged, in practical impact, is more like an expression of opinion than it is like an assertion of fact. It is the kind of hyperbole that must be accepted in the rough and tumble of political argument.

I.

It is plain, I think, that the opinion-fact dichotomy is not as rigid as the various dissents suppose. There is no need to become caught up in a debate about the true nature of the allegedly libelous statement in terms of that dichotomy. The formalistic distinction between the two would be binding on us, sitting as an *en banc* court, only if the Supreme Court had required it. The thought that the Supreme Court has required it rests upon what I believe to be a misapprehension of dicta in *Gertz v. Robert Welch, Inc.,* 418 U.S. 323, 94 S.Ct. 2997, 41 L.Ed.2d 789. The facts of that case are important, if only by contrast with other cases, to an understanding of still-evolving doctrine in this area. Plaintiff Gertz was a lawyer who represented the family of a youth killed by a policeman in civil litigation against the policeman. In his capacity as counsel, Gertz attended the coroner's inquest but otherwise did nothing more than press the civil suit. The defendant, which published a monthly magazine, ran an article that portrayed Gertz as "an architect of the 'frame-up'" against the police officer, implied that Gertz had a lengthy criminal record, called him a "Leninist" and a "Communist-fronter," and identified him as an official of an organization that advocated violent seizure of the government. 418 U.S. at 326, 94 S.Ct. at 3000. None of this was true. The Court introduced its discussion of the governing considerations with an observation that was not necessary to the decision:

We begin with the common ground. Under the First Amendment there is no such thing as a false idea. However pernicious an opinion may seem, we depend for its correction not on the conscience of judges and juries but on the competition of other ideas. But there is no constitutional value in false statements of fact. Neither the intentional lie nor the careless error materially advances society's interest in "uninhibited, robust, and wide-open" debate on public issues. *New York Times Co.* v. *Sullivan,* 376 U.S., at 270 [84 S.Ct. at 721]. They belong to that category of utterances which "are no essential part of any exposition of ideas, and are of such slight social value as a step to truth that any benefit that may be derived from them is clearly outweighed by the social interest in order and morality." *Chaplinsky* v. *New Hampshire,* 315 U.S. 568, 572 [62 S.Ct. 766, 769, 86, L.Ed. 1031] (1942). *Id.,* 418 U.S. at 339–40, 94 S.Ct. at 3007 (footnote omitted).

In *Gertz,* it was obvious that most of the assertions that were the subject of the action purported to be flat statements of fact. The two statements that might arguably have been statements of opinion were that Gertz was a "Leninist" and a "Communist-fronter." 418 U.S. at 326, 94 S.Ct. at 3000. The Court did not discuss their proper categorization. But as Judge Friendly said in *Cianci* v. *New York Times Publishing Co.,* 639 F.2d 54, 61 (2d Cir.1980), these assertions must have been "deemed sufficiently 'factual' to support an action for defamation," since the Supreme Court remanded the case for jury trial.

For this reason, it is instructive to compare the Court's treatment of an even more clearly "factual" assertion in *Greenbelt Cooperative Publishing Association* v. *Bresler,* 398 U.S. 6, 90 S.Ct. 1537, 26 L.Ed.2d 6 (1970). Plaintiff Bresler, a real estate developer and builder, engaged in negotiations with the City Council of Greenbelt, Maryland, for zoning variances so that he could build high-density housing on land he owned. Simultaneously, the city was trying to acquire another tract of land from Bresler to construct a high school. The concurrent negotiations gave each side bargaining leverage. Bresler, of course, could vary the price for the tract depending on the city's attitude toward the variances. A newspaper accurately reported the public debate at city council meetings at which Bresler's negotiating demands were denounced as "blackmail." Bresler sued, alleging that the articles imputed a crime to him. The Court held that this denunciation was a constitutionally protected statement since here the word "blackmail" was no more than "rhetorical hyperbole, a vigorous epithet used by those who considered Bresler's negotiating position extremely unreasonable." *Id.,* 398 U.S. at 14, 90 S.Ct. at 1542. The context in which the words appeared was such that no reader could have thought that Bresler was charged with a crime.

The analytical approach of *Bresler* was reaffirmed in Old Dominion Branch No. 496, *National Association of Letter Carriers* v. *Austin,* 418 U.S. 264, 285–86, 94 S.Ct. 2770, 2'781–82, 41 L.Ed.2d 745 (1974), a case argued and handed down on the same days as *Gertz.* In *Letter Carriers,* a union newsletter, Carrier's Corner, published the names of those, including plaintiffs, who had not joined the union under the heading "List of Scabs." Just above the list the newsletter printed a particularly derogatory definition of the term "scab" attributed to Jack London which included the statement that a scab was "a traitor to his God, his country, his family and his class."[4] The Court quoted the reasoning of *Bresler* about the meaning imparted by context and then said:

> It is similarly impossible to believe that any reader of the Carrier's Corner would have understood the newsletter to be charging the appellees with committing the criminal offense of treason. As in Bresler, Jack London's "definition of a scab" is merely rhetorical hyperbole, a lusty and imaginative expression of the contempt felt by union members towards those who refuse to join. 418 U.S. at 285–86, 94 S.Ct. at 2782 (footnote omitted).

---

4. The statement read in full:

The Scab

"After God had finished the rattlesnake, the toad, and the vampire, He had some awful substance left with which He made a *scab.*

"A scab is a two-legged animal with a corkscrew soul, a water brain, a combination backbone of jelly and glue. Where others have hearts, he carries a tumor of rotten principles.

"When a scab comes down the street, men turn their backs and Angels weep in Heaven, and the Devil shuts the gates of hell to keep him out

"No man (or woman) has a right to scab so long as there is a pool of water to drown his carcass in, or a rope long enough to hang his body with. Judas was a gentleman compared with a scab. For betraying his Master, he had character enough to hang himself. A scab has not.

"Esau sold his birthright for a mess of pottage. Judas sold his Savior for thirty pieces of silver. Benedict Arnold sold his country for a promise of a commission in the British Army. The scab sells his birthright, country, his wife, his children and his fellowmen for an unfulfilled promise from his employer.

"Esau was a traitor to himself; Judas was a traitor to his God; Benedict Arnold was a traitor to his country; a SCAB is a traitor to his God, his country, his family and his class." *Letter Carriers,* 418 U.S. at 268, 94 S.Ct. at 2773.

The decision in *Letter Carriers* was not based on the first amendment but rather on the protection that the federal labor laws extend to communications made in the course of a labor dispute. 418 U.S. at 283 n. 15, 94 S.Ct. at 2781 n. 15. Nevertheless, the Court's interpretation of the labor laws relies heavily on first amendment defamation cases, including *Gertz. Id.* at 282-86, 94 S.Ct. at 2780–82. It therefore seems correct to regard *Letter Carriers* as a further explication of those cases.

A comparison of *Gertz,* on the one hand, with *Bresler* and *Letter Carriers,* on the other, indicates the actual state of the law. The fact that the epithets "Leninist" and "Communist-fronter" were deemed actionable, while the epithets "blackmail," "scab," and "traitor" were not, demonstrates that, when it comes to first amendment analysis, the Supreme Court does not employ a simplistic opinion-fact dichotomy. A statement that, on its face and standing alone, sounds like an assertion of fact may not be actionable. Context is crucial and can turn what, out of context, appears to be a statement of fact into "rhetorical hyperbole," which is not actionable. Thus, it is clear that the Supreme Court, in the service of the first amendment, employs a test which requires consideration of the totality of the circumstances in which a statement appears.[5]

Courts other than the Supreme Court agree that context may make non-actionable statements that are facially assertions of fact. Thus, the Ninth Circuit has said that "even apparent statements of fact may assume the character of statements of opinion, and thus be privileged, when made in public debate, heated labor dispute, or other circumstances in which an 'audience may anticipate efforts by the parties to persuade others to their positions by use of epithets, fiery rhetoric or hyperbole.'" *Information Control Corp.* v. *Genesis One Computer Corp.,* 611 F.2d 781, 784 (9th Cir.1980). Moreover, "the test to be applied in determining whether an allegedly defamatory statement constitutes an actionable statement of fact requires that the court examine the statement in its totality in the context in which it was uttered

---

5. The shadings of particular words may be important, too. Though *Gertz* assumed that "Leninist" and "Communist-fronter" were actionable, in *Buckley* v. *Litteg* 539 F.2d 882, 894 (2d Cir.1976), *cert. denied* 429 U.S. 1062, 97 S.Ct. 785, 50 L.Ed.2d 777 (1977), it was held that the accusation that William F. Buckley Jr., is a "fascist" was a constitutionally protected statement of opinion, and in the panel decision in this case, *Ollman* v. *Evans,* 713 F.2d 838, 850 (D.C.Cir.), *reh. en banc granted,* No. 79-2265 (Oct. 6, 1983), the statement that Ollman is a "Marxist" was held a constitutionally protected statement of opinion. In one sense, these statements were as factual as those held actionable in *Gertz,* but the terms "fascist" and "Marxist" have been so bandied about in debate that their meanings have blurred. We now usually hear those terms as merely blanket denunciations of those with whom the speaker strongly disagrees and who are, respectively, to the right or to the left of him on the political spectrum. They have become equivalent to saying that a person's political outlook is not respectable. The terms used in *Gertz,* however, carry the strong flavor that the person so described is subject to Communist Party discipline. That imputation was strongly reinforced by the false allegation that Gertz was an official of an organization that advocated forcible seizure of the government as well as by the context in which these charges were made: a series of articles, of which that on Gertz was one, that claimed there was "a nationwide conspiracy to discredit local law enforcement agencies and create in their stead a national police force capable of supporting a Communist dictatorship."418 U.S. at 325, 94 S.Ct. at 3000.

or published." *Id.* at 784. It is not unusual to protect false statements of fact where, because of the context, they would have been understood as part of a satire or fiction. In *Myers* v. *Boston Magazine Co.,* 380 Mass. 336, 403 N.E.2d 376 (1980), a magazine called the plaintiff the "worst" sports announcer in Boston and stated that he was "enrolled in a course for remedial speaking." Holding that the distinction between opinion and fact is a question of law, the court said the statement, in context, was one of opinion and would reasonably be understood to suggest that the plaintiff should have been enrolled in such a course. 403 N.E.2d at 379. The remarks about plaintiff appeared in a series of categorizations of various people as the best and worst in their fields. As the court noted, the "pervasive mood" was one of "rough humor." *Id.,* 403 N.E.2d at 377. *See Pring* v. *Penthouse International, Ltd.,* 695 F.2d 438, 443 (10th Cir.), *cert. denied,* —U.S.—, 103 S.Ct. 3112,77 L.Ed.2d 1367 (1983) (in fictional account false statement of facts constitutionally protected "obviously a complete fantasy").[6]

---

6. It should be noted that a number of scholars have sharply criticized the utility of the opinion-fact dichotomy both at common law and in various lower court opinions applying *Gertz.* One respected commentator indicated that "[n]o task undertaken under the law of defamation is any more elusive than distinguishing between the two." R. Sack, *Libel, Slander, and Related Problems* 155 (1980). Another concedes that the opinion-fact distinction has "proved to be a most unsatisfactory and unreliable one, difficult to draw in practice." W. Prosser, *Handbook of the Law of Torts* 820 (4th ed. 1971). This view is echoed by Wigmore who finds "no virtue in any test based on the mere verbal or logical distinction between 'opinion' and 'fact.'" 7 J. Wigmore, *Evidence* § 1919, at 14 (J. Chadbourn rev. ed. 1978). Wigmore goes on to observe:

> In the first place no such distinction is scientifically possible. . . . As soon as we come to analyze and define these terms for the purpose of that accuracy which is necessary in legal rulings, we find that the distinction vanishes. . . . If then our notion of the supposed firm distinction between "opinion" and "fact" is that the one is certain and sure, the other not, surely a just view of their psychological relations serves to demonstrate that in strict truth nothing is certain. Or if we prefer the suggestion of Sir G.C. Lewis that the test is whether "doubt can reasonably exist," then certainly it must be perceived that the multiple doubts which ought to exist would exclude vast masses of indubitably admissible testimony. Or if we prefer the idea that "opinion" is inference and fact is "original perception," then it may be understood that no such distinction can scientifically be made, since the processes of knowledge and the sources of illusion are the same for both.

Id. at 14–16. In sum, the opinion/fact "distinction, without more, primarily furnishes vague familiar terms into which one can pour whatever meaning is desired." Titus, "Statement of Fact Versus Statement of Opinion—A Spurious Dispute in Fair Comment," 15 *Vand.L.Rev.* 1203 (1962). For an excellent discussion of the deficiencies of the opinion/fact distinction see Franklin & Bussel, "The Plaintiff's Burden in Defamation: Awareness and Falsity," 25 *Wm. & Mary L.Rev.* 825, 869-85 (1984). This article suggests that a major purpose served by the dichotomy

I trust I have said enough to demonstrate that in Supreme Court decisions and the decisions of other courts there is no mechanistic rule that requires us to employ hard categories of "opinion" and "fact"—defined by the semantic nature of the individual assertion—in deciding a libel case that touches upon first amendment values.[7]

We must turn instead to the totality of the circumstances of the case to determine whether a statement may be actionable.

---

concerns the relative ease of proof of libelous statements. *See infra* at 983–86.

Scholarly criticism of the opinion/fact distinction is not surprising since even at common law a significant minority of jurisdictions rejected the opinion-fact dichotomy as unworkable and gave more weight to the question whether the public interest in free discussion was implicated. Annot., 110 A.L.R. 412, 435 (1937); *Coleman* v. *MacLennon*, 78 Kan. 711, 98 P. 281 (1908); *Snively* v. *Record Publishing Co.*, 185 Cal. 565, 198 P. 1 (1921). This view was well stated by the Alaska Supreme Court in *Pearson* v. *Fairbanks Publishing Co.*, 413 P.2d 711 (Alaska 1966):

> The distinction between a fact statement and an opinion or comment is so tenuous in most instances, that any attempt to distinguish between the two will lead to needless confusion. The basis for the privilege is that it is in the public interest that there be reasonable freedom of debate and discussion on public issues. One should not be deterred from speaking out through the fear that what he gives as his opinion will be construed by a court as inferring, if not actually amounting to, a mis-statement of fact.

Id. at 714 (footnote omitted); see 1 F. Harper & F. James, *Torts* § 5.28, at 458 (1956). The *Pearson* court ultimately protected as privileged, unless actual malice were shown, an editorial attack on syndicated columnist Drew Pearson in which it was said that an anonymous colleague of Pearson's had summed up Pearson's reputation in Washington by calling him "the garbage man of the fourth estate." 413 P.2d at 717, The parallel between Pearson's case and Ollman's is obvious.

7. Justices Rehnquist and White have indicated as much in their dissent from the denial of certiorari in *Miskovsky* v. *Oklahoma Publishing Co.*, 654 P.2d 587 (Okla.), *cert. denied* 459 U.S. 923, 103 S.Ct. 235, 74 L.Ed.2d 186 (1982) (Rehnquist, J., dissenting). In that case, the Justices suggest that the Supreme Court of Oklahoma erred in relying on a rigid opinion/fact dichotomy to determine the truth or falsity of an allegedly libelous statement. 459 U.S. at 924, 103 S.CL at 236, *citing*, 654 P.2d at 593. The Justices expressed concern that the Oklahoma court may have misapprehended the reach of the Supreme Court's dicta in *Gertz* and believed itself bound to apply too rigid a constitutional standard. They favored granting certiorari to make clear that the *Gertz* dicta should not be applied mechanically given the "'rich and complex history' of the common law's effort to deal with the question of opinion." *Id.*, 459 U.S. at 925, 103 S.Ct. at 236.

In *Miskovsky*, Justices Rehnquist and White appear to have criticized the lower courts' application of the opinion/fact dichotomy because they believed too much protection was being given to certain statements of opinion. This case illustrates a different failing of the mechanistic application of the *Gertz* dichotomy. Here we have a statement of rhetorical hyperbole which is not easily encompassed in rigid categories labeled either "opinion" or "fact."

II.

There are several factors that convince me Ollman cannot maintain this action. These considerations are of the type that the Supreme Court and other courts have deemed important: the danger to first amendment freedoms and the functional meaning of the challenged statement as shown by its context and its qualities as recognizable rhetorical hyperbole. The factors here are: Ollman, by his own actions, entered a political arena in which heated discourse was to be expected and must be protected; the "fact" proposed to be tried is in truth wholly unsuitable for trial, which further imperils free discussion; the statement is not of the kind that would usually be accepted as one of hard fact and appeared in a context that further indicated it was rhetorical hyperbole.

A.

Plaintiff Ollman, as will be shown, placed himself in the political arena and became the subject of heated political debate. That fact has significance in two ways. The first, and more conventional, point is that the existence of a political controversy *is* part of the total context that gives meaning to statements made about Ollman. When we read charges and countercharges about a person in the midst of such controversy we read them as hyperbolic, as part of the combat, and not as factual allegations whose truth we may assume. It will be seen, as the events are recounted, how true that is in Ollman's case.

My second point is less conventional, though by no means ruled out by case law as a next step in the evolution of doctrine in this troubling field. It is this: in order to protect a vigorous marketplace in political ideas and contentions, we ought to accept the proposition that those who place themselves in a political arena must accept a degree of derogation that others need not. Because this would represent a further development of the law I have argued it more fully than the first point. But it is not necessary to accept this proposition in order to accept the first point, that political controversy is part of the context that tends to show that some apparently factual assertions should be treated as rhetorical hyperbole and hence as opinions.

It is common ground that the core function of the first amendment is the preservation of that freedom to think and speak as one pleases which is the "means indispensable to the discovery and spread of political truth." *Whitney v. California,* 274 U.S. 357, 375, 47 S.Ct. 641, 648, 71 L.Ed. 1095 (1927) (Brandeis, J., concurring). Necessary to the preservation of that freedom, of course, is the willingness of those who would speak to be spoken to and, as in this case, to be spoken about. This is not always a pleasant or painless experience, but it cannot be avoided if the political arena is to remain as vigorous and robust as the first amendment and the nature of our polity require.

In deciding a case like this, therefore, one of the most important considerations is whether the person alleging defamation has in some real sense placed himself in an arena where he should expect to be jostled and bumped in a way that a private person need not expect. Where politics and ideas about politics contend, there is a first amendment arena. The individual who deliberately enters that arena must expect that the debate will sometimes be rough and personal. This would not be true of a political scientist who confined himself to academic pursuits and eschewed political proselytizing. Such a person might legitimately expect that, should columnists for some reason become interested in him, any criticism leveled would stick close to his work, and that, if assertions were made about his reputation, they would be actionable if false.

But Ollman has, as is his undoubted right, gone well beyond the role of the cloistered scholar, and he did so before Evans and Novak wrote about him. As the column recounts, and its literal accuracy in these respects is not challenged, Professor Ollman was an active proponent not just of Marxist scholarship but of Marxist politics. He wrote an article called "On Teaching Marxism and Building the Movement," which asserted that his classroom was a place where the students' "bourgeois ideology is being dismantled," that his endeavor was to "make more revolutionaries," and that "radical professors" are important to "the movement." His book approved the "youth rebellion" as helping make possible "a socialist revolution." Twice he put himself forward for election to the council of the American Political Science Association, campaigning on the promise that, "If elected . . . I shall use every means at my disposal to promote the study of Marxism and Marxist approaches to politics throughout the profession." It was plain that Ollman was a political activist and that he saw his academic post as, among other things, a means of advancing his political goals. This is controversial behavior for an academic, no matter what political creed he espoused, and was bound to raise for debate the question whether he used his position as a teacher to indoctrinate the young with his political beliefs.

It was thus inevitable that when Ollman, who was a political figure, put himself forward as a candidate for the chairmanship of the department of politics and government at the University of Maryland there would be a public political controversy. But more took place, both upon Ollman's initiative and the initiatives of others, that confirmed his status as a figure in a political arena before the Evans and Novak column appeared.

A hot public controversy erupted the day after Ollman's nomination for the chairmanship of the department was disclosed. Among the participants in the dispute, which was extensively covered by the news media, were the Republican Acting Governor of Maryland, two members of the university's board of regents, a state senator, a member of the Prince George's County council, the associate general secretary of the American Association of University Professors, the *Washington Post* columnist Richard Cohen, and the three Democratic candidates for governor.[8] Ollman's nomination thus became an issue in the 1978 Maryland gubernatorial race. The debate about his nomination and politics received nationwide press coverage.

In the midst of this controversy, Ollman announced that he had begun to market a new board game called "Class Struggle," which he said he had been working on for seven years. He said, "This game will give our people [a] view of how our society works, and for whom." Players representing workers moved a little hammer around the board; those representing capitalists moved a little top hat. Players moved to the final confrontation—revolution. "'Not a violent overthrow,' Ollman emphasized, 'but a structural change.'"The*Washington Post*, Apr. 28, 1978. The Evans and Novak column appeared on May 4.

The president of the university rejected Ollman's appointment, and the *Washington Post,* in an editorial generally critical of the decision, said:

---

8. The day after the news of Ollman's nomination appeared in a student newspaper at the university, reporters from the general press asked Maryland's Acting Governor Blair Lee about the matter at his weekly news conference. According to a story in the *Washington Post* of April 21, 1978, Lee questioned the wisdom of appointing a Marxist as department head at a public institution. Even before Lee spoke, two members of the university's board of regents had publicly objected to the appointment, and an associate professor who was also a Prince George's County councilman was quoted as saying, "there's going to be a lot of political reaction and public discussion." Lee said the legislature might react by attempting to cut the university's budget and said that one state senator had lodged a formal complaint with him about the nomination.

On April 22, 1978, the *Washington Post* reported that the associate general secretary of the American Association of University Professors had written to Lee to urge that he stop interfering in Ollman's nomination, arguing that academic qualifications, not personal ideology, should be dispositive. The following day, April 23, Richard Cohen's column in the *Washington Post* took the matter up and argued that the principle of academic freedom required that Ollman's politics be treated as irrelevant to his nomination. On April 27, a *Post* story said that three Democratic candidates for governor had criticized Lee for interfering with an academic institution. An aide to one of them was quoted as saying that Ollman was a "golden issue."The story stated that "Academic freedom and Lee's right to make such remarks have been debated at Baltimore forums and Montgomery County coffee klatches all this week. The gubernatorial race has found its first real controversy."

"A teacher's politics may be his own business, but it becomes a legitimate criterion by which to judge his appointment when it calls into question his classroom intentions. In recent weeks, Mr. Ollman's public statements have not made his case more appealing. To many, his remarks have suggested that he is in fact more interested in polemics than in political science." *Washington Post,* July 23, 1978, at C 6, col. 1.

The important point about all of this is that Ollman was not simply a scholar who was suddenly singled out by the press or by Evans and Novak. Whatever the merits of his scholarship, he was also a political man who publicly tried to forward his political goals. He had entered the political arena before he put himself forward for the department chairmanship. That candidacy merely widened the area within which he was known and raised for debate a topic of legitimate political concern, a debate which his further actions fueled. That being so, he must accept the banging and jostling of political debate, in ways that a private person need not, in order to keep the political arena free and vital.

Ollman may not be required to accept the same degree of buffeting that a candidate for a major office must, but when he chose to become a spokesman for Marxism to be implemented politically, when he stated that his teaching effectively converted students to Marxism, when he stated that he wanted to spread Marxist approaches to politics throughout a profession of teachers and writers, when he stated that he favored revolution by structural change, when he marketed a game designed to teach the general public about class struggle, and when he stood for an office that would extend his influence over teaching and writing, and hence over the development of the political views of the young—when Professor Ollman chose that path he became a figure in whom the public might legitimately be interested, and about whose intentions and professional status public questions might legitimately be raised. In a word, when he did those things, Ollman entered a first amendment arena and had to accept the rough treatment that arena affords.

The concept of the public, political arena that I have employed has at least some of the same functional characteristics as the concept of a person who is a public figure for limited purposes. That similarity may prompt the objection that the public figure concept applies only to distinguish between negligence and actual malice for purposes of liability. That is, of course, an accurate statement of current doctrine, but I know of no case holding that the concept may not be put to the use proposed, to assist in deciding how much public bumping a person must accept as a risk of the controversies he chooses to engage in.

Two of the dissenting opinions (Wald and Scalia, JJ.) maintain that commentary about public figures is already adequately protected by the actual malice requirement of *New York Times* v. *Sullivan.* According to this view, there is no reason to go beyond *Sullivan* and accord greater first amendment protection to some false political statements made knowingly and with actual malice. But the Supreme Court has already placed the law in precisely the posture to which the dissent objects. *Gertz,* of course, means that a statement characterized as an opinion cannot be actionable even if made with actual malice and even if it severely damages the person discussed. In such circumstances, society must depend upon the competition of ideas to correct pernicious opinions rather than on "the conscience of judges and juries."

Bresler and *Letter Carriers* make the point even clearer. In both, apparent factual assertions—in *Bresler* that plaintiff engaged in "blackmail"; in *Letter Carriers* that plaintiffs were "scabs" and "traitors"—were held not actionable because, in context, the reader would take them not as assertions of fact but as vigorous hyperbole. In neither case did the Court inquire about actual malice. It assumed that even if these statements were made with actual malice, they were protected because the context in which they appeared alerted the reader that the statements were not to be read as factual allegations. Thus, the Supreme Court has obviously recognized that the actual malice requirement of *Sullivan* does not always provide adequate protection and the Court has provided the additional protection that the First Amendment requires.

In this respect, I am doing no more than following Supreme Court precedent. As I said at the outset of this subsection, part of the context here is the existence of a vigorous political controversy that Ollman himself fueled and which conditions the way a reader understands the kind of charge that Evans and Novak related.

Judge Wald's dissent objects that making the distinction between a person who has stepped into the political arena and one who has not is a task too baffling for judges. The answer is that this is exactly the task that judges must perform in deciding whether a person has become a public figure.

But I have suggested, though it is not essential to my result, that the law consider the existence of political controversy and the concept of a political arena in an additional way. That concept could be used to set a kind of *de minimis* level for rough statements about persons who enter a First Amendment arena and become, in essence, public figures for limited purposes. This is a different spectrum from that of the actual malice-negligence distinction but surely one to which the concept of a public figure or a political individual is relevant. Indeed, though the law has not yet had occasion to consider this point, Americans have a kind of common understanding or social usage that runs along these lines. The United States has just been through an intense political campaign. In this highly charged atmosphere, many cruel and damaging things were said about various candidates for major political offices. Some of the statements made may well meet the law's standards for actual malice—reckless disregard for the truth of the matter asserted. Examples will no doubt spring to mind. Yet if the statement is of the sort that we recognize as rhetorical hyperbole, we would be astonished and highly disapproving if the defamed candidate brought an action for libel. We expect people who engage in controversy to accept that kind of statement as their lot. We think the First Amendment demands a hide that tough. As I have said, Ollman may not be required to be as thick-skinned as a candidate for major political office but, as a political man, he shares some of the same responsibility. I do not say that this point alone is sufficient to decide the case, but it weighs, and, I think, weighs heavily, on the side of holding the statement not actionable.

But, in any event, it is indisputable that this swirling public debate provided a strong context in which charges and countercharges should be assessed. In my view, that context made it much less likely that what Evans and Novak said would be regarded as an assertion of plain fact rather than as part of the judgments expressed by each side on the merits of the proposed appointment.

B.

Particularly troubling in a first amendment context is the kind of fact that is proposed for trial and, on either side's demand, jury determination. Here it is well to recur to one of the functions of the rough division between opinions and facts. It is relatively easy to litigate a false statement of fact; it may be impossible to prove or disprove an opinion. Courts of law may reasonably limit their dockets to questions which they are competent to resolve. Accordingly, the opinion-fact division serves a purpose by confining the category of actionable statements to those which lend themselves to competent judicial resolution of the truthfulness of their content. Viewed from that juridical perspective, the statement in question here is qualitatively more like an opinion than a fact. It is simply not fit for jury determination.

The evidence is mounting that juries do not give adequate attention to limits imposed by the first amendment and are much more likely than judges to find for the plaintiff in a defamation case. It is appropriate for judges, therefore, to take cases from juries when they are convinced that a statement ought to be protected because, among other reasons, the issue it presents is inherently unsusceptible to accurate resolution by a jury. As the Supreme Court said in *Bose Corp.* v. *Consumers Union of United States, Inc.,*—U.S.—, 104 S.Ct. 1949, 80 LEd.2d 502, appellate courts must independently examine the record in first amendment cases to ensure that constitutional values are not endangered. "The requirement of independent appellate review . . . reflects a deeply held conviction that judges—and particularly members of [the Supreme] Court—must exercise such review in order to preserve the precious liberties established and ordained by the Constitution." *Id.,* 104 S.Ct. at 1965. The underlying principle, it seems to me, requires judges to decide when allowing a case to go to a jury would, in the totality of the circumstances, endanger first amendment freedoms. That danger is overwhelming when the issue is of the sort presented here.

The issue the dissents would have tried—the political science academic community's opinion of Professor Ollman's stature as a political scientist—is inherently incapable of being adjudicated with any expectation of accuracy. One dissent (Wald, J.) suggests that "[o]ne could, for instance, devise a poll of American Political Science Association members as to their opinion, on a scale of one to ten, of the scholarly value of Ollman's work. Testimony of prominent political scientists or other measures of reputation would also serve to verify or refute the statement about Ollman's reputation without sending the jury onto a sea of speculation." But this suggestion is itself abstract speculation. Some element of realism is necessary in these matters. Let us try to imagine the nature of the trial and what the jury could make of such evidence.

As every presidential campaign reminds us, there is a great spread in the results of public opinion polls, even in the results of polls taken at the same time by a number of reputable and experienced polling organizations. There are scientific and professional disputes about polling methodology, about the representativeness of the sample or of those who respond to the questionnaire, since it is often true that those who respond have markedly different views from those who do not respond. (The problems of sampling, as will be seen, are very much present with a group whose members are as disparate as political scientists.) There are disputes about the phrasing and the order of the questions put, and whether such matters skewed the results. Indeed, if the column's assertion about his status among academics harmed Ollman's status among academics, the poll would be seriously biased. (If there was no such harm, of course, Ollman would not have much of a case.) All of these disputes would occur about the poll suggested by the dissent, and would be tried with experts in statistics, psychology, and perhaps other disciplines offering the jury conflicting scientific arguments. Perhaps both the plaintiff and defendants would devise and send out questionnaires so that the jury, weighing scientific arguments about which experts cannot agree, would have to decide which poll was the more methodologically sound. I do not think the results of a trial on issues like these could be anything but random and, whatever we might be willing of necessity to allow in a different kind of trial, I would be utterly unwilling to let first amendment freedoms ride upon an outcome determined by chance.

Let us suppose, however, that the jury chooses one poll as methodologically more acceptable than the other. And let us suppose that the results show that most of the scores awarded Ollman range between 2 and 7, with a scattering of 1's and 10's, and a mean of 3.5 and a median of 4. What on earth is a jury to make of that? That Ollman has high status?, that he has low status but not "no status"? If low status, is that close enough to "no status" to afford the statement of "no status" protection as permissible hyperbole? It is not at all clear what the term "no status" connotes. The term is so vague as to suggest little more than general, but not necessarily universal, disapproval. Thus, if the profession were sharply divided so that a fifth of those responding ranked Ollman at 8 and the remainder ranked him at 1, would the jury be permitted to find that, in effect, showed "no status" or would it be instructed that any favorable opinion showed "some status" so that the column's statement was one of false fact?

How is the jury, or an appellate court, to know whether knowledge that the poll was for use in a lawsuit skewed the results? The controversy and this case are widely known, especially among academic political scientists. But the professors who fill out the questionnaires will not be available for examination. Indeed, in order to avoid one kind of bias, they would have to be promised anonymity. How are we to know whether the political stance of the combatants—that Ollman is a Marxist and Evans and Novak are generally regarded as conservatives—skewed the results? Indeed, must not the ideological coloration of the entire political science academic profession become an issue for the jury in evaluating the poll? If that community is conservative, would they rank Ollman lower for purposes of a lawsuit against Evans and Novak than their real estimate of his professional qualities? If that community leans to the left, would its members, for similar political reasons, rank him higher? Would not the investigation into opinions about Ollman necessarily include an investigation of the political opinions of the relevant academic community?

Matters are really worse than this, however. Academic political scientists number in the tens of thousands. With the exception of a few very prominent persons, the quality of no one's work is known throughout the profession. The profession is fragmented and contains many subsets. Knowledge of a professor's work is likely to be confined to one or a few such subsets. Thus, political scientists who view themselves as devoted to value-free empirical studies are unlikely to have any informed estimate of the work done by most persons working in political philosophy. More than this, we are not talking about opinions concerning the professional credentials of a faculty member in the school of engineering or medicine, fields in which ideology plays little or no part in estimations of status. We are talking about an academic specialty which, as anyone remotely familiar with it knows, is politically highly charged and riven. Political outlook may color professional estimation. In this field there are varieties of liberals, conservatives, libertarians, Marxists, and Straussians. Suppose, to put a not wholly unreasonable hypothetical, that on the questionnaire the dissent proposes, Ollman received 9's and 10's from Marxists and 1's and 2's from Straussians. It may be doubted that either set of numbers has any significance that a jury should be entitled to consider. If views of professional status are colored or determined by political or philosophical agreement or disagreement, is that the "status" we are interested in? Presumably, if Ollman has been defamed, it is in relation to a more objective, or less political, status. At least, he puts the matter that way. *See* page 1010, *infra.*

The suggestion that reputation could be verified by the testimony of prominent political scientists cures none of this. If prominent political scientists could be induced to testify, and if those who could be induced represented a fair cross-section of the academic community, both heroic assumptions, the jury would be left with contradictory opinions about opinions. I do not know how the jury could reach any informed judgment unless it were told that any opinion favorable to Ollman meant that the allegation of "no status" was false.

The problem of trying academic reputation to a jury is very similar to the problem a faculty faces when it tries to determine whether to vote to award tenure to a candidate. Judge Winter, himself a veteran of tenure debates, described the situation in *Zahorik* v. *Cornell University,* 729 F.2d 85 (2d Cir.1984):

> [T]enure decisions are a source of unusually great disagreement. Because the stakes are high, the number of relevant variables is great and there is

no common unit of measure by which to judge scholarship, the dispersion of strongly held views is greater in the case of tenure decisions than with employment decisions generally. . . . [A]rguments pro and con are framed in largely conclusory terms which lend themselves to exaggeration, particularly since the stauncher advocates on each side may anticipate and match an expected escalation of rhetoric by their opponents. Moreover, disagreements as to individuals may reflect long standing and heated disputes as to the merits of contending schools of thought or as to the needs of a particular department. . . . [A] file composed of irreconcilable evaluations is not unusual. *Id.* at 93.

I can testify that this description is accurate, though perhaps understated. The faculty member who has not read the candidate's publications himself and formed his own judgment is helpless before the impressive, well-documented but diametrically opposed arguments of others. The jury would certainly be in a far worse position to judge.[9]

Academic reputation, in short, seems to me peculiarly unsuited to a trial at law unless the person in question is one of the few universally acknowledged throughout the profession to be a major figure. Ollman is not claimed to be that. This concern may or may not be weighty enough by itself to deny Ollman access to the jury. I tend to think it may be. But I need not decide that because the points I am making are intended to be cumulative and this point certainly goes to the question of the degree of risk we are willing to impose upon the exercise of political comment.

---

9. Judge Scalia suggests there is not much danger to press freedom here since Ollman would have to prove his case by "clear and convincing evidence." That is next to no protection. If Ollman put three knowledgeable political scientists on the stand to testify that his academic standing was in fact high, and if Evans and Novak put three equally credible witnesses on the stand to testify that Ollman's reputation was low, I fail to see on what theory the trial judge could take the case from the jury. It is not required that a plaintiff produce more witnesses than the defendants. The situation is the classic battle of the experts and the jury will be free to decide which set it finds "clear and convincing." For the reasons given in the text, that decision will bear only a coincidental resemblance to the "fact" of Ollman's real status. Nor is it apparent that Evans and Novak could defeat Ollman's case, as the dissent asserts, simply by showing that the professor they quote did tell them what they printed. If the professor spoke with knowledge that his assertion was false or with reckless disregard for its truth or falsity, publishing the assertion may well be libelous. It is far from clear that journalists discharge their duty so as to escape legal liability by inquiring of a single source when they should know that others have a different version of the "fact." If the printed statement is treated as a fact, despite its context, there will be precious little protection for it at the trial level.

C.

The statement of "no status" is very unlikely to be read as a flat statement of fact. Rather, it strikes the reader primarily as an exaggerated expression of the anonymous professor's own view of Ollman's academic credentials. It is wrong to speak as though there is always a sharp distinction between opinion and fact. There certainly is at the extremes an obvious difference in kind. The assertion that "Jones stole $100 from the church poor box last Friday night," cannot be tortured into an opinion, just as the assertion that "I think Jones is the kind of man who would steal from tire-church poor box" is obviously only a statement of the speaker's opinion of Jones's character. But the statement that "Half the people in this town think Jones is the kind of man who would steal from the poor box" is not quite like either of the first two. It is less harmful than the first and perhaps more damaging than the second. I say "perhaps" because the assertion of what others think always has a ring of hyperbole about it. The hearer knows that what he is being told is, in fact, one man's opinion about others' opinions. It can be called an assertion of fact, which in a sense it is, but it is also the kind of criticism that we are used to hearing and about which we regularly suspend judgment. Told by Smith that Jones actually stole the money, we think that Smith would not dare say such a thing if it were not so. There is a hard quality to the statement it is capable of proof or disproof and it describes a physical action that did or did not take place. Told by Smith that half the town thinks Jones is the kind of fellow who would steal the money, we instantly discount it as an expression of Smith's antipathy to Jones. We think it may or may not be so and we realize that there is very little chance of verifying the truth of the assertion as made.

So it is here with the statement that Ollman has no status within the profession of political scientists, It is one man's impression or opinion relayed by Evans and Novak. The reader does not accept it as a concrete fact. He understands that the speaker thinks poorly of Ollman. He gathers that Ollman is a controversial figure within the profession, which certainly appears to be true. Indeed, the column contains information from which the reader might draw the same conclusion even if Evans and Novak had not made it explicit. Earlier than the passage under discussion, the column stated:

> He [Ollman] twice sought election to the council of the American Politi
> cal Science Association as a candidate of the "Caucus for a New Political
> Science" and finished last out of 16 candidates *each* time. Whether or not
> that represents a professional judgment by his colleagues, as some critics

contend, the verdict clearly rejected his campaign pledge: "If elected . . . I shall use every means at my disposal to promote the study of Marxism and Marxist approaches to politics throughout the profession."

The results of these two elections would certainly appear to be a rejection of Ollman's campaign pledge, and the fact that he made the pledge coupled with the results of the two elections certainly give grounds for supposing that Ollman is an "activist" and that his stature in the profession, or in important segments of the profession, might well be low. Indeed, the column contains accurate quotations from Ollman's writings that would strongly suggest such an assessment, by some members of the profession, might be likely. I have already rehearsed these in connection with Ollman's status as a political actor.

This raises the question of what academic reputation or status is. Men and women engaged in academic life are judged by colleagues on various scales of values. That fact might prove troublesome at trial. But Ollman, interestingly enough, advances a quite conventional standard by which status should be judged: "Plaintiffs occupation is that of scholar and teacher. It is commonly expected that a person in that position will be open-minded and fair-minded, will not attempt to indoctrinate students, and will seek the truth through research and testing and will communicate the results of his search by means of publications which adhere to certain objective canons of scholarship." Brief for Appellant at 6. If the ideal of the scholar seeking truth dispassionately is the standard, as most lay readers of newspapers undoubtedly believe that it is, then the column's quotations from his writings and from his electioneering statements, as well as his own public statements about, and the marketing of, his board game, Class Struggle, indicate that he has upon more than one occasion significantly departed from it. Thus, the anonymous professor's remark that Ollman had "no status" would be taken as a comment upon what the column and the news stories had already revealed.

When we come to the context in which this statement occurred, it becomes even more apparent that few people were likely to perceive it as a direct assertion of fact, to be taken at face value. That context was one of controversy and opinion, and it is known to be such by readers. It is significant, in the first place, that the column appeared on the Op-Ed pages of newspapers. These are pages reserved for the expression of opinion, much of it highly controversial opinion. That does not convert every assertion of fact on the Op-Ed pages into an expression of opinion merely by its placement there. It does alert the reader that he is in the context of controversy and politics, and that what he reads does not even purport to be as balanced, objective, and fair-minded as he has a right to hope to be the case with what is contained in the news columns of the paper. The Op-Ed pages are known to be a forum for controversy, often heated controversy, analogous in many respects to the context of a labor dispute. The latter, of course, was found to impart corrective meaning to the very unpleasant assertions challenged in *Letter Carriers.*

In this case, moreover, the column was identified as written by Evans and Novak, men who are widely known, and certainly known to readers of the Op-Ed pages, as purveyors of opinion who are frequently controversial. More than this, before the reader comes to the passage in question, he will have discovered many times over that Evans and Novak are, to say the least of it, suspicious of Ollman's intentions and that they regard him as a remarkably wayward academic. All of that impression is conveyed in language and expressions of opinion that no one on this court finds actionable. By the time the reader comes to the assertion of an anonymous professor's statement of academic opinion about Ollman, he is, I think, likely to read the remark *as* more of the same. He is most unlikely to regard that assertion as to be trusted automatically. It is an assertion of a kind of fact, it is true, but a hyperbolic "fact" so thoroughly embedded in opinion and tendentiousness that it takes on their qualities.

It is important to be clear about this. It is the totality of these circumstances that show the statement to be rhetorical hyperbole. If the statement were that a person is known by his friends to be an alcoholic or that a professor's written works were plagiarized, then it would be a very different kind of factual assertion from that involved here, one taken more seriously by readers, and not mitigated by context.[10]

---

10. The suggestion is made (Scalia, J.) that my position would enable political commentators "to destroy private reputations at will." The distinction just made in the text should disprove that charge. The question is one of meaning in context. But the extravagance of the charge prompts some reflections about its realism as applied to this case. Ollman's reputation among political scientists is not precisely a "private reputation." As, I have been at some pains to point out, he made his academic intentions and performance a legitimate subject of public controversy. I do not think that the first amendment allows him to have it both ways: acting as a public political man but suing as if he were a private scholar. Moreover, some realism about the world is in order here, too. Among what audiences can the assertion that Ollman's reputation is already low lower his reputation? The general reader forgets his name within days, if not hours, of reading such a column. Academic political scientists who have an opinion of Ollman based on his work are hardly likely to change that opinion because of a quotation from an unnamed professor. Ollman, after all, is not in the position of a physician, an engineer, or a retailer. He does not depend upon public reputation to attract clients or customers. These facts, while they do not themselves deny Ollman a cause of action, provide some perspective for the claims about the destruction of his private reputation.

I have attempted the kind of contextual inquiry that I think the Supreme Court's cases indicate and the rationale of the first amendment mandates. I am persuaded that Ollman may not rest a libel action on the statement contained in the Evans and Novak column.

Lebron v. Washington Metropolitan Area Transit Authority

Michael A. Lebron,
Appellant

v.

Washington Metropolitan Area Transit Authority, et al.
No. 84–5189

749 F.2d 893
United States Court of Appeals,
District of Columbia Circuit.

Argued May 29, 1984
Decided Dec. 14, 1984

Before Bork, Scalia, and Starr, Circuit Judges.

Opinion for the Court filed by Circuit Judge Bork.

Bork, Circuit Judge.

This case arose when the Washington Metropolitan Area Transit Authority ("WMATA" or "Authority") refused to lease display space in its subway stations to Michael A. Lebron, who sought to display a poster critical of the Reagan administration. WMATA refused because in its judgment Mr. Lebron's poster is "deceptive." Mr. Lebron then sued to enjoin WMATA from violating the rights guaranteed him by the First and Fourteenth Amendments to the Constitution and to compel the Authority to let him display his poster. He also sought damages. The district court denied Mr. Lebron relief, agreeing with WMATA that the poster is "deceptive and distorted" and therefore not protected by the First Amendment. A motions panel of this

Court ordered WMATA to show the poster pending this appeal. We reverse the judgment for WMATA.

I.

WMATA was established through a congressionally approved interstate compact to improve public transportation in the Washington, D.C. metropolitan area. One way in which the Authority raises revenue is by leasing the free-standing dioramas inside subway stations for use as advertising space. WMATA accepts both public service and commercial advertisements, although there is a fee difference based upon the type of advertisement.[1] Submitted advertisements are evaluated by WMATA's Director of Marketing, John E. Warrington, based upon guidelines set by the Authority's Board of Directors. Guideline No. 2 states, in part, that "[a]ll copy and artwork should avoid conveying derisive, exaggerated, distorted, deceptive or offensive impressions." Plaintiff's Exh. 3, included in Record Excerpts ("R.E."), as Exhibit A. WMATA has in the past rented display space to groups seeking to convey messages of public interest and about candidates for local political office.[2] *Lebron* v. *Washington Metropolitan Area Transit Authority,* 585 F.Supp. 1461 at 1465 (D.D. C.1984) ("Mem. op.").

In October of 1983, Mr. Lebron, an artist from New York City, asked to rent diorama space to display a political poster. The poster contains text transposed over and below a photomontage. The left side of the photomontage depicts President Reagan and a number of administration officials seated at a table laden with food and drink. All the men are smiling or laughing and President Reagan is pointing to the right side of the poster. Standing on the right side, looking towards the President with expressions of hostility or sullenness, are a number of casually dressed men and women, some of whom are members of racial minorities. Were the photomontage taken to be a single photograph, the President and his men would appear to be laughing at

---

1. Mr. Lebron has at all times offered to pay the higher commercial rates to display his advertisement. Complaint ¶ 17.

2. The district court found that WMATA has "rented subway advertising space for political and social commentary advertisements covering a broad spectrum of political views and ideas." *Lebron* v. *Washington Metropolitan Area Transit Authority,* 585 F.Supp. 1461 at 1464. (D.D.C. Mar. 21, 1984). For example, WMATA has accepted for display advertisements for the pro-nuclear power positions of the Edison Electric Institute, for an anti-abortion group called Birthright of Northern Virginia, for the Rape Crisis Center, and for many religious groups, including the Unification Church and the Founding Church of Scientology. *Gay Activists Alliance* v. *WMATA*, 5 Media L.Rep. (BNA) 1404, 1405 (D.D.C. 1979).

those on the opposite side of the poster. At the top of the poster, emblazoned in yellow (in contrast to the black and white of the photomontage), is the caption "Tired of the JELLYBEAN REPUBLIC?" The bottom of the poster presents text critical of the Reagan administration's policies. The poster is plainly political and was "intended to convey Mr. Lebron's belief about the manner in which certain segments of the American population have reacted to the effects of the Reagan administration's policies on them." Mem. op. at 1463. Mr. Lebron offered to place on the poster the following disclaimer:

> The photographic montage appearing here is a composite, and does not represent an actual encounter between or among the persons depicted. The views expressed are solely those of the author and artist, Michael Lebron, and are not to be attributed to any of the persons depicted hereon, Metro, its employees, TDI, or its employees. Complaint ¶ 24.

He proposed to place this disclaimer in small print in the lower right hand corner of the photomontage.

The preproduction version of the poster Mr. Lebron sent to WMATA's subcontractor for marketing, TDI-Winston Network, Inc.,[3] was forwarded to Mr. Warrington, who rejected the poster on the ground that it did not satisfy WMATA's guidelines. R.E. at Exh. A. Mr. Lebron's counsel requested reconsideration and, after consultation with WMATA's counsel, Mr. Warrington reversed his earlier decision and approved the advertisement.[4]

Concerned about his change of position, Mr. Warrington told WMATA's General Manager about the poster. The General Manager convened a meeting of selected WMATA personnel to discuss the issue, and this group unanimously found the picture deceptive. After this meeting Mr. Warrington informed Mr. Lebron's counsel that "a broader representative group" had determined that the poster "so clearly violate[s] the guidelines . . . that the request must be turned down." Letter from John E. Warrington to Donald Weightman (Jan. 3, 1984); R.E. at Exh. E. This decision, according to the trial court, was not based upon the poster's political message but on the group's judgment that the photomontage was distorted and deceptive. Mem. op. at 1464, 1465.

---

3. TDI-Winston Network, Inc. was originally a named defendant in this action. The suit against it was dropped after it filed a stipulation with the district court agreeing to comply with the court's decision. Stipulation of Dismissal (Jan. 25, 1984).

4. WMATA conceded to the district court that Mr. Lebron relied to his detriment on WMATA's acceptance of the poster and incurred certain expenses in producing the poster. Based upon that reliance, WMATA has agreed that Mr. Lebron is entitled to reimbursement. Mem. op. at 1498.

Mr. Lebron sought preliminary relief on the grounds that WMATA's actions violated 42 U.S.C. § 1983 (1982) and the First Amendment. The district court denied a temporary restraining order on the following day, finding no irreparable injury. The parties agreed to consolidate the motion for a preliminary injunction with trial on the merits. Mem. op. at 1462.

After trial the court held that Mr. Lebron's constitutional rights had not been violated and that the regulation was valid. Specifically, the court found that WMATA had not evaluated the content of the photomontage and rejected it because of its political message. Rather, "WMATA permissibly concluded that the photomontage is deceptive and distorted since it depicts an apparent event which actually did not occur." Mem. op. at 1464 (footnote omitted).[5]

II.

[1] There is no doubt that the poster at issue here conveys a political message; nor is there a question that WMATA has converted its subway stations into public fora by accepting other political advertising. Mem. op. at 1465; see *Gay Activists Alliance* v. *WMATA*, 5 Media L.Rep. (BNA) 1404, 1406–09 (D.D.C.1979). *See also Perry Education Ass'n* v. *Perry Local Educator's Ass'n*, 460 U.S. 37, 45, 103 S.Ct. 948, 954, 74 L.Ed.2d 794 (1983).[6] Because WMATA, a government agency, tried to prevent Mr. Lebron from exhibiting his poster "in advance of actual expression," *Southeastern Promotions, Ltd.* v. *Conrad*, 420 U.S. 546, 553, 95 S.Ct. 1239, 1243, 43 L.Ed.2d 448 (1975), WMATA's action can be characterized as a "prior restraint," *id.*, which comes before us bearing a presumption of unconstitutionality. E.g., *Bantam Books, Inc.* v. *Sulli-*

---

5. The lower court found that the proffered disclaimer would not

> effectively prevent passersby from being deceived into believing that the portrayed derisive confrontation actually did occur. The disclaimer could be read only if a subway passenger took the time to stop and study the entire advertisement at close range. The print size and placement of the disclaimer would not provide adequate notice that the event supposedly being depicted in fact had not occurred. Mem. op. at 1464 (citations and footnotes omitted).

6. Unlike *Lehman* v. *City of Shaker Heights*, 418 U.S. 298, 94 S.Ct. 2714, 41 L.Ed.2d 770 (1974), where the Supreme Court sustained a ban on all political advertising inside a city transit system, the Authority here, by accepting political advertising, has made its subway stations into public fora. *Perry Education Ass'n* v. *Perry Local Educator's Ass'n*, 460 U.S. at 45, 103, S.Ct. at 954 (once "the state has opened [public property] for use by the public as a place for expressive activity," certain exclusions are constitutionally forbidden, even if the state "was not required to create the forum in the first place.)

van, 372 U.S. 58, 70, 83 S.Ct. 631, 639, 9 L.Ed.2d 584 (1963) (citing cases). Subject to a limited number of exceptions—most notably, reasonable time, place, and manner regulations—political speech may not constitutionally be restricted in a public forum. This case does not come within those exceptions and accordingly we reverse the district court and hold that WMATA violated the plaintiffs First Amendment right of free speech.

A.

WMATA's refusal to accept this poster for display because of its content is a clear-cut prior restraint. Here, WMATA has by official action prevented Mr. Lebron from using a public forum to say what he wants to say. *Southeastern Promotions,* 420 U.S. at 553, 95 S.Ct. at 1243. As such, WMATA "carries a heavy burden of showing justification for the imposition of such a restraint." *Organization for a Better Austin* v. *Keefe,* 402 U.S. 415, 419, 91 S.Ct. 1575, 1577, 29 L.Ed.2d 1 (1971). *See New York Times Co.* v. *United States,* 403 U.S. 713, 714, 91 S.Ct. 2140, 2141, 29 L.Ed.2d 822 (1971) (per curiam). We impose this burden on public officials because of "[o]ur distaste for censorship—reflecting the natural distaste of a free people—[which] is deep-written in our law." *Southeastern Promotions,* 420 U.S. at 553, 95 S.Ct. at 1243. As Chief Justice Burger has recently reminded us, however, "to say the [guideline] presents a First Amendment *issue* is not necessarily to say that it constitutes a First Amendment *violation." Metromedia, Inc.* v. *San Diego,* 453 U.S. 490, 561, 101 S.Ct. 2882, 2920, 69 L.Ed.2d 800 (1981) (Burger, C.J., dissenting). All prior restraints are not per se unconstitutional, *Southeastern Promotions,* 420 U.S. at 558, 95 S.Ct. at 1246, for "[i]t has been clear since [the Supreme] Court's earliest decisions concerning the freedom of speech that the state may sometimes curtail speech when necessary to advance a significant and legitimate state interest." *Members of the City Council of Los Angeles* v. *Taxpayers for Vincent,* 466 U.S. 789, 104 S.Ct. 2118, 2128, 80 L.Ed.2d 772 (1984) (citation omitted).

The asserted governmental interests served by Guideline No. 2 are "WMATA's responsibility to the public in preventing purposeful deceptions" and its "proprietary interest in raising revenue from its advertising space." Mem. op. at 1467. The second is subsumed by the first: WMATA's fear is of a "considerable loss of advertisement revenue from those advertisers who will not become associated with untruthful, distorted, or deceptive displays." *Id.,* quoting Defendant's Opposition to Plaintiff's Motion for a Preliminary Injunction at 10. We find that the asserted interest in preventing deception is not served here because, simply put, this poster is not deceptive.

[2] In making this determination, we are guided by the Supreme Court's recent decision in *Bose Corp. v. Consumers Union of United States, Inc.,* 466 U.S. 485, 104 S.Ct. 1949, 1958, 80 L.Ed.2d 502 (1984). In *Bose,* the Court set out the responsibility of an appellate court in cases raising First Amendment issues: "an appellate court has an obligation to make an independent examination of the whole record in order to make sure that the judgment does not constitute a forbidden intrusion on the field of free expression." *Id.* (citations and quotation marks omitted). *See National Association of Letter Carriers v. Austin,* 418 U.S. 264, 282, 94 S.Ct. 2770, 2780, 41 L.Ed.2d 745 (1974); *Greenbelt Cooperative Publishing Ass'n v. Bresler,* 398 U.S. 6, 11, 90 S.Ct. 1537, 1540, 26 L.Ed.2d 6 (1970). This injunction is particularly easy for us to obey in this case for we have the poster in hand, and there are no questions of credibility.[7] The issue is one of judgment only—namely, would a reasonable man believe that this poster depicts an event that actually took place.[8] Carefully inspecting the poster for ourselves, we are "left with the definite and firm-conviction that a mistake has been committed" by the district court. *United States v. Gypsum,* 333 U.S. 364, 395, 68 S.Ct. 525, 541, 92 L.Ed.2d 746 (1948).[9] The poster's text, the utter implausability of the scene portrayed, the difference in lighting between the two halves of the photomontage, the awkward relation of the two groups of figures to one another, the difference in the sizes of the figures in the two groups, and the proffered disclaimer make inevitable this conclusion. No reasonable person could think this a photograph of an actual meeting. In looking at this poster, moreover, the

7. We do not defer to the agency in cases such as these. "When the executive or the administrative process abridges constitutional rights, it is subject to closer scrutiny than otherwise, and ultimately it is the court rather than the agency that must balance the competing interests." *A Quaker Action Group v. Morton,* 516 F.2d 717, 723 (D.C.Cir.1975).

8. That some small number of careless readers might be misled by this poster changes neither our inquiry nor our conclusion. Speakers are not required to indulge the lowest common denominator of the populace; First Amendment protection is not limited only to messages which every reader, no matter how ill-informed or inattentive, can comprehend. *Cf. Butler v. Michigan,* 352 U.S. 380, 383, 77 S.Ct. 524, 525, 1 L.Ed.2d 412 (1957) (striking down a statute "quarantining the general reading public against books not too rugged for grown men and women in order to shield juvenile innocence" because its effect was "to reduce the adult population . . . to reading only what is fit for children").

9. In *Bose,* the Supreme Court discussed those types of facts appellate courts may review in the course of their independent review of the record. 104 S.Ct. at 1959–60 nn. 16–17. The finding of fact at issue here is the kind that is "inseparable from the principles from which it was deduced." *Id.* at 1960 n. 17. The "stakes . . . are too great" in cases implicating the freedom of speech to entrust determinations of falsity in advance of actual expression "finally to the judgment of the trier of fact," and thus to preclude reviewing courts from exercising their own independent judgment. *Id.*

observer's eye is immediately drawn to the bold-faced, bright yellow text reading, "Tired of the JELLYBEAN REPUBLIC?" The message is that of an advocate; it sets the poster's tone and alerts the reader that the message disparages the Reagan administration. There is no pretext of objectivity. Given the context, the reasonable reader will subject the poster's entire content, including the photomontage, to a level and kind of scrutiny different from the scrutiny generally given to messages pretending to be dispassionately informative. Cf. *Greenbelt Cooperative Publishing Ass'n v. Bresler,* 398 U.S. 6, 14, 90 S.Ct. 1537, 1541, 26 L.Ed.2d 6 (1970). Finally, the proffered disclaimer, while perhaps not quite large enough to be immediately noticeable or effective on its own, when combined with the other factors reveals to the observer that the photomontage does not depict an actual event. It is apparent at once that the poster does not purport to show an actual scene but to make a metaphorical political statement.

[3] In fact, the district judge stated that "the photomontage is sufficiently ambiguous to allow a discerning viewer to recognize it as a composite." Mem. op. at 1464 n. 4. Although we think the photomontage recognizable as a composite by persons considerably less acute than a "discerning viewer," the ambiguity specified by the district court is enough to support a finding that WMATA acted unconstitutionally. To assess speech in a public forum some balancing may be necessary, but "the thumb of the [c]ourt [should] be on the speech side of the scales." Kalven, *The Concept of the Public Forum:* Cox v. Louisiana, 1965 Sup.Ct.Rev. 1, 28. *See Cox v. Louisiana,* 379 U.S 536, 578, 85 S.Ct. 453, 468, 13 L.Ed.2d 471 (1965) ("[T]his Court does, and I agree that it should, 'weigh the circumstances' in order to protect, not to destroy, freedom of speech, press and religion.") (Black, J.). In light of the "profound national commitment to the principle that debate on public issues should be uninhibited, robust, and wide-open," *New York Times v. Sullivan,* 376 U.S. 254, 270, 84 S.Ct. 710, 720, 11 L.Ed.2d 686 (1964), courts ought not to restrain speech where the message sought to be communicated is political and is "sufficiently ambiguous to allow a discerning viewer" (or reader) to recognize it as something other than a reproduction of an actual event.

B.

Judge Scalia is of the view, that, while it is a sound judicial practice to avoid passing upon constitutional issues, it is also a sound judicial practice, of even more venerable antiquity, to avoid passing upon the truth or falsity of political pamphleteering or advertising, particularly in the context of prior restraint. He would give the latter policy preference here, and would decline to judge whether Mr. Lebron seeks to publish a political message that is false. He would reverse the district court because a scheme that empowers agencies of a political branch of government to impose prior restraint upon a political message because of its falsity is unconstitutional.

Although Judge Starr would not reach the issue, I agree with this basis of reversal as well. I know of no case that supports an attempt at censorship equivalent to that which has occurred here. Prior administrative restraint of political messages on a content-related basis other than substantive falsity—notably, obscenity—is permissible.[10] *Cf. Freedman* v. *Maryland,* 380 U.S. 51, 58–59, 85 S.Ct. 734, 738–39, 13 L.Ed.2d 649 (1965) (outlining elements that would validate film censorship scheme). And in extreme situations prior judicial restraint on the basis of falsity may be appropriate. *See, e.g., Tomei* v. *Finley,* 512 F.Supp. 695 (N.D.Ill.1981) (granting preliminary injunction prohibiting use in political advertising of the acronym "REP" [Representation for Every Person party] on grounds that it falsely implied affiliation with Republican party). But prior administrative restraint of distinctively political messages on the basis of their alleged deceptiveness is unheard-of—and deservedly so. In. *Vanasco* v. *Schwartz,* 401 FSupp. 87 (S.D.N.Y.1975), a three-judge court struck down as unconstitutional on its face New York's "Fair Campaign Code," which prohibited, *inter alia,* "misrepresentation" of any candidate's qualifications or positions, in part because of lack of judicial involvement in the determination. The Supreme Court summarily affirmed without opinion. 423 U.S. 1041, 96 S.Ct. 763, 46 L.Ed.2d 630 (1976).

[4]WMATA argues, and the district court agreed, that it is not engaged in unlawful censorship but is administering a permissible and reasonable time, place, and manner regulation. But, since WMATA is judging the truth of a political statement, to accept its argument is to destroy the distinction between content-neutral and content-based regulations. Even if WMATA "do[es] not differentiate among political viewpoints in political and social advertisements," mem. op. at 1467, an assessment of the deceptiveness of a message necessarily involves a judgment about the substance and content

---

10. Even then, however—and even when distinctively political speech is *not* involved—the Supreme Court has said that the administrative restraint can only be temporary, for a specified period pending the administrative agency's seeking of a judicial restraint. *Southeastern Promotions,* 420 U.S. at 560, 95 S.Ct. at 1247. Such a requirement seems inconvenient if not unworkable in the context of managing the advertising business of a state-run commercial enterprise such as a bus or subway. As does the principle generally applicable that political speech cannot be required to conform to even rudimentary canons of good taste. *Cohen* v. *California,* 403 U.S. 15, 91 S.Ct. 1780, 29 L.Ed.2d 284 (1971). These are valid reasons to doubt whether such enterprises should be considered mandatory public forums that cannot generically reject political speech.

of that message. Although Guideline No. 2 does not, on its face, favor one viewpoint or idea at the expense of another, *see Defame v. Oregon,* 299 U.S. 353, 356, 57 S.Ct. 255, 256, 81 L.Ed. 278 (1937) (state statute prohibited advocacy of doctrine of "criminal syndicalism"), and does not discriminate on the basis of the subject matter of the speech, *see First National Bank of Boston v. Bellotti,* 435 U.S. 765, 767, 98 S.Ct. 1407, 1411, 55 L.Ed.2d 707 (1978) (state statute barred banks from spending money to influence voting on referendum proposals), it is simply not content-neutral. Applying this guideline involves an exercise of discretion and subjective judgment on the part of WMATA officials. It is not a time, place, and manner restriction. Even if applied pursuant to procedural safeguards, the guideline would be unconstitutionally overbroad as applied to political speech.

I note that this conclusion does not necessarily place WMATA in the position of having to accept and display before its riders deceptive political advertising. If that prospect is repugnant it can possibly be avoided by declining to accept political advertising in general.[11] The availability of that recourse, at least as far as this court is concerned, depends upon whether subway stations are more akin to airports, *see Southwest Africa/Namibia Trade & Cultural Council v. United States,* 708 F.2d 760 (D.C.Cir.1983), or to public buses, *see Lehman v. City of Shaker Heights,* 418 U.S. 298, 94 S.Ct. 2714, 41 L.Ed.2d 770 (1974). *See also Members of the City Council of Los Angeles v. Taxpayers for Vincent,*—U.S.—, 104 S.Ct. 2118, 2134 n. 32, 80 L.Ed.2d 772 (1984). We need not reach that issue here.

For the reasons set forth above, the judgment of the district court is *Reversed.*

---

11. WMATA is apparently concerned that its inability to control the messages displayed in its subway stations would leave it open to defamation actions based upon those messages. Although we need not decide this question to resolve the present case, we note that to the extent that WMATA is duty-bound to carry these messages, exposure to defamation liability is unlikely. In *Farmers Educational & Cooperative Union of America v. WDAY,* 360 U.S. 525, 533–35, 79 S.Ct. 1302, 1307–08, 3 L.Ed.2d 1407 (1959), the Supreme Court held that a radio station was immune from a defamation action where it was forbidden to censor libelous material it was under a statutory obligation to broadcast. That the station could avoid that obligation by refusing to sell time to any candidates did not vitiate the station's immunity. Similarly, here WMATA made an initial decision to accept political advertising. We express no opinion as to whether WMATA was obliged to make that decision— but, having made it, WMATA's power to reject political advertisements is subject to the strict protections the First Amendment extends to political speech in a public forum. Where WMATA has no power to reject a particular advertisement, defamation liability should not follow.

C. ARTICLES

The first section of the following article is, I believe, the first modern exposition of the idea that the Constitution must be interpreted according to the original understanding of its principles by the men who made it law. Early commentators took it more or less for granted that the document should be interpreted as its authors intended. The article reprinted here attempts to demonstrate that there can be no rule of law in constitutional adjudication unless the original understanding of the charter's principles is the magistrate's guide. The second part of the article concerns First Amendment problems. A comment on that topic appears at the end of the article.

Neutral Principles and
Some First Amendment Problems

A persistently disturbing aspect of constitutional law is its lack of theory, a lack which is manifest not merely in the work of the courts but in the public, professional, and even scholarly discussion of the topic. The result, of course, is that courts are without effective criteria and, therefore we have come to expect that the nature of the Constitution will change, often quite dramatically, as the personnel of the Supreme Court change. In the present state of affairs that expectation is inevitable, but it is nevertheless deplorable.

The remarks that follow do not, of course, offer a general theory of constitutional law. They are more properly viewed as ranging shots, an attempt to establish the necessity for theory and to take the argument of how constitutional doctrine should be evolved by courts a step or two further. The first section centers upon the implications of Professor Herbert Wechsler's concept of "neutral principles," and the second attempts to apply those implications to some important and much debated problems in the interpretation of the First Amendment. The style is informal since these remarks were originally lectures and I have not thought it worthwhile to convert these speculations and arguments into a heavily researched, balanced, and thorough presentation, for that would result in a book.

The Supreme Court and the Demand for Principle

The subject of the lengthy and often acrimonious debate about the proper role of the Supreme Court under the Constitution is one that preoccupies many people these days: when is authority legitimate? I find it convenient to discuss that question in the context of the Warren Court and its works simply because the Warren Court posed the issue in acute form. The issue did not disappear along with the era of the Warren Court majorities, however. It arises when any court either exercises or declines to exercise the power to invalidate any act of another branch of government. The Supreme Court is a major power center, and we must ask when its power should be used and when it should be withheld.

Our starting place, inevitably, is Professor Wechsler's argument that the Court must not be merely a "naked power organ," which means that its decisions must be controlled by principle.[1] "A principled decision," according to Wechsler, "is one that rests on reasons with respect to all the issues in a case, reasons that in their generality and their neutrality transcend any immediate result that is involved."[2]

Wechsler chose the term "neutral principles" to capsulate his argument, though he recognizes that the legal principle to be applied is itself never neutral because it embodies a choice of one value rather than another. Wechsler asked for the neutral application of principles, which is a requirement, as Professor Louis L. Jaffe puts it, that the judge, "sincerely believe in the principle upon which he purports to rest his decision." "The judge," says Jaffe, "must believe in the validity of the reasons given for the decision at least in the sense that he is prepared to apply them to a later case which he cannot honestly distinguish."[3] He must not, that is, decide lawlessly. But is the demand for neutrality in judges merely another value choice, one that is no more principled than any other? I think not, but to prove it we must rehearse fundamentals. This is familiar terrain but important and still debated.

The requirement that the Court be principled arises from the resolution of the seeming anomaly of judicial supremacy in a democratic society. If the judiciary really is supreme, able to rule when and as it sees fit, the society is not democratic. The anomaly is dissipated, however, by the model of government embodied in the structure of the Constitution, a model upon which popular consent to limited government by the Supreme Court also rests. This model we may for convenience, though perhaps not with total accuracy, call "Madisonian."[4]

A Madisonian system is not completely democratic, if by "democratic" we mean completely majoritarian. It assumes that in wide areas of life majorities are entitled to rule for no better reason than that they are majorities. We need not pause here to examine the philosophical underpinnings of that assumption since it is a "given" in our society; nor need we worry that

---

1. H. Wechsler, "Toward Neutral Principles of Constitutional Law," *Principles, Politics, and Fundamental Law* 3, 27 (1961) [hereinafter cited as Wechsler].

2. Ibid.

3. L. Jaffe, *English and American Judges as Lawmakers* 38 (1969).

4. See R. Dahl, *A Preface to Democratic Theory* 4–33 (1956).

"majority" is a term of art meaning often no more than the shifting combinations of minorities that add to temporary majorities in the legislature. That majorities are so constituted is inevitable. In any case, one essential premise of the Madisonian model is majoritarianism. The model has also a counter-majoritarian premise, however, for it assumes there are some areas of life a majority should not control. There are some things a majority should not do to us no matter how democratically it decides to do them. These are areas properly left to individual freedom, and coercion by the majority in these aspects of life is tyranny.

Some see the model as containing an inherent, perhaps an insoluble, dilemma.[5] Majority tyranny occurs if the legislation invades the areas properly left to individual freedom. Minority tyranny occurs if the majority is prevented from ruling where its power is legitimate. Yet, quite obviously, neither the majority not the minority can be trusted to define the freedom of the other. This dilemma is resolved in constitutional theory, and in popular understanding, but the Supreme Court's power to define both majority and minority freedom through the interpretation of the Constitution. Society consents to be ruled undemocratically within defined areas by certain enduring principles believed to be stated in, and place beyond the reach of majorities by, the Constitution.

But this resolution of the dilemma imposes severe requirements upon the Court. For it follows that the Court's power is legitimate only if it has, and can demonstrate in reasoned opinions that it has, a valid theory, derived from the Constitution, of the respective spheres of majority and minority freedom. If it does not have such a theory but actually follows its own predilections, the Court violates the postulates of the Madisonian model that alone justifies its power. It then necessarily abets the tyranny either of the majority or of the minority.

This argument is central to the issue of legitimate authority because the Supreme Court's power to govern rests upon the popular acceptance of this model. Evidence that this is, in fact, the basis of the Court's power is to be gleaned everywhere in our culture. We need not canvas here such things as high school civics texts and newspaper commentary, for the most telling evidence may be found in the *U.S. Reports*. The Supreme Court regularly insists that its results, and most particularly its controversial results, do not spring from the mere will of the justices in the majority but are supported, indeed compelled, by a proper understanding of the Constitution of the United States. Value choices are attributed to the Founding Fathers, not to

5. Ibid., 23–24

the Court. The way an institution advertises tells you what it thinks its customers demand.

This is, I think, the ultimate reason the Court must be principled. If it does not have and rigorously adhere to a valid and consistent theory of majority and minority freedom based upon the Constitution, judicial supremacy, given the axioms of our system, is, precisely to that extent, illegitimate. The root of its illegitimacy is that it opens a chasm between the reality of the Court's performance and the constitutional and popular assumptions that give it power.

I do not mean to rest the argument entirely upon the popular understanding of the Court's function. Even if society generally should ultimately perceive what the Court is in fact doing and, having seen, prove content to have major policies determined by the unguided discretion of judges rather than by elected representatives, a principled judge would, I believe, continue to consider himself bound by an obligation to the document and to the structure of government that it prescribes. At least he would be bound so long as any litigant existed who demanded such adherence of him. I do not understand how, on any other theory of judicial obligation, the Court could, as it does now, protect voting rights if a large majority of the relevant constituency were willing to see some groups or individuals deprived of such rights. But even if I am wrong in that, at the very least an honest judge would owe it to the body politic to cease invoking the authority of the Constitution and to make explicit the imposition of his own will, for only then would we know whether the society understood enough of what is taking place to be said to have consented.

Judge J. Skelly Wright, in an argument resting on different premises, has severely criticized the advocates of principle. He defends the value-choosing role of the Warren Court, setting that Court in opposition to something he refers to as "scholarly tradition," which criticizes that Court for its lack of principle.[6] A perceptive reader, sensitive to nuance, may suspect that the judge is rather out of sympathy with that tradition from such hints as his reference to "self-appointed scholastic madarins."[7]

The "mandarins" of the academy anger the judge because they engage in "haughty derision of the Court's powers of analysis and reasoning."[8] Yet, curiously enough, Judge Wright makes no attempt to refute the charge but

---

6. J. S. Wright, "Professor Bickel, the Scholarly Tradition, and the Supreme Court," 84 *Harv. L. Rev.* 769 (1971) [hereinafter cited as Wright].

7. Ibid., 777

8. Ibid., 777–78

rather seems to adopt the technique of confession and avoidance. He seems to be arguing that a Court engaged in choosing fundamental values for society cannot be expected to produce principled decisions at the same time. Decisions first, principles later. One wonders, however, how the Court or the rest of us are to know that the decisions are correct or what they portend for the future if they are not accompanied by the principles that explain and justify them. And it would not be amiss to point out that quite often the principle required of the Warren Court's decisions never did put in an appearance. But Judge Wright's main point appears to be that value choice is the most important function of the Supreme Court, so that if we must take one or the other, and apparently we must, we should prefer a process of selecting values to one of constructing and articulating principles. His argument, I believe, boils down to a syllogism. I. The Supreme Court should "protect our constitutional rights and liberties." II. The Supreme Court must "make fundamental value choices" in order to "protect our constitutional rights and liberties." III. Therefore, the Supreme Court should "make fundamental value choices."[9]

The argument displays an all too common confusion. If we have constitutional rights and liberties already, rights and liberties specified by the Constitution,[10] the Court need make no fundamental value choices in order to protect them, and it certainly need not have difficulty enunciating principles. If, on the other hand, "constitutional rights and liberties" are not in

---

9. This syllogism is implicit in much of Judge Wright's argument. For example, "If it is proper for the Court to make fundamental value choices to protect our constitutional rights and liberties, then it is self-defeating to say that if the Justices cannot come up with a perfectly reasoned and perfectly general opinion now, then they should abstain from decision altogether" *Id.*, 779. The first clause is the important one for present purposed; the others merely caricature the position of commentators who ask for principle.

10. A position Judge Wright also seems to take at times. "Constitutional choices are in fact different from ordinary decisions. The reason is simple: the most important value choices have already been made by the framers of the Constitution" *Id.*, 784. One wonders how the judge squares this with his insistence upon the propriety of the judiciary making "fundamental value choices." One also wonders what degree of specificity is required before the framers may realistically be said to have made the "most important value choices." The Warren Court has chosen to expand the Fourteenth Amendment's theme of equality in ways certainly not foreseen by the framers of that provision. A prior Court expanded the amendment's theme of liberty. Are both Courts to be judged innocent of having made the most important value choices on the ground that the framers mentioned both liberty and equality? If so, the framers must be held to have delegated an almost complete power to govern to the Supreme Court, and it is untrue to say that a constitutional decision is any different from an ordinary governmental decision. Judge Wright simply never faces up to the problem he purports to address: how free is the Court to choose values that will override the values chosen by elected representatives?

some real sense specified by the Constitution but are the rights and liberties the Court chooses, on the basis of its own values, to give to us, then the conclusion was contained entirely in the major premise, and the Judge's syllogism is no more than an assertion of what it purported to prove.

If I am correct so far, no argument that is both coherent and respectable can be made supporting a Supreme Court that "chooses fundamental values" because a Court that makes rather than implements value choices cannot be squared with the presuppositions of a democratic society. The man who understands the issues and nevertheless insists upon the rightness of the Warren Court's performance ought also, if he is candid, to admit that he is prepared to sacrifice democratic process to his own moral views. He claims for the Supreme Court an institutionalized role as perpetrator of limited coups d'etat.

Such a man occupies an impossible philosophic position. What can he say, for instance, of a Court that does not share his politics or his morality? I can think of nothing except the assertion that he will ignore the Court whenever he can get away with it and overthrow it if he can. In his view the Court has no legitimacy, and there is no reason any of us should obey it. And, this being the case, the advocate of a value-choosing Court must answer another difficult question. Why should the Court, a committee of nine lawyers, be the sole agent of change? The man who prefers results to processes has no reason to say that the Court is more legitimate than any other institution. If the Court will not listen, why not argue the case to some other group, say the Joint Chiefs of Staff, a body with rather better means for implementing its decisions?

We are driven to the conclusion that a legitimate Court must be controlled by principles exterior to the will of the justices. As my colleague Professor Alexander Bickel puts it, "The process of the coherent, analytically warranted, principled declaration of general norms alone justifies the Court's function. . . ."[11] Recognition of the need for principle is only the first step, but once that step is taken much more follows. Logic has a life of its own, and devotion to principle requires that we follow where logic leads.

Professor Bickel identifies Justice Frankfurter as the leading judicial proponent of principle but conceded that even Frankfurter never found a "rigorous general accord between judicial supremacy and democratic theory."[12] Judge Wright responds, "The leading commentators of the scholarly tradi-

11. A. Bickel, *The Supreme Court and the Idea of Progress* 96 (1970).
12. Ibid., 34

tion have tried ever since to succeed where the Justice failed."[13] As Judge Wright quite accurately suggests, the commentators have so far had no better luck than the justice.

One reason, I think, is clear. We have not carried the idea of neutrality far enough. We have been talking about neutrality in the *application* of principles. If judges are to avoid imposing their own values upon the rest of us, however, they must be neutral as well in the *definition* and the *derivation* of principles.

It is easy enough to meet the requirement of neutral application by stating a principle so narrowly that no embarrassment need arise in applying it to all cases it subsumes, a tactic often urged by proponents of "judicial restraint." But that solves very little. It certainly does not protect the judge from the intrusion of his own values. The problem may be illustrated by *Griswold* v. *Connecticut*,[14] in many ways a typical decision of the Warren Court. *Griswold* struck down Connecticut's statute making it a crime, even for married couples, to use contraceptive devices. If we take the principle of the decision to be a statement that government may not interfere with any acts done in private, we need not even ask about the principle's dubious origin for we know at once that the Court will not apply it neutrally. The Court, we may confidently predict, is not going to throw constitutional protection around heroin use or sexual acts with a consenting minor. We can gain the possibility of neutral application by reframing the principle as a statement that government may not prohibit the use of contraceptives by married couples, but that is not enough. The question of neutral definition arises: Why does the principle extend only to married couples? Why, out of all forms of sexual behavior, only to sex? The question of neutral derivation also arises. What justifies any limitation upon legislatures in this area? What is the origin of any principle one may state?

To put the matter another way, if a neutral judge must demonstrate why principle *X* applies to cases *A* and *B* but not to case *C* (which is, I believe, the requirement laid down by Professors Wechsler and Jaffe), he must, by the same token, also explain why the principle is defined as *X* rather than as *X minus*, which could also cover *A* but not cases *B* and *C*, or as *X plus*, which would cover all cases, *A*, *B*, and *C*. Similarly, he must explain why *X* is a proper principle of limitation on majority power at all. Why should he not choose *non-X*? If he may not choose lawlessly between cases in applying principle *X*, he may certainly not choose lawlessly in defining *X* or in choosing *X*, for principles

13. Wright, *supra* note 6, 775.
14. 381 U.S. 479 (1965).

are after all only organizations of cases into groups. To choose the principle and define it is to decide the cases.

It follows that the choice of "fundamental values" by the Court cannot be justified. Where constitutional materials do not clearly specify the value to be preferred, there is no principled way to prefer any claimed human value to any other. The judge must stick close to the text and the history, and their fair implications, and not construct new rights. The case just mentioned illustrated the point. The *Griswold* decision has been acclaimed by legal scholars as a major advance in constitutional law, a salutary demonstration of the Court's ability to protect fundamental human values. I regret to have to disagree, and my regret is all the more sincere because I once took the same position and did so in print.[15] In extenuation I can only say that at the time I thought, quite erroneously, that new basic rights could be derived logically by finding and extrapolating a more general principle of individual autonomy underlying the particular guarantees of the Bill of Rights.

The Court's *Griswold* opinion, by Justice Douglas, and the array of concurring opinions, by Justices Goldberg, White, and Harlan, all failed to justify the derivation of any principle used to strike down the Connecticut anti-contraceptive statute or to define the scope of principle. Justice Douglas, to whose opinion I must confine myself, began by pointing out the "specific guarantees in the Bill of Rights have penumbras, formed by emanations from those guarantees that help give them life and substance."[16] Nothing is exceptional there. In the case Justice Douglas cited, *NAACP v. Alabama*,[17] the state was held unable to force disclosure of membership lists because of the chilling effect upon the rights of assembly and political action of the NAACP's members. The penumbra was created solely to preserve a value central to the First Amendment, applied in this case through the Fourteenth Amendment. It has no life of its own as a right independent of the value specified by the First Amendment.

But Justice Douglas then performed a miracle of transubstantiation. He called the First Amendment's penumbra a protection of "privacy" and then asserted that other amendments create "zones of privacy."[18] He had no better reason to use the word "privacy" than that the individual is free within these zones, free to act in public as well as in private. None of the penumbral zones from the First, Third, Fourth, and Fifth Amendments, all of which he

15. R. Bork "The Supreme Court Needs a New Philosophy," *Fortune*, Dec., 1968, 170.
16. 381 U.S. at 484.
17. 357 U.S. 449 (1958).
18. 381 U.S. at 484.

cited, along with the Ninth covered the case before him. One more leap was required. Justice Douglas asserted that these various "zones of privacy" created an independent right of privacy,[19] a right not lying within the penumbra of any specific amendment. He did not disclose, however, how a series of specified rights combined to create a new and unspecified right.

The *Griswold* opinion fails every test of neutrality. The derivation of the principle was utterly specious, and so was its definition. In fact, we are left with no idea of what the principle really forbids. Derivation and definition are interrelated here. Justice Douglas called the amendments and their penumbras "zones of privacy," though of course they are not that at all. They protect both private and public behavior and so would more properly be labeled "zones of freedom." If we follow Justice Douglas in his next step, these zones would then add up to an independent right of freedom, which is to say, a general constitutional right to be free of legal coercion, a manifest impossibility in any imaginable society.

Griswold, then, is an unprincipled decision, both in the way in which it derives new constitutional rights and in the way it defines that right, or rather fails to define it. We are left with no idea of the sweep of the right of privacy and hence no notion of the cases to which it may or may not be applied in the future. The truth is that the Court could not reach its result in *Griswold* through principle. The reason is obvious. Every clash between a minority claiming freedom and a majority claiming power to regulate involves a choice between the gratifications of the two groups. When the Constitution has not spoken, the Court will be able to find no scale, other than its own value preferences, upon which to weigh the respective claims to pleasure. Compare the facts of *Griswold* with a hypothetical suit by an electric utility company and one of its customers to void a smoke pollution ordinance as unconstitutional. The cases are identical.

In *Griswold* a husband and wife assert that they wish to have sexual relations without fear of unwanted children. The law impairs their sexual gratifications. The state can assert, and at one stage in that litigation did assert, that the majority finds the use of contraception immoral. Knowledge that it takes place and that the state makes no effort to inhibit it causes the majority anguish, impairs their gratifications.

The electrical company asserts that it wishes to produce electricity at low cost in order to reach a wide market and make profits. Its customer asserts that he wants a lower cost so that prices can be held low. The smoke pollution regulation impairs his and the company's stockholders' economic

19. Ibid., 485, 486.

gratifications. The state can assert not only that the majority prefer clean air to lower prices, but also that the absence of the regulation impairs the majority's physical and aesthetic gratifications.

Neither case is covered specifically or by obvious implication in the Constitution. Unless we can distinguish forms of gratification, the only course for a principled Court is to let the majority have its way in both cases. It is clear the Court cannot make the necessary distinction. There is no principled way to decide that one man's gratifications are more deserving of respect than another's or that one form of gratification is more worthy than another.[20] Why is sexual gratification nobler than economic gratification? There is no way of deciding these matters other than by reference to some system of moral or ethical values that has no objective or intrinsic validity of its own and about which men can and do differ. Where the Constitution does not embody the moral or ethical choice, the judge has no basis other than his own values upon which to set aside the community judgment embodied in the statute. That, by definition, is an adequate basis for judicial supremacy. The issue of the community's moral and ethical values, the issue of the degree of pain an activity causes, are matters concluded by the passage and enforcement of the laws in question. The judiciary has no role to play other than that of applying the statutes in a fair and impartial manner.

One of my colleagues refers to this conclusion, not without sarcasm, as the "Equal Gratification Clause." The phrase is apt, and I accept it, though not the sarcasm. Equality of human gratifications, where the document does not impose a hierarchy, is an essential part of constitutional doctrine because of the necessity that judges be principled. To be perfectly clear on the subject, I repeat that the principle is not applicable to legislatures. Legislation requires value choice and cannot be principled in the sense under discussion. Courts must accept any value choice the legislature makes unless it clearly runs contrary to a choice made in the framing of the Constitution.

It follows, of course, that broad areas of constitutional law ought to be reformulated. Most obviously, it follows that substantive due process, revived by the *Griswold* case, is and always has been an improper doctrine. Substantive due process requires the Court to say, without guidance from the Constitution, which liberties or gratifications may be infringed by majorities and which may not. This means that *Griswold's* antecedents were also wrongly

---

20. The impossibility is related to that of making interpersonal comparisons of utilities. See L. Robbins, *The Nature and Significance of Economic Science*, ch. 4 (2d ed. 1969); P. Samuelson, *Foundations of Economic Analysis* 243–52 (1965).

decided, e.g., *Meyer* v. *Nebraska*,[21] which struck down a statute forbidding the teaching of subjects in any language other than English; *Pierce* v. *Society of Sisters*,[22] which set aside a statute compelling all Oregon school children to attend public schools; *Adkins* v. *Children's Hospital*,[23] which invalidated a statute of Congress authorizing a board to fix minimum wages for women and children in the District of Columbia; and *Lochner* v. *New York*,[24] which voided a statute fixing maximum hours of work for bakers. With some of these cases I am in political agreement, and perhaps *Pierce's* result could be reached on acceptable grounds, but there is no justification for the Court's methods. In *Lochner*, Justice Peckham, defending liberty from what he conceived as a mere meddlesome interference, asked, "[A]re we all . . . at the mercy of legislative majorities?"[25] The correct answer, where the Constitution does not speak, must be "yes."

The argument so far also indicates that most of substantive equal protection is also improper. The modern Court, we need hardly be reminded, used the equal protection clause the way the old Court used the due process clause. The only change was in the values chosen for protection and the frequency with which the Court struck down laws.

The equal protection clause has two legitimate meanings. It can require formal procedural equality, and, because of its historical origins, it does require that government not discriminate along racial lines. But much more than that cannot properly be read into the clause. The bare concept of equality provides no guide for courts. All law discriminates and thereby creates inequality. The Supreme Court has no principled way of saying which nonracial inequalities are impermissible. What it has done, therefore, is to appeal to simplistic notions of "fairness" or to what it regards as "fundamental" interests in order to demand equality in some cases but not in others, thus choosing values and producing a line of cases as improper and as intellectually empty as *Griswold* v. *Connecticut*. Any casebook lists them, and the differing results cannot be explained on any ground other then the Court's preferences for particular values: *Skinner* v. *Oklahoma*[26] (a forbidden inequality exists when a state undertakes to sterilize robbers but not embezzlers); *Kotch* v. *Board of River Port Pilot Commissioners*[27] (no right to equality is infringed

21. 262 U.S. 390 (1922).
22. 268 U.S. 510 (1925).
23. 261 U.S. 525 (1923).
24. 199 U.S. 45 (1905).
25. Ibid., 59.
26. 316 U.S. 535 (1942).
27. 330 U.S. 552 (1947).

when a state grants pilots' licenses only to persons related by blood to exist-ing pilots and denies licenses to persons otherwise as well qualified); *Goesaert* v. *Cleary*[28] (a state does not deny equality when it refuses to license women as bartenders unless they are the wives or daughters of male owners of licensed liquor establishments); *Railway Express Agency* v. *New York*[29] (a city may forbid truck owners to sell advertising space on their trucks as a distracting hazard to traffic safety though it permits owners to advertise their own business in that way); *Shapiro* v. *Thompson*[30] (a state denies equality if it pays welfare only to persons who have resided in the state for one year); *Levy* v. *Louisiana*[31] (a state may not limit actions for a parent's wrongful death to legitimate chil-dren and deny it to illegitimate children). The list could be extended, but the point is that the cases cannot be reconciled on any basis other than the justices's personal beliefs about what interests or gratifications ought to be protected.

Professor Wechsler notes that Justice Frankfurter expressed "disqui-etude that the line is often very thin between the cases in which the Court felt compelled to abstain from adjudication because of their 'political' na-ture, and the cases that so frequently arise in applying the concepts of 'lib-erty' and 'equality.'"[32] The line is not very thin; it is nonexistent. There is no principled way in which anyone can define the spheres in which liberty is required and the spheres in which equality is required. These are matters of morality, of judgment, of prudence. They belong, therefore, to the political community. In the fullest sense, these are political questions.

We may now be in a position to discuss certain of the problems of legiti-macy raised by Professor Wechsler. Central to his worries was the Supreme Court's decision raised in *Brown* v. *Board of Education*.[33] Wechsler said he had great difficulty framing a neutral principle to support the *Brown* decision, though he thoroughly approved of its result on moral and political grounds. It has long been obvious that the case does not rest upon the grounds advanced in Chief Justice Warren's opinion, the specially harmful effects of enforced school segregation upon black children. That much, as Wechsler and others point out, is made plain by the per curiam decisions that followed outlawing segregated public beaches, public golf courses, and the like. The principle in

28. 335 U.S. 464 (19480).
29. 336 U.S. 106 (1949).
30. 394 U.S. 618 (1969).
31. 391 U.S. 68 (1968).
32. Wechsler, *supra* note 1, at 11, citing Frankfurter, "John Marshall and the Judicial Function," 69 *Harv. L. Rev.* 217, 227–28 (1955).
33. 347 U.S. 483 (1954).

operation may be that government may not employ race as a classification. But the genesis of the principle is unclear.

Wechsler states that his problem with the segregation cases is not that:

> History does not confirm that an agreed purpose of the Fourteenth Amendment was to forbid separate schools or that there is important evidence that many thought contrary; the words are general and leave room for expanding content as time passes and conditions change.[34]

The words are general but surely that would not permit us to escape the framers' intent if it were clear. If the legislative history revealed a consensus about segregation in schooling and all the other relations in life, I do not see how the Court could escape the choice revealed and substitute its own, even though the words are general and conditions have changed. It is the fact that history does not reveal detailed choices concerning such matters that permits, indeed requires, resort to other modes of interpretation.

Wechsler notes that *Brown* has to do with freedom to associate and freedom not to associate, and he thinks that a principle must be found that solves the following dilemma:

> [I]f the freedom of association is denied by segregation, integration forces an association upon those for whom it is unpleasant or repugnant. Is this not the heart of the issue involved, a conflict in human claims of high dimension. . . . Given a situation where the state must practically choose between denying the association to those individuals who wish it or imposing it on those who would avoid it, is there a basis in neutral principles for holding that the Constitution demands that the claims for association should prevail? I should like to think there is, but I confess that I have not yet written the opinion. To write it is for me the challenge of the school-segregation cases.[35]

It is extremely unlikely that Professor Wechsler ever will be able to write that opinion to his own satisfaction. He has framed the issue in insoluble terms by calling it a "conflict between human claims of high dimension," which is to say that it requires a judicial choice between rival gratifications in order to find fundamental human right. So viewed it is the same case as *Griswold* v. *Connecticut* and not susceptible of principled resolution.

A resolution that seems to me more plausible is supported rather than

---

34. Wechsler, *supra* note 1, 43.
35. Ibid., 47.

troubled by the need for neutrality. A court required to decide *Brown* would perceive two crucial facts about the history of the Fourteenth Amendment. First, the men who put the amendment in the Constitution intended that the Supreme Court should secure against government action some large measure of racial equality. That is certainly the core meaning of the amendment. Second, those same men were not agreed about what the concept of racial equality requires. Many or most of them had not even thought the matter through. Almost certainly, even individuals among them held such views as that blacks were entitled to purchase property from any willing seller but not to attend integrated schools, or that they were entitled to serve on juries but not to intermarry with whites, or that they were entitled to equal physical facilities but that the facilities should be separate, and so on through the endless anomalies and inconsistencies with which moral positions so frequently abound. The Court cannot conceivably know how these long dead men would have resolved these issues had they considered, debated and voted on each of them. Perhaps it was precisely because they could not resolve them that they took refuge in the majestic and ambiguous formula: the equal protection of the laws.

But one thing the Court does know: it was intended to enforce a core idea of black equality against governmental discrimination. And the Court, because it must be neutral, cannot pick and choose between competing gratifications and, likewise, cannot write the detailed code the framers omitted, requiring equality in this case but not in another. The Court must, for that reason, choose a general principle of equality that applies to all cases. For the same reason, the Court cannot decide that physical equality is important but psychological equality is not. Thus, the no-state-enforced-discrimination rule of *Brown* must overturn and replace the separate-but-equal doctrine of *Plessy* v. *Ferguson*. The same result might be reached on an alternative ground. If the Court found that it was incapable as an institution of policing the issue of the physical equality of separate facilities, the variables being insufficiently comparable and the cases too many, it might fashion a no-segregation rule as the only feasible means of assuring even physical equality.

In either case, the value choice (or, perhaps more accurately, the value impulse) of the Fourteenth Amendment is fleshed out and made into a legal rule not by moral precept, not by a determination that claims for association prevail over claims for separation as a general matter, still less by consideration of psychological test results, but on purely juridical grounds.

I doubt, however, that it is possible to find neutral principles capable of supporting some of the other decisions that trouble Professor Wechsler. An example is *Shelly* v. *Kramaer*,[36] which held that the Fourteenth Amendment forbids state court enforcement of a private, racially restrictive covenant. Although the amendment speaks only of denials of equal protection of the laws by the state, Chief Justice Vinson's opinion said that judicial enforcement of a private person's discriminatory choice constituted the requisite state action. The decision was, of course, not neutral in that the Court was most clearly not prepared to apply the principle to cases it could not honestly distinguish. Any dispute between private persons about absolutely any aspect of life can be brought to a court by one of the parties; and, if race is involved, the rule of *Shelley* would require the court to deny the freedom of any individual to discriminate in the conduct of any part of his affairs simply because the contrary result would be state enforcement of discrimination. The principle would apply not merely to the cases hypothesized by Professor Wechsler, i.e. the inability of the state to effectuate a will that draws a racial line or to vindicate the privacy of property against a trespasser excluded because of the homeowner's racial preferences, but to any situation in which the person claiming freedom in any relationship had a racial motivation.

That much is the common objection to *Shelley* v. *Kramaer*, but the trouble with the decision goes deeper. Professor Louis Henkin has suggested that we view the case as correctly decided, accept the principle that must necessarily underline it if it is respectable law, and proceed to apply that principle:

> Generally, the equal protection clause precludes state enforcement of private discrimination. There is, however, a small area of liberty favored by the Constitution even over claims to equality. Rights of liberty and property, of privacy and voluntary association, must be balanced in close cases, against the right not to have the state enforce discrimination against the victim. In the few instances in which the right to discriminate is protected or preferred by the Constitution, the state may enforce it.[37]

This attempt to rehabilitate *Shelley* by applying its principle honestly demonstrates rather clearly why neutrality in the application of principle is not enough. Professor Henkin's proposal fails the test of the neutral derivation of principle. It converts an amendment whose text and history clearly show it to be aimed only at governmental discrimination into sweeping prohibition of private discrimination. There is no warrant anywhere for that conversion. The judge's power to govern does not become more legitimate if he is constrained to apply his principle to all cases but is free to make up his own

---

36. 334 U.S. 1 (1948).
37. Henkin, Shelley v. Kramer: "Notes for a Revised Opinion," 110 U. *PA. L. Rev.*

principles. Matters are only made worse by Professor Henkin's suggestion that the judge introduce a small number of exceptions for cases where liberty is more important than equality, for now even the possibility of neutrality in the application of principle is lost. The judge cannot find in the Fourteenth Amendment or its history any choice between equality and freedom in private affairs. The judge, if he were to undertake this task, would be choosing, as in *Griswold* v. *Connecticut*, between competing gratifications without constitutional guidance. Indeed, as Professor Henkin's description of the process shows that the task he would assign is legislative:

> The balance may be struck differently at different times, reflecting differences in prevailing philosophy and the continuing movement from laissez-faire government toward welfare and meliorism. The changes in prevailing philosophy themselves may sum up the judgment of judges as to how the conscience of our society weighs the competing need and claims of liberty and equality in time and context, the adequacy of progress toward equality as a result of social and economic forces, the effect of lack of progress on the life of the Negro and, perhaps, on the image of the United States, and the role of official state forces in advancing or retarding this progress.[38]

In short, after considering everything a legislator might consider, the judge is to write a detailed code of private race relations. Starting with an attempt to justify *Shelley* on grounds of neutral principle, the argument rather curiously arrives at a position in which neutrality in the derivation, definition, and application of principle is impossible and the wrong institution is governing society.

The argument thus far claims that, cases of rare discrimination aside, it is always a mistake for the Court to try to construct substantive individual rights under the due process or the equal protection clause. Such rights cannot be constructed without comparing the worth of individual gratifications, and that comparison cannot be principled. Unfortunately, the rhetoric of constitutional adjudication is increasingly a rhetoric about "fundamental" rights that inhere in humans. That focus does more than lead the Court to construct new rights without adequate guidance from constitutional materials. It also distorts the scope and definition of rights that have claim to protection.

There appear to be two proper methods of deriving rights from the Constitution. The first is to take from the document rather specific values

---

38. Ibid., 494.

that text or history shows the framers actually to have intended and that are capable of being translated into principled rules. We may call these specified rights. The second method derives rights from governmental processes established by the Constitution. These are secondary or derived individual rights. This latter category is extraordinarily important. This method of derivation is essential to the interpretation of the First Amendment, to voting rights, to criminal procedure and to much else.

Secondary or derivative rights are not possessed by the individual because the Constitution has made a value choice about individuals. Neither are they possessed because the Supreme Court thinks them fundamental to all humans. Rather, these rights are located in the individual for the sake of a governmental process that the Constitution outlines and the Court should preserve. They are given to the individual because his enjoyment of them will lead him to defend them in court and thereby preserve the governmental process from legislative or executive deformation.

The distinction between rights that are inherent and rights that are derived from some other value is one that our society worked out long ago with respect to the economic market place, and precisely the same distinction holds and will prove an aid to clear thought with respect to the political market place. A right is a form of property, and our thinking about the category of constitutional property might usefully follow the progress of thought about economic property. We now regard it as thoroughly old hat, passé and in fact downright tiresome to hear rhetoric about an inherent right to economic freedom or to economic property. We no longer believe that economic rights inhere in the individual because he is an individual. The modern intellectual argues the proper location and definition of property rights according to judgments of utility, i.e. the capacity of such rights to forward some other value. We may, for example, wish to maximize the total wealth of society and define property rights in a way we think will advance that goal by making the economic process run more efficiently. As it is with economic property rights, so it should be with constitutional rights relating to governmental processes.

The derivation of rights from government processes is not an easy task, and I do not suggest that a shift in focus will make anything approaching a mechanical jurisprudence possible. I do suggest that, for the reasons already argued, no guidance whatever is available to a court that approaches, say, voting rights or criminal procedures through the concept of substantive equality.

The state legislative reapportionment cases were unsatisfactory precisely because the Court attempted to apply a substantive equal protection approach. Chief Justice Warren's opinions in this series of cases are remarkable for their inability to muster a single respectable supporting argument. The principle of one man, one vote was not neutrally derived: it runs counter to the text of the Fourteenth Amendment, the history surrounding its adoption, and ratification and the political practice of Americans from colonial times up to the day the Court invented the new formula.[39] The principle was not neutrally defined: it presumably rests upon some theory of equal weight for all votes, and yet we have no explanation of why it does not call into question other devices that defeat the principle, such as the executive veto, the committee system, the filibuster, the requirement on some issues of two-thirds majorities and the practice of districting. And, as we all know now, the principle, even as stated, was not neutrally applied.[40]

To approach these cases as involving rights derived from the requirements of our form of government is, of course, to say that they involve guarantee clause claims. Justice Frankfurter opposed the Court's consideration of reapportionment precisely on the ground that the "case involves all the elements that have made the Guarantee Clause cases nonjusticiable," and was a "Guarantee Clause claim masquerading under a different label."[41] Of course, his characterization was accurate, but the same could be said of many voting rights cases he was willing to decide. The guarantee clause, along with the provisions and structure of the Constitution and our political history, at least provide some guidance for a Court. The concept of the primary right of the individual in this area provides none. Whether one chooses to use the guarantee of a republican form of government of Article IV, Section 4 as a peg or to proceed directly to considerations of constitutional structure and political practice probably makes little difference. Madison's writing on the republican forms of government specified by the guarantee clause suggests that representative democracy may properly take many forms, so long as the forms do not become "aristocratic or monarchial."[42] That is certainly less easily translated into the rigid one person, one vote requirement, which rests on a concept of the right of the individual to equality, than into the requirement expressed by Justice Stewart in *Lucas* v. *Forty-Fourth General Assembly*[43] that a legislative apportionment need only be rational and "must be such as

---

39. See the dissents of Justice Frankfurter in *Baker* v. *Carr*, 369 U.S. 186, 266 (1962); Justice Harlan Reynolds in *Reynolds* v. *Sims*, 377 U.S. 533, 589 (1964); and Justice Stewart in *Lucas* v. *Forty-Fourth Gen. ass'y*, 377 U.S. 713, 744 (1964).
40. See *Fortson* v. *Morris*, 385 U.S. 231 (1966).
41. *Baker* v. *Carr*, 369 U.S. 186, 297 (1962).
42. Ibid.
43. *The Federalist* No. 43 (J. Madison).

not to permit the systematic frustration of the will of a majority of the electorate of the state."[44] The latter is a standard derived from the requirements of a democratic process rather than from the rights of individuals. The topic of governmental processes and the rights that may be derived from them is so large that it is best left at this point. It has been raised only as a reminder that there is a legitimate mode of deriving and defining constitutional rights, however difficult intellectually, that is available to replace the present unsatisfactory focus.

At the outset I warned that I did not offer a complete theory of constitutional interpretation. My concern has been to attack a few points that may be regarded as salient in order to clear the way for such a theory. I turn next to a suggestion of what neutrality, the decision of case according to principle, may mean for certain First Amendment problems.

Some First Amendment Problems: The Search for Theory

The law has settled upon no tenable, internally consistent theory of the scope of the constitutional guarantee of free speech. Nor have many such theories been urged upon the courts by lawyers or academicians. Professor Harry Kalven, Jr., one whose work is informed by a search for theory, has expressed wonder that we should feel the need for theory in the area of free speech when we tolerate inconsistencies in other areas of the law so calmly.[45] He answers himself:

> If my puzzle as to the First Amendment is not a true puzzle, it can only be
> for the congenial reason that free speech is so close to the heart of demo-
> cratic organization that if we do not have an appropriate theory for our law
> here, we feel we really do not understand the society in which we live.[46]

Kalven is certainly correct in assigning the First Amendment a central place in our society, and he is also right in attributing that centrality to the importance of speech to democratic organization. Since I share this common ground with Professor Kalven, I find it interesting that my conclusions differ so widely from his.

I am led by the logic of the requirement that judges be principled to the following suggestions. Constitutional protection should be accorded only to speech that is explicitly political. There is no basis for judicial intervention

---

44. Ibid., 753–54.
45. H. Kalven, *The Negro and the First Amendment* 4–5 (1966) [hereinafter cited as Kalven].
46. Ibid., 6.

to protect any other form of expression, be it scientific, literary, or that variety of expression we call obscene or pornographic. Moreover, within that category of speech we ordinarily call political, there should be no constitutional obstruction to laws making criminal any speech that advocates forcible overthrow of the government or the violation of the law.

I am, of course, aware that this theory departs drastically from existing Court-made law, from the views of most academic specialists in the field and this may strike a chill into the hearts of some civil libertarians. But I would insist at the outset that constitutional law, viewed as the set of rules a judge may properly derive from the document and its history, is not an expression of our political sympathies or of our judgments about what expediency and prudence require. When decision making is principled it has nothing to say about the speech we like or the speech we hate; it has a great deal to say about how far democratic discretion can govern without endangering the basis of democratic government. Nothing in my argument goes to the question of what laws should be enacted. I like the freedoms of the individual as well as most, and I would be appalled by many statutes that I am compelled to think would be constitutional if enacted. But I am also persuaded that my generally libertarian commitments have nothing to do with the behavior proper to the Supreme Court.

In framing a theory of free speech the first obstacle is the insistence of many very intelligent people that the "First Amendment is an absolute." Devotees of this position insist, with a literal respect they do not accord other parts of the Constitution, that the framers commanded complete freedom of expression without governmental regulation of any kind. The First Amendment states: "Congress shall make no law . . . abridging the freedom of speech. . . ." Those that take that as an absolute must be reading "speech" to mean any form of verbal communication and "freedom" to mean total absence of governmental restraint.

Any such reading is, of course, impossible. Since it purports to be an absolute position we are entitled to test it with extreme hypotheticals. Is Congress forbidden to prohibit incitement to mutiny aboard a naval vessel engaged in action against an enemy, to prohibit shouted harangues from the visitors' gallery during its own deliberations or to provide any rules for decorum in federal courtrooms? Are the states forbidden, by the incorporation of the Fist Amendment in the Fourteenth, to punish the shouting of obscenities in the streets?

No one, not the most obsessed absolutist, takes any such position, but if one does not, the absolute position is abandoned, revealed as a play on words.

Government cannot function if anyone can say anything anywhere at any time. And so we quickly come to the conclusion that lines must be drawn, differentiations made. Nor does that in any way involve us in a conflict with the wording of the First Amendment. Laymen may perhaps be forgiven for thinking that the literal words of the amendment command complete absence of governmental inhibition upon verbal activity, but what can one say of lawyers who believe any such thing? Anyone skilled in reading language should know that the words are not necessarily absolute. "Freedom of speech" may very well be a term referring to a defined or assumed scope of liberty, and it may be this area of liberty that is not to be "abridged."

If we turn to history, we discover that our suspicions about the wording are correct, except that matters are even worse. The framers seem to have had no coherent theory of free speech and appear not to have been overly concerned with the subject. Professor Leonard Levy's work, *Legacy of Supression,*[47] demonstrates that the men who adopted the First Amendment did not display a strong libertarian stance with respect to speech. Any such position would have been strikingly at odds with the American political tradition. Our forefathers were men accustomed to drawing a line, to us often invisible, between freedom and licentiousness. In colonial times and during and after the Revolution they displayed a determination to punish speech thought dangerous to government, much of it legitimate discourse. Jeffersonians, threatened by the Federalist Sedition Act of 1798, undertook the first American elaboration of a libertarian position in an effort to stay out of jail. Professor Walter Berns offers evidence that even then the position was not widely held.[48] When Jefferson came to power it developed that he read the First Amendment only to limit Congress and he believed suppression to be a proper function of the state governments. He appears to have instigated state prosecutions against Federalists for seditious libel. But these later developments do not tell us what the men who adopted the First Amendment intended, and their discussions tell us very little either. The disagreements that certainly existed were not debated and resolved. The First Amendment, like the rest of the Bill of Rights, appears to have been a hastily drafted document upon which little thought was expended. One reason, as Levy shows, is that the Anti-Federalists complained of the absence of a Bill of Rights less because they cared for individual freedoms than as a tactic to defeat the Constitution. The Federalists promised to submit one in order to get the Constitution rati-

47. L. Levy, *Legacy of Suppression* (1960) [hereinafter cited as Levy].
48. W. Berns, "Freedom of the Press and the Alien and Sedition Laws: A Reappraisal," 1970 *Sup. Ct. Rev.* 109.

fied. The Bill of Rights was then drafted by Federalists, who had opposed it from the beginning; the Anti-Federalists, who were really more interested in preserving the rights of state governments against federal power, had by that time lost interest in the subject.[49]

We are, then, forced to construct our own theory of the constitutional protection of speech. We cannot solve our problems simply by reference to the text or to its history. But we are not without materials for building. The First Amendment indicates that there is something special about speech. We would know that much even without a First Amendment, for the entire structure of the Constitution creates a representative democracy, a form of government that would be meaningless without freedom to discuss government and its policies. Freedom for political speech could and should be inferred even if there were no First Amendment. Further guidance can be gained from the fact that we are looking for a theory fit for enforcement by judges. The principles we seek must, therefore, be neutral in all three meanings of the word: they must be neutrally derived, defined and applied.

The law of free speech we know today grows out of the Supreme Court decisions following World War I, *Schenck* v. *United States*,[50] *Abrams* v. *United States*,[51] *Gitlow* v. *New York*,[52] *Whitney* v. *California*,[53] not out of this majority position but rather from the opinions, mostly dissents. Professor Kalven remarks upon "the almost uncanny power" of these dissents. And it is uncanny, for they have prevailed despite the considerable handicap of being deficient in logic and analysis as well as in history. The great Smith Act cases of the 1950s, *Dennis* v. *United States*,[54] as modified by *Yates* v. *Unites States*,[55] and, more recently, in 1969, *Brandenburg* v. *Ohio*[56] (voiding the Ohio criminal syndicalism statute), mark the triumph of Holmes and Brandeis. And other cases, culminating perhaps in a modified version of *Roth* v. *United States*,[57] have pushed the protections of the First Amendment outward from political speech all the way to the fields of literature, entertainment and what can only be called pornography. Because my concern is general theory I shall not attempt a comprehensive survey of the cases nor engage in theological dispu-

---

49. Levy, *supra* note 47, 224–33
50. 249 U.S. 47 (1919).
51. 250 U.S. 616 (1919).
52. 268 U.S. 642 (1925).
53. 274 U.S. 357 (1927).
54. 341 U.S. 494 (1951).
55. 354 U.S. 298 (1957).
56. 395 U.S. 444 (1969).
57. 354 U.S. 476 (1957).

tation over current doctrinal niceties. I intend to take the position that the law should have been built on Justice Sanford's majority positions in *Gitlow* and *Whitney*. These days such an argument has at least the charm of complete novelty, but I think it has other merits as well.

Before coming to the specific issues in *Gitlow* and *Whitney*, I wish to begin the general discussion of First Amendment theory with consideration of a passage from Justice Brandeis's concurring opinion in the latter case. His *Whitney* concurrence was Brandeis's first attempt to articulate a comprehensive theory of the constitutional protection of speech, and in that attempt he laid down premises which seem to me correct. But those premises seem also to lead to conclusions which Justice Brandeis would have disowned.

As a starting point Brandeis went to fundamentals and attempted to answer the question why speech is protected at all from government regulation. If we overlook his highly romanticized version of history and ignore merely rhetorical flourishes, we shall find Brandeis quite provocative.

> Those who won our independence believed that the final end of the state was to make men free to develop their faculties; and that in its government the deliberative forces should prevail over the arbitrary. They valued liberty both as an end and as a means. They believed liberty to be the secret of happiness and courage to be the secret of liberty. The belief that freedom to think as you will and to speak as you think are means indispensable to the discovery and spread of political truth: that without free speech and assembly discussion would be futile; that with them, discussion affords ordinarily adequate protection against, the dissemination of noxious doctrine. . . . They recognized the risks to which all human institutions are subject. But they knew. . . . that it is hazardous to discourage thought, hope and imagination: that hate menaces stable government: that the path of safety lies in the opportunity to discuss freely supposed grievances and proposed remedies: and that the fitting remedy for evil counsels is good ones.[58]

We begin to see why the dissents of Brandeis and Holmes possessed the power to which Professor Kalven referred. They were rhetoricians of extraordinary potency, and their rhetoric retains the power, almost half a century later, to swamp analysis, to persuade, almost to command assent.

But there is structure beneath the rhetoric, and Brandeis is asserting, though he attributes it all to the Founding Fathers, that there are four benefits to be derived from speech. These are:

---

58. 274 U.S. at 375.

1. The development of the faculties of the individual;
2. The happiness to be derived from engaging in the activity;
3. The provision of a safety valve for society; and,
4. The discovery and spread of political truth.

We may accept these claims as true and as satisfactorily inclusive. When we come to analyze these benefits, however, we discover that in terms of constitutional law they are very different things.

The first two benefits—development of individual faculties and the achievements of pleasure—are or may be found, for both speaker and hearer, in all varieties of speech, from political discourse to shop talk to salacious literature. But the important point is that these benefits do not distinguish speech from any other human activity. An individual may develop his faculties or derive pleasure from trading on the stock market, following his profession as a river port pilot, working as a bartender, engaging in sexual activity, playing tennis, rigging prices, or in any thousands of other endeavors. Speech with only the first two benefits can be preferred to other activities only by ranking forms of personal gratification. These functions or benefits of speech are, therefore, to the principled judge, indistinguishable from the functions or benefits of all other human activity. He cannot, on neutral grounds, choose to protect speech that has only these functions more than he protects any other claimed freedom.

The third benefit of speech mentioned by Brandeis—its safety valve function—is different from the first two. It relates not to the gratification of the individual, at least not directly, but to the welfare of society. The safety valve function raises only issues of expediency or prudence, and, therefore, raises issues to be determined solely by the legislature or, in some cases, by the executive. The legislature may decide not to repress speech advocating the forcible overthrow of the government in some classes of cases because it thinks repression would cause more trouble that it would prevent. Prosecuting attorneys, who must in any event pick and choose among cases, given their limited resources, may similarly decide that some such speech is trivial or that ignoring it would be wisest. But these decisions, involving only the issue of the expedient course, are indistinguishable from thousands of other managerial judgments governments must make daily, though in the extreme case decision may involve the safety of the society as surely as a decision whether or not to take a foreign policy stand that risks war. It seems plain that decisions involving only judgments of expediency are for the political branches and not for the judiciary.

This leaves the fourth function of speech—the "discovery and spread of political truth," its ability to deal explicitly, specifically, and directly with politics and government, is different from any other form of human activity. But the difference exists only with respect to one kind of speech: explicitly and predominantly political speech. This seems to me the only form of speech that a principled judge can prefer to other claimed freedoms. All other forms of speech raise only issues of human gratification and their protection against legislative regulation involves the judge in making decisions of the sort made in *Griswold* v. *Connecticut*.

It is here that I begin to part company with Professor Kalven. Kalven argues that no society in which seditious libel, the criticism of public officials, is a crime can call itself free and democratic.[59] I agree, even though the framers of the First Amendment probably had no clear view of that proposition. Yet they indicated a value when they said that speech in some sense was special and when they wrote the Constitution providing for representative democracy, a form of government that is meaningless without open and vigorous debate about officials and their policies. It is for this reason, the relation of speech to democratic organization, that Professor Alexander Meiklejohn seems correct when he says:

> The First Amendment does not protect a "freedom to speak." It protects the freedom of those activities of thought and communication by which we "govern." It is concerned, not with a private right, but with a public power, a governmental responsibility.[60]

But both Kalven and Meiklejohn go further and would extend the protection of the First Amendment beyond speech that is explicitly political. Meiklejohn argues that the amendment protects:

> Forms of thought and expression within the range of human communications from which the voter derives the knowledge, intelligence, sensitivity to human values: the capacity for sane and objective judgment which, so far as possible, a ballot should express.

He list four such thoughts and expressions:

> 1. Education, in all its phases. . . .
> 2. The achievements of philosophy and the sciences. . . .

---

59. Kalen *supra* note 45, 16.
60. A Meiklejohn, "The First Amendment Is an Absolute," 1961 *Sup. Vt. Rev.* 245, 255.

3. Literature and the arts. . . .

4. Public discussions of public issues. . . .[61]

Kalven, following a similar line, states: "[T]he invitation to follow a dialectic progression from public official to government policy to public policy to matters in the public domain, like art, seems to me to be overwhelming."[62] It is an invitation, I wish to suggest, the principled judge must decline. A dialectic progression I take to be a progression by analogy from one case to the next, an indispensable but perilous method of legal reasoning. The length to which analogy is carried defines the principle, but neutral definition requires that, in terms of the rationale in play, those cases within the principle be more like each other than they are like cases left outside. The dialectical progression must have a principled stopping point. I agree that there is an analogy between criticism of official behavior and the publication of a novel like *Ulysses*, for the latter may form attitudes that ultimately affect politics. But it is an analogy, not an identity. Other human activities and experiences also form personality, teach, and create attitudes just as much as does the novel, but no one would on that account, I take it, suggest that the First Amendment strikes down regulations of economic activity, control entry into trade, laws about sexual behavior, marriage and the like. Yet these activities, in their capacity to create attitudes that ultimately impinge upon the political process, are more like literature and science than literature and science are like political speech. If the dialectical progression is not to become an analogical stampede, the protection of the First Amendment must be cut off when it reaches the outer limits of political speech.

Two types of problems may be supposed to arise with respect to this solution. The first is the difficulty of drawing a line between political and nonpolitical speech. The second is that such a line will leave unprotected much speech that is essential to the life of a civilized community. Neither of these problems seems to me to raise crippling difficulties.

The category of protected speech should consist of speech concerned with governmental behavior, policy or personnel, whether the governmental unit involved is executive, legislative, judicial, or administrative. Explicitly political speech is speech about how we are governed, and the category therefore includes a wide range of evaluation, criticism, electioneering, and propaganda. It does not cover scientific, educational, commercial, or liter-

---

61. Ibid., 256–57.

62. Kalven, "The *New York Times* Case: A Note on 'The Central meaning of the First Amendment,'" 1964 *Sup. Ct. Rev.* 191, 221.

ary expressions as such. A novel may have impact upon attitudes that affect policies, but it would not for that reason receive judicial protection. This is not anomalous, I have tried to suggest, since the rationale of the First Amendment cannot be the protection of all the kinds of activities that influence political attitudes. Any speech may do that, and we have seen that it is impossible to leave all speech unregulated. Moreover, any conduct may affect political attitudes as much as a novel, and we cannot view the First Amendment as a broad denial of the power of government to regulate conduct. The line drawn must, therefore, lie between the explicitly political and all else. Not too much should be made of the undeniable fact that there will be hard cases. Any theory of the First Amendment that does not accord absolute protection for all verbal expression, which is to say any theory worth discussing will require that a spectrum be cut and the location of the cut will always be, arguably, arbitrary. The question is whether the general location of the cut is justified. The existence of close cases is not a reason to refuse to draw a line and so deny majorities the power to govern in areas where their power is legitimate.

The other objection that the political-nonpolitical distinction will leave much valuable speech without constitutional protection is no more troublesome. The notion that all valuable types of speech must be protected by the First Amendment confuses the constitutionality of laws with their wisdom. Freedom of nonpolitical speech rests, as does freedom for other valuable forms of behavior, upon the enlightenment of society and its elected representatives. That is hardly a terrible fate. At least a society like ours ought not to think it so.

The practical effect of confining constitutional protection to political speech would probably go no further than to introduce regulation or prohibition of pornography. The Court would be freed of the stultifying obligation to apply its self-inflicted criteria: whether (a) "the dominant theme of the material taken as a whole appeals to a prurient interest in sex;" (b) the material is patently offensive because it affronts contemporary community standards relating to the description or representation of sexual matters; and (c) the material is utterly without redeeming social value."[63] To take only the last criterion, the determination of "social value" cannot be made in a principled way. Anything some people want has, to that degree, social value, but cannot be the basis for constitutional protection since it would deny regulation of any human activity. The concept of social value neces-

---

63. *A Book Named "John Cleland's Memoirs of a Woman of Pleasure"* v. *Attorney General*, 383 U.S. 413, 418 (1966).

sarily incorporates a judgment about the net effect upon society. There is always the problem that what some people want some other people do not want, or wish actively to banish. A judgment about social value, whether the judge realize it or not, always involves a comparison of competing values and gratifications as well as competing predictions of the effects of the activity. Determination of "social value" is the same thing as determination of what human interests should be classed as "fundamental" and, therefore, cannot be principled or neutral.

To revert to the previous example, pornography is increasingly seen as a problem of pollution of the moral and aesthetic atmosphere precisely analogous to smoke pollution. A majority of the community may foresee the continued availability of pornography to those who want it will inevitably affect the quality of life for those who do not want it, altering, for example, attitudes toward love and sex, the tone of private and public discourse, and the view of social institutions such as marriage and the family. Such a majority surely has as much control over the moral and aesthetic environment as it does over the physical, for such matters may even more severely impinge upon their gratifications. That is why, constitutionally, art and pornography are on a par with industry and smoke pollution. As Professor Walter Berns says, "[A] thoughtful judge is likely to ask how an artistic judgment that is wholly idiosyncratic can be capable of supporting an objection to the law. The objection, 'I like it,' is sufficiently rebutted by 'we don't.'"[64]

We must now return to the core of the First Amendment, speech that is explicitly political. I mean by that criticisms of public officials and policies, proposals for the adoption or repeal of legislation or constitutional provisions and speech addressed to the conduct of any government unit in the country.

A qualification is required, however. Political speech is not any speech that concerns government and law, for there is a category of such speech that must be excluded. This category consists of speech advocating forcible overthrow or violation of law. The reason becomes clear when we return to Brandeis's discussion of the reasons for according constitutional protection of speech.

The fourth function of speech, the one that defines and sets apart political speech, is the "discovery and spread of political truth." To understand what the Court should protect, therefore, we must define "political truth." There seem to me three possible meanings to that term:

---

64. Berns, "Pornography vs. Democracy: The Case for Censorship," *The Public Interest*, Winter, 1971, 23.

1. An absolute set of truths that exist independently of Constitution or statute.

2. A set of values that are protected by constitutional provision from the reach of legislative majorities.

3. Within that area of life which the majority is permitted to govern in accordance with the Madisonian model of representative government, whatever result the majority reaches and maintains at the moment.

The judge can have nothing to do with any absolute set of truths existing independently and depending upon God or the nature of the universe. If a judge should claim to have access to such a body of truths, to possess a volume of the annotated natural law, we would, quite justifiably, suspect that the source of the revelation was really no more exalted than the judge's viscera. In our system there is no absolute set of truths, to which the term "political truth" can refer.

Values protected by the Constitution are one type of political truth. They are, in fact, the highest type since they are placed beyond the reach of simple legislative majorities. They are primarily truths about the way government must operate, that is, procedural truths. But speech aimed at the discovery and spread of political truth is concerned with more than the desirability of constitutional provisions or the manner in which they should be interpreted.

The third meaning of "political truth" extends the category of protected speech. Truth is what the majority thinks it is at any given moment precisely because the majority is permitted to govern and to redefine its values constantly. "Political truth" in this sense must, therefore, be a term of art, a concept defined entirely from a consideration of the system of government which the judge is commissioned to operate and maintain. It has no unchanging content but refers to the temporary outcomes of the democratic process. Political truth is what the majority decided it wants today. It may be something entirely different tomorrow, as truth is rediscovered and the new concept spread.

Speech advocating forcible overthrow of the government contemplates a group less than a majority seizing control of the monopoly power of the state when it cannot gain its ends through speech and political activity. Speech advocating violent overthrow is thus not "political speech" as that term must be defined by a Madisonian system of government. It is not political speech because it violates constitutional truths about processes and because it is not aimed at a new definition of political truth by a legislative majority. Violent overthrow of government breaks the premise of our system concerning the ways in which truth is defined, and yet those premises are the only reasons for protecting political speech. It follows that there is no constitutional reason to protect speech advocating forcible overthrow.

A similar analysis suggests that advocacy of law violation does not qualify as political speech any more then advocacy of forcible overthrow of the government. Advocacy of law violation is a call to set aside the results that political speech has produced. The process of the "discovery and spread of political truth" is damaged or destroyed if the outcome is defeated by a minority that makes law enforcement, and hence the putting of political truth into practice, impossible or less effective. There should, therefore, be no constitutional protection for any speech advocating the violation of law.

I believe these are the only results that can be reached by a neutral judge who takes his values from the Constitution. If we take Brandeis's description of the benefits and functions of speech as our premise, logic and principle appear to drive us to the conclusion that Sanford rather than Brandeis or Holmes was correct in *Gitlow* and *Whitney.*

Benjamin Gitlow was convicted under New York's criminal anarchy statute which made criminal advocacy of the doctrine that organized government should be overthrown by force, violence, or any unlawful means. Gitlow, a member of the left-wing section of the Socialist party, had arranged the printing and distribution of a "Manifesto" deemed to call for violent action and revolution. "There was," Justice Sanford's opinion noted, "no evidence of any effect resulting from the publication and circulation of the Manifesto."[65] Anita Whitney was convicted under California's criminal syndicalism statute, which forbade advocacy of the commission of crime, sabotage, acts of force or violence or terrorism "as a means of accomplishing a change in industrial ownership or control, or effecting any political change." Also made illegal were certain connections with groups advocating such doctrines. Whitney was convicted of assisting in organizing the Communist Labor Party of California, of being a member of it, and of assembling with it.[66] The evidence appears to have been meager, but our current concern is doctrinal.

Justice Sanford's opinions for the majorities in *Gitlow* and *Whitney* held essentially that the Court's function in speech cases was the limited but crucial one of determining whether the legislature had defined a category of forbidden speech which might constitutionally be suppressed.[67] The category

65. 268 U.S. at 656.
66. 274 U.S. at 372 (Brandeis, Ju., dissenting).
67. 268 U.S., at 656.

might be defined by the nature of the speech and need not be limited in other ways. If the category was defined in a permissible way and the defendant's speech or publication fell within the definition, the Court had, it would appear, no other issues to face in order to uphold the conviction. Questions of the fairness of the trial and the sufficiency of the evidence aside, this would appear to be the correct conclusion. The legislatures had struck at speech not aimed at the discovery and spread of political truth but aimed rather at destroying the premises of our political system and the means by which we define political truth. There is no value that judges can independently give such speech in opposition to a legislative determination.

Justice Holmes' dissent in *Gitlow* and Justice Brandeis' concurrence in *Whitney* insisted the Court must also find that, as Brandeis put it, the "speech would produce, or is intended to produce, a clear and imminent danger of some substantive evil which the state consistently may seek to prevent."[68] Neither of them explained why the danger must be "clear and imminent" or, as Holmes had put it in *Schenck*, "clear and present"[69] before a particular instance of speech could be punished. Neither of them made any attempt to answer Justice Sanford's argument on the point:

> [T]he immediate danger [created by advocacy of overthrow of the government] is none the less real and substantial, because the effect of a given utterance cannot be accurately foreseen. The state cannot reasonably be required to measure the danger from every such utterance in the nice balance of a jeweler's scale. A single revolutionary spark may kindle a fire that, smoldering for a time, may burst into a sweeping and destructive conflagration. It cannot be said that the state is acting arbitrarily or unreasonably when in the exercise of its judgment as to the measures necessary to protect the public peace and safety, it seeks to extinguish the spark without waiting until it has enkindled the flame or blazed into conflagration. It cannot reasonably be required to defer the adoption of measures for its own peace and safety until the revolutionary utterances lead to actual disturbances of the public peace or imminent and immediate danger of its own destruction; but it may, in the exercise of its judgment, suppress the threatened danger in its incipiency. . . .[70]

To his point that proof of the effect of speech is inherently unavailable and yet its impact may be real and dangerous, Sanford might have added that

---

68. 274 U.S., 373.
69. 249 U.S., 52.
70. 268 U.S., 669

the legislature is not confined to consideration of a single instance of speech or a single speaker. It fashions a rule to dampen thousands of instances of forcible overthrow advocacy. Cumulatively these may have enormous influence, and yet it may well be impossible to show any effect from any single example. The "clear and present danger" requirement, which has had a long and uneven career in our law, is improper not, as many commentators have thought, because it provides a subjective and an inadequate safeguard against the regulation of speech, but rather because it erects a barrier to legislative rule where none should exist. The speech concerned has no political value within a republican system of government. Whether or not it is prudent to ban advocacy of forcible overthrow and law violation is a different question altogether. Because the judgment is tactical, implicating the safety of the nation, it resembles very closely the judgment that Congress and the President must make about the expediency of waging war, an issue that the Court has wisely thought not fit for judicial determination.

The legislature and the executive might find it wise to permit some rhetoric about law violation and forcible overthrow. I am certain that they would and that they should. Certain of the factors weighted in determining the constitutionality of the Smith Act prosecutions in *Dennis* would, for example, make intelligible statutory, though not constitutional, criteria: the high degree of organization of the Communist Party, the rigid discipline of its members and the party's ideological affinity to foreign powers.[71]

Similar objections apply to the other restrictions Brandeis attempted to impose upon government. I will mention but one more of these restrictions. Justice Brandeis argued that:

> Even imminent danger cannot justify resort to prohibition of these functions essential to effective democracy, unless the evil apprehended is relatively serious. . . . Thus, a state might, in the exercise of its police power, make any trespass upon the land of another a crime, regardless of the results or of the intent or purpose of the trespasser. It might, also, punish an attempt, a conspiracy, or an incitement to commit the trespass. But it is hardly conceivable that this court would hold constitutional a statute which punished as a felony the more voluntary assembly with a society formed to teach that pedestrians had the moral right to cross unenclosed, unposted, waste lands and to advocate their doing so, even if there was imminent danger that advocacy would lead to a trespass. The fact that speech is likely to result in some violence or in destruction of property

---

71. 341 U.S., 511.

is not enough to justify its suppression. There must be the probability of serious injury to the state.[72]

It is difficult to see how a constitutional court could properly draw the distinction proposed. Brandeis offered no analysis to show that advocacy of law violation merited protection by the Court. Worse, the criterion he advanced is the importance, in the judge's eyes, of the law whose violation is urged.

Modern law has followed the general line and the spirit of Brandeis and Holmes rather than of Sanford, and it has become increasingly severe in its limitation of legislative power. *Brandenburg* v. *Ohio*, a 1969 per curiam decision by the Supreme Court, struck down the Ohio criminal syndicalism statute because it punished advocacy of violence, the opinion stating:

> . . . *Whitney* [the majority opinion] has been thoroughly discredited by later decisions. . . . These later decisions have fashioned the principle that the constitutional guarantees of free speech and free press do not permit a State to forbid or proscribe advocacy of the use of force or of law violation except where such advocacy is directed to inciting or producing imminent lawless action and is likely to incite or produce such action.[73]

It is certainly true that Justice Sanford's position in *Whitney* and in *Gitlow* has been completely undercut, or rather abandoned, by later cases, but it is not true that his position has been discredited, or even met, on intellectual grounds. Justice Brandeis failed to accomplish that, and later justices have not mounted a theoretical case comparable to Brandeis.

These remarks are intended to be tentative and exploratory. Yet at this moment I do not see how I can avoid the conclusions stated. The Supreme Court's constitutional role appears to be justified only if the Court applies the principles that are neutrally derived, defined, and applied. And the requirement of neutrality in turn appears to indicate the results I have sketched here.

---

72. 274 U.S., 377–78.
73. 395 U.S., 447.

Discussion with colleagues has led me to abandon the proposition that only political speech should be accorded constitutional protection. This shift of position is only on grounds of practicality, not any difficulty with the underlying principle. The practical difficulty lies in distinguishing political speech from other varieties. Novels, plays, music, and other art forms as well as scientific speech are frequently freighted with political meaning. If judges and juries undertook to sort through masses of such materials, the result would be an administrative and legal nightmare. No speaker or writer could proceed with confidence that the unknown judge and jury he would one day face would draw the political/nonpolitical line correctly or consistently with the determinations of other tribunals. The best that can be done is probably to build on the rule set out in Chaplinsky v. New Hampshire, 315 U.S. 568, 571–2 (1942): *"There are certain well-defined and narrowly limited classes of speech, the prevention and punishment of which have never been thought to raise any Constitutional problem. These include the lewd and obscene, the profane, the libelous, and the insulting or 'fighting' words—those which by their very utterance inflict injury or tend to incite an immediate breach of the peace. It has been well observed that such utterances are no essential part of any exposition of ideas, and are of such slight social value as a step to truth that any benefit that may be derived from them is clearly outweighed by the social interest in order and morality."*

It is a measure of the direction of our legal culture that today the Court upholds freedom to display hardcore pornography while frequently allowing legislatures to enact severe restrictions on political speech. That trend does not bode well for either freedom or morality.

THEIR WILL BE DONE

What do the nomination of a replacement for Sandra Day O'Connor, constitutional law, and moral chaos have to do with one another? A good deal more than you may think.

In *Federalist* 2, John Jay wrote of America that "Providence has been pleased to give this one connected country to one united people—a people descended from the same ancestors, speaking the same language, professing the same religion, attached to the same principles of government, very similar in their manners and customs. . . ." Such a people enjoy the same moral assumptions, the cement that forms a society rather than a cluster of groups. Though Jay's conditions have long been obsolete, until recently Americans did possess a large body of common moral assumptions rooted in our original Anglo-Protestant culture, and expressed in law. Now, however, a variety of disintegrating influences are undermining that unanimity, not least among them is the capture of constitutional law by an extreme liberationist philosophy. America is becoming a cacophony of voices proclaiming different, or no, truths.

Alexis de Tocqueville observed that "If each undertook himself to form all his opinions and to pursue the truth in isolation down paths cleared by him alone, it is not probable that a great number of men would ever unite in any common belief. . . . [W]ithout common ideas there is no common action, and without common action men still exist, but a social body does not."

Contrast Tocqueville with Justices Harry Blackmun and Anthony Kennedy. Blackmun wanted to create a constitutional right to homosexual sodomy because of the asserted "'moral fact' that a person belongs to himself and not others nor to society as a whole." Justice Kennedy, writing for six justices, did invent that right, declaring that "At the heart of [constitutional]

From the *Wall Street Journal*, July 5, 2005.

liberty is the right to define one's own concept of existence, of meaning, of the universe, and of the mystery of human life." Neither of these vaporings has the remotest basis in the actual Constitution and neither has any definable meaning other than that a common morality may not be sustained by law if a majority of justices prefer that each individual follow his own desires.

Once the justices depart, as most of them have, from the original understanding of the principles of the Constitution, they lack any guidance other than their own attempts at moral philosophy, a task for which they have not even minimal skills. Yet when it rules in the name of the Constitution, whether it rules truly or not, the Court is the most powerful branch of government in domestic policy. The combination of absolute power, disdain for the historic Constitution, and philosophical incompetence is lethal.

The Court's philosophy reflects, or rather embodies and advances, the liberationist spirit of our times. In moral matters, each man is a separate sovereignty. In its insistence on radical personal autonomy, the Court assaults what remains of our stock of common moral beliefs. That is all the more insidious because the public and the media take these spurious constitutional rulings as not merely legal conclusions but moral teachings supposedly incarnate in our most sacred civic document. That teaching is the desirability, as the sociologist Robert Nisbet put it, of the "break-up of social molecules into atoms, of a generalized nihilism toward society and culture as the result of individualistic hedonism and the fragmenting effect of both state and economy." He noted that both Edmund Burke and Tocqueville placed much of the blame for such developments on the intellectual class—in our time dominant in, for example, the universities, the media, church bureaucracies, and foundation staffs—a class to which judges belong and to whose opinions they respond. Thus ever-expanding rights continually deplete America's bank of common morality.

Consider just a few of the Court's accomplishments: The justices have weakened the authority of other institutions, public and private, such as schools, businesses, and churches; assisted in sapping the vitality of religion through a transparently false interpretation of the establishment clause; denigrated marriage and family; destroyed taboos about vile language in public; protected as free speech the basest pornography, including computer-simulated child pornography; weakened political parties and permitted prior restraints on political speech, violating the core of the First Amendment's guarantee of freedom of speech; created a right to abortion virtually on demand, invalidating the laws of all 50 states; whittled down capital punishment, on the path, apparently, to abolishing it entirely; mounted a campaign to normalize homosexuality, culminating soon, it seems obvious, in a right to homosexual marriage; permitted racial and gender discrimination at the expense of white males; and made the criminal justice system needlessly slow and complex, tipping the balance in favor of criminals. Justice O'Connor, a warm, down-to-earth, and very likeable person, joined many, though not all, of these bold attempts to remake America. Whatever one may think of these outcomes as matters of policy, not one is authorized by the Constitution and some are directly contrary to it. All of them, however, are consistent with the left-liberal liberationist impulse that advances moral anarchy.

Democratic senators' filibusters of the president's previous judicial nominees demonstrate liberals' determination to retain the court as their political weapon. They claim that conservative critics of the Court threaten the independence of the judiciary, as though independence is a warrant to abandon the Constitution for personal predilection. The Court's critics are not angry without cause; they have been provoked. The Court has converted itself from a legal institution to a political one, and has made so many basic and unsettling changes in American government, life, and culture that a counterattack was inevitable, and long overdue. If the critics' rhetoric is sometimes overheated, it is less so than that of some Democratic senators and their interest-group allies. The leaders of the Democratic Party in the Senate are making it the party of moral anarchy, and they will fight to keep the Court activist and liberal. The struggle over the Supreme Court is not just about law: it is about the future of our culture.

To restore the Court's integrity will require a minimum of three appointments of men and women who have so firm an understanding of the judicial function that they will not drift left once on the bench. Choosing, and fighting for, the right man or woman to replace Justice O'Connor is the place to start. That will be difficult, but the stakes are the legitimate scope of self-government and an end to judicially imposed moral disorder.

STYLES IN CONSTITUTIONAL THEORY

There is probably more debate today than ever before about the duties of judges, and indeed about the freedom of judges, in deciding constitutional cases. Though there is much to be said on the topic of the actual performance of our courts and the theories of adjudication they appear to be following, this paper is not a critique of the courts. I intend to focus instead upon the theorists of constitutional law, the legal intellectuals, these days mostly to be found in the academy. Their styles of argument tell us something about the attitudes of intellectuals not only toward law but also toward the American polity and American society. We may also discern what is being taught in the law schools and, hence, what may be the views of the profession and the judges of the next generation.

Differing styles of constitutional theory are best examined in the context of the Bill of Rights and Fourteenth Amendment, for it is there, in the tension between governmental authority and individual liberty, rather than in questions of governmental structure and operation, that styles differ most radically and that the most interesting inferences are to be drawn.

The problem in this area of constitutional theory always has been, and always will be, the resolution of what has been called the Madisonian dilemma. The United States was founded on what we now call a Madisonian system, one which allows majorities to rule in wide areas of life simply because they are majorities, but which also holds that individuals have some freedoms that must be exempt from majority control. The dilemma is that neither the majority nor the minority can be trusted to define the proper spheres of democratic authority and individual liberty. The first would court tyranny by the majority; the second, tyranny by the minority.

It is not at all clear that the framers assigned the federal judiciary a major role in the resolution of this dilemma. Indeed, it is good for any incipient

From *South Texas Law Journal*, 1985.

judicial hubris to recall that in *Federalist* 78, Hamilton, misquoting Montesquieu only slightly, said that "Of the three powers . . . the judiciary is next to nothing."[1] The framers attempted to balance majorities and minorities primarily by such strategies as enlarging the political unit, federalism, separation of powers, and the structure of representation. But over time it came to be thought that the resolution of the Madisonian problem—the definition of majority power and minority freedom—was primarily the function of the judiciary and, especially, the function of the Supreme Court. That understanding, which now seems a permanent feature of our political arrangements, creates the need for constitutional theory.

For most of our history, theorists found resolution of the Madisonian dilemma no particular problem. Men such as Joseph Story, James Kent, James Bradley Thayer, and Thomas Colley viewed the Constitution as law—a unique form of law, perhaps, one requiring special handling—but law nonetheless. The primary problems were the usual ones of interpretation and construction.

It was not until the latter half of this century, so far as I can tell, that it began to be suggested seriously, and with elaborate argument, that courts had power to create and enforce against the majority will values that were not in some real sense to be found in the Constitution. The distinction between the theory of our first century-and-a-half and the last thirty years is by no means absolute. There have always been suggestions that courts might apply natural justice. Indeed, Chief Justice Marshall may have suggested extra-constitutional powers when he wrote in *Fletcher* v. *Peck*: "It may well be doubted whether the nature of society and of government does not prescribe limits to the legislative power. . . ."[2] And it is certainly true that courts from time to time did create extra-constitutional rights, as the defunct doctrine of economic substantive due process reminds us. But there was no theory of judicial behavior that justified such departures, at least none that I have been able to find. The reigning theory was that the Constitution is law and is to be interpreted.

Today, the reigning theory is that interpretation may be impossible, and is certainly inadequate. The majority of theorists would assign to judges not the task of defining values found in the Constitution but the task of creating new values and hence new rights for individuals against the majority. These value-creating theories are sometimes referred to as non-interpretivism.

There has been a major shift in the styles of constitutional argument. The purpose here is to examine this shift in terms of the content of theory,

---

1. *The Federalist* 78, at 519 n. (A. Hamilton) (P. Ford ed. 1898).
2. *Fletcher* v. *Peck*, 10 US (6 Cranch) 87, 135 (1810).

the mode of discourse, the legitimacy of the theories put forward, the attitude of legal intellectuals toward American society, and, finally, the possible effects upon our constitutional liberties.

In 1833, Joseph Story, an Associate Justice of the Supreme Court of the United States and the Dane Professor of Law at Harvard, could introduce his three-volume *Commentaries on the Constitution of the United States* with the following words:

> The reader must not expect to find in these pages any novel views and novel constructions of the Constitution. I have not the ambition to be the author of any new plan of interpreting the theory of the Constitution, or of enlarging or narrowing its powers, by ingenious subtleties and learned doubts. . . . Upon subjects of government, it has always appeared to me that metaphysical refinements are out of place. A constitution of government is addressed to the common sense of the people; and never was designed for trials of logical skill, or visionary speculation.[3]

When Story came to the role of the courts, he assumed that their task was to interpret: "The first and fundamental rule in the interpretation of all instruments is, to construe them according to the sense of the terms, and the intention of the parties."[4]

The same interpretivist assumption is found in Kent, Cooley, and other writers of the last century and the first half of this century. That assumption was the premise for Thayer's end-of-the-century dictum that a court must not invalidate a statute unless it was convinced not merely that the legislature had probably exceeded its constitutional powers, but that it had made a clear mistake in supposing its act constitutional. Courts must not, he said, "even negatively, undertake to legislate."[5] To quote extensively from the writers of the older tradition in defense of a strictly interpretivist theory of constitutional adjudication is impossible for the simple reason that they took the theory for granted and had no opposing school to rebut. That fact, while it may create a certain imbalance here, underscores the radical and unexpected nature of the shift that has occurred.

---

3. J. Storey, *Commentaries on the Constitution of the United States*, at viii (3rd ed. Boston 1858).
4. Ibid, at 283, § 400.
5. Thayer, "The Origin and Scope of the American Doctrine of Constitutional Law", 7 *Harvard Law Review* (2893), 129, 150. "The courts . . . must not, even negatively, undertake to legislate. And, again, they must not act unless the case is so very clear, because the consequences of setting aside legislation may be so serious." *Id.*

The point at which theorists began to view the constitutional judge as properly a legislator seems not to have achieved its full articulation until well after World War II. The most influential theorist of this new school was my good friend and colleague, Alexander M. Bickel. He did not hesitate to assert that the judge must create rights not found in the Constitution, indeed, should create rights the written Constitution clearly assumes not to exist. The judge was to become the scholar-king. It is little short of astounding to reread today the wide-ranging, free-handed task Bickel would then—he had second thoughts in later years—have assigned to the Supreme Court:

> The function of the Justices . . . is to immerse themselves in the tradition of our society and of kindred societies that have gone before, in history and in the sediment of history which is law, and . . . in the thought and the vision of the philosophers and the poets. The Justices will then be fit to extract "fundamental presuppositions" from their deepest selves, but in fact from the evolving morality of our tradition.[6]

It is tempting to say at this point that nothing could be further from the theories of Story, Cooley, and Thayer than constitutional law, if it can be called that, drawn from prolonged immersion in the visions of poets. It is tempting to say that, but, as you will see, it is possible to get still further away from the old tradition.

One is doubtless familiar with the next stage of theory. Dan Harry Wellington would create new constitutional rights by employing "the *method of philosophy*"[7] to determine the "conventional morality"[8] of our society. Professor Ronald Dworkin sees a "fusion of constitutional law and moral theory."[9] In Dworkin's view, the judge is to determine the principles that underlie and explain the nation's moral judgments, and then apply those principles against any particular moral judgment made by a legislature to decide whether the

---

6. A. Bickel, *The Least Dangerous Branch* (1962), 236.

7. Wellington, "Common Law Rules and Constitutional Double Standards: Some Notes on Adjudication," *Yale Law Journal* 83 919730, 221, 246.

> "Because of its nature—because it is "there," yet changing—the way in which one learns about the conventional morality of a society is to live in it, become sensitive to it, experience [it] widely, read extensively, and ruminate, reflect, and analyze situations that seem to call moral obligations into play. This task may be called the method of philosophy."

8. Ibid, at 243–49, 284.

9. R. Dworkin, *Taking Rights Seriously* (1977), 149.

latter is consistent or aberrational. Professsor Thomas Grey suggests that there is a "higher law" of unwritten "natural rights which courts are to enforce.[10]

Professor Richard Parker promises a new constitutional theory which will "take seriously and work from (while, no doubt, revising) the classical conception of a republic, including its elements of relative equality, mobilization of the citizenry, and civic virtue."[11] This, it seems, is to be constitutional theory as written by the Committee on Public Safety. It is to be hoped Professor Parker has heard of Thermidor.

These are only a few of the theorists of this sort. The groves of legal academe are thick with young philosophers who propose various systems of morality that judges must use to create new constitutional rights. An important feature of these systems is that they not only control democratic choice but that they purport to have sufficient rigor so that they can control the judge. The judge is, the theorists claim, prevented by their systems from simply imposing his view of policy and morality.

The progression by no means stops there. It could not stop there. The nature of the non-interpretive enterprise is such that its theories must end in constitutional nihilism and the imposition of the judge's merely personal values on the rest of us. The reason is that none of these theorists has been able—and I venture to suggest none ever will be able—to build a philosophical structure that starts from accepted premises and logically demonstrates the answers, or the range of allowable answers, to questions not answered by the written Constitution. Nor has anyone managed to connect all the moral judgments embodied in our laws to state more basic principles that themselves decide concrete cases. Nothing less than this power and rigor is required if we are to accept government by judges who are not applying the Constitution. Yet no theologian, no moral philosopher, no social philosopher has achieved that hegemony in the recorded history of human thought. That does not prove conclusively that it cannot be done, perhaps, but it does give some reason to suspect that no law professor is going to accomplish the task anytime soon.

This failure will become apparent—indeed, it is already apparent as each of the non-interpretive theorists convincingly destroys all the others' systems—and that is why the inevitable end to non-interpretivist, value-choosing theory is constitutional nihilism. Professor Paul Brest, a non-in-

---

10. Grey, "Do We Have an Unwritten Constitution?", *Stanford Law Review* 27 (1975), 703.
11. Parker, "The Past of Constitutional Theory—And its Future", *Ohio State Law Journal* 146 (1981), 223, 258.

terpretivist, bravely acknowledges this: "the controversy over the legitimacy of judicial review in a democratic polity . . . is essentially incoherent and unresolvable"[12] since "no defensible criteria exist"[13] "to assess theories of judicial review,"[14] and, therefore, "the Madisonian dilemma is in fact unresolvable."[15]

One might suppose that a constitutional theorist who concludes that value-choosing constitutional theory cannot be coherent, that it cannot satisfy its own criteria of legitimacy, and that all existing theory is debased, one might suppose that such a theorist would entertain the idea of judicial restraint, or judicial modesty, or even judicial abdication in favor of the democratic process. One might suppose that, but one would be quite wrong. Nihilism turns instead to advocacy of opportunistic judicial authoritarianism precisely because what fuels the non-interpretivist impulse in the first place is a desire to change society in ways that legislatures refuse. The desire for results is greater than the respect for process, and, when theory fails, power remains.

Professor Brest seems to call at a minimum for judicial action that serves the public good as he perceives the good, and, apparently still in the context of constitutional theory, he states, "if it would be arrogant to think that we could change the world, it would be even more irresponsible to act as if we couldn't."[16] Professor Brest speaks, approvingly, of working "toward a genuine reconstitution of society."[17] His despairing view of our society seems to couple nihilism with apocalypticism.

A second reason that non-interpretivism ends in nihilism is that it has proved wholly unable to meet a condition most theorists have accepted as indispensable—consistency with democratic control of government. Alexander Bickel explained why that is essential:

> [N]othing can finally depreciate the central function that is assigned in
> democratic theory and practice to the electoral process; nor can it be de-
> nied that the policy-making power of representative institutions, born of

---

12. Brest, "The Fundamental Rights Controversy: The Essential Contradictions of Normative Constitutional Scholarship", *Yale Law Journal* 90 (1980), 1063.

13. Ibid, 1065. "As I turned to the possibilities of non-originalist, substantive, value-oriented constitutional adjudication, I became increasingly uncertain about the criteria we implicitly invoke to assess theories of judicial review. In this article I conclude that no defensible criteria exists."

14. Ibid.

15. Ibid, 1097.

16. Ibid, 1108.

17. Ibid, 1109.

the electoral process, is the distinguishing characteristic of the system. Judicial review works counter to this characteristic. . . .

. . . [D]emocracies do live by the idea, central to the process of gaining the consent of the governed, that the majority has the ultimate power to displace the decision-makers and to reject any part of their policy. With that idea, judicial review must achieve some measure of consonance.[18]

In short, a value-choosing theory must give a satisfactory reason why it is legitimate for a court to impose a new value upon a majority against its wishes.

Bickel not only posed the problem, he essayed an answer which in my opinion no one writing afterward has improved upon. That answer came in two parts. The first was one of relative institutional capacities; courts are simply better than legislatures in dealing with principles of long-run importance as opposed to immediate problems. He said: "[C]ourts have certain capacities for dealing with matters of principle that legislatures and executives do not possess. Judges have, or should have, the leisure, the training, and the insulation to follow the ways of the scholar in pursuing the ends of government."[19]

Other than to heave a wistful sigh, I will pass by this vision of a judge's life without comment.

The second step in Bickel's argument is that the courts' commands are not really final. Speaking of the resistance to the decision in *Brown* v. *Board of Education*, Bickel wrote:

The Supreme Court's law . . . could not in our system prevail—not merely in the very long run, but within the decade—if it ran counter to deeply felt popular needs or convictions, or even if it was opposed by a determined and substantial minority and received with indifference by the rest of the country. This, in the end, is how and why judicial review is consistent with the theory of and practice of political democracy. This is why the Supreme Court is a court of last resort presumptively only.[20]

Bickel is quoted here because he expressed the arguments so well. Others, including Wellington, have employed essentially the same strategies to escape the charge that non-interpretive review is unacceptably anti-democratic.

Both steps in the argument—superior institutional capacity and lack of finality—are essential, but, unfortunately, neither can survive examination.

---

18. A. Bickel, *supra*, note 6, at 19, 27.
19. Ibid, 25–26.
20. Ibid, 258.

Even if we assume that courts have superior capacities for dealing with matters of principle, it does not follow that courts have the right to impose more principle upon us than our elected representatives give us. Governmental decisions will involve a mix of, or a tradeoff between, principle and expediency. By placing decisions in the legislative arena, the Constitution holds that the mix or tradeoff we are entitled to is what the legislature provides. Courts have no mandate to impose a different mix merely because they would arrive at a tradeoff that weighed principle more heavily. This keystone of the Bickel-Wellington thesis must be judged to fail.

A similar failure attends the argument of those who, like Dworkin and Perry, suppose that a system of morality may override legislative outcomes.[21] Democratic decisions are not required to conform to any moral system. If they were, there would be no need for the legislatures contemplated by the Constitution; we would need only moral philosophers. The same may be said for Parker's notion that the nation must move toward something called the "classical conception of a republic" with such revisions as he deems appropriate.[22]

Some theorists seek to avoid this difficulty by claiming that they would have courts make democracy more democratic. Professor, now Dean, John Hart Ely, who is a non-interpretivist whether he knows it or not, takes this tack.[23] The difficulty is that there is neither a constitutional nor an extra-constitutional basis for making the Constitution more democratic than the Constitution is. The Constitution prescribes the outlines of the ways we govern ourselves. Within that frame, we arrange our political processes as we see fit. Nobody has yet made legitimate an authority in the judiciary to stop what the Constitution allows.

The non-interpretivist's contention that the Court is not final and hence is not undemocratic, or at least not unacceptably so, must also be rejected. It is true that an outraged people can, if it persists, overturn a Supreme Court decision. That necessarily means that there would be little democratic control over a non-interpretivist court. Given the number of decisions to be scrutinized, the political process would have to focus upon only two or three decisions or else exist in a state of permanent convulsion. As we know from history, moreover, it may take decades to accomplish the reversal of a single decision. And even then, the reversal cannot be forced if a substantial

---

21. R. Dworkin, *supra* note 9, 149; M. Perry, *The Constitution, The Courts, and Human Rights; An Inquiry Into the Legitimacy of Constitutional Policymaking By the Judiciary* (1982).

22. Parker, *supra* note 11, 258.

23. J. Ely, *Democracy and Distrust* (1980).

minority supports the result. The theory assumes, as one of my clerks put it, that in the long run none of us will be dead.

Professors Charles Black[24] and Michael Perry[25] rest the democratic nature of judicial review upon Congress' power under article III to remove the jurisdiction of the Supreme Court and of the lower federal courts. The support is too slender. Whatever the constitutionality of the proposal, jurisdiction removal is unusable where uniformity is crucial. If a Court proposed to rule upon a war or a draft plan, Congress, no matter how incensed, could hardly use a power that would result in control of the issue by the varying decisions of fifty state supreme courts. Nor would the principle of democratic supremacy be vindicated since the decision would still be lodged in the judiciary, albeit state judiciaries, rather than in the political branches.

Many non-interpretive theorists have responded to this anti-democratic difficulty by simply dropping Bickel's condition from the discussion. Perry, who has begun to suspect that this problem is looming on his horizon and that article III does not provide an adequate nexus between non-interpretivist theory and democratic theory, has added a footnote to his latest effort which runs as follows: "If I were unable to defend constitutional policymaking by the judiciary as consistent with the principle of electorally accountable policymaking, then given my commitment to constitutional policymaking by the judiciary, I would have to question the axiomatic character of the principle of electorally accountable policymaking."[26] In a word, if judicial rule and democracy come into conflict, Perry will have to question the desirability of democracy.

The fact of the matter is that there are no really effective means by which the people of the political branches can respond to constitutional policymaking of which they disapprove. The mechanisms now at hand that might work would have the effect not merely of limiting the Court's capacity for improperly infringing the rights of majorities but also of damaging, perhaps destroying, the rights of minorities. No one wants to do that. In this sense, the Court's vulnerability makes it well-nigh invulnerable.

Though the progression has been sketched briefly here, several trends and themes are discernable in these changes in styles of constitutional theory. The content has moved from conventional legal argument, which relies on text, structure, and legislative history to discern the intent of the framers, to various forms of moral philosophy, reformist demands for more

---

24. C. Black, Jr., *Decision According to Law* (1981), 17–18, 37–39.

25. M. Perry, *supra* note 21.

26. Ibid, 10 n.*.

equality, and more participation. Each of these has not only a distinctive substance but a distinctive rhetorical style. The older writers, with occasional flights of lyricism about American liberties, by and large display a plain, direct, lawyerlike prose. The style of the philosophers, on the other hand, is often abstract, complex, even convoluted. It could hardly be otherwise; it takes laborious analysis to unpack the concepts the philosophers deal with and to show their varying applications to moral problems. This literature is as difficult to read as it must be to write. The reformers' tones vary from dismay to anger; they show disapproval and dislike for the world as it is constituted.

A related change is one of attitudes toward democratic government and politics. The older writers accepted completely that the primary form of policymaking was to be through representative institutions accountable to the electoral process. I do not know whether this was because they were themselves devoted to the majoritarian principle, or because they accepted the Constitution as law and knew that the Constitution, with important exceptions, which are nonetheless exceptions, prescribes representative democracy as the primary mode of making policy.

Certainly the older theorists were not naïve about the defects of democracy. Thayer was not, but he thought that a court must be. In his essay he stated:

> [I]n a court's revision of legislative acts, as in its revision of a jury's acts, it will always assume a duly instructed body; and the question is not merely what persons may rationally do who are such as we often see, in point of fact, in our legislative bodies, persons untaught it may be, indocile, thoughtless, reckless, incompetent,—but what those other persons, competent, well-instructed, sagacious, attentive, intent only on public ends, fit to represent a self-governing people, such as our theory of government assumes to be carrying on our public affairs,—what such persons may reasonably think or do, what is the permissible view for them.[27]

Thayer knows the defects in our representatives but holds that the form of government prescribed by the Constitution requires the judge to ignore the imperfections. Perhaps Thayer thought that for judges to examine and take account of the actual processes of representative government in their constitutional decisions would be to start down a dangerous path leading to judicial oligarchy. If so, the modern theorists tend to prove the soundness of his judgments. The most moderate of the value-choosing theorists,

---

27. Thayer, *supra* note 5, 149.

Bickel and Wellington, make the defects of legislatures and the superiority of judges in matters of principle their starting point.

At times the search for a policymaking body, any policymaking body other than a legislature, displays a strain of desperation. To illustrate the point, I will quote my friend, Dean Wellington, who, on the current academic spectrum, is by no means an extremist in these matters. In analyzing the abortion decisions in the light of conventional morality, which he equates with the criterion for constitutionality, Wellington states that he takes "some comfort" in the fact that his own conclusions agree with those of the American Law Institute, and then states:

> The work of the Institute is a check of sorts. Its conclusions are some evidence of society's moral position on these questions. It is, indeed, better evidence than state legislation, for the Institute, while not free of politics, is not nearly as subject to the pressures of special intrest groups as is a legislature.[28]

I yield to no one in my admiration for the ALI's profound and path-breaking work in such matters as the Restatement, Second, of Property (Donative Transfers) and International Aspects of United States Income Taxation; however, the thought that a small collection of judges, professors, and practitioners is better able to reflect the moral consensus of our entire society than are elected legislatures boggles the mind. To have a court listen to the Institute in preference to the legislature is, by constitutional legerdemain, to make the ALI the legislature.

Other theorists are extreme. Parker finds our present democracy in a state of "corruption," which is warrant enough for courts to remake it.[29] Perry is willing to entertain the idea that judicial governance is better than democratic governance.[30] Brest simply asserts criteria which courts should impose.[31] Brest's position is, in a real sense, the most extreme, being no more than an assertion of will. It is not, in any sense of the words, a "constitutional theory"; indeed, he denies the possibility of any theory. The position is instead both anti-democratic and anti-constitutional, and one need spend no time worrying over its legitimacy or intellectual coherence because it pretends to neither.

---

28. Wellington, *supra* note 7, 311.
29. Parker, *supra* note 11, 259.
30. See M. Perry, *supra* note 21.
31. Brest, *supra* note 12, 1108–09.

A change related to these principles, is that constitutional scholarship has become much more explicitly ideological. This is inevitable when theory becomes non-interpretive, for the theorists must argue for the imposition of new values upon the society and those values will come out of a system of philosophy which, by definition, most of us do not accept. The argument will, therefore, have a distinctive political and moral cast. Because the writer insists upon his all-encompassing philosophical system, it will appear tendentious and highly ideological.

Indeed, one of the interesting things about the modern, non-interpretive theorists is that no matter the source from which they purport to derive new rights, no matter the method of argument they pursue, they all come out at approximately the same place. Their results cluster closely about the same set of social and political values. John Hart Ely purports not to make substantive policy choices, merely to be reinforcing the process of representation, but it is notable that a court following his prescriptions would come out about where a court would come out by following Grey's natural law, Wellington's conventional morality, Dworkin's moral philosophy of our society, or the system of almost any non-interpretivist writer. There is food for thought in this conclusion.

One explanation for this remarkable similarity is that all respectable modes of constitutional theorizing lead to approximately the same place, and that place is a much more egalitarian and socially permissive position than a majority of Americans desire. If this hypothesis is correct, then certainly the American electorate is seriously deficient in its moral sense.

There is, however, an alternative hypothesis. The results of these various constitutional theories are almost entirely compatible with the political and social stance, which, as every study shows, is characteristic of the professoriate. If this correlation between constitutional theories and personal preferences has any significance, it may suggest that, probably unconsciously, many theorists have come to see courts as merely a superior route to the political ascendancy of their own views. Brest seems to adopt this analysis, saying that scholarship in this area is mostly advocacy to persuade courts to adopt the writer's notion of the public good.

It is left to the reader to decide which of these hypotheses best explains the remarkable similarity of the outcomes prescribed by professors who engage in constitutional theorizing.

Finally, consider briefly the effects that may be produced by the dominance of non-interpretive theory among professors of constitutional law. They are, after all, training the lawyers and judges of the next generation.

From this perspective, perhaps the most important shift in the style of Amercian constitutional theory is the change in what the theorists regard as the legitimate underpinning for constitutional liberties. For Story, Kent, Cooley, and Thayer, the source was the intent of the framers and ratifiers, and that was to be discerned from text, history, structure, and precedent. What is important about the non-interpretivists is not that they added moral philosophy but that moral philosophy displaces such traditional sources as text and history and renders them unimportant. That is necessarily the case despite occasional protestations that it is not. Interpreting the Constitution locates certain values that are to be protected and sets limits to the range of circumstance over which those values will be enforced by a court. Moreover, interpretation shows that other values do not have constitutional protection. It is important to the value-creating or non-interpretive theorists, however, to establish the legitimacy of a drastic expansion of a limited value or the creation of a right protecting a value that the framers ignored or intended to leave to the political process. That can only be done if moral philosophy trumps text, history, structure, and precedent. The latter becomes unnecessary to constitutional liberties. Soon, the theorist begins to speak less and less of them, and abstract moral argument comes to be the foundation of constitutional liberties.

It is no small matter to discredit the traditional foundations upon which our constitutional liberties have always rested. Should those liberties come under attack, they would then be sustained only by rather abstract moral philosophy. We have seen how easily abstract reasoning can turn and produce tyranny in the name of the rights of man. Liberties have proved most stable and enduring when they rested on history and long custom and when the area of absolute freedom grew by consensus rather than diktat.

The institutions and traditions of the American republic, including the historic Constitution, are our best chance for happiness and safety. Yet it is precisely these institutions and traditions that are weakened and placed in jeopardy by the habit of abstract philosophizing about the rights of man or the just society. Our institutions and traditions were built by and for real human beings. They incorporate and perpetuate compromises and inconsistencies. They slow change, tame it, deflect and modify principles as well as popular simplicities. In doing that, they provide safety and the mechanism for a morality of process. It follows that real institutions can never be as pure as abstract philosophers demand, and the philosophers' abstractions must always teach a lesson in derogation of our institutions for that reason. This is a dangerous lesson to teach the future lawyers and judges of our republic.

It is at least worth considering that Justice Storey may have had hold of a profound truth when he said that "[u]pon subjects of government . . . metaphysical refinements are out of place. A constitution . . . is addressed to the common sense of the people; and never was designed for trials of logical skill, or visionary speculation."[32]

---

32. J. Storey, *supra* note 3, viii.

ADVERSARY JURISPRUDENCE

The prophecies of what the courts will do in fact, and nothing more pretentious, are what I mean by law.

—Oliver Wendell Holmes

Every law or rule of conduct must, whether its author perceives the fact or not, lay down or rest upon some general principle, and must therefore, if it succeeds in attaining its end, commend the principle to public attention and imitation and thus affect legislative opinion.

—A. V. Dicey

The nightmare of the American intellectual is that the control of public policy should fall into the hands of the American people. . . . [P]olicymaking by the justices of the Supreme Court, intellectuals all, in the name of the Constitution, is the only way in which this can be prevented.

—Lino Graglia

Until recently, the name of Charles Pickering was hardly a household word. That changed the moment President Bush nominated the obscure federal trial judge for a seat on a court of appeals. Overnight, Judge Pickering became the latest casualty of the cultural wars. If there was no compelling reason that Pickering should have been elevated to an appeals court, there was certainly no good reason why he should not have been. Candidates no better qualified have in the past been routinely confirmed by the Senate. He was not. Instead, in a scenario that has become depressingly familiar, he was vilified by the media and anti-Bush partisans. His candidacy was scuffled by a party-line vote in the Judiciary Committee, which denied him consideration by the full Senate where he probably would have been confirmed.

What was surprising about the unfortunate Pickering's travails was the brutality of the campaign against him. We have, alas, become accustomed to such battles over Supreme Court nominees. Until now, however, such

From *The New Criterion*, May 2002

battles had not extended to nominations to the lower courts. The immediate explanation, of course, was that the Democratic Party and its allies—People for the American Way, NOW, NARAL, and other left-wing groups—immolated Pickering to warn George Bush that they had the votes in the Committee to defeat any Supreme Court nominees who bore the slightest resemblance to Justices Antonin Scalia and Clarence Thomas.

The political struggle for control of the courts has become open and savage precisely because it is a major part of the war in our culture, a battle for dominance between opposed moral visions of our future. In that battle, Supreme Court Justices are the major prize, but appeals court nominees are also important because those courts are final for all but the tiny sliver of cases accepted by the Supreme Court for review.

The outcome of the struggle for control of the courts will determine the future of the rule of law and hence the prospects for the survival of traditional American culture. The culture war has been best described by James Davison Hunter, who first adapted the term to the American context. On one side are traditionalists who accord a presumption of legitimacy and worth to longstanding sources of cultural authority, sources whose strength is eroded or whose continued existence is brought into doubt by the clamor for liberation of the individual. On the other side are the emancipationists, who are highly critical of constituted authorities and institutions and wish to liberate the individual will from such restraints. That is a process that must have limits if a coherent culture is to survive. Our courts, however, continually test and frequently transgress those limits. The disagreement is not merely philosophical; it is intensely political and generates furious passions. It may be roughly summarized as a battle between the ethos of the student radicals of the Sixties and that of adherence to bourgeois virtues.

The emancipationist party is led by—in fact it almost entirely consists of—intellectuals, a group that, as Friedrich Hayek noted, "has long been characterized by disillusionment with [the West's] principles, disparagement of its achievements, and exclusive concern with the creation of 'better worlds.'" This destructive utopianism was not too serious as long as intellectuals were an ineffective minority, but they increased in size and influence after World War II, and in the Sixties their values came to predominate.

We are accustomed to manifestations of the liberationist impulse in the institutions controlled by intellectuals: the press (print and electronic), universities, Hollywood, mainline churches, foundations, and other "elite" institutions that engage in shaping or trying to shape our attitudes. Most people, however, do not think of the judiciary—insofar as they think about the judiciary at all—in the same way. They should. Television and motion pictures powerfully influence the direction of our culture but they do not claim to speak with the authority of the Constitution, nor do they possess the judges' power to coerce. In truth, television and motion pictures would not have the unfortunate cultural impact they do if courts had not broken the restraints of enacted law. Behavior and language are now routine that not long ago would have met not only with social disapproval but also with legal sanctions. No doubt public attitudes were changing in any event, but they could not have moved so far and so fast if the courts had not weakened moral curbs and made legal restraint impossible.

As many thinkers have noted, the Enlightenment has had a dark as well as a cheerful legacy. If it bequeathed us greater freedom, it also brought with it an attenuated sense of tradition and weaker attachments to communal, familial, and religious values. Although these disruptions accelerated in the Sixties, their real beginning was the growing view that what one did with one's life was almost entirely a matter of personal choice, owing little to the wishes of family, religion, or community. Today, this disintegration of the culture, and hence of the society, goes by the apparently respectable name of libertarianism, a catchword rather than a philosophy, and one with very unhappy consequences.

To say that this is a general cultural movement that we do not know how to stop or reverse is not to absolve activist courts from their responsibility in causing the damage we see about us. The courts, and especially the Supreme Court, have led the way to cultural dissolution by breaking down the legal barriers that restrain radical individualism. And, in destroying those barriers, an enterprise wicked enough in itself, the Court has also fostered the immoral attitude that the individual will must be completely emancipated, no matter what the cost. The judiciary has in large measure become the enemy of traditional culture. This enterprise of the law deserves the title of adversary jurisprudence.

The political manifestation of the culture war was the 1972 takeover of the Democratic Party by the McGovernites. To put the matter crudely, but by no means inaccurately, since that time the Democratic Party has come to represent the values of the Sixties, while the Republican Party, insofar as it has a pulse, tends to a traditionalist stance on social issues. If it seems odd to refer to politicians as intellectuals, it must be remembered that the term does not signify any particular skill at intellectual work. Ted Turner, Cornel West, and Barbra Streisand qualify; you get the idea. The intelligentsia are influential beyond their numbers because they control the institutions that shape attitudes, ration information, and offer prestige and comfortable lives to the young they recruit. *The New York Times*, Harvard Law School, the Ford Foundation, and NBC's nightly news are a few of many examples.

The performance of the Supreme Court over the past half century follows the agenda of the intelligentsia. The Court majority's spirit is activist and emancipationist: it liberates the individual will in constitutional issues of speech, religion, abortion, sexuality, welfare, public education, and much else. This is what liberalism has become in our time. Judicial activism, a term of abuse flung about freely without much thought, properly refers to the practice of some judges of enunciating principles and reaching conclusions that cannot plausibly be derived from the Constitution they purport to be interpreting. Activism consists in the assumption by the judiciary of powers not entrusted to it by the document which alone justifies its authority. The results are twofold: the erosion of democracy and the movement of the culture in a left-liberal direction. If the text, history, and structure of the Constitution no longer guide and confine the judge, he has nowhere to look but to his own ideas of justice, and these are likely to be formed by the assumptions of the intellectualized elites he has known for most of his life and whose approval he very much wants. When the judge's views are claimed, however implausibly, to be based on the Constitution, the legislators and the public are helpless. For better or for worse, on crucial issues, an activist Court, not the Constitution, leads and shapes the culture.

At the apex of all our courts, federal and state, sits the Supreme Court of the United States. Its rulings are not merely final but are highly visible and influential statements of the principles our most fundamental document is said, not always credibly, to enshrine for our governance and contemplation. Though these principles are the same as those on the intellectual class agenda, it must be said that there is more diversity of opinion on the Court than there is in the faculty lounges of the law schools. That fact makes the liberal Left anxious and determined to control every new appointment. So far they have been successful. No matter how many Justices are appointed by Republican presidents, the works of the Warren Court and the victories of the ACLU are not reversed.

The small sampling of cases that can be discussed here nevertheless constitutes a cornucopia of judicial activism: no court could arrive at such results by reasoning from the text, history, or structure of the Constitution. Here, as elsewhere in our national life, attitude trumps reason.

The First Amendment to the United States Constitution is a major focal point of the culture war.

Consider freedom of speech. The First Amendment to the Constitution, dealing with speech and religion, is central to America's understanding of itself and its freedoms. The first words of the Amendment are: "Congress shall make no law respecting an establishment of religion, or prohibiting the free exercise thereof; or abridging the freedom of speech, or of the press."

The Court has since extended these prohibitions from Congress to all federal, state, and local governments. But that is of secondary importance to the explosive expansion it has given the words "speech" and "establishment." It is indicative both of the Court's radically altered importance in cultural matters and of the late rise of the intellectual class that neither the Speech Clause nor the Establishment Clause, adopted in 1791, occasioned Supreme Court review of official acts until well into the twentieth century.

American law concerning freedom of speech, and perhaps much wider areas of constitutional law, has been deformed by the almost irrebuttable presumption of unswerving rationality and freedom of individual choice embodied in Justice Oliver Wendell Holmes's foolish and dangerous metaphor of the marketplace of ideas. That notion made its debut in 1919 in Holmes's much-lauded dissent in *Abrams* v. *United States*. The Court majority upheld the convictions under the Espionage Act of Russian immigrants, self-proclaimed "revolutionists" who distributed circulars in New York City advocating a general strike and urging that workers stop producing ammunition to be used against the revolutionaries in Russia. The theory of the prosecution was that the strike, though not so intended, would harm the war effort against Germany. Holmes would have set aside the convictions on statutory grounds, which would have been entirely proper, but he went on to introduce into the First Amendment an unfortunate assumption:

> [W]hen men have realized that time has upset many fighting faiths, they may come to believe even more than they believe the very foundations of their own conduct that the ultimate good desired is better reached by free trade in ideas—that the test of truth is the power of thought to get itself accepted in the competition of the market.

Holmes certainly knew that horrible ideas are often accepted in the market. The market for ideas has few of the self-correcting features of the market for goods and services. When he wrote, Holmes of course knew nothing of Soviet Communism or German Naziism, but his own experience in the Civil War demonstrated that when ideas differ sharply enough, the truth of one or the other is not settled in the competition of the market but in the slaughter of the battlefield. Nevertheless, the compelling quality of his prose and the attractiveness to intellectuals of the supposed ultimate supremacy of good ideas has served, down to our own day, to make his absurd notion dominant in First Amendment jurisprudence and, more remotely, in other fields of constitutional law.

The metaphor of the marketplace not only assumes the goodwill and rationality of most men who have to choose among the ideas offered, but also, by the nature of a market, the choices, desires, and gratifications of the individual are of first importance. Given that assumption, it is an easy step to the thought that no idea should be kept from the market. Individualism is placed above the welfare of the community, a theme that runs throughout constitutional law.

But Holmes, joined again by Brandeis, elevated that thought to incoherence. *Gitlow* v. *New York* (1925) upheld a conviction under a criminal anarchy statute for publishing a call for the violent overthrow of the government. "If in the long run [Holmes wrote in dissent] the beliefs expressed in proletarian dictatorship are destined to be accepted by the dominant forces of the community, the only meaning of free speech is that they should be given their chance and have their way." This in a case where the defendant urged violent action by a minority to institute a dictatorship that would put a stop to free speech? What happened to the marketplace of ideas? Why, on Holmes's reasoning, were the dominant forces of the community that enacted the criminal anarchy law not allowed to have their way? That they should, on his reasoning, must be the only meaning of free speech. There is an alarming frivolity in these dissents. "If in the long run the belief, let us say, in genocide is destined to be accepted by the dominant forces of the community, the only meaning of free speech is that it should be given its chance and have its way. Do we believe that?" Alexander Bickel asked. "Do we accept it?" Funny little mustached men wearing raincoats stand on street corners preaching obviously crackpot notions that may one day become the policy of a nation. "Where nothing is unspeakable, nothing is undoable."

The themes of the Holmes-Brandeis dissents were ready at hand for adoption by the intellectualized post-World War II Court. After some wavering, the essence of those dissents became the law in *Brandenberg* v. *Ohio* (1969). The Court there reversed the conviction under the Ohio Criminal Syndicalism statute of a Ku Klux Klan leader who made a speech threatening to blacks and Jews, ruling that "the constitutional guarantees of free speech and free press do not permit a state to forbid or proscribe advocacy of the use of force or of law violation except where such advocacy is directed to inciting or producing imminent lawless action and is likely to produce such action." To wait until violence is imminent, of course, is likely to wait too long to prevent it.

What benefits can such speech have in a country committed to representative democracy? The ideas involved, if such expostulations can be called ideas, could be offered in Holmes's marketplace uncoupled from calls to violence. A nation that fears only violence but is otherwise indifferent to fundamental republican principles, as the *Abrams* and *Gitlow* dissents and *Brandenberg* would have it, is unlikely to show persistent determination in defending its culture.

Individualistic relativism appears even more clearly in cases dealing with vulgarity, pornography, and obscenity. The prime example is *Cohen* v. *California* (1971) which overturned a conviction for disorderly conduct of a man who entered a courthouse wearing a jacket bearing the words "F . . . the Draft" (without the ellipsis). The majority opinion by Justice Powell asked "How is one to distinguish this from any other offensive word?" and answered that no distinction could be made since "one man's vulgarity is another's lyric." The Court would never dream of saying that one man's armed robbery is another's redistribution of wealth in pursuit of social justice. (Although, come to think of it, the Warren Court's solicitude for criminals may have come close to that.)

Cohen was just the beginning. The following year the Court decided *Rosenfeld* v. *New Jersey*, *Lewis* v. *New Orleans*, and *Brown* v. *Oklahoma*. Rosenfeld addressed a school board meeting of about 150 people, including about forty children, and on four occasions used the adjective "motherf . . . ing" to describe the teachers, the school board, the town, and the United States. Lewis shouted the same epithet at police officers who were arresting her son. Brown used the same language in a meeting in a university chapel. None of the convictions—for disorderly conduct, breach of the peace, and use of obscene language in a public place—was allowed to stand. The relativism of these decisions seems to reflect a loss of will to maintain conventional standards. The Court refused to allow punishment for the same obscene and assaultive speech that was tolerated by supine university faculties and administrators in the late 1960s and early 1970s. When the faculties collapsed, the universities were corrupted; when the Supreme Court gave way, the national culture was defiled. Now, of course, such language is routine on television and in motion pictures.

Pervasive vulgarity was guaranteed by *Miller* v. *California* (1973) which laid down the conditions under which a state could regulate obscenity. That test is a maze whose center cannot be reached. The most damaging condition is that the work, taken as a whole, must lack serious literary, artistic, political, or scientific value. How can a jury find that *anything* lacks serious artistic value when museums, our cultural authorities on what is art, exhibit Robert Mapplethorpe's photograph of one man urinating in the mouth of another, a picture of the Virgin Mary spattered with dung, and jars of excrement as works of art? There will, in any event, always be a gaggle of professors eager to testify that the most blatant pornography is actually a profound parable about the horrors of capitalism or the oppressiveness of bourgeois culture.

The themes the Court had been developing reached a crescendo of sorts in *United States* v. *Playboy Entertainment Group, Inc.* (2000). The decision held unconstitutional a congressional statute that required cable television channels "primarily dedicated to sexually-oriented programming" to limit their transmission to hours when children are unlikely to be viewing. The Court majority found the law a restriction on the content of speech that was not justified because there appeared to be less restrictive methods of protecting children.

The Justices, equating sex and speech, said, "Basic speech principles are at stake in this case." That is a peculiar view of fundamentals since Playboy advertised, as Justice Scalia pointed out in dissent, that its channel depicted such things as "female masturbation/external," "girl/girl sex" and "oral sex/cunnilingus." Most of the speech in such entertainment probably consisted of simulated moans of ecstasy which the females are required to utter in order to excite viewers.

The legislation and the Court both focused on the danger that children would be exposed to erotic sounds or pictures. The Court's discussion centered upon the pleasures of adults. No weight was given to the interest of society in preserving some vestige of a moral tone. "Where the designed benefit of a content-based speech restriction is to shield the sensibilities of listeners, the general rule is that the right of expression prevails, even where no less restrictive alternative exists. We are expected to protect our own sensibilities 'simply by averting [our] eyes.'" Many of the people around us will not avert their eyes, and that fact will certainly produce a moral and aesthetic environment which it is impossible to ignore. We are forced to live in an increasingly ugly society.

Indeed, the Court majority refuted its own avert-your-eyes solution when it said: "It is through speech that our convictions and beliefs are influenced, expressed, and tested. It is through speech that we bring those beliefs to bear on Government and society. It is through speech that our personalities are formed and expressed." Try substituting "consuming pornography" or "watching female masturbation/external" for the word "speech" in that passage and see how persuasive it remains.

Apparently aware that this line of cases has been criticized, the majority opinion essays a rebuttal:

> When a student first encounters our free speech jurisprudence, he or she might think it is influenced by the philosophy that one idea is as good as any other, and that in art and literature objective standards of style, taste, decorum, beauty, and esthetics are deemed by the Constitution to be inappropriate, indeed unattainable. Quite the opposite is true. The Constitution no more enforces a relativistic philosophy or moral nihilism than it does any other point of view. The Constitution exists precisely so that opinions and judgments, including esthetic and moral judgments about art and literature, can be formed, tested, and expressed. What the Constitution says is that these judgments are for the individual to make, not for the Government to decree, even with the mandate or approval of a majority.

In a word, what the Constitution says, as interpreted by today's Court, is that one idea *is* as good as another so far as the law is concerned; only the omnipotent individual may judge. A majority may not enact its belief, apparently self-evidently wrong-headed, that the production and consumption of obscenity and pornography work social harms. That is a relativistic philosophy or moral nihilism, if anything is. And it is not the Constitution's philosophy; it is the Court's.

It is not too much to say that the suffocating vulgarity of popular culture is in large measure the work of the Court. The Court did not create vulgarity, but it defeated attempts of communities to contain and minimize vulgarity. Base instincts are always present in humans, but better instincts attempt, through law as well as moral disapproval, to suppress pornography, obscenity, and vulgarity. When the law is declared unfit to survive, not only are base instincts freed, they are also validated.

The triumph of the individual over the community advanced in a new direction in *Texas* v. *Johnson* (1989), a five-to-four decision invalidating federal law and the laws of forty-eight states prohibiting the physical desecration or defilement of the American flag. While chanting insults to the United States, Johnson burned the flag in public to show contempt for this country. He was not prosecuted for his words but only for the burning. Equating an expressive *act* with speech, itself an extremely dubious proposition, Justice Brennan said the government could not prohibit the expression of an idea on the grounds of offensiveness. Unifying symbols are essential to an increasingly divided community, but the strain of individualism in its precedents left the Court majority unable to accept that fact.

The perversion of the First Amendment took the opposite tack when legislative majorities cut at the heart of the Speech Clause by diminishing and biasing political speech.

Buckley v. Valeo (1976) upheld portions of the Federal Election Campaign Act that severely limited individual contributions to political campaigns on the theory that large contributions may lead to the corruption of politics or may create a public impression of corruption. Had limits so severe then been in effect they would have made impossible Eugene McCarthy's primary challenge that led Lyndon Johnson not to run for re-election. Yet freedom of political speech is conceded to lie at the core of the Speech Clause.

Any hope that Buckley was an aberration that the appointment of new justices would cure was dashed by Nixon v. Shrink Missouri Government PAC (2000). Missouri law set limits on campaign contributions for state elections that were considerably more severe than the limits set by the federal law. The Court once more held that corruption or the possible appearance of corruption was an adequate ground to regulate contributions. Justice Stevens concurred, insisting on "one simple point. Money is property; it is not speech." A soapbox is also property, not speech, but the speech of an orator in Hyde Park would be much less effective without it. Television equipment, paid for by contributions, is also property, but speech could not reach a mass audience without it. Justice Breyers concurrence, while conceding that money enables speech, argued that limiting the size of the largest contributions serves "to democratize the influence that money itself may bring to bear upon the electoral process." Real democratization would justify restrictions upon media commentary that is obviously one-sided in support of liberal candidates and policies. Had the speech been pornographic it would have gained greater protection. Those, including the President, who are counting on the Supreme Court to rescue the political process from the excesses of the new campaign finance law may be unpleasantly surprised.

The Court's deformation of the Speech Clause is outdone by its treatment of religion. Tocqueville saw that religion should be "considered as the first of [the Americans'] political institutions; for if it does not give them the taste for freedom, it singularly facilitates their use of it" because it "prevents them from conceiving everything and forbids them to dare everything." That was then. Now the restraints for which Tocqueville praised religion are seen as intolerable limitations on the individual will. The power of religion to prevent and forbid is greatly attenuated and no little part of that decline is due to the Supreme Court's endorsement of intellectual class secularism. This decline, in turn, bears directly upon the Court's interpretation of the freedom of speech, since in that area there is no longer much that cannot be conceived and dared.

The Establishment Clause has spawned a welter of cases, but it is necessary to examine only a few to see the themes that run through them. *Engel* v. *Vitale* (1962) was the first case dealing with a nondenominational prayer initiated by New York school officials. Officially sanctioned prayer had long been a feature of public schooling, but now the Court, perceiving a forbidden establishment of religion, started down a path leading to the official equality of religion and irreligion. In truth, irreligion seems the preferred constitutional value. A year later, *Abington School District* v. *Schempp* (1963) invalidated a Pennsylvania law requiring that the school day begin with a reading of verses from the Bible and student recitation of the Lord's Prayer. Although any student could be excused upon the written request of his parent, the Court said "the breach of [constitutional] neutrality that is today a trickling stream may all too soon become a raging torrent." That was extravagant hyperbole. In all of American constitutional history, the trickling stream has never achieved the status of even a sluggish creek.

The Court said the state must maintain neutrality by "neither aiding nor opposing religion." The long-standing policy, dating back to George Washington's presidency and the first Congress, that the state should favor religion in general was ignored. Faith and atheism may seem now to stand on equal footing, but only faith is barred from official recognition. That may be appealing to many moderns, but it certainly was not the view of those who wrote, the Congress that proposed, and the states that ratified the First Amendment.

So drastic has the antagonism to religion become that *Wallace* v. *Jaffree* (1985) struck down an Alabama statute permitting one minute of silent prayer or meditation in public schools. No one would know whether a student was praying, meditating, or daydreaming. The difficulty, according to Justice Stevens, was that by adding the option of silent prayer, the state characterized prayer as a favored practice.

The Court's treatment of religion became even more draconian in *Lee* v. *Weisman* (1992) which held unconstitutional a rabbi's recitation of a nonsectarian prayer at a middle-school graduation ceremony. Justice Souter disparaged evidence that after adoption of the First Amendment the founding generation encouraged public support for religion, saying that such acts "prove only that public officials, no matter when they serve, can turn a blind eye to constitutional principle." That is an extraordinary dismissal of the evidence that the same Congress that proposed the no-establishment principle also hired chaplains for both Houses and the armed forces, and successfully called upon presidents to declare national days of thanksgiving to God. History is in fact quite clear that the founding generation thought the state could and should encourage religion. The prayer was harmful to plaintiff Deborah Weisman, the Court said, because public or peer pressure might cause her to stand or at least maintain a respectful silence during its reading. She could constitutionally be required to stand or remain silent during the reading of any other material—the *Communist Manifesto*, say, or Darwinian theory—so long as it had no hint of religious content. But then such philosophical trickles which have upon occasion become raging torrents are not religious, at least not in the conventional sense.

One of the most extreme examples of anti-religious animus was presented by *Board of Education of Kiryas Joel Village School District* v. *Grumet* (1994). The Satmar Hasidim, who practiced a strict form of Judaism, established a village that excluded all but Satmars. Their children were educated in private religious schools. Federal law entitled handicapped children "the deaf, mentally retarded, and those suffering from various physical, mental, or emotional disorders" to special education services, but a Supreme Court ruling forced them to attend public schools outside the village. Their parents withdrew the children because of "the panic, fear, and trauma [the children] suffered in leaving their own community and being with people whose ways were so different." The State of New York responded by constituting the village a separate school district to enable it to provide for itself the special services needed.

The Supreme Court, however, in an opinion by Justice Souter, found this to be a forbidden establishment of religion. Justice Stevens, joined by Blackmun and Kennedy, concurred, offering the advice that "the State could have taken steps to alleviate the children's fear by teaching their schoolmates to be tolerant and respectful of Satmar customs." Teaching grade schoolers to be tolerant and respectful of handicapped, strangely dressed classmates who spoke Yiddish and practiced what the classmates would see as a weird religion would be a Sisyphean task at best. The Justices must have forgotten how cruel children can be to those they regard as even mildly eccentric.

"The isolation of these children," the concurrence went on to say, "while it may protect them from 'panic, fear, and trauma' also unquestionably increased the likelihood that they would remain within the fold, faithful adherents of their parents' religious faith." Why families' freedom to raise their children as they think best should be suspect and what relevance the observation had to the Establishment Clause went unexplained. The concurrence spoke for social atomization.

Justice Scalia, in a dissent joined by Chief Justice Rehnquist and Justice Thomas, wrote that the Grand Rebbe, who brought the Satmars from Europe to escape religious persecution, would be "astounded" to learn that the sect was so powerful as to have become an "establishment" of New York State, and the Founding Fathers would be "astonished" that the Establishment Clause was used to prohibit a characteristically American accommodation of the religious practices of a tiny minority sect. "I, however," Scalia continued, "am not surprised. Once this Court has abandoned text and history as guides, nothing prevents it from calling religious toleration the establishment of religion." (Actually, once text and history are jettisoned, nothing prevents the Court from doing anything it chooses with any part of the Constitution.) Souter inadvertently conceded the point by rebuking Scalia for "his inability to accept the fact that this Court has long held that the First Amendment reaches more than classic, eighteenth-century establishments." Unfortunately for that riposte, the Establishment Clause is a product of the eighteenth century.

The same radical individualism determined the result in *Santa Fe Independent School District* v. *Doe* (2000). The school district authorized two student elections, one to decide whether invocations, messages, or statements should be delivered at home football games and a second to select a student to deliver them. The Court held the school district's policy a forbidden establishment of religion. Dislike of majority rule surfaced in Justice Stevens's opinion for the majority: "[T]his student election does nothing to protect minority views but rather places the students who hold such views at the mercy of the majority. School sponsorship of a religious message is impermissible because it sends the ancillary message to members of the audience who are nonadherents 'that they are outsiders, not full members of the political community, and an accompanying message to adherents that they are insiders, favored members of the political community.'" Religious speech must have extraordinary political power. All of us have heard actual *political* speech with which we heartily disagreed without feeling any the less members of the political community. But where religion is concerned, even imaginary discomfort to a hypothetical individual overrides the reasonable desires of the community.

There is also the issue of feminism. *United States* v. *Virginia* (1996) held 7–1 that Virginia Military Institute, which is supported by the state, could not, under the Equal Protection Clause of the Fourteenth Amendment, remain an all-male school. The school was founded in 1839. The Fourteenth Amendment, designed to protect the newly freed slaves, was not ratified until 1868. Nobody at the time suggested that the Amendment banned single-sex education. In fact, it was not until 1971, over a hundred years later, that the Court first applied the Amendment to an irrational distinction between men and women. The ratifiers would have been aghast that a military school could not be all-male.

VMI featured strict discipline, hard physical performance, and an absolute lack of privacy, something, in fact, very like Marine boot camp. The admission of women required modifications, as they have in every military college. VMI's distinctive character, it was pointed out, would be lost. The Court attached no weight to this prospect. The Court insisted on the abstract equality of men and women in all things, undeterred by the historical meaning of the Equal Protection Clause, the value of well over a century of unquestioned excellence and tradition, and most certainly not by the heretical thought that there might be some areas of life suited to masculinity that feminism should not be permitted to destroy. Masculinity is a highly suspect idea in today's elite culture and it cannot, therefore, be expected to find lodgement in the Supreme Court's version of constitutional law.

There is no limit to what the Court can do with the Equal Protection Clause. As Justice Scalia said in dissent, the "current equal-protection jurisprudence . . . regards this Court as free to evaluate everything under the sun." That is exactly right. Every law makes a distinction between lawful and unlawful behavior. Every law, therefore, produces inequality because some conduct is allowed while other conduct is forbidden. The Court's equal protection jurisprudence thus allows scrutiny of all law to see if it meets the Justices' views of appropriate policy.

It might appear that the Court's theme of equality is contrary to the theme of emancipated individualism, but that is a misunderstanding. Equality denies the right of the majority to impose standards that require some individuals to desist from activities they enjoy. When the clause is applied to erase such distinctions, the individual is liberated, even if we think he ought not to be. Emancipation of the will is then quite selective. One is reminded of the folks who deny the existence of any objective truth or moral standard even while fiercely imposing their truths on others. They are not in fact nihilists, since they clearly believe in something, even if it is only the protection of their own prerogatives. Equality can be a means of breaking down traditional authority so that a new morality may be imposed. Though equal rights authoritarians demand non-judgmentalism, they are very judgmental about traditionalists who oppose them. The emancipation of the individual will turns out to be about power.

The intelligentsia are not through with VMI. The college has a tradition of a "brief, nonsectarian, inclusive blessing" before the evening meal. The ACLU persuaded a district court to prohibit even that. VMI's superintendent said, no doubt pensively, "Hearing a brief prayer before supper is no more the establishment of religion than the singing of 'God Bless America.'" True, but he shouldn't have given the ACLU any ideas for an additional lawsuit.

The Court's intervention has also been disruptive in the matter of sexuality. Much of the Court's activism is concerned with sexuality as the abortion cases *Roe* v. *Wade* (1973), *Planned Parenthood* v. *Casey* (1992), and *Stenberg* v. *Carhart* (2000) make clear. The chosen instrument in these cases was the Due Process Clause of the Fourteenth Amendment, which requires that no one be deprived of life, liberty, or property without due process of law. The language obviously requires only fair procedures in the application of substantive law. But in *Dred Scott* v. *Sanford*, a 1857 decision, Chief Justice Roger Taney transformed the identical Due Process Clause of the Fifth Amendment to require that statutes have substantive meanings which judges approve. He and a majority of the Court did not approve of a federal statute which, quite arguably, would have freed a slave taken by his owner to territory where slavery was forbidden. Taney wrote that depriving a man of his property, regardless of procedural regularity, could hardly be called due process. "Substantive due process," an oxymoron, was born.

Regardless of the shame in which it was conceived, and its internal contradiction, substantive due process has proved too valuable for judicial activism to be given up. In 1965, *Griswold* v. *Connecticut* gave birth to the Court-invented and undefined "right of privacy" which in turn spawned *Roe* v. *Wade*, a case which, without even a pretense of legal reasoning, announced a right to abortion. In an opinion of just over fifty-one pages, Justice Harry Blackmun surveyed such subjects as the view of abortion taken in the Persian Empire, the English common law, and by the American Medical Association, before announcing without further ado that the right of privacy was "broad enough" to cover a right to abortion. In *Planned Parenthood* v. *Casey*, the concurring opinion of three Justices, which created a majority to sustain a somewhat modified right to abortion, fashioned a right to "personal dignity and autonomy": "At the heart of liberty"—runs the by-now famous "mystery passage"—"is the right to define one's own concept of existence, of meaning, of the universe, and of the mystery of human life." Though the liberty to be protected is left entirely unclear by this fog-bound rhetoric, the mood is certainly one of radical individualism. The three-justice opinion simply refuses to explain what it is talking about, just as *Roe* v. *Wade* did almost twenty years earlier.

Worse was to come. In *Stenberg* v. *Carhart*, the Court struck down a Nebraska statute banning partial birth abortions, a procedure in which a live baby is almost entirely removed from the mother, its skull pierced and its brain vacuumed out, before the carcass is taken from the birth canal. The procedure is morally indistinguishable from infanticide, but the Court majority held that an exception for cases in which the mother's life was otherwise endangered was not sufficient; there must be an exception to preserve the mother's health. Though it is never true that the mother's health would be adversely affected unless a partial birth abortion were performed, the ruling means that such abortions cannot be banned at all. There will always be an abortionist willing to certify that the procedure is essential to health.

In view of the territory the Court has claimed, it is worth examining the title deed composed in the *Griswold* decision. At issue was an ancient and unenforced statute prohibiting the use of contraceptives. Justice William O. Douglas reasoned that various provisions of the Bill of Rights protected aspects of privacy. That being so, the emanations from such rights formed a penumbra from which a larger, unmentioned right of privacy could be deduced. That reasoning assumes that the framers and ratifiers of the Bill of Rights had a sense that there was a more encompassing right which they were unable to articulate and so had to settle for a list of specific guarantees. In this view, the Court must finish the drafting by discerning a meaning the founders could not. The word "hubris" comes to mind. Bogus as it was, Douglas's sleight of hand seemed harmless, but it became the rhetorical cover for the far more serious decisions that followed. It is on that bastardized version of constitutional reasoning that the entire edifice of so-called "reproductive rights" rests.

The radical individualism of the abortion cases has offshoots. In *Eisenstadt* v. *Baird* (1972), the Court moved beyond the rationale of *Griswold*, which purported to rest upon the marriage relationship, to decide that the same rationale must apply to the distribution of contraceptives to unmarried people. Justice William Brennan announced that "If the right of privacy means anything, it is the right of the *individual*, married or single, to be free from unwarranted governmental intrusion into matters so fundamentally affecting a person as the decision whether to bear or beget a child."

It would be quibbling to point out that the right of privacy does not, in fact, mean anything, except what a majority of the Court wants it to mean on any given day. There was, of course, no explanation why the law in question was an "unwarranted" intrusion. The point to notice is that, once more, individualism triumphed over majority morality.

The Court's concern with sexuality has taken it into the subject of homosexual behavior. Justice Harry Blackmun's dissenting opinion in *Bowers* v. *Hardwick* (1986) is perhaps the leading example of judicial insistence upon an individualism so unconfined as to be useless for any practical purpose other than rhetorical bludgeoning. The majority upheld the constitutionality of making homosexual sodomy a criminal offense. Blackmun's dissent dismissed the relevance of prior cases that seemed to confine the claimed "right of privacy" to the protection of the family: "We protect those rights not because they contribute, in some direct and material way, to the general public welfare, but because they form so central a part of an individual's life." This casual dismissal of the family, heretofore considered the most important unit of society, was in keeping with the modern attitudes of the intellectual class. On Blackmun's reasoning, since the individual is all, no-fault divorce must be a constitutional right. But he immediately went on to make matters worse: "[T]he concept of privacy embodies 'the moral fact that a person belongs to himself and not others nor to society as a whole.'" In short, the individual owes nothing to family, neighborhood, friends, nation, or anything outside his own skin, if that would interfere with his own pleasures. The four justices who signed the dissent cannot really have meant that, of course, but the fact that it could be written at all shows how far committed to individualism some of the justices have become.

Romer v. *Evans* (1996) took the next step and overruled *Bowers* without mentioning that case. By referendum the citizens of Colorado amended the state constitution to prevent localities from adding sexual orientation to the list of characteristics—race, sex, etc.—that were protected from private discrimination. The Court struck down the amendment on the theory that it treated homosexuals differently from other protected groups and thus violated the Equal Protection Clause. The rationale can best be described as incoherent. In order to gain legal immunity from private discrimination, homosexuals would have to seek it at the state level while the other groups would not. The fact is, of course, that all statewide or national laws require some groups to go beyond local government in order to change those laws. The Bill of Rights itself states principles that cannot be changed except by constitutional amendment. The most that can be made of *Romer* is that homosexuality is now a subject of special judicial solicitude. Individuals must be free to engage in homosexual behavior regardless of the community's moral standards.

A number of observers predict that within a few years the Court will announce that the principle of equality requires a constitutional right to same-sex marriage. If Jane is free to marry John, why doesn't equal protection require that Fred be equally able to marry John? Two state courts, of course, have already taken that step, to the intense displeasure of their citizens.

Since the Court is a central prize in the culture war, the fight to control it is political, engaging the White House and the Senate. There is, however, an equally important arena consisting of academic lawyers and pressure groups. These are heavily on the side of the emancipationists or liberals. Their tactic is frequently to insist, contrary to obvious reality, that the Supreme Court is dominated by conservatives.

Harvard's Laurence Tribe, for example, calls the current Justices "the most activist in our history." He said that "the astonishing weakness and vulnerability of the majority opinion in *Bush* v. *Gore*, and of the majority opinions in a number of other democracy-denying decisions in whose mold it was cast, are functions in part of the uniquely narrow spectrum of views . . . covered by the membership of the current Court." It must come as a revelation to the Justices themselves to learn that Stevens and Sourer advance almost the same views as Scalia and Thomas. Tribe describes the Court's makeup as "four justices distinctly on the right, two moderate conservatives, a conservative moderate, two moderates, and no liberals." Cass Sunstein of Chicago states that today's Court has no liberals, which can only be true if he defines liberals as extreme radicals. Yale's Bruce Ackerman urges the Senate not to confirm anyone nominated by George Bush.

It is only on the misunderstanding that the proper function of judges is to advance an ideological agenda that Abner Mikva, once a judge on the court on which I sat and later counsel to President Clinton, can urge the Senate not to confirm any Bush nominees to the Court because that might disturb the "delicate balance on the court on fundamental issues." That "delicate balance" means a Court that is predominantly liberal. In his next sentence, Mikva clarifies the balance he praises by noting, with obvious approval, that the Warren Court, which was heavily liberal, made fundamental changes by substantial majorities. Balance is desirable only when a Republican president might tip the Court in a neutral direction. When liberals say "balance" they mean a Court that will rewrite the Constitution to make it ever more liberal.

It is hard not to think such remarks disingenuous. The Court as a whole lists heavily to the cultural left. A "narrow spectrum of views" hardly describes a Court that though it splits on important cultural issues, almost invariably comes down on the liberal side and whose members regularly denounce one another in heated terms. Tribe himself rebuts his narrow-spectrum description by saying that "the recurring 5–4 majority on the Court on these matters has become a genuine threat to our system of government." How close votes threaten our system of government is unspecified. That Tribe is committed to the judicial activism he decries is demonstrated by his four (at last count) attempts to find an acceptable rationale for *Roe* v. *Wade*. The problem is not that he fails—success is impossible—but that he will not stop trying. Abortion must be a constitutional right even if no one can explain why.

The interest groups of the Left proceed by systematic lying about judicial nominees who adopt the traditional approach of interpreting the Constitution according to its actual meaning. In opposing Judge Pickering, Ralph Neas of the hard-left People for the American Way said, "Achieving ideological domination of the federal judiciary is the top goal of right-wing activists inside and outside the Bush administration." The left wing has discovered an effective tactic of labeling any conventional jurist an ideologue with a right-wing agenda and hence "outside the mainstream."

There is far more diversity of opinion on the Court than is to be found on law school faculties. In the last three decades, as the students of the Sixties became professors, law scholarship has become increasingly left wing and intellectually disordered. Faculties are less and less engaged in scholarship that might conceivably be of use to practitioners and judges or to the reform of legal doctrine. As Harry Edwards, formerly chief judge of the Court of Appeals for the District of Columbia Circuit, put it, "there is a growing disjunction between legal education and the legal profession," which is reflected in the gradual replacement of older, traditional scholars by younger faculty whose work is often so theoretical as to be of little use outside the coterie of like-minded professors who engage in impractical discourse. The division, Edwards says, "is permeated by rancor, contempt and ill will." The newer scholarship is politically motivated: "Many, although not all, of the legal theorists would like to bring about a radical transformation of society. In many cases, their work amounts to an attack on classical liberalism, which they would like to see replaced with a philosophical or political theory that will lead to a much more egalitarian society."

Professor Edgar Hahn, a professor of jurisprudence at Case Western Reserve University, reports, "Reading hundreds of articles in researching a book on legal scholarship confirms that politically correct writing appears with increasing frequency." In the university community, he writes, political correctness "is associated with language modification, oppression studies, race and gender victimization, rejection of the white male canon," which it sees as a culture of "objectivity and rationality." This began with the critical legal studies movement which attempted to deconstruct the intellectual foundations of existing law and traditional legal scholarship, without, however, indicating what might be substituted. A liberal professor states that "critical legal studies is a political location for a group of people on the Left who share the project of supporting and extending the domain of the Left in the legal academy." Hahn says that the advocates of political correctness now come from "Critical Race theorists, composed of Blacks and females, feminists, plus the remnants of the Critical Legal Studies movement." Hahn continues: "One of the more esteemed techniques is the use of personal experiences to convey the emotion and agony of persevering in an alien environment of patriarchy, hierarchy, and objectification." Thus some work of "scholars" consists of storytelling. Their narratives are published in law reviews and have been sufficient for the award of tenure. This intellectual collapse is now praised as "postmodern jurisprudence" a term which itself ought to be an embarrassment to the legal academics involved.

There have emerged almost innumerable competing theories of how the Constitution should be "interpreted." None of these has proved satisfactory to the competing theorists so that now we have reached a state of advanced nihilism in which articles and books are written on the impossibility of all normative theories of constitutional law or the "misguided quest for constitutional foundations." Were these counsels of despair accurate, the only honest conclusion would be that since they cannot make sense of what they are doing, judges should abandon judicial review altogether. That conclusion is never drawn, however. Constitutional law is about power, and professors will never relinquish their bit of that power.

If the legal academy is hopeless, one might suppose that at least some Justices would by now have undertaken a justification for their habitual departures from any conceivable meaning of the Constitution they claim as their authority. But search as one may, the opinions of the Court are utterly devoid of any such attempt. The most the Court has ever offered is the statement that it has never felt its power confined by the original understanding of the document. That much is certainly true, but it is hardly a justification. Persistent invasions of territory belonging to the people and their elected representatives cannot establish an easement across territory that the Constitution assigns to the democratic process.

It is not obvious what, if anything, can be done to bring the American judiciary back to legitimacy in a polity whose basic character is supposed to be democratic. It was once argued that a wayward Court would be corrected by professional criticism. The bar, however, is largely uninterested and academic constitutional commentary is largely intellectually corrupt.

Perhaps there is no remedy for judicial activism, perhaps a preference for immediate victories and short-term gratification of desires is characteristic of the spirit of our times. The public does seem ready to jettison long-term safeguards and the benefits of process for the short-term satisfaction of desires. That is always and everywhere the human temptation. But it is precisely that temptation that a constitution and its judicial spokesmen are supposed to protect us against. Constitutions speak for permanent values and judges are supposed to give those values voice. Instead, representatives of our judiciary are all too often, and increasingly, exemplars of disrespect for the rule of law. That situation is inconsistent with the survival of the culture that has for so long sustained American freedom and well-being. The example of lawless courts teaches a lesson of disrespect for process to all other actors in that system, the lesson that winning outside the rules is legitimate, and that political victory is the only virtue.

Born in Europe, central to the American founding, and fundamental to Western civilization, the ideal of the rule of law no longer commands much more than verbal allegiance. If prophecies of what the Court will do in fact is the meaning of law, then, in cultural matters the law may be predicted by the known personal inclinations of the Justices, nothing more pretentious. That is not the rule of law; it is the rule of judges. It would have been unthinkable until recently that so many areas of our national life would be controlled by judges. What is today unthinkable may well become not only thinkable but also actual in the next half century.

The liberal mindset refuses to recognize that real institutions can never approximate their ideal institutions. The pursuit of the ideal necessarily proceeds by and teaches an abstract, universalistic style of reasoning and legal argument. It leads to an incessant harping on rights that impoverishes political, cultural, and legal discourse. Universalistic rhetoric teaches disrespect for the actual institutions of the nation. Those institutions slow change, allow compromise, tame absolutisms, and thus embody inconsistencies that are, on balance, wholesome. They work, in short, to do things, albeit democratically and therefore messily, that abstract generalizations about the just society bring into contempt.

A Court that in one context after another lays down general principles of emancipation commends that principle to public attention and imitation and thus affects legislative opinion. Many people assume that what is legal is also moral, and they are all too likely to believe that what has been declared unconstitutional is immoral. Resistance to judicial imperialism in the name of the Constitution itself comes to be seen as immoral.

Writing last year in the *Wall Street Journal*, Charles Murray reflected on Arnold Toynbee's thesis about the decline of civilizations. One reliable sign of decline, Toynbee suggested, was when elites began to imitate those at the bottom of society. In robust societies, those at the bottom tend to imitate "their betters"—a phrase whose departure from common usage betokens the degradation Toynbee prophesied. One does not have to look far to see the vulgarization of the elites in contemporary American society. There is no more elite institution in America than the Supreme Court of the United States. The sampling of cases discussed here suggests that the Court is ahead of the general public in approving, and to a degree enforcing, the vulgarization or proletarianization of our culture.

Yet it is precisely that for which the Court is most admired by the intelligentsia and in our law schools. The names of Warren, Douglas, and Brennan are enshrined in the liberal pantheon. Justices who performed their duties more faithfully are often less well-known or even almost entirely forgotten. The career of Chief Justice Morrison Waite is a case in point. Probably not one in twenty law professors and not one in a hundred lawyers even recognizes his name. Yet Professor Felix Frankfurter, in praising Waite, identified the characteristic judicial sin: "When dealing with such large conceptions as the rights and duties of property, judges lacking some governing directions are easily lost in the fog of abstraction." That may be even more true today as the Court multiplies vaguely defined rights.

Frankfurter said that Waite has become

> a dim figure in constitutional history because his opinions are not delectable reading. . . . But the limited appeal of his opinions is due in part to something else—to the fulfillment of one of the greatest duties of a judge, the duty not to enlarge his authority. . . . The distinction between those who are makers of policy and those concerned solely with questions [of the Constitution's allocations] of ultimate power probably marks the deepest cleavage among the men who have sat on the Supreme Bench. . . . The conception of significant achievement on the Supreme Court has been too much identified with largeness of utterance, and too little governed by inquiry into the extent to which judges have fulfilled their professed role in the American constitutional system.

Unless it takes its law from the original understanding of the Constitution's principles, the Court will continue to be an adversary to democratic government and to the morality of our traditional culture.

THE CONSTITUTION, ORIGINAL INTENT, AND ECONOMIC RIGHTS

To approach the subject of economic rights it is necessary to state a general theory about how a judge should deal with cases which require interpretation of the United States Constitution. More specifically, I intend to address the question of whether a judge should consider himself or herself bound by the original intentions of those who framed, proposed, and ratified the Constitution. I think the judge is so bound. I wish to demonstrate that original intent is the only legitimate basis for constitutional decision making. Further, I intend to meet objections that have been made to that proposition.

This issue has been a topic of fierce debate in the law schools for the past thirty years. The controversy shows no sign of subsiding. To the contrary, the torrent of words is freshening. It is odd that the one group whose members rarely discuss the intellectual framework within which they decide cases is the federal judiciary. Judges, by and large, are not much attracted to theory. That is unfortunate, and hopefully it is changing. There are several reasons why it should change.

Law is an intellectual system. If it is to progress at all, it is through continual intellectual exchanges. There is no reason why members of the judiciary should not engage in such discussion. Rather, because theirs is the ultimate responsibility, there is every reason why they should engage in such discussion. The only real control the American people have over their judges is that of criticism—criticism that ought to be informed. Criticism focused not upon the congeniality of political results but upon the judges' faithfulness to their assigned role. Judges ought to make explicit how they perceive their assigned role.

We appear to be at a tipping point in the relationship of judicial power to democracy. The opposing philosophies about the role of judges are being

This article is an adaption of a speech I gave at the first Sharon Siegan Memorial Lecture at the University of San Diego School of Law on November 18, 1985; *San Diego Law Review* (1986).

articulated more clearly. Those who argue that original intention is crucial do so in order to draw a sharp line between judicial power and democratic authority. Their philosophy is called intentionalism or interpretivism. Those who would assign an ever increasing role to judges are called non-intentionalist or non-interpretivist. The future role of the American judiciary will be decided by the victory of one set of ideas over the other.

In this Article, I am not concerned with proving that any particular decision or doctrine is wrong. Rather, I am concerned with the method of reasoning by which constitutional argument should proceed.

The problem for constitutional law always has been and always will be the resolution of what has been called the Madisonian dilemma. The United States was founded as what we now call a Madisonian system, one which allows majorities to rule in wide areas of life simply because they are majorities, but which also holds that individuals have some freedoms that must be exempt from majority control. The dilemma is that neither the majority nor the minority can be trusted to define the proper spheres of democratic authority and individual liberty. The first would court tyranny by the majority; the second, tyranny by the minority.

Over time it has come to be thought that the resolution of the Madisonian problem—the definition of majority power and minority freedom—is primarily the function of the judiciary and, most especially, the function of the Supreme Court. That understanding, which now seems a permanent feature of our political arrangements, creates the need for constitutional theory. The courts must be energetic to protect the rights of individuals, but they must also be scrupulous not to deny the majority's legitimate right to govern. How can that be done?

Any intelligible view of constitutional adjudication starts from the proposition that the Constitution is law. That may sound obvious but in a moment you will see that it is not obvious to a great many people, including law professors. What does it mean to say that the words in a document are law? One of the things it means is that the words constrain judgment. They control judges every bit as much as they control legislators, executives, and citizens.

The provisions of the Bill of Rights and the Civil War amendments not only have contents that protect individual liberties, they also have limits. They do not cover all possible or even all desirable liberties. For example, freedom of speech covers speech, not sexual conduct. Freedom from unreasonable searches and seizures does not protect the power of businesses to set prices. These limits mean that the judge's authority has limits and that outside the designated areas democratic institutions govern.

If this were not so, if judges could govern areas not committed to them by specific clauses of the Constitution, then there would be no law other than the will of the judge. It is common ground that such a situation is not legitimate in a democracy. Justice Brennan recently put the point well: "Justices are not platonic guardians appointed to wield authority according to their personal moral predilections."[1] This means that any defensible theory of constitutional interpretation must demonstrate that it has the capacity to control judges. An observer must be able to say whether or not the judge's result follows fairly from premises given by an authoritative, external source and is not merely a question of taste or opinion.

There are those in the academic world, professors at very prestigious law schools, who deny that the Constitution is law. I will not rehearse their arguments here or rebut them in detail. I note merely that there is one question they do not address. If the Constitution is not law, with the usual areas of ambiguity at the edges, but which nevertheless tolerably tells judges what to do and what not to do—if the Constitution is not law in that sense, what authorizes judges to set at naught the majority judgment of the representatives of the American people? If the Constitution is not law, why is the judge's authority superior to that of the President, the Congress, the armed forces, the departments and agencies, the governors and legislatures of the states, and that of everyone else in the nation? No answer exists.

The answer that is attempted is usually that the judge must be guided by some form of moral philosophy. Not only is moral philosophy typically inadequate to the task but, more fundamentally, there is no legitimating reason that I have seen why the rest of us should be governed by the *judge's* moral visions. Those academics who think the Constitution is not law ought to draw the only conclusion that intellectual honesty leaves to them: that judges must abandon the function of constitutional review. I have yet to hear that suggested.

The only way in which the Constitution can constrain judges is if the judges interpret the document's words according to the intentions of those who drafted, proposed, and ratified its provisions and its various amendments. It is important to be plain at the outset what intentionalism means. It is not the notion that judges may apply a constitutional provision only to circumstances specifically contemplated by the Framers. In such a narrow form the philosophy is useless. Because we cannot know how the Framers would vote on specific cases today, in a very different world from the one

---

1. Speech by William J. Brennan, Georgetown University (Oct. 12, 1985), reprinted in *New York Times*, Oct. 13, 1985, at 36, col.2.

they knew, no intentionalist of any sophistication employs the narrow version just described.

There is a version that is adequate to the task. Dean John Hart Ely has described it:

> What distinguishes interpretivism [or intentionalism] from its opposite is its insistence that the work of the political branches is to be invalidated only in accord with an inference whose starting point, whose underlying premise, is fairly discoverable in the Constitution. That the complete inference will not be found there—because the situation is not likely to have been foreseen—is generally common ground.[2]

In short, all an intentionalist requires is that the text, structure, and history of the Constitution provide him not with a conclusion but with a major premise. That premise states a core value that the Framers intended to protect. The intentionalist judge must then supply the minor premise in order to protect the constitutional freedom in circumstances the Framers could not foresee. Courts perform this function all of the time. Indeed, it is the same function they perform when they apply a statute, a contract, a will, or, indeed, a Supreme Court opinion to a situation the Framers of those documents did not foresee.

Thus, we are usually able to understand the liberties that were intended to be protected. We are able to apply the First Amendment's Free Press Clause to the electronic media and to the changing impact of libel litigation upon all the media; we are able to apply the Fourth Amendment's prohibition on unreasonable searches and seizures to electronic surveillance; we apply the Commerce Clause to state regulations of interstate trucking.

Does this version of intentionalism mean that judges will invariably decide cases the way the Framers would if they were here today? Of course not. But many cases will be decided that way and, at the very least, judges will confine themselves to the principles the Framers put into the Constitution. Entire ranges of problems will be placed off-limits to judges, thus preserving democracy in those areas where the Framers intended democratic government. That is better than any non-intentionalist theory of constitutional adjudication can do. If it is not good enough, judicial review under the Constitution cannot be legitimate. I think it is good enough.

There is one objection to intentionalism that is particularly tiresome. Whenever I speak on the subject someone invariably asks: "But why should we be ruled by men long dead?" The question is never asked about the main

---

2. John Hart Ely, *Democracy and Distrust* 1–2 (1980).

body of the Constitution where we really are ruled by men long dead in such matters as the powers of Congress, the President, and the judiciary. Rather, the question is asked about the amendments that guarantee individual freedoms. The answer as to those amendments is that we are not governed by men long dead unless we wish to cut back those freedoms, which the questioner never does. We are entirely free to create all the additional freedoms we wish by legislation, and the nation has done that frequently. What the questioner is really driving at is why judges, not the public but judges, should be bound to protect only those freedoms actually specified by the Constitution. The objection underlying the question is not to the rule of dead men but to the rule of living majorities.

Moreover, when we understand that the Bill of Rights gives us major premises and not specific conclusions, the document is not at all anachronistic. The major values specified in the Bill of Rights are timeless in the sense that they must be preserved by any government we would regard as free. For that reason, courts must not hesitate to apply only values to new circumstances. A judge who refuses to deal with unforeseen threats to an established constitutional value, and hence provides a crabbed interpretation that robs a provision of its full, fair, and reasonable meaning, fails in his judicial duty.

But there is the opposite danger. Obviously, values and principles can be stated at different levels of abstraction. In stating the value that is to be protected, the judge must not state it with so much generality that he transforms it. When that happens the judge improperly deprives the democratic majority of *its* freedom. The difficulty in choosing the proper level of generality has led some to claim that intentionalism is impossible.

Thus, in speaking about my view of the Fourteenth Amendment's equal protection clause as requiring black equality, Professor Paul Brest of Stanford said,

> The very adoption of such a principle, however, demands an arbitrary choice among levels of abstraction. Just what *is* "the general principle of equality that applies to all cases"? Is it the "core idea of *black* equality" that Bork finds in the original understanding (in which case Alan Bakke did not state a constitutionally cognizable claim), or a broader principle of "*racial* equality" (so that, depending on the precise content of the principle, Bakke might have a case after all), or is it a still broader principle of equality that encompasses discrimination on the basis of gender (or sexual orientation) as well?

> The fact is that all adjudication requires making choices among levels of generality on which to articulate principles, and all such choices are inherently non-neutral. No form of constitutional decisionmaking can be salvaged if its legitimacy depends on satisfying Bork's requirements that principles be "neutrally derived, defined and applied."[3]

I think that Brest's statement is wrong and that an intentionalist can do what Brest says he cannot. Let me use Brest's example as a hypothetical—I am making no statement about the truth of the matter. Assume for the sake of the argument that a judge's study of the evidence shows that both black and general racial equality were clearly intended, but that equality on matters such as sexual orientation was not under discussion.

The intentionalist may conclude that he must enforce black and racial equality but that he has no guidance at all about any higher level of generality. He has, therefore, no warrant to displace a legislative choice that prohibits certain forms of sexual behavior. That result follows from the principle of acceptance of democratic choice where the Constitution is silent. The same sort of analysis could be used to determine whether an amendment imposes black equality only or the broader principle of racial equality. In short, the problem of levels of generality may be solved by choosing no level of generality higher than that which interpretation of the words, structure, and history of the Constitution fairly support.

The power of extreme generalization was demonstrated by Justice William O. Douglas in *Griswold* v. *Connecticut*.[4] In *Griswold* the Court struck down Connecticut's anticontraception statute. Justice Douglas created a constitutional right of privacy that invalidated the state's law against the use of contraceptives. He observed that many provisions of the Bill of Rights could be viewed as protections of aspects of personal privacy. He then generalized these particulars into an overall right of privacy that applies even where no provision of the Bill of Rights does. By choosing that level of abstraction, the Bill of Rights was expanded beyond the known intentions of the Framers. Since there is no constitutional text or history to define the right, privacy becomes an unstructured source of judicial power. I am not arguing that any of the privacy cases were wrongly decided—that is a different question. My

---

3. Brest, "The Fundamental Rights Controversy: The Essential Contradictions of Normative Constitutional Scholarship," *Yale L.J.* 90 (1981), 1063, 1091–92 (footnotes omitted).
4. 381 U.S. 479 (1965).

point is simply that the level of abstraction chosen makes the application of a generalized right of privacy unpredictable. A concept of original intent, one that focuses on each specific provision of the Constitution rather than upon values stated at a high level of abstraction, is essential to prevent courts from invading the proper domain of democratic government.

That proposition is directly relevant to the subject of economic rights and the Constitution. Article I, section 10, provides that no state shall pass any law impairing the obligations of contracts.[5] The Fifth and Fourteenth Amendments prevent either the federal or any state government from taking private property for public use without paying just compensation.[6] The intention underlying these clauses has been a matter of dispute and perhaps they have not been given their proper force. But that is not my concern here because few would deny that original intention should govern the application of these particular clauses.

My concern is with the contention that a more general spirit of libertarianism pervades the original intention underlying the Fourteenth Amendment so that courts may review all regulations of human behavior under the due process clause of that amendment. As Judge Learned Hand understood, economic freedoms are philosophically indistinguishable from other freedoms. Judicial review would extend, therefore, to all economic regulations. The burden of justification would be placed on the government so that all such regulations would start with a presumption of unconstitutionality. Viewed from the standpoint of economic philosophy, and of individual freedom, the idea has many attractions. But viewed from the standpoint of constitutional structures, the idea works a massive shift away from democracy and toward judicial rule.

Professor Siegan has explained what is involved:

> In suit challenging the validity of restraints, the government would have the burden of persuading a court . . . first, that the legislation serves important governmental objectives; second, that the restraint imposed by government is substantially related to the achievement of these objectives, that is, . . . the fit between means and ends must be close; and third, that a similar result cannot be achieved by a less drastic means.[7]

This method of review is familiar to us from case law. It has merit where the court is examining legislation that appears to threaten a right or a value

---

5. U.S. Constitution, art. I, § 1.

6. Ibid, amend. V; ibid, amend. XIV, § 1.

7. B. Siegan, *Economic Liberties and the Constitution* (1980), 324.

specified by a provision of the Constitution. But when employed as a formula for the general review of all restrictions on human freedom without guidance from the historical Constitution, the court is cut loose from any external moorings and required to perform tasks that are not only beyond its competence, but beyond any conceivable judicial function. That assertion is true, I submit, with respect to each of the three steps of the process described.

The first task assigned the government's lawyers is that of carrying the burden of persuading a court that the "legislation serves important governmental objectives."[8] That means, of course, objectives the court regards as important, and importance also connotes legitimacy. It is well to be clear about the stupendous nature of the function that is thus assigned the judiciary. That function is nothing less than working out a complete and coherent philosophy of the proper and improper ends of government with respect to all human activities and relationships. This philosophy must cover all questions: social, economic, sexual, familial, and political.

It must be so detailed and well-articulated, all the major and minor premises in place, that it allows judges to decide infinite numbers of concrete disputes. It must also rest upon more than the individual preferences of judges in order that internal inconsistency be avoided and that the legitimacy of forcing the chosen ends of government upon elected representatives, who have other ends in mind, can be justified. No theory of the proper end of government that possesses all of these characteristics is even conceivable. Certainly no philosopher has ever produced a generally acceptable theory of the sort required, and there is no reason to suppose that such a universal theory is just over the horizon. Yet, to satisfy the requirements of adjudication and the premise that a judge may not override democratic choice without an authority other than his own will, a theory with each of the mentioned qualities is essential.

Suppose that in meeting a challenge to a federal minimum wage law the government's counsel stated that the statute was the outcome of interest group politics, or that it was thought best to moderate the speed of the migration of industry from the north to the south; or that it was part of a policy to aid unions in collective bargaining. How is a court to demonstrate that none of those objectives is important and legitimate? Or, suppose that the lawyer for Connecticut in the *Griswold* case stated that a majority, or even a politically influential minority, regarded it as morally abhorrent that couples capable of procreation should copulate without the intention, or at least the

8. Ibid.

possibility, of conception. Can the court demonstrate that moral abhorrence is not an important and legitimate ground for legislation? I think the answer is that the court can make no such demonstration in either of the supposed cases. Further, though it may be only a confession of my own limitations, I have not the remotest idea of how one would go about constructing the philosophy that would give the necessary answers—to judges. I am quite clear how I would vote as a citizen or a legislator on each of these statutes.

This brings me to the second stage of review, in which the government bears the burden of persuading the court that the challenged law is "substantially related to the achievement of [its] objectives."[9] In the case of most laws about which there is likely to be controversy, the social sciences are simply not up to the task assigned. For example, if the government insists upon arguing that a minimum wage law is designed to improve the lot of workers generally, microeconomic theory and empirical investigation may be adequate to show that the means do not produce the ends. The requisite demonstration will become more complex and eventually impossible as the economic analyses grow more involved. It is well to remember, too, that judge-made economics has not been universally admirable. Much that has been laid down under the antitrust laws testifies to that. Moreover, microeconomics is the best, the most powerful, and the most precise of the social sciences.

What is the court to do when told that a ban on the use of contraceptives in fact reduces the amount of adultery in the population? Or if it is told that slowing the migration of industry to the Sun Belt is good because it is more painful to lose jobs than not to get new jobs? The substantive due process formulation does not directly address cost-benefit analysis, but one might suppose a court employing this kind of review would also ask whether the benefits achieved were worth the costs incurred. Perhaps that is included in the concept of a substantial relationship between ends and means. If so, that introduces into the calculus yet another judgment that can only be legislative and impressionistic.

The third step—that the government must show that a "similar result cannot be achieved by a less drastic means"[10]—is loaded with ambiguities and disguised tradeoffs. A "similar" result may be one along the same lines but not the full result desired by the government. Usually, it would presumably involve a lesser amount of coercion. A court undertaking to judge such matters will have no guidance other than its own sense of leg-

---

9. Ibid.
10. Ibid.

islative prudence about whether the greater result is or is not worth the greater degree of restriction.

There are some general statements by some Framers of the Fourteenth Amendment that seem to support a conception of the judicial function like this one. But it does not appear that the idea was widely shared or that it was understood by the states that ratified the amendment. Such a revolutionary alteration in our constitutional arrangements ought to be more clearly shown to have been intended before it is accepted. This version of judicial review would make judges platonic guardians subject to nothing that can properly be called law.

The conclusion, I think, must be that only by limiting themselves to the historic intentions underlying each clause of the Constitution can judges avoid becoming legislators, avoid enforcing their own moral predilections, and ensure that the Constitution is law. For the subject of economic rights, that means we must turn away from the glamour of abstract philosophic discourse and back to the mundane and difficult task of discovering what the Framers were trying to accomplish with the Contract Clause and the Takings Clause.

THE CASE AGAINST POLITICAL JUDGING

W hat was once the dominant view of constitutional law—that a judge is to apply the Constitution according to the principles intended by those who ratified the document—is now very much out of favor among the theorists of the field. In the legal academies in particular, the philosophy of original understanding is usually viewed as thoroughly passé, probably reactionary, and certainly—the most dreaded indictment of all—"outside the mainstream." That fact says more about the lamentable state of the intellectual life of the law, however, than it does about the merits of the theory.

In truth, only the approach of original understanding meets the criteria that any theory of constitutional adjudication must meet in order to possess democratic legitimacy. Only that approach is consonant with the design of the American Republic.

When we speak of "law," we ordinarily refer to a rule that we have no right to change except through prescribed procedures. That statement assumes that the rule has a meaning independent of our own desires. Otherwise there would be no need to agree on procedures for changing the rule. Statutes, we agree, may be changed by amendment or repeal. The Constitution may be changed by amendment pursuant to the procedures set out in Article V. It is a necessary implication of the prescribed procedures that neither statute nor Constitution should be changed by judges. Though that has been done often enough, it is in no sense proper.

What is the "meaning" of a law, that essence that judges should not change? It is the meaning understood at the time of the law's enactment. What the Constitution's ratifiers understood themselves to be enacting must be taken to be what the public of that time would have understood the words to mean. It is important to be clear about this, because the search is not for a subjective intention. If, for instance, Congress enacted a statute outlawing

From *National Review*, December 8, 1989.

the sale of automatic rifles and did so in the Senate by a vote of 51 to 49, no court would overturn a conviction under the law because two senators in the majority later testified that they had really intended only to prohibit the *use* of such rifles. They said "sale" and "sale" it is. Thus, the common objection to the philosophy of original understanding—that Madison kept his notes of the convention at Philadelphia a secret for many years—is off the mark. He knew that what mattered was public understanding, not subjective intentions.

Law is a public act. Secret reservations or intentions count for nothing. The original understanding is thus manifested in the words used and in secondary materials, such as debates at the conventions, public discussion, newspaper articles, dictionaries in use at the time, and the like.

The search for the intent of the lawmaker is the everyday procedure of lawyers and judges when they apply a statute, a contract, a will, or the opinion of a court. To be sure, there are differences in the way we deal with different legal materials, which was the point of John Marshall's observation in *McCulloch* v. *Maryland* that "we must never forget, that it is a *constitution* we are expounding." By that he meant narrow, legalistic reasoning was not to be applied to the document's broad provisions, a document that could not, by its nature and uses, "partake of the prolixity of a legal code." But in that same opinion he also wrote that a provision must receive a "fair and just interpretation," which means that the judge is to interpret what is in the text and not something else. And, it will be recalled, in *Marbury* v. *Madison* Marshall based the judicial power to invalidate a legislative act upon the fact that a judge was applying the words of a written document. Thus, questions of breadth of approach or of room for play in the joints aside, lawyers and judges seek in the Constitution what they seek in other legal texts: the original meaning of the words.

We would at once criticize a judge who undertook to rewrite a statute or the opinion of a superior court; and yet such judicial rewriting is often correctable by the legislatures or superior courts, whereas the Supreme Court's rewriting of the Constitution is not correctable. At first glance, it seems distinctly peculiar that there should be a great many academic theorists who explicitly defend departures from the understanding of those who ratified the Constitution while agreeing, at least in principle, that there should be no departure from the understanding of those who enacted a statute or joined a majority opinion. A moment's reflection suggests, however, that Supreme Court departures from the original meaning of the Constitution are advocated *precisely because* those departures are not correctable democratically.

The point of the academic exercise is to be free of democracy in order to impose the values of an elite upon the rest of us.

It is here that the concept of neutral principles, which Herbert Wechsler has said are essential if the Supreme Court is not to be a naked power organ, comes into play. Wechsler, in expressing his difficulties with the decision in *Brown* v. *Board of Education,* said that courts must choose principles which they are willing to apply neutrally; to apply, that is, to all cases that may fairly be said to fall within them. This is a safeguard against political judging. No judge will say openly that any particular group or political position is always entitled to win. He will announce a principle that decides the case at hand, and Wechsler has no difficulty with that if the judge is willing to apply the same principles in the next case, even when it means a group favored by the first decision is disfavored by the second.

When a judge finds his principle in the Constitution as originally understood, the problem of neutral derivation of principle is solved. The judge accepts the ratifiers' definition of the appropriate ranges of majority and minority freedom. The "Madisonian dilemma" (essentially, the conflict of majority rule with minority rights) is resolved in the way that the Founders resolved it, and the judge accepts the fact that he is bound by that resolution as law. He need not, and must not, make unguided value judgments of his own.

This means, of course, that a judge, no matter on what court he sits, may never create new constitutional rights or destroy old ones. Any time he does so, he violates the limits of his own authority and, for that reason, also violates the rights of the legislature and the people. When a judge is given a set of constitutional provisions, then, as to anything not covered by those provisions, he is, quite properly, powerless. In the absence of law, a judge is a functionary without a function.

This is not to say, of course, that majorities may not add to minority freedoms by statute, and indeed a great deal of the legislation that comes out of Congress and the state legislature does just that. The only thing majorities may not do is invade the liberties the Constitution specifies. In this sense, the concept of original understanding builds in a bias towards individual freedom. Thus, the Supreme Court properly decided in *Brown* that the equal protection clause of the Fourteenth Amendment forbids racial segregation or discrimination by any arm of government, but, because the Constitution addresses only governmental action, the Court could not address the question of private discrimination. Congress did address it in the Civil Rights Act of 1964 and in subsequent legislation, enlarging minority freedoms beyond those mandated by the Constitution.

The neutral definition of the principle derived from the historic Constitution is also crucial. The Constitution states its principles in majestic generalities that we know cannot be taken as sweepingly as the words alone might suggest. The First Amendment states that "Congress shall make no law . . . abridging the freedom of speech," but no one has ever supposed that Congress could not make some speech unlawful or that it could not make all speech illegal in certain places, at certain times, and under certain circumstances. Justices Hugo Black and William O. Douglas often claimed to be First Amendment absolutists, but even they would permit the punishment of speech if they thought it too closely "brigaded" with illegal action. From the beginning of the Republic to this day, no one has ever thought Congress could not forbid the preaching of mutiny at sea or disruptive proclamations in a courtroom. One may not cry "Fire!" in a crowded theater.

But the question of neutral definition remains and is obviously closely related to neutral application. Neutral application can be gained by defining a principle so narrowly that it will fit only a few cases. Thus, once a principle is derived from the Constitution, its breadth or the level of generality at which it is stated becomes of crucial importance. The judge must not state the principle with so much generality that he transforms it. The difficulty in finding the proper level of generality has led some critics to claim that the application of the original understanding is actually impossible. That sounds fairly abstract, but an example will make clear the point and the answer to it.

In speaking of my view that the Fourteenth Amendment's equal protection clause requires black equality, Dean Paul Brest said:

> The very adoption of such a principle, however, demands an arbitrary choice among levels of abstraction. Just what *is* "the general principle of equality that applies to all cases"? Is it the "core idea of *black* equality" that Bork finds in the original understanding (in which case Allan Bakke [a white who sued because a state medical school gave preference in admissions to other races] did not state a constitutionally cognizable claim), or a broader principle of "*racial* equality" (so that, depending on the precise content of the principle, Bakke might have a case after all), or is it a still broader principle of equality that encompasses discrimination on the basis of gender (or sexual orientation) as well?
>
> . . . The fact is that all the adjudication requires making choices among the levels of generality on which to articulate principles, and all such choices are inherently non-neutral. No form of constitutional decision-making can be salvaged if its legitimacy depends on satisfying Bork's requirements that principles be "neutrally derived, defined, and applied."

If Brest's point about the impossibility of choosing the level of generality upon neutral criteria is correct, we must either resign ourselves to a Court that *is* a "naked power organ" or require the Court to stop making "constitutional" decisions. But Brest's argument seems to me wrong, and I think a judge committed to original understanding can do what Brest says he cannot. We may use Brest's example to demonstrate the point.

The role of a judge committed to the philosophy of original understanding is not to "*choose* a level of abstraction." Rather, it is to find the meaning of a text—a process which includes finding its degree of generality, which is part of its meaning—and to apply that text to a particular situation, which may be difficult if its meaning is unclear. With many if not most textual provisions, the level of generality which is part of their meaning is readily apparent. The problem is most difficult when dealing with the broadly stated provisions of the Bill of Rights. It is to the latter that we confine discussion here. In dealing with such provisions, a judge should state the principle at the level of generality that the text and historical evidence warrant. The equal-protection clause was adopted in order to protect freed slaves, but its language, being general, applies to all persons. As we might expect, the evidence of what the drafters, the Congress that proposed the clause, and the ratifiers understood themselves to be requiring is clearest in the case of race relations. It is there that we may begin looking for evidence of the level of generality intended. Without meaning to suggest what the historical evidence in fact shows, let us assume we find that the ratifiers intended to guarantee that blacks should be treated by law no worse than whites, but that it is unclear whether whites were intended to be protected from discrimination. On such evidence, the judge should protect only blacks from discrimination, and Allan Bakke would not have had a case. The reason is that the next higher level of generality above black equality, which is racial equality, is not shown to be a constitutional principle, and, therefore, there is nothing to be set against a current legislative majority's decision to favor blacks. Democratic choice must be accepted by the judge where the Constitution is silent. The test is the reasonableness of the distinction, and the level of generality chosen by the ratifiers determines that. If the evidence shows the ratifiers understood racial equality to have been the principle they were enacting, then Bakke *would* have a case.

To define a legal proposition or principle involves simultaneously stating its contents and its limits. When, for instance, you state what *is* contained within the clause of the First Amendment guarantee of the free exercise of religion, you necessarily state what is *not* contained within that clause.

Because the First Amendment guarantees freedom of speech, judges are required reasonably to define what is speech and what is its freedom. Where the law stops, the legislator may move on to create more; but where the law stops, the judge must stop.

The neutral or nonpolitical application of principle has been discussed in connection with Wechsler's discussion of *Brown*. It is a requirement, like the others, addressed to the judge's integrity. Having derived and defined the principle to be applied, he must apply it consistently and without regard to his sympathy or lack of sympathy with the parties before him. This does not mean that the judge will never change the principle he has derived and defined. Anybody who has dealt extensively with law knows that a new case may seem to fall within a principle as stated and yet not fall within the rationale underlying it. As new cases present new patterns, the principle will often be restated and redefined. There is nothing wrong with that; it is, in fact, highly desirable. But the judge must be clarifying his own reasoning and verbal formulations and not trimming to arrive at results desired on grounds extraneous to the Constitution. This requires a fair degree of sophistication and self-consciousness on the part of the judge. The only external discipline to which the judge is subject is the scrutiny of professional observers who will be able to tell over a period of time whether or not he is displaying intellectual integrity.

The structure of government the Founders of this nation intended most certainly did not give courts a political role. The debates surrounding the Constitution focused much more upon theories of representation than upon the judiciary, which was thought to be a comparatively insignificant branch. There were, however, repeated attempts at the Constitutional Convention in Philadelphia to give judges a policy-making role. The plan of the Virginia delegation, which, amended and expanded, ultimately became the Constitution of the United States, included a proposal that the new national legislature be controlled by placing a veto power in a Council of Revision consisting of the executive and "a convenient number of the National Judiciary." That proposal was raised four times and defeated each time. Among the reasons, as reported in James Madison's notes, was the objection raised by Elbridge Gerry of Massachusetts that it "was quite foreign from the nature of ye. office to make them judges of policy of public measures." Rufus King, also of Massachusetts, added that judges should "expound the law as it should come before them, free from the bias of having participated in its formation." Judges who create new constitutional rights are judges of the policy of public measures and are biased by having participated in the policy's formation.

The intention of the Convention was accurately described by Alexander Hamilton in *The Federalist* 78: "[T]he judiciary, from the nature of its functions, will always be the least dangerous to the political rights of the Constitution; because it will be least in a capacity to annoy or injure them." The political rights of the Constitution are, of course, the rights that make up democratic self-government. Hamilton obviously did not anticipate a judiciary that would injure those rights by adding to the list of subjects that were removed from democratic control. Thus, he could say that the courts were "beyond comparison the weakest of the three departments of power," and he appended a quotation from the "celebrated Montesquieu": "Of the three powers above mentioned [the others being the legislative and the executive], the judiciary is next to nothing." This was true because judges were, as Rufus King said, merely to "expound" the law.

Even if evidence of what the Founders thought about the judicial role were unavailable, we would have to adopt a rule that judges must stick to the original meaning of the Constitution's words. If that method of interpretation were not common in the law, if James Madison and Justice Joseph Story had never endorsed it, if Chief Justice John Marshall had rejected it, we would have to invent the approach of original understanding in order to save the constitutional design. No other method of constitutional adjudication can confine courts to a defined sphere of authority and thus prevent them from assuming powers whose exercise alters, perhaps radically, the design of the American Republic. The philosophy of original understanding is thus a necessary inference from the structure of government apparent on the face of the U.S. Constitution.

We come now to the question of precedent. It is particularly important because, as Professor Henry Monaghan of Columbia University Law School notes, "much of the existing constitutional order is at variance with what we know of the original understanding." Some commentators have argued from this obvious truth that the approach of original understanding is impossible or fatally compromised, since they suppose it would require the Court to declare paper money unconstitutional and overturn the centralization accomplished by abandoning restrictions on congressional powers during the New Deal. But to say that prior courts have allowed, or initiated, deformations of the Constitution is not enough to create a warrant for present and future courts to do the same thing.

All serious constitutional theory centers upon the duties of judges, and that comes down to the question: What should the judge decide in the case now before him? Obviously, an originalist judge should not deform the Constitution further. Just as obviously, he should not attempt to undo all mistakes made in the past. At the center of the philosophy of original understanding, therefore, must stand some idea of when the judge is bound by prior decisions and when he is not.

Is judicial precedent an ironclad rule? It is not, and never has been. As Felix Frankfurter once explained, "*stare decisis* is a principle of policy and not a mechanical formula of adherence to the latest decision, however recent and questionable, when such adherence involves collision with a prior doctrine more embracing in its scope, intrinsically sounder, and verified by experience." Thus, in Justice Powell's words "[i]t is . . . not only [the Court's] prerogative but also [its] duty to re-examine a precedent where its reasoning or understanding of the Constitution is fairly called into question." The Supreme Court frequently overrules its own precedents. *Plessy* v. *Ferguson,* and the rule of separate-but-equal in racial matters, lasted 58 years before it was dispatched in *Brown* v. *Board of Education.* In a period of 16 years the Court took three different positions with respect to the constitutionality of federal power to impose wage and price regulations on states and localities as employers. Indeed, Justice Blackmun explained in the last of these decisions that prior cases, even of fairly recent vintage, should be reconsidered if they "disserve principles of democratic self-governance." Every year the Court overrules a number of its own precedents.

The practice of overruling precedent is particularly common in constitutional law, the rationale being that it is extremely difficult for an incorrect constitutional ruling to be corrected through the amendment process. Almost all Justices have agreed with Felix Frankfurter's observation that "the ultimate touchstone of constitutionality is the Constitution itself and not what we have said about it." But that, of course, is only a partial truth. It is clear, first, that Frankfurter was talking about the Supreme Court's obligations with respect to its own prior decisions. Lower courts are not free to ignore what the Supreme Court has said about the Constitution, for that would introduce chaos into the legal system as courts of appeal refused to follow Supreme Court rulings and district courts disobeyed their appellate courts orders. Second, what "the Constitution itself" says may, as in the case of paper money, be irretrievable, not simply because of "what [the justices] have said about it," but because of what the nation has done or become on the strength of what the Court said.

To say a decision is so thoroughly embedded in our national life that it should not be overruled, even though clearly wrong, is not necessarily to say that its principle should be followed in the future. Thus, the expansion of Congress's commerce, taxing, and spending powers has reached a point where it is not possible to state that, as a matter of articulated doctrine, there are any limits left. That does not mean, however, that the Court must necessarily repeat its mistake as congressional legislation attempts to reach new subject areas. Cases now on the books would seem to mean that Congress could, for example, displace state law on such subjects as marriage and divorce, thus ending such federalism as remains. But the Court could refuse to extend the commerce power so far, without overruling its prior decisions, thus leaving existing legislation in place but not giving generative power to the faulty principle by which that legislation was originally upheld. It will be said that this is a lawless approach, but that is not at all clear. The past decisions are beyond reach, but there remains a constitutional principle of federalism that should be regarded as law more profound than the implications of the past decisions. They cannot be overruled, but they can be confined to the subject areas they concern. When we cannot recover the transgressions of the past, then the best we can do is say to the Court, "Go and sin no more."

Finally, it should be said that those who adhere to a philosophy of original understanding are more likely to respect precedent than those who do not. As Justice Scalia has said, if revisionists can ignore "the most solemnly and democratically adopted text of the Constitution and its amendments . . . on the basis of current values, what possible basis could there be for enforced adherence to a legal decision of the Supreme Court?" If you do not care about stability, if today's result is all-important, there is no occasion to respect either the constitutional text or the decisions of your predecessors.

The Struggle Over the Role of the Court

Whatever one thinks about the performance of courts today, a subject upon which I shall have nothing to say here, it is quite clear that there have been times in our history when courts have gone well beyond their proper constitutional sphere. When that occurs, democratic government is displaced and the question is how to restore a proper allocation of powers. Absent a constitutional amendment, a general means to ensure that courts stay within the limits the Constitution provides for them can only be intellectual and moral.

That may seem a weak control. It does not seem so to me. Intellectual criticism in the short run may be quite ineffective. In the long run, ideas will be decisive. That is particularly true with respect to courts, more so perhaps than with any other branch of government.

Courts are part of a more general legal-constitutional culture and ultimately are heavily influenced by ideas that develop elsewhere in that culture. It is not too much to say, for example, that the Warren Court was, in a real sense, the culmination of a version of the legal-realist movement that dominated the Yale Law School years before. Similarly, the outcome of a present debate taking place in the law schools will surely affect the courts of today and the future.

A new struggle for intellectual dominance in constitutional theory is under way at this moment. The struggle is about the duty of judges with respect to the Constitution. It is taking place out of public sight, in a sense, because it is carried on almost entirely in the law schools and in the law reviews. But that doesn't mean it won't affect our entire polity in the years ahead. The ideas that win hegemony there will govern the profession, including judges, for at least a generation and perhaps more.

From *National Review*, September 17, 1982

Let me sketch the nature of the debate. The contending schools of thought are called, somewhat unhappily, "interpretivism" and "noninterpretivism." In popular usage, "interpretivism" is often called strict construction. And "noninterpretivism" is what we loosely refer to as activism or imperialism.

John Hart Ely, then of Harvard Law School, described them this way: Interpretivism is the tenet "that judges deciding constitutional issues should confine themselves to enforcing norms that are stated or are clearly implicit in the written Constitution. . . . What distinguishes interpretivism"—or, if you will, strict construction—"from its opposite is its insistence that the work of the political branches is to be invalidated only in accord with the inference whose starting point, whose underlying premise, is fairly discoverable in the Constitution." Noninterpretivism—or activism, if you will—advances "the contrary view, that courts should go beyond that set of references and enforce norms that cannot be discovered within the four corners of the document."

The noninterpretivists, in a word, think that in litigation which is nominally constitutional the courts may—indeed should—remake the Constitution. These theorists are usually careful to say that a judge should not simply enforce his own values. And they variously prescribe as the source of this new law, which is to control the judge, such things as natural law, conventional morality, the understanding of an ideal democracy, or what have you.

There is a curious consistency about these theories. No matter from which base they start, the professors always end up at the same place, prescribing a constitutional law which is considerably more egalitarian and socially permissive than either the written Constitution or the state of legislative opinion in the American public today. That may be the point of the exercise.

My own philosophy is interpretivist. But I must say that this puts me in a distinct minority among law professors. Just how much of a minority may be seen by the fact that a visitor to Yale who expressed interest in debating my position was told by one of my colleagues that the position was so passé that it would be intellectually stultifying to debate it.

By my count, there were in recent years perhaps five interpretivists on the faculties of the ten best-known law schools. And now the President has put four of them on courts of appeals. That is why faculty members who don't like much else about Ronald Reagan regard him as a great reformer of legal education.

If the theory of noninterpretivism—that judges can draw their constitutional rulings from outside the document—achieves entire intellectual hegemony in the law schools, as it is on the brink of doing, the results will be disastrous for the constitutional law of this nation. Judges will feel justified in continually creating new individual rights, and those influential groups which form what might be called the Constitution-making apparatus of the nation—that is, the law professors, the courts, the press, the leaders of the bar—will support the courts in doing this. It will be very hard to rally public opinion against groups so articulate and in control of most of the means of communication. It will be particularly hard since much opposition will be disarmed by being told that this is what the Constitution commands. We are a people with a great and justified veneration for the Constitution.

The hard fact is, however, that there are no guidelines outside the Constitution that can control a judge once he abandons the lawyer's task of interpretation. There may be a natural law, but we are not agreed upon what it is, and there is no such law that gives definite answers to a judge trying to decide a case.

There may be a conventional morality in our society, but on most issues there are likely to be several moralities. They are often regionally defined, which is one reason for federalism. The judge has no way of choosing among differing moralities or competing moralities except in accordance with his own morality.

There may be immanent and unrealized ideals of democracy, but the Constitution does not prescribe a wholly democratic government. It is difficult to see what warrant a judge has for demanding more democracy than either the Constitution requires or the people want.

The truth is that the judge who looks outside the Constitution always looks inside himself and nowhere else.

Noninterpretivism, should it prevail, will have several entirely predictable results. In the first place, the area of judicial power will continually grow and the area of democratic choice will continually contract. We will have a great deal more constitutional law than the Constitution itself contains.

Rights will be created, and they will often conflict with one another, so the courts will find that they must balance them in a process which is indistinguishable from legislation.

There is a good example of this. Recently, a federal court of appeals had occasion to consider a state statute which required a wife to consult with her husband before having an abortion. The husband was given no control over the decision, merely a sort of due-process right to be heard. Naturally, someone claimed that even that violated the Constitution. The court of appeals said that it had to balance the wife's right to privacy against her husband's right to procreation.

Neither of those rights is to be found anywhere in the Constitution. The court upheld the statute, but the point is that a court, without any guidance from the Constitution, or any source other than its own views, had to make an accommodation of values and interests of a sort that used to be entirely the business of the legislature. That will become the general situation if non-interpretivism becomes dominant.

Another result of this theory, which, as I say, is the dominant theory of the law schools—at least it appears to be winning the debate at the moment—will be the nationalization of moral values as state legislative choices are steadily displaced by federal judicial choices. This is directly contrary to the theory of the Constitution, which is that certain moral choices specified in the document are national, but that unless Congress defines a new national consensus, all other moral choices are to be made democratically by the people in their states and in their cities.

Finally, there will occur what I have called the gentrification of the Constitution. The constitutional culture—those who are most intimately involved with the constitutional adjudication and how it is perceived by the public at large: federal judges, law professors, members of the media—is not composed of a cross-section of America, either politically, socially, or morally. If, as I have suggested, noninterpretivism leads a judge to find constitutional values within himself, or in the values of those with whom he is most intimately associated, then the values which might loosely be described as characteristic of the university-educated upper middle class will be those that are imposed.

There is nothing wrong with that class, but there is also no reason why its values shuold be imposed upon everybody else. If that happens, then the Constitution will have been gentrified.

Perhaps I've said enough to show why I think this dominant philosophy in the major law schools must not be allowed to go unchallenged intellectually. But I want to make two last points about the rhetoric of its adherents.

Noninterpretivism—activism—is said to be the means by which courts add to constitutional freedom and never subtract from it. That is wrong. Among our constitutional freedoms or rights, clearly given in the text, is the power to govern ourselves democratically.

Every time a court creates a new constitutional right against government or expands, without warrant, an old one, the constitutional freedom of citizens to control their lives is diminished. Freedom cannot be created by this method; it is merely shifted from a larger group to a smaller group.

G. K. Chesterton might have been addressing this very controversy when he wrote: "What is the good of telling a community it has every liberty except the liberty to make laws? The liberty to make laws is what constitutes a free people."

The claim of noninterpretivists, then, that they will expand rights and freedom is false. They will merely redistribute them.

What is perhaps even more troubling is the lack of candor—and I think it can only be called that—which so often characterizes the public rhetoric of constitutional scholars who subscribe to this theory.

Professor Paul Bator of Harvard put the point very well at the Federalist Society meeting at Yale. He explained that there are two different kinds of arguments that the constitutional in-group uses, depending on its purposes at the moment.

On Monday, while we are arguing for a result in court that would be hard to justify in terms of the written Constitution, we say things like: "Oh well, any sophisticated lawyer understands that the text of the Constitution is really not very clear, its history is often extremely ambiguous, and in many areas simply unknown. That being so, why shouldn't the court just do good as we define the good?"

But on Tuesday, after the decision has been made, we find ourselves talking to a different and much larger group, people who are not constitutional theorists and who may be enraged at what the court has done. These tend to be regarded by the constitutional cognoscenti as the great unwashed. To them, we do not mention the ambiguities, the uncertainties that underlie the decision. We certainly don't mention the political basis for the decision. Instead, we say to them, "Why, you are attacking the Constitution." That, of course, is not what the critics are doing.

If noninterpretivism is to be respectable, its scholars must stop talking this way. When they address the public, they should say, frankly, "No, that decision does not come out of the written or historical Constitution. It is based upon a moral choice the judges made, and here is why it is a good choice, and here is why judges are entitled to make it for you."

That last is going to be a little sticky, but that is what honesty requires. Until the public understands the basis by which constitutional argument moves, there will be little chance for the public to decide what kind of courts it really wants.

These concerns are not new. There is a great deal of dissatisfaction with courts today. It is important, in some sense, to recognize that those concerns, that kind of anger is as old as our Republic. Americans have never been entirely at ease with the concept of judicial supremacy, and they have also never wanted to try democracy without any judicial safeguards.

Thomas Jefferson spoke feelingly of the dangers of judicial power: "The Constitution, on this hypothesis [of judicial supremacy], is a mere thing of wax in the hands of the judiciary, which they may twist, and shape into any form they please. It should be remembered, as an axiom of eternal truth in politics, that whatever power in any government is independent is absolute also. . . . Independence can be trusted nowhere but with the people in mass."

But Alexander Hamilton spoke with equal feeling on the necessity for safeguards enforced by independent judges when he said: "there is no liberty if the power of judging be not separated from the legislative and executive powers. . . . The complete independence of the courts of justice is peculiarly essential in a limited Constitution."

Both Jefferson and Hamilton had powerful points. It seems to be me that only a strictly interpretivist approach to the Constitution, only an approach which says the judge must get from the Constitution what is in that document and in its history and nothing else, can preserve for us the benefits that Hamilton saw, while avoiding the dangers that Jefferson prophesied.

OLYMPIANS ON THE MARCH:
THE COURTS AND THE CULTURE WARS

[T]o be "reactionary" means nothing more than to believe that in some of its aspects, however secondary, the past was better than the present.

—Leszek Kolakowski

Everything has been said before, but since nobody listens we have to keep going back and beginning all over again.

—André Gide

Walter Bagehot said of the English constitution, "[I]n the full activity of an historical constitution, its subjects repeat phrases true in the time of their fathers, and inculcated by those fathers, but now no longer true." So it is with us. We are living with a vision of a Constitution that no longer exists. The reason is apparent. The Constitution, which is, for all practical purposes, the Supreme Court, follows the elite culture. Thus it is that the liberal transformation of the Constitution over the past fifty years has been accomplished by Courts with heavy majorities appointed by Republican presidents (the current count is seven to two).

As cultural dominance passes from one elite to the next, so does the Supreme Court's law change to reflect the views of the new elite. New values are added and old ones abandoned. Not all values, however, can find even remotely plausible support in the historical Constitution. When vagabond values are to be implemented, the Court's declarations that various executive or legislative acts are unconstitutional are often not even colorably related to the charter supposedly being applied. Disregard for text, legislative purpose, and history confers enormous freedom, so that the Court, employing some primitive and often sophomoric version of moral philosophy or natural law, is at liberty to enforce what it chooses. It is not to be expected that lives devoted to lawyers' arts would, upon the donning of black robes, suddenly produce philosophers. We are then governed not by law but by the moods of an unelected, unrepresentative, and unaccountable committee of nine law-

From *The New Criterion*, May 2004.

yers. What they decide is often law only in the sense that we will obey their ukases, even when they split five to four and the four have by far the better arguments. What they decide is not law in the sense that it has its origin, its root, in any legal materials and that the result falls within a range that would be regarded as acceptable by most judges, past, present, and future. Moods shift; fair readings do not.

The progression is clear on the record. In the last third of the nineteenth century and the first third of the twentieth, the dominant culture was that of the business class, and the Court often responded with the invention of constitutional rights favorable to that class, striking down reform legislation which, however unwise, was clearly within the constitutional powers of state and federal legislatures. The Court invented, for example, a right to enter into contracts that is nowhere to be found in the Constitution. *Lochner v. New York,* a 1905 decision, is the classic example. The Court, dividing six to three, struck down a state statute setting maximum hours for bakers as violative of the (nonexistent) right to make contracts. Early New Deal economic regulations were routinely invalidated until a series of retirements and deaths enabled Franklin Roosevelt to remake the Court. The cultural dominance of the business class having been ended by the Great Depression, the new Court freely approved economic regulations and began to prepare the ground for the creation of new rights. An even more momentous shift came with the Court headed by Earl Warren.

The New Deal Court had been philosophically riven. Arthur Schlesinger, Jr., has described the Court as it stood in 1947. The wing occupied by Justices Black and Douglas was "concerned with settling particular cases in accordance with their own social preconceptions," a version of "value jurisprudence" identified largely with the Yale law school. Its dominant theme was equality, as shown by its heavy reliance upon the Equal Protection Clause. Schlesinger, Jr. wrote that "Black and Douglas vote less regularly for doctrines than for interests—for the trade union against the employer, for the government against the large taxpayer, for the administrative agency against the business, for the injured workman, for the unprotected defendant, against the patent holder—so that in the phrase of Professor Thomas Reed Powell 'the less favored in life will be the more favored in law.'" This was a flat contradiction of the judicial oath to "administer justice without respect to persons and do equal right to the poor and to the rich." It was as well an expression of the socialist impulse which, significantly, became the regnant outlook of the Court at a time when the American intelligentsia was socialist. As a consequence of the Warren Court's preference for equal results rather than equal justice, it politicized every branch of the law, statutes as well as the Constitution. Ironically, the Court's favored constitutional implement was the clause of the Fourteenth Amendment promising "equal protection of the laws."

Socialism, however, was then discredited. In practice it produced impoverishment and tyranny so that not even intellectuals could cling to its dream, or at least most of them could not do so publicly. Radicalism took the form of the New Left of the 1960s, which gradually grew more interested in personal freedom unrestricted by law, morals, or even the rules of self-preservation (drugs and filthy living conditions were often considered signs of "authenticity"). The New Left practiced a politics of expression and self-absorption. A vision of radical individual autonomy thus lay at the heart of their world view. There was a good deal of that in their intellectual class elders and now it is the dominant mood of the intelligentsia.

It is not too surprising, then, that a mood of radical autonomy or, if you will, moral relativism began to appear in the jurisprudence of the Supreme Court. The Court, in step with the intellectual class, has dropped the socialist drive of the Warren Court. The difference between the two Courts is shown by the differing fates of the two fields I know best, antitrust and constitutional law. The death of the socialist illusion made possible the use of basic economics to return antitrust to rationality. But the rise of moral relativism—perhaps a better term would be moral chaos—drove constitutional law in a new but no more respectable or rational direction.

Today, a lawyer who appears before the Court in a case involving antitrust, taxation, labor law, or a similar question will find his case is typically dealt with in a straightforward, lawyerly manner. But when the Court is presented with a cultural issue in a constitutional context, the Court majority usually departs from the Constitution, often indeed from any conceivable meaning of the Constitution, in order to enact an item on the modern liberal agenda, generally resulting in the enshrinement of radical individual autonomy as part of the Bill of Rights. That is signified by the Court's heavy use of the Due Process Clause's guarantee of liberty. To some considerable degree, therefore, it seems valid to say that the current Court is dominated by a gentrified form of Sixties radicalism. I do not know how otherwise to account for the absolute mess of our current jurisprudence of individual rights.

Though the justices are properly criticized for abandoning the proper judicial function to follow intellectual class fecklessness, responsibility for the health of the legal order does not, of course, depend entirely upon judges or even upon a reckless intellectual class. Responsibility rests as well with the practicing bar, the law schools, and, ultimately, with the public that elects or delegates to representatives the election of judges. None of these is performing well or even tolerably. The problems, not all of which may be soluble, lie in the nature of legal practice, the way law is taught, the modern conception of legal scholarship, the ideological direction of the courts, the enormously enlarged area of authority and competence appropriated by those courts, the eagerness of factions to circumvent democracy by litigation, and, finally, public incomprehension of what is and is not in our Constitution and so the public's inability to judge the judges. I have had some experience as a practitioner, professor, government lawyer before the Supreme Court, and judge; doubtless my views are colored by that fact.

When college graduation approached and I was trying to decide on a career, law still recruited the young with prettified images of Holmes and Brandeis. It was Holmes who said that it was possible to live greatly in the law, a rather obscure remark that seemed meaningful at the time. A life in the law seemed to promise battle, require devotion, and reward learning—and what idealistic young man would not choose to be warrior, priest, and scholar? The reality proved to be rather different. Economic pressures have made law less of a profession and more of a business, drastically limiting the role the bar can play in maintaining the integrity of the law. Such concerns necessarily give way to an absorption with billable hours. Though it is not quite true, as a British barrister put it, that success in law depends on the ability to eat sawdust without butter, quite a bit of sawdust-munching is required.

Firms have, moreover, entered an era of giantism. When I joined the largest law firm in Chicago, it had fifty-three lawyers with fewer than a dozen more in a Washington branch. Today the firm has over 450 lawyers in Chicago and well over 900 nationwide, and it is by no means the largest in either category. A firm of fifty-three lawyers today would be considered practically a boutique operation. Giantism produces an atmosphere more like a corporate headquarters than a partnership. Corporations are not known for a selfless devotion to sound public policy, nor, it turns out, is the practicing bar. That is not a criticism of either business or the bar, but merely a fact that probably cannot be altered.

At one time we were reconciled to the democratic unaccountability of courts by the promise that their powers would be kept within tolerable limits by the informed criticism of the bar. That has not been borne out. Practitioners have provided very little in-depth analyses of major constitutional doctrines; the organized bar has offered none. Attorneys, by and large, have not the time and energy left over from busy practices to study the fields in which the courts operate or to engage in sustained critiques. My practice was primarily in antitrust, but while it was apparent that the law was a doctrinal mess, there was no time to study it as a field; the problems present themselves case by case so that connecting links are not obvious, nor is it in either the client's or the firm's interest to have lawyers spending time on theoretical inquiries that, in any event, a judge is more likely to find irritating than persuasive. It is probably for that reason that the reform of antitrust law, when it occurred, came from the academy rather than from the practicing bar. Fields such as constitutional law, which rarely arise in ordinary practice, go almost entirely unexamined. Only ideological litigants, like the ACLU which is devoted to distorting constitutional law in the service of cultural leftism, have any occasion to spend a great deal of time on the subject. Moreover, since their success depends on judges, very few lawyers are willing to risk criticizing them. Bar politicians, leaders of the American Bar Association, for example, find it congenial to hobnob with judges and defend them from criticism. (The ABA, while it engages in professional training to some extent, is increasingly a culturally liberal political organization rather than a professional one, passing resolutions favoring a right to abortion, racial preferences, a universal right to food, AIDS needle-exchange programs, campaign finance reform, and opposing laws regulating sexual conduct between adults.) Its presidents make statements favoring judicial activism. Rather than providing an informed critique of the courts' performance, the ABA is a cheerleader for some of the worst tendencies of modern jurisprudence.

The exigencies of law practice discourage inquiries that have no immediate practical use. The last thing an advocate wants to tell a judge is that the case at bar presents a profound, or even a moderately interesting, question. That would suggest the case could be decided either way. His case, the lawyer must say, with every appearance of sincerity, is clear, so simple that it is hardly worth discussing, and must obviously be decided in favor of his client. The cases he cites are controlling whereas those mistakenly, and perhaps disingenuously, relied upon by his opponent are wide of the mark. So, too, with respect to policy arguments and hypothetical instances, both relied upon to show that only beneficial results will follow from accepting his position while his adversary's contentions would plunge the law into chaos and black night. It can be an exhilarating game, but some lawyers eventually find its repetition turns into drudgery. If they are lucky, they find alternatives.

While the time had come to leave the practice, I do not regret in the slightest the eight years I spent there. There was a great deal of satisfaction in winning, the excitement of the contest, the tactical maneuvering, and the camaraderie of a team working on high-stakes and difficult cases. There was the night of the "lost chord" when at 4 A.M. a colleague at last found the perfect precedent for our side and slapped the book triumphantly back on the shelf. We went down the hall for a celebratory coffee, only to discover, upon returning to the library, that we never could find that case again. Or the night in the conference room when I looked up from drafting a difficult paragraph, found that my colleague had disappeared, and finally located him sleeping on the floor underneath the table. There was the romanticism (I don't know how else to put it) of leaving the office in the first gray light before dawn, the old stone buildings of Chicago just beginning to emerge from the blackness beyond the reach of the street lamps, catching a rare cab on Michigan Boulevard to go home to Hyde Park, shower, shave, put on fresh clothes, and, my wife and children still asleep, return downtown for another day's work.

Ultimately, however, that was not the intellectual life the law had seemed to promise. Litigation is a plastic art; only those who were involved remember it at all. Like working a crossword puzzle, it is absorbing while you are doing it, but, when it is done, there is nothing left. In the days and nights, for weeks on end, that a friend and I spent writing and endlessly rewriting a brief about a now-forgotten trust estate worth many millions, we could have produced, I flatter myself, a book of some worth. In the long run, however, the real value of practice to me was that I learned how the court system works. Too many students and professors are inclined to view judges, particularly Supreme Court justices, as philosopher kings. Some experience trying to persuade judges would disabuse the professors, and hence their students, of that notion.

In seeking an academic position, I discovered that eight years of practice made me highly suspect. Some professors apparently thought former practitioners would tell war stories about their cases and teach students how to schmooze with the court clerk. Yale, however, with whatever reservations, appointed me to its law faculty, for which I will always be grateful. The first five years, until the student radicals arrived, were the best years of my professional life. The students were bright and argumentative. Ward Bowman, an economist, provided invaluable discussions about antitrust. Alexander Bickel—whom I count as the best friend I ever had—was equally important to my development of a theory of constitutional interpretation, though we disagreed about it. Together, we taught a seminar in Constitution Theory. Influenced by John Stuart Mill and extrapolating from *Griswold* v. *Connecticut,* the original right of privacy case, I made the preposterous argument that the only harm government should be permitted to prevent was physical injury. Bickel said, "What if I engage in indecent exposure?" I replied that the law already had a doctrine to deal with that. "What doctrine?" Bickel asked. "De minimis non curat lex—the law does not take cognizance of trifles." That was the only time in a long relationship that he was silenced for a minute.

Bickel emphasized tradition as the only effective curb on courts. His judicial philosophy, I told our class on the First Amendment, was a combination of Edmund Burke and *Fiddler on the Roof.* That one he liked. He recognized, however, that the Warren Court had shattered whatever tradition there was left to lean upon. I, in contrast, was searching for a firm theory of when government was permitted to coerce and when it was not. Both of us, I now think, were wrong. The tradition, such as it was, is now gone forever, and I came to realize that Lord Patrick Devlin was right: "it is not possible to set theoretical limits to the power of the State to legislate against immorality."

Teaching is the best way to learn an entire field of law. Practitioners drill deeply into narrow areas in preparing a case. Academics teach across an entire field. Each has advantages, and, when combined, they nourish each other. When not combined, there is in each the danger of sterility. It is unfortunate that these two branches of the profession view each other with suspicion. It is even more unfortunate that sometimes the suspicion on both sides is justified. The aversion of many professors to those who practiced what the professors were supposedly teaching was astonishing. When I spoke at an appointments committee meeting against hiring young men and women just out of school or clerkships, I was met with stony expressions; nobody on the committee and few on the faculty had more than trivial experience with the day-to-day operation of the law. One exceptionally able student, urged to join the faculty, said he would like two or three years of experience first. He was told not to waste his time.

The insularity of legal academia has become a major problem. Many articles published in major law reviews are of no use to practitioners or judges but consist of philosophical exercises (at which law professors are not very good), often on the trilogy familiar in the humanities—race, sex, and class. Some prestigious law schools actually award tenure to those who write stories bereft of any legal analysis about the anguish of living in an oppressive society. It may be tempting to view such follies as no more than raw material for another *Lucky Jim,* but the situation is serious. Many law students are ill-prepared for their careers and potentially dangerous to their clients; they must be socialized and in some cases educated by the law firms that hire them.

Working in tandem with this distrust of professionalism is the strong liberal bias of law faculties. One professor said to another, with the intent that I should overhear, that it was the "shame of the law school" that it had two Republicans when no other department at Yale had any. Two out of about thirty-five was, in his view, too many by two, but he was wrong about the rest of the university: aside from the two excrescences in the law school, there was one other admitted Republican on Yale's faculty of two thousand. There surely must have been more, but they had the sense to keep their heads down.

I would not overstate the matter. There were professors who offered professional training and maintained good relationships with the practicing bar. Nor do I do wish to give the impression that I was in any way ill-treated. Most of the faculty, if somewhat bemused by finding a conservative in their midst, were friendly and willing to hear, if not to adopt, nonliberal views. The problem was that ideas and attitudes were clustered at one end of the spectrum. Students were not exposed to the full range of opinion about law. The addition of former student radicals to faculties, moralistic men and women with harder ideological edges, seems at many schools to have made the few conservatives actually beleaguered. That is particularly true, though not exclusively so, of those who teach and write about constitutional law.

My tenure at Yale was interrupted by service as solicitor general of the United States. The solicitor general must approve any government appeals from adverse decisions in any court, federal, state, or local, and also, along with members of a relatively small staff, argues government cases in the Supreme Court. Contrary to what might be supposed, the Supreme Court is the most enjoyable court to argue before. The justices are prepared and engage in lively questioning. Not all courts are like that. There are few more disheartening experiences than arguing for half an hour or more to a judge who has not read the briefs and who sits silent and impassive throughout.

The solicitor general necessarily comes to know the justices' tendencies and abilities very well. There was then, as there is today, a wide range in both characteristics. Justice Byron White was perhaps the quickest intellectually, often seeing the point well before the advocate got to it. At the other end of that spectrum was Justice Harry Blackmun. The most ideological justice was probably William J. Brennan, Jr., who was also the most charming and friendly member, though his view of the judicial function was as different from my own as could be. He was the real leader of the Court in its adoption of deplorable tendencies. He was an affable man whose compelling attractiveness undoubtedly accounted for much of his influence with other justices. It seems likely that Brennan played a major role in converting Earl Warren, whose strong point was not conceptual thinking, from a moderate conservative into a judicial radical.

Robert Nisbet, a particularly insightful observer, stated the ideological situation in the law schools and the judiciary somewhat dramatically but with considerable accuracy:

> The crusading and coercing roles of the Supreme Court and the federal judiciary . . . have created a new and important model for all those whose primary aim is the wholesale reconstruction of American society. . . . There are more and more judges, more and more lawyers, and more and more law students and professors who have entered easily into a state of mind that sees in the Supreme Court precisely what Rousseau saw in his archetypical legislators and Bentham in his omnipotent magistrate: sovereign forces for permanent revolution.

The ideological movement of constitutional law can be gauged by the changes in the casebooks used in the law schools. When I began teaching the subject in 1964, most of the casebooks concerned the structural features of the Constitution—separation of powers, federalism, the scope of Congress's and the President's powers, the legitimacy and rationale of judicial supremacy, and so on. Cases involving the Bill of Rights took up less than half the book. Indeed, to a modern reader, it is amazing that in Joseph Story's *Commentaries on the Constitution of the United States,* written in 1833, the discussion of the first ten amendments, the Bill of Rights, occupies about one-fiftieth of the pages. In truth, the Bill of Rights, supplemented after the Civil War by the Fourteenth Amendment guaranteeing due process of law and the equal protection of the laws against incursions by state government, did not generate many cases until well into the twentieth century. The pace picked up with the Warren Court and has not slackened since. In the 1997 edition of a leading constitutional law casebook, Bill of Rights cases took up almost four times the space given to the structural Constitution, signifying an enormous shift from interest in the processes of government to the rights of individuals. The Bill of Rights took up about 2 percent of Story's *Commentaries* and about 73 percent of the casebook. The American public regards constitutional law as little more than a list of individual rights, and they may be correct.

The reasons for this shift are no doubt various, including the multiplying confrontations of an increasingly pluralistic society. The judicial response has been to multiply rights. The most important reason for present purposes, however, was the 1954 discovery by the Supreme Court that it could order massive social change (the end of government racial discrimination in *Brown v. Board of Education*) unrelated, so the Court thought, to the meaning of the Constitution, and could prevail over resistance. I have argued elsewhere that *Brown* could have been justified on constitutional principles, but the crucial fact is that the Court did not think so. Encouraged to improve society further, it went on to ordain other major changes in governmental processes and in cultural and moral matters that were clearly not within the Court's constitutional authority. Thus, as Lino Graglia puts it, "The first and foremost thing to know about constitutional law . . . is that it has very little to do with the Constitution." The unpalatable truth is that the Court is making up the Constitution and has been for many years.

Courts below the Supreme Court have less freedom to legislate large new principles, but judges at any level can be consciously influenced by political considerations and personal predilections. In a case with large political implications, our court clearly lacked jurisdiction, but one judge, while privately admitting that to be so, placed his decision on factual grounds because that would leave him free to decide a future case, as a ruling of lack of jurisdiction would not. "You never know," he said, "what may come down the pike next." That was lawlessness. A number of other examples come to mind. I have no doubt that my views and temperament influenced my judging, but that is inevitable, and the influence was never conscious. A number of my colleagues on the bench could honestly say the same thing, and there is a great difference between judges who, knowing it impossible to succeed entirely, do their best to eliminate views that have no proper role in reaching decisions and those who actively enforce their prejudices.

Judges belong to the class that John O'Sullivan first identified as "Olympians." The political philosopher Kenneth Minogue described the philosophy of this class:

> Olympianism is the project of an intellectual elite that believes that it enjoys superior enlightenment and that its business is to spread this benefit to those living on the lower slopes of human achievement. . . . Olympianism burrowed like a parasite into the most powerful institution of the emerging knowledge economy—the universities.

From there the infection spread to other culture-shaping institutions, most notably the Supreme Court which was accused, justly in my opinion, with reasoning backwards from desired results to spurious rationales. "[T]hat is a reality," Alexander Bickel wrote, "if it be true, on which we cannot allow the edifice of judicial review to be based, for if that is all judges do, then their authority over us is totally intolerable and totally irreconcilable with the theory and practice of political democracy." Yet that is the reality upon which judicial review rests today.

The Court's dominant theme is now radical personal autonomy or moral relativism, signified by its emphasis on the liberty mentioned in the Due Process Clause. That reliance, though repeated scores of times, is utterly illegitimate. The clause was clearly meant to guarantee that no one be deprived of liberty without a fair process; it has nothing to say about a fair substance of the law. History as well as the constitutional text proves that. As John Hart Ely wrote, "there is simply no avoiding the fact that the word that follows 'due' is 'process.' . . . [W]e apparently need periodic reminding that 'substantive due process' is a contradiction in terms—sort of like 'green pastel redness.'" Unfortunately, periodic reminding does no good. The Court continues on its way, judging the substance of laws according to the justices' personal opinions of what liberties we should or should not enjoy. There could be no clearer demonstration that the Court regularly and frequently orders our lives changed with a power it has no legitimate claim to wield.

The question arises, why is the movement of judge-made constitutional law in the direction of extreme personal autonomy? It is, of course, the world view of the Olympians, but it has also come to be a feature of popular culture. Look where you will, autonomy erodes discipline everywhere. Religion is a field in many ways very much like law, and both have heresies that threaten to overcome orthodoxy. The phenomenon of "cafeteria Catholics" is well known: despite the Church's doctrine, Catholic rates of contraceptive use and abortion are about the same as those of Protestants and Jews. When the Episcopal Church ordained a practicing homosexual as a bishop, appeals to scripture were brushed aside with amused disdain. A United Methodist lesbian minister was acquitted in a church trial of the charge that lesbianism was incompatible with Christianity, though it clearly is. The restraints of public decency have been abandoned on cable TV and are losing force on over-the-air TV and radio. No small part of these developments is due to the Court's protection of obscenity and its marginalization of religion. But, equally, no small part of the Court's behavior is due to the culture in which it operates. The real doctrines of the Constitution have no more chance to control the Court than do the real doctrines of the churches to control the behavior of its clergy and parishioners.

And why are legal arguments—in law schools as much as in courts—frequently invested with so much anger, an anger that also suffuses and distorts our politics? Law is unlikely, after all, to develop an intense emotional temperature unrelated to the wider world of political and social discourse. To say that the anger is due to the culture war is accurate but hardly an explanation. An explanation that I find eminently plausible is that there is always a segment of the population, usually the intellectuals, that requires meaning in life. The decline of religion, the loss of its redemptive vision, required a new transcendent principle. The obvious, the only, candidate was socialism.

Conservatism offers no comparable utopian goal. As Charles Krauthammer points out, the collapse of the socialist ideal has left Olympians with nothing except anger. Anger at the existing state of society was, of course, always an active ingredient in socialism. Some compensation for the loss of socialism is sought by various angry radicals in the extreme versions of feminism, environmentalism, animal rights, racial and gender preferences, homosexual rights, international control of American actions, and other causes. That anger characterizes the Democratic party, which is the party of the Olympians, and the activist groups that are what's left of socialism.

The debate within the Supreme Court is usually, though not always, more genteel, but the same urge to reconstruct a highly imperfect society is apparent. The Supreme Court is enacting a program of radical personal autonomy, indeed moral chaos, piece by piece, creating new and hitherto unsuspected constitutional rights: rights to abortion, homosexual sodomy (and, coming soon, homosexual marriage), freedom from religion in the public square, racial and sexual preferences. None of these is justified by the actual Bill of Rights.

I could easily multiply examples. But the underlying philosophy of the Olympians—if it deserves so dignified a name as "philosophy"—is wonderfully summed up in the famous "mystery passage" that Justice Anthony Kennedy first articulated in an opinion reaffirming the made-up constitutional right to abortion. "These matters," Justice Kennedy wrote for the Court,

> involving the most intimate and personal choices a person may make in a lifetime [abortion, etc.], choices central to personal dignity and autonomy, are central to the liberty protected by the Fourteenth Amendment. *At the heart of liberty is the right to define one's own concept of existence, of meaning, of the universe, and of the mystery of human life.* Beliefs about these matters could not define the attributes of personhood were they formed under compulsion of the State. [emphasis added]

Although this passage instantly attracted some measure of the ridicule it deserved, Justice Kennedy chose to repeat it in *Lawrence* v. *Texas* (2003), which pretends to discover a constitutional right to homosexual sodomy. What other practices, we may wonder, are now "at the heart of liberty"? Kennedy's aria about "the right to define one's own concept of existence, of meaning," etc., is not simply laughable intellectually; it also tells us something grim about our future, the Court, and a people that supinely accepts such judicial diktats.

Kennedy's rhetoric is loaded with legal and cultural messages. First, and most obviously, the "mystery passage" demonstrates once again that today's Bill of Rights jurisprudence has almost nothing to do with the Bill of Rights. Once more the procedural meaning of the Due Process Clause has been transformed into an unconfined substantive judgment by a majority of the justices. When new rights are not invented out of whole cloth, as in *Lawrence,* real rights are expanded beyond all recognition. The Court is now the Olympians' heavy artillery and panzer divisions in the culture war. The "mystery passage," in particular, and the opinions on social and cultural issues, generally, demonstrate that a majority of the Court is willing to make decisions for which it can offer no intelligible argument. There is thus a sharp decline in intellectual honesty and the integrity of constitutional law. Constitutional law is no longer an intellectual discipline but a series of political impulses. I sometimes feel sorry for the editors of casebooks who accompany each opinion with a series of questions and observations about the doctrines the Court is laying down, modifying, refining, and abandoning. Doctrines don't matter; politics do.

The sanctity of these decisions is not just a litmus test for judicial nominees but an article of faith among Democratic politicians. One of the more dismaying sights of the year was all seven candidates for the Democratic presidential nomination standing before a feminist organization obsequiously pledging allegiance to *Roe* v. *Wade.* The Senate Democrats, along with a few Northeastern Republicans, will not confirm any nominee to the Supreme Court, and very few to any federal court, who does not express wholehearted support for that ghastly decision. To almost all Democratic senators, virtually unrestrained judicial activism in the service of the cultural Left has become the "mainstream."

In the hands of the Court, radical individualism approaches judicial nihilism. Since each individual must be permitted to define meaning for himself, it must follow that there is no allowable truth, legal or moral. Yet, as Lord Devlin observed, "What makes a society of any sort is community of ideas, not only political ideas but also ideas about the way its members should behave and govern their lives; these latter ideas are its morals." Partly as a consequence of the Supreme Court's extra-constitutional adventures, we are losing our community of ideas about moral behavior. The result is a species of legal triumphalism: When law has disintegrated the bonds of society, its common moral assumptions, there will be nothing left but law to sustain us, and law alone cannot bear that weight.

Even the sense of the sacred is now a mocked and withered virtue. To-day's justices seem to have taken their inspiration from the radically liber-tarian John Stuart Mill of *On Liberty*—from the Mill, that is, who endorsed the view that "society has no business *as* society to decide anything to be wrong which concerns only the individual." *This* Mill would have applauded the sentiment if not the logic of Kennedy's "mystery passage." As Gerturde Himmelfarb has pointed out, however, there was another, more sober Mill, a Mill who acknowledged that

> In all political societies which have had a durable existence, there has been some fixed point; something which men agreed in holding sacred; which it might or might not be lawful to contest in theory, but which no one could either fear or hope to see shaken in practice. . . . But when the question-ing of these fundamental principles is (not an occasional disease but) the habitual condition of the body politic . . . the state is virtually in a position of civil war; and can never long remain free from it in act and fact.

That describes our culture war to a T. Examples of the denigration of the formerly sacred are numerous: the symbol of the American flag, the idea of public decency, the centrality of religion, and even traditional marriage—all are clearly threatened if not, indeed, mortally damaged. Of all the institu-tions of society, perhaps only the judiciary and, most especially, the Supreme Court is still regarded as sacred. Certainly, a majority of the justices think of the Court that way, and three of them have been explicit about the sacro-sanct nature of their office. In *Planned Parenthood* v. *Casey* (1992), three of the five justices who voted to retain a right to abortion wrote of Americans who would be "tested" by following the Court's decision:

> [The American people's] belief in themselves as [a] people [who aspire to live according to the rule of law] is not readily separable from their under-standing of the Court invested with the authority to decide their consti-tutional cases and speak before all others for their constitutional ideals. If the Court's legitimacy should be undermined, then so would the country be in its very ability to see itself through its constitutional ideals.

That the people are "tested" by their willingness to follow the puerile moralizing of judges and that their "belief in themselves" is inextricably bound to their obedience to the Court is a piece of hubris that might have been expected to produce a backlash of outrage. That it did not is worth pondering.

Having established virtually unquestioned authority on the domestic front, judges, also without any warrant in the Constitution, appear to be contemplating roles as international statesmen. Justice Stevens, writing for four members of the Court in 1988, relied upon "the views that have been expressed by respected professional organizations, by other nations that share our Anglo-American heritage, and by leading members of the Western European community" to hold it a forbidden cruel and unusual punishment to execute a person for a capital crime committed when he was fifteen years of age. There have been other instances of reliance upon foreign decisions and statutes in interpreting the Constitution of the United States, but perhaps the most intriguing was Justice Steven Breyer's statement in 1999 that he found "useful" decisions concerning allowable delays in executions by the Privy Council of Jamaica, the Supreme Court of India, and the Supreme Court of Zimbabwe. It is puzzling enough to contemplate what decisions handed down by foreign courts in the late twentieth century have to do with an American document written in the late eighteenth century; it passes understanding how the Bill of Rights drafted by James Madison is illuminated by the decisions of judges controlled by Robert Mugabe, the African tyrant and mass murderer.

The citation of foreign decisions in American constitutional opinions may be irritating, but it may also be only window-dressing: the Court would probably reach the same results without the aid of the Supreme Court of Zimbabwe. Still, Justice Sandra Day O'Connor suggests the justices will go further. She said in a recent speech that decisions by the courts of other countries could be persuasive authority in American courts. At a time, she said, when 30 percent of the United States' gross national product is internationally derived, "No institution of government can afford to ignore the rest of the world." It might seem that the one institution of government that *should* ignore the rest of the world is the one that derives its sole authority from a purely domestic source, the United States Constitution. It got worse. Justice O'Connor said the Court had found persuasive an amicus brief submitted by American diplomats saying that their jobs in foreign countries were made difficult by the practice of capital punishment in the United States. Rather than representing us to foreign nations, the diplomats were representing foreign countries in our Court. This internationalizing trend is so delightful to Olympians—though they might draw the line at Zimbabwe—that Linda Greenhouse could write with apparent approval in *The New York Times* that "it is not surprising that the justices have begun to see themselves as participants in a worldwide constitutional conversation." It would be more accurate to say that they are participants in a worldwide constitutional convention.

Perhaps we should have seen this coming. For as Minogue pointed out, "We may define Olympianism as a vision of human betterment to be achieved on a global scale by forging the peoples of the world into a single community based on the universal enjoyment of appropriate human rights. . . . Olympians instruct people, they do not obey them." And Olympians require constitutional courts to make certain their instructions stick. They may succeed. The idea of international law is catnip to some people, particularly to the intelligentsia. They may sell the notion to much of the public because it is often supposed that removing disputes from the arenas of diplomacy and force is to substitute high principle for the clash of crass interests. Those who make and ratify our treaties ought not to place authority in international courts without considering what we know about judges. Added to the usual tendency of courts with vague charters to enlarge their powers beyond anything anticipated by the law writers, there is the additional, and insoluble, problem of conflicting national interests and animosities, particularly animosity to the West in general and to the United States in particular. Nevertheless, the process of internationalizing law is taking place in our and in foreign courts without the consent of representative institutions.

In short, what we are witnessing is the homogenization of the constitutional laws of the nations of the West. And, since constitutional law is increasingly made by judges without reference to the actual constitutions they purport to be applying, there is developing an international constitutional common law. That is made possible by the fact that judges in almost all Western nations share Olympian values. Thus, we tend to see indifference or hostility to religion, the embrace of sexual permissiveness, the normalization of homosexuality, the creation of abortion rights, the classification of pornography and extreme vulgarity as protected free speech, hostility to traditional authorities, and special rights for favored ethnic minorities and, often, for women. All this leads to the Balkanization of society and the weakening of social discipline based upon a shared morality. It is difficult to say what the next developments in the judicial reconstruction of society will be. No one could have foreseen many of the developments just listed early in the twentieth century: many were not anticipated even ten or fifteen years ago. Who even a decade ago could have concluded that "homosexual marriage" was a right guaranteed by the Massachusetts state constitution (a document written by John Adams)?

It sometimes seems that there is nothing left for judges to invent. But then one recalls the cautionary tale of the patent office commissioner who resigned in the nineteenth century because he believed all significant inventions had already been made. We may rely upon the apparently endless creativity of judges to continue to find new socially disintegrating rights in various federal, state, and foreign constitutions.

Though it may seem a matter for wonder that the public and its elected representatives accept all this with so little resistance, they are in fact almost completely helpless. Those who devised and ratified the Constitution had no idea what courts could become and so they built no safeguards against imperialistic judges. The framers carefully provided means for Congress to check the President and for the President to restrain Congress, but they provided no means for either of those branches to check the judiciary. Impeachment is utterly impracticable. The Jeffersonians tried that in order to replace the Federalist Supreme Court and failed. Impeachment is almost never successful unless bribery is involved. Some commentators suggest reliance on the congressional power under the Constitution to make exceptions to the Supreme Court's appellate jurisdiction. But even if the Court would accept the subtraction of its authority over a class of cases—and it is by no means certain that it would—the Constitution also provides that jurisdiction over federal constitutional questions lodges in state courts, many of which are at least as activist as the U.S. Court, and neither Congress nor state legislatures could remove it.

Only a draconian response to unconstitutional court decisions remains. The Massachusetts Supreme Judicial Court has ordered the state's legislature to amend its statutory law to permit homosexual marriage. It is, or should seem, extraordinary that a court should order a legislature to amend and enact laws. The underlying decision is so self-evidently an act of judicial usurpation of the legislative function, and so wrong as a matter of constitutional interpretation, that it might seem that any self-respecting legislature would simply refuse to comply, and if it did comply, that the governor would veto the bill. So accustomed have we become to judicial supremacy, however, that such a course sounds revolutionary. Yet there must be some means of standing up to a court that itself is behaving unconstitutionally in very serious matters.

The classic hypothetical supposes that in 1860 the southern states had claimed a constitutional right to secede (they would have had a plausible argument) and that the Court, most of whose members were southerners, had agreed and ordered Lincoln to let the states go peacefully. Should Lincoln have obediently removed federal troops from Fort Sumter and ordered the armed forces not to interfere with the secession? The question answers itself. Some issues are too important for courts to determine national policy. We may disagree about which issues are that crucial, but that there must be a line beyond which courts must not go and demand obedience seems incontrovertible. At present, we have no criteria for drawing such lines. The Court has employed the political question doctrine to discipline itself, but that doctrine rests with the discretion of the Court.

It is understandable that no legislature or governor has taken such action in the past. (Lincoln provides an exception. During the Civil War he suspended the writ of habeas corpus before Congress, which alone had the authority to do so, acted to ratify what he had done.) We have become so used to the supremacy of the courts that it might be politically dangerous for legislators to stand against judges. Defying a court's constitutional ruling, moreover, might set a dangerous precedent. The power of courts rests entirely upon moral authority granted by the perception that they stand on principle. Our sense of their fragility and fear of harming their capacity to do good restrains us. Thus the vulnerability of courts paradoxically renders them almost invulnerable. But what has happened in Massachusetts, and is likely to happen nationally, is so outrageous that a stand against an imperialistic court might be popular, and it would certainly be wise, because it would be a last-stand defense of the constitutional order.

The problems with all efforts to rein in runaway courts, including the appointment of restrained judges, are manifold, but two require mention. The first is that there is a large and powerful constituency for activist courts. The Olympians, who control virtually all the means of opinion formation, are also powerful in the Senate and will resist by any means available, including, as they are now demonstrating, the filibuster, to stop any effort to attempt to restrict courts to their proper constitutional function. In that they will be supported by a large portion of the non-Olympian public, which simply does not know what is in the Constitution. The judiciary, and most especially the Supreme Court, is held in higher esteem, with the possible exception of the churches, than any other institution, public or private. And this seems true in all Western nations where judges have acquired the power of judicial review.

One reason, oddly enough, is that the Court is held in high esteem precisely because it is unelected, unrepresentative, and unaccountable—which is to say that the justices are not seen as politicians. To survive and to get anything done, politicians have to make expedient compromises. Judges, or so it is mistakenly believed, are not politicians but men and women of principle, untarnished by compromise. The public does not stop to consider that compromise gives all the players some of what they want while judicial principle usually turns out to be a zero-sum game, and, moreover that the non-elite majority is usually the loser in ideological litigation. The preference for judges over legislators seems to signify a weariness with and distrust of democracy. If so, that is an ominous development and one encouraged by judges who have insisted not only upon their supremacy but upon their superior virtue. The appearance of other authoritarians stronger even than the Court would be an expensive cure for the ills of radical autonomy. We may come at last, though perhaps too late, to see the wisdom of Judge Learned Hand's observation about "the fatuity of the system which grants such powers to men it insists shall be independent of popular control."

REINS ON JUDGES: A LONG TRADITION

To the Editor:

Bob Herbert (column, Dec. 4) refers to my proposal, since withdrawn, that Congress be empowered to overturn judicial decisions as "right-wing radicalism run wild."

In fact, there is a long and respectable history of attempts to curb courts that run wild: Thomas Jefferson tried impeachment of the Supreme Court justices, but his first attempt narrowly failed in the Senate. Robert La Follette proposed overriding the court by a two-thirds vote in Congress. Judge Learned Hand thought of amending the Constitution to limit the court; Franklin D. Roosevelt tried to "pack" the court with new justices to change the court's direction.

Mr. Herbert must be dismayed by the persistence of such right-wing radicals as these in trying to tame unchecked judicial power.

More recently, Canada, hardly a right-wing country, adopted a constitutional provision like the one I suggested. Its ineffectiveness caused me to abandon my own proposal.

Concerns about imperialistic courts are not part of a "relentless conservative assault" but the continuation of a tradition created by both liberals and conservatives who value the historic meaning of the Constitution more than they do the power of judges to make the Constitution mean whatever they wish.

From the *New York Times*, December 12, 2000

Natural Law and the Constitution

The notion of injecting "natural law" into constitutional interpretation is the conservative version of the liberals' "living Constitution," which is to be informed by "moral philosophy." The conservative version is no more reputable than the liberal. Both are simply means of amending the Constitution to bring it into closer alignment with one's preferred world view. This is not to deny that there are regulations of behavior that can be viewed as natural law. This is the case with all animals that live in communities.

The basic rules are probably those essential to the survival of a group or community. Animals that live in communities must develop regulations of cooperation and restraint that govern the behavior of community members toward each other—rules about food gathering and sharing, the protection and training of the young, the sexual availability of females, etc. Philosophers tend not to like such mundane explanations. I once debated the subject with Alan Bloom before an audience of Yale students. By way of illustration, and to encourage a degree of humility, I pointed out that wild dog packs have rules of this sort. Bloom responded that men are not wild dogs. I knew I had lost the audience when the Yalies responded with yips and howls and beating their forepaws together.

Natural law seems an unlikely topic for extensive television coverage, nor would one expect United States senators to develop high anxiety over the subject. Yet the confirmation hearings of Justice Clarence Thomas brought both of those improbable events to pass. Thomas and Senator Joseph Biden grappled repeatedly with the concept of natural law and its relation to constitutional law. The educational benefits, however, cannot be said to

From *First Things*, March 1992.

have been great, or even modest. Most commentators thought the subject remained "murky."

The sudden popularity of so arcane and elusive a topic was due to Thomas's past writing that justices could use natural law to alter the Constitution. It was hoped by some and feared by others that this meant he would vote to remake the Constitution in a conservative direction. Liberal professors and commentators at once feigned hysteria at the thought that a justice might invoke extra-constitutional principles. The anathema "out of the mainstream" was once more solemnly intoned. This, from people who pronounced Justices William Brennan and Thurgood Marshall "great" precisely because they repeatedly departed from any conceivable meaning of the historic Constitution, was a bit hard to take. Nevertheless, their hypocrisy aside, the liberals have a point.

Now that there is reason to hope for the imminent demise of left-liberal activism by the Supreme Court, we must ask what our real objection was to the era that seems to be passing. Did we think that the illegitimacy of the Court's performance lay in its liberalism or in its activism, its politics, or its contempt for law? Having endured for half a century a Court that seized authority not confided to it to lay down as unalterable law a liberal social agenda nowhere to be found in the actual Constitution of the United States, conservatives must decide whether they want a Court that behaves in the same way but in the service of *their* agenda.

These thoughts are prompted by proposals that the Court should strike down, on the basis of natural law, statutes that contravene nothing in the Constitution. That idea is more popular with conservatives than I had supposed. There is a growing literature, but Hadley Arkes's recent book *Beyond the Constitution*, and articles by Russell Hittinger and William Bentley Ball[1] may provide a representative sample. All three take me to task for excluding natural law as a source of new principles in constitutional adjudication.

"Natural law." The words have an attractive, even a seductive, resonance. They refer to principles about ultimate right and wrong that transcend particular nations and cultures and are true for all people at all times. Most of us feel intuitively that natural law exists, though we differ, both as to its source and its content. For some, it is ordained by God; for others, it arises from the nature of human beings, even if we are evolutionary accidents; or it may simply express the requirements for anything recogniz-

---

1. Hittinger, "Liberalism and the American Natural Tradition," 25 *Wake Forest Law Review* 429 (1990); Ball, "The Tempting of Robert Bork: What's a Constitution Without Natural Law?" *Crisis*, June 1990.

able as a society. Whatever its source, natural law's content is discovered by reason.

In contrast, "cultural relativism," which Professor Arkes equates with legal positivism, holds that there are "no moral truths which hold their validity across cultures. . . . [So that statutes or constitutional provisions] have the standing of law only because they are 'posited' or set down by the authorities in any country." Arkes appears to think legal positivism implies cultural or moral relativism. But of course, on his own statement, that is not so. It is quite possible, indeed quite sensible, to think that there are moral truths but that statutes and constitutions have standing as law, law to be applied by judges and enforced by the police, only because the authorities have said so.

Given the general tendency to confuse the two, it is important to understand the limited sense in which natural law or moral philosophy is useful, indeed indispensable, to constitutional adjudication, and the larger, more free-hand sense in which it is pernicious.

Arkes is particularly valuable in his exploration of the limited use of philosophy as he discusses the moral principles that necessarily underlie many of the most important constitutional decisions. One wishes that more of our jurists would take to heart his demonstration that "the various clauses of the Constitution and the Bill of Rights can be established, in their meaning, only by attaching them to the properties of a moral argument. And when we do that, we find ourselves tracing these clauses back to the structure of moral understanding that must lie behind the text of the Constitution." The Constitution, in some of its most important provisions, is quite general, not meant to be taken in full literalness, and therefore dangerous in the hands of those who do not interpret such provisions in the light of the principles that underlie and animate them.

The point is easily illustrated. The First Amendment states that "Congress shall make no law . . . abridging the freedom of speech." The words sound absolute. As Justice Black was fond of saying, "no law means no law"; there are no exceptions. The Court has expanded "speech" to mean "expression" so that it would appear that government may inhibit no expressive conduct. This, of course, is nonsense, and not even Justice Black ever took such a position. When there was danger that speech might provoke violence, for example, Black would find that the speech could be suppressed on the ground that it was "brigaded" with action.

But if the First Amendment is not an absolute, how are judges to know which speech is protected and which is not? By discerning the principle that underlies the speech clause, Arkes responds, and that, of course, is far wiser than proceeding by slogans or verbal formulas applied mechanically. It is a needed admonition and one I agree with. In arguing that moral philosophy should not be used to place in the Constitution what is not already there, I have been careful to say that I did not "mean that moral philosophy is alien to law and must be shunned in adjudication, but I do mean that it is valuable only at the retail level and disastrous at the wholesale. Moral reasoning can make judges aware of complexities and of the likenesses and dissimilarities of situations, all of which is essential in applying the ratifiers' principles to new situations. . . . The role it has to play is assisting judges in the continuing task of deciding whether a new case is inside or outside an old principle."

That much is common ground, and it is to be wished that Professor Arkes had stopped with that claim and illustrated the folly of ignoring it more copiously. Had the Supreme Court thought in the terms he suggests, it seems likely, for example, that the flag-burning cases would have come out differently. Certainly, eight justices could not have concluded that the First Amendment was relevant to nude dancing in the Kitty Kat Lounge. If they had been forced by Arkes to articulate their principle, it would have been entertaining to read the explanation of what idea was being expressed by the young ladies in question.

It is Professor Arkes's larger claims for a natural law constitutional juris-prudence—claims advanced by Professor Hittinger and Mr. Ball as well—that, it seems to me, land the whole enterprise in trouble. Arkes contends that moral reasoning not only illuminates the proper reach of existing con-stitutional principles but may properly be employed by judges to create new constitutional principles. A natural law judge would make positive laws out of his own perception of universal moral principles. Those moral postulates would then become just as binding on the polity as the written law of the Constitution. That is where we legal positivists get off.

Arkes writes that his object is to restore the connection between morals and law that the Founders and our early jurists understood. This understand-ing has been destroyed, he believes, by the pestilence of legal positivism, the idea that right and wrong have no existence or meaning apart from the provisions of law. I am among those cited both as holding "an extravagant skepticism toward the very notions of moral truths and natural rights" and as "regard[ing] any appeal to 'natural rights'—any appeal beyond the text of the Constitution—as a pretext for evading the discipline of the Constitu-tion." Well, no and yes, in that order. It seems impossible to live any sort of decent life without ideas about moral truth, just as it seems a corruption of the judge's function to confuse those ideas with the law to be applied.

Arkes praises the elder Justice Harlan for his dissent in *Plessy* v. *Ferguson*. The Court majority upheld state legislation requiring that blacks and whites occupy different railroad cars, so long as the physical facilities were equal. What elicits Arkes' approval is Harlan's suggestion that, the post-Civil War amendments aside, segregation could be condemned on the basis of the clauses in the original Constitution of 1787 guaranteeing the states a republican form of government and stating that the Constitution is the supreme law of the land. (It is dangerous to rely upon the insights of the elder Harlan. Holmes provided a tolerably accurate assessment when he said that he never troubled himself when that great man shied since Harlan's mind was a powerful vise, the jaws of which could not be gotten within two inches of each other.)

If there can be imported into the guarantee of a republican form of government a moral content to condemn segregation, it is difficult to understand why the same moral reasoning would not have enabled the pre-Civil War Court to end slavery. Here moral reasoning is used not to explicate provisions of the Constitution but to transform them. The difficulty is that the existence of slavery under state law was acknowledged by the original Constitution. The idea that the same Constitution could be used to end the institution is similar to the argument, favored by Justices Brennan and Marshall, that the death penalty violates the Constitution despite the fact that the document explicitly assumes that punishment's availability. It is difficult to justify a reading of the Constitution that denies what it says. Much the same problem arises when Arkes argues that certain principles of the Bill of Rights essential to the idea of law could have been applied to the states even though the Bill of Rights was clearly intended only to bind the federal government.

Hittinger assures us that "natural law reasoning is unavoidable" for three reasons. First, "the framers and ratifiers of the Bill of Rights intended at least some of the amendments to secure natural rights." Second, judicial review under the Constitution makes possible the entry of natural law theory into litigation. Third, "the Court has repeatedly vindicated individual rights on the basis of extra-textual appeals." The first reason merely requires the judge to discern what the framers and ratifiers meant, not to make up new rights the judge regards as "natural." The second and third are certainly true but do not justify the practice. If natural law reasoning is, in truth, unavoidable in constitutional adjudication, the reason is the temptation of men to use power not legitimately theirs when there is no effective method of resistance. To call what the Court has done, from *Dred Scott* to *Lochner* to *Roe*, "natural law reasoning" is to confer unwarranted dignity on a series of results resting on nothing more than assertion.

Professor Hittinger seems to think that natural law reasoning in deciding cases has safeguards: "Virtually no one holds that natural law can be a tool of legal interpretation completely independent of texts and history." But what is the relationship of natural law and history to the text when Chief Justice Taney could find in the due process clause a constitutional right to own slaves and Justice Blackmun, with the concurrence of six of his colleagues, found in the same clause a right to an abortion? Using a provision as a mere textual peg avoids all limits. Praising a series of justices, Hittinger says that they "did not mean by fundamental rights a blank check that could be filled in by judicial discretion." Perhaps the check was not entirely blank but the justices did assert the discretion to fill in the names of the payor and payee and the amount. The only thing not blank was the name of the institution to which the claimant must come to cash in his fundamental right—the Supreme Court of the United States.

Ball also believes that judges may properly amend the Constitution with their version of natural law. Thus, the due process clauses of the Fifth and Fourteenth Amendments, which were intended to be guarantees of fair procedures, not of good statutes, should be employed to strike down laws that restrict a "liberty" the judges, and Mr. Ball, would rather not be restricted. There is little argument to support the legitimacy of that practice, other than a mention of some cases whose outcome Ball approves on moral grounds. There are, of course, a great many cases, beginning with *Dred Scott*, that use the same due process technique to reach results Ball abhors. On purely moral issues, judges are no more competent or trustworthy, as Justice Scalia observed in *Cruzan*, the Missouri "right to die" case, than "nine people picked at random from the Kansas City telephone directory." Moral approval of results, an approval that will never be unanimous and will frequently be a minority view, is not of itself sufficient to justify judges in overriding the moral choices of elected legislatures.

The first and most serious problem with natural law judging, therefore, is its dubious morality. To find a principle through the natural law reasoning of judges that makes the Constitution mean something other than, sometimes opposite to, what those who voted to make it law understood themselves to mean can hardly be sound moral argument. The only reason the Constitution exists, and hence that judges have any power to void democratic choices, is that the ratifiers could agree upon certain principles. Some of those principles (the allowance of slavery, for example) were undoubtedly base. Some (freedom of speech and religion) were undoubtedly noble. But whatever their moral status, they were what was agreed to and what persuaded men to vote for them. Had the ratifiers known what a natural law judge might do to their Constitution, the principles would not have been adopted to begin with. To change the principles of the document later, and to do so in the name of the same document, is a piece of trickery hardly worthy to be called moral reasoning.

Indeed, Arkes recognizes as much elsewhere in his argument, for he writes with approval: "During the First Congress, James Madison remarked that the natural right of human beings to be governed only with their consent was an 'absolute truth.' Lincoln would later insist, in the same vein, that this doctrine of self-government was 'absolutely and eternally right.'" Government by the Constitution that was voted into law is far closer to self-government than government by judges who find principles in the document that the voters never dreamed of and would not have ratified if they had.

One need not be skeptical about the existence of moral truths and natural rights to think that appeals, by judges, to natural rights, appeals beyond the text of the Constitution, are a pretext for evading the discipline of the Constitution. Of course, there are, as Arkes and Ball insist, moral truths beyond the Constitution and moral truths antecedent to the Constitution, or the Constitution would not exist or, if existing, would not be of significantly more interest than the law of decedents' estates.

The formulation and expression of moral truths as positive law is, in our system of government, a system based on consent, a task confided to the people and their elected representatives. The judge, when he judges, must be, it is his sworn duty to be, a legal positivist. When he acts as a citizen, he, like all other citizens, must not be a legal positivist, but must seek moral truth. Otherwise, there is no way for anybody to say what the law should be, what should be enacted and what repealed. Or, at least, there would be no way other than to express one's personal interests, which no one with a differing interest is likely to find in the least persuasive.

The point is made in Arkes' discussion of Lincoln's debate with Douglas about slavery. Lincoln argued that new states and territories ought not be allowed to adopt slavery because the institution was wrong. He destroyed Douglas' argument that the matter should be left to local choice. Indifference to what choice was made necessarily assumed that slavery was neither right nor wrong but only a matter of taste. That, of course, was nonsense if slavery was a moral wrong, as Lincoln, arguing from the principles of the Declaration of Independence, demonstrated that it was. But Lincoln never suggested that the Supreme Court end slavery. If he had, he would have been untrue to his own principles of self-government.

The amendment of the Constitution according to a judge's perception of moral truth is itself so obviously morally wrong that it seems almost superfluous to add that, in any event, Arkes and Ball would not get the results they want. Ball is quite unrealistic on the point: "But do I not thus argue for the kind of despotic judiciary which gave us *Roe v. Wade?* Indeed, not. The remedy for that is not to deprive the judiciary of its power to do right, but to install in it justices who espouse the moral principles of our tradition." This ignores the fact that, from *Dred Scott* to *Roe,* we have signally failed to do so. In any event, the proposal envisions confirmation hearings in which the nominee is required to pledge allegiance to a conservative agenda rather than a liberal one. To accomplish that we need only replace our present senators with senators of whom Mr. Ball approves. We may also have to replace part of the electorate. The prospect of "correct" natural law judging is a chimera.

Arkes seems to share Ball's optimism, since he assumes that good natural law will drive out the bad. He takes me to task for saying, "There may be a natural law, but we are not agreed upon what it is, and there is no such law that gives definite answers to a judge trying to decide a case." He responds, "The translation has become familiar: The mere presence of disagreement on matters of moral consequence is taken as proof for the claim that there are no moral truths (or 'natural law')." The passage bears no such construction. It is evident that people do disagree and, though there may be natural law, so long as we are unable to convince one another of its content, there will be no agreed-upon moral truths that will give judges definite answers. What we will get, as law binding upon us and impossible to change democratically, is the moral truth of a majority of nine justices. Mr. Arkes may be certain about some moral truths, but if he imagines that he can always persuade five out of nine justices to the same knowledge, he should reflect upon those occasions when, using moral reasoning, he attempted to persuade a faculty meeting of a point that ran counter to the professors' views. And no matter how long and cogently he argues, Arkes will never convince Justice Blackmun that abortion is not a natural right. This certainty that one possesses such truths and that they can be demonstrated to everyone's satisfaction reminds me of a brief encounter with Mortimer Adler. He had compared me unfavorably to Justice Blackmun on the ground that I was a legal positivist while Blackmun was a natural law judge. I asked Adler why he thought judges were entitled to enforce the natural law. He said, "It doesn't take long to learn."

Since I am tired of explaining to my wife that, contrary to Arkes and Hittinger, I am not a moral skeptic, I am grateful to Mr. Ball for understanding that I have merely been urging moral modesty on judges: "I hope there is no need to stress that Bork rejects neither God nor God's laws; he simply doesn't want earthly judges barging into God's act!" Precisely. When a judge barges into God's act, he is all too likely to confuse who has the leading role.

A final word should be said on the relation of judging under the Constitution to larger political or ideological issues. Arkes advances the surprising contention that "the cause of conservatism in politics has been attached to 'positivism' in the law, and that kind of marriage will be the undoing of political conservatism. For it will insure that, in jurisprudence, conservatism will be brittle and unworkable, and that on matters of moral consequence conservative jurisprudence will have nothing to say." I wish he had developed that argument further since, as it stands, I do not follow it. There is no apparent reason why the vitality of political conservatism depends upon abandoning a jurisprudence of legal positivism. Political conservatism can strive for conservative legislation and legal positivist judges will faithfully apply it, just as they would apply legislation embodying liberal principles. This is merely the recognition that, in our system of government, it is not judges but the people and their elected representatives who are to make major policy decisions.

There is nothing "brittle" or "unworkable" about that. Conservative jurisprudence, if that is what legal positivism is, will, on matters of moral consequence, say what the American people direct judges to say. The morality of the consequence will be the morality of those who made the Constitution law and those who agree to abide by that law today. Natural law, morality, is the stuff out of which legislation and constitutions are made. Positive law is the application of those legal documents to decide specific controversies in court. This division of labor between the judicial branch and the political branches is a major aspect of the separation of powers, and, far from being the undoing of political conservatism, it is the foundation of the Republic.

Ball makes a somewhat similar point, saying that "however praiseworthy we may find Bork's criticism of judicial liberalism, his criticism is basically not that of a conservative." In a way, that is quite true. A number of liberals agree with my view that the judge should be politically neutral. My view of law is conservative only in that what is being conserved is the constitutional design of our government. But Ball means that criticism of law is not conservative unless it proceeds from a natural law perspective, and, in the process, he reads a great many people out of the camp of political conservatism. He approves Russell Kirk's dictum that there is no conservatism without natural law: "The 'first canon' of conservative thought is: 'belief in a transcendent order, or body of natural law, which rules society as well as conscience.'" Ball should be wary of that thought. Belief in a transcendent order could as easily, and as misleadingly, be described as the "first canon" of liberal thought. As Hittinger makes clear, much liberal jurisprudence that is unrelated to the Constitution can only be described as natural law. The dictum is also inaccurate for it arbitrarily disqualifies as conservatives people who accept and struggle to preserve every conservative value but who do not believe that such values derive from a transcendent order. It is entirely possible to think that we live in a meaningless universe, to be, if you will, a secular humanist, but also to believe, on essentially empirical grounds, that, given our culture and history, we will be healthier and happier if we live by conservative values. No useful purpose is served by denying that such friends are conservatives. We have few enough allies without thinning the ranks further.

The proper question in judging under the Constitution is not political conservatism or liberalism but the legitimacy of authority: who has the right to decide particular issues? I share many of the views that Arkes, Hittinger, and Ball express, but that does not make the imposition of those views by judges legitimate. Should these gentlemen persuade judges that natural law is their domain, the theorists will find that they have merely given judges rein to lay down their own moral and political predilections as the law of the Constitution. Once that happens, the moral reasoning of the rest of us is made irrelevant.

Natural Law and the Law: An Exchange

Introduction

The March issue of First Things *featured an essay by Robert H. Bork, "Natural Law and the Constitution." In that essay, Judge Bork responded to criticisms of his views on the topic by Hadley Arkes, Russell Hittinger, and William Bentley Ball. Because of the significance of the subject, the Editors decided to extend the discussion by inviting Messrs. Arkes, Hittinger, and Ball to respond to Mr. Bork's response to them and, finally, by allowing Mr. Bork a (for now) concluding reply to his critics.*

Hadley Arkes

In his generous nature, Robert Bork was willing to bring out the threads that connect us, even though he has borne serious reservations about the kind of argument that runs through my book *Beyond the Constitution*. As ever, he has shown an uncommon willingness to think anew about his own arguments, and for my own part, I will reflect again about the points of his reluctance to join my argument. He reveals, in his piece, points of substantial disagreement, and they may be the subject of a conversation carried on with more profit over the years, because it may be carried on as a conversation among friends. But in the aftermath of his commentary, it is worth considering briefly some of the issues that linger in the center of the debate and that touch the concerns of this journal.

As Robert Bork knows, every exponent of natural law, from Aquinas to Abraham Lincoln, understood the necessity of having "positive law." We might have a sense, for example, of the principle that would justify the protection of life from reckless endangerment. When that principle is applied to our highways, it needs to be expressed in regulations of "positive law" that

From *First Things*, May 1992.

bear on the conditions of our lives. And so the law may impose a speed limit of 55 m.p.h., or it may prescribe "breathalyzer" tests, along with roadblocks, to check on the sobriety of drivers. Natural law would provide the principle that justifies measures of this kind, but natural law would not require any one of these measures to the exclusion of others. And that is why a generation of jurists schooled in natural law found it easier to follow a regimen of judicial restraint: when judges understood more clearly the difference between natural law and positive law, they understood more readily that the mission of judges would not encompass the management of the schools or the allocation of public housing.

The proponents of natural law, then, understood the need for positive law, but that did not make them "positivists" in the current understanding. The lawyers and jurists who have earned that title are the people who have argued that there are no standards of moral judgment apart from the standards that are "posited," or set down, in the law. Hence Chief Justice Rehnquist, who has written that the "value judgments" of individuals "take on a form of moral goodness *because* they have been enacted into positive law. *It is the fact of their enactment that gives them whatever moral claim they have upon us as a society"* (emphasis added).

Judge Bork has sought to put a benign haze over this matter, but is easily dissolved: any moral principle that does not *bind* is not a moral principle. If there are no binding propositions on right and wrong apart from the law, then there is no morality outside the positive law. And if a positive law is made only through the stipulations of a local majority, then there is no right or wrong apart from the preferences of a local majority. We may be talking now about some of our friends, but the fact is that anyone who satisfies this strict understanding of a "positivist" has amply satisfied the requirements of a "cultural relativist." He may affect a respect for something he calls "moral principles," but he has committed himself to a view that acknowledges no moral truth apart from the opinions of right and wrong that are dominant in any country (i.e., the opinions that are held by a majority).

That is a position that Robert Bork came near to incorporating many years ago. "Truth," he once said, "is what the majority thinks it is at any given moment precisely because the majority is permitted to govern and to redefine its values constantly." If he has strained to persuade his friends that he is not a moral skeptic, it may be because they remember lines of that kind. Nor is it exactly settling when he seeks to make a confirming gesture about moral truth and he can deliver himself only of this sentiment: that "it seems impossible to live any sort of decent life without *ideas* about moral truth" (emphasis added). That merely tells us, of course, that there is utility in having these ideas, not that the ideas are true. But his inclination has been to move steadily away from skepticism, and he has even endorsed the notion that, in interpreting the Bill of Rights and other parts of the Constitution, it will often be necessary to trace our judgments back to "the structure of moral understanding that must lie behind the text of the Constitution."

Still, that moral understanding seems a bit cloudy to him, and he admits a critical doubt about the "source" and "content" of natural law. "For some," he says, "it is ordained by God; for others, it arises from the nature of human beings, even if we are evolutionary accidents." But here he has preserved a venerable confusion that the exponents of natural law dispelled long ago. As "the judicious" Richard Hooker explained quite clearly in 1593, the law that comes to us through revelation is the divine law. But the natural law is the law that is accessible to us simply through the reason that marks the nature of human beings: "Law rational therefore, which men commonly use to call the law of nature, meaning thereby the law which human nature knoweth itself in reason universally bound unto, which also for that cause may be termed most fitly the law of reason."

Natural law began, then, with that very nature of human beings that creates the possibilities of law: namely, that human beings are the only beings who can give reasons over matters of right and wrong. That was the understanding of Aristotle and the American Founders; but in an interesting slip, that was not part of Bork's account of human "nature." We may be, as he says, "evolutionary accidents," but the founders of law noted, in the first instance, that this primate conjugated verbs and framed justifications.

Hooker understood that the natural law began with those "laws of reason" that were accessible to creatures gifted with reason. Our first generation of jurists in this country understood that they were "doing" natural law when they wove those laws of reason through their judicial opinions. Those axioms of the law seemed so self-evident and compelling that we could often forget that we were in the presence of the first principles of law. Bork himself has applied those axioms of reasoning acutely in his own writings but without the sense that he has been speaking the language of natural law. And yet he has complained that "a natural law judge would make positive laws out of his own perception of universal moral principles. Those moral postulates would then become just as binding on the polity as the written law of the Constitution. That is where we legal positivists get off."

But when the Founders—and Bork—invoked the axioms of reason, there was no sense that the truth of these propositions depended merely on "perceptions." Consider: Justice Story often cited the maxim that what may not be done directly may not be done indirectly. If it is wrong to commit a murder, it is wrong also to hire or incite another party to perform the same killing. If the federal government cannot reach a subject directly, it may not use the taxing power as surrogate, and legislate through the guise of taxing. Chief Justice Marshall offered this dictum in *Cohens* v. *Virginia* (1821): "The judicial power of every well constituted government must be co-extensive with the legislative, and must be capable of deciding every judicial question which grows out of the constitution and laws." Corollary: any question or subject that may come, properly, within the authority of the courts must come properly within the jurisdiction of the legislature. How could it be then that the Congress is not empowered to legislate on the subject of abortion when the federal courts claim the competence to reach that subject in all of its dimensions?

These implications are scarcely trivial, and yet they flow from propositions that have a "necessary" force of axioms in the law. Marshall and Story did not see these axioms as depending in any way on their own "perceptions." They understood, rather, that the axioms were part of the "principles of law" and the discipline of judging. And for that reason, it could hardly be a question for them—as it is for Bork—of whether these axioms were "as binding on the polity as the written law of the Constitution": these axioms were utterly necessary to the coherence of the law, and any part of the law that ran counter to them simply could not have coherence as a proposition and the standing of "law." If they were axioms, they would be necessary and binding, regardless of whether they had been set down in the Constitution. A lawyer recently arguing before the Supreme Court made the common mistake of claiming a right, "under the Constitution," to a presumption of innocence. Every schoolboy apparently knows that defendants should be presumed innocent until proven guilty. And yet nowhere in the Constitution is that proposition set down. What is the ground, then, on which we have come to treat it as a principle of our law? Could it have something to do with the fact that any contrary proposition becomes untenable?

When an earlier generation of jurists noted these axioms or drew out their corollaries, they did not have the sense that they were creating "new constitutional principles." They saw themselves, rather, as drawing out the implications that arose from the axioms of law. Bork himself, as a writer and a judge, has engaged in the same exercise with considerable effect, and on this head, there is no example more telling than the argument he has advanced as his central teaching: namely, that positive law must take precedence over natural law. Natural law may indeed offer a collection of lofty thoughts, but the principles of natural law would not be binding in our law unless they are formally incorporated through the positive law. This understanding is put forward as a rule of construction—but more than that, as a premise that anchors his jurisprudence. And yet, that premise is nowhere to be found in the text of the Constitution. On what basis, then, would it claim our credence as a rule to be followed in our law—and indeed, on what basis would we even claim to know that it is true?

Robert Bork is evidently persuaded that this understanding appeals to a sense of the fitness of things or perhaps even to the "logic of law." But either way, he would be appealing to a principle of reasoning that would not depend for its truth on whether it happened to be mentioned in the Constitution. In other words, we would be back to the axioms of the law: we would have discovered, yet again, the principles of natural law.

It is a curious question as to why Bork has adopted the premises of his adversaries: why does he assume that, if we speak seriously about natural law, we must be assigning more power to the judges? My own book was directed as much to legislators and executives, who also bear a responsibility to deliberate on the constitutionality of their own acts. But Bork has been disposed to support the claim of the judges to act as the sole interpreters of the Constitution. And he has resisted the understanding held by Lincoln that the political branches may work through ordinary legislation to limit and even reverse the decisions of the courts. The defenders of natural law have not sought to protect, in that way, the power of courts. But it does not appear quite yet that Bork has made the connection: the proponents of natural law have been drawn to him precisely because he has supported in his teaching a discipline of restraint for judges.

Robert Bork, as a jurist, was the most sensible and disciplined of judges. I remarked to him once that he is very much a child of the University of Chicago, and he has spoken the language of natural justice all his life. And that is another reason why his absence from the Supreme Court has been a grievous loss. If he were there, we would now have on that tribunal two judges who have brooded at length over natural law: one who has proclaimed his dedication to it, while professing that it has only the faintest bearing on the cases before him; and another who has practiced natural law even while professing with a proper diffidence that it cannot be done.

And yet, there is one reflex that continues to run counter to this pattern. Bork expressed his dubiety about the argument made by Justice Harlan that the segregation of the races might be challenged under that clause in the Constitution which guarantees to each State "a republican form of government." He found it "difficult to understand why the same moral reasoning would not have enabled the pre-Civil War court to end slavery." The task for the judges then would have been comparable, he thought, to the task managed by Justices Brennan and Marshall on the death penalty: *viz.,* to flex their genius in showing "that the death penalty violates the Constitution despite the fact that the document explicitly assumes that punishment's availability."

But here, Bork runs the risk of falling into the same mistake made by Chief Justice Taney in the *Dred Scott* case: there is no explicit endorsement of slavery in the Constitution comparable to the explicit mention of "capital" crimes and punishments. And as Bork knows, that was not an accident. The Founders made their accommodation with slavery, but they took care that the name of that hateful institution would not be imprinted in the Constitution where it could stand as a lingering embarrassment when slavery had come to an end. The silences of the Constitution in this respect were a mark of the original understanding: that slavery would be tolerated for prudential reasons, but it could never be endorsed in principle. Even Founders from the South recognized that slavery was incompatible in principle with a polity founded on the right of human beings to be governed only with their own consent. I cannot imagine that Bork should find it extravagant in any degree that a judge would acknowledge that same understanding.

What is at issue is whether judges could have taken it upon themselves to upset the political compromise on slavery that was necessary to the creation of the Union. Judges tutored in natural rights and committed to a "government of consent" had been quite cautious not to snatch this responsibility from the hands of officers elected by the people. A court composed of judges of that character could have helped to avert a political crisis by avoiding the mistake made by Chief Justice Taney: they would not have fallen into the error of finding that "the right of property in a slave is distinctly and expressly affirmed in the Constitution."

They would have been more alert to that point precisely because they would have understood the principles of natural right that stood behind the Constitution, and guided even its compromises. The aim of my book was to remind us of the way in which jurists and statesmen in an earlier day were able to trace their judgments back to those first principles "beyond the Constitution." Just what those principles were and how they reasoned about them forms the issue in dispute even among friends. And it is a reflection of Robert Bork, in his sense of engagement, that the question provides for him and his friends the steadiest of work.

Russell Hittinger

Judge Bork reminds us that ideology should have no place in constitutional interpretation. In *Federalist* 78, Alexander Hamilton maintained that the judiciary "may truly be said to have neither Force nor Will, but merely judgment. . . ." This holds not only for the institution of the judiciary, which has no immediate authority over the sword or the purse and enjoys no legislative powers, but also for the judge whose responsibility is to interpret the law, to exercise judgment rather than legislative will. Whatever the merits or demerits of a particular philosophy *about* law, the law cannot be regarded as an instrument, outcome, or implication of the judge's private theory. Here there is no significant disagreement between Judge Bork and his critics.

Moreover, no one who has carefully considered the history of the Supreme Court over the past several decades can fail to agree with Judge Bork's general admonition about the clumsy and sometimes mischievous uses of natural law theory. In the first place, whatever the state of eighteenth-century opinion on the issue, today there is no general agreement about the meaning of "natural law." In the second place, the concept is useless unless it is applied to particular disputes. While there is an impressive amount of case law influenced by one or another natural law theory, philosophically speaking, the results hardly constitute a consistent body of law. In the third place, since the late nineteenth century, judicial uses of natural law (more often than not) have been ideological. Rather than being an instrument in the service of clarifying the moral principles embedded in our law, natural law theory has been used to obscure a willful and often ignorant political or social agenda favored by the judiciary.

To my knowledge, most so-called "conservative" proponents of natural law are in agreement with Judge Bork about this problem. In reference to my article in the *Wake Forest Law Review* 429 (1990), Judge Bork neglects to point out that one of my chief points is that liberal natural law theory has been something close to an unmitigated disaster. I argue that it has proved to be neither a faithful steward of the tradition of American natural law jurisprudence, nor an articulate vehicle for defending the rule of law. Though Bork correctly cites me as saying that natural law theory is "unavoidable," I certainly never suggested that the Douglas-Brennan-Blackmun school of natural law should be regarded as an unavoidable fixture of our constitutional jurisprudence. The whole point of the article is to show precisely where it has gone wrong, how it has capitulated to ideology, and perforce why it ought to be rejected.

Curiously, Judge Bork writes as though he is on the defensive on this issue of natural law. But the truth of the matter is that *he* has set the terms of the discussion. Having issued a very powerful criticism of judicial activism, he has put natural law jurisprudence in the position of having to justify itself—at the very least in the position of having to distinguish itself from the run-amok activism of the contemporary court. As he says: "Having endured for half a century a Court that seized authority not confided to it to lay down as unalterable law a liberal social agenda nowhere to be found in the actual Constitution of the United States, conservatives must decide whether they want a Court that behaves in the same way but in the service of *their* agenda." Judge Bork's concern is intelligible and fair.

The problem is that the issue is not a tidy one. It necessarily involves analysis of historical, philosophical, and hermeneutical issues that cannot be undertaken in a careful way in a brief essay, much less in a reply to such an essay. On this score, I am not sure that Judge Bork has really tackled the strongest arguments or the most perplexing questions raised in the writings of either Professor Arkes or myself. The complex issues are flattened out and reduced to the problem of judicial review. Whatever the extent or depth of the problem of natural law, it is something more than what can be accurately encapsulated in the debate over judicial review or the performance of the activist Court.

Moreover, the waters of this debate are muddied because Judge Bork has not adequately, or at least not entirely, elucidated his own understanding of these matters. For example, he admits that a judge can be expected to address natural law in the course of discerning "what the framers and ratifiers meant"—a discernment, he says, that must be distinguished from making up "new rights the judge regards as 'natural.'" I agree. Although Clarence Thomas ran from the issue of natural law during the Senate hearings, he too finally agreed with the proposition that it is proper for a judge to attend to natural law theory if it is a conspicuous element in the statute or constitutional text under dispute. Indeed, for an American to rule out some conjunction between original intent and natural law would be nothing less than an ideological, if not Orwellian, rewriting of history.

In a certain sense, the entire issue rests upon what can be included in, or excluded by, this discernment about the intent of the framers and ratifiers. They had strong convictions about natural law—convictions that influenced not only their understanding of the natural principles of justice underlying the Constitution as a whole, but that also shaped their understanding of certain clauses of the Constitution, the Bill of Rights, and section one of the Fourteenth Amendment. Granted that the judge must never read his private theory of "nature" or "justice" into the Constitution, the question is

(1) whether one is already there, and (2) whether it sets a norm for interpretation of the law.

Simply put, does Judge Bork believe that a responsible method of original intent can locate a natural law of rights or political institutions embedded in our Constitution? If so, does Judge Bork believe that this can have any bearing upon the judge's interpretation and application of the law? If the answer to these two questions is yes, then there is probably some common ground between Judge Bork and his conservative critics. Judge Bork gives indications that this common ground exists, even though his approach to natural law often appears to be exclusively devoted to debunking judicial activism, whether of the left or the right.

A judge who focuses upon the natural law intent of the framers might be a clumsy hermeneuticist; he might be a maladroit jurisprude when he tries to apply the principles to the case at hand; indeed, for lack of either philosophical or legal training, he might make a complete mess of things; but he cannot be called a judicial activist. He can only be called a judicial activist if we have already determined, ahead of the game as it were, that there is no judicially cognizable natural law theory to be found in the legal texts or in the intent of the framers. If one has reason to believe that this is so, then Judge Bork is correct when he suggests that conservative proponents of natural law are up to nothing essentially different than the liberal activists. Both would be reading a theory "into" the law. And even if one theory is better on its own merits, it would still amount to an imposition of a judge's private opinion. But if one has reason to believe that the fundamental law bespeaks *some* natural principles of justice, then the superficial symmetry between liberal and conservative activists does not necessarily follow. For what *might* distinguish these two schools is whether or not one or the other comports with the original intent of the framers and ratifiers. That, I maintain, is an important difference.

The charge of "activism" on the part of a natural lawyer cannot be anything other than polemical assertion until we settle this matter. Judge Bork sometimes appears to leave the door ajar to the possibility that one or another understanding of natural law comports with the intent of the founders (and hence the possibility of a principled distinction between sound and unsound theories and users of natural law), while at other times he seems to suggest that judicial uses of natural law theory are necessarily impositions of the judge's private worldview (and hence the distinction between sound and unsound theories has no point as to what judges do).

Granted the wide array of theoretical and practical problems that attend natural law theory as a method of constitutional interpretation, it is nevertheless important to keep in mind that it is not the only species of willful, ignorant, or ideological jurisprudence. Arguably, more mischief has been done in the name of one or another doctrine of original intent or "originalism" than under the rubric natural law. For example, three notorious and pernicious cases were due almost entirely to misguided efforts to resolve constitutional disputes via original intent.

In *Dred Scott* v. *Sanford* (1857), Justice Taney referred to the "natural" inferiority of the blacks. Yet his opinion, in his own words, sought to discern the status of the question "within the meaning of the Constitution." Taney bounced from one clause of the Constitution to another, from the privileges and immunities and diverse citizenship clauses to the Fifth Amendment; and he solemnly cited a wide array of statutes pertaining to slavery in search of legislative precedent and intent. The salient point is that he expressly rejected any moral or legal opinion that would "induce the Court to give to the words of the Constitution a more liberal construction in their favor than they were intended to bear when the instrument was framed and adopted." In ascertaining the intent of the framers, Taney avowed fidelity to the "plain words," to the "intent" of the framers, and styled himself as a strict constructionist.

In *Everson* v. *Board (1947)*, Justice Black, an inveterate foe of natural law reasoning, summarily undid the principles of church-state jurisprudence that had been in place for well over a century. On the basis of what was a phantasmal history of colonial opinions on the matter, and relying upon an exegesis of a private letter in which Thomas Jefferson referred to the "wall of separation," Justice Black construed the Establishment Clause to mean that government is prohibited from aiding and promoting religion. The Court's jurisprudence of the Establishment Clause has been in disrepair ever since.

And regarding *Roe* v. *Wade* (1973), we can agree with Judge Bork that Justice Blackmun sought to augment and expand an alleged natural right to privacy that covers a unilateral decision to procure an abortion. But we can also point out that the case pivoted upon Justice Blackmun's survey of the history of statutory law, common law, and constitutional case law. For it was his assessment of these that led him to claim that the fetus does not enjoy rights to be balanced against those of the mother. Laws against abortion were only intended, he argued, to protect the health of the woman. While Blackmun's exegesis of the legislative and constitutional history was as superficial as Taney's in *Dred Scott,* we should not fail to see that the opinion was based upon a misguided method of original intent, not natural law.

The rhetorical and dialectical point I want to make is that it makes no more sense to jettison a method of original intent because it has been used with disastrous results than it does to throw out natural law because frequently it has been a foil for ideological jurisprudence. Willful and ideologically disposed judges are just as liable to tell false stories regarding original intent as they are to concoct false theories about human nature. I myself no more trust Justice Black's historical imagination than I trust Justice Brennan's philosophical understanding of natural law. But banishing historical imagination and moral philosophy from judicial interpretation of the law is no solution to the problem of remedying the errors they make.

There is no other (scholarly) way to respond to willful, ignorant, and ideological uses of a method than carefully and patiently to distinguish between its sound and unsound formulations, and between its responsible and irresponsible uses. One can agree that the theoretical tool of natural law is problematic; one can even agree that in the climate of today's legal culture it is especially apt to be used in a way that causes more harm that good. But it is quite another thing to set up an uncompromising either-or between fidelity to original intent and judicial respect for natural principles of justice. I don't buy this either-or proposition. It is too easy, and is itself prone to ideological distortion. Rather than reading theories "into" the Constitution, it can read theories "out." A judge has no more authority to do the one than the other.

Finally, I should say that I have never said that Judge Bork is himself a "moral skeptic" or relativist—only that his judicial philosophy too quickly and completely rules out natural law. I believe he was a first-rate judge and remains a timely and effective critic of judicial activism. Although I think that his formulation of what is at stake in natural law theory is one-sided, I for one am indebted to what he has had to say on these matters.

William Bentley Ball

Judge Bork's essay says much that is important and appealing. Once again, it is fun to see him taking swings at the liberal-left (and connecting). And it is refreshing to read a legal positivist who, unlike so many of that persuasion, is open and upfront with his convictions. He takes exception to my article in the June 1990 *Crisis*. I think it useful for *First Things* readers that, first, I discuss the genesis of that article.

I had tried a case in Wisconsin in which I sought to prevent the jailing of Amish parents and the governmental obliteration of their religious way of life. I argued (in trial court and ultimately before the Supreme Court [*Wisconsin v. Yoder*, 1972]) that the state's criminal prosecution of these people for refusing, on religious grounds, to enroll their children in public high schools violated the Free Exercise Clause of the First Amendment. The Supreme Court agreed. That federal clause had long been held by the Court to be applicable to the states through the Due Process Clause of the Fourteenth Amendment. The Court's reasoning was that "due process" is a term embracing "substantive," as opposed to merely "procedural," rights. "Substantive," the Court said, describes rights "so rooted in the traditions and conscience of our people as to be ranked as fundamental." The free exercise of religion, said the Court, is one such right. Going back to medieval times, English courts had recognized a power in judges to go beyond the letter of the law "where equity fulfills its spirit, which is justice." The American Constitution did not disturb this natural law principle.

Judge Bork blasted the *Yoder* decision on two grounds: (1) that the Court's upholding of the Amish really constituted an "establishment" of their religion, and (2) that its resort to the "due process" (natural law) foundation for its ruling was in error. In *Crisis,* I took on Bork in reference to both points, but I now see that I had better take up the second again.

Contrary to Bork's charge, I have not engaged in any proposal that "the Court should strike down, on the basis of natural law, statutes that contravene nothing in the Constitution." In *Yoder,* I urged courts to strike down a statute precisely because, as applied to the Amish, it did contravene the Constitution. In dozens of cases in twenty-two states, I have contended against statutes which, because they violate fundamental liberties or natural rights, violate due process. Bork's hang-up with me on this point arises from his view that "due process of law," as given in the Fifth and Fourteenth Amendments, refers solely to guarantees of fair procedure. As Bork well illustrates in *The Tempting of America,* this conception has been consistently rejected (he would say "violated") by the Court. Back in 1819, the Court said that the source of our "due process" concept was the Magna Charta, a declaration of rights indeed not limited to procedural rights. But it is important to see what is implied in limiting due process to "fair procedures."

Suppose that, in response to population-control pressure groups, Maryland (and Maryland would be just the state to do it) enacts a statute requiring the aborting of a third child born of any low-income woman who already has two. Nothing in the black print of the Maryland and federal constitutions *except* their due process clauses protects such a woman's liberty to give birth or the right to life of the unborn child. The "right to life, liberty, and property" phrasing is found solely in those clauses. But those are substantive, or natural, rights, and Bork says that such rights are not protected by those clauses.

Procedural rights are indeed important, and Bork will allow (nay, insist) that the Maryland lady have procedural due process. So she will be entitled to the right papers, various forms of notice, with adequate numbers of copies in due form, a hearing, etc. But that is all she will take from the due process clauses. After such procedures are properly carried out, the abortion procedure will also be. The day-to-day keepers of due process, in this view, are the court clerks and the process servers. Of course, this woman, in the Bork view, can try to get the state or federal constitutions suitably amended or get a protective statute enacted. And while she raises funds to that end, organizes a PAC, and establishes a political force to effect change, women like her will keep getting aborted.

I am sure Judge Bork will call that a bizarre example of his principle, but example of his principle it truly is. He himself has supplied another that is equally hair-raising. In 1927, in *Buck* v. *Bell,* the Court upheld a Virginia statute authorizing the sterilizing of mental "defectives." The great legal positivist, Justice Holmes, remarked that in his opinion "three generations of imbeciles are enough." As to this and a related case, Bork, in *The Tempting of America,* says that "nothing in the Constitution made the state of being fertile a civil right." True enough, if judges may not resort to substantive due process.

Contrary to what Bork says, I have not expressed the belief "that judges may properly amend the Constitution with their version of natural law," or with any version of anything. (Nor, I think, have Judge Thomas, Russell Kirk, Professor Arkes, or Professor Hittinger.) That is like saying, "*Since Catholics worship images, they disobey biblical strictures.*" The trick in the phrasing is the premise that they worship images. The trick in Bork's phrasing is the premise that natural rights are not protected by the Due Process Clause. The tradition is otherwise. Bork, in *The Tempting,* quotes Justice Marshall as suggesting that "the nature of society" may prescribe limits on the legislative power. That was in 1810. Bork says that Marshall adopted the idea of "principles of natural justice as a source of judicial power." This Marshall was John, not Thurgood. John was affirming natural law before Thurgood ever tried his hand at it.

Finally, we come to an important question relating to who's who. Bork says that Professor Arkes and I want the Supreme Court (and presumably all benches) to be filled with judges who share our moral views. Speaking for myself, he is exactly right. But I well realize what nags Bork. That is the fact that, for example, seven justices in *Roe* v. *Wade* reached out into the realm of fantasy to summon a "right of privacy" as a basis for killing people. But these were his brother legal positivists. They can scarcely be accused of having resorted to Higher Law. They resorted to what one can properly call Lower

Law or Unnatural Law. I agree that, under their reading and my reading of "due process," they could do that. But the answer is not to constrict due process to procedure (thus leaving us largely at the mercy of majorities). Instead it is to labor for the seating of judges who, respectful of the legislative will, nevertheless embrace the saving concept of a transcendent order.

Robert H. Bork

It is, of course, flattering to have one's ideas about the relationship of constitutional adjudication to natural law taken seriously by so distinguished a trio, and it is cheering that the discussion proceeds in a civilized and thoughtful manner, which is not invariably the case in these matters. Some, though by no means all of the differences expressed seem to spring from confusion about what I said. I must take the responsibility for that, so I will attempt, outdoing Richard Nixon, to make about a half-dozen things perfectly clear.

It sometimes feels as if Hadley Arkes and I are, in the most agreeable way, talking right past each other. Let me see if I can dispel the "benign haze" that Arkes perceives. I wrote about the duties of judges with respect to the Constitution and denied that a judge is entitled to discover and enforce natural law principles that are not found in the Constitution. When he is at work, his concern must be with positive law and positive law only. A moral principle binds, as Arkes puts it, but it binds morally. If the people have enacted an immoral law, it is the judge's duty to enforce it or resign. He may resign because he agrees, as he should, that there is "morality outside the positive law," but that morality is not his business while on the bench.

That is why I wrote, just over twenty years ago, the sentence that disturbs Professor Arkes: "Truth is what the majority thinks it is at any given moment precisely because the majority is permitted to govern and to redefine its values constantly." I never wrote a better line. And it has nothing to do with moral or cultural relativism, the view that there is no moral truth apart from the opinions of the majority; it has to do with democracy. The article ("Neutral Principles and Same First Amendment Problems," *Indiana Law Journal* 47 [1971]) was discussing Brandeis's statement that one of the functions of speech protected by the First Amendment is the "discovery and spread of political truth." The highest political truth for a judge is the Constitution of the United States, but if a statute does not contravene the Constitution, it contains the "truth" the judge must apply, because the people govern. It is kind of Hailey Arkes to speak of my "inclination to move steadily away from skepticism," but the truth is that I have never been a skeptic and have not moved. The misperception arises because when I speak of the judge's obligation to rid his judging of moral principles not found in the law, some readers think I am denying that there are such principles.

There appears to be a similar confusion about my statement that people differ over the source and content of natural law. As an empirical observation, that seems undoubtedly correct. Nor does Richard Hooker dispel any confusion, since there is none. Natural law may be "ordained by God" and yet not be divine law because discoverable by reason rather than by revelation. If one believes that God created man and then reasons from the nature of man to natural law, the ultimate source of natural law would appear to be God.

Arkes advances the "axioms of reason" as natural law in constitutional adjudication. It seems a bit imperialistic to claim the field of logic for natural law. The meaning of natural law is in danger of severe dilution if so much is placed within its boundaries. There is certainly no objection to the use of reason to decide that a principle in the Constitution has necessary corollaries. Much reasoning, legal and nonlegal, proceeds in that fashion. Though I do not think, as some of my interlocutors appear to, that Chief Justice John Marshall is the final word on matters legal, this method of reasoning from the implications of written constitutional principles to subsidiary principles is indispensable and was brilliantly demonstrated by Marshall's opinion in *McCulloch* v. *Maryland*. If logical reasoning is natural law I hereby welcome it into the courtroom and wish that it were more frequently to be found there.

It came as something of a shock to learn that my view that natural law is binding on a judge only when incorporated in positive law is itself natural law. I must decline the honor. That view does not rest on the "fitness of things" or the "logic of the law" but rather upon the statements at the founding of what the duties of courts are and upon the design of our government. If there was evidence that the framers and ratifiers intended judges to apply natural law, I would accept that judges had to proceed in that fashion. When an institution is intended and designed to operate in a particular way, when its members take an oath to operate in that way, it seems appropriate that the institution and its members should do so. I suppose it could be said that this duty of fulfilling an obligation is itself natural law. If so, it is a piece of natural law that requires the judge to confine himself to positive law in all else.

To Russell Hittinger's complaint that in my piece, "The complex issues [of natural law] are flattened out, and reduced to the problem of judicial review," I must reply that I addressed natural law in relation to judicial review only because Hittinger, Arkes, and William Bentley Ball did so. I had no intention, and for purposes of this discussion no need, to explore the "extent or depth of the problem of natural law" more generally.

The questions Hittinger puts—do I believe that "a responsible method of original intent can locate a natural law of rights or political institutions embedded in our Constitution?" and, if so, do I believe that "this can have any bearing upon the judge's interpretation and application of the law?"— tend to be swallowed up when he goes on to say that the question of deciding between two schools of natural law jurisprudence is "whether or not one or the other comports with the original intent of the framers and ratifiers."

We discern the original intent by asking what the words of the Constitution meant to reasonable men at the time of the ratification. In that inquiry, we have not only the text itself but the assistance of a great many secondary materials, such as the records of the Philadelphia Convention and the debates of the time. If we thus determine the original understanding of a provision, the question of which school of natural law best comports with that understanding is greatly diminished in importance—indeed, becomes academic. The only case I can imagine in which a judge would want to know about natural law would be if he learned that a particular version of natural law demonstrated that the text's words meant something other than we might think today and, further, that that version of natural law was widely held by the framers and ratifiers.

Hittinger's claim that possibly "more mischief has been done in the name of one or another doctrine of original intent or 'originalism' than under the rubric natural law" is misleading. He states that the *Dred Scott, Everson,* and *Roe* opinions, which he correctly describes as "notorious and pernicious," were "misguided efforts to resolve constitutional disputes via original intent."

Roe, contrary to Hittinger's reading, did not pivot on Blackmun's survey of past law to show that the fetus does not enjoy rights to be balanced against those of the mother. The case pivoted on the decision that the "right to privacy" included a right to an abortion—both natural right concepts—for, without the right to an abortion, there would have been no occasion to discuss the rights of the fetus. Moreover, the suggestion that the fetus has rights under the Due Process Clause of the Fourteenth Amendment is incorrect; the ratifiers were not addressing that problem at all. The Constitution has nothing to say about abortion, either way. That is a subject for moral debate and moral choice by the American people.

Insofar as those opinions spoke in the name of originalism, moreover, their efforts were not "misguided" but disingenuous. Those were natural law decisions (in the sense that they rested on nothing in the Constitution) disguised as decisions based on the original understanding. Because originalism—applying the words as they were meant by the ratifiers—better fits our notion of what law is, judges who wish to arrive at results they prefer will, whenever possible, dress their personal views in the language of the original understanding. Any judge can speak in the name of originalism; that does not mean he is being guided by the original understanding, and the authors of those three opinions were not. No announcement of a philosophy, be it natural law or originalism, can control a lawless judge. The difference is that a natural law approach invites the judge to be lawless, while originalism requires that he actively dissemble in order to be lawless.

Perhaps Mr. Ball will one day accept the fact, which I have pointed out to him before, that I never "blasted" *Wisconsin* v. *Yoder,* the case he is proud of winning. I made the simple, and entirely unoriginal, point that the Supreme Court exempted Amish children from Wisconsin's compulsory education law in the name of the Free Exercise Clause of the First Amendment, but that if Wisconsin had created the same exemption by statute, the Court would have struck it down in the name of the Establishment Clause of the same amendment. I then said: "This is not to say that *Yoder* was wrongly decided. It is to say that something has been wrongly decided when the two religion clauses have by interpretation been brought to a collision." An unexceptional proposition, one would have thought.

Ball first denies proposing that "the Court should strike down, on the basis of natural law, statutes that contravene nothing in the Constitution," or, a little later, "with any version of anything," but, in between, he proposes precisely that. He finds that a hypothetical forced-abortion statute violates nothing in the Constitution except the Due Process Clause because the law violates a woman's natural rights. Natural rights perform for Ball the same function natural law serves for Arkes: a means to strike down statutes that contravene nothing in the Constitution. No natural rights were put into the Due Process Clause by the framers and ratifiers. Ball, and many other people, prefer to overlook the embarrassment that the word "due" modifies "process," not "substance."

Nor is he aided in attributing substance to the clause by his observation that "the source of our 'due process' concept was Magna Charta, a declaration of rights indeed not limited to procedural rights." Our due process concept derives from the provision of Magna Charta that says, "No freed man shall be taken, imprisoned, disseised [dispossessed of real property], outlawed, banished, or in any way destroyed, nor will we proceed against or prosecute him, except by the lawful judgment of his peers and by the law of the land." The right to be tried by "the law of the land" in time became the right to "due process of law." The derivation Ball relies on is from one phrasing of a procedural guarantee to another. In any event, one can ransack the entire Magna Charta without finding anything of assistance to Ball's unfortunate hypothetical woman.

There is little point in positing unlimited judicial power on the ground that majorities may run amok. So may judges, and they have. I would rather entrust the making of laws to a majority of the people rather than to a smaller majority—five out of nine. It is not clear why Mr. Ball thinks the people cannot be trusted to make decent laws but can be trusted to choose judges who will be faithful to a good (but largely unspecified) transcendent order. Any constitutional theory that lodges in judges the power to strike down all bad laws actually grants them power to strike down any law *they* think bad, regardless of what you and I and a majority of our fellow citizens think.

The Due Process Clause has no substantive meaning. Nobody knows what will turn out to be in the clause until a judge pulls out the rabbit he has put there. Or it may be something quite different from a rabbit, and rather more sinister. If Mr. Ball authorizes judges to go on the bench with their own individual annotated volumes of the transcendent order, the decisions may veer to the right or to the left, no one can say in advance. But one thing is certain: we are going to get the judicial equivalents of *Roe* v. *Wade,* again, and again—forever.

I hope this exchange has been useful to the debate over the role of judges in a democracy. It has been useful to me, and I suspect that the exchange will continue. May I always have such congenial and worthy adversaries.

MR. JAFFA'S CONSTITUTION

A review of *Original Intent and the Framers of the Constitution: A Disputed Question,* by Harry V. Jaffa (Regnery, 1993)

The meaning of the Constitution of the United States, it turns out, is no more and no less than one's heart's desire. Both constitutional jurisprudence and constitutional scholarship are largely exercises in wish fulfillment. That conservative intellectuals are as guilty of this as liberal intellectuals probably means that a jurisprudence of the actual principles of the Constitution as those were understood by the men who made them law is impossible for the foreseeable future.

There is one way to tell the liberals and conservatives apart at a glance. On picking up a book on constitutional theory—if, for some reason, you should wish to do that—look for the animating catchphrase. If the author says "moral reasoning," he is a liberal; if he says "natural law," he is a conservative. In either case, he will find things in the Constitution that are not there. Whichever, put the book down at once and go on to something useful.

These somber thoughts are inspired by Professor Harry Jaffa's new book, *Original Intent and the Framers of the Constitution: A Disputed Question.* The book reprints various essays by Mr. Jaffa and by some of his milder critics. To the uninitiated, the title may offer hope. At last, such an innocent might think, we are to get an historical account of what the Framers did intend and a demonstration of why their intentions are the only legitimate basis for constitutional jurisprudence. Alas, that reader will soon find that Mr. Jaffa is no more committed to the original understanding than the rest of the consti-

From *National Review,* February 7, 1994.

tutional clerisy: he defines original intent so that it rises above the meaning of the Constitution itself.

Before turning to the substance of the essays, it must be said that one of the book's notable qualities is the venom with which Professor Jaffa addresses those he regards as adversaries, just about all of them conservatives: Jeane Kirkpatrick, Irving Kristol, Edwin Meese, Russell Kirk, Oliver Wendell Holmes Jr., William Rehnquist, and, I rejoice to say, given the company to which I am assigned, me. It turns out, for reasons that are not entirely clear, that most of us are disciples of the late, unlamented John C. Calhoun. At other times we are identified with Karl Marx. Mr. Jaffa claims Thomas Jefferson, James Madison, and Abraham Lincoln for himself, thus gaining a sizable head start in the debate.

Putting aside what would be a very considerable quibble over intellectual antecedents, when Mr. Jaffa launches into his argument he quickly dissipates the advantage he has awarded himself. His reasoning runs like this: The Declaration of Independence enunciates truths of natural law; the principles of the Declaration inform the Constitution; and, for that reason, the Constitution must be interpreted as if those principles had been written into it. (I have discussed three rather more temperate theorists who adopt similar positions in "Natural Law and the Constitution," *First Things,* March 1992, and "Natural Law and the Law: An Exchange," *First Things,* May 1992 (found on page 305 in this volume).

Natural law appears in the first paragraph of the Declaration in the claim that Americans are entitled to separate from Great Britain and to assume "the separate and equal station to which the Laws of Nature and of Nature's God entitle them." These laws begin the second paragraph:

> We hold these truths to be self-evident, that all men are created equal, that they are endowed by their Creator with certain unalienable Rights, that among these, are Life, Liberty, and the pursuit of Happiness. That, to secure these rights, Governments are instituted among Men, deriving their just Powers from the consent of the governed.

These are noble words, words of high aspiration, but it is unclear what they add to our reading of the Constitution. We know, for example, that the "unalienable Rights" did not become constitutional absolutes: the Bill of Rights expressly contemplates the punishment of crimes by the deprivation of liberty and life, both of which certainly tend to interfere with the pursuit of happiness. The upshot is that, so far as the Constitution is concerned, these rights are unalienable unless society has reason to take them away.

Mr. Jaffa takes me severely to task for having said that "our constitutional liberties arose out of historical experience. . . . They do not rest upon any general theory." Citing the Declaration once more and a number of state constitutions asserting that all men are born free and equal, etc., he wonders whether I have "ever read a single document of our Founding." Well, I suppose the Constitution qualifies as one. The liberties to be found there clearly derive from historical experience with the British Crown and the states' fear of the new federal power. The First Amendment's prohibition of the establishment of religion reflected not only the fact that various denominations feared a federal choice of one but that six states had established religions which they did not want Congress to supplant. The Second Amendment's right to bear arms was supposed to protect against any tyrannizing tendencies of the central government. The Third Amendment's prohibition of the quartering of troops in private homes in peacetime was a reaction to the British practice in the colonies, as was the Fourth Amendment's ban of unreasonable searches and seizures and general warrants. And so it goes. One wonders, for example, what natural-law theory produced the Seventh Amendment's guarantee of a jury trial in common-law suits involving more than twenty dollars.

Nor is the original Constitution much more help to the proponent of a general theory of human liberty. The writ of habeas corpus is guaranteed and bills of attainder prohibited, again based on historical experience. The ban on state laws impairing the obligation of contracts reacted to the practice of relieving debtors of their obligation to repay. There is simply no point in nattering on about declarations of freedom and equality as though they constituted a general theory of liberty that was written into the Constitution. They don't and it wasn't.

It is the proposition that "all men are created equal" that Mr. Jaffa finds particularly enlightening for purposes of constitutional interpretation. It is not clear, however, what the principle means for modern problems. Equality was not explicitly incorporated in the Constitution (as the "equal protection of the laws") until the Fourteenth Amendment was ratified in 1868. The history of its judicial interpretation reminds us that "equality" is a most ambiguous concept, one whose content fluctuates with the mores and fads of the times. It is not at all clear how the tenet that all men are created equal would bear upon issues such as women in combat, abortion, homosexual rights, affirmative action, the death penalty, or other topics that vex us and the courts today. This suggests that the Declaration offers a very limited glimpse of natural law and hence, even on Mr. Jaffa's terms, offers little guidance for constitutional interpretation.

The subject he most wishes to discuss, and does so over and over again, is the bearing of the Declaration, and hence the Constitution, on slavery. Here, his argument is startling. Though the Framers left slavery untouched out of a prudent desire to form a Union, Mr. Jaffa thinks the Supreme Court could, nevertheless, properly have used their document, without benefit of any federal legislation, to extinguish slavery in the federal territories. Mr. Jaffa focuses on *Dred Scott* v. *Sandford*. The facts are familiar. Scott, a slave, was taken by his master from a slave state, Missouri, to federal territory where Congress had forbidden slavery in the Missouri Compromise of 1820, and then back to Missouri. Scott sued for his freedom on the theory that he became free when on land where slavery was outlawed. The Supreme Court, in an opinion by Chief Justice Roger Taney, ruled against Scott and in the process held that the Missouri Compromise's outlawing of slavery in federal territory was unconstitutional. That effectively denied the Federal Government the power to prohibit slavery not only in federal lands but in new states admitted to the Union.

In a passage that infuriates Mr. Jaffa, I have written that Taney created a constitutional right to own slaves in federal territories although there is no such right to be found in the Constitution. Taney created such a right by converting the due process clause of the Fifth Amendment from a guarantee of fair procedures to a guarantee of what he regarded as fair substance: "an act of Congress which deprives a citizen of the United States of his liberty or property, merely because he came himself or brought his property into a particular Territory of the United States, and who had committed no offense against the laws, could hardly be dignified with the name of due process of law." Hence Scott remained a slave.

Mr. Jaffa attacks my analysis in terms that might, if one wished to be generous, be called offensive. He argues that the Constitution recognizes a right to own slaves in the clauses requiring states to return fugitive slaves to their owners, providing for state representation in the House by adding to the number of free persons three fifths of all others, and preventing Congress from prohibiting the importation of slaves prior to 1808. Thus, he concludes, I made my "case against Taney only by the most shameless expurgating and bowdlerizing of the Constitution's text." Let us examine that claim.

The Constitution certainly recognized that slaves were held pursuant to the laws of some states, but the Constitution most emphatically did not guarantee such a right. The obligation of states to return fugitive slaves did not mean that Congress could not forbid slavery in territories it governed any more than the state obliged to return the fugitives was forbidden to outlaw slavery on its own territory. The three-fifths clause was designed to limit slave-state representation in Congress. The importation clause was a compromise that delayed a federal ban on the importation of slaves for twenty years. How any of this adds up to justifying Taney's invention of a constitutional right to own slaves in federal territory remains a complete mystery.

At the time of *Dred Scott,* slavery was left to state laws, which could protect or prohibit the institution. Congress has legislative power over territories more complete than a state legislature has over its state, for the state legislature may not interfere with the exercise of federal power. There can be nothing constitutionally wrong, therefore, if Congress defines what may or may not be property within a federal territory. In the Missouri Compromise, Congress said that persons could not be property in a designated part of federal territory. That is why *Dred Scott* was a usurpation of congressional power accomplished, Mr. Jaffa to the contrary notwithstanding, through Taney's invention of substantive due process.

The most that can be made of the unexpurgated and unbowdlerized text is that the Constitution did not of its own force forbid slavery. That is why it is startling to see Mr. Jaffa reverse his field and, in a mirror image of Taney's opinion, pour his own substance into a purely procedural provision in order to state that the due-process clause of the Fifth Amendment accomplished just that. Taney went wrong, he says, because that clause prevents a person from being deprived of liberty without due process of law, which slaves were not afforded. This reflects "the laws of nature and nature's God," so that the "positive law of slavery might overrule the law of nature in the slave states, but it could not extend beyond their boundaries, except for the reclaiming of fugitives."

That is, quite literally, an incredible proposition. It produces two preposterous results. If a slave and his owner entered a Northern territory where slavery was forbidden by the Missouri Compromise, the due-process clause would have no effect whatever because that clause forbids only the Federal Government from depriving a person of liberty. It has no application to private individuals. Thus, Dred Scott, who was not deprived of liberty by any federal law, could not have been freed by the due-process clause. Mr. Jaffa's position collapses. He has rewritten the Constitution to transform a prohibition of government action into a prohibition of private action.

But matters are worse even than that. Mr. Jaffa's argument means that if Scott had been taken to a southern territory where the Missouri Compromise allowed slavery, he *would* have been able to claim freedom under the due-process clause because the Compromise was federal law that deprived him of liberty. Thus, the Missouri Compromise was unconstitutional not, as Taney thought, because it barred slavery in the northern part of the Louisiana Territory, but, following Mr. Jaffa's argument, because it allowed slavery in the southern part. Not even Lincoln made that claim. But perhaps he did not understand the Constitution's incorporation of the Declaration of Independence as well as Professor Jaffa does.

Mr. Jaffa asks us to believe that the men of the Philadelphia Convention who wrote the Constitution, those in Congress who proposed the Constitution and the Bill of Rights, and those in the states who ratified both laid down principles which they clearly had no intention of endorsing and which are contradicted by the words of the document itself. There would have been no Constitution and no Fifth Amendment due-process clause if the ratifying southern states had understood that a later natural-law sleight of hand could deprive them of what they had bargained for.

One of Mr. Jaffa's many difficulties is that he, like the liberal activists he resembles, displays no awareness of the difference between politics and law. My writings, which he savages, dealt with the duty of the judiciary in applying existing law, not with the declaration of political principles. Thus, he is wrong when he says that my position "rejects, root and branch," a resolution of the 1860 Republican Platform proclaiming that the principles of the Declaration of Independence embodied in the Constitution, which are quoted above, are "essential to the preservation of our Republican institutions." He also quotes, without noticing the contradiction, another part of that platform promising not to interfere with states' control of their own institutions. Moreover, if Mr. Jaffa thinks that slavery was somehow guaranteed by the Constitution, it is he who rejects the first resolution.

Again and again, Mr. Jaffa quotes Jefferson, Madison, and others about the principles of equality, liberty, and natural rights. "No one can at one and the same time be a legal positivist and an adherent of the original intentions of the Framers. For the Framers were very far from being either moral skeptics or legal positivists. Their commitment to the natural rights and natural law doctrine of the Declaration of Independence represented the most profound of their original intentions." That observation is simply silly. The Framers were not legal positivists for the very good reason that no one who makes law can be. The lawgiver must have ideas of right and wrong that antecede the law he makes. The Framers wrote law, presumably embodying as much of their thinking on natural rights as prudence allowed, and the judge is bound to follow that law no matter what *he* thinks of its correspondence to natural law. That means that, in his judicial capacity though in no other, the judge must be a legal positivist. Which further means, contrary to Mr. Jaffa, that only a legal positivist judge can be an adherent of the Framers' original intent.

Written in dyspeptic prose, *Original Intent and the Framers of the Constitution* is one of the least coherent, least consequential, and most disingenuous pieces of constitutional theorizing on record: incoherent because Mr. Jaffa offers conclusions that cannot possibly be tortured out of constitutional text, history, or structure; inconsequential because, so far as is apparent, his argument has application only to one pre-Civil War case; disingenuous because he misrepresents not only that case but the Constitution itself. This may sound unduly harsh. I have tried to show that it is only duly harsh.

Jaffa v. Bork: An Exchange

Harry Jaffa

Judge Bork concludes his discourse in *NR's* February 7 issue as follows:

> Written in dyspeptic prose, *Original Intent and the Framers of the Constitution* is one of the least coherent, least consequential, and most disingenuous pieces of constitutional theorizing on record: incoherent because Mr. Jaffa offers conclusions that cannot possibly be tortured out of constitutional text, history, or structure; inconsequential because, so far as is apparent, his argument has applicability only to one pre-Civil War case; disingenuous because he misrepresents not only that case but the Constitution itself. This may sound unduly harsh. I have tried to show that it is only duly harsh.

I have been writing for *National Review* for nearly thirty years, and I believe its readers are sophisticated enough to tell a book review from a temper tantrum. No one before has pronounced my prose "dyspeptic," although clearly it has given Judge Bork heartburn. It is not difficult to know why.

The July 9, 1991, issue of *National Review* published an article entitled "The Closing of the Conservative Mind: A Dissenting Opinion on Judge Robert H. Bork." In it I offered a critique of the central thesis of Judge Bork's then recently published book, *The Tempting of America: The Political Seduction of the Law.* In the intervening two and a half years Judge Bork has studiously ignored that critique, but now that it is incorporated in *Original Intent and the Framers of the Constitution,* he has condescended to descend from his pedestal.

Bork's book is built around the proposition that liberal judges write their own subjective opinions into constitutional law. They attribute to the Constitution rights that are the judges' own invention, and then devise rem-

From *National Review*, March 21, 1994.

edies on the ground that the Constitution requires them. Judge Bork and I are agreed that that is wrong and bad. I don't like liberal judicial activism any more than he does.

According to Bork, however (in *Tempting)*, the first case in which this occurred was that of *Dred Scott* v. *Sandford,* in which Chief Justice Taney, in his opinion for the Court, discovered a constitutional right of slave ownership, which "right is nowhere in the Constitution." Because of this alleged right, says Bork, Taney pronounced the Missouri Compromise ban on slavery, or any prospective congressional ban on slavery in any United States territory, to be unconstitutional. According to Bork,

> this was the first appearance in American constitutional law of "substantive due process," and that concept has been used countless times since by judges who want to write their personal beliefs into a document that, most inconveniently, does not contain such beliefs.

The only trouble with this analysis is that Taney did *not* invent a right to slave ownership that is "nowhere to be found in the Constitution." The recognition of the right of slave ownership is massively present within the Constitution of 1787. Taney did not, as Bork says, read a right of slave ownership *into* the Constitution.

This is not the only example of Bork re-writing the Constitution to suit his purposes. He does the same thing to the Ninth Amendment, which reads: "The enumeration in the Constitution of certain rights shall not be construed to deny or disparage others retained by the people." Professor Douglas Kmiec of Notre Dame University Law School, who was head of the Office of Legal Counsel in the Meese Justice Department, takes Bork to task for arguing that these words "are a meaningless 'inkblot.'" In *The Attorney General's Lawyer* (1992, 35–37), Kmiec writes that "Bork's inkblot assertion cannot stand. If the Constitution is law, no part of it can be unenforced." Kmiec also writes that "Madison . . . perceived the Ninth Amendment as incorporating natural law . . ." which is of course why Bork de-incorporates it from the Constitution. So much for the advocate of a jurisprudence of "original understanding"!

It is just as illegitimate for a conservative to deny rights that are recognized by the Constitution as it is for liberals to invent rights not recognized by it. I wrote that no one, so far as I knew, in two hundred years (that is, before Judge Bork) had ever denied that the Constitution of 1787 recognized the lawfulness of slave property. This is why I said that Bork had bowdlerized the Constitution.

Judge Bork now admits that

> The Constitution certainly recognized that slaves were held pursuant to
> the laws of some states, but the Constitution most emphatically did not
> guarantee such a right.

It bears repeating that in his book Judge Bork asserted categorically that
recognition of a right of slave ownership was "nowhere to be found" in the
Constitution. Now he admits that the Constitution of 1787 "certainly recognized" such a right. But he pours out his invective upon me for discovering
his error.

Judge Bork compounds his error, even while denying it. He says that
the Constitution did nothing to guarantee slave property. But consider the
words of Article IV, Section 2:

> No person held to service or labor in one state, under the laws thereof, es-
> caping into another, shall, in consequence of any law or regulation there-
> in, be discharged from such service or labor, but shall be delivered up on
> claim of the party to whom such service or labor may be due.

Contrary to what Bork says elsewhere, the Constitution does not say that
fugitives are to be returned by the states. A good indication of the "original
understanding" of this clause is the fact that the first federal fugitive-slave law
was passed in 1793, and remained in effect until a much more stringent law
was passed in 1850. Returning fugitive slaves was therefore recognized as a
federal responsibility during almost all of the period between the adoption
of the Constitution and the adoption of the Thirteenth Amendment. Even
after the Emancipation Proclamation the fugitive slave law continued in effect—legally if not practically—in slave-holding counties that were loyal to
the Union. Thus there can be no question but that the Constitution of 1787
made the Federal Government an active agent in preserving and protecting
slavery.

Bork writes that the "three-fifths clause [Article 1, Section 2] was designed to limit slave-state representation." But consider: A man in antebellum Pennsylvania owns property in land and buildings and livestock. Another man, in Virginia, owns property of the same value; but the Virginian's
property is invested in part in five slaves. The Virginian in effect casts one
vote for himself and three more for his five slaves. (Of course, the Virginian would have liked to have five more votes, rather than three. Perhaps
this is what Judge Bork meant by limiting slave-state representation. All the
Virginian had to do to have his slaves counted as whole persons, rather than

three-fifths of persons, was to free them. But then he could not have cast their votes.) And these additional votes were registered in representation in the Electoral College as well as in the federal Congress. If Judge Bork had read any of the antebellum debates over slavery, he would have found this to be one of the leading free-state grievances, and one of the reasons for their opposition to adding more slave states to the Union.

Judge Bork writes that

> The importation clause [Article I, Section 9] was a compromise that delayed a federal ban on the importation of slaves for twenty years.

This article merits more notice than Judge Bork's passing glance. Taney relied upon it when he wrote that under the Constitution of 1787

> the negro . . . was bought and sold and treated as an ordinary article of merchandise and traffic, when ever a profit could be made by it.

Consider that, contrary to Judge Bork, the Constitution says nothing about delaying a ban. Article I, Section 9, only forbids a ban. This clause constitutes an exception to the power of Congress "to regulate commerce with foreign nations and among the several states. . . ." And it is a powerful exception, so powerful that Article V of the Constitution says that this clause may not be amended. It is true that when the twenty years had elapsed, the *foreign* slave trade was in fact banned. But the *interstate* slave trade was never banned, nor was any serious attempt ever made to regulate it, despite repeated efforts of antislavery societies to promote legislation requiring humane and sanitary treatment of the Negroes. Moreover, at least one reason why the foreign slave trade was banned in 1808 was that states like Virginia and Kentucky were exporting their surplus slaves to newer slave states which could more profitably employ them. Cheap African imports lowered the price at which they could sell their homegrown products on the domestic market. The banning of the foreign slave trade was a protectionist measure as well as a humanitarian one. (The protectionist interest in limiting foreign competition is also apparent in Article I, Section 9, in which it is said that a duty may be imposed on each imported slave, "not exceeding ten dollars for each person.") In short, even after 1808 there was that in the "original understanding" of the Constitution which justified Taney in saying that the Constitution recognized slaves not only as chattels, but as ordinary commercial property.

Judge Bork has now admitted at least three conspicuous clauses of the Constitution of 1787 that recognize a right of slave ownership. But, he says,

> How any of this adds up to justifying Taney's invention of a constitutional
> right to own slaves in federal territory remains a complete mystery.

Bork then asserts that

> Congress has legislative power over territories more complete than a state
> legislature has over its state, for the state legislature may not interfere
> with the exercise of federal power. There can be nothing constitutionally
> wrong, therefore, if Congress defines what may or may not be property
> within a federal territory. In the Missouri Compromise, Congress said
> that persons could not be property in a designated part of federal terri-
> tory. That is why *Dred Scott* was a usurpation of congressional power ac-
> complished, Mr. Jaffa to the contrary notwithstanding, through Taney's
> invention of substantive due process.

Judge Bork writes as if Taney's opinion in *Dred Scott* was merely a judicial
idiosyncrasy. In fact, it was an outcome of the firestorm over slavery in
the territories that began during the Mexican War and that culminated in
the Civil War, Judge Bork says that there "can be nothing constitutionally
wrong . . . if Congress defines what may or may not be property within a
federal territory." That may be true today, but in the generation before the
Civil War, no resolution to that effect could have passed Congress. In fact,
during the Mexican War, just such a resolution—the Wilmot Proviso— repeatedly passed the House and just as repeatedly was defeated in the Senate.
(The Wilmot Proviso—for Judge Bork's information—said that in all the
territory acquired from Mexico as a result of the war, slavery would be prohibited. Abraham Lincoln said, somewhat hyperbolically, that as a member of
Congress he had voted for the Wilmot Proviso "as good as forty times.") The
1862 law that finally banned slavery in all United States territories passed
during the Civil War only because the representatives of 11 slave states had
withdrawn from Congress.

Long before Taney joined the Supreme Court, the Missouri Compromise ban of 1820 was widely regarded in the South as unconstitutional. It
was permitted to pass, however, as a concession necessary to have Missouri
admitted as a slave state. Moreover, at the time it appeared to be a settlement of all outstanding constitutional questions in regard to slavery. With
the acquisition of vast new territories conquered from Mexico, all previous
concessions were rescinded. In the 1850 territorial laws for Utah and New
Mexico, Congress could not agree either to permit or to ban slavery. It provided that any states formed from these territories might be admitted into

the Union, with or without slavery, as their constitutions might prescribe. But the crucial question was: What would be the status of slavery in the territories *before* the time for adoption of a state constitution? This would determine whether such constitutions would or would not sanction slavery. And on this question Congress, like the country, was irreconcilably divided. Hence it was written into the territorial laws of 1850 that any dispute about the status of slavery in any territory could be appealed directly from the Supreme Court of the territory to the Supreme Court of the United States. In short, Congress itself, and not any gratuitous intervention by the Court, handed the Court the question of the constitutional status of slavery in the territories. Of all this, Bork appears to know nothing.

In 1854 Congress passed the Kansas-Nebraska Act, which said that the Missouri ban of 1820 was inconsistent with the policy of the 1850 laws, and was therefore "inoperative and void." Senator Douglas, the author of the Kansas-Nebraska Act, always claimed that the policy of the 1850 laws was one of congressional non-intervention. The hard-line Southerners, who had a dominating influence on both the Presidents who preceded Lincoln, as well as on the Senate during the same period, were not satisfied with Douglas's "popular sovereignty," which left the decision on slavery in each territory to the local inhabitants. They wanted guarantees that slave property, no less than any other kind of property, would have the protection it needed. When Taney wrote that the only power conferred by the Constitution on Congress in the territories "is the power, coupled with the duty, of guarding and pro-tecting the owner in his rights" they finally got it.

On the eve of the decision in March 1857, both the outgoing and the incoming Presidents (Pierce and Buchanan) exhorted the American people to accept the forthcoming decision of the Supreme Court as a final resolution of the question of the status of slavery in the territories. There is little doubt that these "doughface" Presidents were in some kind of collusion with Taney. When the Court acted as it did, it was attempting to cut the Gordian knot which had immobilized the political process. The decision, and Taney's opin-ion, were evidence that the Southern Democrats at that moment dominated the Presidency, the Senate, and the Supreme Court. But the rising tide of Republicanism marked the imminent end of that dominance. *Dred Scott* was a desperate attempt to transform a moral and political question into a legal and constitutional one. But it was political, not legal forces, that produced the result. "Substantive due process" had absolutely nothing to do with it.

Judge Bork finds it a "complete mystery" how the constitutional recogni-tion of the right of slave ownership "adds up . . . to a constitutional right to own slaves in federal territory." The mystery is solved once one understands that the debate over slavery in the territories was also a debate between two theories of the nature of the Union and the Constitution. This was also a debate between two rival opinions about the "original intent" of the Constitution. The Civil War itself was nothing more or less than a continuation of this debate "by other means."

The architect of the Southern view of the Constitution was John C. Calhoun. Although he died in 1850, he is rightly regarded as the Moses of the Confederacy, the lawgiver who showed the South the promised land. Jefferson Davis was his disciple. Roger B. Taney was his disciple. (In *NR's* history, Willmoore Kendall, Frank Meyer, Garry Wills, Mel Bradford, and Russell Kirk are among those who have subscribed to the view of Calhoun as the supreme sage of American constitutionalism.) Public opinion in the states that seceded in 1860–61 was influenced decisively by Calhoun. It is nearly impossible to imagine the Civil War except in the light of the Southern mind as shaped by Calhoun.

Calhoun's idea of states' rights was the cornerstone of his constitutional architecture. Each state, he held, became a member of the Union under the Constitution of 1787 solely by virtue of its ratification of the Constitution. The Constitution was a "compact" among the states so ratifying. Each state was an equal partner in this compact. The territories of the United States belonged equally to all the states. The Federal Government was their agent, deriving all its authority from their acts of ratification. It had no power to govern the territories, except as that power had been delegated to it by the states in the Constitution. The constitutional equality of the states forbade the Congress, as the common agent of the states, from discriminating among the property rights recognized as lawful by any of the states. It therefore had no lawful power to discriminate against slave property, or to offer it less protection than other property. Hence, the Missouri law was unconstitutional. This was the Calhounian theory behind Taney's opinion.

This is a powerful argument. If it is true, then the Missouri law was in fact unconstitutional. And if that law was unconstitutional, then Taney was correct in saying that anyone deprived of his slave property because of it, and who had committed no punishable offense, had been deprived of his property without due process. "Substantive due process" does not enter into the argument.

The only question is whether the theory of states' rights, whose truth is assumed by Taney, is in fact true. Suffice it to say that the theory of states' rights stands in opposition to the theory of natural rights. In the true doctrine of original understanding, as held by the Framers and ratifiers of the Constitution, all rights of all legitimate civil societies are derived from the consent of the governed. And the consent of the governed arises from the equality of the natural rights of all human beings, under "the laws of nature and of nature's God." The states severally, and the Union as a whole, exist to secure man's natural rights. States' rights are therefore derived from natural rights. Circumstances arising from British rule during the colonial period may have justified slavery as a necessary evil where it already was deeply rooted, at the time the Constitution was ratified. But there could be no justification for extending that evil to virgin territory. Hence Congress did have the right to outlaw slavery in any or all of the territories.

The natural-rights theory enables us to distinguish the *principles* of the Constitution from the *compromises* of the Constitution. In *Original Intent and the Framers of the Constitution* I have tried to show how understanding this distinction in *Dred Scott* unravels many of the mysteries surrounding the equal-protection clause of the Fourteenth Amendment today. Judge Bork, as a legal positivist, is no more able than Calhoun to distinguish the Constitution's principles from its compromises. Judge Bork tries to draw Lincoln's conclusion—plenary congressional power over property rights in the territories—from Calhoun's premises. But such plenary power can be inferred only from the doctrine of natural rights. Calhoun, and Taney, reached their conclusions only by severing the doctrine of states' rights—and hence of constitutional power—from its original foundation in natural rights. Judge Bork has done the same. O.K., Judge, the ball is in your court!

Mr. Bork Responds

Not really. After Professor Jaffa's latest effort, the ball has disappeared over the fence and is lying in the weeds, far from any court. Rarely has historical learning been deployed to so little effect. I am pleased Professor Jaffa has quoted my assessment of his book as "incoherent, inconsequential, and disingenuous." It cannot be said too often. His response ignores most of the points made in my review of his book in order simply to repeat two of his most obvious errors.

The odd notion, which Jaffa shares with Taney, that the Constitution contained a right, good against the Federal Government, to own slaves rests entirely upon a few provisions that attempt to cope with the brute fact that slaves were held in the Southern states and that the North could do nothing about that if a nation was to be created. Robert Goldwin has pointed out, quite correctly, that the Framers assiduously avoided giving slavery constitutional standing. Thus, there was no "evidence in the original Constitution of the kind of thinking ascribed to the founders by Chief Justice Taney in the *Dred Scott* case . . . there is no such racism to be found in the Constitution, then or now, not a word of it" (*Why Blacks, Women, and Jews Are Not Mentioned in the Constitution, and Other Unorthodox Views*). So far as the Constitution was concerned, slavery was a fact that had, for the time being at least, to be endured, not the guaranteed right that Taney made it.

Even more peculiar is Professor Jaffa's insistence that substantive due process had nothing to do with the *Dred Scott* decision. Here he parts company with Taney, and about time, too. Taney advanced many arguments for slavery but he also said quite clearly that depriving a man of his property (a slave) merely because he brought his property into a particular territory of the United States (where slavery was forbidden by the Missouri Compromise) "could hardly be dignified with the name of due process of law." As Professor David Currie has written, Taney's *Dred Scott* opinion "was at least very possibly the first application of substantive due process in the Supreme Court, the original precedent for *Lochner* v. *New York* and *Roe* v. *Wade*."

By now every reader must be heartily sick of arguments about the correct interpretation of an opinion almost 140 years old. It is time to bring this bootless discussion to a close. In doing so, I would remind Professor Jaffa that the first discussant to resort to the *ad hominem*, which is his standard style of argument, has no standing to complain if he is treated severely in return.

Constitutional Persons:
An Exchange on Abortion

Nathan Schlueter

R eaders of *First Things* should by now be well-acquainted with the heated national debate—in part inspired by these very pages—over the role and legitimacy of the modern Supreme Court, armed with the power of judicial review, in a country that proclaims itself to be self-governing. Under the influence of a progressive jurisprudence the modern Court has issued controversial and innovative rulings on topics ranging from criminal due process to school prayer, rulings that often conflict with both the text and context of the Constitution, and with the history and traditional practices of our nation. But perhaps no issue better illustrates—and indeed magnifies—this conflict than abortion. *Roe* v. *Wade* and its progeny not only challenge the legitimacy of the Court, with their highly partisan and tendentious reading of the Constitution, they challenge the legitimacy of the entire government, a government that tolerates, and often even encourages, the mass destruction of those human beings who are most innocent and defenseless.

It is surprising, therefore, that on this most central constitutional and moral issue a preponderance of pro-life advocates and legal scholars continually misinterpret the Constitution. According to them, a proper reading of the Constitution would reject the concept of a privacy right to abortion, and thus return the nation to the pre-*Roe* status quo in which the decision of when, whether, and how to regulate abortion was left to the states. In offering this "restoration interpretation," they ignore or reject the proper interpretation, which would extend the protections of the Fourteenth Amendment to unborn persons. This is what I will call in this essay the "unborn person interpretation." They continue to do this despite the fact that both the majority in *Roe* and the appellants to the case conceded that if the per-

From *First Things*, January 2003 With Nathan Schlueter

sonhood of the unborn could be established, "the appellant's case, of course, collapses, for the fetus's right to life would then be guaranteed specifically by the Amendment."

To gauge the pervasiveness of the restoration interpretation among life advocates, one need only consult these pages. Forty-five leading pro-life advocates, including Gary Bauer of the Family Research Council, James Dobson of Focus on the Family, Clarke Forsythe of Americans United for Life, Wanda Franz of the National Right to Life Committee, and Ralph Reed of the Christian Coalition, signed a much heralded joint "Statement of Pro-Life Principle and Concern" published in *First Things* in 1996 in which the primary legal complaint was made that *Roe* "wounded American democracy" by removing the issue of abortion from "democratic concern." The statement suggested two legal remedies: first, the Supreme Court could reverse *Roe,* returning the issue to the states; second, the nation could pass a constitutional amendment that would extend Fifth and Fourteenth Amendment due process protection to unborn persons. The statement does not even hint at the possibility of a Supreme Court ruling that would extend due process and equal protection to unborn persons. The *First Things* statement seems to reflect the unanimous opinion of those Justices on the Supreme Court who have urged reversing *Roe,* not one of whom has attempted to make or even respond in their opinions to the unborn person interpretation.

However well-intentioned, the arguments of the restoration advocates are usually grounded in an epistemological skepticism that is alien to normal constitutional interpretation and harmful to the political morality on which free government is based. While I don't object to a constitutional amendment that would extend special protection to unborn persons—especially since such an amendment would presumably lodge protection for the unborn beyond the discretion of partisan courts, and also dispose of any potential problems with respect to state action—such an amendment is constitutionally superfluous. The issue of protecting the basic rights of persons from hostile or indifferent state governments was constitutionally resolved almost one hundred and fifty years ago in the Fourteenth Amendment, purchased with the blood of hundreds of thousands of American lives in the awful crucible of the Civil War. The constitutional debate over abortion, then, is ultimately a rehearsal of the very same questions that shook the nation during the Civil War.

To see why the restoration argument, while certainly more honest and legally plausible than the opinion in *Roe* v. *Wade,* is both constitutionally flawed and politically problematic, we must first consider the arguments that have been made on its behalf. The core of the restoration argument consists of an attack on the contention that the right of a woman to terminate her pregnancy is a personal privacy right protected by the Constitution. Such a right is—to use the words of the Court—neither "implicit in the concept of ordered liberty," nor is it "a principle of justice so rooted in the traditions and conscience of our people as to be ranked fundamental." To the contrary, there is a strong historical and legal tradition in America condemning and prohibiting abortion as a violation of the rights of the unborn. Moreover, the alleged privacy protected in *Roe* differs in kind from the other privacy precedents insofar as the right necessarily affects the interests of another human life, the fetus, and insofar as the abortion procedure has a decidedly public expression.

So far as it goes, this is an acceptable argument. But it leaves out of the equation the paramount question of the status of the unborn child. The Justices write as if this question can be ignored or constitutes merely a "value judgment" about which reasonable people can disagree. Justice Antonin Scalia himself explicitly asserts this latter position in his dissenting opinion to the *Casey* decision: "There is of course no way to determine that [i.e., whether the human fetus is a human life] as a legal matter; it is in fact a value judgment. Some societies have considered newborn children not yet human, or the incompetent elderly no longer so." But if the status of the unborn child is merely a value judgment, then there is at least a plausible argument that the states have no right prohibiting abortion, especially when one considers the considerable burden an unexpected, unwanted, or dangerous pregnancy can place on a woman. Indeed, Justice Scalia's arguments have a frightening moral and epistemological agnosticism at their center.

> The states may, if they wish, permit abortion on demand, but the Constitution does not *require* them to do so. The permissibility of abortion, and the limitations upon it, are to be resolved like most important questions in our democracy; by citizens trying to persuade one another and then voting. As the Court acknowledges, "Where reasonable people can disagree the government can adopt one position or the other."

By making the determination of human life a value judgment, Justice Scalia forecloses the possibility that any scientific proof or rational demonstration can establish that an unborn child is a human being. Indeed, he ultimately forecloses the possibility that there can be any rational discussion of the matter at all, insofar as values by their very nature are subjectively determined. Taken to an extreme, as Justice Scalia's legal positivism in this matter seems to do, democracy becomes the simple exercise whereby the powerful define for themselves their "own concept of existence, of meaning, of the universe, and the mystery of life," to use the famous words of the majority opinion in the *Casey* decision. In such a universe, constitutional government is superfluous. One is strongly reminded of Lincoln's arguments with respect to slavery: "If [the Negro] is *not* a man, why in that case, he who *is* a man may, as a matter of self-government, do just as he pleases with him. But if the Negro *is* a man, is it not to that extent a total destruction of self-government to say that he too shall not govern *himself?*"

It cannot be too strongly emphasized that whether or not an unborn child is a human being is *the* critical question in this debate, and the question was definitively answered decades ago. Whatever might be said for an earlier time, today there can be no scientific disagreement as to the biological beginning of human life. Embryology, fetology, and medical science all attest to the basic facts of human growth and development, and medical textbooks for decades have declared that distinct and individual human life begins at conception. Contrary to Justice Scalia's assertion, this is not a value question any more than that of whether an acorn is an oak tree. It is indeed both telling and disturbing that while self-proclaimed postmodernist Stanley Fish can concede that the scientific evidence is clearly on the side of the pro-life movement, Justice Scalia continues to insist that this is a value judgment. The value decision only concerns whether we will protect all persons, or only those we have judged worthy of protection through the democratic process.

Perhaps even more disturbing is Justice Scalia's moral agnosticism, revealed in his pragmatic arguments against *Roe*. He rightly objects with scorn to the plea by the majority in *Casey* to the "contending sides of a national controversy to end their national division by accepting a common mandate rooted in the Constitution," as if the Court did not create the national controversy in the first place with its controversial ruling. And he quotes Lincoln's warning in his First Inaugural Address against deferring decisions of policy "upon vital questions affecting the whole people" to the Supreme Court, and thus resigning the power of self-government. Of course, Lincoln was referring to the ignominious *Dred Scott* decision in which the Court ruled not only that blacks were ineligible for national citizenship and thus had no legal access to federal courts, but also that slaves constituted property protected by the Fifth Amendment due process clause against congressional prohibition of slavery in the territories. It was in part in order to overturn this ruling that Lincoln pressed for, Congress passed, and the nation ratified the Thirteenth and Fourteenth Amendments to the Constitution extending due process and equal protection rights to all persons under United States jurisdiction.

According to Justice Scalia, the restoration argument would return the issue of abortion to the states, and thus remove it as a national issue. "As with many other issues, the division of sentiment within each state was not as closely balanced as it was among the population of the nation as a whole, meaning not only that more people would be satisfied with the results of state by state resolution, but also that those results would be more stable."

Stable for whom? Certainly not unborn children in states with permissive abortion laws. Couldn't Justice Scalia have added to those dicta some condemnation of the practice of abortion, despite his perceived constitutional obligations? One wonders whether restoration is Scalia's preference, and not merely his constitutional interpretation. In any case, the irony of Justice Scalia's position should not be lost: his argument sounds disturbingly similar to the "popular sovereignty" position of Stephen Douglas, Abraham Lincoln's bitter adversary, in both its professed agnosticism about the moral issue of abortion, as well as its proposed solution to the conflict. With Lincoln, we must see this argument for what it is: a dangerous threat to self-government insofar as it undermines the very public opinion that makes self-government possible, the belief in the transcendent dignity of all human beings from the moment of conception to natural death. Any attempt to define human worth or value with a smaller category than the general field of human beings, as Lincoln rightly saw, is necessarily arbitrary and sets forth a principle that itself undermines the principal foundation for self-government.

Not all advocates of the restoration argument, however, express Scalia's epistemological and moral skepticism so boldly. Christopher Wolfe, for example, attempts to make a similar argument while at the same time affirming the moral evil of abortion. His argument runs some of the same dangers as that of Scalia however, in that while recognizing the strength of many of the arguments for absolute prohibition of abortion, Wolfe concedes that, "given the fact that many people did and do in fact doubt (however wrongly, in fact) whether a human person exists from the time of human conception . . . the Constitution lacks the kind of clarity that would be necessary for a judge to strike down a law permitting abortion." So Wolfe's position, like Scalia's, is based ultimately upon conceding that the status of unborn children is open to doubt.

But we must ask: Why allow anti-life advocates to continue this deceptive argument that the ontological status of an unborn child is open to doubt, that it is based upon religion, or values, or some other subjective standard, and that it is a point over which reasonable people can disagree? Why does Professor Wolfe leave open to doubt what is obvious to so skeptical a man as Stanley Fish? We must be clear: if the ontological status of the unborn child is open to question, then objective knowledge itself is open to question. So long as life advocates concede that this is an open question the battle over abortion, and perhaps democracy itself, is lost.

To be sure, as the *End of Democracy?* symposium in *First Things* (November 1996) revealed, there is ample reason for reticence about the unborn person interpretation. The last half-century of "living constitutionalism" and its subsequent judicial license has left a badly scarred Constitution in its wake, severely undermining the delicate balance of powers that was part of the Founders' original design. The "least dangerous branch" of *Federalist* 78 has arguably become the "most dangerous branch" of Brutus 15. As many liberals are beginning to discover, the surrender of self-government to the Supreme Court is a double-edged sword that can cut both ways. We must be cautious, therefore, about seeking unwarranted readings of our privileged moral principles into the Constitution. For the purposes of this essay I will assume without argument that the proper reading of the Constitution is a *textualist* reading as that term is used by Justice Scalia in his book *A Matter of Interpretation*. A textualist reading assumes that the primary guidance for interpreting the Constitution comes from text and context. As Justice Scalia describes it, "A text should not be construed strictly, and it should not be construed leniently; it should be construed reasonably, to contain all that it fairly means." This principle excludes both "living Constitution" jurisprudence as well as "natural law" jurisprudence. According to this textualist jurisprudence, it seems to me, the unborn person reading is the most honest and legitimate, despite Justice Scalia's claims to the contrary.

The simple syllogism for my argument can be stated as follows. The word "person" in the due process and equal protection clauses of the Fourteenth Amendment includes all human beings. Unborn children are human beings. Therefore, the due process and equal protection clauses of the Fourteenth Amendment protect unborn children. To refute this syllogism, advocates of the restoration interpretation must either deny the major premise, that the legal person of the Fourteenth Amendment includes all human beings, or deny the minor premise, that an unborn child is a human being. Because virtually none of the life advocates are willing to deny the minor premise, the main point of contention must be the major premise.

So, do the due process and equal protection clauses of the Fourteenth Amendment include all human beings? Based on the text of the Constitution, its repeated construction prior to *Roe,* explicit statements of the framers of the Fourteenth Amendment, and valid inferences from state practices toward abortion, we can answer this question in the affirmative.

The first section of the Fourteenth Amendment states: "Nor shall any state deprive any person of life, liberty, or property, without due process of law; nor deny to any person within its jurisdiction the equal protection of the laws." The problem is that the Constitution never defines the word "person." Justice Scalia, among others, rightly looks to context for guidance on the meaning of this term, and he finds no evidence that the word was intended to include unborn persons. In a speech delivered at Notre Dame in 1997 he pointed out that none of the references to "person" in the Constitution have prenatal application. For example, the second section of the Fourteenth Amendment states that "representatives shall be apportioned among the several states according to their respective numbers, counting the whole number of persons in each state, excluding Indians not taxed." Because there is no evidence that the framers contemplated counting unborn persons for purposes of apportioning representatives. Scalia argues, they must not have understood "person" to include "unborn person."

There are serious flaws in this argument, flaws that are attached to any contextual attempt to understand the meaning of the word "person" in the Constitution for due process purposes. The reason for this is that apart from the Fifth and Fourteenth Amendments every reference to person is context dependent—that is, each reference is intended to accomplish a particular limited purpose. Take Justice Scalia's example. The means for determining numbers of persons in each state is regulated by the second section of the first Article of the Constitution. According to this passage, "actual enumeration" shall be made by Congress every ten years "in such manner as they shall by law direct." In other words, Congress can determine by statute those who should be counted in the census for purposes of allocating representatives. Surely Congress could constitutionally include unborn persons in the census count, and with good reason, as the count might be more accurate. On the other hand, this might be an impractical enterprise. A clearer example illustrating this contextual problem is the eligibility requirement for holding office in the House of Representatives. The Constitution states, "No person shall be a representative who shall not have attained to the age of twenty-five years." Does this mean that no persons under the age of twenty-five are protected by the due process clause? Of course not.

It is quite clear from the history of the Amendment that its framers did *not* intend to give Congress the power to determine personhood for due process and equal protection purposes. An early draft of the Amendment stated: "Congress shall have the power to make all laws which shall be necessary and proper to secure the citizens of each state all privileges and immunities of citizens in the several states, and to all persons in the several states equal protection in the rights of life, liberty, and property." Several Republicans objected to this language because it would merely "effect a general transfer of sovereignty over civil rights from the states to the federal government, while effectively failing to limit the exercise of state power that had produced the black codes." Instead, the framers of the Amendment chose to lodge the prohibition in the Amendment itself, while leaving Congress *corrective* power. The Amendment clearly does not give Congress plenary power over the meaning of the first section of the Fourteenth Amendment. The strong implication of the text and history is that the courts would have a strong hand in enforcing its provisions. Scalia's interpretation is implausible and would effectively emasculate the Amendment.

Another prevalent and yet erroneous interpretation of the Fourteenth Amendment holds that its provisions are limited exclusively to blacks. This reading is supported by neither the text of the Amendment, the history of its framing, nor its subsequent application. The Amendment was aimed not only at the "black codes" of various states, which sought to effectively reduce freedmen to slavery while technically obeying the provisions of the Thirteenth Amendment, but also at the entire constitutional apparatus that placed the rights of persons at the mercy of oppressive state governments. (Remember, whites that supported blacks in their quest for freedom were also in danger of retaliation.) In other words, the framers were seeking a constitutional remedy for protecting the rights of persons when the states failed to do so. For this reason, they chose to use the term "person" rather than "blacks" as the object of protection in the text of the Constitution.

Abundant evidence from the congressional debates over the Fourteenth Amendment indicates that the framers intended the word "person" to include all human beings. For example, the author of section one of the Fourteenth Amendment, John Bingham, stated that "before that great law the only question to be asked of a creature claiming its protection is this: Is he a man? Every man is entitled to the protection of American law, because its divine spirit of equality declares that all men are created equal." And Senator Lyman Trumball declared that the Amendment would have the "great object of securing to every human being within the jurisdiction of the Republic equal rights before the law."

The history of enforcement of the provisions of due process and equal protection clauses supports the argument that the provisions were not intended exclusively for freedmen. Indeed, the vast majority of Fourteenth Amendment due process cases that later came before the Court, even in the late nineteenth century, involved economic issues. The word "person" accordingly has been given a very liberal construction by the Supreme Court to include all human beings, be they minors, prisoners, aliens, enemies of the state, and even corporations. Indeed, apart from *Roe,* the Court has *never once* differentiated between "person" and "human being," nor has it ever excluded a human being from the due process protections of the Fourteenth Amendment. So it is a fair legal inference to say that if it can be demonstrated that an unborn child is a human being, then that child will constitute a "person" for Fourteenth Amendment purposes.

Notice that the minor premise of the syllogism above is only marginally contingent upon historical analysis. The primary issue is ontological, not historical. Just as "the freedom of speech"—to use Justice Scalia's example in *A Matter of Interpretation*—includes movies, radio, television, and computers, so the Fourteenth Amendment includes human persons whose personhood was not fully "discovered" when the due process and equal protection clauses of the Amendment were written. In other words, it doesn't ultimately matter what past people thought about *when* human life begins, so long as they agreed—as they did—that at whatever point it begins, this is the point at which the protective powers of the state must be introduced. They did not have enough access to the scientific and biological facts of human reproduction and embryology to know for certain when life begins. But in a time of 4-D ultrasound technology, when infants can be operated on while still in the womb, there is no room for dispute about the status of the fetus.

One objection to the unborn person interpretation is the lack of precedent to support it. The common law basis of our system embodied in the principle of *stare decisis* and the just requirements of consistency in applying the law demand a respect for precedent. To this objection I offer two replies. First, there *was* a federal court precedent for the unborn person reading of the Fourteenth Amendment before *Roe* v. *Wade,* though this fact was virtually ignored by Justice Harry Blackmun and the *Roe* Court. In *Stenberg* v. *Brown* (1970) a three-judge federal district court upheld an anti-abortion statute, stating that privacy rights "must inevitably fall in conflict with express provisions of the Fifth and Fourteenth Amendments that no person shall be deprived of life without due process of law." After relating the biological facts of fetal development, the court stated that "those decisions which strike down state abortion statutes by equating contraception and abortion pay no attention to the facts of biology." "Once new life has commenced," the court wrote, "the constitutional protections found in the Fifth and Fourteenth Amendments impose upon the state the duty of safeguarding it." Yet in commenting on the unborn person argument in *Roe,* Justice Blackmun wrote that "the appellee conceded on reargument that no case could be cited that holds that a fetus is a person within the meaning of the Fourteenth Amendment." He did so despite the fact that he had cited the case just five paragraphs earlier! The failure of both appellees and the Court to treat this case is both unfortunate and inexplicable. Second, while our system is based upon a reasonable and healthy respect for precedent, this has never prevented the Court from revisiting and modifying precedent when the erroneous foundation and unjust results of that precedent become manifest. Such is the case with respect to abortion and the Fourteenth Amendment.

The historical practices of the states both before and during the time the Fourteenth Amendment was ratified can serve as evidence of what the framers of that Amendment thought about its meaning. Clarification of this matter will also help clarify why the unborn person interpretation is different in kind from a "living Constitution" or "natural law" jurisprudence. The principle can be stated simply: the killing of an unborn human being has been universally condemned by Christendom, was a crime at common law, and was made a felony through all stages of pregnancy by the vast majority of the states in the latter half of the nineteenth century. There was virtually no debate about the principle; the only question concerned the facts: When does human life begin? What began as a standard of "quickening," or the first perception of fetal movement (which, by the way, had nothing to do with "viability"—a term which is ultimately grounded in utilitarian notions of "meaningful life") eventually became "conception," as medical science revealed the nature of human reproduction, growth, and development.

Thus, at the urging of the American Medical Association, among others, states began to revise their statutes to accommodate the new scientific knowledge. As Justice William Relinquist pointed out in his dissent in *Roe,* "By the time of the adoption of the Fourteenth Amendment in 1868, there were at least thirty-six laws enacted by state or territorial legislatures limiting abortion." From this he concluded that "there apparently was no question concerning the validity of this provision or of any other state statutes when the Fourteenth Amendment was adopted." As Justice Scalia himself points out. "By the turn of the nineteenth century virtually every state had a law prohibiting or restricting abortion on its books." Significantly—and contrary to the assertions of several historians and legal scholars who were relied upon in *Roe*—abundant evidence indicates that these restrictions on abortion were passed with the primary purpose of protecting unborn children, and not merely to protect the health of the mother.

While this argument appears to provide stronger support to the "restoration argument" than to the "unborn person" argument, the appearance is only superficial. The framers of the Fourteenth Amendment did not intend to supplant the criminal codes of the various states. They merely intended to set conditions to those codes, the enforcement of which would be worked out primarily in litigation and secondarily in congressional enforcement. By the time the Fourteenth Amendment was ratified the states were well on their way toward enforcing its provisions with respect to unborn children. Moreover, other pressing concerns dominated the attention of the time period. *Roe* was the first case in which the issue of abortion had come directly before the Supreme Court, and it would have been a perfectly appropriate time for the Court to affirm the proper extension of the protections of the Fourteenth Amendment to unborn persons.

Thus, the unborn person interpretation has nothing to do with broadening or narrowing legal concepts to meet ever-evolving standards of morality accessible only to privileged elites. In such cases judges usually broaden or contract the meaning of the legal concept itself, as when they argue, for example, that the right to "liberty" includes an absolute right to engage in behavior once regarded as legitimately subject to state "police power" regulations covering the right to contract, to view obscene materials, or to use contraception. In the argument above, the legal concept—the protection of all human beings—remains unchanged. The only change comes from the clear development in scientific knowledge about when human beings come into existence.

A final consideration goes beyond the scope of this paper, but deserves mention. One could concede the entire argument above and still object that the practical effect of the unborn person interpretation on the protection of unborn children would be minimal due to the "state action" doctrine. According to the extreme formulation of this doctrine, the Fourteenth Amendment only places limits upon state action, and does not reach private action. I will only state here that the narrow reading is not plausible, and is not supported by the continuous reading of that Amendment. Congress is clearly given the power in Section Five of the Fourteenth Amendment to remedy both hostile state action and state failure to secure the constitutionally protected rights of persons. The unborn person reading would make it constitutionally incumbent upon states to secure the basic rights of all persons in their jurisdiction without discrimination, and would enable Congress to pass remedial legislation protecting those same rights in states that fail to do so.

This would be a bold affirmation of the democracy our nation suffered through the agony of the Civil War to achieve, and whose principle is enshrined in the Fourteenth Amendment. If, then, as seems likely to happen in the near future. Congress passes and the President signs a ban on partial-birth abortion, the issue of abortion and the Constitution will again come to the forefront of national attention. We must not let this opportunity pass to boldly challenge the prevailing jurisprudence and its attendant epistemological and moral skepticism with respect to abortion.

In sum, we must be cautious that our legitimate fears of an overweening Court and "living constitutionalism" do not blind us to the proper constitutional and political response to the problem of abortion. Metaphysical realism regarding both the identity and the dignity of the human person is the fixed point around which our political order revolves. Without it, there can be no resistance to the ever-encroaching influence of pragmatic and utilitarian conceptions of human dignity. This principle was given strong affirmation in the Fourteenth Amendment. While this Amendment was not intended to redress every social ill, its legitimate purposes certainly extend to the protection of unborn persons. We cannot afford to feign skepticism about the personhood of unborn children any more than an earlier age could afford to feign skepticism about the personhood of African-Americans.

Robert H. Bork

Professor Nathan Schlueter belongs to the "heart's desire" school of constitutional jurisprudence: if you want something passionately enough, it is guaranteed by the Constitution. No need to fiddle around gathering votes from recalcitrant citizens. He is by no means alone. His school counts among its members a majority of the Justices of the Supreme Court as well as professors of constitutional law, but Schlueter's closest counterpart is perhaps Justice Harry Blackmun of *Roe* v. *Wade* fame or ignominy, depending on your point of view. Blackmun and Schlueter have announced diametrically opposed constitutional rights, but both are made out of whole cloth. Blackmun invented a right to abortion, just as Schlueter has invented a complete prohibition of abortion. Though neither would care to admit the relationship, they are brothers under the parchment.

A dash of reality may be in order at the outset. The exercise in which Schlueter engages, while interesting and nobly inspired, is entirely irrelevant to the future course of the law. *Roe* had nothing whatever to do with constitutional interpretation. The utter emptiness of the opinion has been demonstrated time and again, but that, too, is irrelevant. The decision and its later reaffirmations simply enforce the cultural prejudices of a particular class in American society, nothing more and nothing less. For that reason, *Roe* is impervious to logical or historical argument; it is what some people, including a majority of the Justices, want, and that is that. If Mr. Schlueter were entirely correct in his constitutional argument, nothing would change. Only a shift in the culture, reflected in our politics, can make a change. Perhaps *Roe* may one day be whittled away by new appointees to the Court, though unless an unforeseeable cultural-political shift occurs, such candidates will have great difficulty in winning Senate approval. Dim as are the prospects for the demise of *Roe,* it is not imaginable that any Justice, let alone five of them, would rule that the Constitution prohibits all abortion, no exceptions. Schlueter's argument will never be more than a curiosity.

The main outline of Schlueter's position is familiar. Again and again, prolife advocates have said that the constitutional guarantee that life not be taken without due process of law, found in both the Fifth Amendment, ratified in 1791, and the Fourteenth Amendment, ratified in 1868, means, properly interpreted, that unborn children may not be deprived of life by abortion. That reading seems to me absurd. I think it clear that the Constitution has nothing to say about abortion, one way or the other, leaving the issue, as the Constitution leaves most moral questions, to democratic determination. I am, therefore, one of those whom Mr. Schlueter criticizes as restorationists: *Roe* should be overruled and the issue of abortion returned to the moral sense and the democratic choice of the American people.

The constitutional question is not what biological science tells us today about when human life begins. No doubt conception is the moment. The issue, instead, is what the proponents and ratifiers of the Fifth and Fourteenth Amendments understood themselves to be doing. It is clear that the Fifth Amendment's due process clause was intended to guarantee that no one be deprived by the federal government of life, liberty, or property without regular procedures. The Fourteenth Amendment made that guarantee applicable against the states.

Can those guarantees of fair and regular procedures be read as applying to unborn children who are deprived of life? Certainly not. When the two Amendments were proposed and ratified, abortion was known, had been known for millennia, and there had been arguments about whether life began at quickening or some other stage prior to birth. No one concerned in the adoption of these Amendments could have been ignorant of the fact that life did or could exist at some time prior to birth. Thus, if they intended to protect all human life, they would have known that the Amendments did, or very probably would, prohibit some category of abortions. It passes belief that nobody would have said so or raised the question for discussion, but the records are bare of any such question or discussion. The conclusion can only be that those who adopted these Amendments addressed only the rights of persons who had been born.

Indeed, the language of the Amendments strongly supports that understanding. The Fifth Amendment states that no "person" shall be held to answer for a capital or otherwise infamous crime except on presentment or indictment of a grand jury. Moreover, no "person" shall suffer double jeopardy for the same crime or be compelled to be a witness against himself. These all quite clearly apply only to persons who have been born since it is difficult to imagine an unborn child being charged with an infamous crime, or being tried twice for the same crime, or being required to be a witness against himself. The due process clause follows immediately after those guarantees and refers to the same persons mentioned in the preceding clauses. Not even the most tortured interpretation of the due process clause in the Fifth Amendment can make it apply to the unborn.

The Fourteenth Amendment starts by referring to "all persons born or naturalized in the United States" and provides that they are citizens of the United States and of the state in which they reside. In the same section, it is provided that no state shall "deprive any person of life . . . without due process of law." Since this due process clause was carried forward from that of the Fifth Amendment, one would think it referred to the same persons. That inference is supported by the Amendment's speaking of persons born or naturalized. None of these categories include unborn children. Thus, both the history and the texts of the two due process clauses demonstrate that they have nothing to do with the issue of abortion.

Schlueter's claim of historical support for his position fails; in fact, the material he cites cuts against that claim. He asserts that abortion was universally condemned by Christendom, a crime at common law, and a felony in the vast majority of states in the latter half of the nineteenth century. This is a curious argument. If all those assertions were true, that would say nothing about what the ratifiers of the Fifth and Fourteenth Amendments meant. Armed robbery was even more universally condemned, certainly condemned by Christendom, a crime at common law, and a felony in every state. That does not mean that the Amendments in question outlawed armed robbery.

Worse, Schlueter quotes then-Justice William Rehnquist's dissent in *Roe,* apparently not noticing that the words undermine his argument. Rehnquist said: "By the time of the adoption of the Fourteenth Amendment in 1868, there were at least thirty-six laws enacted by state or territorial legislatures limiting abortion." The crucial word is *limiting.* To limit conduct is to prohibit only some aspects of it while allowing the rest. It is impossible to suppose that the states ratified an Amendment they understood to outlaw all abortions but simultaneously left in place their laws permitting some abortions. If it is answered that people of the time thought that life began at some specific point after conception but before birth, and that that understanding was written into the due process clause, then the laws they left on the books should uniformly reflect that understanding. Schlueter makes no claim that the laws displayed any such uniformity, nor, so far as I know, does anyone else.

No better is the argument that the ratifiers meant to protect anybody who should later be discovered to be a person just as the commerce clause was subsequently applied to trucks that the ratifiers knew nothing of. There is no equivalence. We have already seen that there is not the slightest scintilla of evidence for the proposition that the Amendments were designed to protect all human life, including the unborn. The commerce clause was designed to keep open trade between the states, and naturally it did not matter what instruments were used to conduct that trade. Interstate movements of trucks clearly fall within the principle the commerce clause was designed to vindicate. It is abundantly clear from text and history that abortion had nothing to do with the principle the due process clause was intended to establish.

When all else fails, it is always good to quote Lincoln. In this case, Schlueter quotes Lincoln about the evils of slavery and the rights of all men to self-government. The example is ill-chosen. Lincoln was not addressing a court or expounding the meaning of the due process clause. He was addressing the moral sentiments of the nation. Though it would have been highly useful to him, he never suggested that the Supreme Court could abolish slavery by a proper interpretation of the Fifth Amendment. At the time he spoke, the District of Columbia and some territories, all governed by Congress and so subject to the due process clause, had laws permitting and protecting slavery. Apparently no one, including Lincoln, imagined that that clause gave the federal courts the power to prohibit slavery. Yet a slave was surely as much a person as an unborn child.

If there were no other objections to Schlueter's reading of the due process clauses, it should be enough that for two hundred years, in one case, and almost a century and a half, in the other, nobody suspected that those clauses meant what Schlueter would have them mean, not the men who proposed them or those who ratified them. The presumption is overwhelmingly against any revolutionary interpretation of the Constitution that occurs this late in the day.

Schlueter correctly recognizes that he has a problem with the fact that the due process clause limits governmental action and not the actions of private individuals. Abortions are killings by private persons. Without some additional constitutional action, there is no way around this other than to say that what the state fails to forbid, the state affirmatively orders. That would make all private action state action. It would follow that no area of individual freedom is exempt from judicial control. Suppose you establish trusts for two of your three children, but, for reasons satisfactory to you, leave the third child out. He sues you for depriving him of property without due process of law and, because you favored the other children, of denying him the equal protection of the laws. If private action is state action, he has a colorable constitutional case, and the courts will decide whether your reasons for discriminating pass constitutional muster. The same thing would be true with respect to any other actions of yours that somebody happened not to like. There is no exercise of individual freedom that could not be challenged under such a regime. The courts would make the rules for private conduct and legislatures would become largely irrelevant. That would turn the constitutional allocation of powers on its head.

Schlueter's solution is to have the Supreme Court declare all abortions violations of the due process clauses, and then have Congress enforce the ruling by legislating under section five of the Fourteenth Amendment. Aside from misuse of the due process clause involved, that solution assumes a judicial and social consensus antagonistic to all abortions so broad and intense as hardly to require such drastic action by Congress and the courts. *Roe* would be jettisoned and state legislatures would outlaw abortions. But the notion that any such anti-abortion consensus lies in any foreseeable future is a fantasy.

It is wrong to play word games with the text of the Constitution. Reading the word "person" to encompass all human life and thus to make abortion illegal is exactly like arguing that the Thirteenth Amendment's prohibition of "involuntary servitude" makes the military draft unconstitutional. A person drafted into the army against his desires is placed in a condition that looks and feels very much like involuntary servitude. Every so often a beginning law student of libertarian bent discovers this argument but is defeated by the fact that Congress continued to vote for conscription with not the remotest notion that it had already made the draft unconstitutional. Context governs. The Thirteenth Amendment was adopted to prohibit slavery or its equivalent. Not every obligation placed upon the individual by government or by other individuals amounts to involuntary servitude.

Schlueter persistently confuses science with law. Science and rational demonstration prove that a human exists from the moment of conception. What they do not prove is that existing law, addressed to different problems, must change with every advance of science. Minimum wage laws have been demonstrated by economics and empirical proof to cause unemployment or to price certain classes of people out of certain occupations. Rent control diminishes the amount of housing available and skews the occupancy of existing housing. In both cases, people may be said to be deprived of liberty or property without due process of law. Nevertheless, for reasons that may be thought discreditable, legislatures keep enacting such laws and there is no constitutional reason to say they may not.

Schlueter tries, wholly without success, to distinguish his position from "living Constitution" or "natural law" jurisprudence. But he ignores the plain text of the Fifth and Fourteenth Amendments and offers a patently irrelevant version of history. Any judge who followed his prescription would be guilty of judicial activism at least equal to Roger Taney's in *Dred Scott* and Harry Blackman's in *Roe*. Once we fall into the habit of sacrificing the integrity of law in the service of moral passions bad things are certain to follow, as our history abundantly demonstrates.

It will be best to notice only briefly Schlueter's remarks about Justice Antonin Scalia. As my argument to this point suggests, Scalia is quite right that the Constitution has nothing to say about abortion. He is also right that different persons and different societies make different value judgments about when life begins or when a fetus is entitled to moral respect. There is no point in ignoring that fact. Value judgments, contrary to Schlueter, are subject to rational discourse and people do change their minds as a result. I have changed my mind about abortion as a result of discussion. Though I am fairly sure that Scalia does not regard the beginning of life as an open question, a proper regard for the restraint proper to a judge prevents him from denouncing abortion in his opinions, as Schlueter thinks he should. Scalia needs no defense from me, but Schlueter should reflect that the proclivity to assault one's closest allies as insufficiently pure may be a symptom of the onset of fanaticism.

The Impossibility of Finding
Welfare Rights in the Constitution

There is a certain difficulty today—one, I think, of communication. Professor Michelman and I tend to operate in different universes of constitutional discourse. His universe is somewhat more abstract and philosophical than mine, and considerably more egalitarian, in keeping with the Zeitgeist. I would claim, although I think Professor Michelman would deny it, that the argument for welfare rights is unconnected with either the Constitution or its history. The welfare-rights theory, therefore, offers inadequate guidelines and so requires political decision making by the judiciary. If that is not true—if there are criteria other than social and political sympathies—I certainly do not see the legal sources from which Professor Michelman's form of constitutional argumentation arises.

I represent that school of thought which insists that the judiciary invalidate the work of the political branches only in accordance with an inference whose underlying premise is fairly discoverable in the Constitution itself. That leaves room, of course, not only for textual analysis, but also for historical discourse and interpretation according to the Constitution's structure and function. The latter approach is the judicial method of *McCulloch* v. *Maryland*,[1] for example, and it has been well analyzed by my colleague Professor Charles Black in his book, *Structure and Relationship in Constitutional Law*.[2]

Given these limits to what I conceive to be the proper method of constitutional interpretation, it is not surprising that I disagree with the thesis that welfare rights derive in any sense from the Constitution or that courts may legitimately place them there. The effect of Professor Michelman's style of argument, which has quite a number of devotees on the faculties of both Yale and Harvard, is to create rights by arguments from moral philosophy rather

---

1. 17 U.S. (4 Wheat.) 316 (1819).
2. C. Black, *Structure and Relationship in Constitutional Law* (1969).

From *Washington University Law Quarterly*, 1979.

than from constitutional text, history, and structure. The end result would be to convert our government from one by representative assembly to one by judiciary. That result seems to me unfortunate for a variety of reasons.

The impossibility of the enterprise is but one reason that this development is unfortunate. There is a certain seductiveness to the notion of judges gathered in conference and engaged in the sort of subtle philosophical analysis advanced by Professor Michelman. But the hard truth is that this kind of reasoning is impossible for committees. The violent disagreements among the legal philosophers alone demonstrate that there is no single path down which philosophical reasoning must lead. On arguments of this type, one can demonstrate that the obligation to pay for welfare is a violation of a right as easily as that there is a constitutional right to receive welfare. Under these impossible circumstances, courts—perhaps philosophers, also—will reason toward conclusions that appeal to them for reasons other than those expressed. Judicial government, at best, will be government according to the prevailing intellectual fashion and, perhaps, government according to quite idiosyncratic political and social views.

The consequence of this philosophical approach to constitutional law almost certainly would be the destruction of the idea of law. Once freed of text, history, and structure, this mode of argument can reach any result. Conventional modes of interpretation do not give precise results, but if honestly applied, they narrow the range of permissible results to a much greater extent than do arguments from moral philosophy. What is at stake, therefore, in "The Quest for Equality" through the judiciary is the answer to the question of who governs. A traditional court must leave open a wide range for democratic processes; a philosophical court in the new manner need not.

Professor Michelman has chosen to rest his argument in part upon the ongoing work of Professor John Ely.[3] The premise of their joint argument, as I understand it, is that interpretation of the Constitution cannot be confined to an "interpretivist" approach, which I and others suggest, because particular constitutional provisions—the Ninth Amendment and the privileges-or-immunities-clause among them—command judges to look beyond conventional sources and to create new rights. That argument seems unpersuasive for a number of reasons.

---

3. See Ely, "The Supreme Court, 1977 Term—Foreword: On Discovering Fundamental Values," 92 *Harv. L. Rev.* 5 (1978); Ely, "Constitutional Interpretivism: Its Allure and Impossibility," 53 *IND. L.J.* 399 (1978); Ely, "Toward a Representation—Reinforcing Mode of Judicial Review," 37 *MD. L. Rev.* 451 (1978).

In the first place, not even a scintilla of evidence supports the argument that the framers and the ratifiers of the various amendments intended the judiciary to develop new individual rights, which correspondingly create new disabilities for democratic government. Although we do not know precisely what the phrase "privileges or immunities" meant to the framers, a variety of explanations exist for its open-endedness other than 'that the framers intended to delegate to courts the power to make up the privileges or immunities in the clause.

The obvious possibility, of course, is that the people who framed the privileges-or-immunities clause did have an idea of what they meant, but that their idea has been irretrievably lost in the mists of history. If that is true, it is hardly a ground for judicial extrapolation from the clause.

Perhaps a more likely explanation is that the framers and ratifiers themselves were not certain of their intentions. Although the judiciary must give content to vague phrases, it need not go well beyond what the framers and ratifiers reasonably could be supposed to have had in mind. If the framers really intended to delegate to judges the function of creating new rights by the method of moral philosophy, one would expect that they would have said so. They could have resolved their uncertainty by writing a Ninth Amendment that declared: "The Supreme Court shall, from time to time, find and enforce such additional rights as may be determined by moral philosophy, or by consideration of the dominant ideas of republican government." But if that was what they really intended, they were remarkably adroit in managing not to say so.

It should give theorists of the open-ended Constitution pause, moreover, that not even the most activist courts have ever grounded their claims for legitimacy in arguments along those lines. Courts closest in time to the adoption of the Constitution and various amendments, who might have been expected to know what powers had been delegated to them, never offered argument along the line advance by Professor Michelman. The Supreme Court, in fact, has been attacked repeatedly throughout its history for exceeding its delegated powers; yet this line of defense seems never to have occurred to its members. For these reasons I remain unpersuaded that the interpretivist argument can be escaped.

For purposes of further discussion, however, let us assume that the interpretivist argument has been escaped; that the Court may read new rights into the Constitution. Even so, the welfare-rights thesis is a long way from home. Professor Michelman, so far as I can tell, rests the argument for his thesis on two bases: first, on a cluster of Supreme Court decisions; second, on Professor Ely's discovery of a transcendent value in the Constitution that vests courts with the power and function called "representation-reinforce-ment." I think neither argument supports the theory.

The most obvious problem with Professor Michelman's argument from case law is one that he recognizes. The cases, as he admits, are confusing and internally contradictory. This absence of a clear pattern is less suggestive of an emerging constitutional right to basic needs than it is of a politically divided Court that has wandered so far from constitutional moorings that some of its members are engaging in free votes. Moreover, even if a right to basic needs clearly emerged from the cases, the questions would remain whether these decisions were constitutionally legitimate.

That question brings us to Professor Michelman's basic argument for the legitimacy of representation-reinforcement—the idea that people will have better access to the political process if their basic needs are met. This argument raises at least two problems: one concerns justification of repre-sentation-reinforcement as a value courts are entitled to press beyond that representation provided in the written Constitution and statutes; the other relates to the factual accuracy of the assertion that persons at the lower end of the economic spectrum need assistance to be represented adequately.

It would not do to derive the legitimacy of representation-reinforcement from such material as, for example, the one-man-one-vote cases because those cases themselves require justification and cannot be taken to support the principle advanced to support them. Nor would it do to rest the concept of representation-reinforcement on the American history of steadily expand-ing suffrage. That expansion was accomplished politically, and the existence of a political trend cannot of itself give the Court a warrant to carry the trend beyond its own limits. How far the people decide not to go is as im-portant as how far they do go.

The idea of representation-reinforcement, therefore, is internally con-tradictory. As a concept it tends to devour itself. It calls upon the judiciary to deny representation to those who have voted in a particular way to en-hance the representation of others. Thus, what is reinforced is less demo-cratic representation than judicial power and the trend toward redistribution of goods. If I were looking at the Constitution for a suffusing principle that judges were entitled to enforce even though it was not explicitly stated, that principle would be the separation of powers or the limited political authority of courts. That principle, of course, would run the argument in a direction opposite to Professor Michelman's. In truth, the notion of a representation-reinforcement finds no support as a constitutional value beyond those guar-antees written into the document.

Let us pass over that hurdle, however, to ask what kind of a function the courts would perform to reinforce representation. The effort to apply that value would completely transform the nature and role of courts. Aside from the enforcement problem that limits the application of the value, a theoretical problem plagues the theory. Professor Michelman apparently concludes that a claimant cannot go into a court and demand a welfare program as a constitutional right, but if a welfare program already exists, he can demand that it be broadened. The right to broadening rests upon the premise that there is a basic right to the program. If so, why cannot the Court order a program to start up from scratch? In part it seems to be a remedial problem—how to order the United States Congress, for example, to establish a medical health insurance program—but that is not entirely convincing. If a constitutional right is at stake, why should the Court not issue a declaratory judgment, at least to exert a hortatory effect upon the legislature? A constitutional lawyer with the boldness to suggest a constitutional right to welfare ought not to shy at remedial difficulties.

It might be useful to consider what a court would have to decide in a constitutional claim to a welfare right. Suppose a claimant represented by Professor Michelman came to the Supreme Court, alleged that the state of X had just repealed its welfare statutes, and asked for an authoritative judgment that he and all similarly situated persons are entitled to welfare so that they could better participate in the political process. Because they would not have to devote all their energies to making a living, they not only would have a better opportunity for participation in the political process, but also would not be stigmatized as a poor powerless group. The justices might find this plausible. Suppose, however, that the attorney general for the state of X then stands up and argues that the state, in repealing the welfare laws, acted precisely for the purpose of reinforcing representation. The legislature had at last become convinced that welfare payments tend to relegate entire groups to a condition of permanent dependency so that they are not the active and independent political agents that they ought to be; moreover, these groups had lost political influence because they had been stigmatized as people on welfare. Experience had convinced the legislature that it would be better for people of that class, and for their participation in the political process, to struggle without state support as other poor groups have done successfully in our history.

What is the Court to do when faced with two arguments of this sort, neither of them obviously true or untrue? Is the Court to make a sociological estimate of which actions will, in fact, reinforce representation in society? And what of the possibility that payment of welfare benefits today may reinforce representation, but ten or twenty years from now welfare payments will have the opposite effect? In a judicial context, the problem is hopeless. Courts simply are not equipped, much less authorized, to make such decisions. There are almost no limits to where this concept of representation-reinforcement will lead the courts. If, for example, the concept of representation-reinforcement justifies the demand for welfare, why might it not also justify judicial invalidation of the minimum wage and the collective bargaining laws? Counsel could show theoretically and empirically that those laws create unemployment, that they do so primarily among the poor and disproportionately among the young black population, and that unemployment harms these groups' capacity to participate in the political process. Representation-reinforcement could take us back to *Lochner*.[4]

You may view this as ribaldry if you wish, but if Harvard theorists succeed in establishing representation-reinforcement as a constitutional right, we ought to consider suing the United States for an increase in defense expenditures, because the Soviets clearly intend domination, and if *they* succeed, our representation, among other things, will be drastically curtailed. It is preposterous that the Supreme Courts should control the defense budget to reinforce or safeguard access to a democratic political process, but not much more preposterous than the suggestion that the Court control the nondefense budget to the same end.

There are any number of difficulties with the welfare-rights theory. For instance, why should the Court or any other nondemocratic body define basic needs? A welfare recipient might tell the Court that he would be better able to participate in the democratic process if the government provided him with something better than the existing package of public housing, food stamps, and health insurance; that he would feel more dignified or would be less stigmatized if he looked like everybody else; *i.e.,* had more disposable income. The solution is a negative income tax. How could the Court legitimately tell the claimant either that he is wrong about himself or that, if he is right, he still has no case?

I will conclude with a consideration that is increasingly beneath the notice of the abstract, philosophical style of argument: the factual premises of the constitutional position seem deficient. The premise that the poor or the black are underrepresented politically is quite dubious. In the past two decades we have witnessed an explosion of welfare legislation, massive income redistributions, and civil rights laws of all kinds. The poor and the minori-

---

4. *Lochner* v. *New York*, 198 U.S. 45 (1905).

ties have had access to the political process and have done very well through it. In addition to its other defects, then, welfare-rights theory rests less on demonstrated fact than on a liberal shibboleth.

Perhaps we should be discussing not "The Quest for Equality," but the question of how much equality in what areas of life is desirable. Equality is not the only value in society; we must balance degrees of it against other values. That balance is preeminently a matter for the political process, not for the courts.

GETTING OVER THE WALL

Review of *Separation of Church and State*, by Philip Hamburger (Harvard University Press, 2002)

This year is the two hundredth anniversary of Thomas Jefferson's letter to the Danbury Baptist Association that asserted that the Constitution erected a "wall of separation between church and state." So profoundly has that metaphor affected American attitudes toward religious liberty and religion's dangers that most of us, including a majority of the Supreme Court, have forgotten that the "wall" is a constitutional myth without support in the words or actions of the Framers. Dissenting justices have pointed out that the First Congress, which proposed the First Amendment for ratification, also employed chaplains for the House, Senate, and armed forces, required that churches be built in the Northwest Territory, and called upon presidents to proclaim days of Thanksgiving to God (only Jefferson refused).

Justice David Souter, an enthusiastic separationist, argues that "those practices prove, at best, that the Framers simply did not share a common understanding of the Establishment Clause, and, at worst, that they, like other politicians, could raise constitutional ideals one day and turn their backs on them the next." That is no small accusation to level against the Framers, and it ought to be supported by very strong historical evidence. However, the evidence runs overwhelmingly the other way.

In *Separation of Church and State*, Philip Hamburger, a legal historian at the University of Chicago Law School, demonstrates conclusively that separation of church and state was no part of the intention underlying the First Amendment's Establishment Clause, "Congress shall make no law respect-

From *The Public Interest*, Fall 2002.

ing an establishment of religion." What the religious dissenters who heavily influenced the adoption of the Amendment wanted, and what the plain text of the Amendment gave them, was simply the prohibition of an established national church. Separation was radically different from what early Americans considered the true meaning of religious liberty.

James Madison's role is instructive. In his 1785 "Memorial and Remonstrance," he argued that religion and government should have nothing to do with each other. But that was not the position he took in his drafting of the First Amendment. As Hamburger explains, "Madison reconciled himself to language less sweeping than that he had used in 1785, and Congress adopted a moderated version of the no-cognizance standard, which did not forbid all legislation respecting religion."

The evidence for strict separation comes down to little more than Jefferson's 1802 letter to the Danbury Baptist Association, containing his famous wall-of-separation rhetoric. The Baptist Association, consisting of some 26 churches in the Connecticut Valley, sought Jefferson's views on religious liberty, hoping to use his response in their efforts to end their state's establishment. But the Baptists did not publish or use the letter in any way, since separation was incompatible with their understanding of Christianity's importance.

It was in fact not until 1840, when Protestants and Catholics in New York City clashed over the use of public school funds, that the idea of separation of church and state first attracted broad support and national attention. A second wave of separationist agitation began in the late nineteenth century, supported by Protestants, nativists, secularists, and anti-Christian secularists (known as "Liberals"). Opposed to all clerical hierarchies, all churches, and all religions—especially Christianity—the Liberals, as Hamburger points out, "insisted upon a purely secular version of separation that would segregate government not only from any one church but also, more broadly, from all distinct religions." Convinced that the Establishment Clause did not by itself completely separate church and state, these groups sought to amend the Constitution. They wanted to isolate or even prohibit Catholic parochial schools while the public schools continued to inculcate a generic Protestantism.

Only later, when their amendment efforts failed, did the separationists conveniently "discover" that the Establishment Clause already embodied the separation principle, and they turned to the courts to obtain what the democratic process had denied them. The story is one of intense and recurrent anti-Catholicism. When, in the 1928 presidential election, the Catholic

Al Smith was soundly beaten, largely because of his religion, the joke went round that he sent a one-word telegram to the Pope: "Unpack."

The modern separationist myth, as Hamburger shows, leaps from Jefferson's 1802 letter to Justice Hugo Black's 1947 *Everson* opinion, which adopted the "wall" as a constitutional doctrine and omits "any discussion of nativist sentiment in America and, above all, omits any mention of the Ku Klux Klan," which helped lead the fight for separation. The myth also omits many details about Hugo Black, who was not only anti-Catholic but also a Klan leader, not the naive, young lawyer he later made himself out to be. It is impossible to read the separationist opinions of the Court from that time forward without recognizing what Chief Justice Rehnquist called a "bitter hostility" toward any government recognition of religion. As American society became increasingly secular and groups indifferent or actively hostile to religion grew in numbers, the antipathy toward Catholicism became a more general antipathy to all religion. Eventually, many Protestants realized, as Hamburger notes, that "they faced a greater threat from secularism and separation than from Catholicism." And indeed, Protestant and Jewish institutions and practices have since come under the increasingly antagonistic scrutiny of the courts.

Separation is popularly taken to imply that clergy and religious organizations may not properly attempt to influence voters or governments. This view, most commonly directed by liberals against the Catholic church, contains considerable hypocrisy. Liberals enthusiastically welcomed the role of black churches during the civil-rights movement—a role that included political speeches from the pulpits—and castigated the Catholic church for its public opposition to abortion. Religious argument is thus reduced to politics, and judged according to one's partisan stance.

Though the Establishment Clause was intended to prevent government discrimination among religions, it is clear, Hamburger notes, that the separation doctrine of the Supreme Court cannot help but discriminate among religions. Those whose religion demands communal expression are disfavored, while those who prefer private individual religiosity are favored.

Although the privatization of religion by the courts further diminishes the role of religion in public life, the secular society desired by many on the left certainly does not lack in religious fervor. Hamburger notes, as others have, that the groups that most vigorously condemn church participation in politics simultaneously bring a religious passion to their egalitarian politics. This began with Jefferson's Republicans, and it persists today. "It surely is no coincidence," writes Hamburger, that many of the very groups that have sought to exclude churches from politics have pursued their political goals by appealing to religious passions and aspirations. . . . Perhaps the powerful emotions and desires associated with religion are unavoidable and, if not channeled through conventional religious institutions, are likely to find other outlets. . . . Yet it remains unclear whether powerful yearnings for purity and transcendence are less dangerous when focused on this world than on another.

Hamburger's tone throughout this book is unfailingly moderate; he never overstates his evidence. Yet I wish he had taken a few pages to dissect the thoughtlessness of judges who assure us, with no better support then Jefferson's idiosyncratic views, that strict separation has always been the understanding of the First Amendment, as well as to illustrate the current madness, in which it is held to be a forbidden establishment of religion if a student is offended by hearing others say "under God" as part of the pledge of allegiance. The examples are endless—and mindless.

Hamburger does, however, rightly stress the fraudulent and unpleasant origins of the doctrine: "Precisely because of its history—both its lack of constitutional authority and its development in response to prejudice—the idea of separation should, at best, be viewed with suspicion." As constitutional doctrine, the myth should be viewed with contempt. *Separation of Church and State,* to the extent that law and public discourse retain any degree of intellectual integrity, should begin the process of changing our thinking and that of our magistrates. Whether or not this occurs, Hamburger has made a major contribution to historical scholarship.

THE SANCTITY OF SMUT

How did "virtual child porn" end up with constitutional protection?

The Supreme Court is not testing the limits of free "speech" so much as it is obliterating them. The latest example is *Ashcroft* v. *Free Speech Coalition,* a decision holding that Congress may not prohibit child pornography created by using adults who look like minors or by using computer imaging. Justice Anthony Kennedy's majority opinion described the Child Pornography Prevention Act of 1996 as "proscrib[ing] a significant universe of speech" that fell "within the First Amendment's vast and privileged sphere." Since such speech was not "obscene" under the court's prior definition and did not involve real children in its production, the court found that the government had no constitutionally adequate grounds to suppress it.

To anyone unfamiliar with the court's extraordinarily permissive rulings in the past, it might seem that any depiction of children in a variety of sexual acts could be, and certainly should be, prohibited. The government, however, was limited by those rulings to arguing on grounds that virtually ensured its defeat.

To the suggestion that child pornography might be used to lure children into sexual encounters or might tip adults teetering on the verge of pedophilia over the line the court responded, "The prospect of crime . . . by itself does not justify laws suppressing protected speech."

The importance of the *Free Speech Coalition* decision is less in its particular rejections of the government's necessarily limited rationales, however, than in the light the case throws upon the entire direction of First Amendment decisions that have brought the court to this point. There was, to put the matter bluntly, no good reason to throw free speech protections around pornography, nude dancing, raw profanity, and calls for law violation in the

From the *Wall Street Journal*, April 23, 2002.

first place. Our jurisprudence has gone so far astray that there appears to be a right to display a picture of the Virgin Mary festooned with pornographic pictures and cow dung; but the presence of a crèche on government property is a forbidden establishment of religion under the same amendment.

There is nothing about the First Amendment that requires these results. That until relatively recently pornographers did not even raise the First Amendment in defending their sordid trade indicates how far we have come. It would seem merely common sense to think that graphic depictions of children in sexual acts would likely result in some action by pedophiles. The court finesses that problem with the statement that its "precedents establish . . . that speech within the rights of adults to hear may not be silenced completely in an attempt to shield children from it." Quite right. But why is pornography within the rights of adults to hear and see?

And why—to take only one category of speech undeserving of the court's solicitude—are the rawest forms of profanity exempt from regulation? Cable television is saturated with words never before used in public, and the broadcast networks are racing to catch up. *The New York Times* reports that in "A Season on the Brink," the character playing basketball coach Bobby Knight "drops the F-word 15 times in the first 15 minutes," and that the characters in "South Park" used a "well-known word for excrement 162 times in 30 minutes." The industry response to criticism on this score is that such words give the programs authenticity because this is the way people talk. In reality, however, the arrow probably points in the other direction.

People increasingly talk this way because they hear the words on television, and they hear the words on television because the Supreme Court's rulings have deprived the government of any effective sanctions for profanity. In justifying its decision here, the court actually said, "The right to think is the beginning of freedom, and speech must be protected from the government because speech is the beginning of thought." One wonders what valuable thoughts are triggered by child pornography or by nude dancing and profanity. The point is not that the court should outlaw such things; it has no power to do so. But it ought not to deny society the power to curb speech of no social value, indeed capable of inflicting great social harm.

In cases like *Free Speech Coalition,* the court, far from enhancing the value of thought, makes thought more difficult. The reduction of speech to the barracks-room level actively destroys thought that displays any subtlety, gradation, or nuance. All that is protected is the right of the individual to satisfy his desires, no matter how base, without regard to the rights of others or the health of the society.

One justice who knows better justified his vote on these lines with the remark that too many precedents would have to be overturned in order to give the First Amendment its proper scope. That is certainly true, but the precedents that would have to be jettisoned were themselves innovations. There is no constitutional justification for a ratchet effect that progressively liberates the worst in our natures. By destroying limits to speech, the court severely handicaps the community's efforts to retain a morally and aesthetically satisfying environment.

Sanctimony Serving Politics:
The Florida Fiasco

A great deal more than the name of the new president was at stake in *Bush v. Gore*. As columnist Tony Blankley wrote in the *Washington Times* on November 11,

> [W]hat is sticking in the craw this time is the brazen, slick, daylight heisting of the votes. . . . In this regard, Mr. Gore has learned from Mr. Clinton that when he violates the nation's values in front of the public—staring us down, daring us to do something about it—our failure to defend ourselves morally weakens us for the next time. And there will always be a next time.

In that sense, the Supreme Court, at considerable cost to itself, saved us, at least momentarily, from a further precipitous decline in our public morality.

Few events illustrate so starkly the debased state of America's political and legal culture as did Vice President Gore's frenzied attempts to overturn Governor Bush's narrow victory in the Florida presidential election. Almost no one and no institution emerged unscathed from the toxic mixture of unrestrained personal ambition and liberal ideology that forced the contest to ultimate resolution in the United States Supreme Court. Yet the lessons of that unseemly brawl have been obscured by the welter of recriminations, celebrations, and invincibly ignorant punditry that have followed.

The battle for Florida's twenty-five electoral votes, and hence for the presidency, involved so many lawsuits on different theories in both state and federal courts, as well as the possibilities of action by the Florida legislature and Congress, that it was impossible for a time to calculate all the possible outcomes of the chaos. Only in retrospect did the story line become clear.

As the entire world now knows, the disputed Florida votes were cast by punching out a chad opposite the preferred candidate's name. The votes, cast on November 7 and counted by machine, gave Bush the victory and, it

From *The New Criterion*, March 2001.

seemed, the presidency. The closeness of the contest automatically triggered a machine recount, which confirmed the outcome, albeit by a narrower margin. Gore then sought a manual recount of all "undervotes" (ballots on which the machines had detected no vote for president) in four heavily Democratic counties. Florida's secretary of state, to whom the returns were to be made, refused to waive the November 14 statutory deadline, however, which left too little time for the recount and the inevitable challenges in court. But the Florida Supreme Court, composed of six Democrats and one independent, acting on its own motion, enjoined the certification of the vote. Citing the necessity of determining the "will of the people" (a phrase with ominous associations) and the need not to be deterred by a "hypertechnical reliance upon statutory provisions," the unanimous court ordered that the recount proceed to find the "intent" of the unknown persons who had not fully dislodged the chads on their ballots. Purporting to exercise its "equitable powers," the court extended the deadline to November 26, a date unrelated to any statute and apparently chosen simply to help Gore.

The U.S. Supreme Court, to the surprise of almost all court-watchers, took the case, unanimously stayed the recount, and remanded the case to the Florida court for clarification of the basis for its decision. Now divided four to three, the Florida court reinstated the November 26 deadline and held that all Florida counties must be recounted. Yet the court also said that votes counted after November 26 could be included, thus, in defiance of Florida law and its own opinion, creating a flexible "deadline" to give Gore the maximum opportunity to win. The shamelessness of this performance practically forced the U.S. Supreme Court to accept Bush's appeal. In an opinion issued on December 12, the court fractured. Five justices held that the deadline was that same day, that the Equal Protection Clause of the Fourteenth Amendment was violated by the disparate standards used by the recounters to determine the "intent" underlying each ballot, found the time (which amounted to a few hours) too short to conduct a proper recount, and ordered the process stopped. Two justices agreed to the equal protection ruling but thought the deadline was December 18, when the electors were to meet, and would have allowed the state the extra six days to attempt the surely impossible task of adopting adequate standards, completing a recount in all counties, and deciding all court challenges. Two justices would simply have affirmed the Florida court. Though the decision appears to be five to four, seven justices agreed that a violation of equal protection was in progress and, since a valid recount could not have been completed even by December 18, Bush had, in practical effect, won seven to two.

The conclusion that the Equal Protection Clause had been violated raises serious difficulties, however. At first glance, it seems hard to deny that an essentially standardless process by which some votes are valid and other, identical, votes are not raises equal protection problems. Some recounters considered only partially detached chads a vote while others settled for a dent or a crease, and these differences occurred not only from county to county but also within counties and between recounters. But these and similar disparities have always existed within states under our semi-chaotic election processes. By raising that to the level of a constitutional violation, the court federalized state election laws. The opportunities for uncertainty, litigation, and delay in close elections seem endless, which is probably why federal courts have never entered this particular briar patch before. Once the Equal Protection Clause is unleashed, it will apply to every federal, state, and local election in the country. Ironically, several justices known for their concern about the independence of states struck a blow against federalism.

Three justices—Rehnquist, Scalia, and Thomas—offered a better rationale in their concurring opinion. They relied on Article II, Section 1, Clause 2 of the Constitution, which provides that "Each State shall appoint, in such manner as the Legislature thereof may direct, a Number of Electors" and on Section 5 of Title 3 of the United States Code which requires that the laws governing an election must be made beforehand. The Florida court violated these requirements by changing after the election both the final date for certification and the responsibilities of the various state agencies as the legislature had defined them. Counsel for Gore was put in the untenable position at oral argument of contending that the Florida court could make post-election changes in the law that the legislature could not. Had two of the other four justices who relied upon equal protection gone along with this analysis, the decision would have been sounder and much future difficulty avoided. Article II and Section 5 of Title 3 speak only to presidential elections and do not rule out every difference in election procedures within a state. But that rationale did not command a majority, perhaps because the other four justices found the familiar rhetoric of equal protection more comfortable.

So fraught with complications and dangers is the court's equal protection rationale that some commentators have expressed the hope that it will prove to be like a railroad ticket good for this day and train only. If so, that would merely reveal the inadequacy of the original ruling, and, in any event, courts are not supposed to issue decisions that cannot be shown to be aspects of more general principles. But the hope of inconsistency is probably forlorn anyway. If the Supreme Court intends to back away from equal protection in future election cases, that fact will not be known in advance to lower court judges who may proceed to federalize state election laws as the seven justices in *Bush* v. *Gore* suggest they should. In order to stop that trend, the court may have to shift to the different ground offered in the concurring opinion. That said, it must be remembered, in extenuation, that the justices were working under tremendous pressure of time and public scrutiny. It is no easy thing to hammer out a legal brief in one or two days, and the task is made almost impossible if several law firms are involved. The justices, each with four clerks, operate as nine separate law firms. Herding cats isn't even in it.

Though the majority has been criticized for setting the cutoff date on the twelfth rather than the eighteenth of December, that seems a minor sin given the fact that neither date could realistically have been met. We are entitled to speculate that, with good reason, the majority so distrusted the recount process in Florida and the state's courts that it seemed better to end the matter on the twelfth rather than put the country and the court through six more days of legal chicanery and useless turmoil.

Cruder commentators, with which the print and electronic media and law school faculties are amply supplied, put the decision down to raw political partisanship. But the idea that each of the seven justices who found a constitutional violation and the five who voted to end the recounts immediately were voting for a Bush presidency is a bit too crass to be credited, particularly if you know the people involved.

The more likely explanation is that the justices saw an election being stolen in Florida and that the Supreme Court of Florida was not only complicit but also willing to defy the U.S. Supreme Court. Yet the court majority could not agree on a valid constitutional doctrine to remedy an incipient constitutional crisis. The justices could hardly admit that they shared Justice Steven's version of the Bush position:

> What must underlie the petitioners' entire federal assault on the Florida election procedures is an unstated lack of confidence in the impartiality and capacity of the state judges who would make the critical decisions if the vote were to proceed.

Stevens was arguing that the court had no right to entertain such misgivings. But there were excellent reasons to do just that. One might add that there was a justified lack of confidence in those who would do the actual recounting. Canvassing boards regularly split two to one along party lines in finding valid votes for Gore. Once the boards decided that a dimple or a crease on a chad could indicate a voter's intent, an impossibly subjective element was introduced. (A crease may be created, of course, by the thumbnail of the recounter.) Scalia noted, moreover, that it was "generally agreed that each manual recount produces a degradation of the ballots, which renders a subsequent recount inaccurate."

The court's choice was between an inadequate majority opinion and permitting the stealing of a presidential election. It does not help a great deal to say, as some have, that the court's performance was statesmanlike. That is an excellent quality in other branches of government but it is not a primary aspect of judicial virtue. Adherence to law is. It is just as well, therefore, that there is a valid rationale for what the majority did even if only three justices subscribed to it. The defiance shown by the Florida Supreme Court coupled with the obvious purpose of the repeated recounts of selected counties to produce a victory for Al Gore cried out for someone or some institution to save the integrity of the electoral process. That the U.S. Supreme Court did.

The majority opinion raises a further question: whether a desirable result can ever be an adequate reason for law-bending. That seems to depend on one's political sympathy. The question lay at the heart of the court's ruling in *United States* v. *Nixon* requiring the president to comply with the special prosecutor's subpoena of White House tapes. Strictly speaking, the case was not justiciable, for it involved a dispute between the head of the executive branch and a subordinate officer. Such disputes can be resolved definitively by an order from the president to the subordinate, which means that there is not the "case" or "controversy" that Article III of the Constitution requires for the exercise of judicial power. James St. Clair, Mr. Nixon's attorney, tried to make that argument to the Supreme Court but Justice Potter Stewart responded that in the ordinary case that would be true, but here the president, through the acting attorney general, me, had given the prosecutor a charter that guaranteed his right to go to court. That was not, of course, a complete answer. The case would not have been different if a president gave a charter to the secretary of defense promising not to interfere in military decisions and then sued to make a reluctant secretary order the invasion of Grenada. No court, in the ordinary course, would have entertained that suit since, charter or not, the president has the constitutional power as commander in chief to control the military. The issue would be as nonjusticiable a question as can be imagined. St. Clair, however, did not respond to the charter argument, and the court relied upon it in deciding the case against Nixon.

The court was, however, under enormous "hydraulic pressure." The Watergate scandal had reached the highest pitch of public emotion, and it was unthinkable to the public that the court would refuse to decide; the general outrage that there seemed to be no way to get the (expected) incriminating evidence from the White House, that the Watergate controversy was unresolvable, was more than the court could be expected to bear. So it was with the ongoing subversion of the presidential election in the seemingly endless demand for selective recounts in Florida. With a difference: when, jurisdiction or no jurisdiction, the tapes case went against Nixon, there was no suggestion by liberals, and little enough by anybody else, that the decision was illegitimate. Instead, there was general satisfaction. But when a decision that may be criticized goes against a Democrat, as this one did against Gore, there is widespread denunciation of the court as having behaved politically.

It is possible to be at once critical of the majority's legal performance in *Bush* v. *Gore* and yet recognize that such performances are inevitable, or at least almost irresistible, when the pressure is high enough. Very few people today are critical of the court's 1803 decision in *Marbury* v. *Madison,* though this first broad assertion of the power of judicial review came in a case over which the Supreme Court had no jurisdiction and which required the willful misconstruction of a congressional statute in order to gin up a bogus constitutional issue. John Marshall was combating the centrifugal force of the Jeffersonians, who held the presidency and a congressional majority and who sought to weaken the national government so that the United States would once more resemble a confederacy rather than a unified nation. That may not be an adequate justification, but the case is now regarded as sacred writ.

Some of the fiercest attacks upon the *Bush* v. *Gore* majority came from within the court. Justice Stevens announced that the "loser" is "the nation's confidence" in the judiciary "as an impartial guardian of the rule of law." The judiciary, and in particular the court upon which Stevens sits, has not been an impartial guardian of, or even particularly interested in, the rule of law. Stevens is himself a leader of the most political wing of the court, regularly finding policies in the Constitution that are really only items on the liberal agenda for the nation.

Public comments on the case, some of them thoughtful, more of them intemperate, virtually all missed the point that there was a solid rationale for the decision even though only three Justices articulated it. Stuart Taylor, Jr., one of the more thoughtful commentators, said in *National Journal* on December 16 that

> the U.S. and Florida Supreme Courts have done very little to make the law respectable. If this cloud has a silver lining, it comes as a reminder to a court-worshipping nation that judges are as fallible (and sometimes as political) as politicians.

Aside from the fact that the nation is very likely to go on worshipping courts, what, exactly, could the nation do if it got over its worshipping ways? The courts might modify their adventurism somewhat if public opinion turned decisively against them, but that is unlikely. Too many influential groups—law school and university faculties, print and electronic journalists, Hollywood, all of our faux intelligentsia—support and encourage the court's political role because it usually results in the political results they like.

Taylor also holds out a hope that seems to me forlorn:

> [F]orceful criticism of unstatesmanlike decisions such as this one—and of the Florida court's hubristic, judicial imperialism—is a vital antidote to the tendency of judges of all political stripes to aggrandize their own power. Indeed, if judges cannot be persuaded to restrain themselves, they risk a dangerous and destabilizing popular backlash.

It is unclear what would be dangerous and destabilizing about a popular backlash against judges who undertake to rule without a warrant. The questions to be asked are whether the courts are not now themselves a dangerous and destabilizing force in our polity and whether a popular backlash could produce a result worse than the continuing displacement of popular self-government by judges. Indeed, it is not at all clear what a backlash could accomplish. We are hardly likely to deprive courts of their power of judicial review. Perhaps for that reason, repeated warnings of an effective backlash have never been borne out.

During the era of the Warren Court, the contempt for law and the desire to make major policy were so blatant that even the court's supporters repeatedly warned that results reached with so little respect for craftsmanship and candor made the court vulnerable. We have learned that those failings, however egregious, have not lessened the power of the court to do what it wants. There is, unfortunately, no particular reason to believe that will change. Indeed, Earl Warren, the exemplar of lawless judges, is now celebrated as a great and humane jurist.

The New York Times reporter Linda Greenhouse, who has covered the court for years, cautions that the need for the court to explain its actions in terms the public can understand and accept "is arguably greater than ever when the court can be perceived as stepping over the fine but nonetheless still distinct line that separates law and politics." "Beyond debate" she said, "is the fact that the court has now placed itself in the midst of a political thicket where it has always most doubted its institutional competence and where as a personal matter the justices have always appeared least comfortable." That would be a remarkably obtuse observation for any observer of the court's adventures. But it is a particularly astounding admonition coming from a woman who marched in pro-abortion demonstrations to the Supreme Court to support abortion and *Roe* v. *Wade.* She should have no illusions about the political thicket the court long ago entered, with her enthusiastic approval.

The most strident attacks on the court's performance, however, came from Jeffrey Rosen of *The New Republic* and the lawyer-novelist Scott Turow. In an article with the title "Disgrace: The Supreme Court commits suicide," Rosen wrote that the five justices in the majority have "made it impossible for citizens of the United States to sustain any kind of faith in the rule of law as something larger than the self-interested political preferences" of the five. "We've had," Mr. Rosen informs us, "quite enough of judicial saviors." He thinks "The appropriate response [to *Bush* v. *Gore*] is to appoint genuinely restrained judges, in the model of Ginsburg and Breyer, who will use their power cautiously, if at all, and will dismantle the federal judiciary's imperious usurpation of American democracy." That sentence produces intellectual whiplash. Ginsburg? Breyer? Those are two of the four activist liberal judges on the court. They regularly ignore the Constitution as those who wrote and ratified it understood its principles, substituting instead their own extremely liberal social and cultural preferences. Justice Ginsburg wrote *U.S.* v. *Virginia et al.,* suddenly finding that after a century and a quarter of peaceful coexistence, the Fourteenth Amendment and the maintenance of the Virginia Military Institute as all-male were in irreconcilable conflict. Justice Breyer, as the junior member of the court, has been assigned few major opinions but has joined, with Justice Ginsburg, in cases such as *VMI, Romer* v. *Evans*—creating special voting rights for homosexuals—*Stenberg* v. *Carhart*—striking down a ban on partial birth abortions—and *Santa Fe School District* v. *Doe*—holding unconstitutional student elections permitting speech that might be used for prayer prior to high school football games. Sadly for Mr. Rosen's panegyric to the judicial left, the only justices who in any way resemble, though in different degrees, a restrained judiciary are the very justices he denounces as lawless.

Turow wrote in the *Washington Post* that the court's decision "to stay the hand count of undervote ballots was the most overtly politicized action by a court that I have seen in 22 years of practicing law. It was an act of judicial lawlessness that effectively terminated Gore's chance to win the presidency." The prize for sanctimony in the service of politics, however, must be awarded jointly to the 554 law professors whose full-page ad in *The New York Times,* paid for by the left-wing People for the American Way Foundation, declared that

> By stopping the vote count in Florida, the U.S. Supreme Court used its
> power to act as political partisans, not judges of a court of law. . . . By
> taking power from the voters, the Supreme Court has tarnished its own
> legitimacy. As teachers whose lives have been dedicated to the rule of law,
> we protest.

The insufferable smugness of this statement is difficult to top. It is to be
doubted, given the notorious politicization of the nation's law schools, that
there are anything close to five-hundred professors whose lives are dedicated
to the rule of law. There are many times that number, including many who
signed the ad, whose professional careers have been devoted to seeing that
the rule of law does not hamper judicial advancement of the liberal agenda.

Even more extreme and shrill was Alan Dershowitz's labelling the Florida Secretary of State Katherine Harris a "crook" aiding and abetting the
Bush campaign. Character assassination is merely part of the ultra-liberal
repertoire. More dangerous was Jesse Jackson's and the congressional Black
Caucus's claims that Bush's victory had been won by fraud, intimidation of
black voters, a partisan Republican Supreme Court, and that racism infected the whole process. This added racial tension to an already emotionally
charged controversy could only intensify the damaging sense of perpetual
victimization that such leaders rely upon for their continuing power.

Such hypocrisy did not, fortunately, go entirely unmasked. Fred Bar-
bash, a *Washington Post* columnist, wrote,

> The shock expressed by partisan critics, their portrayal of a once-pristine
> court now forever sullied, drips with irony. Liberals counted on, and ex-
> ploited, ideologically predictable court voting patterns for decades.

Randy E. Barnett, a professor at Boston University School of Law, also put
paid to the liberal commentators' nonsense. Writing in the *Wall Street Journal,* he noted that

> we are urged that conservative judges must exercise the restraint they say
> they believe in. It is a convenient argument indeed. A kind of intellectual
> jujitsu that tries to turn an opponent's own thrusts against him. Activist
> judges are acting true to their principles when they escape the bounds of
> the law, while conservative justices are hypocrites if they abandon their
> principles of 'restraint' to bring wayward courts back to earth. Heads,
> activist justices win; tails, conservative justices lose.

The reaction and ferocity of the liberal assaults upon the court majority were stunning. Conservatives in the modern era have never mounted anything comparable. It is clear that liberals do not view conservatives as legitimate adversaries but rather as vermin—sexist, racist, hysterical about homosexuality—in short, primitives who are not entitled to govern, who win elections solely because large portions of the American public are equally corrupt. It follows that conservatism has no legitimate role in our politics or law, and, since civilization is at stake, any weapon may be used.

Liberal viciousness and mendacity in its current virulence may be traced to the election of Ronald Reagan in 1980. Since several prominent leftish Democratic senators went down to defeat along with Jimmy Carter, some of us made the mistake of thinking that the election represented a decisive shift in American culture. We could not have been more mistaken. That was the point at which the liberals became vicious, and their fury seems only to have intensified since. The Eighties was the time when the 1960s generation became active in national politics, and they brought their intransigence, intolerance, and irrationality (including a disregard for facts) with them from the campuses to politics and to a swarm of activist organizations. Hatred and intolerance migrated from the campuses to the national scene.

Republicans and conservatives (overlapping but by no means identical categories) behaved as the university faculties and administrations had before them: they went on the defensive and made concessions in futile attempts at appeasement. When they resist, they do so apologetically, rarely with the vigor and relentlessness necessary to meet the liberal attack. As Richard Brookhiser wittily if wistfully said of Republicans, "In their hearts they know they're wrong."

The attacks on Katherine Harris and others demonstrated that the politics of personal destruction, an invention of the Democratic Party, is alive and flourishing. I know something of that technique as do Clarence Thomas, Kenneth Starr, Henry Hyde and the House managers in the Clinton impeachment proceedings, and now John Ashcroft. It is by no means confined to politicians but is the common tactic of much of the media, of academics, and of the luminaries, so to speak, of the entertainment world. America is engaged in a religious war: a contest about culture and the proper ways to live. Judges, though this court-worshipping nation does not realize it, are combatants and extremely powerful ones. The activists, however, know what the public does not. Courts today are, more often than not, the heavy artillery of liberalism, engaged, for example, in creating and expanding a right to abortion, normalizing homosexuality, and driving religion from our public life.

It is not too surprising that the vast majority of Americans do not understand the role of courts or when they go astray. Constitutional law is like inside baseball: only those who play the game have any chance of real understanding. There is no point in bemoaning the fact that schools and colleges do not teach about constitutional law. Imagine trying to teach the intricacies of just one case, *Bush* v. *Gore,* explaining the comparative merits of basing the decision on the Fourteenth Amendment's Equal Protection Clause or Article II of the Constitution and Section 5 of Title 3 of the U.S. Code. There is no hope whatever that many laymen can be taught to judge the performance of the court across the range of important constitutional issues. The vast majority of us are uninformed about this extremely, and increasingly, powerful branch of government. That ignorance, which seems incurable, does not bode well for American democracy. The American judiciary, both federal and state, has done more to shape our future than any outcome of the 2000 election could possibly have done. That is part of the case for restrained judges: they will leave to the people what belongs to the people, whether the people know it or not. Blankley's warning about Gore's tactics applies equally well to imperialistic courts: they stare us down, daring us to do something about their usurpations, weakening us morally for the next time, and there will always be a next time. The "next time" now comes several times a year in the Supreme Court. And, so long as the result pleases liberals, there is not even a ripple of backlash.

Viewing the win-at-any-cost temper of the Gore forces in Florida, I and others quoted Learned Hand's familiar passage:

> This much I think I do know—that a society so riven that the spirit of moderation is gone, no court *can* save; that a society where that spirit flourishes, no court *need* save; that in a society which evades its responsibility by thrusting upon the courts the nurture of that spirit, that spirit in the end will perish.

True enough, but those words do not quite fit our situation today. Too often overlooked is Hand's immediately following observation. Speaking of the temper of moderation and faith in the sacredness of the individual, he said:

> If you ask me how such a temper and such a faith are bred and fostered, I cannot answer. They are the last flowers of civilization, delicate and easily overrun by the weeds of our sinful human nature; we may even now be witnessing their uprooting and disappearance until in the progress of the ages their seeds can once more find some friendly soil.

Hand was prescient in suggesting that even in his day America might be witnessing the suffocation of the last flowers of civilization by the weeds of our nature. What we see, then, is not courts powerless to enforce moderation but courts too often actively destroying that indispensable virtue. *Bush v. Gore* was a valiant effort, legitimate in law, to rein in runaway political passions and a lawless state court those passions had captured.

Travesty Time, Again

*In its death penalty decision, The Supreme Court
hits a new low*

There are plenty of reasons to deplore *Roper* v. *Simmons,* the Supreme Court's decision that a murderer under the age of 18 when he committed his crime cannot be given the death penalty. The Court majority once more exhibited for all to see that dazzling combination of lawlessness and moral presumption which increasingly characterizes its Bill of Rights jurisprudence.

The opinion starts unpromisingly, informing us that by "protecting even those convicted of heinous crimes, the Eighth Amendment reaffirms the duty of the government to respect the dignity of all persons." Readers may wonder about the dignity of the victim. Christopher Simmons, then 17, discussed with two companions his desire to murder someone, saying they could "get away with it" because they were minors. He and a juvenile confederate broke into the house of Shirley Crook, covered her eyes and mouth, and bound her hands with duct tape. They drove her to a state park, walked her onto a bridge, tied her hands and feet together with electrical wire, completely covered her whole face with duct tape, and threw her into the Meramec River, where, helpless, she drowned. Simmons bragged about the killing to friends, telling them he had killed a woman "because the bitch seen my face." Arrested, he confessed, and was sentenced to death.

The Supreme Court, though conceding that retribution and deterrence are valid functions of the death penalty, intoned that "we have established the propriety and affirmed the necessity of referring to 'the evolving standards of decency that mark the progress of a maturing society' to determine which punishments are so disproportionate as to be cruel and unusual." That means the justices' views evolve, which is, by definition, progress. Justice

Anthony Kennedy's opinion attempted to mask this unpalatable reality by claiming that the meaning of the Eighth Amendment had changed owing to a new "national consensus" against executing under-18 killers. This assertion of a "national consensus," however, was derived from the example of just 18 states that had faced the issue of granting an exemption to juvenile murderers out of the 38 with the death penalty. This dubious escalator means that the founders who allowed such punishments fall well short of our superior understanding of decency, as do the 20 states that today permit the execution of those younger than 18. In Simmons's case, it took the Missouri legislature, the governor, a unanimous jury, and a judge to bring him to death row. All now stand branded, five to four, as morally indecent. The majority did not, and could not, explain why any state is forbidden to make a policy choice—denied its constitutional sovereignty—because other states disagree with it.

Trying its hand at psychology, the *Roper* majority argued that neither deterrence nor retribution supported the death penalty for killers under the age of 18. As for deterrence, the Court said, the likelihood that teenagers engage in cost-benefit analysis that attaches any weight to the possibility of execution is so remote as to be virtually non-existent. This in a case where the murderer counted on his minority to "get away with it." This from a Court that finds teenage girls sufficiently mature to decide on abortion without parental knowledge or consent. Retribution was discounted on the theory that young killers, apparently without exception, are less culpable than presumably more thoughtful adult murderers. The Court ignored the fact that juries, unlike the Court, do not decide such issues categorically but by evaluation of the individual and must take youth into account as one mitigating factor.

Retribution was also ruled out without considering its indispensable role in the criminal-justice system. The mixture of reprobation and expiation in retribution is sometimes required as a dramatic mark of our sense of great evil and to reinforce our respect for ourselves and the dignity of others. None of this was examined by the Court. Its steady piecemeal restriction of the death penalty—now "reserved for a narrow category of crimes and offenders"—suggests that the Court is on a path to abolish capital punishment altogether even though the Constitution four times explicitly assumes its legitimacy.

The most ominous aspect of *Roper*, however, is the Court majority's reliance upon foreign decisions and unratified treaties. The opinion cited "the stark reality that the United States is the only country in the world that continues to give official sanction to the juvenile death penalty," a fact the Court

found "instructive" in interpreting the American Constitution. Since the nations of Europe have, among others, abolished the death penalty, the Court
seems to be suggesting that we (or rather the justices) should do likewise.
After all, "[w]e have previously recognized the relevance of the views of the
international community in determining whether a punishment is cruel and
unusual." If the meaning of a document over 200 years old can be affected by
the current state of world opinion, James Madison and his colleagues labored
in vain.

Article 37 of the United Nations Convention on the Rights of the Child,
we are reminded, expressly prohibits capital punishment for those under 18.
The United States—almost uniquely among countries—did not ratify it.
Indeed, this country has never accepted any international covenant containing the prohibition in Article 37. "In sum, it is fair to say that the United
States now stands alone in a world that has turned its face against the juvenile
death penalty." To accept such covenants would, of course, be attempting to
alter our Constitution by treaty. Perhaps that is why the Court hedged: "The
opinion of the world community, while not controlling our outcome, does
provide respected and significant confirmation for our own conclusions."
This "underscores the centrality of those same rights within our own heritage of freedom." That comes pretty close to accepting foreign control of the
American Constitution.

What is really alarming about *Roper* and other cases citing foreign law
(six justices now engage in that practice) is that the Court, in tacit coordination with foreign courts, is moving toward a global bill of rights. Neither our
courts nor the foreign courts are bound by actual constitutions. Prof. Lino
Graglia was quite right when he said that "the first and most important thing
to know about American constitutional law is that it has virtually nothing to
do with the Constitution." That is certainly the case with the Bill of Rights.
From abortion to homosexual sodomy, from religion to political speech and
pornography, from capital punishment to discrimination on the basis of race
and sex, the Court is steadily remaking American political, social, and cultural life. As Justice Antonin Scalia once said in dissent, "Day by day, case
by case, [the Court] is busy designing a Constitution for a country I do not
recognize."

The courts of the United Kingdom, Canada, Israel, and almost all Western countries are doing the same thing, replacing the meaning of their charters with their own preferences. Nor are these judicial alterations random.
The culture war evident in the United States is being waged internationally,
both within individual nations and in international institutions and tribunals.

It is a war for dominance between two moral visions of the future. One is the liberal-elite preference for radical personal autonomy and the other is the general public's desire for some greater degree of community and social authority. Elite views are fairly uniform across national boundaries, and since American and foreign judges belong to elites and respond to elite views, judge-made constitutions tend to converge. It hardly matters what particular constitutions say or were understood to mean by those who adopted them.

Judges are not, of course, the only forces for a new elite global morality. Governments and non-governmental organizations are actively promoting treaties, conventions, and new institutions (the International Criminal Court, for example) that embody their view that sovereignty and nation-states are outmoded and that we must move toward regional or even global governance. American self-government and sovereignty would be submerged in a web of international regulations. The Supreme Court, in decisions like *Roper,* adds constitutional law to the web. That is the one strand, given our current acceptance of judicial supremacy, that cannot be rejected democratically. What is clear is that foreign elites understand the importance of having the Supreme Court on their side, which is precisely why their human-rights organizations have begun filing amicus briefs urging our Supreme Court to adopt the foreign, elite view of the American Constitution.

Roper is one more reason that it is urgent that the president nominate and battle for justices who will rein in a Court run amok.

Tradition and Morality
in Constitutional Law

When a judge undertakes to speak in public about any subject that might be of more interest than the law of incorporeal hereditaments he embarks upon a perilous enterprise. There is always, as I have learned with some pain, someone who will write a story finding it sensational that a judge should say anything. There is some sort of notion that judges have no general ideas about law or, if they do, that, like pornography, ideas are shameful and ought not to be displayed in public to shock the squeamish. For that reason, I come before you, metaphorically at least, clad in a plain brown wrapper.

One common style of speech on occasions such as this is that which paints a bleak picture, identifies even bleaker trends, and then ends on a note of strong and, from the evidence presented, wholly unwarranted optimism. I hope to avoid both extremes while talking about sharply divergent ideas that are struggling for dominance within the legal culture. While I think it serious and potentially of crisis proportions, I speak less to thrill you with the prospect of doom—which is always good fun—than to suggest to you that law is an arena of ideas that is too often ignored by intellectuals interested in public policy. Though it was not always so, legal thought has become something of an intellectual enclave. Too few people are aware of the trends there and the importance of those trends for public policy.

It is said that, at a dinner given in his honor, the English jurist Baron Parke was asked what gave him the greatest pleasure in the law. He answered that his greatest joy was to write a "strong opinion." Asked what that might be, the baron said, "It is an opinion in which, by reasoning with strictly legal concepts, I arrive at a result no layman could conceivably have anticipated."

That was an age of formalism in the law. We have come a long way since then. The law and its acolytes have since become steadily more ideological and more explicit about that fact. That is not necessarily a bad thing: there

1984 AEI Francis Boyer Lecture on Public Policy

are ideologies suitable, indeed indispensable, for judges, just as there are ideologies that are subversive of the very idea of the rule of law. It is the sharp recent growth in the latter that is worrisome for the future.

We are entering, I believe, a period in which our legal culture and constitutional law may be transformed, with even more power accruing to judges than is presently the case. There are two reasons for that. One is that constitutional law has very little theory of its own and hence is almost pathologically lacking in immune defenses against the intellectual fevers of the larger society as well as against the disorders generated by its own internal organs.

The second is that the institutions of the law, in particular the schools, are becoming increasingly converted to an ideology of the Constitution that demands just such an infusion of extraconstitutional moral and political notions. A not untypical example of the first is the entry into the law of the First Amendment of the old, and incorrect, view that the only kinds of harm that a community is entitled to suppress are physical and economic injuries. Moral harms are not to be counted because to do so would interfere with the autonomy of the individual. That is an indefensible definition of what people are entitled to regard as harms.

The result of discounting moral harm is the privatization of morality, which requires the law of the community to practice moral relativism. It is thought that individuals are entitled to their moral beliefs but may not gather as a community to express those moral beliefs in law. Once an idea of that sort takes hold in the intellectual world, it is very likely to find lodgment in constitutional theory and then in constitutional law. The walls of the law have proved excessively permeable to intellectual osmosis. Out of prudence, I will give but one example of the many that might be cited.

A state attempted to apply its obscenity statute to a public display of an obscene word. The Supreme Court majority struck down the conviction on the grounds that regulation is a slippery slope and that moral relativism is a constitutional command. The opinion said, "The principle contended for by the State seems inherently boundless. How is one to distinguish this from any other offensive word?" One might as well say that the negligence standard of tort law is inherently boundless, for how is one to distinguish the reckless driver from the safe one. The answer in both cases is, by the common sense of the community. Almost all judgments in the law are ones of degree, and the law does not flinch from such judgments except when, as in the case of morals, it seriously doubts the community's right to define harms. Moral relativism was even more explicit in the majority opinion, however, for the Court observed, apparently thinking the observation decisive: "One man's vulgarity is another's lyric." On that ground, it is difficult to see how law on any subject can be permitted to exist.

But the Court immediately went further, reducing the whole question to one of private preference, saying: "We think it is largely because governmental officials cannot make principled distinctions in this area that the Constitution leaves matters of taste and style so largely to the individual." Thus, the community's moral and aesthetic judgments are reduced to questions of style and those are then said to be privatized by the Constitution. It testifies all the more clearly to the power of ideas floating in the general culture to alter the Constitution that this opinion was written by a justice generally regarded as moderate to conservative in his constitutional views.

George Orwell reminded us long ago about the power of language to corrupt thought and the consequent baleful effects upon politics. The same deterioration is certainly possible in morality. But I am not concerned about the constitutional protection cast about an obscene word. Of more concern is the constitutionalizing of the notion that moral harm is not harm legislators are entitled to consider. As Lord Devlin said, "What makes a society is a community of ideas, not political ideas alone but also ideas about the way its members should behave and govern their lives." A society that ceases to be a community increases the danger that weariness with turmoil and relativism may bring about an order in which many more, and more valuable, freedoms are lost than those we thought we were protecting.

I do not know the origin of the notion that moral harms are not properly legally cognizable harms, but it has certainly been given powerful impetus in our culture by John Stuart Mill's book *On Liberty*. Mill, however, was a man of two minds and, as Gertrude Himmelfarb has demonstrated, Mill himself usually knew better than this. Miss Himmelfarb traces the intellectual themes of *On Liberty* to Mill's wife. It would be ironic, to put it no higher, if we owed major features of modern American constitutional doctrine to Harriet Taylor Mill, who was not, as best I can remember, one of the framers at Philadelphia.

It is unlikely, of course, that a general constitutional doctrine of the impermissibility of legislating moral standards will ever be framed. So the development I have cited, though troubling, is really only an instance of a yet more worrisome phenomenon, and that is the capacity of ideas that originate outside the Constitution to influence judges, usually without their being aware of it, so that those ideas are elevated to constitutional doctrine. We have seen that repeatedly in our history. If one may complain today that the Constitution did not adopt John Stuart Mill's *On Liberty*, it was only a few judicial generations ago, when economic laissez faire somehow got into the Constitution, that Justice Holmes wrote in dissent that the Constitution "does not enact Mr. Herbert Spencer's Social Statics."

Why should this be so? Why should constitutional law constantly be catching colds from the intellectual fevers of the general society?

The fact is that the law has little intellectual or structural resistance to outside influences, influences that should properly remain outside. The striking, and peculiar, fact about a field of study so old and so intensively cultivated by men and women of first-rate intelligence is that the law possesses very little theory about itself. I once heard George Stigler remark with some astonishment: "You lawyers have nothing of your own. You borrow from the social sciences, but you have no discipline, no core, of your own." And, a few scattered insights here and there aside, he was right. This theoretical emptiness at its center makes law, particularly constitutional law, unstable, a ship with a great deal of sail but a very shallow keel, vulnerable to the winds of intellectual or moral fashion, which it then validates as the commands of our most basic compact.

This weakness in the law's intellectual structure may be exploited by new theories of moral relativism and egalitarianism now the dominant mode of constitutional thinking in a number of leading law schools. The attack of these theories upon older assumptions has been described by one Harvard law professor as a "battle of cultures," and so it is. It is fair to think, then, that the outcome of this confused battle may strongly affect the constitutional law of the future and hence the way in which we are governed.

The constitutional ideologies growing in the law schools display three worrisome characteristics. They are increasingly abstract and philosophical; they are sometimes nihilistic; they always lack what law requires, democratic legitimacy. These tendencies are new, much stronger now than they were even ten years ago, and certainly nothing like them appeared in our past.

Up to a few years ago most professors of constitutional law would probably have agreed with Joseph Story's dictum in 1833: "Upon subjects of government, it has always appeared to me, that metaphysical refinements are out of place. A constitution of government is addressed to the common-sense of the people, and never was designed for trials of logical skill or visionary speculation." But listen to how Nathan Glazer today perceives the lawyer's task, no doubt because of the professors he knows: "As a political philosopher or a lawyer, I would try to find basic principles of justice that can be defended and argued against all other principles. As a sociologist, I look at the concrete consequences, for concrete societies."

Glazer's perception of what more and more lawyers are doing is entirely accurate. That reality is disturbing. Academic lawyers are not going to solve the age-old problems of political and moral philosophy any time soon, but the articulated premise of their abstract enterprise is that judges may properly reason to constitutional decisions in that way. But judges have no mandate to govern in the name of contractarian or utilitarian or what-have-you philosophy rather than according to the historical Constitution. Judges of this generation, and much more, of the next generation, are being educated to engage in really heroic adventures in policy making.

This abstract, universalistic style of legal thought has a number of dangers. For one thing, it teaches disrespect for the actual institutions of the American polity. These institutions are designed to achieve compromise, to slow change, to dilute absolutisms. They embody wholesome inconsistencies. They are designed, in short, to do things that abstract generalizations about the just society tend to bring into contempt.

More than this, the attempt to define individual liberties by abstract reasoning, though intended to broaden liberties, is actually likely to make them more vulnerable.

Our constitutional liberties arose out of historical experience and out of political, moral, and religious sentiment. They do not rest upon any general theory. Attempts to frame a theory that removes from democratic control areas of life the framers intended to leave there can only succeed if abstractions are regarded as overriding the constitutional text and structure, judicial precedent, and the history that gives our rights life, rootedness, and meaning. It is no small matter to discredit the foundations upon which our constitutional freedoms have always been sustained and substitute as a bulwark only abstractions of moral philosophy. The difference in approach parallels the difference between the American and the French revolutions, and the outcome for liberty was much less happy under the regime of "the rights of man."

It is perhaps not surprising that abstract, philosophical approaches to law often produce constitutional nihilism. Some of the legal philosophers have begun to see that there is no overarching theory that can satisfy the criteria that are required. It may be, as Hayek suggested, that nihilism naturally results from sudden disillusion when high expectations about the powers of abstract reasoning collapse. The theorists, unable to settle for practical wisdom, must have a single theoretical construct or nothing. In any event, one of the leading scholars has announced, in a widely admired article, that all normative constitutional theories, including the theory that judges must only interpret the law, are necessarily incoherent. The apparently necessary conclusion—judicial review is, in that case, illegitimate—is never drawn. Instead, it is proposed that judges simply enforce good values, or rather the values that seem to the professor good. The desire for results appears to be stronger than the respect for legitimacy, and, when theory fails, the desire to use judicial power remains.

This brings into the open the fundamental antipathy to democracy to be seen in much of the new legal scholarship. The original Constitution was devoted primarily to the mechanisms of democratic choice. Constitutional scholarship today is dominated by the creation of arguments that will encourage judges to thwart democratic choice. Though the arguments are, as you might suspect, cast in terms of expanding individual freedom, that is not their result. One of the freedoms, the major freedom, of our kind of society is the freedom to choose to have a public morality. As Chesterton put it, "What is the good of telling a community that it has every liberty except the liberty to make laws? The liberty to make laws is what constitutes a free people." The makers of our Constitution thought so too, for they provided wide powers to representative assemblies and ruled only a few subjects off limits by the Constitution.

The new legal view disagrees both with the historical Constitution and with the majority of living Americans about where the balance between individual freedom and social order lies.

Leading legal academics are increasingly absorbed with what they call "legal theory." That would be welcome, if it were real, but what is generally meant is not theory about the sources of law, or its capacities and limits, or the prerequisites for its vitality, but rather the endless exploration of abstract philosophical principles. One would suppose that we can decide nothing unless we first settle the ultimate questions of the basis of political obligation, the merits of contractarianism, rule or act utilitarianism, the nature of the just society, and the like. Not surprisingly, the politics of the professors becomes the command of the Constitution. As Richard John Neuhaus puts it, "the theorists' quest for universality becomes simply the parochialism of a few intellectuals," and he notes "the limitations of theories of justice that cannot sustain a democratic consensus regarding the legitimacy of law."

Sometimes I am reminded of developments in another, perhaps parallel, field. I recall one evening listening to a rather traditional theologian bemoan the intellectual fads that were sweeping his field. Since I had a very unsophisticated view of theology, I remarked with some surprise that his church seemed to have remarkably little doctrine capable of resisting these trends.

He was offended and said there had always been tradition. Both of our fields purport to rest upon sacred texts, and it seemed odd that in both the main bulwark against heresy should be only tradition. Law is certainly like that. We never elaborated much of a theory—as distinguished from mere attitudes—about the behavior proper to constitutional judges. As Alexander Bickel observed, all we ever had was a tradition, and in the last thirty years that has been shattered.

Now we need theory, theory that relates the framers' values to today's world. That is not an impossible task by any means, but it is a good deal more complex than slogans such as "strict construction" or "judicial restraint" might lead you to think. It is necessary to establish the proposition that the framers' intentions with respect to freedoms are the sole legitimate premise from which constitutional analysis may proceed. It is true that a willful judge can often clothe his legislation in sophistical argument and the misuse of history. But hypocrisy has its value. General acceptance of correct theory can force the judge to hypocrisy and, to that extent, curb his freedom. The theorists of moral abstraction are devoted precisely to removing the judge's guilt at legislating and so removing the necessity for hypocrisy. Worse still, they would free the intellectually honest judge from constraints he would otherwise recognize and honor.

It is well to be clear about the role moral discourse should play in law. Neuhaus is entirely correct in saying whatever else law may be, it is a human enterprise in response to human behavior, and human behavior is stubbornly entangled with beliefs about right and wrong. Law that is recognized as legitimate is therefore related to—even organically related to, if you will—the larger universe of moral discourse that helps shape human behavior. In short, if law is not also a moral enterprise, it is without legitimacy or binding force.

To that excellent statement I would add only that it is crucial to bear in mind what kind of law, and which legal institutions, we are talking about. In a constitutional democracy the moral content of law must be given by the morality of the framer or the legislator, never by the morality of the judge. The sole task of the latter—and it is a task quite large enough for anyone's wisdom, skill, and virtue—is to translate the framer's or the legislator's morality into a rule to govern unforeseen circumstances. That abstinence from giving his own desires free play, that continuing and self-conscious renunciation of power, that is the morality of the jurist.

II.

ANTITRUST LAW

A. Articles

The Crisis in Antitrust

Long-standing contradictions at the root of antitrust doctrine have today brought it to a crisis of policy. From its inception with the passage
of the Sherman Act in 1890, antitrust has vacillated between the policy of
preserving competition and the policy of preserving competitors from their
more energetic and efficient rivals. It is the rapid acceleration of the latter "protectionist" trends in antitrust that has brought on the present crisis.
Anti-free-market forces now have the upper hand and are steadily broadening and consolidating their victory. The continued acceptance and expansion
of their doctrine, which now constitutes antitrust's growing edge, threaten
within the foreseeable future to destroy the antitrust laws as guarantors of a
competitive economy.

The situation would be sufficiently serious if antitrust were merely a
set of economic prescriptions applicable to a sector of the economy, but it is
much more than that; it is also an expression of a social philosophy, an edu-
cative force, and a political symbol of extraordinary potency. Its capture by
the opponents of the free market is thus likely to have effects far beyond the
confines of antitrust itself.

The very existence of this crisis—and the basic societal changes it por-
tends—seems unsuspected by most Americans. Even the general business
community, which will be most directly affected, though it is conscious of
hostility, appears to understand neither the nature nor the immediacy of the
threat. To be sure, businessmen and their lawyers may frequently be heard
inveighing against some particular action of the courts or of the governmental enforcement agencies. Calls from industry for mutual reasonableness
and understanding between government and business are common. But such
responses to the situation are dangerously beside the point. The problem is

From *Fortune*, December 1963. With Ward S. Bowman Jr.

not created by a temporary aberration of the courts or the unreasonableness of a particular set of officials who can be jollied out of it or, if not, who will eventually be replaced with a more reasonable crew. The danger arises from a fundamental and widespread misconception of the nature and virtues of the competitive process. This misconception, coupled occasionally with real hostility toward the free market, exists in varying degrees in the courts, in the governmental enforcement agencies, and in the Congress, with the result that in crucial areas the doctrines of antitrust are performing a 180-degree turn away from competition.

The nature of the present crisis in the law can be demonstrated by comparing the law concerning price fixing and the developing law of mergers. The comparison illustrates the schizophrenia afflicting basic antitrust policy.

The rule that price fixing and similar cartel arrangements are illegal per se, that is, incapable of legal justification, must be ranked one of the greatest accomplishments of antitrust. Though its wisdom may seem obvious now, it was not always apparent that this was the correct rule or that the courts would adopt it. The first price-fixing case to reach the Supreme Court (in 1897) was the government's Sherman Act suit against the Trans-Missouri Freight Association, an association of railroads that agreed upon rates to be charged shippers. Both the trial court and the court of appeals agreed that the government's bill should be dismissed because the agreement provided for "reasonable" rates and the new Sherman Act only struck down unreasonable restraints of trade. The Supreme Court, by a five-to-four vote, rejected this view. If one vote had been cast the other way the "reasonableness" of the price agreed upon would have determined legality and the Sherman Act might easily have become not the symbol of the free market but a judicial version of the NRA. To many observers at the time the Supreme Court's Trans-Missouri decision seemed disastrous. Were businessmen to be helpless to defend themselves by reasonable agreement from "ruinous competition"? Would not the small and perhaps less efficient producer be at the mercy of the more efficient? The Supreme Court majority rejected such arguments for judicially supervised cartels. A year later William Howard Taft, then a circuit-court judge, rejected a similar defense in the *Addyston Pipe & Steel* case, saying that to adopt such a standard was to "set sail on a sea of doubt" and that courts that had done it had "assumed the power to say . . . how much restraint of competition is in the public interest, and how much is not." Since then, with very few exceptions, the Supreme Court has hewed to the rule of per se illegality for cartel agreements.

The reason behind the characterization of this rule as one of the supreme achievements of antitrust goes straight to fundamentals. Why should we want to preserve competition anyway? The answer is simply that it is the chief glory of competition that it gives society the maximum output that can be achieved at any given time with the resources at its command. Under a competitive regime productive resources are combined and separated, shuffled and reshuffled ever anew in the endless search for greater profits through greater efficiency. Each productive resource moves to that employment where the value of its marginal product, and hence the return paid to it, is greatest. Output is seen to be maximized because there is no possible rearrangement of resources that could increase the value to consumers of total output. We want competition, then, because we want our society to be as rich as possible and because we want individual consumers to determine by their actions what goods and services they want most. This preference for material prosperity requires no apology. Aside from its obvious advantages, prosperity is important both in our long-run competition with the Communist world and for humanitarian reasons. There is much justifiable concern about relative poverty in our society and about particular groups that are thought to be disadvantaged in one way or another. It should be obvious that such groups will achieve major gains in prosperity only by sharing in the general increase of wealth. Competition allows us to use our resources most effectively to this end.

Price fixing is antisocial precisely because it lessens the total output of the society. When competitors agree on higher prices and put them into effect, they necessarily restrict output and so reduce total wealth. Some of the resources in the industry are then unused or are forced to migrate to other employment where the value placed on them by consumers is not so high. Over time, of course, such resources will move back into the industry as new firms, attracted by the higher rate of return there, move in. Usually the only way for the cartelists to prevent that is to persuade the government to impose legal barriers on entry into the industry, but that is not always possible. The tendency of competition to erode cartels does not, however, disprove the value of the rule against price fixing. Though its life is limited, the cartel may last long enough to cause a substantial loss in output.

The per se rule fashioned by the Supreme Court is thus a model antitrust law. It is at once a clear, workable rule and the expression of sound social policy. In dismal contrast has been the record of the courts in the field of mergers and of practices that are thought to injure competition by injuring competitors. Such practices as exclusive dealing and price discrimination fall within this latter category. It is here that antitrust has gone awry and that the immediate cause of its crisis lies. In order to understand the crisis, it is essential to understand the doctrines that underlie the courts' performance. These consist primarily of the theories of: (1) monopoly-gaining or exclusionary practices; (2) incipiency; and (3) the "social" purposes of the antitrust law. Though they enjoy nearly universal acceptance and provide the impetus and intellectual support for the law's current growth, these doctrines in their present form are demonstrably fallacious in concept and visibly hurtful in application.

Economic theory indicates that present notions of the exclusionary practices are fallacious. This was first perceived by Professor Aaron Director, of the University of Chicago Law School, who noted that practices conventionally labeled "exclusionary"—notably, price discrimination, vertical mergers, exclusive-dealing contracts, and the like—appeared to be either competitive tactics equally available to all firms or means of maximizing the returns from a market position already held. Director's analysis indicates that, absent special factors which have not been shown to exist, so-called exclusionary practices are not means of injuring the competitive process. The example of requirements contracts (i.e., contracts by which a customer agrees to take all his requirements of a product from a particular supplier) can be used to illustrate the point. The theory of exclusionary tactics underlying the law appears to be that firm X, which already has 10 percent of the market, can sign up more than 10 percent of the retailers, perhaps 20 percent, and, by thus "foreclosing" rivals from retail outlets, obtain a larger share of the market. One must then ask why so many retailers are willing to limit themselves to selling X's product. Why do not 90 percent of them turn to X's rivals? Because X has greater market acceptance? But then X's share of the market would grow for that reason and the requirements contracts have nothing to do with it. Because X offers them some extra inducement? But that sounds like competition, it is equivalent to a price cut, and surely X's competitors can be relied upon to meet competition.

The theory of exclusionary practices, here exemplified in the use of requirements contracts, seems to require one of two additional assumptions to be made theoretically plausible. One is the assumption that there are practices by which a competitor can impose greater costs upon his rivals than upon himself. That would mean that X could somehow make it more expensive for his rivals to sign retailers to requirements contracts than it is for X to do so. It would be as though X could offer a retailer a $1 price reduction and it would cost any rival $2 to match the offer. It is difficult to imagine that such a mechanism exists in the case of requirements contracts, price cutting, or the usual examples of predatory or exclusionary practices, but it is perhaps conceivable. One possibility, though of limited applicability, would be the case where the only seller of a full line required retailers to deal with him exclusively or not at all. He might be able to get more retailers than his initial market share would seem to command if it would be difficult or impossible for the retailers to assemble a full line from the remaining suppliers.

The other assumption upon which the theory of exclusionary practices might rest is that there are imperfections in or difficulties of access to the capital market that enable X to offer a $1 inducement (it has a bankroll) and prevent its rivals from responding (they have no bankroll and, though the offering of the inducement is a responsible business tactic, for some reason cannot borrow the money). No general case has been made showing that imperfections of this type exist in the capital market.

Myth and Fact in the Standard Oil case

Professor Director's reasoning applies to all practices thought to be exclusionary or monopoly gaining. A moment's thought indicates, moreover, that the notion of exclusionary practices is not merely theoretically weak but is, for such a widely accepted idea, remarkably lacking in factual support. Has anybody ever seen a firm gain a monopoly or anything like one through the use of requirements contracts? Or through price discrimination? One may begin to suspect that antitrust is less a science than an elaborate mythology, that it has operated for years on hearsay and legends rather than on reality. The few supposedly verified cases of the successful use of exclusionary tactics to achieve monopoly are primarily in the early history of antitrust. The story of the old Standard Oil trust is probably the classic example. The Supreme Court's 1911 *Standard Oil* opinion is pivotal not merely because it is thought to have launched the famous "rule of reason," nor because it decreed dissolution which made the oil industry more competitive. Its greatest significance is that it gave weight, substance, and seeming historical veracity to the whole theory of exclusionary and monopoly-gaining techniques. It thus provided much of the impetus for the passage of the Clayton and Federal Trade Commission acts in 1914. Such intellectual support as can be mustered for the law against price discrimination derives primarily from the lessons supposedly taught by that case.

The factual accuracy of the Standard Oil legend is under attack and is coming to seem as dubious as the theory that it is thought to support. Professor John McGee, an economist now at Duke University, reviewed the entire case record of the Standard Oil litigation and reported that there is not one clear episode of the successful use by Standard Oil of local price cutting or other predatory practices. The other supposed instances of monopolies gained through such tactics deserve similar investigation.

It would be claiming too much to say that there is no merit to the theory of exclusionary practices, but it is fair to say that that theory has been seriously challenged at both the theoretical and the empirical levels. Perhaps a sound theoretical base can be constructed. The law could then be directed at those practices that in particular settings may be exclusionary. So far as is known, however, this task has not been undertaken or even recognized by the Antitrust Division, the Federal Trade Commission, or any court.

The trees don't grow up to the sky

The incipiency theory starts from the idea that it is possible to nip restraints of trade and monopolies in the bud before they blossom to Sherman Act proportions. It underlies the Clayton Act, the Robinson-Patman Act, and the Federal Trade Commission Act. Though the idea initially sounds plausible, its consequences have proved calamitous. The courts have used the incipiency notion as a license for almost unlimited extrapolation, reasoning from any trend toward concentration in an industry that there is an incipient lessening of competition. The difficulty with stopping a trend toward a more concentrated condition at a very early stage is that the existence of the trend is prima facie evidence that greater concentration is socially desirable. The trend indicates that there are emerging efficiencies or economies of scale—whether due to engineering and production developments or to new control and management techniques—which make larger size more efficient. This increased efficiency is valuable to the society at large, for it means that fewer of our available resources are being used to accomplish the same amount of production and distribution. By striking at such trends in their very earliest stages the concept of incipiency prevents the realization of those very efficiencies that competition is supposed to encourage. But it is when the incipiency concept works in tandem with the unsophisticated theory of exclusionary practices currently in use that its results are most anticompetitive. Where a court or the Federal Trade Commission lacks the means to distinguish between tactics that impose greater costs on rivals and those that are normal means of competing, what evidence can it look to in its effort to discern an incipient lessening of competition? The obvious resort is to evidence that a competitor has been injured, for it is through the infliction of injury upon competitors that the exclusionary devices are thought ultimately to injure the competitive process itself. There seems no way to tell that a competitor has been "injured," however, except that he has lost business. And this is precisely the meaning that the statutory test of incipient lessening of competition or tendency toward monopoly is coming to have. In case after case the FTC, for example, nails down its finding that competition is injured with the testimony of competitors of the respondent that his activities and aggressiveness may or have cost them sales. The conduct that threatens such "injury" is then prohibited. That this result is itself profoundly anticompetitive seems never to occur to the commission or to most courts.

When the anti-efficiency impact of the law is occasionally perceived, the third theory—the social purpose of the antitrust laws—is called upon to provide a rationalization. Judge Learned Hand's *Alcoa* opinion contains the most famous exposition of this view. Hand suggested that Congress, in passing the Sherman Act, had not necessarily been actuated by economic motives alone, and continued: "It is possible, because of its indirect social or moral effect, to prefer a system of small producers, each dependent for his success upon his own skill and character, to one in which the great mass of those engaged must accept the direction of a few." He went on to say: "Throughout the history of these statutes it has been constantly assumed that one of their purposes was to perpetuate and preserve, for its own sake and in spite of possible cost, an organization of industry in small units which can effectively compete with each other."

Hand's rhetoric has commended itself to most commentators on the topic, but it seems clear upon reflection that it is a position which is inaccurate as a description of congressional intent, dubious as social policy, and impossible as antitrust doctrine.

It is simply not accurate to say that Congress ever squarely decided to prefer the preservation of small business to the preservation of a free market in which the forces of competition worked themselves out. There was much rhetoric in Congress about the virtues of small business but no clear indication that antitrust should create shelters for the inefficient. In fact, the statutory language of all the major antitrust laws after the Sherman Act explicitly requires the preservation of *competition*. That places an enormous burden of persuasion upon those who purport to find in the legislative history a direction to value small business above competition.

Hand's notion, moreover, is dubious, and indeed radical, social policy. It would be hard to demonstrate that the independent druggist or groceryman is any more solid and virtuous a citizen than the local manager of a chain operation. The notion that such persons are entitled to special consideration has typified some of the ugliest European social movements. It hardly seems suited to the U.S., whose dominant ideal, though doubtless often enough flouted in practice, has been that each business should survive only by serving consumers as they want to be served. If that ideal is to be departed from here, if antitrust is to turn from its role as the maintainer of free markets to become the industrial and commercial equivalent of the farm price-support program, then we are entitled to an unequivocal policy choice by Congress and not to vague philosophizing by judges who lack the qualifications and the mandate to behave as philosopher kings.

It is clear, in addition, that the "social purpose" concept is impossible as antitrust doctrine. It runs into head-on conflict with the per se rules against cartel agreements. Those rules leave it entirely to the play of competitive forces to determine which competitors shall grow and which shall shrink and disappear. If the social-policy argument makes sense, then we had better drop the per se rule in favor of one permitting the defense that cartels benefit small businessmen. Co-existence of the social-policy argument with the pro-competitive rules would introduce so vague a factor that prediction of the courts' behavior would become little more than a guessing game. How could one know in a particular case whether the court would apply a rigorously pro-competitive rule or the social policy of preserving small business units from aggressive behavior? When the person whose conduct is to be judged is in doubt concerning which of two completely contradictory policies will be applied, the system hardly deserves the name of law.

The crash of merger policy

The three theories discussed are active in many areas of antitrust, but perhaps they may be best illustrated in the law that is now developing under the antimerger statute, amended Section 7 of the Clayton Act. Their collaboration produced the crash of antitrust merger policy in Chief Justice Warren's opinion for the Supreme Court in *Brown Shoe Co. v. United States*. The Court there held illegal the merger of Brown, primarily a shoe manufacturer, with the G. R. Kinney Co., primarily a retailer. Their respective shares of the nation's shoe output were 4 percent and 0.5 percent. Kinney had 1.2 percent of total national retail shoe sales by dollar volume (no figure was given for Brown), and together the companies had 2.3 percent of total retail shoe outlets. With over 800 shoe manufacturers, the industry was as close to pure competition as is possible outside a classroom model. Yet the seven Justices participating in the case managed to see a threat to competition at both the manufacturing and the retailing levels, and they did so by using the three concepts already discussed.

The Court held the merger illegal for both its vertical and its horizontal aspects. The Court generally views vertical integration as a form of exclusionary practice, since it is always possible that the manufacturing level will sell to the retail level of the same firm and thereby "foreclose" a share of the retail market otherwise open to competing manufacturers. In the *Brown Shoe* case the Court said the share of the market foreclosed was not enough by itself to make the merger illegal but that it became illegal when two other factors were examined: " . . . the trend toward vertical integration in the shoe industry, [and] . . . Brown's avowed policy of forcing its own shoes upon its retail subsidiaries . . ." It is enlightening to examine the facts upon which that conclusion rests. The "trend toward vertical integration" was seen in the fact that a number of manufacturers had acquired retailing chains. The district court found that the thirteen largest shoe manufacturers, for example, operated 21 percent of the census shoe stores. Accepting that figure for the moment, it is impossible to see any harm to competition. On a straight extrapolation, there would be room for over sixty manufacturers of equal size to integrate to the same extent, and that would result in as pure competition as is conceivable. In fact, since these were the largest shoe manufacturers, there would be room for many more manufacturers. But that is by no means all; the category of census shoe stores includes only those that make at least half their income from selling shoes. It thus leaves out about two-thirds of the outlets that actually sell shoes, including such key ones as department and clothing stores. Even if, as there was no reason to expect, complete vertical integration took place in the industry, there would obviously be room for hundreds of shoe manufacturers, and, given the ease of entry into shoe retailing, no basis for imagining that any new manufacturer could not find or create outlets any time he chose. The Court's cited "trend toward vertical integration" was thus impossible to visualize as a threat to competition.

Imaginary *"foreclosure"*

Brown's "avowed policy of forcing its own shoes upon its retail subsidiaries" turns out, upon inspection of the Court's footnotes, to spring from the testimony of its president that Brown's motive in making the deal was to get distribution in a range of prices it was not covering, and also, as Kinney moved into stores in higher income neighborhoods and needed to upgrade and add new lines, " . . . it would give us an opportunity, we hoped, to be able to sell them in that category." The empirical evidence of coercion was no more impressive than this "avowal." At the time of the merger Kinney bought no shoes from Brown, but two years later Brown was supplying 7.9 percent of Kinney's needs. (Brown's sales to its other outlets apparently had risen no higher than 33 percent of requirements, except in one case in which Brown supplied over 50 percent.) The "trend toward vertical integration" and the "avowed policy of forcing its own shoes upon its retail subsidiaries" were thus almost entirely imaginary. But even if they were accepted at face value, it ought to be noted that, since Kinney supplied about 20 percent of its own retail requirements, less than 1 percent of the nation's total retail shoe sales was open to "foreclosure" by Brown through this merger and it had actually "foreclosed" slightly less than one-tenth of 1 percent. The idea of vertical integration as an exclusionary device had to be coupled with almost unlimited extrapolation in the name of incipiency to reach the incredible result that the Court achieved on the vertical aspect of the case.

"It is competition . . . the Act protects. But . . . "

The horizontal aspect—the putting together of Brown's and Kinney's retail outlets—was held illegal on similar reasoning. The Court found the creation of market shares of as low as 5 percent of shoe retailing in any city illegal, stating: "If a merger achieving 5 percent control were now approved, we might be required to approve future merger efforts by Brown's competitors seeking similar market shares. The oligopoly Congress sought to avoid would then be furthered . . ." On this reasoning every merger "furthers" oligopoly no matter how small a share of the market is taken over. To imagine that every firm would then merge up to 5 percent is to indulge in sheer conjecture, and in any event the result would be competition. Twenty firms in an industry is far too many to act as oligopolists. Given the ease and rapidity of entry into shoe retailing, the Supreme Court's fear of oligopoly is simply incomprehensible.

Then, apparently without realizing the inconsistency with its earlier prediction that Brown would "force" its shoes upon Kinney, the Court suggested that the merger was also bad because Kinney's new ability to get Brown's shoes more cheaply would give it an advantage over other retailers. "The retail outlets of integrated companies, by eliminating wholesalers and by increasing the volume of purchases from the manufacturing division of the enterprise, can market their own brands at prices below those of competing independent retailers." The merger was therefore bad both because Brown might "force" Kinney and because Kinney wanted to be "forced." This fascinating holding creates an antitrust analogue to the crime of statutory rape.

Apparently concerned that the achievement of efficiency and low prices through merger seemed to be illegal under this formulation, the Court then stated: "Of course, some of the results of large integrated or chain operations are beneficial to consumers. Their expansion is not rendered unlawful by the mere fact that small independent stores may be adversely affected. It is competition, not competitors, which the Act protects. But we cannot fail to recognize Congress' desire to promote competition through the protection of viable, small, locally owned businesses. Congress appreciated that occasional higher costs and prices might result from the maintenance of fragmented industries and markets. It resolved these competing considerations in favor of decentralization." No matter how many times you read it, that passage states: Although mergers are not rendered unlawful by the mere fact that small independent stores may be adversely affected, we must recognize that mergers are unlawful when small independent stores may be adversely affected.

The *Brown Shoe* case employed the theory of exclusionary practices to outlaw vertical integration that promised lower prices, the theory of incipiency to foresee danger in a presumably desirable trend that was barely started, and the theory of "social purpose" to justify the fact that it prevented the realization of efficiencies by a merger that, realistically viewed, did not even remotely threaten competition.

The attack on conglomerates

The FTC and some of the lower federal courts are now pushing these doctrines to their logical conclusion—an attack on efficiency itself as anticompetitive. This is seen most clearly in the rash of suits challenging conglomerate mergers. A conglomerate merger is one between parties that are neither competitors nor related as supplier and customer, an example being the acquisition by a locomotive manufacturer of an underwear maker. It neither increases any firm's share of a market nor forecloses anybody from a market or source of supply. The government's attack on such mergers, therefore, has had to be on the theory that they create a "competitive advantage" which may enable the new firm to injure rivals. The competitive advantage, upon inspection, turns out to be efficiency. Thus a district court recently entered a preliminary injunction at the government's request restraining Ingersoll-Rand Co. from acquiring three manufacturers of underground coal-mining machinery and equipment. Though the opinion rested in part upon the competing status of the acquired companies, it stressed the conglomerate aspects of the merger. One of the court's explicit fears was that the merger would create "economies of scale" (efficiencies due to size) which would put other companies at a competitive disadvantage. The court of appeals affirmed, noting as anticompetitive the fact that Ingersoll-Rand would be able "to offer a complete line of equipment to its consumers and to further enhance its position and dominance in the market by extending consumer financing to prospective purchasers through its wholly owned subsidiary finance company." This is a decision that illegality attaches when the merger enables better service to consumers.

On a similar theory the FTC is attacking Procter & Gamble's acquisition of the Clorox Chemical Co. The hearing examiner has held the acquisition illegal, assigning as major reasons the fact that, by integrating Clorox advertising with its own, P. & G. had realized substantial savings over what Clorox alone had had to spend, and the supposition that P. & G. might sell Clorox through its own existing sales force and thus lower the costs of distribution. The examiner thought the creation of such efficiencies anticompetitive because they might hurt the sales of other liquid-bleach manufacturers. Neither the *Ingersoll-Rand* case nor the *Procter & Gamble* decision considers that the creation of just such efficiencies is the main benefit competition has to offer society. If it now takes fewer salesmen and distribution personnel to move a product from the factory to the consumer than it used to, that is a net gain to society. We are all richer to that extent. Multiply that by hundreds and thousands of transactions and an enormously important social phenomenon is perceived. Any law that makes the creation of efficiency the touchstone of illegality can only tend to impoverish us as a nation.

Preserving the dodoes

Too few people understand that it is the essential mechanism of competition and its prime virtue that more efficient firms take business away from the less efficient. Some businesses will shrink and some will disappear. Competition is an evolutionary process. Evolution requires the extinction of some species as well as the survival of others. The business equivalents of the dodoes, the dinosaurs, and the great ground sloths are in for a bad time—and they should be. It is fortunate for all of us that there was no Federal Biological Commission around when the first small furry mammals appeared and began eating dinosaur eggs. The commission would undoubtedly have perceived a "competitive advantage," labeled it an "unfair method of evolution," and stopped the whole process right there.

It is important to try to understand why this anticompetitive strain has developed in antitrust. The institutions primarily responsible are the Supreme Court, the enforcement agencies, and Congress.

It would be difficult to overestimate the role of the Supreme Court. Though not compelled by the wording or the legislative history of the laws, the Court has with increasing frequency taken extreme anticompetitive positions. In many cases the Court has materially changed the law as it had previously been understood. This means that the Court is making major social policy, and the policy it chooses to make today is predominantly anticompetitive. It is naive to imagine that Congress can always correct the Court when it legislates in this fashion. When the Court, consciously or unconsciously, changes the meaning of a statute or the direction of a body of law, it may very well accomplish a change that Congress was politically incapable of making but is equally incapable of reversing. In fact, the prestige of the Court is so high that by taking the lead in formulating new policy it may make further legislative change in the same direction much easier. The propriety of this process and of the Court's rather unrestrained use of its power and influence depends of course upon one's view of the correct roles and relationships of the judiciary and the legislature. It seems at least highly doubtful that it is appropriate for major policy shifts to come through the judicial process when they could not initially have been arrived at by the political process.

The Antitrust Division and the FTC have also played leading parts in pushing the law in the direction it has taken. This is to be expected because of the natural partisan feeling that springs up in any group of men who are always on one side of litigation as well as the fact that such specialized agencies are likely to attract and hold men who take personal satisfaction in prosecuting "business culprits." Then, too, there is the tendency of men to see what they are told is there. If a congressional committee were to suggest to the FTC that vampires were injuring competition, the Government Purchasing Office would shortly be asked to lay in a supply of holly stakes.

When the head of the Antitrust Division or the FTC reports to a congressional committee, protocol requires that he wear a suitable number of bloody scalps of businessmen at his belt. It would be unthinkable, moreover, that he report no need for fresh powers. It is established ritual that there is always grave danger to the American economy, if indeed it is not already too late, and that new restrictions are imperative. If an antitrust chieftain did not bring in the scalps and follow the ritual, his own scalp would shortly be hanging from the committee's lodgepole. Scolding the enforcement agencies, therefore, while it is highly diverting sport at bar-association meetings a sort of sedentary version of bull-baiting suitable for middle-aged lawyers is ultimately rather beside the point.

Congress, through legislation and through pressure on the enforcement agencies, is a prime source of the tendencies we are discussing. The men who seek and receive the key posts in congressional committees concerned with antitrust generally display an active dislike of large business units and antipathy toward the free market. The old native Populist strain in American thought, which identifies virtue with the small local businessman and evil with the banks, the railroads, and big corporations, has been strongly represented in recent Congresses by Wright Patman, Hubert Humphrey, the late Senator Kefauver, and many others.

The present trend in Congress is shown by the antitrust bills now pending. They uniformly seek less competition. The so-called quality-stabilization bill, now likely to become law, is nothing more than a federal resale price-fixing law. Its aim is to prevent volume distributors from selling to the public at lower prices than less efficient outlets charge. Senator Humphrey is sponsoring a bill that would make the vague, little-used prohibitions of Section 3 of the Robinson-Patman Act, now solely a criminal statute, available to private triple-damage litigants and for government civil suits. Humphrey proclaims as virtues that the bill would outlaw not only "unreasonably low prices," whatever they might be, but would also prevent a seller who offered one customer a lower price than another from defending himself, as he may under present law, on the ground that he did so only to meet the equally low price of a rival seller. The destruction of that defense would mean, of course, that the seller might have to lower all his prices everywhere or let the customer go. If sellers must lower all prices or none, it is an excellent bet that consumers in general are going to pay higher prices. If consumers are required to subsidize inefficiency, antitrust is on its way to becoming the businessman's version of the farm price-support program.

Incantations Won't Help

What can be done to arrest and reverse these trends? The basic difficulty is lack of understanding of the competitive process, and this failure exists not merely in the courts, the federal agencies, and the Congress but also in the nation at large. We have inherited a marvelously responsive and intricate mechanism, the free market, which we do not understand or appreciate, and so, like savages left a tractor, we poke and rip at it, hit it with clubs and mutter incantations, all in the vain hope of improving its performance. The courts and the legislature preside like a body of medicine men, giving the tribe a new set of chants and directing that yet another piston rod be ripped out or spark plug smashed in order to make the mysterious mechanism behave. This pattern of behavior will take a long time to correct. An educational process of such magnitude is necessarily slow, particularly when there are strong know-nothing forces in the society who will vehemently oppose and vilify the ideas themselves.

The best short-run hope is the more active and direct participation of the business community in those aspects of congressional activity that bear upon the free market. Efficient businesses will lose most directly by the "protectionist" trend of antitrust, for they will be denied the returns that accrue in a competitive economy to initiative, imagination, and good management. If the business community does not inform itself of what is taking place and take an active, intelligent role in the political arena in support of competition, the antitrust laws are condemned to become parodies of themselves and the most potent political symbol of the free market ever known to our society will be lost to the forces of economic regimentation.

Statement of Robert H. Bork

M y name is Robert H. Bork. I am Chancellor Kent Professor of Law at Yale University. I appreciate the opportunity afforded by your invitation to discuss the proposal laid before you by Professor John J. Flynn to shorten antitrust trials by eliminating evidence of conduct when a firm is charged with having monopoly power.

Under the proposed statute, the government would merely prove "monopoly power" in any relevant market and rest its case. Proceedings would then move to the remedy phase, and dissolution of the firm into as many viable entities as possible would be the preferred remedy. The defendant could avert that outcome only by proving that dissolution or other structural relief would entail the "loss of substantial economies of scale." That defense is included, one assumes, in recognition of the fact that dissolution which destroys efficiencies is harmful to consumers, and that, apparently, is not the object of the proposed exercise. The existence of the defense shows that consumer welfare is the dominant consideration underlying this proposal.

Professor Flynn's theory, as I understand it, is that his statute would merely state the law as it is, that cases like *Alcoa* and *United Shoe* were, in fact, decided solely on the defendant's possession of monopoly power, that that criterion is a proper and sufficient one, and that much time and energy could be saved by ignoring the issue of conduct.

The proposed statute seems to me to have three major flaws. First, it would be unlikely appreciably to shorten trials. Second, if it did so, it would succeed at the cost of eliminating the relevant evidence. Third, the remedy would produce the economic evils the statute is designed to cure. I will discuss these points in turn.

There are a number of reasons why the proposed law would not be likely to shorten trials. Evidence of conduct now comes into an antitrust

From the National Commission for the Review of Antitrust Laws and Procedures, 1978–9.

case because the government is trying to show that some factor other than efficiency accounts for the defendant's market share and the defendant is trying to show that efficiency is the cause of its success. If market share alone is made sufficient for dissolution, the theory goes, neither side will have any incentive to probe the details of conduct and, should they try it, the trial judge would exclude the evidence. This seems to me an unrealistic expectation.

A statute that may result in the dissolution of a highly efficient firm will make many judges quite anxious because the dissolution will prove costly to consumers, shareholders, employees, and if such policy mistakes are repeated often enough, to our national strength. If, therefore, the government offers evidence to show that the company has engaged in predatory behavior, the judge will want to hear it. If the defendant offers evidence of a blameless path to large size, the judge will probably want to hear that also. But I will put that assessment of human nature and common sense to one side, since the statute itself provides obvious opportunities to try the issue of conduct.

The first is the prohibition of "monopoly power." If that includes, as it does under present law, the power to exclude competitors, an element of proof will be the conduct of the firm. The existence of power is best shown by the fact that it has been exercised.

But let us assume that the statute is explicitly rewritten so that it does not prohibit monopoly power but some stated share of the relevant market, perhaps something on the order of 85 or 90 percent and above. Then conduct evidence will reappear when the issue of market definition is tried. One of the best ways of determining whether two products are part of the same market is to study the behavior of the firms that make those products toward each other. Do they react and how do they react to each other's price changes, product changes, promotional campaigns, and so on? Are they reacting to one another or to other forces and events in the market?

The government, presumably, will claim that the firms are behaving without reference to each other in order to show that they are in different markets. The defendant will be showing the reverse, because to establish that the firms are rivals and in the same market is to lower the defendant's market share. This is precisely the type of analysis the dissenting Justices employed in the *Cellophane* case to show that cellophane was not regarded by DuPont as competitive with other flexible wrapping materials. On that issue, the dissent was undoubtedly correct, and the conduct evidence was relevant to market definition.

Evidence of conduct is also likely to come in during the trial of defendant's inevitable claim of economies of scale. The argument will be that defendant's market behavior is evidence that economies of scale exist, and the government will have to counter that evidence. It might be possible by rewriting the statute or by arranging its legislative history to make it clear that the defense of economies of scale refers solely to efficiencies of mass production, the lowering of costs associated with high volume output. The defense would then be confined to something like time-and-motion studies to demonstrate lower costs, and would be most unlikely to succeed. But it would be difficult during the process of getting such a statute enacted to admit that your purpose was to get evidence of the most important efficiencies that might be destroyed by the remedy excluded from the hearing on remedies. That would be an admission that shortness of trials is to be purchased at the expense of rational outcomes. It would be like shortening robbery trials by passing a statute that the only defense to an indictment is an alibi and the only alibis that may be placed in evidence must show the defendant was more than 100 miles from the scene of the crime. That would move a lot of trials faster. It would also send a lot of good citizens to jail.

More troubling than the likelihood that the statute would not shorten trials is the certainty that it would produce injustice to defendants and economic harm to consumers. The single most important factor in deciding whether a large market share, one large enough to make output restriction a realistic possibility, ought to be interfered with by law is the way in which that market share was gained. Yet it is precisely that most probative factor that this proposal would make irrelevant. In the absence of patent monopoly, a legal license from the government, or control of a unique natural resource, there are only three ways for a firm to attain anything resembling monopoly position in a market: (1) merger; (2) deliberate predation; and (3) superior efficiency. Mergers are already covered by Section 7 of the Clayton Act. That leaves the possibilities of predation or superior efficiency. Professor Flynn's proposal would deprive the law of the ability to try to distinguish between those two, although that is obviously the most important distinction in deciding whether firm size is pro-consumer or anti-consumer.

If a firm achieves monopoly power by predation, the results are bad for consumers because they get monopoly resource misallocation without the compensating benefit of efficiency. But if a firm obtains monopoly power by superior efficiency, the results, on balance, favor consumers. The firm has no room to exploit its monopoly position except to the degree that it is more efficient than actual or potential rivals. This means that its power to restrict prices is almost certainly very small. We are not talking about either a frequent or a very serious problem. But to the degree that this situation exists, it is obvious that the firm's efficiency outweighs its capacity to restrict output. The efficiency effects outweigh the monopoly effects. If that were not true, rivals would expand and new entrants would appear because, even given superior efficiency, the price would be high enough to allow others to make normal or supernormal profits.

It would make sense to ignore the distinction between predation and efficiency in the law only if we were convinced that size approaching the monopolistic was usually attained by predation and not by efficiency. There is no reason at all to suppose any such thing. Economic studies are beginning to conclude that predation is a relatively rare occurrence. That is also predictable on theoretical grounds because most practices thought to be possible techniques of predation turn out, upon examination, to hurt the predator more than his supposed victim. This is not to say that predation never occurs. It is to say that it is much less common than folklore suggests, and is certainly not the predominant explanation for large corporate size. This means that it is essential to study conduct in a monopoly power case. Otherwise, the law will do much more harm than good. The no-fault divestiture proposal advanced by Professor Flynn is a prescription for doing precisely that.

The remedy of dissolution would destroy many socially valuable efficiencies and the defense of substantial economies of scale would prove a futile safeguard. Any firm that has grown to large size without the employment of predatory practices has demonstrated its superior efficiency. It has not demonstrated that it is efficient in some absolute sense, that it never makes mistakes, that it always produces the ideal product at the ideal price. It has just proved that it is better at pleasing consumers than its rivals are. It makes no sense to talk about market failure in the sense of default by competitors any more than it makes sense to denigrate the performance of a winning runner on the ground that his rivals did not run fast enough to beat him. On that day, in that race, he was the fastest, and anything that worsens his performance hurts those who value it. It is the same with the superior firm. It may not be the best imaginable, but it is the best we have.

Dissolution is certain to destroy important efficiencies. The proposal before you is thoroughly misguided in that it supposes the only really valuable efficiencies are economies of scale. That is not the case. Economies of scale are perhaps among the least valuable of efficiencies in the ordinary industrial or commercial context. An economy of scale is defined as the return the firm obtains because it is large; it does not in any way account for the firm being large in the first place. If economies of scale were decisive, every firm could overtake the industry leader simply by building a larger plant and organization. The reason smaller firms do not typically take so simple a route to success is that they know very well that there is much more to success than that. They may not be able to manage the larger operation at an acceptable cost or the public may not be willing to take a larger output of the product of that firm. The efficiencies that lead to large size are the important ones, and, by definition, they cannot be economies of scale.

This means that the defense provided by the statute excludes all the really important efficiencies and further guarantees that the statute will have a pernicious impact. This subject could be discussed at length, but in the interest of brevity I will mention only that efficiency which seems to be obviously the most important in the economic world. I refer to efficient management. Everything else follows from that: superior product design; superior manufacturing techniques; superior labor performance; superior estimates of consumer desires and market trends; superior distribution practices. The list could be extended almost endlessly. But the point is clear; all success depends upon decisions that are better than those made by competitors, and those decisions are made by management over a period of time. The dissolution of firms will damage the management team that made it successful, damage the organization that past management decisions have built, and prevent management from having as wide a beneficial impact in the future.

But there is more to the point than that. The passage of a statute such as the one proposed, and the dissolution of a few firms under it, would inform every business approaching the range where it might conceivably be prosecuted under the law that it is much better to hold back production and take higher prices in order to avoid the possibility of fatal involvement with the law. The threat of the law would produce the evils of monopoly that the law was supposed to cure. That is to say, the threat of this statute would produce restriction of output and prices above the competitive level.

There is a problem with the protracted monopoly case. The problem has its root in the disposition of government to attack large, successful firms that should not be under attack. The trial of conduct issues is interminable because [to a] very little [extent a corporation's] large size [is] accounted for by improper conduct and enormous effort is spent trying to find something, anything, that sounds improper. What we are suffering from is an unwillingness to accept the fact that most industrial success through internal growth, almost all of it, is deserved and is beneficial to consumers. Only in the rare case of successful predation is that not true.

The problem of the enormous structural case is that far too many of them are brought, not that they should be decided more rapidly and always against the defendant.

ANTITRUST AND MONOPOLY:
THE GOALS OF ANTITRUST POLICY

The life of antitrust law—meaning by that its areas of policy growth—is, in contrast to Holmes's dictum about common law, neither logic nor experience but bad economics and worse jurisprudence. The economics consists of a woefully unsophisticated theory of the means by which firms can gain monopolies, or at any rate injure the competitive process and so injure consumers, by attacking or foreclosing their rivals.[1] The jurisprudence, which is the topic of my paper, consists of the notion that under existing antitrust statutes the courts may properly implement a variety of mutually inconsistent goals, most notably the goals of consumer welfare and small business welfare. Together, these ideas are creating a broad trend of policy directed less to the interest of consumers in free markets than to the interest of inefficient producers in safe markets. The question is whether this trend is either necessary or proper. I think it is neither.

The subject has been debated in a variety of ways. It may be helpful for a lawyer to argue the neglected point that the larger goals of antitrust policy are necessarily affected, in fact determined, by the institutional arrangements we have chosen to implement the policy.

My thesis is that existing statutes can be legitimately interpreted only according to the canons of consumer welfare, defined as minimizing restrictions of output and permitting efficiency, however gained, to have its way. That much I think is required under present statutes by the nature of the judicial process. You will notice, however, that the implications of my argument sometimes overflow the bounds of existing institutions and would sup-

---

1. "The controlling article is Director and Levi, Law and the Future: Trade Regulation," 52 *Nw. U.L. Rev.* 282 (1956). See also Bork and Bowman, "The Crisis in Antitrust," 65 *Columbia Law Rev.* 363 (1965), and "Contrasts in Antitrust Theory: I and II," id. At 401 and 417.

From *The American Economic Review*, May 1967.

port the view that no revision of antitrust should, as a question of legislative wisdom, depart from the consumer welfare premise.

If I am correct, reform is needed, but it need not come from Congress. Antitrust policy is determined, far more than most people realize, by the Supreme Court. Reform is as likely to come through change in the intellectual world which ultimately reaches the Court as by any other means. Reform by the Supreme Court, moreover, is more likely to achieve clean theoretical lines than reform achieved through the political process. The existence of an unelected, somewhat elitist, and undemocratic judicial institution thus makes theory more important than it might otherwise be in our governing processes. I am not suggesting a judicial coup d'etat. Rather, I intend to argue that an exclusive adherence to a consumer welfare test is the only legitimate policy for the Supreme Court under present statutes precisely because of the Court's elitist, unrepresentative nature.

Economics may be a science best confined to analysis and shunning the normative. The lawyer who ignores norms, however, is likely to descend to the level of gossip. Lawyers are properly concerned, not merely with the ways legal institutions behave in fact, but with models of how they ought to behave and how their behavior can be brought closer to the model. The time has come for lawyers to lessen their traditional preoccupation with what courts do in fact and to construct normative models off judicial behavior. Courts as institutions are not fully subject to the discipline of either an economic or a political marketplace. We can attempt to remedy that by constructing an intellectual marketplace which disciplines judicial power through informed criticism. For that task we need a model from which deviations can be measured. This paper attempts to state part of the model appropriate for courts enforcing the antitrust laws.

Social values other than consumer welfare have always played a part in, at least, the rhetoric of antitrust. As early as 1897 the Supreme Court expressed concern over combinations that reduced prices through efficiency, saying, "trade or commerce . . . may . . . be badly and unfortunately restrained by the driving out of business the small dealers and worthy men whose lives have been spent therein, and who might be unable to readjust themselves to their altered surroundings."[2] More recently Judge learned Hand informed us that "one of [the] purposes of [the antitrust statutes] was to perpetuate and preserve, for its own sake and in spite of possible cost, an organization of industry in small units which can effectively compete with each other."[3] He

---

2. *United States* v. *Trans-Missouri Freight Ass'n*, 166 U.S. 290, 323 (1897).

3. *United States* v. *Aluminum Co. of America*, 148 F.2d 416, 429 (2d Cir. 1945).

believed social and moral considerations could properly override consumers' economic welfare. These strains in the law have grown and prospered. They are virulent in decisions under the Robinson-Patman Act and the anti-merger, amended section 7 of the Clayton Act. In the *Von's Grocery* case[4] a majority of the Supreme Court was willing to outlaw a merger which did not conceivably threaten consumers in order to help preserve small groceries in the Los Angeles area against the superior efficiency of the chains.

Consumer welfare is the only legitimate goal of antitrust, not because antitrust is economics, but because it is law. At the risk of provoking hilarity in Professor Director, I invoke the cliché that the law has a life of its own. I appeal to three unrelated aspects of the legal process which most of us assume:

1. The functions of courts and legislatures are different, the latter making major political choices. Courts inevitably make policy, but where Congress has written a statue, the policy movements of the courts are ideally molecular rather than molar.

2. An important function of the courts, performed in a variety of ways, is to help keep the legislative process responsible by ensuring, so far as possible, that major policy decisions by the legislature are deliberately and openly made.

3. The judicial process itself must be responsible. That requires the decision of cases upon criteria which are judicially administrable, give fair warning to those required to obey the law, permit sufficient predictability so that desirable conduct is not needlessly inhibited, and permit rational explanation of the application of the criteria so that judicial performance may be evaluated and controlled.

The first two principles imply that it is the task of the courts under the antitrust laws to determine what policy choice the Congress has made and to apply it, but, if the Congress has not made its choice clear, to press that institution to live up to its responsibility. An examination of the language and legislative history of the antitrust laws makes it clear that consumer welfare was at a minimum a primary intended value. For my argument I do not need to contend that it was the sole intended value, since I will attempt to show the impropriety both of any other single value and of multiple values.

The first place to look for the policy choice of the legislature is in the words of the statutes. The language of the Sherman Act tells us little, but every major antitrust statute after the Sherman Act speaks in economic terms. Section 7 of the Clayton Act makes illegal corporate mergers "where . . . the

---

4. *United States v. Von's Grocery Co.*, 384 U.S. 270 (1966).

effect . . . may be substantially to lessen competition, or to tend to create monopoly . . ." Very nearly identical language is used in section 3 of the Clayton Act with respect to requirements contracts, exclusive dealing contracts, and the like. Even the Robinson-Patman Act prohibits price discrimination only "where the effect of such discrimination may be substantially to lessen competition or tend to create a monopoly . . . or to injure, destroy, or prevent competition with any person . . ."

The polar models employed by these statutes are thus "competition" and "monopoly." These are models developed by economists rather than sociologists and appear therefore to frame a law to which economic analysis, and not much else, is relevant. As models, competition and monopoly indicate different outcomes for resource allocation. The preference for competitive rather than monopolistic resource allocation is most clearly explained and firmly based upon a desire to maximize output as consumers value it. The language of the statutes, then, clearly implies a consumer welfare policy.

The legislative history of the Sherman Act shows an intention that the courts implement only a consumer welfare policy.[5] Later statutes are less clear, some congressmen displaying both a consumer-welfare premise and an intention that the protection of small business be accomplished through antitrust, often without realizing the conflict. What should a court do? Suppose that the unfocused, sloganistic intent to help small business could be implemented only by a statutory interpretation which would have serious deleterious effects upon national wealth. Would any court really be justified in translating such vaporings into hard results probably never foreseen even by the rhetorician, and certainly not by many of his colleagues? Given the courts' function of assisting the legislature to perceive and face the choice that must be made, the courts can and should use the language of the antitrust statutes and the other aspect of legislative history to hold to a consumer welfare policy. This will force Congress, if it wished to change that policy or create exceptions to it, to face the real issues, the benefits and costs of alternative policies, and to make the legislative choice.

Some people suggest that the legislative intent was not really unfocused, that Congress really intended to sacrifice consumers to small business but found it politically expedient to phrase the statutes in the language of competition. Courts, it seems to be suggested, should rely not upon the straight-faced statutory command but upon the discreet congressional wink. But the purpose of a wink is to indicate the opposite of what one is saying in order to

5. My argument on this point appears in an article entitled "Legislative Intent and the Policy of the Sherman Act," Vol. IX of the *J. of Law and Econ.*

deceive a third party who hears only the words. The third party to a dialogue between the Congress and the federal courts is the electorate. There is surely a strong case that the courts should take to Congress at its word, and require that body, if it really wants contrary results, to phrase its law in words that make the political decision and its costs apparent, not only to the courts, but to the electorate and the legislators themselves. Otherwise the legislative process becomes something of a fraud, and the courts are accessories.

The third aspect of the legal process—judicial responsibility—is by far the most important for my argument. Courts simply cannot achieve the elements of responsibility already mentioned if they decide each case according to an essentially unstructured choice between consumers and inefficient producers. There exists no social science, no set of criteria, which could guide the choice in the particular case. Courts could achieve some of the elements of responsibility (e.g., administrable criteria, predictability) by opting either to protect only consumers or to protect only inefficient producers. The latter choice is not legitimately open to the courts, however. It would run contrary, not only to the competition language of the statutes and the legislative history, but would require destruction of such long-standing features of antitrust as the rule of per se illegality for cartels. In effect, the courts, to be consistent, would have to outlaw all creations or expressions of efficiency and to sanction all cartels. No one thinks that is a legitimate interpretation of the goals underlying the antitrust laws. We are left, then, with a choice between strict adherence to a consumer welfare rationale or a case-by-case compromise between consumer and producer interests.

In my view, the desideratum of judicial responsibility is so crucial that even if Congress had written statutes which explicitly ordered the federal courts to balance consumer and small business interests in each case, which it did not, I think the courts should flatly refuse to accept the delegation. Indeed, if the situation were put that badly, I think the courts would refuse. A court is not the proper institution, either by equipment, responsiveness to the electorate, or specialization of function, to write *ab initio* detailed specifications of political compromise between conflicting and incommensurable values. I am at a loss why anyone thinks courts should dictate the terms of a compromise in antitrust any more than they should have written the tariff laws, the code of labor relations, or chosen the rate of progression for the income tax.

My belief that the Court, if it recognized the issue, would refuse to make political choices between the small business and consumers is reinforced by the history of the Court's behavior. Defendants in the first Sherman Act price-fixing case to reach the Supreme Court urged that they be judged according to the "reasonableness" of the price they fixed.[6] A reasonable price, according to important common law precedent, was one fair to both the participants in the cartel and to the public.[7] The formula was thus one for judicial mediation between conflicting producer and consumer interests. The Court declined this invitation to case-by-case legislation and instead adopted a rule of per se illiegality.[8] As Judge Taft phrased it the following year, a reasonable-price test forces judges to "set sail on a sea of doubt"[9] with no guide "except the vague and varying opinion of judges as to how much, on principles of political economy, men ought to be allowed to restrain competition."[10]

In the case of criminal statutes, at least, the problem takes in constitutional dimensions. For example, the Court in *United States* v. *Cohen Grocery Co.*[11] struck down as void for vagueness section 4 of the Lever Act which provided "that it is hereby made unlawful for any person willfully . . . to make any unjust or unreasonable rate or charge in handling or dealing in or with any necessaries; to conspire, combine, agree, or arrange with any other person . . . (i.e.) to exact excessive prices for any necessaries . . ." The Supreme Court said, in terms precisely applicable to the suggested balancing of consumer, producer, and other social interests: "To attempt to enforce the section would be the exact equivalent of an effort to carry out a statute which in terms merely penalized and punished all acts detrimental to the public interest when unjust and unreasonable in the estimation of the court and jury"[12]

Similarly, in *Cline* v. *Frink Dairy Co.*[13] the Supreme Court held the Colorado Antitrust Act unconstitutionally vague because it made the lawfulness of certain conspiracies and combinations turn upon a determination of "reasonable profit." An in *United States* v. *Trenton Potteries Co.* the Court once more rejected the reasonable-price test, stating: "In the absence of express legislation requiring it, we should hesitate to adopt a construction making

---

6. *United States* v. *Trans-Missouri Freight Ass'n*, 166 U.S. 290 (1897).

7. E.g., *Nordenfelt* v. *Maxim Nordenfelt Guns and Ammunition Co.* [1894] App. Cas. 535, 565. The application of the common law formula emasculated an Australian antitrust statute similar to the Sherman Act in *Attorney General of Australia* v. *Adelaide S.S. Co. Ltd.* [1913] App. Cas. 781.

8. 166 U.S. 290, 342 (1897).

9. *United States* v. *Addyston Pipe & Steel Co.*, 85 Fed. 271, 283–284 (6th Cir. 1898).

10. *Id*. at 283.

11. 255 U.S. 81 (1921).

12. *Id*. at 89.

13. 274 U.S. 445 (1927).

the difference between legal and illegal conduct in the field of business relations depend upon so uncertain a test as whether prices are reasonable—a determination which can be satisfactorily made only after a complete survey of our economic organization and a choice between rival philosophies."[14]

Yet, without express legislation requiring it, this is precisely what the Court does do every time it undertakes to decide a particular case by weighing the social value of small business against the value of increased wealth to consumers.

United States v. *National Dairy Products Corp.*,[15] a 1963 case, demonstrates both that the Supreme Court continues to be concerned with the vagueness of a reasonable-price test and that it has other approaches than a declaration of unconstitutionality to employ in its dialogue with Congress, in this case the device of statutory construction. The Court majority saved section 3 of the Robinson-Patman Act, which makes it a criminal offense to sell goods at "unreasonable low prices for the purpose of destroying competition or eliminating a competitor," only by interpreting it to prohibit sales below cost made with predatory intent. This reading transformed a reasonable-price test, requiring a compromise between inconsistent values, into a wholly consumer-oriented statute using cost and intent as tests. The long-standing function of the concept of predatory intent in antitrust law has been to assure the courts—whether rightly or wrongly is beside the present point—that a particular practice is not an expression of efficiency but reflects merely the desire to gain monopoly harmful to consumers. A three-member minority was not satisfied with this solution to the statute's vagueness and voted to hold it void.

As a matter of history, the Supreme Court has employed the void-for-vagueness doctrine only where criminal statutes were challenged. But that certainly cannot be taken to indicate that the same absence of criteria are unobjectionable where civil sanctions are involved. This is particularly true of antitrust where civil sanctions—triple damages, divestiture, and broad injunctions—are likely to be at least as hurtful as the available criminal penalties.

Apparently the present Supreme Court has not fully perceived that any attempt to write political compromises between consumers and producers involves the judicial improprieties that the Court has so wisely avoided in rejecting the reasonable-price test. If there is any doubt that the problem is real, it should be laid to rest by the Court's *Brown Shoe* opinion holding il-

---

14. 273 U.S. 392, 298 (1927).
15. 372 U.S. 29 (1963).

legal the acquisition of a shoe retailing chain by a sole manufacturer, partly because of the anticipated adverse impact upon smaller shoe retailers: "Of course, some of the results of large integrated or chain operations are beneficial to consumers. Their expansion is not rendered unlawful by the mere fact that small independent stores may be adversely affected. It is competition, not competitors, which the Act protects. But we cannot fail to recognize Congress' desire to promote competition through the protection of viable, small, locally owned businesses. Congress appreciated that occasional high costs and prices might result from the maintenance of fragmented industries and markets. It resolved these competing considerations in favor of decentralization."[16] No matter how many times you read it, that passage states: although mergers are not unlawful merely because small independent stores may be adversely affected, we must recognize that mergers are unlawful when small independent stores may be adversely affected.

Given the fragmented nature of the shoe industry, particularly in retailing, the ease of entry, and the obvious fact that the acquisition was motivated by a search for increased efficiency, the Court must either have been saying that any efficiency-creating merger is illegal because it threatens less efficient rivals or that, for reasons it could not articulate, this particular merger threatened social values other than consumer welfare. The former statement is, of course, illegitimate. Except where a special neutral motive, such as a quirk in the tax laws, is operative, all mergers are presumably motivated either by a desire to increase efficiency or to gain a position making output restriction profitable. Mergers of the latter type are clearly illegal. If mergers of the former type are also illegal, then virtually all mergers are outlawed, and that is a law Congress plainly did not write.

But if the Court was not announcing the per se illegality of mergers, then the incoherence of this passage from *Brown Shoe* demonstrates that the introduction of producer protection goals into antitrust subverts judicial virtue and responsibility. I believe no one could successfully maintain that the "criteria" laid down by the quoted passage are judicially administrable, give fair warning, avoid the needless inhibition of desirable mergers, or fulfill the Court's obligation, arising from its elitist, unrepresentative nature, to demonstrate the reasoned derivation of its decisions from known premises.

The requirements of space permit me merely to touch upon a variety of objections which are sometimes raised to my argument. One arises from the observations that courts often behave in the way I have characterized as improper. A sufficient answer to that may be that even in law long usage

---

16. *Brown Shoe Co.* v. *United States*, 370 U.S. 294, 344 (1962).

does not always conclusively establish propriety. Courts can hardly be said to have established an easement into the field of legislation, and the value of *stare decisis* is that the courts, even when wrong, are at least wrong predictably while here unpredictability is a primary feature of their behavior. We are searching for a model of proper judicial conduct, not trying to describe past conduct. To rest upon the observation that courts have always done the things objected to (though of course the cases discussed show that they have also refused to do them) is like telling a stockholder trying to introduce better cost accounting techniques that his firm has always failed to maximize profits.

In any event, many of the examples of contrary judicial behavior are explainable in other terms or according to other models. In constitutional law, for example, courts are sometimes forced to engage in unstructured political decisions precisely because they are dealing with values and principles which are by definition to be kept out of the hands of legislature. Even in constitutional law, however, it is recognized as desirable that the Court, so far as the subject matter permits, should achieve the elements of judicial responsibility.[17] The common law is frequently cited as an accepted example of continuing judicial legislation. I do not think the common law today contains as much of the free balancing of contradictory values in it as people suppose. To the extent that it does it is very bad law. Much of modern common law, moreover, consists of rules built up by courts many years, even centuries ago. The policy movements of today's common law courts are often merely interstitial, arising from the necessity to choose between conflicting values only in peripheral cases where it is not clear what rule governs. The major rules themselves were legislated by courts of a very different era, during a time when society was far less democratic and the legislature had not risen to its modern place as the direct representative of the people and the primary organ of policy making and political choice. The model of judicial behavior suitable to such an era is not appropriate to ours. A third example is the modern administrative process, but this does not provide a compelling analogy. It is common knowledge that the administrative process is performing poorly and one of the reasons is that legislatures and courts have not yet learned to make the agencies responsible by separating their executive, legislative, and adjudicative functions and requiring them to perform according to models appropriate for each. Our present administrative process is thus not a model for emulation but a warning of what the judicial process many become if courts persist in mixing grossly legislative and adjudicative functions.

17. See "Neal, *Baker* v. *Carr*: Politics In Search of Law," 1962 *Sup. Ct. Rev.*, 252.

Courts do not appear to be comfortable making case-by-case political judgments. They are likely, if they adopt a theory that seems to require such ad hoc decision making, to seek an escape either by framing hard, arbitrary rules[18] or by placing the real decision-making function in some other agency. The latter technique may account for the rule in recent years that "the government always wins." The Supreme Court, encumbered by an incoherent economic theory of injury to competition through injury to competitors, the mystery of market definition, and the impossibility of reconciling rationally the contradictory values of consumer and small business welfare, may have turned the problem over to the Antitrust Division and may now be contenting itself with ratifying the decisions of the government.[19] This, of course, relieves the Court of operating with unadministrable criteria but it does not achieve judicial responsibility, for it creates a legislative agency where Congress intended none. The lawyers and economists of the Antitrust Division, moreover, are no more capable of solving the problems of antitrust policy than is the Court if they adhere to the Court's economic theory and its theory of the propriety of case-by-case political compromise between irreconcilable goals. Delegation of the problem to the Antitrust Division solves nothing. It merely puts the inherent irresponsibility of the decision-making process out of sight.

I have talked primarily about the impropriety of the goal of preserving small business under present statutes, but it should be clear that the introduction of any goal which conflicts with consumer welfare would be equally pernicious. I will briefly mention three which Professors Kaysen and Turner have classified:[20] (1) the attainment of desirable economic performance by individual firms and ultimately by the economy as a whole (by which they mean primarily economic efficiency and progressiveness); (2) the achievement and maintenance of competitive processes as an end in itself; and (3) a code of "fair" competition or conduct in the marketplace.

Each of these goals is partially or wholly inconsistent with the policy of maximizing consumer want satisfaction. The first goal stated is partially consistent since I take "efficiency" to be defined in terms of meeting consumer desires. I do not know how else one could measure the value of output. But the propriety of "progressiveness" as an antitrust criterion is not obvious. As defined by Kaysen and Turner, "progress consists in increasing output, in in-

---

18. *Id.* at 300–27.

19. See Simon, "A Partial Search for Affirmative Antitrust Answers," in *Basic Antitrust Questions in the Middle Sixties* (Nat. Indus. Conf. Bd., 1966), 31.

20. Kaysen and Turner, *Antitrust Policy* (1959), 11–18.

creasing output per unit of input by the development of new techniques, and in producing new and better products."[21] Progress in this sense is obviously not costless to consumers. It requires the devotion of resources to research and development that would otherwise be devoted to the production of other goods and services. Progress will occur even without special consideration by the law, but the rate will be that which consumers choose by the degree to which they make it profitable to engage in the activity of producing progress. Courts have no criteria for establishing compromise deviations from consumer welfare here either. Such deviations should come from specific legislative direction, as in the patent statutes, subsidies, or tax relief.

The second possible goal listed—the achievement and maintenance of competitive processes—presumably means something other than a consumer welfare standard which is already stated in the goal of efficiency. If it means preserving the rivalry for its own sake, there seems no point in it. If it means maximizing competition, it does not state a goal that is even conceivable. A policy of maximizing competition would, as Justice Holmes pointed out in his Northern Securities dissent,[22] require the dissolution of virtually all industrial and commercial organizations. It is a prescription for the annihilation of our society and most of the individuals in it. Even a policy of pushing to a condition that a majority of economists would agree constituted pure competition would involve a vast destruction of the wealth of our society. And "workable competition" seems a meaningless concept unless it is merely another term for guessing about the impact upon consumers of moving from a given situation to an alternative. Then it becomes the consumer welfare standard.

The adoption of a code of "fair" competition, the third alternative, seems to mean the prohibition of certain commercial conduct on moral or ethical grounds. Antitrust, that is to say, could be in whole or in part a tort law. But the tort law concept of antitrust has serious difficulties built into it. When a tort rule prohibits a method of competing or creating efficiency, its effect is to favor some producers at the expense of other producers and at the expense of all consumers. That is unlike any tort law that I know of because the activity inhibited is entirely beneficial to the community. There is, in addition, the very real difficulty of defining tortious business behavior without reference to consumer welfare. The business community could not be expected to provide a useful consensus. Businessmen themselves have long been in disagreement, for example, as to whether vigorous price competition is "ethical."

21. *Id.* at page 13.
22. *Northern Securities Co.* v. *United States*, 193 U.S. 197, 400 (1904).

The difficulty, in any event, of stating a general standard for tortious economic behavior, is illustrated by Kaysen and Turner's definition of economic "coercion" which might be the tort prohibited: "Typically, then, coercion consists in the ability of a firm with market power to impose terms in a bargain which the other party would refuse, were there an alternative transactor with whom he could deal more advantageously."[23] This definition of a tort standard demonstrates the inutility of such concepts. The requirement of "market power" either means that the tort exists only when present law would see illegal monopoly, in which case we are back to using a consumer welfare policy, or that any firm in a less than purely competitive market must somehow guess what terms and condition it could get if the market were purely competitive. If "market power" does not mean one of these things, then, under the definition given, every market transaction involves coercion—and by both parties simultaneously.

Nor is it any more helpful to employ other suggested standards, such as the equal treatment of parties in similar positions. If the parties are really equally situated, the market will treat them equally, for that will be the most profitable way to treat them. This truism can be avoided only by giving equality and ethical content which does not correspond to economic categories, and that raises once more the difficulty of defining "ethical" competition without reference to consumer welfare, and the question of why it is "ethical" for government to prefer one set of businessmen over another set and over the entire set of consumers.

These considerations lead me to conclude that the introduction of goals other than consumer welfare into antitrust is destructive of antitrust as law. Confining antitrust to consumer welfare, on the other hand, permits courts to employ the teachings of economic analysis to estimate whether the net effect of a particular structure, act, or agreement is likely to be an increase or a decrease in output. The judgment must often prove rough and may change over time as economic understanding progresses. But these kinds of uncertainty we must always live with in a legal system. One is uncertainty about where a spectrum will be cut. The other uncertainty arises from doubt as to the state of the courts' intellectual sophistication concerning the phenomena to be dealt with. Neither of these kinds of uncertainty can ever be eliminated in a legal system that undertakes to deal with matters of any complexity. The kind of uncertainty which a legal system ought not to tolerate, particularly where statutes are involved, is that which arises because judges are making case-by-case and *ex post facto* the political choices. We have in Congress a

---

23. Kaysen and Turner, *supra*, note 20, at page 17.

body of politicians elected to make political choices and to write them into prospective rules of general application.

Much more could be said on the topic of the goals of antitrust in a longer paper. But it seems to me both that the claims of the judicial process in this field have gone almost unnoticed and that they constitute the single most decisive argument in favor of confining antitrust to a consumer welfare goal.

THE SUPREME COURT VERSUS
CORPORATE EFFICIENCY

The Supreme Court handed down last April an antitrust decision with grave—indeed, ominous—implications for business, and for the public. What the court ruled on was Procter & Gamble's 1957 acquisition of Clorox Chemical Co., a merger that the Federal Trade Commission had chosen for attack. "This," said the government's petition to the Court, "is a pilot case of major significance. . . ." Indeed it was, for in holding the acquisition of Clorox illegal, the Supreme Court came very close to declaring, contrary to what reason and common sense tell us, that a gain in a corporation's efficiency is a bad thing, against the public interest.

The *Procter & Gamble* decision brings us to the threshold of new and severe antitrust policy toward corporate diversification by merger. And the decision's shadow may stretch backward as well as forward in time. Under current Supreme Court doctrine, mergers may be challenged years later (Du Pont's purchase of 23 percent of General Motors stock was successfully attacked thirty years after the event). Worse, the relevant facts for judgment are not those existing at the time of the merger but those prevailing when the suit is brought, even if the changed facts resulted not from the merger but from other causes. The backward sweep of doctrines now developing may, therefore, dismantle diversified corporations put together before the new theories were more than a glint in a trustbuster's eye.

P. & G., of course, is a giant company, the biggest in its field, and at the time of the merger Clorox itself was the dominant company in *its* market, household liquid bleach; not all mergers are closely comparable. But basic principles established in such test cases are often pushed far beyond the sort of fact situation in which they first gained acceptance. In its 1962 decision in the *Brown Shoe* ease, the Supreme Court said that the creation by horizontal merger of a 5 percent market share was unlawful, even in a business as

From *Fortune*, August 1967.

easy to enter as shoe retailing. Similar reasoning as to conglomerate mergers could extend the principles of *Procter & Gamble* to an enormous number of diversification mergers, past as well as future.

The history of antitrust also teaches that ideas have a way of leapfrogging statutory categories. In this case, the Court applied the merger section of the Clayton Act (enacted in 1914, amended in 1950). If the notions the Court expressed are carried over to the antimonopoly provisions of the older Sherman Act (1890), we may see new limitations upon corporate growth by internal expansion. And, given the power of Supreme Court pronouncements to affect government policies, it is not utterly farfetched to suggest that the rationale of *Procter & Gamble* may soon form the basis of proposals for direct government regulation of the types of business activity there viewed as suspect, particularly advertising.

Though it opens new vistas of antitrust enforcement, *Procter & Gamble* is in a sense a manifestation of long term trends in antitrust. For roughly the last thirty years, in one antitrust context after another—mergers, exclusive dealerships, patent-license restrictions, price discrimination, and so on and on—the Supreme Court has steadily and drastically reshaped the law to protect the inefficient producer at the expense of consumers. (See "The Crisis in Antitrust," *Fortune*, December 1963.) This development has, no doubt, quite complex causes, but one cause surely has been the failure of the business community to comprehend the values at stake and bring before the Supreme Court reasoned arguments concerning the proper goals of antitrust policy and the nature of economic reality.

P. & G.'s long, expensive, and unsuccessful fight to save its Clorox acquisition was consistent with this regrettable pattern. The litigation illustrates once more how, in the making of antitrust policy by the Supreme Court, concepts of extremely dubious merit suddenly become the law of the land without passing the test of vigorous adversary debate. The deplorable inadequacies of this little-noticed process are anomalous in a democratic society, and raise a question whether rational antitrust policy is even a possibility. Perhaps the most important lesson to be learned from *Procter & Gamble,* then, is that all parties concerned in the evolution of antitrust law, and particularly the business community and its attorneys, should re-examine their roles and responsibilities.

From a business viewpoint, P. & G.'s 1957 acquisition of Clorox was a natural. Clorox, the only nationally distributed brand of household liquid bleach, was the best-selling brand by far, and its market share had been growing in each of the five years prior to the merger. The company made no other product. Clorox' principal shareholders were reaching retirement age, and wishing to convert their stock for that of a flourishing company with a marketable security, they initiated negotiations with Procter & Gamble. P. & G. had no entry in the market for household liquid bleach, but made and sold a wide spectrum of related cleaning products, so Clorox bleach fit into the product line like a missing part in a puzzle.

At the time, there may have seemed to be little antitrust peril in the merger since it was neither horizontal nor vertical. That is, P. & G. and Clorox were not competitors; and neither were they in the relationship of customer and supplier, so their union did not present the danger, to which the Court is highly sensitive, that any rival would be "foreclosed" from a source of supply or a market. But P. & G.'s purchase of Clorox provided a test case for the FTC's emerging theories on conglomerate mergers, and the commission soon afterward issued a complaint.

The road to the Supreme Court was tortuous. After sixty-two days of hearings spread over fourteen months, an FTC hearing examiner decided that P. & G. had violated Section 7 of the Clayton Act. That section makes it unlawful for one corporation to acquire stock or assets of another where "the effect of such acquisition may be substantially to lessen competition, or to tend to create a monopoly." The full commission, however, found the record inadequate to support the conclusion, and directed the examiner to consider post-acquisition developments. The examiner did so, and once more held the merger illegal. This time the commission, with two new members out of five, said post-acquisition evidence was irrelevant and held the merger unlawful on the original record. The court of appeals reversed the commission, holding that the record did not support the claimed probability of anticompetitive effects in the liquid-bleach industry.

The case had now reached a critical stage. The FTC was no longer in full control; it was up to the solicitor general, Thurgood Marshall, to decide whether to ask for Supreme Court review. In making such decisions the solicitor general routinely consults the head of the Antitrust Division of the Department of Justice, currently Donald Turner. The collaboration of three offices was thus involved in determining whether to petition for review and what position to take before the Court. The agreement of the FTC, the solicitor general, and the Antitrust Division that P. & G.'s merger with Clorox should be struck down means that the case represents deliberate, broadly formulated government policy, and that more such cases are sure to come. The Court's opinion upholding the government thus deserves careful parsing.

A Seemingly Fantastic Reversal

Justice William O. Douglas wrote the opinion. Douglas has a tendency from time to time to assert without explanation and to treat conclusions as self-evident. Even Justice John Marshall Harlan, who concurred in the 7-0 decision, was moved to complain that the Douglas opinion "leaves the Commission, lawyers, and businessmen at large as to what is to be expected of them in future cases of this kind." It is a just comment.

But lurking in the ambiguities and uncertainties of the Douglas opinion we may, nevertheless, perceive the shape of policies and prosecutions to come. Law—ill-defined, unstructured, unexplained, but law nonetheless—is being made. If the new doctrines follow the course already traveled by other antitrust theories, they will start as a series of highly debatable assumptions that, by virtue of repetition in other cases, acquire the patina of verified truth, and then expand according to their inner logic to become something like rules of per se illegality.

The elements of Justice Douglas's argument ran like this: Clorox, with 49 percent of total sales (even higher percentages in some regional markets), was the dominant firm in a highly concentrated, "oligopolistic" industry. Clorox and its largest rival, Purex, together accounted for almost 65 percent of national sales, and the top six firms for almost 80 percent. Since "all liquid bleach is chemically identical, 'Clorox' dominance rested on heavy expenditures for advertising and promotion. Procter & Gamble's acquisition of Clorox (which was, strictly speaking, a "product-extension" merger) would probably injure competition because "the substitution of the powerful acquiring firm for the smaller, but already dominant, firm may substantially reduce the competitive structure of the industry by raising entry barriers and by dissuading the smaller firms from aggressively competing. . . ."

Justice Douglas did not define "entry barriers." A careful study of the opinion, however, indicates that he meant the merger would make Clorox more efficient. The creation of new efficiency by merger is thus illegal, at least when the industry in which the efficiency is created is already "concentrated." Efficiency and concentration are subjects worth tarrying over for a moment. The curious treatment of them by the parties and the Court illuminates much of the present direction of antitrust.

Prior to the merger, Procter & Gamble anticipated making Clorox more efficient in various ways. P. & G.'s promotion department stressed these additional economies as factors favoring the acquisition. In 1955, in a report recommending acquisition of Clorox, the department said: "We feel that with our sales, distribution and manufacturing setup, we could effect a number of savings that could possibly increase the net profit of [Clorox'] business considerably. . . ." And in 1957 another report by that department stated: "We are advised that Clorox spent $2,660,000 in the last half of 1956 for advertising, or at the rate of $5,320,000 a year. We believe that P. & G. advertising philosophies and economies applied to an advertising expenditure of this size can be expected to further advance the Clorox business." Those unfamiliar with the incredible perversities of current antitrust doctrine might have expected Procter & Gamble to base its defense on the value of these efficiencies to consumers. Once the litigation began, however, it was the government that pointed triumphantly to P. & G.'s expectation of cost savings, while P. & G. insisted there was no substantial evidence that Clorox received any benefits from the merger.

This seemingly fantastic reversal of tactics was dictated by legal trends already far advanced when the government challenged the acquisition. The antitrust enforcement agencies had long before faced defenses claiming enhanced efficiency and had developed a highly successful countergambit. Government attorneys took to calling efficiencies "competitive advantages" and arguing that they threatened competition. Defendants' attorneys at once adopted the conservative, lawyer-like line of denying everything alleged, including "competitive advantages." One watched with mounting exasperation as in case after case defendants denied that their contracts, mergers, or whatever could conceivably create a single efficiency. This placed them neatly in a vise. Defendants were never able to explain with any credibility what had motivated their challenged conduct. Moreover, they were never able to mount an affirmative case for their actions in terms of public benefit; all they could do was deny the government's case against. In this way an absurd idea became firmly embedded in the law.

While Procter & Gamble's tactics were in keeping with the illogic of the legal doctrine it faced, the denial of any gain in efficiency had the inevitable consequence of making the company's position before the Supreme Court untenable. The Justices may justifiably have wondered why, if the merger created no advantages, P. & G. had bothered to buy Clorox. Had P. & G.'s executives spent so many years trying to anticipate the whims of the American housewife that they themselves had become addicted to impulse buying? Was it sheer coincidence that Clorox approached P. & G. instead of I. T. T. or Republic Steel?

How Efficiency Becomes a Terrible Thing

The astounding fact is that the only good word said for efficiency in the Supreme Court came from the government. Though denying that the principle was applicable to this case, the government's brief stated that "in general, advantages afforded by a merger which reflect simply greater efficiency ought not to be a basis for holding the merger illegal; efficiency is, after all, a prime goal of antitrust." One suspects that this sentence originated with Donald Turner, who had written the same thought as a Harvard law professor before taking on his present job at the Antitrust Division. But the Court is less reasonable on this issue than is Turner. Justice Douglas simply pronounced efficiencies irrelevant. "Possible economies," he said, "cannot be used as a defense to illegality." That in itself is an unfortunate notion, but Justice Douglas went even further. To support his assertion, he cited a passage from the Supreme Court's *Brown Shoe* decision. Though "beneficial to consumers," the passage ran, the cost savings resulting from that merger were a threat to "the protection of viable, small, locally-owned businesses." Moreover, Justice Douglas's own line of argument in *Procter & Gamble* proceeded from efficiencies to illegality. Thus he clearly meant more than that economies "cannot be used as a defense": he meant, in fact, that economies weigh on the side of illegality.

The opinion cited three kinds of efficiencies that might raise barriers to entry: (1) Procter & Gamble's great capital resources could supplement Clorox' limited advertising budget; (2) Clorox would share in volume discounts on advertising rates granted P. & G. by television networks and magazines; and (3) Clorox would obtain, in advertising and promotion, the advantages of a multiproduct firm (e.g., featuring several products in a single mailing or on a single network television program would cut the cost for each product). Procter & Gamble, the nation's largest advertiser and a prime example of the multiproduct corporation, would appear to have a very substantial stake in battling the notion that these efficiencies could be anticompetitive, yet it confined itself to arguing that the FTC had not proved such efficiencies existed.

It would have been possible to attack the issues on a more fundamental level. The pivotal issue in *Procter & Gamble* was the meaning of the word "competition." Section 7 of the Clayton Act prohibits mergers only when the effect "may be substantially to lessen competition, or to tend to create a monopoly." The FTC opinion condemning the merger defined competition essentially in terms of the number of competitors in a market and the ease with which outside firms could enter. The Supreme Court accepted that definition, P. & G. did not challenge it, and the illegality of the merger followed logically. By making Clorox more effective, the argument ran, the merger would increase Clorox' "dominance" in an already "concentrated" industry. The more effective Clorox became, the less likely would be the entry of new firms.

The logical conclusion of this line of reasoning is grotesque, for it follows that anything that contributes to Clorox' efficiency is anticompetitive. Efficiency becomes that terrible thing, "a barrier to entry." That is the crux of the *Procter & Gamble* decision. It is applied here to a merger. It has been applied, and will be applied again, to other forms of business behavior: contracts, pricing practices, cooperative action, and internal growth.

We are in the presence of an antitrust paradox. If ease of entry is the hallmark of competition, it should be lawful for Clorox and its rivals to rig prices—the higher the prevailing price of bleach, after all, the easier it is for outside firms to enter the market. On the same reasoning, we should have applauded rather than punished the price-fixing conspiracy in the electrical-equipment industry a few years back.

Losing the Magical Potency

Barriers to entry treated by superior efficiency or ability abound in the world and attempts to lower them only make matters worse. Some of us in the general population find that our slowness afoot, lagging reflexes, and intense dislike for having our ligaments torn and bones broken operate as decisive barriers to entry into the lucrative and exciting business of professional football. The result is that skilled football players have the industry to themselves and make a great deal of money. The Court's reasoning in *Procter & Gamble* teaches us that competition in the quarterback market would be improved, and the public thereby benefited, if Joe Namath's knees were twisted before every game and Fran Tarkenton required to wear snowshoes.

The concept of "competition" obviously requires redefinition. Justice Harlan's concurring opinion was on the right track in stating that "economic efficiencies produced by the merger must be weighed against anticompetitive consequences." He was focusing on benefits to *consumers* rather than to less efficient producers. On such an analysis, he and the Court should have found P. & G.'s acquisition lawful. Why is it not a socially valuable efficiency for Clorox to share in the advertising and promotional cost savings that accrue to a firm with more than one product? Why is it improper to Clorox to share in the volume discounts offered large advertisers by national media? Why is it not a benefit to society if Procter & Gamble's large capital resources contribute to Clorox' efficiency? These issues were neither explored nor explained by the Court.

Under a consumer-oriented analysis, the talismanic words "oligopoly" and "barriers to entry" lose their magical potency and the issue becomes one of alternatives. Are consumers benefited or injured if Procter & Gamble is permitted to bring new efficiencies to Clorox? If Clorox' management found ways of cutting costs without merger, it would clearly not be sound public policy to put a stop to that. The result might be to make Clorox even more "dominant," but the increased market share could be gained and held only if Clorox served consumers at least as well as its rivals. Any attempt to restrict output and raise prices would lead to a decline in market position. The presumption, then, must be that increased efficiency is always pro-consumer and pro-competitive.

This kind of analysis lies at the historic root of American antitrust policy. The Senate debates of 1890 preceding passage of the Sherman Act made it absolutely clear that the measure was not meant to interfere with efficiency, even if it resulted in monopoly. Senator George Hoar of Massachusetts, who explained the Judiciary Committee's final draft of the bill to the Senate, declared that a man who "got the whole business because nobody could do it as well as he could" would not violate the Sherman Act. *Procter & Gamble* runs counter to this salutary principle.

A Package That Includes Hope

There are those, however, who will defend *Procter & Gamble* on the ground that the economies involved were of a suspect nature: they related to advertising. The Supreme Court's rationale was broader, but the Federal Trade Commission's opinion clearly evinced hostility to advertising as such. There is abroad the notion that advertising is socially wasteful, and in this case that view was reinforced by the fact that Clorox had often been able to persuade consumers to pay a cent or two more per bottle for a product chemically identical with other bleaches. This is not the occasion for a disquisition on the social role of advertising, but the problem is surely more complex than the FTC appears to think.

The objection, of course, is that advertising such as Clorox' does not set forth "objective" differences in the product but merely serves to entrench the advertiser's brand. But the advertiser, even one selling an "identical" commodity, offers more than a physical product. He is selling a package that also includes intangible services, some of which are provided by the advertising itself, such as information (what the general product does, where it may be purchased, etc.) and even entertainment. He often sells ego gratification. Youth, sophistication, charisma, and sexual attractiveness come with soft drinks, cigarettes, ale, and cosmetics. Charles Revson, chairman of Revlon, Inc., has said, "We sell hope." There appears to be no reason for the law to tell consumers they cannot buy these things in the marketplace, or to tell advertisers they cannot provide them.

To the degree that *Procter & Gamble* rests on suspicion of advertising, as it clearly did at the commission level, we seem faced with an incipient policy of governmental intervention in an economic and social process that the intervenors have not begun to understand. One must hope that realistic analysis and rigorous discussion will occur before the necessity for broad intervention becomes another self-evident dogma.

In addition to his argument concerning entry barriers, Justice Douglas raised an entirely separate point—that the merger removed Procter & Gamble as the most likely entrant into the liquid-bleach industry, and that the potential benefits of competition between P.&G. and Clorox were thus lost. This reasoning cannot stand scrutiny. The government offered no evidence that P.&G. had any intention of getting into the bleach business in competition with Clorox; the only hard evidence on the point was that P.&G.'s promotion department had recommended *against* independent entry. Moreover, Lever Brothers and Colgate-Palmolive are easily identifiable potential entrants.

Sound or not, there it is—dubious reasoning become law. And having become law, it will have consequences. The Court's potential-competition theory would appear to cast a Section 7 cloud over any acquisition of a large company in a concentrated industry by a company making related products. And the Court's ability to see incipient oligopoly in a 5 percent market share, as in *Brown Shoe,* suggests that we may be in for some shocks when we learn what industries the Court considers "concentrated."

Shaky but Unchallenged

Perhaps the most thought-provoking aspect of all this is that these basic themes—the goals of antitrust and the nature and value of efficiency—were never argued by Procter & Gamble in the Supreme Court. This would hardly be worth noting if Procter & Gamble were unique in this respect, but the dismaying fact is that the business community and its lawyers have not urged the basic ideas of the free market in the courts. In failing to do that, they have not represented us well. I say "us" because the antitrust lawyer, whether he represents the government or the defendant, represents also ideas that are contending for acceptance. No body of men could conceivably attain expertise in the widely varied, highly complex fields in which the Supreme Court must decide cases. The Justices must to a considerable degree rely upon what the lawyers bring before them. It is important, therefore, that both sides debate the larger issues, the fitness of the rules.

The failure of the antitrust defense bar to debate basic principles has certainly contributed to the Court's acceptance of dubious and even pernicious notions. The theories that prevailed and became law in *Procter & Gamble* provide cases in point. The idea that conglomerate mergers might be a threat to competition was almost unheard of until it was advanced in the late 1940's by an economist, Professor Corwin Edwards, then at Northwestern University (he formerly held a high staff position at the FTC). To this day the theory remains shaky, if not totally untenable, but the defense bar has failed to challenge it. Without the rigorous examination that only adversary debate can provide, an idea of little, if any, validity has been placed at the core of a body of law about to undergo rapid expansion.

The same story can be told of "barriers to entry." The idea was put forward in 1956 in a book by Joe S. Bain, a professor of economics at the University of California, Berkeley. This notion, too, went unchallenged by the defense bar. As a result, anything that makes entry into an industry more difficult—including the increased efficiency of the firms composing it—has come to be regarded as anticompetitive. And now we appear to be witnessing the beginning of the same sort of process with the notion that there is something antisocial and anticompetitive about advertising.

The causes of the defense bar's default are no doubt complex, but one is surely a lack of adequate economic sophistication. The great antitrust cases, those that set trends and establish principles, inevitably turn on inferences drawn from economic analysis. Many otherwise excellent lawyers simply have not grasped that micro-economics is now their province, and that they cannot discharge their responsibilities by hiring an economist as an expert witness at a trial. The specialist in antitrust should have as much command of basic price theory as specialists in other fields of law have of forensic medicine or tax accounting or the principles of chemistry.

Another factor is the differing structures of the contending interests. The government is represented by the Antitrust Division and the Federal Trade Commission, permanent bodies with long-range interests and points of view. The government, therefore, is concerned more with the establishment of basic principles than with the outcome of particular cases. On the other side, each antitrust defendant tends to regard the litigation not as an opportunity to establish a principle but as a nonrecurring catastrophe. He looks only for a way out, and the obvious strategy is to accept the direction of the law and attempt to show that the facts of the particular transaction do not fit the theory. The defense lawyer who takes a rare case to the Supreme Court is similarly motivated. Moreover, the successful advocate is almost invariably the one who aligns himself with the court's predilections, not the one who challenges them.

These tactics are disastrously out of place in today's antitrust litigation. Defendants are simply not winning cases they should win in the Supreme Court. No defendant has won a merger case there since Congress amended Section 7 of the Clayton Act seventeen years ago. As Justice Potter Stewart said in his dissent in an antitrust case early this year: "The sole consistency that I can find is that in litigation under [Section] 7, the Government always wins." The situation in other fields of antitrust is almost equally bleak. Cases can still sometimes be won in lower courts by conventional argument, but the record shows that when a case is appealed to the Supreme Court the defendant would usually have nothing to lose by talking fundamentals.

At Least a Basis for the Future

I do not mean to suggest that such a switch in tactics would begin to win cases immediately. The situation is too far deteriorated for that. Antitrust is a subcategory of ideology, and a majority of today's Supreme Court is in the grip of an economic and social ideology that leads it to prefer protection of the inefficient to competitive vigor. Yet it is possible to demonstrate that this approach to antitrust has resulted in irreconcilable contradictions among antitrust policies and rulings, and that it also requires courts to make political judgments that belong only to Congress. If arguments of this kind were developed before the Court, then, at the very least, we might expect more dissents that could form the basis for a rational antitrust law in the future. The presentation of such arguments, moreover, would help change the terms of discourse in professional, business, and academic circles. This in turn would alter the intellectual environment in which the Court, even more than most policy-making institutions, lives, and to which, ultimately, it responds.

The Court is a fallible human institution, but it is accessible to reason. It may change slowly, but change it does, and it changes, in part at least, in response to the arguments put before it. The conventional arguments of the antitrust defendant and his lawyer have been losing with monotonous regularity. For rational, pro-consumer antitrust policy, time is running out. A long pass may not win the game, but then continuing to fall on the ball so as not to offend anybody is not, in the circumstances, a brilliant play either.

Antitrust in Dubious Battle

In antitrust policy the Nixon Administration has sprinted away to a fast start in the wrong direction. The Antitrust Division of the Department of Justice appears in danger of not only missing a rare and invaluable opportunity to reform this sadly decayed field, but—if its unreflective assault on conglomerate mergers is a taste of the future—making a bad situation much worse. If it wishes to pursue a course that is responsible and constructive, this Administration had better pause and take serious thought about the proper goals of antitrust and the means by which they can be achieved.

There has grown up in recent years the pernicious notion that antitrust is some sort of open warrant for prosecutors to roam the business world like knights-errant, deciding for themselves, often in defiance of conventional anatomical indicia, which are the damsels and which the dragons. Right now the chief of the Antitrust Division, Richard W. McLaren, seems to think he sees a lot of conglomerate mergers exhaling flames. Before he slays them, it is fair to ask his reasons, since he sometimes sounds as if the antitrust laws were his mandate to pursue every social policy except the prevention of lascivious carriage.

Among other things, he has mentioned that conglomerate acquisitions may be tax-motivated, may involve the issuance of dubious securities, are causing something called a "radical restructuring" of the economy, and result in "human dislocations." Valid or not, these objections have nothing to do with antitrust policy. Take "human dislocations," for example. What precisely, does McLaren have in mind? "When the headquarters of one or two large companies are removed from the nation's smaller cities to New York or Chicago or Los Angeles, I think we all recognize that there is a serious impact upon the community. The loss is felt by its banks, its merchants, its professional, and service people—accountants, lawyers, advertising agen-

From *Fortune*, September 1969.

cies. The community loses some of it its best-educated, most energetic and public-spirited citizens. I am concerned that even some of our larger centers may become 'branch house cities,' whose major business affairs are directed by absentee managers. As I have indicated earlier, these are results which contravene the national policy as repeatedly expressed by Congress."

Every lawyer loves a skillful gambit, and attributing to Congress a clear-cut policy it never voted on has always been considered good, clean legal fun, the sort of ink cloud you shoot out when neither the statute nor the facts of the case support your position. But this is going a little too far. McLaren is now more than an advocate: he is a policy-making official.

It is time somebody spoke the magic words "law and order." Members of this Administration must certainly display a positive reaction to that phrase, and law, we surely need not remind them, imposes restraints upon prosecutors and courts quite as much as upon ordinary citizens. The creative flair of the Antitrust Division must be kept within the bounds of the statutes it has been given to enforce. Congress has never, much less "repeatedly," enacted a keep-'em-down-on-the-farm statute that makes the illegality of a merger depend upon its contribution to some interstate brain drain.

It may be admitted that the opinions expressed in the congressional debates on the merger statute, Section 7 of the Clayton Act as amended in 1950, display the same richness of variety as the contents of a fruitcake, so that you can pry a fragment of almost any social policy out of them. But the statute Congress actually voted on calls solely for the preservation of "competition" and the avoidance of "monopoly." It forbids acquisition of one company by another, that is, only where the effect "may be substantially to lessen competition or tend to create a monopoly." With the aid of a little basic economics, you can make a law out of that—taking the terms, as is natural and sensible, to refer to the desirability of efficient use of economic resources in the interest of consumers. But should the Antitrust Division attempt to judge conglomerate mergers by weighing gains in efficiency and competitive vigor (which McLaren admits are relevant) against losses to the certified public accountants of Keokuk, mixing in sociological speculation whether that city or Chicago more urgently needs a particular lot of public-spirited citizens, the result can only be uniformed, ad hoc political guesswork, not anything remotely recognizable as law.

Such a result would violate not merely the wording of the statute but, more fundamental, the ideal of law. Antitrust is a hybrid policy science, being composed of both law and economics. I use the word "science" deliberately. We are too little accustomed to thinking of law as a science, and indeed in current practice there is little enough to suggest the concept, but it should be obvious that law must develop the characteristic of policy science if the ideal of the rule of law is even to be approximated. At the center of any science of law must stand a normative model of judicial behavior, which is to say a system of understood constraints upon the values judges may consider in deciding cases and the methods by which they may reason from proper values to the decision of specific controversies. To a large extent that model must be based upon the specialized function of courts as against the explicitly political role of the legislature.

Antitrust, unlike many other fields of law, already possesses the rudiments of such a science, but failure to follow its principles consistently has led to much that is wrong, and even perverse, in current judge-made law. To start with the bright side, the Supreme Court has resolutely refused to judge the legality of pricing agreements by the general "reasonableness" of the prices charged. To do so would have mired the Court, without criteria fit for judicial use, in a grossly political balancing of the interest of consumers in low prices against the interest of producers in high prices. Any such compromise between the conflicting claims of interest groups belongs to the legislature. But the Court in recent years has failed to recognize that it commits the very error it avoided in pricing cases when it undertakes to balance the interest of consumers in increased efficiency against the interest of what the Court calls "viable, small, locally owned businesses. "That is what the Supreme Court has done in some merger cases. This case-by-case legislative compromise is not only an improper function for courts applying statutes, but also one at which they are not at all adept. In antitrust, when inconsistent values have been let in, it has been the consumer interest that has gone under. And yet this is the primary value that antitrust's protection of competition is intended to serve

The First Requisite of Reform

It hardly needs saying that the same value constraints are relevant to prosecutors. If, for example, a judge is not properly free under amended Section 7 of the Clayron Act to determine the legality of a corporate acquisition according to the dollar worth of the corporation's assets. It is certainly not proper for a prosecutor either to try to persuade the judge to do just that, or to bring actions, motivated by such considerations, that will at the least have harassing effects. That amalgam of muddled thinking, social mythology, and sentimental rhetoric known to its intimates as "the social purposes of antitrust," however sonorously it may ring upon ritual occasions for mock-Jeffersonian oratory, must be excluded from judicial and prosecutorial decisions about actual cases. The first requisite of antitrust reform, therefore, is the identification of and principled adherence to proper goals. *The only legitimate goal of our present statutes is the maximization of consumer welfare.* And that is true, I stress, not because antitrust is economics, but because it must be, first and foremost, deserving of the name of law.

Businessmen can seek profits in two quite different ways that impinge upon consumer welfare. One is the method of monopoly—gaining market control in order to increase net return by restraining output and raising prices. Monopoly misallocates resources with the result that the economy as a whole produces less than it otherwise could, a clear disservice to consumers. The other and altogether different method is the creation of efficiency—by cutting costs, opening new markets, offering new or modified products and services, or in other ways vying successfully for consumer dollars. The whole task of a consumer-oriented antitrust policy is to estimate which of these opposing effects predominates in any specific market behavior or structure.

Since neither misallocation of resources nor efficiency can be directly measured, there is absolutely no merit to the common proposal to decide cases by studying all relevant performance factors. To illustrate, we cannot begin to quantify a claimed future improvement (or decline) in the performance of Jones & Laughlin resulting from its acquisition by Ling-Temco-Vought, because that would require, among other impossibilities, precise statements about differences in quality of future decisions concerning problems that cannot now even be identified.

The Philo Vance Approach

Correct analysis employs what has been called, with misplaced sarcasm, "the Philo Vance approach to antitrust." Since courts cannot measure efficiency or misallocation directly, they must rely on probabilities, framing general rules on the basis of economics. Where economic theory tells us that certain business behavior is likely to result in monopoly profits and misallocation of resources, such behavior should be illegal. All other behavior should be lawful so far as antitrust is concerned, since, in relation to consumer welfare, it is either neutral or motivated by considerations of efficiency. A tax-propelled conglomerate merger, for example, is neutral since courts have no means of judging what impact, if any, it will have upon consumer welfare. They should, therefore, leave the situation to the tax laws or to any other statutes Congress may enact. *Efficiency-motivated mergers deserve the law's protection. The market will penalize those that do not in fact create efficiency.*

Economics provides one other lesson that should be written in red letters across every antitrust prosecutor's bathroom mirror: injury to *competitors* is irrelevant to the question of injury to competition and consumer welfare. Much antitrust argument today seizes upon the fact of competitor injury and treats it as not merely relevant but decisive. The antitrust enforcer, with a massive *non sequitur*, leaps from observed fact to inferred significance as nimbly as did the apocryphal fundamentalist: "Believe in baptism? Why, man, I've seen it done!"

You may see injury to a competitor; you will never see, as raw fact, injury to competition. The presence of the latter can be inferred only on the basis of economic theory. A company's loss of sales—which is all that is ever meant by injury to a competitor—is fully consistent with a gain in efficiency by a rival company. Because antitrust law has confused the fact with the inference, many of its most cherished doctrines strike directly at efficiency as a threat to competition. In such cases, and they are increasing in number, the law itself inflicts upon consumers the kinds of losses that it is intended to prevent.

Unhappily for those of us who make a living out of antitrust's mysteries, the truth is that the law almost always, regardless of context, uses one of two basic theories of how competition may be injured:

1) Competitors may agree to remove the rivalry existing between themselves; or

2) Competitors may inflict injury on rivals and thereby ultimately injure the competitive process.

Cartels and large horizontal mergers fall within the first theory, which, though it has been drastically overextended, contains an important core of validity. The second theory—that of supposedly "exclusionary" practices—is the sole support for the present stern rules concerning vertical mergers, tying arrangements, exclusive dealing contracts, and price discrimination, as well as for the developing harsh treatment of conglomerate mergers and reciprocal buying. This large and growing structure of law rests upon an exceedingly flimsy foundation, for in the version used by the law the idea of exclusionary practices as a threat to competition is fallacious.

Add Two and Zero and Get Four

The fallacy lies in counting the same thing twice—in this case, the same market power. The nature of the error, which is basic to antitrust's current confusions, can be simply illustrated. Frank Carruthers, let us suppose, owns the only motion-picture theater in the remote hamlet of Lakeville,

Connecticut. Having a monopoly, he drives the price of films down to $800 while exhibitors in New Haven must pay $1,000 for a film of equal quality. Carruthers expands by purchasing one of the New Haven theatres, thinks the situation over, and telephones a distributor to announce that he wants better-quality films for his newly acquired theatre in order to gain an advantage over the opposition. "Delighted," the distributor replies, "I can let you have them for $1,200 each."

"You don't understand," says Carruthers. "I want the better films in New Haven for $1,000 or I won't show any of your films in Lakeville."

According to prevalent antitrust thinking, the distributor has no choice but to say yes to this demand, but I think we may confidently rely upon him to say no. Of course, it is worth something to the distributor not to be excluded from Lakeville. But—and this the overlooked point—Carruthers has already exacted that something, in the form of the $200 discount of $1,000 films. Carruthers cannot eat his cake in Lakeville and have it in New Haven too. In demanding a $200 discount in Lakeville and a $200 discount in New Haven, he is demanding that the distributor pay for the same thing twice, pay $400 for a market advantage worth $200. It won't work.

Presumably, Carruthers could, if he choose, give up the discount in Lakeville in exchange for a $200 discount on better films in New Haven, but that would bring him no unfair advantage. Rival exhibitors in New Haven would have to pay $1,200 for better films, and so would Carruthers—$1,000 plus the $200 given up in Lakeville.

Under one guise or another, the fallacy of counting the same market power twice pervades antitrust law. It turns up, for example, in the precedent-making suit that the Antitrust Division filed against I.B.M. in the closing days of the Johnson Administration. The charge, laid under Section 2 of the Sherman Act, is monopolization. I.B.M.'s share of industry revenues has varied, according to the complaint, from about 69 to 80 percent in recent years. These figures suggest superior efficiency, but the complaint attempts to avoid this natural inference by alleging that I.B.M. denied its rivals the opportunity to compete.

I.B.M. did this, it is alleged, through such devices as quoting a single price for computers and software. But since I.B.M. can charge all its computer is worth in the price of the computer, it cannot get more than the combined worth of the computer and software by selling them together, any more than Carruthers could get more than the combined worth of his positions in Lakeville and New Haven by negotiating for them together. Does the selling of computer and software together improperly inhibit the ability of rival computer makers to compete? Of course not. If they can compete with I.B.M. in computers, they can either produce the necessary software themselves or find other companies that can. Then the customer can choose the package he likes best. To assume that competitive software is not available to I.B.M.'s rivals is to assume that I.B.M.'s market strength lies not in computers but in software, and, therefore, that the government has the case backward. Chances are I.B.M's single-price package was a convenience or contributed to the total service the company sold, in either case a form of efficiency—which does, to be sure, make life harder for rivals. But it is impossible to see the practice as a means of improperly preventing competition, and with that idea out of the way, the government's suit stands revealed as an attack on outstanding commercial success as such.

Although numerous economists point to the double counting of market power as an obvious error, antitrust prosecutors continue to assert, in one context after another, the equivalent of the proposition that a seller can add $200 and zero and get $400. Clearly, this peculiar form of new math is wrong—the questioned behavior has other motivations and other effects. Since double counting forms the mainspring of antitrust reasoning about exclusionary effects, a large body of antitrust doctrine, including the existing and emerging rules against vertical and conglomerate mergers must be considered to stand unjustified.

Conglomerate Mergers—Phantom Threat

The Nixon Administration's announced determination to wage war on conglomerate mergers—with special but by no means exclusive attention to the acquisitions of the top 200 manufacturing companies—must rank as one of the bleakest, most disappointing developments in antitrust history. An Administration that could have initiated pro-consumer reforms has chosen instead to accentuate and extend some of antitrust's most irrational economic theories. The campaign against conglomerate mergers is launched in the teeth of the conclusion reached by the task force that President Nixon himself appointed to study and report on antitrust policy. The task force, headed by George J. Stigler, professor of economics at the University of Chicago, said of conglomerate mergers: "Vigorous action on the basis of our present knowledge is not defensible." It most certainly isn't. And yet since the submission of that report we have had not only announcements that vigorous action is to come, but also the filing of suits against L-T-V's acquisition of Jones & Laughlin, I.T.T.'s acquisition of

Canteen Corp., and Northwest Industries' attempt to purchase effective control of Goodrich.

If McLaren succeeds in sustaining the theories of these cases in court—and in recent years the Antitrust Division has been able to get almost any theory upheld in the Supreme Court—he may have succeeded in destroying the last vestiges of rationality in the antitrust laws. If conglomerate mergers can be held a threat to competition, an antitrust attack upon conglomerate mergers raise a variety of debaters' points that can, I believe, be characterized as essentially frivolous. The most commonly urged points against conglomerate mergers are that they increase a general concentration of ownership in the American economy, raise the possibility of reciprocal buying, and create—dread phrase—"barriers to entry." The first of these points is, at its strongest, irrelevant; the second describes a practice that is either harmless or beneficial; and the third raises a specter that is just that, an incorporeal apparition.

A Prophecy That Never Ceases to Frighten

The imminent concentration of all ownership in a few giant corporations, with the accompanying demise of sturdy, locally owned small business, is the standard, Mark I, all-weather antitrust hobgoblin. It serves not only against conglomerate mergers, of course, but against any merger involving a very large company, even where the acquired company is far from large. This congealing of the economy has been prophesied freely at least since 1890 on the basis of perceived trends, and it never happens. It also never ceases to frighten people. The evil of the predicted economy-wide concentration is supposed to be both so self-evident and so enormous that counter-argument is overwhelmed. Nothing about the prediction is self-evident, not the statistics, the correctness of the extrapolation, or the assumed sociological, political, or economic consequences.

These all deserve examination, but the point to be emphasized here is that the superconcentration issue, whether genuine or synthetic in other aspects, is a *bogus antitrust issue*. It has no proper place whatever in enforcement decisions under the present statutes, because it is irrelevant to competition in particular markets and to the allocation of resources by the market mechanism. Consistent with the consumer-welfare standard, it is *market* concentration, not economy-wide concentration, that is the subject of the Clayton Act's provisions concerning "competition" and "monopoly." Congress could write a statute about the sociological implications of economy-wide concentration achieved through mergers—a statute that would perhaps be phrased in terms of the size of merging companies' assets. But Congress has not done so. If superconcentration is a matter of concern, Administration officials should appear before the appropriate congressional committees to ask for a political decision, expressed in the form of a statute, on how superconcentration should be dealt with, and how much economic benefit we are willing to sacrifice in the process.

Another hobgoblin is reciprocity, the business practice of buying from those who buy from you. Though it has probably been going on since men traded arrowheads for mammoth hides, it has only recently been discovered to be anticompetitive. The discovery comes at an opportune time for the anti-conglomerate campaign—the more diversified a firm becomes, the more likely that somewhere in its complex dealing it will find the chance to practice reciprocity. Attorney General John N. Mitchell has indicated that the potential for reciprocity will be a key argument in the attack on conglomerate mergers. He characterized the practice as "one of the most easily understandable dangers posed by the conglomerate merger."

On the contrary, in economic terms the "danger" is not understandable at all, much less easily. As the Stigler task force reported, the "economic threat to competition from reciprocity (reciprocal buying arrangements) is either small or nonexistent." The objection to reciprocity involves the Carruthers fallacy—counting a quantity of market power more than once. If a company is using its position as an important customer to bargain the best possible prices from its suppliers, then that company has no market power left to force the suppliers to buy from it on noncompetitive terms.

The rhetoric of "barriers to entry" is the latest conceptual fig leaf used by the enforcement agencies to hide the obtrusive fact of life that commercial success is usually due to superior efficiency. So far this rhetoric, too, has been highly successful. It persuaded the Supreme Court to strike down Procter & Gamble's acquisition of Clorox on the theory that any addition to Clorox's effectiveness in the market for household liquid bleach would raise barriers to entry. (See "The Supreme Court versus Corporate Efficiency," *Fortune*, August, 1967.) In the long course of that litigation, nobody—not the FTC, the Antitrust Division, the Solicitor General, or the Court—ever explained even once how a "barrier to entry" differed from superior efficiency.

The case centered on the "barrier" that would be created if Clorox shared in the quantity discounts that Procter was supposed to receive from the television networks. Nobody ever showed why the ability to get such discounts should not be considered an efficiency. And now, the most humiliating development of all, it begins to appear from the separate researches of David

Blank, a vice president of C.B.S., and John L. Peterman, a professor at the University of Chicago law school, that the crucial quantity discounts may have suffered from the even more serious defect of not existing. This whole episode has an air of satire: a major merger was dissolved, an unsound concept was embedded in the law, and a vital precedent was established—all on the application of an erroneous theory to an apparently nonexistent "fact."

The only way a company can make entry more difficult through a conglomerate acquisition is by increasing efficiency, and that is beneficial. But if the Antitrust Division succeeds in inhibiting conglomerate mergers with these theories, it will have erected real, and truly anticompetitive, barriers to entry. A successful legal attack would deny us the benefits these mergers can confer: revitalizing sluggish companies and industries; improving management efficiency, either through replacement of mediocre executives or reinforcement of good ones with aids such as superior data retrieval or more effective financial-control systems; transferring technical and marketing know-how across traditional industry lines; meshing research or distribution; increasing ability to ride out fluctuations; adding needed capital; and providing owner-managers of successful small companies with a market for selling the enterprises they have created, thus encouraging other men to go into businesses of their own.

Mistaking horizontal for vertical

The same sort of confusion that characterizes antitrust arguments against conglomerate mergers also shows up in arguments against vertical mergers. A vertical merger, of course, is one in which the acquired company is, actually or potentially, a customer or supplier of the acquiring company. The courts, at the urging of the Antitrust Division, treat vertical mergers with a ferocity wholly unjustified by economic analysis. The law supposes that a manufacturer, M, with 5 percent of a market, can "foreclose" his rivals and "lever" himself to a competitively unjustified market share by acquiring a retailer, R, who has 1 percent of the market and has been selling other manufacturers' products. This is the Carruthers double-counting fallacy again. The theory assumes that R can both enjoy whatever market position it had established and simultaneously transfer its enjoyment to M. It is assumed, in other words, that by forcing its goods on R, M picks up an additional 1 percent of the market in manufacturing, while R keeps its 1 percent in retailing.

But whatever considerations of price, quality, consumer preference, etc., had previously persuaded R not to specialize in M's goods are still operative. If M's goods are forced on R, then the retailer loses the profits that the manufacturer gains. The law's theory of foreclosure, then, turns out to be mistaken. The only sensible explanation for the vertical merger of M and R is that through economies in distribution, management, and the like, it creates profitable efficiencies, which are socially beneficial.

Apologists for tough rules against such mergers (joining manufacturers and merchants in the same line of goods) usually prefer to argue an extreme case. Suppose M should buy 100 percent of the retailers, they say; that surely confers the ability to gain a manufacturing monopoly. As an objection to vertical merger, this argument is spurious—the case as stated is horizontal, not vertical. The problem in such a situation is not the foreclosure of rival manufacturers but the elimination of rivalry at the retail level. To be clear about that, ask yourself whether the situation would be any better if, instead of M, a complete stranger to the industry had bought all the retailers. The answer, clearly, is no: in either case a horizontal monopoly has been created at the retail level.

What I am suggesting is that vertical mergers should be judged by horizontal-merger standards. Thus any acquisition by a manufacturer of a single retail firm should be lawful, because it does not increase market power at the retail level. If the manufacturer acquires two or more retailing companies, horizontal merger standards should be applied to the share created in retailing. I am further suggesting that a manufacturer's acquisition of retailers in the same line of goods should be judged by the same standards as would apply to their acquisition by a newcomer to the industry.

Avoiding Both Kinds of Misallocation

Size or market concentration created by horizontal merger (merger between actual or probable rivals) is a completely different animal from size achieved by internal growth or by conglomerate or vertical merger. Growth demonstrates superior efficiency; horizontal merger to a very large market share does not—it may have been motivated primarily or even solely by a desire to reap monopoly profits. Conglomerate and vertical mergers cannot create the ability to increase profits with restricted output; large horizontal mergers can. On the other side, however, monopoly profit cannot be the motivation for horizontal mergers that add up to only a small share of a market.

To take a clear case: when companies each having 1 percent of a fragmented industry merge, they cannot be supposed to have monopoly profit in mind. As in the case of conglomerate and vertical mergers, their motivation must be either increased efficiency or some effect irrelevant to antitrust. It is, therefore, intelligible policy to set limits on market shares achievable by horizontal merger, but the limits must not be so narrow that their predominant effect is to ban mergers motivated by valid business considerations. Error in either direction will be costly. Allowing horizontal mergers that are too large invites resource misallocation through deliberate restriction of output. Allowing only horizontal mergers that are very small enforces resource misallocation through lowered efficiency.

We are dealing with a spectrum, and it must be confessed that the proper place to cut it is not at all clear. Unfortunately, our guidelines are few and uncertain. But rough observations are enough, I think, to indicate that present law about horizontal mergers is far too harsh.

A Concession to a Phobia

The purpose of limiting horizontal mergers to market shares far smaller than those that would be required for monopoly profits is to guard against "oligopolistic" erosion of competition, i.e., the possibility that a few dominant companies may restrict output through noncollusive mutual restraint. (The term "noncollusive" is essential here, for collusive restraint of competition is illegal per se.) In a concentrated industry, according to some theories of how oligopolies work, it is possible for supposed rivals to soften rivalry through "conscious parallelism." By following an industry leader, or by acting in accordance with what they know of each other's policies, it is said, these companies move in lockstep in matters of production levels and pricing without actually communicating with each other.

But even if one assumes this picture to be accurate for some industries, that still does not justify the stringency of the present rules on horizontal mergers. Judging from such indications as the eagerness of oligopolists to engage in actual collusion despite the considerable legal dangers, the frequency with which even elaborately negotiated and policed collusive schemes break down under the temptations and pressures of the marketplace, and the dramatic drop in prices that often occurs when even a two-company situation replaces a one-company situation, I would estimate that noncollusive restriction of output is usually not a serious problem where there are as many as three substantial companies in a particular market. (I am not asserting that it is necessarily a serious problem where there are only two.)

As a tactical concession to current oligopoly phobia, I am willing to weaken the conclusion that should follow from that and propose a rule permitting horizontal mergers up to market shares that would allow for other mergers of similar size and still leave four significant companies in the market. In a fragmented market, this would indicate a maximum share attainable by merger of about 30 percent. In a market where one company already has more than 30 percent, the maximum would be scaled down somewhat. For example, where one company has 50 percent, no other company could go above about 20 percent by merger (barring some exceptional case, such as the imminent failure of one of the merger partners).

I do not claim that such a rule, or any other I might devise, would either completely prevent noncollusive restriction of output or completely avoid needless destruction of efficiencies. Some such welfare losses are inevitable in any policy that can be framed with respect to horizontal mergers. But I am reasonably confident that this rule, whatever its imperfections, would strike a much better balance between the factors impinging upon consumer welfare than the present judge-made proscription of horizontal mergers creating market shares as small as 5 percent. The harmful effects of that rule upon consumers may be imagined if one realizes it is equivalent to saying that when there are a hundred lawyers in a town no law firm may contain as many as five. Such a rule obviously cuts far too deep into the efficiencies of integration.

The rules on mergers, it should be clear, urgently require reform. And the need for antitrust reform extends beyond merger rules, to fields it has not been possible to discuss here. To put the matter bluntly, we have now reached a stage where the antitrust laws, as they are being interpreted and applied, are simply not intellectually respectable. They are not respectable as law or as economics, and, because they proceed to stifle competition while pretending to protect it, they are not even respectable politics.

The Missing Discussion

Most of the rules that should be changed were made over the years by the Supreme Court, usually at the urging of the Antitrust Division, and reform can quite legitimately come in the same way. The antitrust statutes lay down very little hard law. The courts remain free to change the subsidiary rules they constructed, and the head of the Antitrust Division should play a key role in that process.

Reform should have an ideal in view, and an ideal consumer-oriented law would, for the most part, strike at large horizontal mergers and at cartel agreements among competitors. I agree with the recommendation of the Stigler task force that more resources and ingenuity should be devoted to a drive against price-fixing and market-division cartels, since there appear to be many that enforcement of the law does not now reach. An enforcement drive against collusion in national, regional, and local markets would pay high dividends in consumer welfare; particularly since cartels, being subject to a rule of per se illegality, are among the least difficult and least expensive offenses to prosecute.

Beyond the reformation of existing antitrust law there is a broader and potentially far more important role that lies waiting to be seized, by a bold and creative antitrust administration. The original antitrust philosophy of open markets and free competition that underlies the rule against cartels should be steadily expanded to cover other fields of economic behavior where control of entry, price-fixing, and similar eliminations of competition now occur *with governmental blessing.* The Antitrust Division should make itself the spokesman for antitrust ideals throughout the economy, by testifying on proposed legislation, by intervening in federal and state regulatory processes, and by other means. The opportunities are innumerable—in the regulation of trucking, banking, communications, drug retailing, and in many other fields where regulation often acts less to protect consumers than to preserve business fiefdoms from competitive challenge. A positive antitrust program such as this would elicit enough outraged screams from protected companies to dispel any notion that the policy is narrowly "pro-business."

Some readers may suppose that the views I have expressed here are extreme. They are not. Far from being personal or idiosyncratic they represent, in their general outline, a broad and growing school of thought about antitrust policy. Views in many respects, quite similar to mine are presented, for example, in the Stigler report, which the Administration has so far assiduously ignored. Reform is a necessity, and, regardless of his own views, Richard McLaren could contribute greatly by using his office to start and focus a systematic discussion of antitrust goals and economics. Without reappraisal and reform, antitrust is likely to go on fighting—and, worse, winning—ever more dubious battles.

Antitrust in Transition: The Role of the Courts in Applying Economics

M r. Whiting, your ambition was anticipated. Some years ago, a judge wrote an opinion in which he cited, in order, an article by Betty Bock, an article by Derek Bok, and an article by me. The printer took one look at it, decided there was clearly something wrong, and changed all of the names to Bork—and actually, one of those articles I didn't want credit for.

Contrary to popular belief, being on the D.C. Circuit has advantages, as well as penalties. As an example of one or the other—I won't say which—I haven't seen an antitrust case since I got there. Now, the absence of antitrust cases may be peculiar to our circuit, or it may lend some credibility to the rumor that antitrust policy is dead, probably as a result of foul play, and that the carcass is buried. As to the truth of that rumor, I cannot testify, but it's very pleasant, I can tell you, to share once more a platform with some of the usual suspects.

The title of this talk is "The Role of the Courts in Applying Economics." When I saw it, I called Jim Halverson and asked him what it meant. He said it meant that I could say anything I wanted to. That is a libertarian answer I think thoroughly in keeping with the new spirit of antitrust. Actually, it's not a bad description of what I intend to talk about.

One of the most startling, and I think beneficial, developments in the law has been the relatively recent spread of economic learning among judges (even more perhaps among their clerks), among professors in law schools, among practitioners—this list is not in descending order of importance—and in many other segments of the policymaking and law-making world. I don't want to overstate this. Few, if any, judges qualify as economists. I certainly do not come close, and I have no aspirations in that direction. But, in a way, that is precisely what is most important about the development. It's the spread of basic economic concepts and the awareness of economic ideas to noneconomists that is so unexpected and so promising. One does not have to be a real economist to benefit, because microeconomics is a field in which the simple ideas are the most powerful ideas.

Now, there are two reactions to this new importance of economics in law: One is an enthusiasm so overdone that it leads to the delusion that all of the law's problems can usefully be analyzed through economics. At the opposite end of the spectrum, there is the nihilistic delusion that price theory is so far removed from a science that it is virtually useless anywhere in the law. We have only one end of that spectrum represented here today.

In any event, I appear here to rescue law and economics both from the overly ardent and from the excessively frigid. The notion that economics can be applied to all areas of law seems to me to rest on the curious premise that there are no such things as apples and oranges. It is, of course, possible to state every legal problem in economic language, and thus to leave the impression that you are applying economic analysis. But economics is not a set of words; it is a method of reasoning, and it works only when you are dealing with things that are comparable. That is why economics has produced its most valuable results and insights when dealing with the behavior of persons and firms in real markets, where dollars may be used as measuring units. Fields such as antitrust have, for that reason, benefited most from the application of economics to their problems. If Fred Rowe will just hold on to his seat for a few minutes, I will return to that topic and to him.

Economic reasoning is not being employed merely because a judge uses words like "cost/benefit analysis." It has long been known that, in constitutional law for example, judges are required to weight competing values. When a motion is made to close a courtroom, the judge must weight the competing claims of the defendant's right to a fair trial and the press's right to report matters of public interest. When a law banning obscenity is applied, the judge is required to weigh the interest of the individual in expression against the interest of the community in upholding its moral values. When a military regulation against wearing headgear indoors is applied to the wearing of a yarmulka by a naval officer, the court must weight the value of the free exercise of religion against the demands of military discipline. In each of those examples, the judge may find the weighing process difficult. He will certainly be unable to assign numerical weights—and if he should try that, we will know at once that the apparent precision is spurious.

Ask yourself how much is really gained in rigor, in sophistication, in precision, or in enlightenment, by restating any of those problems in terms of cost/benefit analysis. The answer is, I think, nothing. We knew before we used those terms that going either way would give us the benefit of extending one value and impose the cost of contracting the other. We are still left with the philosophical problem of values that have no common denominator—values that are, as dollars are not, incommensurable.

Now, I want to go to the other end of the spectrum, which is antitrust. There, economic decisions about competition have essentially been delegated by Congress to judges. Only recently, however, has "real" economics, as opposed to "folk" economics, been brought to bear upon the law, and it has worked not a revolution, but that most blessed of events, a counterrevolution. To be precise, it has done so only partially and incompletely, and one must hope that the process will continue until this body of law becomes completely economically rational.

One who holds these sentiments is very likely, as I have for a period of 30 years, to meet Fred Rowe coming in the other direction. One may gather Fred's sentiments from the title of that last article, "The Decline of Antitrust and the Delusions of Models: The Faustian Pact of Law and Economics."[1] I gather that Fred disapproves of the counterrevolution.

In the brief time I intend to take, I want to make two points. The first is that, under the present antitrust statutes as they are written, the pact between law and economics, whether it is Faustian or made in heaven, is inevitable. There is no other way for courts to proceed and produce beneficial results—or, indeed, to produce anything that deserves the name of law. The second point is one I've been trying to convince Fred of, as I say, for 30 years, since we first gathered at the coffee machine in the Kirkland firm. I haven't succeeded yet, but that's no reason to stop trying. The point is simply that Fred, I think, misunderstands the nature of price theory and the contributions it has made and will continue to make to rational policy.

Faustian pact or not, antitrust has no alternative, as I have said, to do anything but rest on economics. That proposition does not itself rest upon economics, but upon a theory of the judicial function in a country that is basically democratic. This is an argument I have made repeatedly, but, for reasons I do not care to examine too closely, an argument to which nobody ever responds. I like to think that the problem may be that the suggestion that law has any intellectual discipline of its own is regarded as too fantastic to be entertained.

The antitrust laws, by and large, give no specific directions to judges other than to preserve competition. In looking to the legislative history, one discerns repeated concern for the welfare of consumers and also for the wel-

---

1. Rowe, "The Decline of Antitrust and the Delusions of Models: The Faustian Pact of Law and Economics", 72 *GEO. L.J.* 1511 (1984).

fare of small business and for various other values—a potpourri of other values. So far as I'm aware, Congress, in enacting these statutes, never faced the problem of what to do when values come into conflict in specific cases. Legislators appear to have assumed, as it is most comfortable to assume, that all good things are always compatible. They did, however, make certain choices that suggest that in cases of conflict consumer welfare is to be preferred to small producer welfare, as well as to all other values. For example, the clear indication that price-fixing rings are to be unlawful, and that monopoly gained through superior efficiency is to be lawful, are indicators of that.

In any case, courts are not, I believe, entitled to balance such things as consumer welfare against small business welfare without engaging in a task that is so unconfinedly legislative as to be unconstitutional. That is why I think, given the way our present antitrust laws are written—they could be written otherwise—courts must adopt consumer welfare as their sole guide in deciding cases. That conclusion calls for price theory, and it calls for those rules, and only those rules, that can be justified in terms of price theory.

Now, I have listened to Fred attentively today, and I have read him assiduously for years, and I am sincere when I say he is a great antitrust theorist. But today, for dramatic reasons, I intend to stress the area of our disagreement.

Those of you who are familiar with Fred's rhetorical style will know that he is given to referring to those of us who think economics important in religious terms. He has, for example, in the past referred to me as the "Ayatollah East of the Chicago School." And in his article, he refers to an unnamed group, which I take to include Bill Baxter and Phil Areeda, as "engaging in the seance of a sodality," as having "undergone religous conversions," and as "reveling in Talmudic subtleties." That is just Fred's way of denying that there is only one God. He is, I think, the leading Pantheist of antitrust. But, since I enjoy this sort of thing, I began to look for another way to characterize Fred's views, and I decided that he is the Antitrust Section's Ned Ludd. You remember Ned Ludd, he's the man for whom the Luddites were named. The dictionary defines Luddites as "a group of workers in England from 1811–1816 who smashed new labor-saving machinery in protest against reduced wages and unemployment." You can see why an antitrust lawyer of the old school would be a Luddite—reduced wages and unemployment having become endemic in this field of law due to new labor-saving analysis. But, I think the Luddism of antitrust, like its historical precursor, is essentially a rearguard action.

I won't argue with Fred in any detail about his view of economics, but I will note that if his assault upon that discipline is correct, he is well on his way to intellectual immortality. He has undertaken to characterize as really essentially worthless an intellectual tradition that begins with Adam Smith and continues through Ricardo and Alfred Marshall and Milton Friedman and George Stigler, and so on. If that tradition can be overthrown, it ought not to be in an antitrust article; a slim book on economics would be an intellectual revolution, something of a sort we have not seen in a long time.

Fred says that economics is nothing more than a series of metaphors of particular times and cultures, and that economic truths fail when conditions change. I think not, and I think Professor Baxter has already pointed out why. Fred refers to the oligopoly model, which dominated antitrust for awhile; then what he calls the efficiency model, which has now come into dominance; and finally, to the learning curve model. In fact, the oligopoly model and the learning curve model are merely particular explanations of how things work that are within the efficiency model. The oligopoly theory that once was dominant in antitrust was shaky even then, and I would suggest that it never did describe conditions in the real world. It wasn't a change in conditions that undid the oligopoly model; it was the realization that it was theoretically incoherent and that there was no observable market in which its conclusions held good.

All of these things, all of the models or theories we are talking about, are simply stages in the intellectual evolution of what Fred calls the efficiency model. Steadily, as that intellectual evolution takes place, antitrust is becoming more and more beneficial to the American public. A lot of people are responsible for that. Bill Baxter is one of those primarily responsible. But, I think it would have been politically impossible for a person like Professor Baxter to have done what he did, had there not been an intellectual shift in the underpinnings of antitrust, a shift in which he took part before he came to office.

Courts have since gotten better at such things as mergers and vertical relationships. They are still really quite horrible, at times, at such matters as identifying price-fixing or collusion from circumstantial evidence; there is still a lot of work to be done.

Antitrust, to use Fred Rowe's words, may be in search of itself, but I think it is increasingly, after almost a century, beginning to find itself and becoming a much better policy.

What Antitrust Is All About

Rarely does a prospective antitrust case roil public passion. But since it became known that I represent a company urging the Justice Department to challenge certain of Microsoft's business practices, my mail has certainly livened up. One letter writer complained that I had sold my "sole." His spelling aside, that writer was at least kinder than the one who labeled me senile.

There seems to be a widespread impression that the Microsoft controversy should be resolved by an ideological litmus test: liberals are bent on punishing success, and conservatives must defend Bill Gates's company from any application of the antitrust laws. But the question is not one of politics or ideology; it is one of law and economics. And that is why an outspoken free marketeer like me can be found arguing against Microsoft.

Indeed, in Congress and among the players, liberals and conservatives, Democrats and Republicans are found on each side of the controversy. What, then, is the complaint of the many companies that are urging action by the Justice Department?

These companies—customers as well as rivals of Microsoft—challenge some of Microsoft's business practices as predatory, intended to preserve the company's monopoly of personal computer operating systems through practices that exclude or severely hinder rivals but do not benefit consumers. Microsoft's effort to maintain and expand a market dominance that now stands at 90 to 95 percent violates traditional antitrust principles. Specifically, it violates Section 2 of the Sherman Act, territory visited decades ago by the Supreme Court.

The case, from 1951, was *Lorain Journal Company* v. *United States*, and the Court's ruling is directly on point. The Journal, in the Court's description of the case, "enjoyed a substantial monopoly in Lorain, Ohio, of the mass

From the *New York Times*, May 4, 1998.

dissemination of news and advertising." The daily newspaper had 99 percent coverage in the town.

"Those factors," the Court said, "made The Journal an indispensable medium of advertising for many Lorain concerns." A minor threat to The Journal's monopoly arose, however, with the establishment of radio station WEOL in a nearby town. The newspaper responded by refusing to accept local advertising from any Lorain County advertiser that used WEOL.

The Supreme Court called that an attempt to monopolize, illegal under Section 2 of the Sherman Act. There being no apparent efficiency justification for The Journal's action—that is, no evidence that it resulted in an operation whose efficiency somehow benefited consumers—it was deemed predatory. To those who say I have altered my longstanding position to represent an opponent of Microsoft, I'm happy to note that 20 years ago I wrote that the Lorain Journal case had been correctly decided.

The parallel between The Journal's action and Microsoft's behavior is exact. Microsoft has a similarly overwhelming market share, and it imposes conditions on those with whom it deals that exclude rivals without any apparent justification on the grounds of efficiency. In fact, the case against Microsoft is stronger, for there are many documents in the public domain that make clear that Microsoft specifically intended to crush competition.

We may not yet know all of the exclusionary practices, but we do know many. Here's a sampler:

* Microsoft's operating system licenses have forbidden "original equipment manufacturers"—makers of personal computers—to alter the first display screen from that required by Microsoft. Microsoft thus controls what the consumer sees. This restriction also hampers consumers' use of competing browsers to search the Internet or to serve as an alternative platform for other programs.

* Microsoft has restrained Internet service providers and on-line services, which are forced to deal with Microsoft because of its monopoly in the Windows system. For instance, it has forbidden service providers to advertise or promote any non-Microsoft Web browser or even mention that such a browser is available. Netscape and others are denied an important distribution channel to consumers.

* Companies that provide content on the Internet, to gain access to Microsoft's screen display, have been forced to agree not to promote content developed for competing platforms.

When a monopolist employs practices and makes agreements that exclude competitors and does so without the justification that the practices and agreements benefit consumers, the company is guilty, as was The Lorain Journal, of an attempt to monopolize in violation of Section 2 of the Sherman Act. When its own documents display a clear intent to monopolize through such means, the case is cold.

Netscape and the other companies seeking an end to these practices are not asking the Justice Department to take any action that would interfere in the slightest with Microsoft's ability to innovate. The department is simply being asked to stop Microsoft from stifling the innovations of others. The object is to create a level playing field benefiting consumers. That is what antitrust is about—a view that should require no one to sell his "sole."

TRUST THE TRUSTBUSTERS:
WHY CONSERVATIVES ARE WRONG ABOUT ANTITRUST

The current debauched state of political discourse is illustrated in micro-cosm by the debate over antitrust enforcement. Time and again, I have found myself in conversation with conservatives about cases brought by the current administration; the consensus is invariably that the cases against, for instance, Microsoft and Visa/MasterCard are wrongheaded. These folk, to be sure, know very little about antitrust policy or the principles that guide it; what they think they do know is that the Clinton Department of Justice is thoroughly corrupt, and that the Antitrust Division is the most corrupt of all. I have heard and read that Joel Klein, the former division head, was merely advancing his career at the expense of heroes of free enterprise, that the judge who decided against Microsoft (a Reagan appointee, by the way) is a toady for the Justice Department, that the cases are nothing more than payoffs to trial lawyers or to Vernon Jordan, and that the companies that complained of Microsoft's and Visa/MasterCard's tactics are whining losers in the competitive marketplace. The true conservative position, it appears, is that antitrust is always Big Government trying to crush individual initiative and success.

Now I take a back seat to no one in my detestation of Bill Clinton, who would, in a well-ordered society, long ago have been hung upside down in a dungeon. But uneducated attacks on antitrust—as merely a politics of envy or populism or what have you—are almost equally distasteful.

Sad to say, not even *National Review* is immune to these fevers. The lat-est example is Michael Catanzaro's piece, "The Antitrust Club" (Sept. 25), which opens with the sinister fact that Vernon Jordan is a board member of American Express and a friend of Joel Klein's, ergo . . . Ergo, what? Well, after all, Jordan tried to get Monica Lewinsky a job at American Express. Of course, she was offered no job, but that is still supposedly probative of

From *National Review*, October 23, 2000.

influence peddling in the case against Visa/MasterCard. It is not even alleged that Jordan played any role whatever in encouraging that lawsuit, but still . . . The bipartisan commission Jordan was on (cochaired by James Rill, antitrust chief in the Bush administration) did not even advise about specific antitrust cases—but so what? Richard Nixon once used antitrust politically against the television networks, which proves . . .

When he gets past all this unsupported innuendo to the actual cases, Mr. Catanzaro is completely wrong about the issues. He uses the same tactic Visa/MasterCard has employed: changing the subject. Mr. Catanzaro argues that the credit-card industry is "already fiercely competitive" because there are thousands of credit-card issuers. A study—by Visa's public-relations firm—of consumer reactions to the case set out the line Visa has employed ever since. The study found that, to consumers with knowledge of the case,

> the [Justice Department's] basic case seems fair: banks *should* be allowed to do whatever they want. Similarly, even some of those who see the industry as competitive are willing to say that there is nothing wrong with it being even more competitive. That is a fundamental problem for Visa, and the main reason we need to keep people from focusing on the specifics of this case. If we cannot keep the topic to the competitiveness of the industry [card issuing, not network competition], and the facts supporting our claims, th[e]n we should divert and put the focus on American Express. We tell many of our clients who are candidates for office, when your arguments get weaker the more people know, never put yourself in a defensive position, divert and attack. The same good advice is applicable here.

Unfortunately for that diversionary tactic, this case is not about competition among bank-card issuers but about the credit-card networks that sell indispensable products and services to the banks. There are four of these networks, and two of them—Visa and MasterCard, which, admittedly, have not competed vigorously with one another—account for 75 percent of the dollar volume. Suppose that a manufacturer held 75 percent of the market and, when accused of monopolization, defended himself by saying he sold to 25,000 retailers. The fatuity of the defense would be apparent at once; so it is with Visa/MasterCard.

When antitrust enforcers look at a company's exclusionary behavior, they ask: Is the exclusion competitive, in that it creates efficiencies valuable to consumers? Or is it simply harmful to rivals, with anticonsumer results? Visa/MasterCard's conduct falls in the latter category. They have adopted rules or policies mandating that any bank that deals with American Express,

Discover, or any other competitor of Visa/MasterCard will be expelled from their systems. No bank can afford that. It would have to tell all its cardholders that their Visa and MasterCard cards were suddenly useless.

The Visa/MasterCard policies fit a pattern familiar to antitrust law: They are concerted refusals to deal, or boycotts. All the banks must agree not to deal with any competitor of those networks. This is a horizontal (between competitors) agreement, made and enforced through the central agencies of Visa and MasterCard (on whose boards sit officials from the major banks) not to compete among themselves by dealing with American Express or Discover. The cases condemning such arrangements are numerous and uniform. The market size of the defendant networks is alone sufficient to condemn the agreement. So is the fact that neither Visa nor MasterCard has been able to point to any efficiency created by the agreements, other than the "efficiency" of not having to compete with American Express and Discover.

Suppose that a law firm in a city had 75 percent of the city's clients and then announced that it would cut off any client that dealt with another firm on any matter. The firm would be organizing and compelling an agreement among its clients not to compete with one another by using any lawyer not a member of the firm. The firm could not cite any efficiency gain other than holding all its clients. That would clearly be unlawful, and the analogy to the Visa/MasterCard policies is exact.

Mr. Catanzaro makes much of the fact that representatives of American Express met with members of the Antitrust Division. He neglects to mention that Visa and MasterCard repeatedly met with those same officials, but failed to convince them of the legality of their boycott. He also neglects to mention that the CEOs of American Express and Netscape were prominent Republicans, who could hardly be expected to exercise a lot of political influence over the Justice Department of a Democratic administration.

The Antitrust Division is, in fact, alerted to most of the cases it eventually brings by injured competitors or customers; in a huge and complex economy, there is no other equally useful source of information. But the division is very careful to winnow valid concerns from mere attempts to hobble rivals.

Mr. Catanzaro likens the Visa/MasterCard case to that against Microsoft, the supposed point of similarity being that other companies "encouraged" the Justice Department to proceed with its investigation. Of course, it is equally true that Microsoft and its allies encouraged the Justice Department to give the company a pass. I have made the case against Microsoft in this magazine ("Against Microsoft," Feb. 7) and the trial court's findings amply bear out the conclusion that Microsoft has indeed been guilty of monopolization.

Visa/MasterCard, Microsoft, and their various apologists commonly make the argument that the government has not proven consumer harm from the practices attacked as illegal. This reflects a fundamental misunderstanding. Consumer harm is not an element of a Sherman Act offense that must be proved independently of the law violation. Antitrust conclusively *presumes* consumer harm when unlawful behavior is shown. If a plaintiff proves, for example, that defendants have fixed prices, that is enough; there is no need to prove that prices would have been lower but for the agreement. If, in a monopolization case, the defendant is shown to have employed exclusionary tactics that did not create efficiency, consumer harm is also conclusively presumed. In both the Microsoft and Visa/MasterCard cases, it is clear, in any event, that innovation has been stifled and price competition softened or eliminated.

Neither is it useful to compare the raw figures for numbers of mergers investigated and turned down, or approved with modifications, from one time period to another. Mergers often come in waves and enforcement activity increases as a result. Nor is it helpful to lump together the activities of the Justice Department, the Federal Trade Commission, and the Federal Communications Commission in an effort to prove something about the cases against Visa/MasterCard and Microsoft. These are very different agencies with differing views. Some are more prone to unjustified activism than others. The Antitrust Division of the Justice Department, while by no means infallible, is, in my opinion, the best of the three.

No one would contend that antitrust enforcers and courts never make mistakes. The history of the policy is replete with economic fiascos, but as better economic analysis has been brought to bear over the past three decades, the law has steadily improved. Mistakes are still made, particularly in private antitrust actions, but mistakes are not the general rule. Contrary to the belief apparently common among conservatives and liberals alike, there is an intellectual structure underlying antitrust. It would be better to understand that structure and evaluate each case individually, instead of relying upon a scandal theory to account for every prosecution.

On Vertical Price Fixing:
A Reply to Professors Gould and Yamey

In replying to Professor Gould and Professor Yamey, I must necessarily assume that the reader is generally familiar with the main outlines of my previous article.[1] It may be useful, nevertheless, to restate the core of my argument very briefly. In the previous article, I urged the legality of certain types of price fixing and market division, both horizontal and vertical. Professors Gould and Yamey are concerned here only with one aspect of that article's thesis: my assertion that vertical price fixing or resale price maintenance, when it is not used as the tool of a cartel among resellers or among manufacturers, can only result from the manufacturer's desire to increase efficiency, and, further, that courts should accept that motivation as conclusive of the effect of such resale price maintenance. (Hereafter, unless otherwise indicated, references to resale price maintenance, or r.p.m., should be taken to indicate only this variety of manufacturer-desired r.p.m.)

In its briefest terms, my argument runs as follows: No manufacturer will desire r.p.m. for the mere purpose of giving his resellers a greater-than-competitive return. The extra return would be money out of his pocket and we may safely assume that manufacturers are rarely moved to engage in that variety of philanthropy. The manufacturer who imposes r.p.m., therefore, must be attempting to purchase something for it. What he gets is usually increased activity by the reseller in providing information, promotional services, and the like. These are means of increasing distributive efficiency and should be permitted on grounds of efficient resource allocation. The case is no different than if the manufacturer owned the resellers and required his

---

1. Bork, "The Rule of Reason and the Per Se Concept: Price Fixing and Market Division II," 75 *Yale L. J.* 373 (1966). The first installment of this article, which appeared at 74 *Yale L. J.* 775 (1965), is of only peripheral relevance to the present discussion.

From *The Yale Law Journal*, March 1967.

reseller employees to perform the same functions. R.p.m. is simply a partial integration and is often more efficient than full integration by ownership or contract.[2]

Since we have isolated a practice which is engaged in for the purpose of creating efficiency, courts and legislatures ought to view r.p.m. as no different from any other normal business decision. Courts and legislatures are no more competent to judge the manufacturer's self-interest in this case than they are in any other, e.g., the purchase of machinery for a particular plant.[3]

Professor Gould and Professor Yamey agree that r.p.m. may create efficiency but they argue that it does not necessarily do so. I will attempt to reply to their specific objections in sections which parallel the divisions of their paper. But I would suggest preliminarily that their objections, even if valid, do not constitute adequate support for their policy recommendation. Since Gould and Yamey think manufacturer-desired r.p.m., depending on the circumstances, may either increase or decrease output, their first task should be to ask whether these varieties can be segregated and handled differently at an enforcement cost which is justified by the benefits. If not, their second task should be to estimate whether on balance consumers would be benefited by outlawing all manufacturer-desired r.p.m. or none. Professors Gould and Yamey do not appear to have built this bridge between their objections to my thesis and their suggested public policy.

I turn next to an examination of Gould and Yamey's specific objections.

I.

The first section of the Gould and Yamey paper offers four "counter-examples" to show that r.p.m. can restrict output. Analysis demonstrates, however, that these counter-examples do not make the showing the authors suppose.

The first counter-example supposes a manufacturer contemplating an advertising campaign through trade journals and the institution of r.p.m. as alternative means of gaining reseller support. Gould and Yamey contend that the advertising campaign, being a "fixed cost" because independent of out-

---

2. These arguments are set out more fully at 75 *Yale L. J.* 373, 397–405 (concerning the absence of restriction of output), and 453–65 (concerning the efficiencies that may be created by price fixing).

3. *Id.* at 404.

put, could not lead to a reduction in the number of items sold, while r.p.m., being an addition to marginal cost, could.

This argument contains, I believe, two fallacies: (a) that the advertising campaign is a fixed cost; and (b) that in the r.p.m. example, a restriction of output has occurred.

The costs of the advertising campaign seem clearly classifiable as marginal. The manufacturer hypothesized by Gould and Yamey is certainly not faced with a stated and invariable expense for his advertising. His alternatives will range from a single one-line notice to multi-page, color advertisements running in every issue of the trade journal. The manufacturer will attempt to choose that combination which will result in an equation of his marginal costs and marginal revenue. In predicting this result, he will necessarily take into account the different costs of the different amounts of advertising. Within the limits allowed by his agreement with the trade journal, moreover, he will vary the amount of his advertising as the campaign proceeds and results exceed or fall below his expectations. Thus, advertising outlay will vary with sales. The added advertising cost of selling additional items must be calculated in making the total output decision. The same is concededly true of r.p.m. used as an inducement for retailers to provide additional promotional efforts. Both advertising and the purchase of promotional efforts through r.p.m., therefore, deserve to be classified as marginal costs.

Assuming success, both an advertising campaign and r.p.m. will shift the final demand and marginal revenue curves up and to the right and the manufacturer's total marginal cost curve (including the reseller's costs and markup) up and to the left. The new intersection of marginal cost and marginal revenue seems likely, on intuitive grounds it must be admitted, to lie to the right of the old intersection, signifying a larger production and sale of the manufactured article. My argument, however, does not depend upon the probability of this result. Admittedly, the curves can be drawn so that the new intersection is to the left of the old, signifying a smaller production and sale of the manufactured article. This situation may, moreover, be more profitable to the manufacturer. It follows that, in some circumstances, both advertising and r.p.m. might conceivably lead to fewer sales of the manufactured article, and individual consumers would then pay more, than if advertising and r.p.m. had not been used. It does *not* follow, however, that output is lower or prices higher. The composition of the product has changed. Using r.p.m. as the example, the manufacturer has purchased and added to his manufactured article the information and promotion supplied by the reseller. This change in the composition of the product offered the consumer will require that resources be bid away from other employments. Perhaps some resources will be released to other employments. But if the new product proves more profitable it means that consumers prefer the new allocation of resources. That in turn means the output of the economy has increased.[4]

Such changes in product composition are a general means of economic progress. Thus, when a truck manufacturer switches from selling trucks to selling trucks plus reseller-provided information, it is precisely the same thing as if he had switched from offering a stripped-down model to a model with a variety of extra features. This, in turn, is no different from the changeover in the razor blade industry from carbon steel to stainless steel blades. Perhaps these changes would in some cases lead to the sale of fewer trucks and fewer razor blades, but it would be fallacious to contend that output had been restricted and that the law should require the manufacturers to switch back to the stripped-down truck and the carbon steel razor blade. The analysis is the same when r.p.m. is used to get resellers to perform functions they would not otherwise perform.[5]

The second counter-example assumes a case in which all manufacturers independently use r.p.m. as a sales-increasing device but find that they have neutralized each other's efforts so that industry sales and profitability decline. The fallacy of this counter-example lies, I believe, in the assumption that the new, less profitable situation can be stable. Since we have assumed that all manufacturers are worse off after the institution of r.p.m., the situation portrayed must be one in which not all consumer demand is primarily

---

4. A source of confusion here is the failure to distinguish between cases in which it is meaningful to regard the production and sale of fewer items as a restriction of output and those in which it is not. We speak of a cartel as restricting output, but we are referring to the means by which it creates or increases a divergence between price and marginal cost and so makes the value of the marginal product of resources in the cartelized industry higher than their value elsewhere. This misallocation of resources does not occur when the number of units produced declines because of a change in the composition of the product with a concomitant increase in its price. In such cases, the relevant output change is not that of the industry, but that of the economy, and that change is inevitably upward. (The theory of second best suggests exceptions to this statement, but I attempt to show at 740–42, *infra*, why second best must be regarded as irrelevant to the enforcement of the antitrust laws.)

5. In note 6 of their paper, Gould and Yamey state that r.p.m. may push outward the upper part of the demand curve and make it less price-elastic. They conclude incorrectly that this permits the possibility that the profitable institution of r.p.m. leads to a lower output. They have overlooked here the same point discussed in the text: the addition of services creating prestige or giving information is a change in the composition of the product the consumer buys. In this example, too, the number of physical items sold may conceivably decrease, but the total output of the economy will increase.

information- or promotion-elastic; rather, a significant segment of demand must be primarily price-elastic. It will, therefore, pay at least some manufacturers and some retailers to offer some articles without r.p.m. Some manufacturers may, as is common, take advantage of both segments of consumer demand by offering one brand that is price maintained and one that is not. Many retailers will find it profitable to carry both types of goods, reserving their selling effort for the price-maintained brands. It is hardly to be believed that where a significant price-elastic demand exists both manufacturers and retailers will refuse to maximize returns by meeting it.[6]

The third counter-example is designed to show that "a monopolist manufacturer can use r.p.m. to preserve or strengthen his monopoly position and so restrict output." I do not think the case is made. Gould and Yamey advance the argument that the manufacturer may use r.p.m. to slow the growth or impede the entry of large-scale resellers, who can prevent him from extracting monopoly returns by threatening to develop alternative sources of supply. In such a situation, one may agree, the monopolist manufacturer would like to impede the entry or further growth of large-scale resellers. But r.p.m. seems an inappropriate tool for that purpose. The possibility of entry at both the manufacturing and retailing levels is necessarily assumed, and the use of r.p.m. seems, if anything, likely to hasten such entry.

The fallacy of this counter-example is seen most clearly if we look at a case in which, but for alleged entry-barring effects, the monopolist manufacturer would not use r.p.m. because his product is best sold by price appeal alone. The least costly method would be to set the resale price so that small resellers were given only a competitive return. Large-scale resellers, who by hypothesis are able to pay less to the monopolist but are subject to the same resale price restrictions, would then make a greater-than-competitive return on each unit sold. Both classes of resellers, however, would welcome a new entrant in manufacturing.

Small resellers would prefer a new entrant because rivalry in manufacturing would lower the price they pay. Gould and Yamey do not explain why such resellers are not able to encourage alternative sources of supply. Nor do they explain why encouragement is needed. The existence of a monopoly return on sales to small resellers should be encouragement enough to potential entrants in manufacturing. Large-scale resellers, though enjoying a higher

---

6. In an aside, Gould and Yamey (at note 7 of their paper) remark that my statement that "reseller pressure for a manufacturer-imposed restraint" cannot be effective "without actual reseller cartelization" is "not convincing." It could conceivably be bias, but upon rereading my argument (75 *Yale L. J.* 373, 410 n.73), I find it compelling.

margin per unit, would be unable because of r.p.m. to use lower resale prices to achieve the large volume which was the sole purpose of their large scale. Many of these resellers will want a supplier of non-price-maintained goods. The monopolist manufacturer's use of r.p.m. in these circumstances would appear to be a blunder since it would make small resellers no less receptive to a new entrant and large-scale resellers more so.

Nor is the analysis changed if the large-scale resellers have not appeared but are about to do so. Such outlets (e.g., discount stores) typically sell a wide range of items and the existence in some lines of monopolist manufacturers using r.p.m. should merely whet their appetites to enter, develop alternative sources of supply (their ability to do so is crucial to Gould and Yamey's counter-example), and take advantage of all resellers encumbered by r.p.m.

The monopolist manufacturer's use of r.p.m. might also make entry more attractive at the manufacturing level. The manufacturing entrant's resellers would be able to undersell the r.p.m.-encumbered resellers of the ex-monopolist and hence expand the new manufacturer's share of the market more rapidly. If the potential entrant foresaw that the monopolist manufacturer would abandon r.p.m. as soon as a rival appeared, the use of r.p.m. would be neutral. Thus, in no case does r.p.m. seem to discourage entry and in some it seems likely to make entry more rapid.[7]

---

7. The analysis here also disposes of the suggestion in note 8 to Gould and Yamey's paper that oligopolists might non-collusively employ r.p.m. to impede entry.

In note 9 Gould and Yamey cite *Monopolies Commission, Report on the Supply of Wallpaper* (London 1964) for "a discussion of a different way in which r.p.m. practised by a monopolist can serve to preserve a monopoly position." The facts offered by the Commission, however, suggest that the "monopoly" in one mode of distribution was due to the superior efficiency attributable to r.p.m. and the scale of operation of the dominant manufacturer. Wallpaper is sold to the English public through decorators and through retail shops. A purchaser from a decorator chooses from a pattern book and the decorator orders the chosen design from a pattern book merchant, paying retail price less a discount, and charging his client retail price. The dominant wallpaper manufacturer fixes the price at which its paper is sold by the merchant to the decorator. The reason seems plain from the description of the merchant's functions. The merchant buys the wallpaper for his pattern books, pays for printing a number and price on the back of each pattern, pays for covering and binding the books, and distributes them free of charge to decorators. The pattern books remain current for two years and during that period the merchant accepts the obligation to supply decorators on short notice with room-size quantities of any pattern in the book. He also accepts the loss of selling off at very low prices any stock left on hand at the end of the period. R.p.m. seems the most efficient way the manufacturer can make sure the merchant is compensated for performing these functions. He would surely not perform them if decorators could accept his services and then purchase elsewhere at lower prices from a merchant who had incurred no such costs. This is the familiar use of r.p.m. to prevent the "free ride." See citation in note 8 *infra*.

Perhaps Professors Gould and Yamey have misinterpreted the common phenomenon of a manufacturer struggling to enforce r.p.m. upon new discount houses. Unfortunately for their explanation, many such manufacturers can, by no stretch of the imagination, be called monopolists. A more likely explanation than theirs is that the manufacturers involved were attempting to obtain promotional efforts through r.p.m. which the discounters were not geared to provide. The discounters obtained a free ride on the efforts of other resellers and the effect was to decrease the reseller sales effort below the level desired by the manufacturers.[8]

The fourth counter-example is said to show that oligopolistic manufacturers may employ r.p.m. non-collusively to eliminate the alleged instability in the manufacturers' price level arising from competition at the retail level. Gould and Yamey appear generally to agree with my argument that r.p.m. would rarely be used as a means of policing a manufacturers' cartel. Yet the argument against the collusive use of r.p.m. to police a cartel is essentially the same as the argument against the non-collusive but consciously parallel adoption of r.p.m. to stabilize oligopolistic pricing. In fact, the use of r.p.m. in the latter case is even less likely since the added returns to oligopoly behavior are probably less than the returns added by cartel behavior and the costs of r.p.m. may be greater in the oligopoly situation.[9]

The Commission objected to the dominant manufacturer's use of r.p.m. for two reasons: (1) Smaller manufacturers with fewer patterns could not readily set some aside for price-maintained distribution through pattern book merchants to decorators; and (2) this form of distribution was declining rapidly and r.p.m. should not be permitted to prop it up. The first objection is to an economy of scale. From a consumer viewpoint it makes no sense to destroy the efficiency of a particular mode of distribution merely because only one manufacturer has the resources to engage in it. Such a policy forces the results of monopoly upon consumers for the sake of avoiding the appearance of monopoly. The Commission's second point contradicts its first, for we are told decorator distribution is losing the competitive struggle with retail shop distribution. If so, the amount of decorator distribution at any given moment still reflects the preference of some consumers for the services thus provided. There is no intelligible reason to destroy the efficiency of that mode of distribution on the ground that only a minority of consumers want it. The Commission ignores the market's function of satisfying minority as well as majority preferences.

The Monopolies Commission's discussion does not make the point Gould and Yamey suggest. Rather it provides an example of the creation of efficiency by r.p.m. and of a mistaken governmental policy of destroying that efficiency for the sake of smaller manufacturers.

8. 75 *Yale L. J.* 373, 453–54, 430–38.

9. Returns are likely to be less because rational oligopolistic behavior without collusion is hardly likely to arrive at the best output and price decisions. Not only is this theoretically true but it derives empirical support from the instances in which oligopolistic firms, presumably enjoying the added returns of oligopolistic behavior, find it worthwhile nonetheless to engage in illegal explicit collusion. Costs are likely to be higher because consciously parallel behavior will be less

The argument in both the oligopoly and the cartel situation against the likelihood of producers using r.p.m. to stabilize non-competitive situations has two aspects. First, r.p.m. would not satisfactorily eliminate competition among retailers for consumer patronage or among manufacturers for favorable treatment by retailers. R.p.m.'s value to manufacturers lies precisely in the fact that retailers who may not compete on price are induced or forced to compete by offering information, promotional services, and the like. This automatic effect gives r.p.m. its value as an efficiency-creating device and tends to destroy its value as a competition-suppressing technique. Since competition at the retailer level would continue, any resultant instability at the manufacturing level would also persist. A manufacturer tempted to shade prices to help retailers meet price competition would be tempted under r.p.m. to shade prices to induce retailers to engage in promotional and other competition on his behalf. In the second place, the use of r.p.m. solely to eliminate competition would be attended by serious costs likely to swamp any slight gains in stabilization. To cite only two instances, some retailers would be getting more-than-competitive returns at the manufacturers' expense and adjustments to changing market conditions would be delayed and complicated by the necessity of arriving at a new, difficult-to-predict, oligopoly solution.

These arguments closely parallel those made in my prior article about the use of r.p.m. to stabilize a manufacturers' cartel[10] and I will not lengthen this reply by repeating them in full. The modifications necessary to adopt the arguments to the oligopoly situation suggested by Gould and Yamey seem minor and obvious.

The four counter-examples deployed by Professors Gould and Yamey do not, it seems to me, withstand analysis. I believe, therefore, that they leave intact my thesis that manufacturer-desired r.p.m. does not reduce output and should be lawful.

II.

In the second section of their paper, Gould and Yamey advance four arguments to support the propriety of judicial supervision of r.p.m. even where it is practiced with the purpose of creating efficiency. The four arguments are:

---

likely to adjust r.p.m. as rapidly or as accurately to changing demand and cost conditions as could be accomplished by actual collusion.

10. *Id.* at 411–15.

(1) Courts may properly supervise and correct the decision of a manufacturer to use r.p.m. because r.p.m. involves manufacturer supervision of reseller business decisions; (2) though r.p.m. may create efficiency when first instituted, it may be difficult for the manufacturer to get rid of when changing conditions make it inefficient; (3) if all manufacturers in an industry use r.p.m., none of them is experimenting with other modes of distribution; and (4) manufacturers who institute r.p.m. are usually, perhaps even always, wrong about their own best interests. I will discuss these points in order.

(1) Gould and Yamey appear to have misconceived my argument on this point. My thesis is that the decision to use r.p.m. in order to attain distributive efficiency is like any other management decision related to the most efficient method of production or sales. Courts are hardly equipped to act as super managements and ratify or reject normal business judgments. Such a notion, generally applied, would turn the antitrust laws into a mandate for the judiciary, of all inconceivable institutions, to manage the now private sector of the economy. Antitrust can only perform a useful function if the courts confine themselves to striking down such practices as appear likely to restrict output. When analysis suggests the practice has no such potentiality the courts should not attempt to instruct business managements on how to maximize net revenues.

Judicial supervision of managements' normal business judgment is in no way the same phenomenon as manufacturer control of resellers' prices. When the manufacturer finds r.p.m. profitable, r.p.m. is in the best interest of the consumers. The fact that some resellers would prefer to be free of r.p.m. in such cases is of no significance since each reseller's interest is parochial. The manufacturer's more general judgment should prevail. This argument rests upon the idea of consumer sovereignty. It does not depend in any way upon a notion that the resellers may be said to have "agreed" to r.p.m. Not only should non-signer clauses be lawful but the manufacturer should be permitted to control resale prices by notice without the purely symbolic act of signing an r.p.m. agreement with at least one reseller.

(2) This objection rests on two assumptions: that manufacturers will probably make long-range mistakes about the efficiency of r.p.m.; and that when altered conditions make r.p.m. inefficient manufacturers will be unable to abandon it. Both of these assumptions seem invalid. It is, it seems to me, completely implausible that we know better than business management how they may best serve their own interests. Should a particular r.p.m. system become inefficient due to unforeseen changes, moreover, it will be to the interest of resellers as a group, as well as the manufacturer, to discon-

tinue the practice. I fail to see the impossibility of getting rid of r.p.m. under such circumstances.

There may, of course, be some reseller resistance to the abolition of r.p.m. on a product, but so may there be to the institution of r.p.m. I see no reason why the resistance is likely to be more difficult to overcome in one case than in the other. The fact that incorrect decisions cannot be reversed painlessly and costlessly is no argument against leaving businessmen power to make decisions. I would suppose that an unwise investment in plant facilities would often prove more costly to reverse than an unwise decision to try r.p.m.

(3) Where all manufacturers in an industry use r.p.m. it is by definition true that none of them is currently experimenting with non-r.p.m. What that proves I do not know. It might also be remarked that where the law forbids r.p.m. none of the manufacturers is experimenting with r.p.m. At least in the former situation any manufacturer is free to try another policy any time he thinks the experiment worthwhile, and he may do so in selected areas or on a distinct brand without committing himself generally. That seems infinitely preferable to a rule, argued in terms of discovery of information, which prohibits the discovery of information.

(4) I confess I do not know what to make of the suggestion that manufacturers are persistently wrong in using r.p.m. Gould and Yamey cite no evidence of such invariable error. If that were true, one should expect only gratitude and relief from businessmen who have had their r.p.m. systems dismantled by law. Instead, one often finds such businessmen curiously eager to repeat their "mistake" and striving to use other legal devices, such as agency and consignment sales, to achieve control of their outlets' prices. If r.p.m. really is always a mistake, we can account for this repetitive self-destructive behavior only by postulating for businessmen some instinctual force that draws them to r.p.m. the way lemmings are drawn into the sea.

III.

Professors Gould and Yamey suggest that the criterion I use for judging the desirability of r.p.m.—its effect upon output—is too simple. I argued in the first installment of my article that output effect is a valid criterion because it is related to consumer welfare and provides rules suitable for principled administration by courts.[11] Gould and Yamey note that I have grounded this test in welfare economics but object that I did not "make sufficiently clear . . . the

---

11. See 74 *Yale L. J.* 775, 829–47.

restrictive nature of the assumptions underpinning this welfare proposition." They note that the "necessary qualifications" to the output-effect criterion are "numerous and their discussion highly technical and somewhat esoteric." Though the authors do not indicate what the "necessary qualifications" are or how they would modify my policy conclusions, I take them to be suggesting that welfare economics would require expansion of my criterion to account for income effects and second best theory. For several reasons, I believe this suggestion should be rejected.

I do not, of course, claim that effect upon output is the sole test supported by welfare economics. I do contend that it is the only appropriate criterion for antitrust law. I will attempt very briefly to show why that is true.

Every action or inaction in the business world has income effects, that is, alters or confirms the existing distribution of income. Antitrust law could not deal with income effects without undertaking to judge every business action (plant location, machinery purchase, wage determination, inventory control, and so on). Several insuperable objections to an income-effect criterion in antitrust are at once apparent: the present structure of antitrust does not contemplate judicial regulation of all aspects of business activity; detailed judicial regulation of this variety would be disastrous for the economy; courts do not have the equipment to trace income effects; and a court is not the appropriate organ of government to make the intensely political determination of which income effects are desirable and which undesirable, that is, how income should be redistributed in our society. The political choice between potential income recipients is obviously a task for the legislature, and that body has tools, such as taxes and subsidies, which are far more direct, comprehensive, and effective in dealing with income distribution than antitrust can ever be.

The theory of second best indicates that some restrictions of output may be beneficial because they narrow relative divergences between price and marginal cost. The difficulty is that we are unable to apply this insight to specific cases. Take a manufacturer's use of r.p.m. as an illustration. In order to apply second best theory, the court would first have to measure the gap between price and marginal cost. That would be an exceedingly difficult task—probably one that is generally impossible since the measurement of marginal cost with any accuracy is usually impossible. Next, the court would have to inquire whether prohibiting r.p.m. would be likely to widen or narrow the divergence, thus adding utter conjecture to its initially suspect measurement. Third, the court would have to inquire whether there existed divergences between marginal cost and price in all industries making substitutes or complements and in all industries to and from which resources might move if r.p.m. in the case before it were struck down, and whether the divergences in such industries would thereby be increased or lessened. Finally, the court would have to judge whether the new equilibrium, across all affected industries, was likely to be better or worse for society. This, I suggest, is a task courts could not conceivably perform. I do not believe any institution could. To bring second best into antitrust, therefore, would accomplish nothing of value but would make the discovery and trial process so interminable and expensive that antitrust would be largely unenforceable.

I find it rather odd that Professors Gould and Yamey should recommend a rule against all r.p.m. because r.p.m. may restrict output, and, in the same paper, object that my thesis fails to take into account a theory which suggests that such restrictions may be desirable. Perhaps their remarks on welfare economics are simply a digression and not offered as relevant to the issue of r.p.m. If so, I hope I have adequately explained why, despite the qualifications one might wish were feasible, the output-effect criterion is the only criterion related to consumer welfare which is suitable for judicial employment.

Two further points are made by Gould and Yamey: (1) r.p.m. inhibits the freedom of resellers to experiment with new forms of retailing, thereby interfering with innovation and experiment; and (2) r.p.m. restricts the range of consumer choice.

The first point is a curious one, for Gould and Yamey urge the need for innovation and experiment in retailing in support of a rule against r.p.m. which chokes off innovation and experiment.[12] The consideration they raise really supports the rule I propose: making r.p.m. optional for the manufacturer. The manufacturer's interest in distributive efficiency is the same as the consumer's. When he decides whether to use r.p.m., the manufacturer must weigh the gains against the losses, including the loss of reseller experimentation. The courts should accept the manufacturer's judgment on the question as they should whenever a judgment as to comparative efficiencies is all that is involved. Under the rule I propose, moreover, innovation and experimentation by resellers need not be cut off. The manufacturer may, if he wishes, permit reseller experimentation in test markets or on particular products. Under the rule proposed by Gould and Yamey all experimentation involving r.p.m. would be closed off.

The second point raised by Gould and Yamey, the restriction of consumer choice, rests on the peculiar thought that only those consumers who

---

12. This is essentially the same point as the third argument set forth by Gould and Yamey under section II.

prefer a product without r.p.m. are entitled to freedom of choice. If we admit that all consumers are entitled to vote with their dollars, we see that consumer choice will dictate the use or non-use of r.p.m. When r.p.m. is the more profitable course for the manufacturer of product x, we know that consumers as a whole prefer product x with the reseller-provided information and service that is purchased by r.p.m. It is the point about the composition of the product all over again. When a detergent manufacturer adds bleach crystals to his product those consumers who prefer his detergent without bleach have had their choice restricted. But if the change proves profitable to the manufacturer, we may assume that consumers as a whole are better satisfied.[13] A law prohibiting the addition of bleach crystals would not widen the range of consumer choice but would restrict it. The same analysis applies to r.p.m. and the addition of reseller effort to the physical product.[14] The consideration of consumer choice supports the proposal to legalize manufacturer-desired r.p.m.

13. *See* note 4 *supra* and accompanying text.
14. *See* 75 *Yale L. J.* 373, 473.

Ancillary Restraints and the Sherman Act

For 250 years the common law has upheld and enforced agreements not to compete if they were ancillary to valid main transactions. By "ancillary" the common law meant subordinate or collateral to another transaction and necessary to make that transaction effective. The doctrine of ancillary restraints is commonly believed to have application to the Sherman Act but, since neither litigation nor commentary has developed the topic, the area and method of that application are in considerable doubt.

This paper is an attempt to suggest the relationship of the common law doctrine of ancillary restraints and section 1 of the Sherman Act. The adaptation of a concept developed at common law to the Sherman Act is very difficult in some areas. The topic is, moreover, a large one. This paper therefore is a preliminary study confined for the most part to an examination of two types of ancillary restraints

1. The agreement of the seller of a business not to compete with the business sold; and

2. the agreement of the participant in a joint venture not to compete with that venture.

The attempt to apply the doctrine of ancillary restraints to the Sherman Act throws light on the nature of the rule of reason as it operates under section 1 of the Act and also poses difficult questions concerning the proper scope of the category of restraints said to be illegal per se. In general, section 1 of the Sherman Act strikes down a restraint only if it has an adverse effect upon competition or was intended to have such an effect. The likelihood of an adverse effect is often found where the parties or one of them has some appreciable degree of market power. Per se doctrines have arisen with respect to agreements to fix prices and to divide markets because such agree-

From *American Bar Association*, Volume 23 (1959). The author acknowledges the assistance of Howard G. Krane in the preparation of this article.

ments necessarily tend or are intended to restrain competition. The doctrine of ancillarity operates to bring the ancillary market division out of the per se category and under the Act's criteria of effect and intent. Thus, an ancillary agreement to stay out of a market is good unless the parties possess market power or intend by the agreement or the transaction it protects to affect competition in the general market adversely. The ancillary restraint is thus tested in the same manner as all other non-per se restraints. The function of ancillarity, then, is to remove the per se label from restraints otherwise falling within that category.

A study of the origin of the doctrine of ancillary restraints shows that its birth in *Mitchel* v. *Reynolds*[1] was also the birth of the test of reasonableness in the restraint of trade area and hence that the doctrine was the forerunner of the Sherman Act's rule of reason. In fact, even today the rule of reason in the area of horizontal agreements not to compete appears to be nothing more than the doctrine of ancillary restraints. If this is true, such agreements are illegal under the Sherman Act unless they are ancillary to valid main transactions.[2]

In the area of the two types of ancillary restraints to be discussed (the agreement not to compete of the seller of a business and of the participant in a joint venture), the reasoning set forth here suggests that the common law doctrine of ancillary restraints, with the modifications required by the different purposes of the antitrust statute, is today a useful concept for Sherman Act analysis in such diverse situations as corporate acquisitions, the organization of jointly held subsidiaries to engage in foreign and domestic trade, and professional league sports such as baseball and football.

The significance of the concept of ancillarity for modern problems of antitrust is best understood after a review of the concept's origin at common law and an understanding of the function it performed in that system of law.

---

1. P. Wms. 181, 24 E. R. 347 (1711).

2. This formulation and the history of the common law also suggest a possible corollary: agreements outside the class of agreements not to compete are not per se illegal under section 1. Thus, boycotts, not being classified as agreements not to compete, would not be illegal unless shown to affect competition in the general market adversely or designed to do so. In *Union Circulation Co.* v. *Federal Trade Commission*, 241 F. 2d 652, 656–57 (C. A. 2d, 1957), Judge Waterman pointed out that the per se label is applied only to those boycotts which on their face have or are intended to have a deleterious effect upon competition. Other boycotts are judged by the effect they are proved to have on the market. Judge Waterman's gloss, which seems accurate, amounts to saying that boycotts are not illegal per se.

The Common Law Doctrine of Ancillary Restraints

The doctrine of ancillarity was born to define an exception to the common law's per se rule against agreements not to practice a trade. The common law initially held such agreements void. The famous *Dyer's Case*[3] decided in 1415, appears to have proceeded on such a rule in holding void the bond of a dyer not to pursue his calling in a certain town for six months. This rule was grounded in the guild economy then prevailing.[4] If a man agreed not to practice the trade in which he was apprenticed, he might not be able to make a living at any other. The rule thus appears to have had, at least in its inception, nothing to do with a desire to preserve competition, but rather only with a desire to prevent men from bargaining away their livelihoods.

It must have been obvious from the beginning that the flat ban against such restraints of trade covered more than the rationale of the rule required. The rule might prevent desirable transfers of property. The most valuable asset of a business might be the good will of the public toward its owner. Should he wish to sell the business the owner could not get a price reflecting the asset of good will or the true going concern value of his business unless he could promise the purchaser not to return to compete with the business sold.[5] Such promises not to practice a trade were obviously outside the rationale of the rule against restraints since they did not raise the danger of a man losing his livelihood but permitted him to sell the business he had developed at its true value. The courts began to uphold such restraints[6] but it was three centuries after the *Dyer's Case* before the exception was rationalized in a case involving a lease rather than a sale of a business.

---

3. Year Book, 2 *Hen. V*, vol 5, pl. 26 (1415).

4. Letwin, "The English Common Law Concerning Monopolies," *U. of Chi. L. Rev.* No. 21 (1954), 355, 374–75. Parker, C. J., in *Mitchel* v. *Reynolds* (1711), 1. P. Wms. 181, 24 E. R. 347, 350, stated that a major objection to covenants not to compete had been "the mischief which may arise from them, 1st, to the party, by the loss of his livelihood, and the subsistence of his family; 2dly, to the publick, by depriving it of an useful member." Judge Taft, in *United States V. Addyston Pipe & Steel Co.*, 85 Fed. 271, 280 (C. A. 6th, 1908) notes that the "changed conditions under which men have ceased to be so entirely dependent for a livelihood on pursuing one trade, have rendered" these two considerations less important than in previous centuries. For a collection of materials on the guild system and its effect on this area of the law, consult Handler, *Cases and Materials on Trade Regulation* 49–59, 102 at n. 1 (1937). See also *Hall Mfg. Co.* v. *Western Steel & Iron Works*, 227 Fed. 588, 591–92 (C. A. 7th, 1915).

5. 6 Corbin on Contracts, §1385, 485 (1951).

6. *Broad* v. *Jollyfe*, 79 E. R. 509 (1620); Anon. 82 E. R. 419 (1641); *Prugnell* v. *Gosse*, 82 E. R. 919 (1648).

In 1711 in *Mitchel* v. *Reynolds*[7] the Court of King's Bench upheld an agreement not to practice a trade on the ground that the restraint imposed was reasonable. Defendant had leased to plaintiff for five years a bakehouse in London and had given his bond not to exercise the trade of baker within the parish during the term of the lease. When defendant reentered the trade plaintiff sued upon the bond and the court, over defendant's contention that his promise was void as a restraint of trade, held the agreement good, being limited in time and place, and exactly proportioned to the term of the lease.

The common law adopted the reasoning of *Mitchel* v. *Reynolds* to justify a number of agreements not to compete. The rationale has been applied to the promise of a partner not to compete after he leaves the partnership, to the promise of a purchaser of property not to use it in competition with the seller, to the promise of an employee not to compete with his employer after the termination of the employment contract, and in other situations.[8]

The ancillary agreements not to compete upheld by the common law were primarily of the market division type. This would seem to have been so not because the common law had any hostility toward price fixing—it did not—but because parties intent on protecting the good will of a business sold or the integrity of a partnership will find a promise not to compete within a given territory more appropriate to the end to be accomplished than a promise to maintain prices.[9]

The Relationship of the Common Law and the Sherman Act

The common law doctrine of ancillary restraints was almost 200 years old when the Sherman Act was passed in 1890. The relationship of the Sherman Act to the antecedent common law was a matter of considerable debate but even those who believed that the Act outlawed all restraints of trade, whether reasonable or unreasonable at common law, conceded that ancillary

---

7. 1 P. Wms. 181, 24 E. R. 347 (1711).

8. Some of the categories are set out by Judge Taft in *United States V. Addyston Pipe & Steel Co.*, 85 Fed. 271, 281–82 (C. A. 6th, 1898).

9. A price fix was upheld as ancillary at common law in *Hultsman* v. *Carroll*, 177 Ark. 432, 6 S. W. 2d 551 (1928). There the owner of a gas station sold it and promised not to sell gasoline in the garage he retained at a price equal to or lower than the price charged by the purchaser of the gas station. This appears to have been a method of confining the garage owner to accommodation sales of gasoline to garage customers so that he could not compete with the gas station business he had sold.

agreements not to compete remained lawful. The Supreme Court made that clear in the early *Trans-Missouri*[10] and *Joint Traffic Association*[11] decisions.

Perhaps the most influential opinion in adapting the common law to the Sherman Act, however, was that of Judge Taft in *Addyston Pipe & Steel Co.*[12] Taft's gloss may have distorted the common law, as some claim,[13] but his formulation is in large part the one adopted by the Sherman Act. Taft stated that all nonancillary agreements not to compete were unenforceable at common law. The only valid agreements not to compete, he said, were those ancillary to a main purpose. Taft warned against a rule which would permit courts to uphold nonancillary agreements not to compete since there would be no standard "except the vague and varying opinion of judges as to how much, on principles of political economy, men ought to be allowed to restrain competition."[14] To adopt such a standard, said Judge Taft, was to "set sail on a sea of doubt."[15]

The Sherman Act has largely accepted this branch of the *Addyston* opinion. Market division and price fixing agreements are illegal without more,[16] as Taft said they should be. But the other half of Taft's thesis, the legality of ancillary restraints of trade, has remained undeveloped under the Sherman Act. We have the authority, not only of *Addyston Pipe & Steel*, but of the Supreme Court in *Standard Oil*[17] and *Apex Hosiery*,[18] that the Sherman Act has adopted the common law. Presumably, then, the common law concerning ancillary restraints is applicable to the Sherman Act.

Unfortunately for this neat, mechanistic approach, the concepts and criteria of the common law may not be transferred directly to the Sherman Act. There is more to the Sherman Act than the common law it absorbed. The

---

10. *United States* v. *Trans-Missouri Freight Association*, 166 U.S. 290, 329 (1897).

11. 171 U.S. 505, 568 (1898); see also *Cincinnati, Portsmouth, Big Sandy and Pomeroy Packet Co.* v. *Bay*, 200 U.S. 179, 185 (1906).

12. 85 Fed. 271 (C. A. 6th, 1898).

13. Peppin, "Price Fixing Agreements Under the Sherman Antitrust Law," *Cal. L. Rev.* no. 28 (1940), 297, 677.

14. 85 Fed. 271, 283 (C.A. 6th, 1898).

15. 85 Fed. 271, 284 (C.A. 6th, 1898).

16. *Kiefer-Stewart Co.* v. *Joseph E. Seagram & Sons, Inc.*, 340 U.S. 211 (1951), probably stands for the per se illegality of price fixing regardless of the market position of the participants. For a discussion of the cases on market divisions see *Report of the Attorney General's National Committee to Study the Antitrust Laws*, (1955), 26; and see *United States* v. *Imperial Chemical Industries, Ltd.*, 100 F. Supp. 504, 593 (S.D.N.Y., 1951).

17. *Standard Oil Co. of New Jersey* v. *United States*, 221 U.S. 1, 60 (1911).

18. *Apex Hosiery Co.* v. *Leader*, 310 U.S. 469, 498 (1940). See also *Cline* v. *Prink Dairy Co.*, 274 U.S. 445, 460–61 (1927).

statute, moreover, has transformed the common law concepts. The reason for this is clear. The common law and Sherman Act rules against restraints spring from different social policies and hence are actually quite different rules. The similarity in their wording is misleading.

The common law rule, as previously noted, was apparently originally designed to prevent a man from trading away his livelihood in a society where state and guild restrictions might prevent him from finding comparable employment. The Sherman Act rule is designed to preserve competition as the regulator of the market. It is natural that rules with such different purposes, though cast in the same verbal formula, would often treat the same things differently.[19]

It is not sufficient, therefore, to seek to know the common law, even though the Sherman Act is said to embody it. The statute, through the rule of reason, has evolved its own common law; it has given new content to the old forms. Appeals to the common law for direct authority are therefore fruitless. We must not seek in the common law cases or concepts to be transplanted directly to the Sherman Act. We must seek rather to know the reason and function of the common law rules and then to discover whether those reasons and functions are valid and useful for the purposes of the Sherman Act.

Just as the rule against restraints has undergone a change in its movement from the common law to the Sherman Act, so the doctrine of ancillary restraints must take on a different content under the antitrust statute. Moreover, even at common law the concept of ancillarity eventually lost much of its original distinctness. With the decay of the medieval society that gave rise to the rule against restraints the common law saw less reason to prohibit agreements not to compete. The decline of the countervailing policy led to increasing laxness in the application of the concept of ancillarity until the New York Court of Appeals, for example, could burlesque the rule by finding that a promise by one party not to compete was reasonably ancillary to the payment of money by the other party.[20]

The common law doctrine of ancillary restraints offers the Sherman Act not content but form: a method of preserving socially valuable transactions

---

19. Compare *e.g., Attorney General of Australia* v. *Adelaide S. S. Co. Ltd.*, (1913) A.C. 781, 109 L.T. 258, and *United States* v. *Socony-Vacuum Oil Co.*, 310 U.S. 150 (1940). The *Adelaide S. S. Co.* case involved the Australian antitrust statute but was decided on common law principles and was afterwards treated by the English courts as common law precedent. e.g., *Palmolive Co.* v. *Freedman*, (1928) Ch. 264. The *Adelaide* case approved a cartel agreement on the ground that a restraint reasonable as to the parties was presumptively reasonable as to the public.

20. *Leslie* v. *Lorillard*, 110 N.Y. 519, 18 N.E. 363 (1888).

by defining an exception to an otherwise rigid ban on agreements not to compete, and a formula for confining the exception to the area of its reason for existence.

The Role of the Doctrine of Ancillary Restraints under the Sherman Act

The initial problem in defining the role of the doctrine of ancillary restraints at the Sherman Act is whether the doctrine has any proper place at all. The typical ancillary restraint after all is an agreement to stay out of a defined market and such agreements are usually said to be illegal per se under section 1 of the Sherman Act. Is there anything in the fact that an agreement is ancillary which should lift it out of the per se category?

The reason the ordinary market division or price fix is not justifiable is that its sole purpose is to suppress competition and it therefore has no value for society. This is not true of the non-per se restraints. The promise of a manufacturer to sell exclusively to one distributor, for example, may aid the efficient utilization of resources and organization of business affairs. Such restraints are therefore condemned by the rule of reason only where an effect or intent adverse to competition is perceived.[21]

In choosing whether to assimilate the ancillary agreement not to compete to the area of per se illegality or to the area of restraints judged by their reasonableness the courts must ask whether the ancillary restraint contains the possibility of serving a valuable social purpose. The covenant by the seller of a going business not to compete with that business may do so. It permits the seller to be paid for the good will of his business and thus makes salable properties of a type which might otherwise be impossible to transfer save by descent. The transferability of such properties permits the market to assess them and assign them to the use in which they have greatest value. The ancillary covenant not to compete accomplishes this at little or no cost to society since it must also pass the tests of effect and intent applicable to other restraints of trade. The restraint, moreover, must be no broader than necessary to accomplish the protection required to transfer the asset in question.

Similarly, the agreement of participants in a joint venture not to compete with the venture has desirable characteristics which appear to remove it from the per se category. The salient feature of joint ventures is that they involve a coalescing or merging of part of the capital or resources or abilities

---

21. See *Bascom Launder Corp.* v. *Telecoin Corp.*, 204 F. 2d 331, 335 (C.A. 2d, 1953), *cert. den.* 345 U.S. 994 (1953).

of the participants. They are thus like partial mergers of the participants. Mergers may involve the elimination of competition, but they may in addition contribute to the more efficient utilization of society's resources. The Sherman Act therefore applies a test of reasonableness to mergers, and even the more stringent Clayton Act requires only that the result of a merger be not "substantially to lessen competition" in the market.[22] Those considerations of public benefit which cause us to apply a rule of reason to mergers apply equally to those partial mergers which are called joint ventures. The ancillary agreement not to compete may be necessary in order that each participant may be safe in contributing his best efforts and his resources to the joint enterprise.

The common law requires that the main transaction protected by an ancillary restraint be valid.[23] The joint venture capable of supporting an ancillary covenant not to compete must itself be valid by Sherman Act standards. As Justice Black noted in the *Timken* decision, agreements between legally separate persons to suppress competition may not be justified by labeling the project a "joint venture."[24] Thus, the joint effort of the oil companies in *SoconyVacuum*[25] to stabilize prices by removing oil from the market could not be considered a valid main transaction capable of supporting any ancillary restraints.

In applying the doctrine of ancillarity, courts will sometimes be troubled with the problem of determining whether the agreement is ancillary in the sense that it is subordinate to a valid main transaction or whether it is itself the primary purpose of the parties. In the latter case of course the agreement is illegal. The problem of distinction does not seem acute, however.

---

22. 15 U.S. C.A. §18 (Clayton Act, §7).

23. This is the classic formulation given the common law in *United States* v. *Addyston Pipe & Steel Co.*, 85 Fed, 271, 282–83 (C.A. 6th, 1898). See *Darius Cole Transp. Co.* v. *White Star Line*, 186 Fed. 63 (C.A. 6th, 1911), where the validity of the main transaction was the primary question for the validity of an ancillary restraint under both the common law and the Sherman Act.

24. *Timken Roller Bearing Co.* v. *United States*, 341 U.S. 593, 598 (1951). Justice Black rejected the joint venture contention on the ground that the dominant purpose of the restrictions present was to suppress competition among American, British and French Timken and with others. But regardless of that, he said, "agreements providing for an aggregation of trade restraints such as those existing in this case are illegal under the Act." This may be taken as a statement that market divisions and similar restraints are illegal on their face whether or not ancillary to a valid joint venture, or it may mean only that an "aggregation" of market division and price fixing agreements such as those found in Timken could never be justified. In fact, the restraints found were not of the type which would be entered into by parties whose intent was to protect a joint venture

25. *United States* v. *Socony-Vacuum Oil Co.*, 310 U.S. 150 (1940).

A primary restraint is unlikely to pass as ancillary because to be effective such a restraint would have to involve parties with sufficient market power to affect competition. But the fact of such power would itself condemn the agreement. Other indicia of improper intent would be excessive breadth of the restraint or the making of restrictive agreements not necessary to the main transaction.[26]

Though this paper is limited to consideration of ancillary restraints supporting sales of businesses and joint ventures, it may be well to note that some ancillary restraints known to the common law may find no proper place under the Sherman Act. The common law upheld the agreement of the purchaser of property not to use the property in competition with the business of the seller.[27] It may be doubted that such a covenant serves a purpose which should be respected by the Sherman Act. It does not enable the transfer of any intangible asset. The seller can extract the full value of the property sold in the price charged; there appears no reason to allow him to take part of the price in the form of an agreement to stay out of his market. The Supreme Court in a pre-Sherman Act decision upheld a covenant by the purchasers of a steamship not to use it in waters on which the seller continued to operate a transportation service.[28] This precedent has been followed recently by the Court of Appeals for the Fifth Circuit applying the Sherman Act to a similar covenant by the purchaser of a ship.[29] The decision followed the common law without regard to the different values of the Sherman Act. The case illustrates the danger that insistance upon the literal rules of the common law will discredit the entire doctrine of ancillarity as a tool for Sherman Act analysis. That would be a disservice to the Sherman Act, lessening its capacity to distinguish between cases which differ in their impact upon competition.

We now turn to some concrete applications of the concept of ancillarity under the Sherman Act.

---

26. In *United States* v. *Great Lakes Towing Co.*, 208 Fed. 733, 742 (N.D. Ohio, 1913), for example, restraints were held illegal under the Sherman Act because the covenants obtained in connection with the purchase of a number of towing businesses covered all harbors on four of the Great Lakes while the businesses purchased were local, usually confined to a single harbor.

27. *Hitchcock* v. *Anthony*, 83 Fed. 779 (C.A. 6th, 1897); *Hodge* v. *Sloan*, 107 N.Y. 244, 17 N.E. 335 (1887); *Huntley* v. *Stanchfield*, 168 Wisc. 119, 169 N.W. 276 (1918); *Lampson Lumber Co.* v. *Caporale*, 140 Conn. 679, 102 A. 2d 875 (1954); Restatement, Contracts, §516 (b) (1932).

28. *Oregon Steam Navigation Co.* v. *Winsor*, 87 U.S. 64 (1873).

29. *Tri-Continental Financial Corp.* v. *Tropical Marine Enterprises, Inc.*, 265 F. 2d 619 (C.A. 5th, 1959), affirming 164 F. Supp. 1 (S.D. Fla., J.D., 1958).

Restraints Ancillary to Sales of Businesses

In the sale of business cases both the utility of the doctrine of ancillary restraints and its method of application seem clear. Some examples may aid discussion.

Suppose a chemical company owning a subsidiary engaged in manufacturing industrial solvents saw that another chemical company was about to enter the field and paid a sum of money in return for the second chemical company's agreement not to compete with the subsidiary. On those facts, the agreement is plainly illegal under section 1 of the Sherman Act.

It seems clear, however, that a chemical company wishing to enter the field of industrial solvents could purchase a subsidiary engaged in that business from a petrochemical concern and take from the seller a valid covenant not to compete in industrial solvents. Potential competition may be restrained, but it may be that the acquisition itself ended potential competition in the field of industrial solvents between the two companies. If the acquisition was lawful, the restraint of potential competition seems a thin objection to a covenant which does no more than protect the acquisition.

The common law requires that the main transaction be valid and that the ancillary restraint afford no more protection than that reasonably required to protect the purchaser in the enjoyment of his purchase. The main purpose in the sale of an industrial solvents subsidiary to a chemical company is a corporate acquisition. The common law requirement of a lawful main transaction here would seem to dictate the employment of the standards of section 7 of the Clayton Act. Section 7's criteria would be controlling for this purpose even though the challenge to the agreement not to compete were made under section 1 of the Sherman Act.

The section 7 test will pose little problem in most cases where the acquiring and acquired company are not competitors. It will of course be more of a problem where a chemical company with an industrial solvents business purchases a second industrial solvents concern and takes a covenant from the seller not to compete in that business. Factors familiar in Clayton 7 litigation, such as market percentages and ease of entry into the industry, come into play to determine the lawfulness of the acquisition and hence the validity of the accompanying restraint.

The fact that enforcement of the agreement not to compete is likely to be sought some time after the acquisition means that the court may be called upon to judge the legality of the acquisition when circumstances differ considerably from those existing at the time it was consummated. To take an extreme example, suppose that at the time of a merger each of the companies involved had eight percent of the market but that the resulting firm grew in a few years to occupy 65% of the market, and the only likely new entry into the industry is by the company that originally sold out. Even if the court's assessment of the original merger is not colored by the facts of the later dates[30] and it holds the acquisition lawful, it may nevertheless refuse to enforce the covenant. In these circumstances, the interests of the purchaser may have to give way to the interest of the public in the preservation of a competitive market. Indeed, if the purchaser has expanded the merged firms to a point where an antitrust problem is present, he probably needs little protection against the firm that sold to him.

Even where the underlying acquisition is lawful, however, the restraint itself must still pass the common law tests of reasonableness. The scope of the restraint must give only that protection reasonably required by the main transaction. As *Mitchel* v. *Reynolds*, the case which originated the doctrine, put it: "What does it signify to a tradesman in London, what another does at Newcastle?"[31] This test also applies under the Sherman Act in order that no more competition be eliminated than necessary to permit the sale and purchase of the going concern value of a business.

The permissible breadth of the restraint is measured by the assets to be protected. The main asset of course is good will.[32] Good will is not merely the reputation of the business among the general public. Purchasers of industrial solvents, for example, being knowledgeable consumers, may be highly appreciative of the technical assistance provided by the supplier, and the good will engendered among such purchasers may persist for a considerable period. Situations may also be imagined where one of the most valuable assets of the business sold is its personnel. The buying company may be counting on the retention of those personnel. This asset might support not only a covenant not to reenter the field of the business sold but a covenant not to hire away any of that business's key personnel. There should be no Sherman Act objections to such an agreement unless the two firms involved are so dominant in the market as employers of such personnel that their agreement would preclude competition in the hiring of such employees. Once the asset

---

30. *United States* v. *E. I. duPont de Nemours & Co.*, 353 U.S. 586 (1957), illustrates the tendency to judge the original acquisition by the market facts at the time the case is heard.

31. 24 E.R. 347, 350 (1711).

32. If the purchaser does not continue the business purchased, as where a manufacturer purchases a competitor's plant and closes it down, it would seem that a covenant not to compete should be void, since a non-operating business has no goodwill to protect.

to be protected is identified, the question becomes the reasonableness of the protection promised.

An ancillary restraint has three dimensions: space, time, and product. In many jurisdictions there are no longer any specific limitations upon the breadth of restraints. The dominant rule at common law is that an ancillary restraint may be as inclusive as necessary to protect the main transaction.

The old common law rule that the spatial dimension of a restraint might not encompass an entire sovereignty, often interpreted in America to mean the entire state, has been on the decline since the landmark case of *Nordenfeldt* v. *Maxim Nordenfeldt Guns & Ammunition Co.*[33] was decided in 1894. The House of Lords there upheld a restraint covering the entire world on the ground that the business sold was worldwide.[34] Today some courts measure the proper area of a restraint by the geographical extent of the business at the time it was sold.[35] Others permit the restraint to cover in addition any area into which the business seemed likely to expand at the time it was sold.[36] The latter view may accord with the expectations of the parties as reflected in the purchase price. Such assets as good will, moreover, may exist beyond the precise area in which the business was actually carried on in the past.

The permissible time dimension of a restraint varies greatly from case to case. Restraints of five years and longer are frequently held reasonable in the

---

33. [1894] App. Cas. 535.

34. On the same principle many courts today permit area restraints as broad as the business sold. *Burton, Parsons & Co.* v. *Parsons*, 146 F. Supp. 114 (D.D.C., 1956) (United States); *William T. Wiegand Glass Co.* v. *Wiegand*, 105 N.J. Eq. 434, 148 Atl. 174 (1930) (United States); *National Enameling & Stamping Co.* v. *Haberman*, 120 Fed. 415 (D. Conn., 1903) (United States); *Prame* v. *Ferrell*, 166 Fed. 702 (C.A. 6th, 1909), cert. den, 215 U.S. 605 (United States); *Voices, Inc.* v. *Metal Tone Mfg. Co.*, 119 N.J. Eq. 324, 182 Atl. 880, aff'd 120 N.J. Eq. 618, 187 Atl. 370 (1936) (United States); *Watertown Thermometer Co.* v. *Pool*, 51 Hun. 157, 4 N.Y. Supp. 861 (1889) (United States). There are two exhaustive annotations involving time and area restrictions in restraints ancillary to the sale of a business: Annotation, Enforceability of covenant against competition, ancillary to sale or other transfer of business, practice, or property, as affected by duration of restriction, 45 A. L R. 2d 77 (1956); Annotation, Enforceability of covenant against competition, ancillary to sale or other transfer of business, practice or property, as affected by territorial extent of restriction, 46 A. R. 2d 119 (1956). See also the extensive annotation in *Arthur Murray Dance Studios of Cleveland, Inc.* v. *Witter*, 105 N.E. 2d 685 (Ct. Common Pleas Ohio, 1952). These annotations contain many authorities relevant to this, and subsequent, footnotes.

35. *Davis* v. *A. Booth & Co.*, 131 Fed. 31 (C.A. 6th, 1904), *cert. den.* 195 U.S. 636; *Fisheries Co.* v. *Lennen*, 116 Fed. 217 (D. Conn. 1902), *aff'd* 130 Fed. 533 (C.A. 2d, 1903); *Trenton Potteries Co.* v. *Oliphant*, 58 N.J. Eq, 507, 43 Atl. 723 (1899).

36. *Knapp* v. *S. Jarvis Adams Co.*, 135 Fed. 1008 (C.A. 6th, 1905); *Prame* v. *Ferrell*, 166 Fed. 702 (C.A. 6th, 1909), *cert. den.* 215 U.S. 605; *North Shore Dye House, Inc.* v. *Rosenfield*, 53 R.I. 279, 166 Atl. 346 (1933).

common law cases.[37] Some courts permit the restraint to last as long as the purchaser of the business or his successors operate the business purchased.[38] It is difficult to lay down general rules regarding the permissible time period of an ancillary agreement not to compete. The term permitted will depend upon such factors as the importance of consumer good will in the particular industry and its probable persistence.[39]

The third dimension of a restraint is that of product. Obviously, the seller may agree not to make the same product as that made by the business sold. He should also be permitted to agree not to sell any competitive products, since by doing so he could recapture much of the good will he sold.[40] By analogy to the geographical expansion cases, the seller of the business should be permitted to agree not to compete in products whose manufacture or sale the business sold seems likely to undertake.

Because the criteria of reasonableness are necessarily general and vary in application from case to case, many restraints will be held by the courts to be too broad. The problem then is whether the entire restraint must fall or whether the court may enforce so much of it as is valid. The common law

---

37. *Walker* v. *Lawrence*, 177 Fed. 363 (C.A. 4th, 1910) (6 years); *Hendrick* v. *Perry*, 102 F. Al 802 (C.A. 10th, 1939)(10 years); *Checket-Columbia Co.* v. *Lipman*, 201 Md. 494, 94 A. 2d 433 (1953) (10 years); *Ditus* v. *Beahm*, 123 Colo. 550, 232 P. 2d 184 (1951) (50 years); *Diamond Match Co.* v. *Roeber*, 106 N.Y. 473, 13 N.E. 419 (1887) (99 years); *Thoms* v. *Sutherland*, 52 F. 2d 592 (C.A. 3d, 1931) (100 years); *Heuer* v. *Rubin*, 62 A. 2d 812 (S. Ct., N.J. 1949) (unlimited); *William T. Wiegand Glass Co.* v. *Wiegand*, 105 N.J. Eq. 434, 148 Atl. 174 (1930) (unlimited).

38. *Wawak* v. *Kaiser*, 90 F. 2d 694 (C.A. 7th, 1937); *Tarry* v. *Johnston*, 114 Neb. 496, 208 N.W. 615 (1926); *Styles* v. *Lyon*, 86 Atl. 564, 87 Conn. 23 (1913). Corbin states: "It is not necessary or reasonable for the restraint to continue as long as the business continues; but only as long as the personal business and customer relationships of the seller are still such that his re-entry into the business will draw business from the buyer by reason of their continuance." 6 Corbin, *Contracts*, §1391, 506 (1951).

39. In *Marshall* v. *Irby*, 203 Ark. 795, 158 S.W. 2d 693 (1942), the court refused to enforce a five year covenant between two dentists on the ground that there was more business for dentists in the area involved than there were dentists. In short, goodwill is not especially important where there is more than enough business to go around. Compare *William T. Wiegand Glass Co.* v. *Wiegand*, 105 N.J. Eq. 434, 148 Atl. 174 (1930), where the business sold was a specialty business catering to a select group of customers throughout the United States. Good will being of great importance, the court upheld a covenant covering the entire United States.

40. The common law is thus required to deal with the problem of market definition. Consult *Loftin* v. *Parker*, 42 S. 2d 824 (S. Ct. Ala., 1949) where the gradations in quality of ready-to-wear goods were an issue; consult also *John T. Stanley Co.* v. *Lagomarsino*, 53 F. 2d 112, 113 (S. D. N. Y., 1931), where a seller of fats, grease and bones agreed not to deal in "fats, grease, bones, soaps of any kind, or any commodity kindred or allied to same." The covenant was held valid only as to the products the seller had dealt in.

has also addressed itself to this problem. Let us suppose that one chemical
company sells its industrial solvents business to another. The business sold
was confined to the New England states, had no plans or prospects of geographical expansion, and was unknown outside its market area. The selling
chemical company, however, agreed not to compete in industrial solvents
anywhere in the United States. If that restraint is unreasonably broad, is the
entire restraint void so that the selling chemical company may reenter the
industrial solvents business in New England, even though a restraint covering that area alone would have been valid? At the old common law that
was often the result,[41] and some courts adhere to the rule today.[42] The tendency, however, is to seek a reasonable portion of the total covenant which
is severable and susceptible of separate enforcement.[43] This search for indicia
of severability often involves the courts in highly artificial construction of
contracts. Some courts have abandoned the test of severability and frankly
enforce the restraints so far as necessary to accomplish their object: freedom
for a purchaser of a business, from competition by the seller.[44] This approach
seems the most fair and least artificial. The objection that courts should not
enforce contracts to which the parties have not consented seems specious.
The party seeking to enforce the covenant not to compete would far rather
have the promise enforced in part than not at all. The resisting party can
hardly complain if his promise is cut down to so much as would have been
reasonable in the first instance.

41. *Mitchel* v. *Reynolds*, 1 P. Wms. 181, 24 E. R. 347 (1711); *Althen* v. *Vreeland*, 36 Atl. 479 (N.J.
Eq., 1897); *Alger* v. *Thacker*, 19 Pick. (Mass.) 51 (1833).
42. *Beit* v. *Beit*, 135 Conn. 195, 63 A. 2d 161, 10 A. L. R. 2d 734, (1948), *rearg. den.* 65 A. 2d
171 (1949); *Stevens & Thompson Paper Co.* v. *Brady*, 151 Ad. 92, 110 N.J. Eq. 566 (1932). This is
the rule adopted by the Restatement, *Contracts*, §518 (1932).
43. *Edwards* v. *Mullin*, 220 Cal. 379, 30 P. 2d 997 (1934); *North Shore Dye House, Inc.,* v. *Rosenfield*,
53 R.I. 279, 166 Atl. 346 (1933); *Bennet* v. *Carmichael Produce Co.*, 64 Ind. App. 341, 115 N.E.
793 (1917); *Fleckenstein Bros. Co.* v. *Fleckenstein*, 76 N. J. L. 613, 71 Atl. 265 (1908); *Trenton Potteries Co.* v. *Oliphant*, 53 N.J. Eq. 507, 43 Atl. 423 (1899).
44. *John T. Stanley Co.* v. *Lagomarsino*, 53 F. 2d 112 (S. D. N. Y., 1931); *Hill* v. *Central West Public
Service Co.*, 37 F. 2d 451 (C.A. 5th, 1930); *Ceresia* v. *Mitchell*, 242 S.W. 2d 359 (S. Ct., Ky 1951);
Thomas v. *Parker*, 327 Mass. 339, 98 N.E. 2d 640 (1951); *Yost* v. *Patrick*, 245 Atl. 275, 17 S. 2d 240
(1944); *Metropolitan Ice Co.* v. *Ducas*, 291 Mass. 403, 196 N.E. 856 (1935); *Edgecomb* v. *Edmonston*,
257 Mass. 12, 153 N.E. 99 (1926).

Restraints Ancillary to Joint Ventures

Perhaps the most fruitful area for the application of the common law of ancillary restraints to the Sherman Act is in the analysis of restraints ancillary to joint ventures.[45]

The analysis here is not limited to explicit agreements by the participants not to compete with the joint venture. The very existence of joint ventures of certain types would seem to imply an agreement by the participants not to compete with it. Persons engaged in such ventures cannot compete with each other without destroying the basis for their joint efforts. Certain types of joint undertakings are therefore almost invariably accompanied by an ancillary restraint, express or implied.

It has already been argued that joint ventures are in a real sense mergers—partial, often short-lived, but mergers nonetheless—and it is appropriate therefore to judge them and their ancillary restraints by merger standards. This is a standard which protects the interest of society in competition and yet permits desirable combinations of capital, technologies, and other resources. Here, however, section 7 of the Clayton Act may not be employed automatically. Section 7 does not apply to joint ventures where there is no acquisition of stock or assets. The courts must develop tests of market power for such situations. They are free to evolve a standard from the market power cases under section 1 of the Sherman Act, from section 2 monopoly cases, and from the relevant lessons of Clayton 7 litigation.

Decisions dealing with joint ventures and permissible ancillary restraints are few. One which suggests important problems in the area is *United States v. Bausch & Lomb Optical Co.*[46] There the Soft-Lite Lens Co. distributed unpatented, pink-tinted lenses. Originally Soft-Lite bought the glass abroad and had it ground in the United States. Eventually it turned to Bausch & Lomb, first as a grinder, later as sole manufacturer of the glass. The parties agreed that Bausch & Lomb would manufacture pink-tinted glass only for Soft-Lite and that it would not compete with Soft-Lite in the sale of pink-tinted lenses. The government attacked this agreement as violative of the Sherman Act. Judge Rifkind in the district court thought that the restraint was ancillary and reasonable. He stated:

---

45. As used here the phrase "joint venture" refers to any joint effort or endeavor whether the relationship between the parties is that of partnership, stockholders in a joint subsidiary, sharers of a physical facility, or some other form.

46. 45 F. Supp. 387 (S. D. N. Y., 1942), affirmed as modified 321 U.S. 707 (1944).

> In the case at bar the main purpose of the contract is to provide a source of supply for Soft-Lite. The restraining covenant is for the protection of the purchaser who is spending large sums to develop his good will and enlarge the public patronage of a relatively new article of commerce. The arrangement, though not a partnership in legal form, is functionally a joint enterprise in which one will produce and the other market the commodity.[47]

The opinion did not make entirely clear the factors relevant to the decision. But the court did feel it important to state that Bausch & Lomb had no monopoly in the manufacture of glass for lenses, whether pink or otherwise. The facts also showed that others had entered the pink glass field in competition with Soft-Lite, and that there had been competition as well from other tints and from untinted lenses. Though the opinion is not explicit, Judge Rifkind apparently applied a market position test to the agreement not to compete.

The *Bausch & Lomb* case raises the difficult question of how broad the concepts of joint venture and ancillarity are. The relationship between the parties was also that of buyer and seller under an exclusive dealing contract. To deal with the case as a joint venture is perhaps to say that all exclusive dealing contracts are joint ventures and that the promise of each not to deal with the other is an ancillary restraint. This may be a way of analyzing exclusive dealing contracts but the concepts of joint venture and ancillarity seem in danger of covering so much that they lose their value. On the other hand, it is difficult to draw a distinction between joint ventures and exclusive dealing contracts of the type involved in *Bausch & Lomb*. If Bausch & Lomb and Soft-Lite had formed a subsidiary corporation to make and sell pink-tinted lenses, there would be no doubt that they were engaged in a joint venture. Their actual arrangement was the same thing functionally and it may be proper to call it a joint venture. That analysis would view the agreement of the manufacturer not to sell in competition with his purchaser as a division of markets requiring the justification of ancillarity to escape per se illegality. Perhaps the promise not to sell to competitors of the purchaser could be viewed in the same way. Turning the situation around, however, what of the promise of the purchaser not to purchase from others? In a word, may the

---

47. 45 F. Supp. at page 398. This aspect of the case was affirmed by an equally divided Supreme Court. 321 U.S. 707, 719 (1944). The Supreme Court's opinion says nothing of this issue and so we do not know whether any of the four justices who voted to reverse thought the ancillary covenant illegal of itself, or whether they thought it infected, as the government argued, by the illegal system of restraints and resale price maintenance present in the case.

Standard Stations[48] case be viewed as involving a joint venture with an ancillary covenant? There is no need to explore here all the possibilities of the doctrine of ancillary restraints nor to decide how far it can meaningfully be extended.[49]

It seems best, however, to restrict the use of the concept of ancillarity to those horizontal restraints—agreements to divide markets and to fix prices—which are usually thought of as illegal per se. The concept of ancillarity has little to add to the analysis of vertical restraints.

Aside from resale price fixing, vertical restraints are not illegal per se so that the doctrine of ancillary restraints could not perform the function of creating an exception to a per se rule. Economic analysis, moreover, may indicate that, except for certain special situations, vertical restraints such as exclusive dealing should not be subject to antitrust law at all.[50] The employment of the doctrine of ancillarity in the area therefore directs attention to the wrong question. The suggestion here, then, is that the sole function of the concept of ancillarity under the Sherman Act should be to point out instances when per se illegality should not attach and to confine the exceptions thus made to their proper scope.

The *Bausch & Lomb* case, however, is instructive outside the exclusive dealing situation. It suggests the lawfulness of joining the complementary technologies or resources of two firms and justifies their agreement not to compete even though they are potential competitors. Suppose, for example, that a boat-building company sees that plastic hulls are a distinct improvement in construction. The company, however, has no experience in the field of plastics and would find it difficult, expensive, and time-consuming to acquire the necessary equipment and skill to make its own plastic hulls. At the same time a plastics company, experienced in the processes of molding and extrusion, casting about for new end uses for its products, decides to go into

---

48. *Standard Oil Co. of California* v. *United States*, 337 U.S. 293 (1949).

49. Other difficult problems include whether motion picture clearance systems may properly be viewed as ancillary restraints [*United States* v. *Paramount Pictures, Inc.*, 66 F. Supp. 323, 341 (S. D. N. Y., 1946), *affirmed in part, reversed in part* 334 U.S. 131 (1948)], and whether the members of a securities underwriting syndicate should be said to be engaged in a joint venture which will support an ancillary agreement on prices [*United States* v. *Morgan*, 118 F. Supp. 621, 690 (S. D. N. Y., 1953)]. Perhaps the concepts of joint venture and ancillary restraint are applicable to agreements by members of organized exchanges not to do business outside the exchange or not to develop a market price outside the exchange. *Cf. Board of Trade* v. *United States*, 246 U.S. 231 (1918).

50. Director and Levi, "Trade Regulation (Symposium on Law and the Future)," 51 *Nw. U. L. Rev.* 281, 292–93 (1956).

boat building. The plastics company, however, is deterred by lack of skill and experience in boat design and construction as well as lack of distributive facilities.

The obvious solution is for the boat and plastics companies to pool their facilities and skills. The plastics firm could agree to manufacture for the boat company exclusively, or the two concerns could create a jointly owned subsidiary to produce plastic boats. The teaching of the *Bausch & Lomb* opinion is that either of these arrangements justifies the promise of the boat and plastics companies not to compete. The covenant must be limited, however. If the boat company also makes prefabricated houses, the creation of a joint subsidiary to make plastic boats clearly will not justify an agreement by the plastics company to stay out of the housing industry.

The joint subsidiary may agree to stay out of the business retained by its parents. In the absence of such a covenant, express or implicit, the parents would hardly contribute their know-how and resources. This may be particularly important where one parent is a minority stockholder.

The same problems concerning the proper scope of the restraints arise in connection with joint ventures as were discussed in connection with acquisitions. The geographical area covered may be amended from time to time as the market area of the joint subsidiary expands. The product dimension can be as wide as the range of competitive products, if the parties desire. The restraint can certainly last as long as the joint venture. But can the plastics company agree to stay out of boat building after the joint venture is over? That may be the only way the boat company can protect its know-how from the possibility that the plastics company will pull out and go into competition. On the other hand, it is doubtful whether the protection of know-how furnishes a basis for extended agreements not to compete.[51] Probably a covenant for a limited period after the demise of the joint venture would be valid. A parallel is provided by the enforceable promise of a partner not to compete with the partnership after his withdrawal from it.

The analysis suggested would validate the numerous joint ventures and ancillary restraints, express or implied, being entered by companies which are not competitors but which have complementary resources and technologies. A more serious problem arises when competitors join to undertake activities together.

---

51. Judge Freed's opinion in *United States* v. *Timken Roller Bearing Co.*, 83 F. Supp. 284, 313–14 (N.D. Ohio, E.D., (1949), cast considerable doubt upon know-how as a basis for ancillary restraints: "If lawful restraints and monopolies could be predicated on the ownership of know-how they could last ad infinitum. This court cannot subscribe to such unharnessed privilege."

To take the difficult case, suppose that the boat company, in order to achieve more economical distribution, sets up joint marketing facilities with a competitor. Perhaps the venture will take the form of a common selling agency or subsidiary. Since joint marketing may involve a restraint on prices, the situation may be thought to involve a per se illegality. As already argued, however, joint facilities, though they may result in the elimination of competition between the participants, may lead to the achievement of socially desirable efficiencies in the use of resources. This consideration should lead, as in the case of full mergers, to a rule of reason approach to joint marketing facilities with their inherent restraint against competition from the participants. Thus, in assessing the legality of a common marketing agency between two boat building companies, the court would have to ask the combined market percentages of the two firms and whether any control over market price was created. Where such control is absent, the joint marketing should be lawful and with it the implied or explicit ancillary agreement not to compete.[52]

Before leaving this phase of the topic it should be noted that certain joint undertakings do not require and hence cannot justify ancillary covenants not to compete. Take a case where a waste product from a manufacturing process is available and two competing companies are able to use the waste product in their own operations. Neither of them, however, can afford to build a plant of the size necessary to take full advantage of the waste product available. If the competitors decide to erect a jointly owned plant to utilize the waste product in their own manufacturing, but continue to compete in the marketing of their product, there will be no need for a covenant not to compete. If the competitors entered such an agreement, therefore, it would not be reasonably ancillary to their joint manufacturing venture, and would probably be illegal—certainly unenforceable—regardless of their market position. But this reasoning cuts the other way as well. Since the joint manufacturing facility does not require an ancillary restraint to make it effective, no restraint should be implied from the mere fact of the joint facility's existence. The absence of an implied or inherent restraint should mean that the joint facility raises no problem under section 1 of the Sherman Act regardless of the market size of the participants. Difficulties would arise only if the joint facility gave the participants such a competitive advantage as to invoke the strictures against monopolizing contained in section 2 of the Sherman Act.

The problem of joint ventures and permissible ancillary restraints varies somewhat in the field of foreign trade because of the difference in application

---

52. This does not imply a return to *Appalachian Coals, Inc.* v. *United States*, 288 U.S. 344 (1933). The parties there intended to affect market price and apparently had the power to do so.

of the Sherman Act. Suppose that an American chemical company wants to reach European markets more effectively with industrial solvents. For a variety of reasons, some economic, some political, some social, the American firm decides that those markets can best be reached by forming a joint subsidiary with an English company. Though the safest course would have been for the American company to choose a noncompetitive firm as a partner, let us suppose that the English company is itself a large producer of industrial solvents. Both parents agree that their joint subsidiary shall operate in continental Europe and that neither parent will sell any industrial solvents there.

The covenant of the English firm of course raises no problem under the antitrust laws of the United States. A foreign company can agree with the American concern that it will not sell in Africa, or Europe, or even South America or Canada. That market allocation agreement does not affect the foreign trade of the United States and hence does not fall within the reach of the Sherman Act.

The agreement of the American chemical company not to export solvents to continental Europe in competition with the joint subsidiary does affect the foreign trade of the United States. The agreement therefore requires justification. It is clearly ancillary to a joint venture abroad. In the absence of some further factor, the agreement should be lawful. The American firm could properly have set up a wholly owned subsidiary on the continent of Europe and could thereafter have refrained from selling in the area served by the subsidiary.[53] The fact that the same effect occurs where the subsidiary is jointly held with an English firm should make no difference. Nor should the relative stockholdings of the English and American companies have any bearing upon the problem so long as the joint venture is in good faith and not a mere cover for a market allocation agreement.

The market size of the American and English firms should not affect the problem at all, so long as the English firm remains free to import industrial solvents into the United States. The market size of the English firm would be irrelevant to the American company's promise not to export to continental Europe and would not affect imports to the United States since they would continue. The sole factor possibly affected by the European joint venture of the two companies would be competition in continental Europe.

---

53. *United States* v. *Minnesota Mining & Manufacturing Co.*, 92 F. Supp. 947, 962–63 (D. Mass., 1950). *Timken Roller Bearing Co.* v. *United States*, 341 U.S. 593 (1951), does not appear to hold the contrary despite the concern expressed by Justice Jackson in dissent. Timken did not create a British subsidiary but bought stock in a large British competitor and then joined with that competitor to create a jointly held French subsidiary.

Such competition is of course no concern of the antitrust laws of the United States.

A second restraint almost necessarily involved would be the promise of the European subsidiary not to sell outside its assigned continental European market. Again, there seems no Sherman Act objection. As mentioned, the Sherman Act has no application to the agreement of a foreign company to stay out of countries other than the United States. As to the United States, no trade has been cut off that previously existed. The agreement is necessary, however, to induce the American company to contribute its capital and know how to the joint subsidiary.

It is suggested above that a general agreement by the English and American parents not to compete would not be necessary to their joint venture and so would not be valid. A difficult question may arise in this regard. Suppose that the English parent seems likely to acquire the know how supplied by the joint subsidiary and use it in importing into the United States. Would that consideration justify a covenant by the English parent not to export industrial solvents to the United States?

The answer is uncertain. Perhaps it is impossible to support restraints as necessary to protect know how. But even if know how can support ancillary restraints, the promise of the foreign parent not to export to the United States may appear too remote from the joint venture itself. Moreover, there may be alternative methods of protecting the American company's know how. Perhaps agreements can be taken from the foreign parent and from the subsidiary that the former will not take nor the latter offer know how received from the American concern. A violation might then permit the recovery of damages and even an injunction against imports by the foreign parent.

The decisions in the area of foreign joint ventures and ancillary restraints are few. The approach suggested here does not conflict with the few decisions, such as *Timken*[54] and *ICI*,[55] that we have. The restraints on competition in those cases were found to be primary purposes of the parties and not merely ancillary to lawful joint enterprises. Needless to say, such restraints are not sheltered from the Sherman Act.

---

54. *Timken Roller Bearing Co.* v. *United States*, 341 U.S. 593 (1951).
55. *United States* v. *Imperial Chemical Industries, Ltd.*, 100 F. Supp. 504 (S. D. N. Y., 1951). *See also,* *United States* v. *General Dyestuff Corp.*, 57 F. Supp. 642 (S. D. N. Y., 1944).

League Sports

The doctrine of ancillary restraints may be of assistance in the difficult area of the application of the antitrust laws to professional league sports such as football and baseball. There has been a good deal of confusion in the attempt to apply the Sherman Act to these businesses and the problem appears to pose a severe test for the rule of reason.

A market allocation agreement—the franchise system—lies at the heart of all professional league sports. Typically, these businesses abound with other restraints, such as agreements not to compete for players and to allocate areas for the sale of television and radio rights. In the ordinary business context such restraints are illegal on their face. Many persons feel that major-league baseball and football are not comparable to other business, but they lack a respectable antitrust concept to express the distinction. The Supreme Court avoided the difficulty with the *Toolson*[56] decision. Now Congress is being asked for special legislation to solve the problem. There may be nothing wrong with such legislation, but we should be hesitant to admit that the rule of reason is not capable of analyzing and coping with the difficulties presented by an unusual business situation.

The case of league sport poses a difficult problem for the Sherman Act and the rule of reason because of the choices apparently open to a court called upon to judge, say, the franchise system, the reserve clause, and an allocation of territories for sale of television rights. The judge may take one of three courses. First, he may note that each of these restraints is an agreement not to compete (respectively, in the sale of admissions, purchase of services, and in the sale of television rights) and hold each illegal per se. Second, the judge may decide that league sports are like joint ventures, and that the agreements not to compete are to be treated as restraints ancillary to the joint venture. Third, the judge may examine the effect of each restraint and attempt to judge it by whether he regards that effect as proper.

The third method is one which the Sherman Act has up to now rejected. The law has been loathe to permit a judge to go through an industry deciding how much competition is good and how much may properly be eliminated.[57] It is equivalent to judging the lawfulness of a price fix by the reasonableness of the price arrived at.

An example of the difficulties which arise when a court attempts such a task is provided by the district court's opinion in *United States* v. *National*

---

56. *Toolson* v. *New York Yankees, Inc.*, 346 U.S. 356 (1953).

57. *United States* v. *Trenton Potteries Co.*, 273 U.S. 392, 395–402 (1927).

Football League.[58] The government there challenged certain restrictions on telecasts and broadcasts of professional football games as market allocation agreements illegal under section 1 of the Sherman Act. The judge rejected the concept of ancillarity without explanation. He felt, however, that a league was not like other businesses and that its special needs would justify some lessening of competition by agreement. The only conceptual position left open to him was that market divisions generally are not illegal per se but are subject to justification. This position is almost certainly wrong; certainly it is wrong where the parties to the agreement have market power.

Now adrift conceptually, the court required a standard by which to judge the restraints involved and chose the effect of each restraint on home game attendance. If a restraint on broadcasting or telecasting protected home game attendance, it was reasonable; otherwise, not. The court offered no reason why the need of a league to keep its individual members financially sound should justify the protection of revenue from home game attendance but not from the sale of radio and television rights. The court was engaged, whether it realized it or not, in deciding how much competition was good for the industry. This is the corruption of the rule of reason against which Judge Taft warned in *Addyston Pipe and Steel.*

A judge faced with the restraints of league sports seems to have only the first and second choices mentioned above properly open to him. He may strike down all the restraints as inherently unreasonable. But if he once admits the principle that a league is not like other businesses and that some degree of lessening of competition is inherent in it, then the logic of the rule of reason as it has developed in section 1 cases, the need to avoid the "sea of doubt," may forbid him to decide what degree of competition is appropriate. It is here that the concept of ancillarity may provide a way out of the difficulty which is consistent with the historical development and logic of the rule of reason.

If the analysis of section 1 of the Sherman Act presented here is correct, then the numerous agreements not to compete which form the structure of professional league sports must be ancillary to some valid main purpose or else be held illegal on their face.

Perhaps a realistic approach to the problem is to recognize that the fact of league organization sets certain professional sports apart from other industries. The members of a league cannot compete in the way that members of other industries can. It is neither in the interests of the members of the league nor of the public generally that the more efficient teams should drive

58. *United States* v. *National Football League*, 116 F. Supp. 319 (E.D. Pa., 1953).

out the less efficient. If one team goes out of business, all are endangered. This suggests that the concept of business competition may be irrelevant as applied to the relationships between members of a league. Functionally the league appears to be a joint enterprise for the production of amusement spectacles. Unlike members of other industries, the members of a league have no alternative way of doing business except in the joint enterprise form.

Viewing the league as a joint venture results in making lawful as reasonably ancillary to the joint venture all agreements between the members which do no more than eliminate business competition among themselves.[59] The presence of market power in this situation would not defeat the defense of ancillarity. The members of the National Football League, for example, may be thought to comprise a separate industry. Under the general analysis of this paper the members of an entire industry could never participate in a valid ancillary division of territories. The difference again is in the nature of a league. Once the preservation of business competition between teams is viewed as irrelevant, the concept of market power, which is merely a way of assessing probable effect upon competition, becomes equally beside the point.

The foregoing suggestions, it should be noted, do not rest upon any assertion that league sports could not survive without the agreements not to compete which they have adopted. It is rather a suggestion that when parties are engaged in a lawful activity which necessarily takes the form of a joint enterprise—as league sports do—it may be anomalous to introduce the concept of competition to govern their relationships with each other. In any event, the doctrine of ancillary restraints provides a method of differentiating between the restraints of league sports and those of other businesses which seem consistent with traditional antitrust concepts. It provides conceptual justification for the apparent desire of the courts to avoid application of per se rules to league sports. The concept of ancillarity thereby provides a way of avoiding serious distortions in the rule of reason. Perhaps the law is capable of developing other criteria for judging the restraints in league sports which may be more discriminating than those of joint venture and ancillarity. Such concepts are not now available, however, and the consistency of either a per se approach or the analysis suggested here appears preferable to the vague standards employed in the *National Football League* case.

The foregoing is not intended as a definitive statement of the relationship of the concept of ancillarity and the Sherman Act. This paper attempts only

---

59. A similar rationale may be applicable to the restraints governing the relationships of leagues of equal status and of major and minor leagues.

to suggest that the doctrine of ancillarity restraints may have a valuable role to play under section 1 of the Sherman Act and that its possibilities have too long awaited exploitation. Only two types of ancillary agreements have been discussed here. Other types may also have utility for antitrust analysis. The rationale of the doctrine of ancillarity as well as the vast body of precedent built up at common law since *Mitchel* v. *Reynolds* lie ready for imaginative application to the problems of the Sherman Act.

B. Opinions

The groundwork for the following opinion was laid twenty-seven years ear-lier in the article on ancillary restraints immediately above. In the article and the opinion, I attempted to resurrect the concept of ancillarity dis-cussed by William Howard Taft, then a court of appeals judge, in United States v. Addyston Pipe and Steel Co., 85 Fed. 271 (1898). *The revival of this apparently forgotten dictum was essential to rescue antitrust from a legally incoherent and economically damaging doctrine that had developed over the intervening years.*

Rothery Storage & Van Co., et. al.,
Appellants
v.
Atlas Van Lines, Inc.
No. 84–5845
792 F.2d 210

United States Court of Appeals,
District of Columbia Circuit.
Argued Oct. 16, 1985
Decided June 3, 1986

Before Wald, Ginsburg and Bork, Circuit Judges.

Opinion for the Court filed by Circuit Judge Bork.

Concurring Opinion filed by Circuit Judge Wald.

Bork, Circuit Judge:

Appellants, plaintiffs below, seek review of the district court's decision dismissing their antitrust action against Atlas Van Lines, Inc. ("Atlas"). *See Rothery Storage & Van Co.* v. *Atlas Van Lines, Inc.*, 597 F.Supp. 217 (D.D.C.1984). Appellants are Atlas. For convenience, we will frequently refer to them by the name of the first-named appellant, Rothery Storage & Co. ("Rothery"). Rothery claims that Atlas and several of the carrier agents affiliated with, Atlas adopted a policy constituting a "group boycott" in violation of section 1 of the Sherman Act, 15 U.S.C. ¶ 1 (1982), which prohibits "[e]very contract, combination . . . or conspiracy . . . in restraint of trade." The trial court granted Atlas's motion for summary judgment on several alternative grounds. *See infra* pages 213–14. Because we find that Atlas's policy is designed to make the van line more efficient rather than to decrease the output of its services and raise rates, we affirm.

I.

Atlas operates as a a nationwide common carrier of used household goods under authority granted by the Interstate Commerce Commission. It contracts to provide moving services to individuals and to businesses transferring employees. Like most national moving companies, Atlas exercises its interstate authority by employing independent moving companies throughout the country *as* its agents. These companies execute a standard agency contract with Atlas, agreeing to adhere, when making shipments on Atlas's authority, to such things *as* standard operating procedures, maintenance and painting specifications, and uniform rates. Typically, such an agreement will contain a provision barring an agent affiliated with a particular van line from dealing with any other line. The agency agreement is supplemented by Atlas's bylaws, rules, and regulations governing the agents' interstate operations.

Some of these independent moving companies, the "non-carrier agents," have no interstate authority of their own and can move goods interstate only on Atlas's authority. Until recently, other companies, the "carrier agents," possessed their own interstate authority and could move goods to the extent of that independent authority as principals for their own accounts. Both types of agent may engage in intrastate carriage without Atlas's permission or governance. A carrier agent, however, could act in interstate commerce both as an agent of the van line it serves and as a competitor of that van line. The carrier agents could, and some did, use Atlas equipment, training, and the like for interstate carriage under their own authorities and pay Atlas nothing.

A van line and its agents constitute an enterprise on a scale not easily obtainable by a single carrier. Atlas, which is the sixth largest van line in the nation, provides a network of 490 agents capable of carrying household goods between any two points in the nation. Atlas coordinates and supports the agents' operations. The use of agents spares a van line the necessity of obtaining enormous amounts of capital to perform the same services and, quite possibly, avoids diseconomies of scale, i.e., the inefficiencies of a single management large and complex enough to perform all the functions that are now divided between the van line and its agents. The agents find customers and do the packing, loading, hauling, and storage. Atlas sets the rates, dispatches shipments, chooses routes, arranges backhauls so the agent's truck need not return empty, arranges services at the origin and destination of shipments, collects all revenues and pays the agents, establishes uniform rules for the appearance and quality of equipment, trains salespeople and drivers, purchases and finances equipment for use by the agents, and maintains insurance on all shipments made under Atlas's authority. In addition, Atlas conducts national advertising and promotional forums. With the assistance of agents, it handles customer claims. In short, Atlas, and its agents make up an enterprise or firm integrated by contracts, one which is indistinguishable in economic analysis from a complex partnership.

The ability of the carrier agents to exercise their independent authority traditionally has been governed by "pooling agreements" that dictate the business relationship between a van line and a carrier agent affiliated with it. The van line could, of course, set the rates at which its agents carried goods on its authority. ICC regulations required that carrier agents use the same rates as their van line principal when carrying shipments under independent authority. Because the relationship between—a carrier agent and a van line constitutes an agreement between competitors, Congress provided antitrust immunity for any such relationship governed by a pooling agreement approved by the ICC. *See* 49 U.S.C. §§ 11341–11342 (1982). In 49 U.S.C. 10934(d) (1982), Congress also allowed agents to sit on the boards of their van lines without antitrust liability.

The deregulation of the moving industry, beginning in 1979, produced changes that had a profound impact on the relationship between van lines and their agents. Prior to the regulatory changes, independent moving companies had little ability to obtain their own interstate transportation authority. The ICC's Policy Statement on Motor Carrier Regulation, 44 Fed. Reg. 60, 296 (1979), and the Motor Carrier Act of 1980, Pub.L.No. 96–296, 94 Stat. 793, greatly increased the ability of common carriers to obtain interstate moving authority. In 1981, moreover, the ICC repealed its requirement that carrier agents charge the same rate for agency shipments and shipments carried on their own accounts. *See North American Van Lines, Inc. v. ICC,* 666 F.2d 1087, 1094–96 (7th Cir.1981). Thus, agents could obtain interstate authority and could cut prices to attract business for their own accounts that otherwise might have constituted agency shipments for the van line's account.

This increased potential for the diversion of interstate business to its carrier agents posed two potential problems for Atlas. Each of these problems is a version of what has been called the "free ride." A free ride occurs when one party to an arrangement reaps benefits for which another party pays, though that transfer of wealth is not part of the agreement between them. The free ride can become a serious problem for a partnership or joint venture because the party that provides capital and services without receiving compensation has a strong incentive to provide less, thus rendering the common enterprise less effective. The first problem occurs because, by statute, a van line incurs strict liability for acts of its agents exercising "actual or apparent authority." 49 U.S.C. § 10934(a) (1982). Thus, an increase of shipments made on the agents' independent authority, but using Atlas's equipment, uniforms, and services would create the risk of increased liability for Atlas although Atlas received no revenue from those shipments. Second, because carrier agents could utilize Atlas services and equipment on non-Atlas interstate shipments, the possible increase of such shipments meant that Atlas might make large outlays for which it received no return. We return to the free-ride problem in Part IV of this opinion.

To meet these problems, Atlas could have amended its pooling agreement to redefine the terms on which it allowed its carrier agents to compete with the principal company. Had Atlas chosen this course and obtained ICC approval of its amended pooling agreement, the new agreement would have enjoyed antitrust immunity under 49 U.S.C. §§ 11341–11342 (1982). Instead, on February 11, 1982, Atlas announced that it would exercise its statutory right to cancel its pooling agreement and would terminate the agency contract of any affiliated company that persisted in handling interstate carriage on its own account as well as for Atlas. Under the new policy, any carrier agent already affiliated with Atlas could continue to exercise independent interstate authority only by transferring its independent interstate authority to a separate corporation with a new name. These new entities could not use the facilities or services of Atlas or any of its affiliates.

II.

Because Atlas and its affiliates refuse to deal with any carrier agent that does not comply, several Atlas carrier agents, appellants here, charged that Atlas's new policy constitutes a "group boycott." They filed this action, and after the completion of discovery on the issue of liability, both sides filed cross motions for summary judgment.

The district court granted summary judgment to Atlas on alternative grounds. First, relying on *Copperweld Corp.* v. *Independence Tube Corp.*, 467 U.S. 752, 104 S.Ct. 2731, 2741 n. 15, 81 L.Ed.2d 628 (1984), the court held that, because the challenged policy was promulgated by Atlas's board of directors, the plurality of actors essential to a finding of conspiracy did not exist. *See* 597 F.Supp. at 225. The court rejected Rothery's argument that *Copperweld* did not apply because some of the directors represented carrier agents and, therefore, might have a separate interest in adopting the new policy. *See id.* at 227–29; *see also Greenville Publishing Co.* v. *Daily Reflector, Inc.,* 496 F.2d 391, 399 (4th Cir.1974) (stating that when a corporation's officers have an "independent personal stake in achieving the corporation's illegal objective," it constitutes an exception to the rule that a corporation cannot conspire with its own officers) (citations omitted).

Second, the court rested on 49 U.S.C. § 10934(d)(4)(1982), which provides antitrust immunity for "discussions or agreements between a motor common carrier . . . and its agents . . . related solely to . . . owner- ship of a motor common carrier . . . by an agent or membership on the board of directors of any such motor common carrier by an agent." *See* 597 F.Supp. at 226. Because the "discussions, voting, and agreement" leading up to the challenged policy involves the terms under which Atlas agents themselves can own independent motor common carriers in interstate service, the court found that policy immune from antitrust liability. *See id.* at 227–28.

The court's third reason went to the merits of the antitrust claim. In the absence of "'considerable' and 'unambiguous'" experience with relation- ships between carrier agents and van lines and the impact of deregulation on those relationships, the court declined to treat the Atlas policy as illegal per se. *See* 597 F.Supp. at 231. Shifting to a rule-of-reason analysis, the court held that Atlas acted reasonably in adopting a policy that ended the carrier agents' ability to benefit from the "diversion" of Atlas's "business infrastruc- ture" to shipments made on their own accounts. *See id.* at 233. The court found it significant that Atlas adopted the less restrictive alternative of forc- ing affiliated carrier agents to exercise their independent authority through a separate company, rather than prohibiting any exercise of such authority by carrier agents. *See id.* at 234. The court also noted that any reduction in competition between Atlas and its carrier agents had to be weighed against procompetitive effects the new policy would have on inter-brand competi- tion. *See id.* at 235.

While we do not agree that the challenged arrangement lacks the elements of a horizontal agreement, we uphold the trial judge's conclusion that Atlas's new policy does not offend the antitrust laws. The challenged restraint is ancillary to the economic integration of Atlas and its agents so that the rule of per se illegality does not apply. Neither are the other tests of the rule of reason offended since Atlas's market share is far too small for the restraint to threaten competition or to have been intended to do so. Because the reasonableness of the restraint is so clear, we do not reach the question of whether the challenged arrangement falls within the statutory exemption from antitrust liability contained in 49 U.S.C. § 10934(d) (1982).

III.

Before turning to considerations we think dispositive, we deal with arguments that Atlas and Rothery each consider decisive. Atlas contends that there is no agreement between actual or potential competitors and hence no violation of section 1 of the Sherman Act. Rothery argues that Atlas's policy constitutes a boycott that is per se illegal. We think neither argument well-founded.

A.

[1] Section 1 of the Sherman Act condemns only those restraints of trade achieved by contracts, combinations, or conspiracies. Thus, only agreements between legally separate entities are covered. The argument that the Atlas board of directors was incapable of conspiring for Sherman Act purposes depends on the legal principle, laid down in *Copperweld Corp.* v. *Independence Tube Corp.*, 467 U.S. 725, 104 S.Ct. 2731, 81 L.Ed.2d 628 (1984), that an agreement within a single enterprise is not an agreement contemplated by the Act. That principle is inapplicable here.

When the Atlas policy challenged in this case went into effect, every agent in the system was an actual or potential competitor of Atlas. The carrier agents were actual competitors and the non-carrier agents, because of the ICC's increased willingness to grant interstate moving authority, were potential competitors. Every carrier that stayed in the Atlas network adhered to a policy of ending or lessening its competition with Atlas (by abandoning its interstate authority or transferring that authority to a separate company with a new trade name) or of not entering into full competition with Atlas (by not obtaining interstate authority). Agents required to ship on Atlas's interstate authority must, of course, abide by Atlas's rates. Thus, all of these legally separate corporations agreed to a policy that restricted competition.

The Supreme Court dealt with an analogous arrangement in *National Collegiate Athletic Association* v. *Board of Regents,* 468 U.S. 85, 104 S.Ct. 2948, 82 L.Ed.2d 70 (1984) *("NCAA").* In order to remain members of the NCAA in good standing, universities had to adhere to the NCAA's policy with respect to the televising of football games. The Court said:

> By participating in an association which prevents member institutions from competing against each other on the basis of price or kind of television rights that can be offered to broadcasters, the NCAA member institutions have created a horizontal restraint—an agreement among competitors on the way in which they will compete with one another. *Id.* at 2959 (footnote omitted). That reasoning controls here.

If it is deemed important, it may be noted that the Atlas Board of Directors consisted of actual or potential competitors of Atlas and that is also sufficient to take this case out of the *Copperweld* rule. *See United States v. Sealy Corp.,* 388 U.S. 350, 87 S.Ct. 1847, 18 L.Ed.2d 1238 (1967); *see also Topco Associates, Inc. v. United States,* 405 U.S. 596, 92 S.Ct. 1126, 31 L.Ed.2d 515 (1972). The two non-carrier agents represented on the eleven-person Board when Atlas adopted the policy were capable of competing by acquiring interstate authority. The four carrier agents represented on the Board at the time were actual competitors of Atlas. Three of the remaining members of the board were officers of Atlas. Thus, all but two members of the board represented separate legal entities that competed in interstate commerce. This brings the case within the rule of *Sealy* and *Topco* and shows the existence of a horizontal restraint. That conclusion does not mean, however, that the restraint is illegal.

B.

[2] Since the restraint on competition within the Atlas system involves an agreement not to deal with those who do not comply with Atlas's policy, and so may be characterized as a boycott, or a concerted refusal to deal, Rothery contends that Supreme Court decisions require a holding of per se illegality. It cannot be denied that the Court has often enunciated that broad proposition. *See, e.g., Arizona v. Maricopa County Medical Society,* 457 U.S. 332, 344 n. 15, 102 S.Ct. 2466, 2473 n. 15, 73 L.Ed.2d 48 (1982); *Klor's, Inc. v. Broadway-Hale Stores,* 359 U.S. 207, 212, 79 S.Ct. 705, 709, 3 L.Ed.2d 741 (1959); *Northern Pacific R.R. v. United States,* 356 U.S. 1, 5, 78 S.Ct. 514, 518, 2 L.Ed.2d 545 (1958); *Fashion Originators' Guild of America v. FTC,* 312 U.S. 457, 468, 61 S.Ct 703, 708, 85 L.Ed. 949 (1941). Other cases, such as *Associated Press v. United States,* 326 U.S. 1, 65 S.Ct. 1416, 89 L.Ed. 2013 (1945), seem to indicate that not even the presence of a joint venture or economic integration to which the agreement against competition is ancillary can save a boycott from per se illegality.

Despite the seeming inflexibility of the rule as enunciated by the Court, it has always been clear that boycotts are not, and cannot ever be, per se illegal.

To apply so rigid and simplistic an approach would be to destroy many common and entirely beneficial business arrangements. As one commentator put it, "all agreements to deal on specified terms mean refusal to deal on other terms," and the literal application of per se illegality to any situation involving a concerted refusal to deal would mean in practical effect "that every restraint is illegal." *See* Rahl, *Per Se Rules and Boycotts Under the Sherman Act: Some Reflections and the Klor's Case,* 45 Va.L.Rev. 1165, 1172 (1959). For that reason, "any comprehensible per se rule for [group] boycotts . . . is out of the question." *Id.* at 1173.[1] Lower courts have long agreed with that assessment. *See Phil Tolkan Datsun, Inc.* v. *Greater Milwaukee Datsun Dealers' Advertising Association,* 672 F.2d 1280 (7th Cir.1982) (excluding an auto dealer from membership in an advertising association lacking market power did not constitute a per se violation of section 1 of the Sherman Act); *United States Trotting Association* v. *Chicago Downs Association, Inc.,* 665 F.2d 781 (7th Cir.1981) *(en banc)* (finding that it was not per se unlawful for an organization of rival harness racing operations to prevent free riding on its informational and standard-promulgation services by sanctioning members who allowed their horses to participate in events sponsored by non-affiliates of the organization); *United States* v. *Realty Multi-List,* 629 F.2d 1351 (5th Cir.1980) (refusing to apply the per se rule where membership requirements had served to foreclose plaintiff from participating with rival realtors in a service providing multiple listing of properties); *Smith* v. *Pro Football, Inc.,* 593 F.2d 1173 (D.C.Cir.1978) (eschewing a per se approach in a challenge to the NFL player draft because of a lack of "purpose to exclude competition"); *E.A. McQuade Tours, Inc.* v. *Consolidated Air Tour Manual Committee,* 467 F.2d 178 (5th Cir. 1972) (rejecting per se analysis of the refusal of airlines to list plaintiff air tour operator in air tour manual after plaintiff failed to meet listing criteria), *cert. denied,* 409 U.S. 1109, 93 S.Ct. 912, 34 L.Ed.2d 690 *Association,* 358 F.2d 165

---

1. The truth of this may be easily demonstrated. When a law firm refuses to hire an applicant there is a concerted refusal to deal since the lawyers in the firm are separate legal entities and capable of practicing law independently. It is also a boycott if the Ivy League refuses to admit a new college to membership or the American League refuses to admit a baseball team. It is no less a boycott if any of these groups refuses to deal because the applicant's grades are too low, or its football program has standards unacceptable to the Ivy League, or the would-be baseball franchise is currently a slow-pitch softball team in an industrial league. A ruling that concerted refusals to deal are per se illegal would mean that Atlas not only must retain carrier agents that compete with it but must admit as an agent any trucker who applied regardless of the need for an additional agent, the trucker's financial condition, its safety record, or its ability to serve customers. That is what a per se rule means: no group may impose a standard of any kind as a condition of dealing. That nonsensical requirement would destroy all of the groups concerned or force them into one ownership in order to claim the immunity of the *Copperweld* rule.

(9th Cir.) (upholding the exclusion of a professional golfer with poor scores from tournament participation), *cert. denied,* 385 U.S. 846, 87 S.Ct. 72, 17 L.Ed.2d 76 (1966); *Molinas* v. *National Basketball Association,* 190 F.Supp. 241 (S.D.N.Y.1961) (holding that a league could adopt and enforce a rule prohibiting any of its teams from employing a player suspended for gambling).[2]

The Supreme Court has now made explicit what had always been understood. In *Northwest Wholesale Stationers, Inc.* v. *Pacific Stationery & Printing Co.,—U.S.* 105 S.Ct. 2613, 86 L.Ed.2d 202 (1985), the plaintiff, a stationer, challenged as per se illegal its expulsion from a wholesale purchasing cooperative for violating the group's bylaws. The Court said that "not all concerted refusals to deal should be accorded *per se* treatment." *Id.* at 2621. We analyze *Pacific Stationery* below at somewhat greater length. *See infra* pages 228–29. It is sufficient for present purposes to note that appellants' contention about the per se illegality of all boycotts has now been squarely rejected by the Supreme Court.

IV.

[4] Appellants contend, however, that Atlas's restraints include horizontal price maintenance since the agents must ship on rates established by Atlas. We take this to be a claim that the horizontal elimination of competition within

---

2. *Accord Brenner* v. *World Boxing Council,* 675 F.2d 445, 455 (2d. Cir.) (suspension of a fight promoter from promoting World Boxing Council fights for "failure to comply with his commitments") (applying the rule of reason unless the restraint at issue can serve "no purpose beyond the stifling of competition), *cert. denied,* 459 U.S. 835, 103 S.Ct. 79, 74 L.Ed.2d 76 (1982); *Las Vegas Sun, Inc.* v. *Summa Corp.,* 610 F.2d 614, 619 (9th Cir. 1979) (cancellation of newspaper advertising by those who had received unfavorable coverage by that newspaper) (holding that the rule of reason applies "[w]here an agreement between competitors 'having a primary purpose and direct effect of accomplishing a legitimate business objective is also alleged to have had an incidental and indirect adverse effect upon the business of some competitors'"), *cert. denied,* 447 U.S. 906, 100 S.Ct. 2988, 64 L.Ed.2d 855 (1980). The rationales employed have varied, with some cases relying upon recent Supreme Court precedent concerning the per se rule, *see, e.g., Realty Multi-List,* 629 F.2d at 1367; *see also* Part V–C *infra* at pages 33–41, some relying upon the dicta in *Silver* v. *New York Stock Exchange,* 373 U.S. 341, 348–49, 83 S.Ct. 1246, 1252, 10 L.Ed.2d 389 (1963), to the effect that a group boycott may be justified by reference to the policies of another federal statute "or otherwise," *see, e.g. Brenner,* 675 F.2d at 454, and some relying upon both rationales, *see, e.g., Phil Tolkan Datsun,* 672 F.2d at 1284–84. The proposition that not all concerted refusals to deal are to be treated as per se illegal has found considerable support among commentators as well. *See, e.g.,* L. Sullivan, *Antitrust* § 89, at 253–56 (1977); 2 J. Von Kalinowski, *Antitrust Laws and Trade Regulation* § 6C.02[2], at 6C-25 to 6C-27 & n. 68 (1986); Bauer, "Per Se Illegality of Concerted Refusals to Deal: A Rule Ripe for Reexamination", 79 *Colum. L. Rev.* 685 (1979).

the system is illegal per se or, failing that, is nevertheless unlawful under a rule-of-reason analysis.

Before turning to the case law, we analyze the economic nature and effects of the system Atlas has created. It will be seen to be a system of a very familiar type, one commonly used in many fields of commercial endeavor.

Atlas has required that any moving company doing business as its agent must not conduct independent interstate carrier operations. Thus, a carrier agent, in order to continue as an Atlas agent, must either abandon its independent interstate authority and operate only under Atlas's authority or create a new corporation (a "carrier affiliate") to conduct interstate carriage separate from its operation as an Atlas agent. Atlas's agents may deal only with Atlas or other Atlas agents.

The result of this is an interstate system for the carriage of household goods in which legally separate companies integrate their activities by contract. In this way the participants achieve many of the same benefits or efficiencies that would be available if they were integrated through ownership by Atlas. At the outset of this opinion, *supra* pages 211–12, we set out the functions performed by Atlas and by the agents and stated that the system is a contract integration, one identical, in economic terms, to a partnership formed by agreement. Analysis might begin and end with the observation that Atlas and its agents command between 5.1 and 6% of the relevant market, which is the interstate carriage of used household goods.[3] It is impossible to believe that an agreement to eliminate competition within a group of that size can produce any of the evils of monopoly. *See, e.g.,* 3 J. Von Kalinowski, *Antitrust Laws and Trade Regulation* 8.0431 at 8–34 to 8–34.2 & n. 71 (1986). A monopolist (or those acting together to achieve monopoly results) enhances its revenues by raising the market price. It can do that only if its share of the market is so large that by reducing its output of goods or services the amount offered by the industry is substantially reduced so that the price is bid up. If a group of Atlas's size reduced its output of services, there would be no effect upon market price because firms making up the other 94% of the market would simply take over the abandoned business. The only effect would be a loss of revenues to Atlas. Indeed, so impotent to raise prices is

---

3. The interstate household goods industry consists of 1100 to 1300 interstate carriers, of which the 15 largest constitute 70% of the market. These carriers employ roughly 8,000 agents. Based on data compiled for 1981, Atlas was the sixth largest interstate carrier, with a 5.86% market share. The market share tapered gradually, from the largest firm's 13.3% share to Atlas's position, after which shares dropped precipitously to 3.19% and 1.99% for the seventh and eighth largest firms. *See* Plaintiff's Statement of Genuine Issues ¶ 69, at 97 ("PSGI"). Thus, the market cannot be said to be heavily concentrated and Atlas is by no means a dominant force in the market.

a firm with a market share of 5 or 6% that any attempt by it to engage in a monopolistic restriction of output would be little short of suicidal.

Appellants argue that Atlas's 6% national market share understates the market power of Atlas and its agents to impose an anticompetitive result because appellants introduced evidence of the existence of distinct product geographic submarkets and because of evidence that the national market "approximates a tight oligopoly." Reply Brief of Appellants at 19–20. Each of these propositions is wrong. With respect to the existence of submarkets, plaintiffs conceded the existence of a nationwide market and did not offer the district court any evidence that created a genuine issue of material fact as to the existence of submarkets. The district judge, therefore, had only the national market before him. Indeed, so clear is the state of the evidence that we would affirm on this basis even if we thought it was not the rationale of the district court's decision. *See Jaffke v. Dunham,* 352 U.S. 280, 281, 77 S.Ct. 307, 308, 1 L.Ed.2d 314 (1957) *(per curiam); United States v. General Motors Corp.,* 518 F.2d 420, 441 (D.C.Cir.1975) (Leventhal, J.); 10 C. Wright, A. Miller & M. Kane, *Federal Practice and Procedure: Civil 2d* § 2716, at 658 (1983).

The criteria for defining markets are well-known. Because the ability of consumers to turn to other suppliers restrains a firm from raising prices above the competitive level, the definition of the "relevant market" rests on a determination of available substitutes. As Professor Sullivan has stated:

> To define a market in product and geographic terms is to say that if prices were appreciably raised or volume appreciably curtailed for the product within a given area, while demand held constant, supply from other sources could not be expected to enter promptly enough and in large enough amounts to restore the old price and volume. L. Sullivan, Antitrust § 12, at 41 (1977); see *United States v. E.I. du Pont de Nemours & Co.,* 351 U.S. 377, 395, 76 S.Ct. 994, 1007, 100 L.Ed. 1264 (1956); *Satellite Television & Associated Resources, Inc.* v. *Continental Cablevision of Virginia, Inc.,* 714 F.2d 351, 356 (5th Cir.1983), *cert. denied,* 465 U.S. 1027, 104 S.Ct. 1285, 79 L.Ed.2d 688 (1984).

The degree to which a similar product will be substituted for the product in question is said to measure the cross-elasticity of demand, while the capability of other production facilities to be converted to produce a substitutable product is referred to as the cross-elasticity of supply. The higher these cross-elasticities, the more likely it is that similar products or the capacity of production facilities now used for other purposes are to be counted in the relevant market.

Brown Shoe Co. v. *United States,* 370 U.S. 294, 82 S.Ct. 1502, 8 L.Ed.2d 510 (1962), introduced into merger law the concept of submarkets within the relevant market. The Supreme Court identified several "practical indicia" that may be used to delineate submarkets, such as "industry or public recognition of the submarket as a separate economic entity, the product's peculiar characteristics and uses, unique production facilities, distinct customers, distinct prices, sensitivity to price changes, and specialized vendors." *Id.* at 325, 82 S.Ct. at 1524. These indicia seem to be evidentiary proxies for direct proof of substitutability. *Brown Shoe* said as much: "Because § 7 of the Clayton Act prohibits any merger which may substantially lessen competition 'in *any* line of commerce' (emphasis supplied), it is necessary to examine the effects of a merger in each such economically significant submarket to determine if there is a reasonable probability that the merger will substantially lessen competition." *Id.* at 325, 82 S.Ct. at 1524.[4] That view of submarket analysis is also mandated by the purpose of the antitrust laws: the promotion of consumer welfare. *See Reiter* v. *Sonotone Corp,* 442 U.S. 330, 343, 99 S.Ct. 2326, 2333, 60 L.Ed.2d 931 (1979). When submarket indicia are viewed as proxies for cross-elasticities they assist in predicting a firm's ability to restrict output and hence to harm consumers.

Under no recognized definition of submarkets did appellants offer evidence sufficient to raise an issue of material fact. Plaintiffs did not offer evidence that prices in alleged submarkets move independently of prices in

---

4. The first group of indicia mentioned in *Brown Shoe* relates to the ability of the consumer to obtain substitutes for a product and, therefore, goes directly to the economic criteria that make one market distinct from another. One factor is "unique production facilities." If a product requires unique production facilities, and the producer raises the price above the competitive level, the ability of other producers to shift resources to make the product would be limited, and the market definition should be likewise limited. "Distinct prices" and "sensitivity to price changes" also relate directly to the economic definition of a market. The first suggests that cross-elasticity of demand is low, and the second that it is high.

The second set of indicia bear less directly upon the economic definition of a market, representing observations about what one ordinarily observes when a market is distinct. The "industry or public recognition of the submarket as a separate economic" unit matters because we assume that economic actors actually have accurate perceptions of economic realities. The "product's peculiar characteristics" refers to the general truth that substitutes in a market often have a strong physical and functional relationship. Both "distinct customers" and "specialized vendors" may indicate unique product attributes, which refers again to the fact that products with distinct physical and functional attributes tend to be priced differently. These factors may be helpful where the other indicia are ambiguous. *See generally* 3 J. Von Kalinowski, *Antitrust Laws and Trade Regulation* § 8.02[2], at 8–27 (1986) (stating that *Brown Shoe* does not provide "a new test" for determining the relevant market, but merely provides "several new factors" in discovering "interchangeability between different products").

surrounding areas or that, if prices were appreciably raised or volume appreciably curtailed in some areas, supply from other sources would not promptly restore the original price and volume. Nor did plaintiffs offer any evidence that any of the *Brown Shoe* "practical indicia" of submarkets are present. Plaintiffs offered instead only assertions that Atlas had high shares of the market in a few cities. Such testimony does not show low cross-elasticities of demand or supply. It does not serve as evidence that these cities were segregable markets in which Atlas could raise prices appreciably without attracting competitors' trucks from adjacent territories. Aside from this, plaintiffs offered only two casual remarks by carrier agents, one stating that its various offices constitute "distinct market area[s]" and the other merely alluding to "geographic and product markets and submarkets." These general comments were not evidence of anything, and, in particular, they were certainly not evidence that the industry recognized some specific submarket as a "separate economic entity."[5] It is clear that these conclusory remarks, which are all plaintiffs offered, would not suffice to create an issue for a jury, and the trial judge would have to direct a verdict for defendant on the question of submarkets. *See* 10 C. Wright, A. Miller, & M. Kane, *supra,* § 2713.1, at 616. The plaintiffs in this case simply did not furnish any evidence "'fairly arguable and of a substantial character,'" *General Motors Corp.*, 518 F.2d at 442, of *Brown Shoe* factors indicating the existence of distinct submarkets.[6]

---

5. Indeed, other statements by plaintiffs demonstrate that there could hardly be such an industry recognition since plaintiffs as a group had no common recognition of submarkets. Thus, in support of its claim of a nationwide market, the defendant cited, among other things, the deposition of the owner of one of the plaintiff carrier agents. *See* Defendant's Statement of Material Facts as to Which There Is No Genuine Dispute ¶ 69, at 60; *see also* Memorandum of Points and Authorities in Support of Defendant's Motion for Summary Judgment at 62. This plaintiff testified that the carrier agent is licensed to operate throughout the United States, that is trucks will go wherever there is a "good shipment coming back," and that shorter hauls are preferred but "it doesn't work out that way." Deposition of "Z" at 34. That plaintiff further stated:

> By geography[,] [a] great deal of our business is generated in the local market-place. My sales market area is the whole world, however.

Id. at 120.

6. Thought we do not rely upon this observation in reaching our decision, it seems apparent why plaintiffs did not offer evidence of real submarkets and why they barely mentioned the point and then in their reply brief only. In an industry in which the supply of the product, space in truck trailers, is among the most mobile factors of production imaginable, and the nature of the business causes these factors of production to be constantly moving throughout the country, it is inconceivable that any showing of submarkets could be made. Any attempt in one city to raise prices above competitive levels would be met by other van lines sending in trucks and trailers at a lower price. This view is supported by a plaintiff's deposition testimony. *See supra* note 5.

After that was before the district court, and all that is before us, therefore, is a nationwide market. Atlas, it is agreed, did 6% of the business in
that market. And the relevance of this figure as a measure of market power
is in no way diminished by appellants' fanciful claims of "tight oligopoly" in
the national market.

Given the fact, shown in note 3, that this industry consists of 1100 to
1300 interstate carriers, employing about 8000 agents, it would seem to be
impossible to entertain any notion of market power. What plaintiffs offered
to support their theory of "tight oligopoly" was a list of van lines and market shares that affirmatively proved their market power contention to be
chimerical. Market concentration, and hence presumed power, is commonly
measured according to the Herfindahl-Hirschman Index ("HHI"). As the
U.S. Department of Justice Merger Guidelines explain, "[t]he HHI is calculated by summing the squares of the individual market shares of all the firms
included in the market. . . . Unlike the traditional four-firm concentration
ratio, the HHI reflects both the distribution of the market shares of the top
four firms and the composition of the market outside the top four firms."
U.S. Department of Justice Merger Guidelines at 13–14 (1984) (footnote
omitted) ("Merger Guidelines").

The Department of Justice divides market concentration into three categories and characterizes a market with an HHI below 1000 as "unconcentrated." Merger Guidelines at 15. When the HHI is between 1000 and
1800, the market is "moderately concentrated," and above 1800, "highly
concentrated." Id. One would suppose that a "tight oligopoly" is a market
that is "highly concentrated." In fact, when the market shares plaintiffs
provided are squared, the van line market has an HHI of approximately
520.[7] It is thus *low* on the range of *unconcentrated* markets. The Guidelines

---

7. The 1981 national market shares for the top fifteen van lines were as follows:

	Share
1. Allied Van Lines, Inc.	13.30%
2. North American Van Lines, Inc.	13.07
3. United Van Lines, Inc.	11.41
4. Aero-Mayflower Transit Co.	8.46
5. Bekins Van Lines, Co.	6.76
6. Atlas Van Lines, Inc.	5.86
7. Global Van Lines, Inc.	3.19
8. Burnham Van Services, Inc.	1.99
9. Wheaton Van Lines, Inc.	1.81
10. American Red Ball Transit	1.18
11. Neptune World Wide Transit	1.06
12. National Van Lines, Inc.	.76

state that "the Department will not challenge mergers falling in this region [below 1000], except in extraordinary circumstances." *Id.* No extraordinary circumstances have been shown, or even suggested, in this case.

We do not mean to suggest that if the HHI were higher and within one of the more concentrated categories, the arrangement would necessarily be illegal. It must be recalled that the Guidelines apply to mergers tested under section 7 of the Clayton Act, a statute aimed at halting "incipient monopolies and trade restraints outside the scope of the Sherman Act," *Brown Shoe,* 370 U.S. at 318 n. 32, 82 S.Ct. at 1520 n. 32, and which therefore applies a much more stringent test than does rule-of-reason analysis under section 1 of the Sherman Act. It must also be recalled that the Guidelines apply to mergers between firms that ordinarily have no internal competition. Here we are dealing with firms that are merely limiting internal competition and are not merging to eliminate competition between firms. Indeed, if every van line in this industry eliminated all internal competition and then the largest two van lines merged, the resulting HHI would be only 868, still well below the top border for "unconcentrated markets."[8] Plaintiffs did not offer evidence that this market approximates a tight oligopoly. They offered evidence that makes

---

13. Pan American Van Lines, Inc.	.56
14. Cartwright Van Lines, Inc.	.52
15. Interstate Van Lines, Inc.	.43

PSGI ¶ 69, at 97. We base our calculation of the HHI on these figures. Although we do not have at our disposal the market share of every firm in the industry, it is only the marginal or "fringe" firms for which we lack data, and the Guidelines explicitly and correctly state that "lack of information about small fringe firms is not critical because such firms do not affect the HHI significantly." Merger Guidelines at 14 n.14.

8. The Supreme Court has shown that interbrand competition, which is intense in the van line industry, can prevent the manifestation of anticompetitive effects from a firm's internal restraints. In *Continental T.V., Inc.* v. *GTE Sylvania Inc.* 433 U.S. 36, 52 n. 19, 97 S.Ct. 2549, 2558 n. 19, 53 L.Ed.2d 568 (1977), the Court stated:

> Interbrand competition is the competition among the manufacturers of the same generic product . . . and is the primary concern of antitrust law. The extreme example of a deficiency of interbrand competition is monopoly, where there is only one manufacturer. In contrast, intrabrand competition is the competition between the distributors—wholesale or retail—of the product of a particular manufacturer.
>
> The degree of intrabrand competition is wholly independent of the level of interbrand competition confronting the manufacturer. Thus, there may be fierce intrabrand competition among the distributors of a product produced by a monopolist and no intrabrand competition among the distributors of a product produced by a firm in a highly competitive industry. But when interbrand competition exists, . . . it provides a significant check on the exploitation of intrabrand market power because of the ability of consumers to substitute a different brand of the same product.

such a characterization merely absurd and which demonstrates the absence of market power in any van line, much less in Atlas, the sixth largest van line.

We might well rest, therefore, upon the absence of market power as demonstrated both by Atlas's 6% national market share and by the structure of the market. If it is clear that Atlas and its agents by eliminating competition among themselves are not attempting to restrict industry output, then their agreement must be designed to make the conduct of their business more effective. No third possibility suggests itself. But we need not rely entirely upon that inference because the record made in the district court demonstrates that the challenged agreement enhances the efficiency of the van line. The chief efficiency, as already noted, is the elimination of the problem of the free ride.

A carrier agent can attract customers because of Atlas's "national image" and can use Atlas's equipment and order forms when undertaking carriage for its own account. Plaintiffs' Statement of Genuine Issues ¶26, at 40 ("PSGI"). The carrier agents "benefit from use of the services of moving and storage firms affiliated with Atlas, for origin or destination work at remote locations, when operating independently of Atlas." *Id.* II 27, at 41. This benefit involves not only the availability of a reliable network of firms providing such services, but also includes the benefit of Atlas's "mediating collection matters" among its affiliates. *Id.* II 27, at 42. To the degree that a carrier agent uses Atlas's reputation, equipment, facilities, and services in conducting business for its own profit, the agent enjoys a free ride at Atlas's expense. The problem is that the van line's incentive to spend for reputation, equipment, facilities, and services declines as it receives less of the benefit from them. That produces a deterioration of the system's efficiency because the things consumers desire are not provided in the amounts they are willing to pay for. In the extreme case, the system as a whole could collapse.

By their own assertions, appellants establish that the carrier agents in the Atlas organization have benefited from Atlas's business infrastructure in carrying shipments made for their own accounts. Rothery suggests free riding does not occur, and that the district court erred in concluding that it did. *See* Brief for Rothery at 29–30. That argument, however, cannot withstand scrutiny, for Rothery has conceded that the carrier agents associated with Atlas do derive significant benefits from Atlas in dealing with customers for their own profit.[9] We find the district court's conclusion that

---

9. Rothery's brief has substantially mischaracterized ¶ V–C of its Statement of Material Undisputed Facts below. Rothery cites this paragraph for the proposition that "[w]hen a carrier agent makes a shipment on its own authority, it uses its own trucks, employees, packing materials, and

free riding existed to be amply supported and by no means clearly erroneous.

A few examples will suffice. Plaintiff-appellants conceded below that
the carrier agents "benefited" from their association with Atlas's "national
image." PSGI 11 26, at 40. We cannot rationally infer that this consumer
identification advantage did not benefit the carrier agents in operating on
their own accounts while using Atlas equipment and personnel trained
by Atlas. Rothery also allowed that, while the carrier agents bore the bulk
of costs associated with their operations, Atlas did make "some small
contributions" to the group advertising programs and "some contributions"
to the painting of trucks on which the Atlas logo appeared. *See* Statement of
Material Undisputed Facts in Support of Plaintiffs' Motion for Partial Summary Judgment as to Liability II V-C, at 15 ("Plaintiffs' Statement of Material Undisputed Facts").

Rothery also credited Atlas with providing a dispatching service, a
clearinghouse service for the settlement of accounts among its affiliates,
assistance in settling claims among affiliates, certain written forms, sales
meetings to provide exposure to national customers, driver and employee
training programs, and the screening of the quality and reliability of affiliated
firms that provided origin and destination services for the carrier agents. *See*
Plaintiffs' Statement of Material Undisputed Facts 11V-D, at 15–17.

Rothery did not assert in its Statement of Material Undisputed Facts,
nor may we infer, that the carrier agents could not avail themselves of
the benefits derived from these services when operating for their own
accounts. Many of these services confer intangible advantages that redound
to the benefit of the carrier agent as a whole, and do not admit of easy segrega-

---

other needed facilities." Brief for Rothery at 29–30. In fact, the paragraph cited by Rothery does
not support this sweeping assertion. It concedes that the carrier agents pay only "the bulk . . . costs
associated with their operations," and it admits that Atlas made contributions covering some of
the costs of operation. Nowhere does the cited paragraph suggest that contributions made by Atlas to the carrier agents benefited only Atlas shipments and not those undertaken for the carrier
agents' own accounts. Indeed, the only part of the cited paragraph that even resembles anything
for which Rothery cites it is a quotation from the Atlas rules stating that Atlas's operations were
to be "conducted primarily with the facilities, drivers, and equipment of the agents of the Company." *See* Statement of Material Undisputed Facts in Support of Plaintiff's Motion for Partial
Summary Judgment as to Liability ¶ V–C, at 15. This amounts to no more than a non-sequitur.
It describes the manner by which shipments on Atlas's interstate authority are to be made, and
in no way precludes the conclusion that Atlas contributes to the carrier agents' business facilities
and that those contributions benefit the carrier agents in carriage on their own authority and
for their own accounts. It goes beyond acceptable advocacy for Rothery to cite ¶ V–C for the
proposition that appears in its brief.

tion as between shipments on Atlas's interstate authority and shipments on the carrier agent's authority. For example, if Atlas provides superior training to the employees of its carrier agents, that training improves the quality of work not only on shipments undertaken for Atlas but also on shipments made on the carrier agent's own interstate authority. And because carrier agents may elect to use their own or Atlas's interstate authority for a given shipment, *see* Plaintiffs' Statement of Material Undisputed Facts 11 I-E, at 3, exposure to national clients at Atlas's sales meetings can provide them with interstate customers for their own, as well as for Atlas's, accounts.

These examples are not exhaustive, but they illustrate the point. Even though entitled to every favorable inference, *see United States* v. *General Motors* Corp., 565 F.2d 754 (D.C.Cir.1977), Rothery, in light of the facts it deemed undisputed below, could not seriously contend that the carrier agents' association with Atlas did not provide them with benefits that aided them in conducting business in competition with Atlas. Thus, because the plaintiff-appellants asserted that the carrier agents paid Atlas only for its clearinghouse service and for the provision of written forms, we agree with the district court's finding that many of the services supplied as part of Atlas's arrangement with the carrier agents' arrangement resulted in Atlas subsidizing its competitors. *See* 597 F.Supp. at 233.

If the carrier agents could persist in competing with Atlas while deriving the advantages of their Atlas affiliation, Atlas might well have found it desirable, or even essential, to decrease or abandon many such services. *See Continental T. V., Inc.* v. *GTE* Sylvania *Inc.,* 433 U.S. 36, 55, 97 S.Ct. 2549, 2560, 53 L.Ed.2d 568 (1977) ("Because of market imperfections such as the so-called 'free rider' effect, [certain] services might not be provided . . . in a purely competitive situation. . . ."). Of that tendency there can be no doubt. When a person or business providing goods or services begins to receive declining revenues, then, other things being equal, that person or firm will provide fewer goods or services. As marginal revenue drops, so does output. Thus, when Atlas's centralized services, equipment, and national image amount to a subsidy of competing carrier agents, this cuts down the marginal revenue derived from the provision of such things so that less will be offered than the market would reward.

On the other side, the firm, receiving a subsidized good or service will take more of it. As cost declines, then, other things being equal, demand increases. Carrier agents, that is, will increase the use of Atlas's services, etc., on interstate carriage for their own accounts, over-consuming that which they can obtain at less than its true cost. In this way, free riding distorts the economic signals within the system so that the van line loses effectiveness in serving consumers. The restraint at issue in this case, therefore, is a classic attempt to counter the perceived menace that free riding poses. By compelling carrier agents to transfer their interstate authority to a separate entity, Atlas can continue providing services at optimal levels, confident that it will be paid for those services.

The Atlas agreements thus produce none of the evils of monopoly but enhance consumer welfare by creating efficiency. There seems no reason in the rationale of the Sherman Act, or in any comprehensible policy, to invalidate such agreements. Nevertheless, at one, intermediate, point in the history of antitrust, Supreme Court decisions seemed to require just that result. It seems clear, however, that the law has returned to the original understanding so that the agreements before us are plainly lawful. Current decisional law is best understood if placed in historical context.

V.

The law concerning contract integrations and the restraints of trade that augment their effectiveness has been a variable growth. At times, courts have thought integrations or partnerships with restraints like Atlas's obviously not only lawful but desirable. At other times, courts have treated the restraints as illegal per se, beyond any possibility of justification. The question is the state of the law today. We begin with the law's earliest analysis of such restraints, then discuss later cases that implicitly repudiated that analysis, and, finally, seek to discover the degree to which the law has now returned to its original formulation.

A.

From the inception of antitrust policy, the Supreme Court has recognized that the elimination of rivalry by the joinder of rivals into a larger economic unit is not, per se, an unlawful restraint of trade. After framing a rule of per se illegality for naked price fixing among competitors in *United States v. Trans-Missouri Freight Association,* 166 U.S. 290, 17 S.Ct. 540, 41 L.Ed. 1007 (1897), the Supreme Court in *United States v. Joint Traffic Association,* 171 U.S. 505, 19 S.Ct. 25, 43 L.Ed. 259 (1898), responded to the objection that condemning every restraint would destroy the most ordinary and indispensable contracts and integrations since they restrained the competition of the parties. The Court majority replied that neither the formation of a corporation or a contract of partnership had ever "been regarded in the nature of a contract in restraint of trade or commerce." 171 U.S. at 567, 19 S.Ct. at 31. Though the verbal formulation of the law has changed, it remains true that the lessening of actual or potential rivalry inherent in the formation of every corporation and every partnership has never been held or said to be illegal per se by the Supreme Court. As Justice Holmes put it in dissent in *Northern Securities Co.* v. *United States,* 193 U.S. 197, 411, 24 S.Ct. 436, 472, 48 L.Ed. 679 (1904) (misconstruing the rule applied by the majority), any such interpretation of the Sherman Act "would make eternal the *bellum omnium contra omnes* and disintegrate society so far as it could into individual atoms." No such construction of the Act is thinkable.

Appellants here do not challenge the formation or existence of the Atlas system. They complain only of the agreement that prevents them from maintaining an independent interstate carrier operation in the same corporation that acts as an agent of Atlas. The law has had more difficulty with agreements of this sort than it has had with the underlying integration or partnership. We begin by examining the Sherman Act's earliest position with respect to such agreements.

In *United States* v. *Addyston Pipe & Steel Co.,* 85 F. 271 (6th Cir.1898), *aff'd,* 175 U.S. 211, 20 S.Ct. 96, 44 L.Ed. 136 (1899), Judge (later Chief Justice) William Howard Taft framed a rule of per se illegality for "naked" price-fixing and market-dividing agreements, i.e., agreements between competitors who cooperated in no other integrated economic activity. But Taft recognized that such a rule would not do where fusions or integrations of economic activity occurred and, further, that agreements eliminating rivalry within such an enterprise were means of enhancing the firm's efficiency. He explained the reasons for the validity of an agreement "by a partner pending the partnership not to do anything to interfere, by competition or otherwise, with the business of the firm":

> [W]hen two men became partners in a business, although their union might reduce competition, this effect was only an incident to the main purpose of a union of their capital, enterprise, and energy to carry on a successful business, and one useful to the community. Restrictions in the articles of partnership upon the business activity of the members, with a view of securing their entire effort in the common enterprise, were, of course, only ancillary to the main end of the union, and were to be encouraged. *United States* v. *Addyston Pipe & Steel Co.,* 85 F. at 280.

To be ancillary, and hence exempt from the per se rule, an agreement eliminating competition must be subordinate and collateral to a separate, legitimate transaction. The ancillary restraint is subordinate and collateral in the sense that it serves to make the main transaction more effective in accomplishing its purpose. Of course, the restraint imposed must be related to the efficiency sought to be achieved. If it is so broad that part of the restraint suppresses competition without creating efficiency, the restraint is, to that extent, not ancillary. Taft added the further obvious qualification that even restraints ancillary in form are illegal if they are part of a general plan to gain monopoly control of a market. 85 F. at 282–83.

If Taft's formulation is the law today, it is obvious that the Atlas agreements are legal, for *Addyston Pipe & Steel's* analysis of ancillary restraints fits this case exactly.[10] The Atlas network involves a union of the parties' enterprise to carry on a useful business, the challenged agreements are ancillary in that they enhance the efficiency of that union by eliminating the problem of the free ride, and, given Atlas's small market share, the agreements cannot be part of a plan to gain monopoly control of the market.

B.

The argument that horizontal eliminations of competition among legally independent persons or companies are automatically illegal, even though the restraint is ancillary to a partnership or a joint venture, rests primarily upon *United States* v. *Topco Associates, Inc.,* 405 U.S. 596, 92 S.Ct. 1126, 31 L.Ed.2d 515 (1972). The business arrangement in *Topco* very closely resembles Atlas's policy.

Topco was a cooperative association of twenty-five small and medium-sized regional supermarket chains operating stores in thirty-three states. Topco functioned as a purchasing agent for its members, ensured quality control on purchased products, developed specifications for certain types of products, and performed other tasks that gave members the efficiencies

---

10. A hypothetical was posed as oral argument which seems instructive. If there were a number of law firms in a given location of a size distribution like that of the van lines in this case, the extraction of a promise by each partnership that its members and associates not compete with the firm could, by no one's estimation, be construed as running afoul of § 1 of the Sherman Act. Indeed it is with respect to the legal profession that the law has properly distinguished between lawful ancillary and unlawful naked restraints. Although literally price fixing among competitors, fee schedules imposed by a law partnership are accepted, even taken for granted. Yet in *Goldfarb* v. *Virginia State Bar*, 421 U.S. 773, 95, S.Ct. 2004, 44 L.Ed.2d 572 (1975), the Supreme Court held that a minimum fee schedule applicable to the entire bar of a state violated § 1 of the Sherman Act. Thus, in its actual operation, the law has recognized the propriety of horizontal restraints ancillary to an efficiency-producing economic integration as distinct from the imposition of such restraints by competitors who have integrated none of their productive endeavors.

usually attainable only by large chains. Topco's stock was owned by its member chains. They were geographically dispersed and, in their various areas, had market shares ranging from 1.5% to 16%, with the average being about 6%.

The legal challenges centered on Topco's private-label program. Topco members had difficulty competing with larger chains and this problem was to some degree attributable to the larger chain's ability to develop their own private labels. The Court's opinion set out some of the efficiencies of private labeling:

> Private-label products differ from other brand-name products in that they are sold at a limited number of easily ascertainable stores. A&P, for example, was a pioneer in developing a series of products that were sold under an A&P label and that were only available in A&P stores. It is obvious that by using private-label products, a chain can achieve significant cost economies in purchasing, transportation, warehousing, promotion, and advertising. These economies may afford the chain opportunities for offering private-label products at lower prices than other brand-name products. This, in turn, provides many advantages of which some of the more important are: a store can offer national-brand products at the same price as other stores, while simultaneously offering a desirable, lower priced alternative; or, if the profit margin is sufficiently high on private brand goods, national-brand products may be sold at reduced price. Other advantages include: enabling a chain to bargain more favorably with national-brand manufacturers by creating a broader supply base of manufacturers, thereby decreasing dependence on a few, large national-brand manufacturers; enabling a chain to create a "price-mix" whereby prices on special items can be lowered to attract customers while profits are maintained on other items; and creation of general goodwill by offering lower priced, higher quality goods. *United States* v. *Topco Associates,* 405 U.S. at 599 n. 3, 92 S.Ct. at 1129 n. 3.

Thus, Topco, like Atlas, was a contractual integration of legally independent businesses designed to achieve efficiencies unavailable to its members separately. Also like Atlas, however, Topco had an ancillary horizontal restraint designed to make the integration more effective. Members could sell Topco-brand products only in designated, and usually exclusive, territories. Member chains were free to expand into each other's territories, and did, but they could not sell the Topco brand in the new territory if another member held the rights there. This restraint had a clear relationship to marketing effectiveness. As Topco said, "private label merchandising is a way of economic life in the food retailing industry, and exclusivity is the essence of a private label program; without exclusivity, a private label would not be private.'" 405 U.S. at 604, 92 S.Ct. at 1132. It noted that every national and large regional chain had its own exclusive private-label products. "'Each such chain relies upon the exclusivity of its own private label line to differentiate its private products from those of its competitors and to attract and retain the repeat business and loyalty of consumers.'" *Id.* at 604–605, 92 S.Ct. at 1132. Smaller chains had to have their own lines to compete with larger chains, which accounted for the Topco program, and needed similar exclusivity for advertising and promotional purposes, which accounted for the market division with respect to the Topco label.

The Supreme Court said, however, "[w]e think that it is clear that the restraint in this case is a horizontal one, and, therefore, a per se violation of § 1 [of the Sherman Act]." 405 U.S. at 608, 92 S.Ct at 1134 The *Topco* opinion also clarified *United States* v. *Sealy Corp.,* 388 U.S. 350, 87 S.Ct. 1847, 18 L.Ed.2d 1238 (1967), which had appeared to hold illegal a very similar set of restraints among mattress manufacturers that wished to market a national brand because both price fixing and market division were involved. *Sealy* was now said to hold that horizontal territorial limitations by themselves were per se unlawful. *See* 405 U.S. at 609, 92 S.Ct. at 1134.

If *Topco* and *Sealy,* rather than *Addyston Pipe & Steel,* state the law of horizontal restraints, the restraints imposed by Atlas would appear to be a per se violation of the Sherman Act. An examination of more recent Supreme Court decisions, however, demonstrates that, to the extent that *Topco* and *Sealy* stand for the proposition that all horizontal restraints are illegal per se, they must be regarded as effectively overruled.

C.

The Supreme Court reformed the law of horizontal restraints in *Broadcast Music, Inc.* v. *Columbia Broadcasting System,* 441 U.S. 1, 99 S.Ct. 1551, 60 L.Ed.2d 1 (1979) ("BMI"), *National Collegiate Athletic Association* v. *Board of Regents,* 468 U.S. 85, 104 S.Ct. 2948, 82 L.Ed.2d 70 (1984) ("NCAA"), and *Northern Wholesale Stationers, Inc.* v. *Pacific Stationery & Printing Co.,*— U.S.—, 105 S.Ct 2613, 86 L.Ed.2d 202 (1985) *("Pacific Stationery")*.

In *BMI*, CBS brought suit to challenge the blanket licenses to perform copyrighted musical compositions issued by BMI and by the American Society of Composers, Authors and Publishers ("ASCAP"). Each blanket license gave the licensee the right to perform any and all of the compositions owned by members and affiliates of the performing rights organization for a stated period of time. Since EMI and ASCAP negotiated the price of their blanket licenses and distributed royalties to the copyright owners, the charge, upheld by the court of appeals, was that the blanket license was a form of price fixing between the copyright owners and so was a horizontal restraint illegal per se under the Sherman Act.

The Supreme Court rejected a "literal approach" to price-fixing because that approach, by itself, does not establish whether a particular practice is of a type that is plainly anticompetitive and very likely without redeeming virtue.

> Literalness is overly simplistic and often overbroad. When two partners set the price of their goods or services they are literally "price fixing," but they are not *per se* in violation of the Sherman Act. See *United States* v. *Addyston Pipe & Steel Co.,* 85 F. 271, 280 (CA6 1898), affd 175 U.S. 211 [20 S.Ct. 96,44 LE&136] (1899).

BMI, 441 U.S. at 9, 99 S.Ct. at 1557. That observation is significant for it shows that the *BMI* Court recognized that partnerships, one form of integration by contract, involve horizontal restraints that are not per se illegal. It also demonstrates, contrary to appellants' claims here, that "price fixing" within a contract integration does not necessarily violate the antitrust law. But the Court's analysis of whether the per se label was appropriate in *BMI* has even more significance for the present case.

The Court began by noting the existence of consent decrees the government had worked out with ASCAP and BMI, said the decrees, though they did not immunize the blanket license from third parties' suits, did indicate that "the challenged practice may have redeeming competitive virtues," so that the decrees could not be ignored completely in analyzing the practice of blanket licensing. *See* 441 U.S. at 13, 99 S.Ct. at 1559. Moreover, Congress, albeit in other performances contexts, had created compulsory blanket licenses, reflecting an opinion that blanket licenses "are economically beneficial in at least some circumstances." *Id* at 16, 99 S.Ct. at 1560.

These observations have their analogues in the present case. That the challenged practice of agent exclusivity "may have redeeming competitive virtues" is shown by the fact that all van lines use the practice, *see* 597 F.Supp. at 222, and that the Interstate Commerce Commission routinely approves the practice, without even requiring a hearing. *See Three Way Corp.* v. *United States,* 792 F.2d 232 (D.C.Cir. 1986). The constraints the consent decrees placed on

ASCAP, *BMI,* 441 U.S. at 24, 99 S.Ct. at 1564, which has a great majority of the most desired music played in the United States, are analogous to the restraints the free market places on Atlas, which does less than 6% of the business in its market. Moreover, just as Congress recognized the utility of the blanket license, so Congress recognized the utility of restraints of the sort Atlas imposes. That is shown by the congressional provision of antitrust immunity for ICC-approved pooling agreements containing such restrictions and is further evidenced by the Senate Committee on Commerce, Science, and Transportation statements concerning restrictions imposed outside a pooling agreement:

> During the course of its deliberations, *the Committee considered* a proposal to include within the immunity section [49 U.S.C. § 10934(d)] *language that would grant immunity to agreements concerning exclusive agency representation, or the fiduciary duty of loyalty of an agent not to compete with the principal concerning the subject matter of the agency.* The Committee determined that *this type of relationship is not a violation of the antitrust laws and is standard agency law* as expressed in Section 393 of the Restatement of the Law of Agencies section. The Committee felt that inclusion of such language could imply that such relationships are a violation of the antitrust laws in the absence of immunity. Thus, the Committee determined not to include such language in the bill. S.Rep. No. 497, 96th Cong., 1st Seas. 8 (1979) (emphasis added).

Though, like the Court in *BMI,* we are not bound by Congress's opinion, it does suggest that agency exclusivity is "economically beneficial in at least some circumstances."

These parallels between *BMI* and Atlas's practice are specific to the two cases. They may be enough to take this particular practice out of the category of per se illegality. But there is in BMI reasoning of more general application which indicates that *Topco* does not state the modern rule as to horizontal restraints. There is, first, the Court's favorable citation of *Addyston Pipe & Steel's* example of partners who eliminate price competition between themselves. If *Topco* meant, as it seemed to, that the existence of a joint venture could not justify an agreement eliminating competition between the joint venturers, the *BMI* Court must be read as overruling *Topco* to that extent.

The opinion pointed out that the practices of ASCAP and BMI were necessary to secure for copyright owners the right to control and profit from the public performance of their musical compositions. The Court said, "we would not expect that any market arrangements reasonably necessary to effectuate the rights that are granted would be deemed a per se violation of the Sherman Act." *BMI*, 441 U.S. at 19, 99 S.Ct. at 1562. In the present case, there is authority to conduct interstate carriage granted by the ICC. Atlas holds that authority but would have a difficult time using it but for its arrangements with its agents. Atlas is not in a position to conduct all of the carriage involved itself. The restraints it imposes are reasonably necessary to the business it is authorized to conduct. One may quibble about whether the ASCAP blanket license is more necessary to the conduct of that business than the agent exclusivity arrangement is to the conduct of Atlas's business. We do not believe, however, that, in choosing the words it did, the Supreme Court intended that lower courts should calibrate degrees of reasonable necessity. That would make the lawfulness of conduct turn upon judgments of degrees of efficiency. There is no reason in logic why the question of degree should be important.

That conclusion is buttressed by the Court's next observation, that

> inquiry must focus on whether the effect and, here because it tends to show effect, . . . the purpose of the practice are to threaten the proper operation of our predominantly free-market economy—that is, *whether the practice facially appears to be one that would* always or almost always *tend to restrict competition and decrease output . . . or instead one designed to "increase economic efficiency* and render markets more, rather than less, competitive." *BMI,* 441 U.S. at 19–20, 99 S.Ct. at 1562 (emphasis added) (citations omitted).

This inquiry implements the Court's designation of consumer welfare as the policy goal of the Sherman Act. *Reiter* v. *Sonotone* Corp., 442 U.S. 330, 343, 99 S.Ct. 2326, 2333, 60 L.Ed.2d 931 (1979). The Court concluded that the blanket license, though it involved price fixing in a literal sense, was not per se unlawful and remanded the case for further rule-of-reason analysis.

The Supreme Court's *NCAA* decision confirms the analytical approach adopted in *BMI*. The NCAA, as part of its regulation of intercollegiate athletics, adopted a plan for the televising of member institutions' football games. The plan limited the number of intercollegiate contests that could be televised and the number of times any one college could televise. No college could sell television rights independently. NCAA negotiated with two networks and arranged a specified price for categories of games. Colleges dissatisfied with the plan's limitations on their ability to sell television rights brought suit, challenging the restraints under section 1 of the Sherman Act. The Supreme Court ruled that section 1 was violated but, significantly for the present case, refused to apply a per se rule.

In language we have already quoted, *supra* page 215, the Court held that the NCAA plan created a horizontal restraint on price competition, 104 S.Ct. at 2959, but nevertheless explicitly refused to apply the per se rule, *id.* at 2960. It did so on the ground that horizontal restraints were necessary if the product was to be available. *Id.* at 2961. Moreover, the Court cited *Continental T.V., Inc.* v. *GTE Sylvania Inc.*, 433 U.S. 36, 51–57, 97 S.Ct. 2549, 2558–61, 53 L.Ed.2d 568 (1977), for the proposition that "a restraint in a limited aspect of a market may actually enhance marketwide competition." 104 S.Ct. at 2961–62. *Sylvania* held a rule of per se illegality inappropriate to a manufacturer's division of its dealers' territories. The Court reasoned that the restraint addressed the problem of the free ride, *see* 433 U.S. at 55, 97 S.Ct. at 2560—if dealers could locate in each other's territories, those who spent on advertising and promotion might not be able to recover their investment. Some dealers, with no advertising and promotion costs, could charge lower prices and capture the customers created by others' expenditures. By applying *GTE Sylvania* in a horizontal case as "requir[ing] consideration of the NCAA's justifications for the restraints, 104 S.Ct. at 2962, the Supreme Court made it clear that elimination of the free ride *is* an efficiency justification available to horizontal restraints that are ancillary to a contract integration. Following *BMI,* the Court reserved the per se rule for practices that, on their face, appear to be of the type that "'would always or almost always tend to restrict competition and decrease output.'" *Id.* at 2960 (citing *BMI,* 441 U.S. at 19–20, 99 S.Ct. at 1562). When per se treatment is inappropriate, the court must consider the justifications advanced for the restraint. 104 S.Ct at 2962. After noting that consumer welfare is the goal of the Sherman Act, the Court said:

> A restraint that has the effect of reducing the importance of consumer preference in setting price and output is not consistent with this fundamental goal of antitrust law. Restrictions on price and output are the paradigmatic examples of restraints of trade that the Sherman Act was intended to prohibit. *Id.* at 2964 (footnote omitted).

Upon considering the justifications advanced by the NCAA, the Court concluded that the restraint did not increase efficiency but decreased output and so violated section 1 of the Sherman Act.

Pacific Stationery applies to boycotts the general formula stated in *BMI* and *NCAA*—that the per se rule is confined to practices of the type that almost always decrease output rather than increasing efficiency—and so confirms, if confirmation were needed, that the formula applies to all horizontal restraints. *Pacific Stationery, as* already noted, involved the expulsion of a stationer from a wholesale purchasing cooperative for violation of the bylaws. The Court noted the efficiencies attainable through such cooperative ventures and said that a joint venture "must establish and enforce reasonable rules in order to function effectively." 105 S.Ct. at 2620. This is a recognition that ancillary restraints are essential to the efficiency of a contract integration. An anticompetitive effect is to be presumed only if the plaintiff makes a "threshold showing" that the group "possesses market power or exclusive access to an element essential to effective competition." *Id.* This statement of the law of ancillary restraints is so close to that of *Addyston Pipe & Steel as* to be virtually indistinguishable. *BMI, NCAA,* and *Pacific Stationery* dictate the result in this case. All horizontal restraints are alike in that they eliminate some degree of rivalry between persons or firms who are actual or potential competitors. This similarity means that the rules applicable to all horizontal restraints should be the same. At one time, as we have seen, the Supreme Court stated in *Topco* and *Sealy* that the rule for all horizontal restraints was one of per se illegality. The difficulty was that such a rule could not be enforced consistently because it would have meant the outlawing of very normal agreements (such as that of law partners not to practice law outside the firm) that obviously contributed to economic efficiency. The alternative formulation was that of Judge Taft in *Addyston Pipe & Steel:* a naked horizontal restraint, one that does not accompany a contract integration, can have no purpose other than restricting output and raising prices, and so is illegal per se; an ancillary horizontal restraint, one that is part of an integration of the economic activities of the parties and appears capable of enhancing the group's efficiency, is to be judged according to its purpose and effect. In *BMI, NCAA,* and *Pacific Stationery,* the Supreme Court returned the law to the formulation of *Addyston Pipe & Steel* and thus effectively overruled *Topco* and *Sealy* as to the per se illegality of all horizontal restraints.

The application of these principles to Atlas's restraints is obvious because, as we have seen, *supra* pages 211–12, 221–23, these restraints are ancillary to the contract integration or joint venture that constitutes the Atlas van line. The restraints preserve the efficiencies of the nationwide van line by eliminating the problem of the free ride. There is, on the other hand, no possibility that the restraints can suppress market competition and so decrease output. Atlas has 6% or less of the relevant market, far too little to make even conceivable an adverse effect upon output. If Atlas should reduce its output, it would merely shrink in size without having any impact upon market price. *See supra* page 217. Under the rule of *Addyston Pipe & Steel, BMI, NCAA,* and *Pacific Stationery,* therefore, it follows that the Atlas agreements do not violate section 1 of the Sherman Act.[11]

A joint venture made more efficient by ancillary restraints, is a fusion of the productive capacities of the members of the venture. That, in economic terms, is the same thing as a corporate merger. Merger policy has always proceeded by drawing lines about allowable market shares and these lines are based on rough estimates of effects because that is all the nature of the problem allows. If Atlas bought the stock of all its carrier agents, the merger would not even be challenged under the Department of Justice Merger Guidelines because of inferences drawn from Atlas's market share and the structure of the market. We can think of no good reason not to apply the same inferences to Atlas's ancillary restraints.

The judgment of the district court is
Affirmed.

---

11. Two additional points should be made. First, we do not think it significant to the outcome that Atlas's policy allowed agents to exercise their own interstate authority through separate corporations. Once it is clear that restraints can only be intended to enhance efficiency rather than to restrict output, the degree of restraint is a matter of business rather than legal judgment. Second, though it is sometimes said that, in the case of restraints like these, it is necessary to weigh procompetitive effects against anticompetitive effects, we do not think that a useable formula if it implies an ability to quantify the two effects and compare the values found. Here, there are no anticompetitive effects and so there is nothing to place on that side of the scale. If the underlying contract integration is lawful, *i.e.* not of such size as to violate the Sherman Act, restraints ancillary to the integration, in the sense we have described, should be lawful. Weighing effects in any direct sense will usually be beyond judicial capabilities but predictions about effects may be reflected in rules about allowable size. The concurrence appears to suggest that the district court conducted a balancing of effects in some fashion other than by drawing inferences from market share and structure. If so, the district court did not explain its alternative method and made no findings on the subject. Nor does the concurrence articulate an alternative means of weighing procompetitive and anticompetitive effects. Antitrust adjudication has always proceeded through inferences about market power drawn from market shares. *See, e.g. Consultants & Designers, Inc. v. Butler Service Group, Inc.*, 720 F.2d 1553, 1562–63 (11th Cir. 1983) (holding under § 1 that when a defendant has "a relatively small portion of the . . . [relevant] market," imposition of a restraint cannot be construed "impermissibly [to] hurt either . . . competitors or competition"); *Smith v. Pro-Football, Inc.*, 593 F.2d 1173, 1185–86 (D.C. Cir. 1978) (applying § 1 and finding "predictable effect" of a restraint imposed by 100% of the teams was "significantly anticompetitive"); *United States v. Aluminum Company of America*, 148 F.2d 416, (2d Cir. 1945) (L. Hand, J.) (a § 2 case holding that "[ninety] percent[ ]is enough to constitute a monopoly; it is doubtful whether sixty or sixty-four percent would be enough; and certainly thirty-three percent is not").

Considerations of space precluded reprinting the following articles in full: Vertical Integration and the Sherman Act: The Legal History of an Economic Misconception, 22 The University of Chicago Law Review 157 *(1954); The Rule of Reason and the Per Se Concept: Price Fixing and Market Division I,* 74 Yale Law Journal 775 *(1965); The Rule of Reason and the Per Se Concept: Price Fixing and Market Division II,* 75 Yale Law Journal 373 *(1966).*

III.

INTERNATIONAL LAW

The Limits of "International Law"

On October 25, 1983, armed forces of the United States invaded Grenada. President Reagan at once stated that our purpose was not only to protect Americans there but to "help in the restoration of democratic institutions" in a country where "a brutal group of leftist thugs violently seized power." Both the President and Secretary of State George P. Shultz said the operation was fully consistent with international law.

Senator Daniel Patrick Moynihan disagreed: "I don't know that you restore democracy at the point of a bayonet." He said we had clearly violated international law. (Moynihan is the public official who most persistently invokes this law and his views deserve attention.) Soon, Harvard law professor Abram Chayes, who had served as legal adviser to the State Department in the Kennedy administration, wrote in the *New York Times* that among international law experts there existed "remarkably broad agreement that the United States' invasion was flagrant violation of international law." On the same page, Eugene V. Rostow, a professor and former dean of the Yale Law School, wrote that "the American and allied campaign in Grenada is legitimized by classic precedents in international law, notably the Cuban missile crisis of 1962."

The American public, to the degree that it paid any attention, must have been quite mystified. High public officials and an undefined group of "experts in international law" were bitterly divided over the legality of what the United States had done. The pattern is familiar. Whenever an American President uses or subsidizes force against another country, the halls of Congress resound and the pages of the newspapers sizzle with pronouncements by his political opponents (and his allies) that he is (and is not) a lawbreaker. Some months later articles arguing both sides appear in scholarly journals. Since the public is assured that there is a law of nations but have no idea what

From *The National Interest*, Winter 1989–90

it is, they are almost certain to come away with the impression that, according to a substantial segment of informed opinion, the United States is a habitual lawbreaker. Indeed the U.S. appears to be recidivist. That is no small matter. People who deliberately break known laws are immoral. So it must be with nations. Or must it? The word "law" is a capacious one and before we accept a sense of guilt it would be will to inquire further.

What, exactly, is international law? Is it law at all? What purpose does it serve?

In some of its branches, it is law in a conventional sense. If two nations dispute fishing rights in the sea under a treaty, they may submit the matter to an international tribunal and agree to abide by the decision. In addition, there are international conventions, some of long standing, that govern the treatment of prisoners of war, of diplomats, of the rights of neutrals, etc. But this is not the kind of international law about which politicians and scholars grow passionate.

In its grandest (or most grandiose) form, international law is about the use or support of armed force against another nation. Concerning that subject, there are a great many statements of principle that *purport* to be law. They may be found, for example, in the Charter of the United Nations, in the Charter of the Organizations of American States, in any number of bilateral and multilateral treaties, and in custom. The rules of customary law, indeed, supposedly derived from the actual practices of nations, are said to be just as binding as any charter.

Most people find this rather perplexing. Nations regularly act in ways that, we are assured by politicians and scholars, constitute clear violations of international law . . . and nothing happens. No police force goes into action, no grand jury indicts, no petit jury sits, no verdict is announced by a court or, if one is, the convicted party ignores it. Articles and books gradually appear contending vociferously, and sometimes learnedly, that there was, or that there was not, a law violation. What can it mean to say that rules like that are in some sense, in any sense, "law"?

Senator Moynihan has no doubts on that subject: "International law *exists*. It is not an option. It is a fact." Others are less sure; and it is not merely laymen who feel unease. Treatises on international law commonly open by addressing the question whether the subject contains much that can properly be called "law." Most writers seem a touch defensive, but they assure the reader that there is "law" there. Yet the explanations themselves tend to be more than a trifle elusive and often romantic. A very prominent international lawyer, Philip Jessup, once offered an argument better than most:

> The layman and the common lawyer who find it difficult to fit interna-
> tional law into their concept of "law" . . . usually are alike in asserting that
> there isn't any international law. They forget that law has many meanings.
> There is the law of gravity, the Sherman Anti-Trust law, the law of supply
> and demand, international law.

The passage confuses rather than clarifies. The law of gravity describes a
force in the natural universe. The law of supply and demand is an observation about human behavior in markets. One who attempts levitation or tries
to purchase more than anyone is willing to sell at a particular price would
not be called a law violator. The Sherman Act is a rule made by a legislature
with conceded political authority and is enforced by courts though damages,
fines, and even imprisonment. The fact that all of these things are called
"laws" demonstrates only that the word has been applied to things that have
little or nothing in common.

Professor Michael Reisman of Yale notes that "Law is perforce a system of authorized coercion, and it can neither be conceived of nor operate
without a supportive political system or power process. In the absence of a
centralization of authoritative force and an effective monopoly over who can
use it to maintain community order and values, individual actors must look
to their own resources." Jessup recognized this problem but tried nonetheless to edge international law closer to the Sherman Act:

> In most cases the layman is impressed by the reality of breaches of inter-
> national law and is not sufficiently aware of the reality of reliance upon it.
> He does not pause to wonder why foreign offices bother to maintain legal
> staffs, which are an expense and sometimes a hindrance to the execution
> of policy.

But the existence of legal staffs poring over issues of international law proves
little about a law relating to international violence. Thousands of mundane
commercial and political matters arise in international settings, where the
meaning of "international law" is itself not a focus of controversy. But so long
as there purports to be international law *about the use of force*, the most cynical
and predatory government will employ a legal staff to engage in international
"shystering" as the need arises. Jessup finally resorted to the argument that,
since people called international lawyers are doing something, what they are
doing must be international law:

> Impotent to restrain a great nation which has no decent respect for the
> opinion of mankind, failing in its severest test of serving as a substitute for

war, international law plods on its way, followed automatically in routine affairs, invoked, flouted, codified, flouted again but yet again invoked. The legal Adviser of the United States Department of State still sits at his desk . . . in Washington and his counterparts sit at Downing Street, the Quai d'Orsay and the Wilhelmstrasse. It is not their task to frame policies. But can one say that the international law with which they deal has no reality?

In January of 1940, when Jessup's article appeared, one might have been inclined to say precisely that. One might have said it scores or hundreds of times since. The Soviets used force to crush movements toward freedom in Hungary, Czechoslovakia, and East Germany, and to seize Afghanistan. But it is not just a great power such as the Soviet Union that is immune to the blandishments of international law. Cuba and Nicaragua have armed and supported insurgency movements attempting to destroy democratic governments in Central America. China overran Tibet, India seized the Portuguese colony of Goa. The least one can say is that, in such cases, whatever reality this wraith called international law possesses is not visible to the non-expert.

This is not to deny that the *idea* of international law has real-world effects. It does. To see what those effects are, it is helpful to examine a pair of recent instances in which actions of the United States raised issues of international law. Two of the most spectacular such examples were the invasion of Grenada and our support of contra forces fighting the Sandinista regime in Nicaragua. The relevant facts cannot reasonably be disputed in either case.

The Nicaraguan revolution that deposed the dictator Anastasio Somoza in 1979 was made by a broad coalition, including the church, organized labor, professional and business groups, and peasants. Cuba, however, armed and advised the Marxist-Leninist Sandinistas who gradually removed democrats from positions of power, suppressed civil, political, and religious rights, and built a powerful army with arms and assistance from the Soviets and their allies. Nicaragua itself began supporting armed insurgencies designed to overthrow other democratic regimes. El Salvador was a particular target.

Alarmed, the United States began to support the Nicaraguan insurgency of the contras and to take other actions, such as the mining of harbors. Nicaragua struck back, using, among other tactics, international law. When the U.S. learned in the spring of 1984 that Nicaragua would file a claim in the International Court of Justice (or World Court), a body established by the Charter of the United Nations as the UN's "principle judicial organ" and composed of judges from various nations, our government suspended its acceptance of the ICJ's jurisdiction as to disputes with any Central American state. The Court nevertheless decided that it retained jurisdiction and the United States then announces that it would not participate further because the dispute involved "an inherently political problem that is not appropriate for judicial resolution." The U.S. then terminated its qualified 1946 acceptance of the Court's compulsory jurisdiction.

This was hardly novel. At the time, only 47 of the 162 nations entitled to accept that compulsory jurisdiction did so—and nine of the fifteen judges on the ICJ came from nations that did not! The Court proceeded to hear only Nicaragua because the U.S. was absent and El Salvador's petition to intervene had been denied—although the ICJ's own statute gave El Salvador that right. At that point, it should have been obvious to anyone what the outcome of the case would be.

In the event, the fears of the United States were realized. The case proceeded in an odd way. Assuming that it had any jurisdiction to begin with, the ICJ clearly had none under the treaties invoked by Nicaragua—the Charters of the United Nations and the Organization of the American States—because the U.S. had long before excepted issues arising under multilateral treaties unless *all* signatories were present. The Court claimed, nonetheless, that it could apply customary international law to the dispute. It found these principles binding despite their incorporation in provisions of the treaties that could not be applied. Customary international law is supposed to reflect the actual practices of nations, but the principles the Court applied were distinguished more for their continual violation by nations than for being followed. They were, moreover, principles hotly disputed among the scholars of international law. Despite these difficulties which, perhaps separately but certainly in combination, would seem to be insuperable, the Court went forward, making law as it went.

The ultimate difficulty with the ICJ's performance, however, was that the principles it fashioned turned out to be one-sided, wooden, and wholly unsuited to the realities of international conflict. The Court decided that merely arming rebels, even in combination with providing military advice and sanctuary for rebel leaders, does not constitute an "armed attack" and that only such an attack bring the issue of individual or collective self-defense into play.

Having found that Nicaragua had not engaged in an armed attack against El Salvador, according to the ICJ's definition, there was no reason whatever for the Court to go on to address the United State's claim that it was exercising the well-established right of collective self-defense. But the Court chose to do so and found this defense legally insufficient for a very odd reason:

> [I]t is the State which is the victim of an armed attack which must form
> and declare the view that it has been so attacked. There is no rule in cus-
> tomary international law permitting another State to exercise the right of
> collective self-defense on the basis of its own assessment of the situation

This was an entirely new procedural requirement, and it means that, even if El Salvador was under attack by Nicaragua and the entire world knew it, if El Salvador, for understandable reasons of prudence, did not wish to make a formal declaration of that fact, the United States could not respond by doing to Nicaragua what that country was doing to El Salvador. The ruling was triply odd since El Salvador had asked the U.S. to assist in its defense, President Duarte had repeatedly mentioned the Nicaraguan attack in press conferences, and El Salvador's rejected petition to intervene in the Court's proceedings had declared the existence of an attack.

It is customary for even those scholars who have pointed out the manifold deficiencies of the ICJ's performance—in its assumption of jurisdiction, its fact-finding, and its legal argument—to deny that they see bias or incompetence. But one must wonder whether an international tribunal can ever be entirely free of the foreign policy interests of the nations whose jurists sit on the tribunal. The ICJ judges, moreover, are elected by the UN's General Assembly and Security Council, often after a highly political process. In explaining the U.S. decision to terminate our acceptance of the Court's jurisdiction, Abraham D. Sofaer, the legal adviser to the State Department, said: "One reasonably may expect at least some judges to be sensitive to the impact of their decisions on their standing with the UN majority." He continued, in rampant understatement, that the UN "majority often opposes the United States on important international questions." It did so on the question of our conduct with respect to Nicaragua.

Every lawyer with a national practice knows that if his corporate client is sued by a local plaintiff in certain state courts, the client is likely to have to eat what the bar calls "home cookin'." The lawyers for the commissioner of baseball were recently reminded of that. So, it would appear, was the United States in the International Court of Justice.

But there appears to have been more to the matter than a politically-inspired but perhaps aberrational decision. As Professor Reisman points out, the

> International law-making process has itself undergone change and has sub-
> tly, but steadily, sought to change international law with regard to certain
> unilateral uses of force. While it has not totally succeeded, it has accom-

plished enough to have made expectations of who and how the law is made and what the law *is* less certain than in the past.

This has much to do with the change in the nature of the UN General Assembly as many new nations were admitted. The Assembly began to operate on the assumption that what was said there was international law or evidence of it. These were largely have-not nations and they want an international law that implements their desires. The result, as Reisman says, is the inversion of many established rules about the use of force. The decision in *Nicaragua* v. *United States* is a case in point.

In any event, the entire episode of *Nicaragua* v. *United States* had a distinctly odd feel for those who fall into the category of what Jessup called the "common lawyer." No court of the United States would entertain a suit challenging the legality of our actions with respect to Nicaragua. Various radical groups tried to litigate our involvement there and elsewhere in Central America, but were not successful. Our courts, under one legal rubric or another, essentially agreed that this was an inherently political dispute, not fit for judicial resolution.

As much could be said for all disputes about the use of force by one nation against another—but that is exactly my point about international law. We have not entrusted matters so gravely affecting our national interests, security, and foreign policy to American judges. Yet many argue that we should entrust such matters to a Court sitting on another continent, made up predominantly of jurists from foreign nations, and elected by an international body dominated on such issues by Communist bloc and Third World nations. Perhaps the administration's objection to the proceedings should have been couched differently: "This is an inherently political problem which we are unwilling to submit to political judgment outside the American political process."

The U.S., of course, refused to honor the judgment of the ICJ by paying damages to Nicaragua. But that does not mean that no harm was done. Even before the Court's decision, Carlos Arguello, Nicaragua's ambassador to the Netherlands who filed the case in the ICJ, announced that a decision against the United States would "be a serious political and moral blow to them." And so it proved. That was true in the U.S. as well as abroad. International law scholarship, along with the rest of the American academic community, was partially politicized and for every professor who criticized the Court's opinion another castigated the United States.

Thus, Herbert W. Briggs, an emeritus professor at Cornell, wrote in the *American Journal of International Law* that "An administration in Washington that takes satisfaction in invading Grenada, hijacking foreign planes in the Mediterranean, bombing people in Libya and attempting to overthrow foreign governments is unlikely to regard making the United Sates of America a fugitive from justice, dodging a Court decision, as a serious matter. In each case, the end is supposed to justify the means." The fact that the Mediterranean hijacking brought to justice in Italy PLO terrorists who had themselves hijacked the cruise ship *Achille Lauro* and murdered an American, or that the bombing of Libya was designed to (and did) deter Qaddafi's support of international terrorism—all this was deemed irrelevant. To which one can only reply that if the U.S. is a fugitive from justice for rejecting the jurisdiction of a biased court over matters vital to its security, then a large majority of the world's nations are in flight.

Except that there was no judgment by the World Court, much the same situation arose when the United States invaded Grenada. Grenada, a recently independent small island nation, had its government overthrown in a coup by Maurice Bishop and his revolutionary party in 1979. Developments followed much the same pattern seen earlier in Cuba and later in Nicaragua: the end to elections, freedom of the press, other political freedoms, and habeas corpus. A large number of political prisoners were held and the new regime engaged in rapid and heavy militarization with the assistance of arms and advisers from the Soviet Union, Cuba, and other nations of the Communist bloc. Grenada's neighbors, the other six island nations of the Organization of Eastern Caribbean States, were alarmed, since Grenada's military forces exceeded all of theirs combined and seemed to have no possible purpose other than to support subversion in order to overthrow their democratic governments.

Factions existed within the Grenadan ruling party, however, and on October 13, 1983, Bishop was arrested and subsequently murdered, along with three of his cabinet and certain union leaders. It is thought that this coup may have been the work of even more hard-line Marxist-Leninists, but, in any case, chaos followed as no group seemed in control. Rioting, looting, demonstrations, shootings, and a round-the-clock curfew on the civilian population, enforced by threats to shoot on sight, left the island without a real government. The other nations of the OECS expressed serious concern, and the United States was concerned as well, for there were about one thousand Americans on the island, many of them medical students. As Richard Chency, then a member of the congressional mission that later investigated, wrote: "Cut off from the outside world, dependent on the People's Revolutionary Army for food and water, and confined to their quarters on pain of death, they were, the State Department employee [who had been trying without success to arrange their evacuation] believed, already hostages."

The OECS member nations, along with Barbados and Jamaica, met and decided to take military action, provided the United States would assist the effort, since their own military forces were meager. The U.S. agreed, and on October 25 the OECS mission, supported by Barbados and Jamaica, but consisting almost entirely of U.S. forces, invaded. When the fighting was over, a CBS News poll found that 91 percent of Grenadans were glad the U.S. troops had come. By December 15, the U.S. armed forces had left the island, order had been restored, American and Grenadan lives very probably saved, and plans were underway for free elections so that the people of Grenada could choose their own government. One would have thought that outside the Communist bloc the American action would have been joyfully received.

One would have been quite wrong. Already, early in November, the UN General Assembly voted to condemn the action as a violation of international law. The majority was larger than that which had condemned the Soviet invasion of Afghanistan! The vote had been taken, moreover, without even allowing the nations of the OECS and the United States to present their case. Yet once more many of the U.S. international law academics responded in their own political fashion. No less than nine professors of international law, including Professor Chayes, signed a short article finding the U.S. "in egregious violation of international law" and stating that the lack of the "imprimatur" of the Organization of the American States would "raise serious doubts concerning the international legitimacy of any successor government." That the government ousted was a Communist dictatorship and that its successor would be feely chosen by the Grenadan people apparently raised no question in the professors' minds about the legitimacy of the former or the asserted doubtful legitimacy of the latter. The professors were not alone, of course. A number of politicians, along with Senator Moynihan, announced a U.S. violation of international law.

What are we to think about these pronouncements? Did the U.S. violate international law so that we are right to condemn the Reagan administration's international lawlessness? Are there known rules that lead reasonable people to firm conclusions about our actions in Nicaragua and Grenada? Or about Soviet and other nations' behavior around the world?

If there are such rules that lead to firm conclusions, this fact is well hidden. *The American Journal of International Law* ran separate symposia on the Grenada invasion and our support of the Nicaraguan contras. The various experts took almost every position imaginable, from the assertion that the United States is a dangerous international outlaw to the contention that everything done exemplified our devotion to the rule of law. Some arguments, such as those by Professor John Norton Moore of the University of Virginia Law School, in defense of our action, seemed to be far more persuasive than others, but I quickly realized that I was judging not on grounds that might be called "legal" but rather on political and moral considerations. The "law" itself seemed infinitely flexible and indeterminate.

This is due to a contradiction at the heart of the subject. Moynihan states the contradiction without seeming to realize that it is fatal to his idea that there is a solid body of law to which the United States must adhere:

> Manifestly, we cannot hold the rest of the world to a good many of the propositions relating to their internal conduct that we wrote into covenants and charters and declarations with such earnestness in the first half of this century. An ancient doctrine (going back at least to Grotius) is *rebus sic stantibus*, which denotes "a tacit condition, said to attach to all treaties, that they shall cease to be obligatory as soon as the state of facts and conditions upon which they were founded has substantially changed" (*Black's Law Dictionary*). For all that Chapter II of the charter of the Organization of the American States requires of members "the effective exercise of representative democracy," this is not going to be the political norm of this hemisphere or this world during the foreseeable future. It had once looked that way; it no longer does. Circumstances have changed. What has not changed—what the United States must strive to make clear has not changed—is the first rule of international law: *Pacta sunt servanda*, agreements must be kept.

But if the condition upon which the United States agreed to the OAS Charter—that the members would be democracies—has changed, why does not *rebus sic stantibus* relieve us of the obligation to keep the rest of the agreement? Moynihan's argument lacks all coherence.

The major difficulty with international law is that it converts what are essentially problems of international morality, as defined by a particular political community, into arguments about law that are largely drained of morality. I once listened to a professor of international law defend the United States' actions in Grenada. The argument seemed tortured and artificial, the most important considerations omitted. When he had done, I asked whether three factors that most Americans deemed relevant counted in international law. (1) The Grenadan government consisted of a minority that seized control by violence and maintained it by terror. (2) It was a Marxist-Leninist regime and represented a further advance in this hemisphere of a power that threaten freedom and democracy throughout the world. (3) Finally, the people of Grenada were ecstatic at being relieved of tyranny and the ever-present threat of violence. The expert replied, somewhat sadly, that these considerations had not weight in international law.

A moment's reflection makes it clear that, in the real world, they can not. In order to be international, rules about the use of force between nations must be acceptable to regimes that operate on different—often contradictory—moral premises. The rules themselves must not express a preference for freedom over tyranny or for elections over domestic violence as the means of coming to power. This moral equivalence is embodied in international charters. The charters must be neutral and the easiest neutral principle is: No force. The fact that the principle will not be observed by those who simply see international law as another foreign policy instrument does not affect the matter.

But even the principle of neutrality is now being altered to the disadvantage of the United States and other democracies. The UN General Assembly, as Reisman notes, has begun to redefine the unlawful use of force so that those whom the General Assembly chooses to regard as struggling for "freedom and independence" may legally attack their own government, another nation may legally provide bases from which the attacks are launched—but the targeted state behaves illegally if it then attacks those bases! This reverses the older rule to the benefit, primarily, of Communist insurgencies supported by nations in the Communist bloc and to the detriment of the United States when it aids the nation under attack.

It might be said that we must accept moral equivalence in international law in order to have rules that are acceptable to, and therefore may deter, Communist bloc nations and others from the use of armed force. The notion that it is worth keeping alive this idea of law in the power relations of nations because eventually that idea may tame the drives of aggressors is a bit like preaching the ideal of the rule of law to the Medellin cartel in the hope that one day the drug lords will be worn down by the rhetoric of idealism and submit to the law of Colombia. Even if one might hope that the aspiration of international law might one day lessen the amount of aggression in the world, there is the present reality that it does not, and that it imposes costs disproportionately on liberal, democratic nations.

The major cost is that, by eliminating morality from its calculus, internationallaw actually makes moral action appear immoral. It can hardly be doubted that, in the American view, it would be a moral act to help a people overthrow a dictatorship that had replaced a democratic government by force, and to restore democracy and freedom to such people. Yet when our leaders act for such moral reasons, they are forced into contrived explanations. The implausibility of such explanations then reverses the moral stance of the parties.

International law thus serves, both internationally and domestically, as a basis for a rhetoric of recrimination directed at the United States. Those who disapprove of a President's actions on the merits, but who fear they may prove popular, can transform the dispute from one about substance to one about legality. The President can be painted as a lawbreaker and perhaps drawn into a legalistic defense of his actions. The effect is to raise doubts and lower American morale. The Soviets and other nations have no such problem.

As currently defined, then, international law about the use of force is not even a piety; it is a net loss for Western democracies. Senator Moynihan, speaking of international relations in Woodrow Wilson's time, said, approvingly, that "the idea of law persisted, even when it did not prevail." That is precisely the problem. Since it does not prevail, the persistence of the idea that it exists can be pernicious. There can be no authentic rule of law among nations until nations have a common political morality or are under a common sovereignty. A glance at the real world suggests we have a while to wait.

Comments on the Articles on the Legality of the United States Action in Cambodia

The following article is adapted from comments I made on a panel discussing "The Cambodian Incursion and International Law" in June 1970.

The Cambodian incursion and its aftermath do raise important Constitutional questions, but they do not seem to me the questions posed by some of the other panelists. I think there is no reason to doubt that President Nixon had ample Constitutional authority to order the attack upon the sanctuaries in Cambodia seized by North Vietnamese and Viet Cong forces. That authority arises both from the inherent powers of the Presidency and from Congressional authorization. The real question in this situation is whether Congress has the Constitutional authority to limit the President's discretion with respect to this attack. Any detailed intervention by Congress in the conduct of the Vietnamese conflict constitutes a trespass upon powers the Constitution reposes exclusively in the President.

The application of Constitutional principles necessarily depends upon circumstances, and when President Nixon took office he faced two unavoidable facts that bear upon the Constitutional propriety of his subsequent actions. The first fact was the presence of United States troops engaged in combat in Vietnam. The President's responsibility for their safety invokes his great powers as Commander-in-Chief of our armed forces under Article II, Section 2, of the Constitution. The second fact was the engagement in Vietnam of our national interests. The President's ability to carry out his general policy of phased withdrawal as the South Vietnamese took over the war—a policy Congress has not in any way repudiated—will affect in many ways, both direct and indirect, the position of the United States in world affairs. The necessity for judgment and choice in carrying out that policy effectively

From *The American Journal of International Law*, January 1971.

invokes the President's powers as Chief Executive with primary responsibility for the conduct of foreign affairs.

These inherent powers of the President are themselves sufficient to support his order to attack the Cambodian sanctuaries seized by the enemy. It is completely clear that the President has complete and exclusive power to order tactical moves in an existing conflict, and it seems to me equally clear that the Cambodian incursion was a tactical maneuver and nothing more. The circumstances demonstrate that. The United States was conducting, with Congress's approval, armed hostilities in Vietnam, the enemy had extended the combat zone by seizing Cambodian territory and using it as a base for attacks upon American and South Vietnamese troops within South Vietnam, the Cambodian Government was unable to eject the North Vietnamese and Viet Cong who thus misused Cambodian territory, and the Government of Cambodia welcomed the American and South Vietnamese attack to clear out the enemy bases in Cambodia. The President's order did not begin a war with Cambodia or with anyone else. The decision to attack the sanctuaries was thus as clearly a tactical decision as is a directive to attack specified enemy bases within South Vietnam itself.

An attempt has been made to counter this argument by claiming that its logical extension places the entire war power in the hands of the President, that he could, for example, cite the need to defend the safety of American troops in Vietnam as justification for an order to bomb supply depots in China. This is a familiar but unsound form of argument. Its premise is that no principle can be accepted if it can be extrapolated to an undesirable result. That would be true only in those relatively rare cases in human affairs where only one principle or consideration is in play. That is not the case here. The Constitutional division of the war power between the President and the Congress creates a spectrum in which those decisions that approach the tactical and managerial are for the President, while the major questions of war or peace are, in the last analysis, confined to the Congress. The example posed—the decision to bomb Chinese depots—is at one extreme of the spectrum, since it would involve the decision to initiate a major war, while the actual case before us, attacks made with the full approval of the Cambodian Government upon bases being used by the enemy in an existing conflict, is at the opposite end of the spectrum. The counter-example offered thus actually emphasizes the tactical nature of the President's decision.

In addition to the inherent powers of the President, there was Congressional authorization for the course he took. The most obvious authorization was in the Tonkin Gulf Resolution. We have heard an attempt to distinguish that document away, but Section 1 expressly authorizes the President "to take all necessary measures to repel any armed attack against the forces of the United States *and* to prevent further aggression." (Emphasis added.) Both branches of that authorization cover the Cambodian incursion. Our forces were under armed attack mounted from and based upon the Cambodian sanctuaries, and the stated purpose of President Nixon's action was to repel that attack and to prevent further aggression. Lest there be any doubt of the intended breadth of the Tonkin Gulf Resolution, it should be recalled that Senator Fulbright, who led in its adoption, said at that time the resolution was tantamount to a declaration of war. In a war the Commander-in-Chief certainly has the power, at an absolute minimum, to order troops across a border to attack an enemy operating from there, particularly when the move is welcomed by the government whose border is crossed.

It is perfectly clear that a President may conduct armed hostilities without a formal declaration of war by Congress and that Congress may authorize such action without such a declaration. Congress's power "to declare war" does not, even semantically, exclude such a course, and the Constitution has been interpreted in this fashion repeatedly throughout our history. The Korean War is the most recent major precedent, and there President Truman went much further than President Nixon, for he committed our troops to a new war without prior Congressional approval. The suggestion that Korea is not a precedent because President Truman acted with the sanction of the United Nations is without merit. The United Nations cannot give an American President any warmaking power not entrusted to him by our Constitution. Moreover, the approval of the United Nations was obtained only because the Soviet Union happened to be boycotting the Security Council at the time, and the President's Constitutional powers can hardly be said to ebb and flow with the veto of the Soviet Union in the Security Council.

I arrive, therefore, at the conclusion that President Nixon had full Constitutional power to order the Cambodian incursion, and that Congress cannot, with Constitutional propriety, undertake to control the details of that incursion. This conclusion in no way detracts from Congress's war powers, for that body retains control of the issue of war or peace. It can end our armed involvement in Southeast Asia and it can forbid entry into new wars to defend governments there. But it ought not try to exercise Executive discretion in the carrying out of a general policy it approves.

WHOSE CONSTITUTION IS IT, ANYWAY?

What is going on here? Justice Sandra Day O'Connor in a recent speech said that decisions of other countries' courts could be persuasive authority in American courts. At a time when 30 percent of the U.S. gross national product is internationally derived, she said, "no institution of government can afford to ignore the rest of the world."

She is by no means alone on the Supreme Court. Six of that Court's nine members have either written or joined in opinions citing foreign authorities. The most astonishing, or risible, so far was Justice Stephen Breyer's opinion arguing that he found "useful" in interpreting our Constitution decisions by the Privy Council of Jamaica, and the Supreme Courts of India and Zimbabwe. Jamaica and India are far-fetched enough. But Zimbabwe—the country devastated by the blood-stained dictator Robert Mugabe! We might as well learn our constitutional law from Saddam Hussein's Iraq or Fidel Castro's Cuba.

Since the mid 1950s we have been in a third great period of constitution-making. Unlike the first two (1787 to 1791 and 1865 to 1870), this one is the work of judges, which achieves efficiency by cutting out the middlemen, the American people acting through their state conventions and legislatures. The efficiency gain is clear, but those hung up on technicalities complain of a lack of legitimacy. Justice Scalia commented on one of the Supreme Court's more imaginative improvements on the Founders' work: "Day by day, case by case, [the Court] is busy designing a Constitution for a country I do not recognize."

Yet even Scalia at his gloomiest probably did not foresee that the new country might be designed bit by bit from European, Asian, and African models. In *Lawrence* v. *Texas,* the decision creating a constitutional right to homosexual sodomy, Justice Kennedy cited a decision of the European Court of Human Rights. In a concurring opinion in *Grutter* v. *Bollinger,* a case up-

From *National Review*, December 8, 2003.

holding a law school's minority preferences in admissions, Justice Ginsburg, joined by Justice Breyer, rejoiced that the decision was in line with the International Convention on the Elimination of All Forms of Racial Discrimination. In *Thompson* v. *Oklahoma,* Justice John Paul Stevens, writing for four members of a divided Court, cited the approval "by other nations that share our Anglo-American heritage, and by the leading members of the Western European Community," as well as foreign legislation and three human-rights treaties, two of which had not been ratified by the United States.

Down from Olympus

We should not have been taken unaware by this absurd turn in our jurisprudence. Most members of the Court belong to that brand of intellectuals that John O'Sullivan has termed "Olympians." Kenneth Minogue added that "Olympianism is the project of an intellectual elite that believes that it enjoys superior enlightenment and that its business is to spread this benefit to those living on the lower slopes of human achievement." Hence the steady stream of Court decisions striking down various restrictions on abortion, on the telecasting of sex acts, and on computer-simulated child pornography; and outlawing any aspect of religion even remotely bearing on government. The Olympians' aspirations are universal. As Minogue put it: "Olympianism [is] a vision of human betterment to be achieved on a global scale by forging the peoples of the world into a single community based on the universal enjoyment of appropriate human rights. . . . Olympians instruct mortals, they do not obey them."

It is hardly surprising, then, that Linda Greenhouse would write in the *New York Times* with complacent approval that "justices have begun to see themselves as participants in a worldwide constitutional conversation." It might be more accurate to say that they see themselves as participants in a worldwide constitutional convention. Constitutions, ours and others', are being remade without reference to the principles actually embodied in them. It seems highly unlikely, to say the least, that the meaning of our Constitution, created by Americans primarily in the 18th and 19th centuries, should turn out to be the cultural fads of Frenchmen and Germans today.

The justices now regard themselves as statesmen. Justice O'Connor, referring to a 2002 decision holding the execution of a mentally retarded man unconstitutional, said that the Court took note of the world community's overwhelming disapproval of the practice. She said that the "impressions we create in this world are important." She went on to say that the Court found influential an amicus brief filed by American diplomats discussing the difficulties they confront in their foreign missions because of U.S. death-penalty practices. Of course, the European elites are enraged by any death penalty, which means the diplomats will continue to be vexed so long as the federal or any state government has capital punishment. Logically applied, as one must hope it will not be, this should mean that concern for the good opinion of Europeans and the comfort of our diplomats would persuade the Court to declare the death penalty unconstitutional altogether, despite the fact that the Constitution several times explicitly recognizes the availability of that punishment.

A "worldwide constitutional conversation" means that the rest of the world should learn from us as well as we from them. But they may be learning the wrong lessons: I have heard alarming reports that European judges are earnestly inquiring how Chief Justice John Marshall managed to centralize power in the federal government in order to learn how they could better diminish the remaining independence of the European Union's more fractious member states.

Our federal courts of appeals have now taken up the task of instructing the peoples of the world in "appropriate human rights." The Alien Tort Claims Act, adopted in 1789, permits aliens to sue in federal courts for torts committed in violation of the law of nations. The law of nations, back then, referred to relations between sovereign states, including the safety of ambassadors, and to piracy. Human rights were not a part of that law. For the most part, this area of law lay dormant for almost two centuries—until it was suddenly resurrected and expanded by a court of appeals that ruled that a suit for damages could be brought here in the U.S. *for the murder by a Paraguayan of a Paraguayan in Paraguay.* The court, as Prof. Jeremy Rabkin put it, "cheered on by a host of international law scholars, insisted . . . that 'customary international law' has greatly expanded and now incorporates an international law of human rights." There are now many such suits, including one in which it is alleged to be a violation of the law of nations when an American company refuses to bargain collectively with its workers in a foreign country.

The courts that countenance such lawsuits are making up the law of nations out of their own notions of appropriate human rights. They are undertaking to instruct the world on how the citizens of all nations must behave. This modern abuse of the Alien Tort Claims Act is judicial imperialism—indeed moral presumption—at its highest pitch. The Supreme Court has yet to deal with this misuse of the statute, and it's not clear what it will do about it; but in the meantime our lower-court Olympians are preaching their morality to the world.

The Arrogance of Power

What these courts are doing closely resembles Belgium's concept of "universal jurisdiction," under which its courts were asserting the authority to try criminally people involved in actions that have no connection to Belgium. A Belgian court tried and convicted Rwandan nuns for their actions during a massacre in Rwanda. The Belgian Supreme Court ruled in 2002 that Israeli prime minister Ariel Sharon may be tried after he leaves office for alleged war crimes in Lebanon 20 years earlier when he was head of Israel's army. Since massacres by Arabs are not prosecuted, it is difficult to disagree with Israelis who see anti-Semitism as an explanation for the difference. That is to be expected. International law in its higher reaches is usually heavily biased and political. As the Muslim populations of continental European nations rapidly increase, it is also to be expected that biased rulings will run heavily against Israel and the U.S. On the evidence of their behavior in the Pinochet affair, the United Kingdom and Spain may be adopting a version of universal jurisdiction.

International-law specialists David Rivkin and Lee Casey have remarked that the modern notion of universal jurisdiction would "permit the courts of any state to prosecute and punish the leadership of any other state for violations of international humanitarian norms." But "proponents should keep in mind that any independent state, not just 'right thinking' Western ones, would be entitled to prosecute." Yugoslavian courts convicted the NATO leaders for the 1999 bombing of Serbia, and Bill Clinton (tried in absentia, of course) was sentenced to 20 years' imprisonment.

To say, as Justice O'Connor did, that "the differences between our nations are fewer and less important than our similarities" is a serious mistake. We have few ideas about law and human rights in common with radical Islam, Russia, China, most of Africa, Cuba, and much of South America. The "impressions we create in [the] world" by abandoning our Constitution may be favorable in Europe, but that is all. Nor is there any good reason to cultivate the good will of European elites by importing their vapid notions of advanced social policy to replace the principles of our Constitution.

We have experimented with bringing into our universities neo-Marxist, feminist, and post-modernist philosophies, primarily out of Germany and France. The result has been wreckage in the study of the humanities. Why anyone would want to replicate that experience in law, as some judges, professors, and interest groups do, is a subject for the study of intellectual pathologies. Postmodernism has been defined as an uneasy alliance between nihilism and the politics of the Left. Radical individualism, which denies the possibility of objective moral standards, is a version of nihilism and the Court's social doctrine, now supplemented by foreign—primarily European—judicial decisions, has steadily moved our culture to the left.

Something larger than the justices' vulnerability to foreign law is in play. Internationalism is all the rage among Olympians. A heavy admixture of internationalism is urged as essential in our foreign policy and our employment of armed force. That may be seen in the proliferation of international tribunals such as the European Court of Human Rights and—more recently, and more ominously—the International Criminal Court, which intends to judge the behavior of citizens of all nations, even those that have not ratified the treaty establishing the court. Many Americans and most Europeans appear to think that morality requires submission of U.S. military responses to threats abroad to the United Nations and its Security Council. The result of these extreme forms of internationalism can only be a serious reduction of our sovereignty and our freedom. In large part, that is precisely what is intended by internationalism's enthusiasts, foreign and domestic. Consciously intended or not, it will also be the tendency of the internationalization of American law by American judges. That ought to be resisted strenuously, in the law as elsewhere.

Having Their Day in (a Military) Court: How Best to Prosecute Terrorists

The debate over the president's order creating military tribunals to try suspected terrorists consists largely of warring slogans and overripe rhetoric: "shredding our Constitution," "seizing dictatorial power," etc., on the one hand, and some version of "the bastards don't deserve any better" on the other. Analysis is in short supply. The issue of the balance between security and civil liberties will be with us, in various guises, for a long time to come. The reality we face means that no resolution of such issues will be wholly satisfactory.

When the issue is trying terrorists, there appear to be only four options: trial in a federal court; trial before an international tribunal; trial before a military tribunal; or setting the captives free. No body this side of a psychiatric ward will choose the last option. But the first and second don't win any prizes either.

Trials in federal courts have features that make them totally inappropriate for the trial of terrorists. Jurors often respond to emotional appeals, and, in any event, would have good reason to fear for their and their families' safety if they convicted. Criminal trials have been adorned by judges with a full panoply of procedural hurdles that guarantee a trial of many months. Appeals and petitions for habeas corpus can take years, and should the death sentence be given, the ACLU has shown how to delay execution for ten years or more through appeals followed by one habeas corpus petition after another. An open trial and proceedings of that length, covered by television, would be an ideal stage for an Osama bin Laden to spread his propaganda to all the Muslims in the world. Many Islamic governments would likely find that aroused mobs make it impossible to continue cooperating with the U.S.

The conclusive argument, however, is that in open trials our government would inevitably have to reveal much of our intelligence information, and

From *National Review*, December 17, 2001.

about the means by which it is gathered. Charles Krauthammer notes that in the trial of the bombers of our embassies in Africa, the prosecution had to reveal that American intelligence intercepted bin Laden's satellite phone calls: "As soon as that testimony was published, Osama stopped using the satellite system and went silent. We lost him. Until Sept. 11." Disclosures in open court would inform not only Middle Eastern terrorists but all the intelligence services of the world of our methods and sources.

Trials before an international tribunal would have all of these defects and more. Picking the members of the court would itself be a diplomatic nightmare. It would be politically impossible to keep judges from Islamic countries off the court. In the past, moreover, international courts have often shown a pronounced anti-American bias. Our prosecutor would be helpless to avoid a propaganda circus and the disclosure of our intelligence capabilities and methods. In the end, convictions would be highly uncertain, but, if obtained, impassioned dissents and the martyrdom of the terrorists would be certain. We should be wary of international tribunals in any event since their establishment seems part of a more general move to erode U.S. sovereignty by subjecting our actions to control by other nations.

Military tribunals avoid or at least mitigate these problems. Propaganda by televised speeches would be impossible and any required disclosure of intelligence methods and successes would be secret. Since trials could move far more efficiently and appeals are cut off by the president's order, punishment of the guilty would be prompt. One of the prices we pay for an all-volunteer military is that for most Americans their armed forces are an unknown world about which it is possible to imagine all sorts of evils; but military tribunals are not, as they have been called, "kangaroo courts" or "drumhead tribunals." Much of the public is probably frightened by visions of defendants convicted out of hand and bustled off to firing squads.

During the Korean War, the officers in my battalion took turns prosecuting and defending. (I had a notable lack of success in both roles.) I sat on the court, and never saw an innocent man convicted but did see a guilty man acquitted. (I prosecuted that one and it still rankles.) Even then, before the widespread reform of the military justice system, military courts manned by officers, in my opinion and that of many others, were superior to the run of civilian courts, more scrupulous in examining the evidence and following the plain import of the law. If I were guilty, I would prefer a civilian jury; if innocent, a military court.

These virtues would be irrelevant if military tribunals were of dubious constitutionality. They are not. The constitutional issue reached the Supreme Court in *Ex parte Quirin* (1942). German saboteurs had entered the United States illegally to destroy war industries and facilities. Arrested by the FBI before they could act, they sought to file for writs of habeas corpus, contending they had a right to trial before regular courts rather than a military commission. The presidential proclamation establishing the commission denied them access to those courts.

The Court denied the petition, judging it irrelevant that one of the defendants might be an American citizen. In its decision, the Court made clear the separate constitutional tracks of the two forms of justice: "Presentment by a grand jury and trial by a jury . . . were at the time of the adoption of the Constitution familiar parts of the machinery for criminal trials in the civil courts. But they were procedures unknown to military tribunals which are not courts in the sense of the Judiciary Articles" of the Constitution. Consistent with that understanding, military tribunals have been used by several presidents in time of war. In the Revolutionary War, before there was a Constitution, George Washington employed such tribunals freely, as did Abraham Lincoln in the Civil War, and Franklin Roosevelt in World War II. We remember the Nuremberg trial, with many of the trappings of a civilian court, as an attempt (failed in my view) to establish an international rule of law in open proceedings. That trial is not a model for the problem we face now. There were, of course, no problems of intelligence disclosures, but, more important, the open trial was not regarded by the allies as the only, or in all cases the preferred, method of proceeding. According to Mark Martins, a respected scholar and military lawyer, "German regular army soldiers were also defendants in many of the thousands of military courts and commissions convened by the Allies after the war in different zones of occupation."

If there is a problem with Bush's order, it is the exemption of U.S. citizens from trials before military tribunals. *Quirin* held that Americans can be tried there, and it is clear that they should. The trial of American terrorists in criminal court would pose all the problems of trying foreign terrorists there: The prosecution would have to choose between safeguarding our intelligence capacity and trying the terrorist. The terrorists could well go free.

Contrary to some heated reactions, military tribunals are well within our tradition. They are needed now more than ever.

Congress and the Bush Administration adopted the use of military tribunals to try terrorists; however, this practice has been, in part, nullified by recent Supreme Court decisions.

IV.

Politics and Public Policy

Hard Truths About the Culture War

What began to concern me more and more were the clear signs of rot and decadence germinating within American society—a rot and decadence that was no longer the consequence of liberalism but was the actual agenda of contemporary liberalism. . . . Sector after sector of American life has been ruthlessly corrupted by the liberal ethos. It is an ethos that aims simultaneously at political and social collectivism on the one hand, and moral anarchy on the other.

—Irving Kristol, "My Cold War"

Equivocation has never been Irving Kristol's strong suit. About the fact of rot and decadence there can be no dispute, except from those who deny that such terms have meaning, and who are, for that reason, major contributors to rot and decadence. We are accustomed to lamentations about American crime rates, the devastation wrought by drugs, rising illegitimacy, the decline of civility, and the increasing vulgarity of popular entertainment. But the manifestations of American cultural decline are even more widespread, ranging across virtually the entire society, from the violent underclass of the inner cities to our cultural and political elites, from rap music to literary studies, from pornography to law, from journalism to scholarship, from union halls to universities. Wherever one looks, the traditional virtues of this culture are being lost, its vices multiplied, its values degraded—in short, the culture itself is unraveling.

These can hardly be random or isolated developments. A degeneration so universal, afflicting so many seemingly disparate areas, must proceed from common causes. That supposition is strengthened by the observation that similar trends seem to be occurring in nearly all Western industrialized democracies. The main features of these trends are vulgarity and a persistent

From *First Things*, June/July 1995.

left-wing bias, the latter being particularly evident among the semi-skilled intellectuals—academics, bureaucrats, and the like—that Kristol calls the New Class.

But why should this be happening? The short answer is the one Kristol gives: the rise of modern liberalism. (The extent to which he would agree with the following argument about the sources and future of modern liberalism, I do not know.) Modern liberalism grew out of classical liberalism by expanding its central ideals—liberty and equality—while progressively jettisoning the restraints of religion, morality, and law even as technology lowered the constraint of hard work imposed by economic necessity. Those ideals, along with the right to pursue happiness, are what we said we were about at the beginning, in the Declaration of Independence. Stirring as rallying cries for rebellion, less useful, because indeterminate, for the purpose of arranging political and cultural matters, they become positively dangerous when taken, without very serious qualifications, as social ideals.

The qualifications assumed by the founders' generation, but unexpressed in the Declaration (it would rather have spoiled the rhetoric to have added "up to a point"), have gradually been peeled away so that today liberalism has reached an extreme, though not one fears its ultimate, stage. "Equality" has become radical egalitarianism (the equality of outcomes rather than of opportunities), and "liberty" takes the form of radical individualism (a refusal to admit limits to the gratifications of the self). In these extreme forms, they are partly produced by, and partly produce, the shattering of fraternity (or community) that modern liberals simultaneously long for and destroy.

Individualism and egalitarianism may seem an odd pair, since liberty in any degree produces inequality, while equality of outcomes requires coercion that destroys liberty. If they are to operate simultaneously, radical egalitarianism and radical individualism, where they do not complement one another, must operate in different areas of life, and that is precisely what we see in today's culture. Radical egalitarianism advances, on the one hand, in areas of life and society where superior achievement is possible and would be rewarded but for coerced equality: quotas, affirmative action, income redistribution through progressive taxation for some, entitlement programs for others, and the tyranny of political correctness spreading through universities, primary and secondary schools, government, and even the private sector. Radical individualism, on the other hand, is demanded when there is no danger that achievement will produce inequality and people wish to be unhindered in the pursuit of pleasure. This finds expression particularly in the areas of sexuality and violence, and their vicarious enjoyment in popular entertainment.

Individualism and egalitarianism do not always divide the labor of producing cultural decay. Often enough they collaborate. When egalitarianism reinforces individualism, denying the possibility that one culture or moral view can be superior to another, the result is cultural and moral relativism, whose end products include multiculturalism, sexual license, obscenity in the popular arts, an unwillingness to punish crime adequately and, sometimes, even to convict the obviously guilty. Both the individualist and the egalitarian (usually in the same skin) are antagonistic to society's traditional hierarchies or lines of authority—the one because his pleasures can be maximized only by freedom from authority, the other because he resents any distinction among people or forms of behavior that suggests superiority in one or the other.

The universality of these forces is indicated by the fact that they are prominent features of two institutions at opposite ends of the cultural spectrum: the Supreme Court of the United States and rock music.

The Court reflects modern cultural trends most obviously when it invents new rights of the individual against the decisions of the political community, but it also does so in the expansion of rights expressed in the Constitution beyond anything the drafters and ratifiers could have intended. Radical individualism surfaced when the Court created a right of privacy, supposedly about the sanctity of the marital bedchamber, which soon explicitly became a right of individual autonomy unconnected to privacy. Four justices subsequently pronounced it a "moral fact that a person belongs to himself and not others nor to society as a whole"—a "fact" which means that a person has no obligations outside his own skin. The same tendency is seen in the Court's drive to privatize religion, as when a girl is held to have a First Amendment right not to have to sit at graduation through a short prayer because it might offend her sensibilities. The list could be extended almost indefinitely. The autonomy the Court requires, of course, is necessarily selective, almost invariably consisting of the freedoms preferred by modern liberalism.

The Court's commitment to egalitarianism is so strong that it overrode the explicit language and legislative history of the 1964 Civil Rights Act to allow preferences for blacks and women. The Court usually argued that the preferences were for prior discrimination, discrimination not against the individuals now benefited but against other members of their race or sex in the past. Even that requirement was dropped when the Court allowed preferences for minorities in the grant of station licenses by the Federal Communications Commission, despite the lack of any evidence that such grants had ever been tainted by discrimination. In these ways the Court reflects, and hence illegitimately legitimates, the thrusts of modern liberal culture.

To point the parallel: in a book appropriately titled *The Triumph of Vulgarity,* Robert Pattison points out that rock music celebrates the unconstrained self: "The extrovert, the madman, the criminal, the suicide, or the exhibitionist can rise to heroic stature in rock for the same reasons that Byron or Raskolnikov became romantic heroes—profligacy and murder are expressions of an emotional intensity that defies the limits imposed by nature and society." Rock culture teaches egalitarianism as well, not only in its frequent advocacy of revolution, but in its refusal to make distinctions about morality or aesthetics based upon any transcendent principle. There is no such principle, only sensation, energy, the pleasure of the moment, and the expansion of the self.

Vulgarity and obscenity are, of course, rife in popular culture. Rock is followed by rap; television situation comedies and magazine advertising increasingly rely on explicit sex; such cultural icons as Roseanne Barr and Michael Jackson can be seen on family-oriented television clutching their crotches. The prospect is for more and worse. Companies are now doing billions of dollars' worth of business in pornographic videos, and volume is increasing rapidly. They are acquiring inventories of the videos for cable television; and a nationwide chain of pornographic video and retail stores is in the works. One pay-per-view network operator says, "This thing is a freight train."

It is likely to become a rocket ship soon if, as George Gilder predicts, computers replace television, allowing viewers to call up digital films and files of news, art, and multimedia from around the world. He dismisses conservatives' fears that "the boob tube will give way to what H. L. Mencken might have termed a new Boobissimus, as the liberated children rush away from the network nurse, chasing Pied Piper pederasts, snuff-film sadists, and other trolls of cyberspace." Gilder concedes, "Under the sway of television, democratic capitalism enshrines a Gresham's law; bad culture drives out good, and ultimately porn and prurience, violence and blasphemy prevail everywhere from the dimwitted 'news' shows to the lugubrious movies." But he blames that on the nature of broadcast technology, which requires central control and reduces the audience to its lowest common denominator of tastes and responses.

But the computer will give everyone his own channel: "The creator of a program on a specialized subject—from Canaletto's art to chaos theory, from GM car transmission repair to cowboy poetry, from Szechuan restaurant finance to C++ computer codes—will be able to reach everyone in the industrialized world who shares the interest."

Perhaps. But there seems little reason to think there will not also be an enormous increase in obscene and violent programs. Many places already have fifty or more cable channels, including some very good educational channels, but there are still MTV's music videos, and the porn channels are coming on line. The more private viewing becomes, the more likely that salacious and perverted tastes will be indulged. That is suggested by the explosion of pornographic film titles and profits when videocassettes enabled customers to avoid going to "adult" theaters. Another boom should occur when those customers don't even have to ask for the cassettes in a store. The new technology, while it may bring the wonders Gilder predicts, will almost certainly make our culture more vulgar and violent.

The leader of the revolution in pornographic video, referred to admiringly by a competitor as the Ted Turner of the business, offers the usual defenses of decadence: "Adults have a right to see [pornography] if they want to. If it offends you, don't buy it." Modern liberalism employs the rhetoric of "rights" incessantly to delegitimize restraints on individuals by communities. It is a pernicious rhetoric because it asserts a right without giving reasons. If there is to be anything that can be called a community, the case for previously unrecognized individual freedoms must be thought through, and "rights" cannot win every time.

The second notion—"If it offends you, don't buy it"—is both lulling and destructive. Whether you buy it or not, you will be greatly affected by those who do. The aesthetic and moral environment in which you and your family live will be coarsened and brutalized. There are economists who confuse the idea that markets should be free with the idea that everything should be on the market. The first idea rests on the efficiency of the free market in satisfying wants; the second raises the question of which wants it is moral to satisfy. The latter question brings up the topic of externalities: you are free not to make steel, but you will be affected by the air pollution of those who do make it. To complaints about pornography and violence on television, libertarians reply, "All you have to do is hit the remote control and change channels." But, like the person who chooses not to make steel, you and your family will be affected by the people who do not change the channel. As Michael Medved puts it, "To say that if you don't like the popular culture then turn it off, is like saying, if you don't like the smog, stop breathing. . . . There are Amish kids in Pennsylvania who know about Madonna." And their parents can do nothing about that.

Can there be any doubt that as pornography and violence become increasingly popular and accessible entertainment, attitudes about marriage, fidelity, divorce, obligations to children, the use of force, and permissible public behavior and language will change, and with the change of attitudes will come changes in conduct, both public and private? The contrary view must assume that people are unaffected by what they see and hear. Advertisers bet billions the other way. Advocates of liberal arts education assure us those studies improve character; it is not very likely that only uplifting culture affects attitudes and behavior. "Don't buy it" and "Change the channel" are simply advice to accept a degenerating culture and its consequences.

Modern liberalism also presses our politics to the left because egalitarianism is hostile to the authorities and hierarchies—moral, religious, social, economic, and intellectual—that are characteristic of a bourgeois or traditional culture and a capitalist economy. Yet modern liberalism is not hostile to hierarchy as such. Egalitarianism requires hierarchy because equality of condition cannot be achieved or approximated without coercion. The coercers will be bureaucrats and politicians who will, and already do, form a new elite class. Political and governmental authority replace the authorities of family, church, profession, and business. The project is to sap the strength of these latter institutions so that individuals stand bare before the state, which, liberals assume with considerable justification, they will administer. We will be coerced into virtue, as modern liberals define virtue: a ruthlessly egalitarian society. This agenda is, of course, already well advanced.

Both diminished performance and personal injustice are accomplished through radically egalitarian measures. Quotas and affirmative action, for example, are common and increasing not only in the workplace but in university admissions, faculty hiring, and promotion. The excuse is past discrimination, but the result is that individuals who have never been discriminated against are preferred to individuals who have never discriminated, regardless of their respective achievements. Predictably, the result is anger on both sides and an increasingly polarized society. After years of struggle to emplace the principle of reward according to achievement, the achievement principle is being jettisoned for one of reward according to birth once more.

Remarkably little thought attends this process. The demand is always for more equality, but no egalitarian ever specifies how much equality will be enough. And so the leveling process grinds insensately on. The *Wall Street Journal* recently reprinted a Kurt Vonnegut story, which the paper retitled "It Seemed Like Fiction" because it was written "in 1961, before the passage of the Equal Pay Act (1963), the Civil Rights Act (1964), the Age Discrimination in Employment Act (1967), the Equal Employment Opportunity Act (1972), the Rehabilitation Act (1973), the Americans with Disabilities Act

(1990), the Older Workers' Benefit Protection Act (1990), and the Civil Rights Act (1991)." At the time of reprinting, Congress was preparing hearings on "The Employment Nondiscrimination Act of 1994" and was considering additional amendments to the Civil Rights Act. Even before all this, Vonnegut saw the trend and envisioned the day when Americans would achieve perfect equality: persons of superior intelligence required to wear mental handicap radios that emit a sharp noise every twenty seconds to keep them from taking unfair advantage of their brains, persons of superior strength or grace burdened with weights, those of uncommon beauty forced to wear masks. Why not?

Modern liberalism is most particularly a disease of our cultural elites, the people who control the institutions that manufacture or disseminate ideas, attitudes, and symbols—universities, some churches, Hollywood, the national press (print and electronic), much of the congressional Democratic party and some of the congressional Republicans as well, large sections of the judiciary, foundation staffs, and almost all the "public interest" organizations that exercise a profound if largely unseen effect on public policy. So pervasive is the influence of those who occupy the commanding heights of our culture that it is not entirely accurate to call the United States a majoritarian democracy. The elites of modern liberalism do not win all the battles, but despite their relatively small numbers, they win more than their share and move the culture always in one direction.

This is not a conspiracy but a syndrome. These are people who view the world from a common perspective, a perspective to the left of the attitudes of the general public. Two explanations for this phenomenon have been advanced. Both seem accurate. One is a heretical version of Marxism, a theory of class warfare; the other might be called a heretical version of religion, a theory of the hunger for spirituality, for a meaning to life.

Joseph Schumpeter first articulated the idea that capitalism requires and hence produces a large intellectual class. The members of that class are not necessarily very good at intellectual work; they are merely people who work with or transmit ideas at wholesale or retail, the folks collectively referred to above as the New Class (also known as the "knowledge class," the "class of semiskilled intellectuals," or the "chattering class").

Why should the New Class be hostile to traditional or bourgeois society? The answer, according to the class warfare theory, is that capitalism bestows its favors, money, and prestige on the business class. The New Class, filled with resentment and envy, seeks to enhance its own power and prestige by attacking capitalism, its institutions, and its morality. It is necessary to attack from the left because America has never had an aristocratic ethos and because the weapons at hand are by their nature suited to the left. The ideas are held not for their merit but because they are weapons.

There is probably a good deal to this, but it seems not quite sufficient. For one thing, it does not account for the Hollywood left. These are folks with no need whatever to envy the CEO of General Motors his prestige or financial rewards. And no one, to my knowledge, has ever classified Barbra Streisand, Jane Fonda, Ed Asner, and Norman Lear as intellectuals.

There is, however, an additional theory. Max Weber noted the predicament of intellectuals in a world from which "ultimate and sublime values" have been withdrawn: "The salvation sought by an intellectual is always based on inner need. . . . The intellectual seeks in various ways, the casuistry of which extends to infinity, to endow his life with a pervasive meaning." The subsidence of religion leaves a void that must be filled. Richard Grenier observes that among those intellectuals "most subject to longings for meaning, Max Weber listed, prophetically: university professors, clergymen, government officials . . . 'coupon clippers' . . . journalists, school teachers, 'wandering poets.'" By "coupon clippers," I take it, Weber meant the generations that inherit the wealth of the men who made it, which would explain why so many foundations created by wealthy conservatives become liberal when the children or grandchildren take over. And for "wandering poets," read the likes of Robert Redford and Warren Beatty. The epitome of Weber's university professors is John Rawls, whose egalitarian theory of justice swept the academy. Among other odd notions, Rawls laid it down that no inequalities are just unless they benefit the most disadvantaged members of society. There is, of course, no good reason for such a rule, and it is a prescription for permanent hostility to actual societies, and most particularly that of the United States, which can never operate in that fashion. No vital society could.

What we are seeing in modern liberalism is the ultimate triumph of the New Left of the 1960s—the New Left that collapsed as a unified political movement and splintered into a multitude of intense, single-issue groups. We now have, to name but a few, radical feminists, black extremists, animal rights groups, radical environmentalists, activist homosexual groups, multiculturalists, People for the American Way, Planned Parenthood, the American Civil Liberties Union, and many more. In a real sense, however, the New Left did not collapse. Each of its splinters pursues a leftist agenda, but there is no publicly announced overarching philosophy that enables people to see easily that the separate groups and causes add up to a general radical left philosophy. The groups support one another and come together easily on many issues. In that sense, the splintering of the New Left made it less visible and therefore more powerful, its goals more attainable, than ever before.

In their final stages, radical egalitarianism becomes tyranny and radical individualism descends into hedonism. These translate as bread and circuses. Government grows larger and more intrusive in order to direct the distribution of goods and services in an ever more equal fashion, while people are diverted, led to believe that their freedoms are increasing, by a great variety of entertainments featuring violence and sex. David Frum argues that the root of our trouble is big government, but the root of big government is the egalitarian passion, which intimidates even many conservatives. So long as that passion persists, government is likely only to get bigger and more intrusive.

We sometimes console ourselves with the thought that our current moral anarchy and statism are merely one phase of a pendulum's swing, that in time the pendulum will swing the other way. No doubt such movements and countermovements are often observable, but it is entirely possible that they are merely ephiphenomena that do not affect the larger movement of the culture. After each swing the bottom of the pendulum's arc is always further to the cultural and political left. Certainly, in the United States, we have never experienced a period of cultural depravity and governmental intrusiveness to rival today's condition.

The prospects look bleak, moreover, if we reflect on the sources of modern liberalism's components. The root of egalitarianism lies in envy and insecurity, which are in turn products of self-pity, arguably the most pervasive and powerful emotion known to mankind. The root of individualism lies in self-interest, not always expressed as a desire for money but also for power, celebrity, pleasures, and titillations of all varieties. Western civilization, of course, has been uniquely individualistic. Envy and self-interest often have socially beneficial results, but when fully unleashed, freed of constraints, their consequences are rot, decadence, and statism.

Because they arise out of fundamental human emotions, it is obvious that individualism and egalitarianism were not invented in the 1960s. They have been working inexorably through Western civilization for centuries, perhaps for millennia, but they have only recently overcome almost all obstacles to their full realization. These forces were beneficent for most of their careers; they produced the glories of our civilization and, freed of the restraints of the past, became malignant only in this century. We are delighted that the restraints that afflicted men in the classical world, in the Middle Ages, even in the last century and much of this have been weakened or removed. Our names for particular events and eras celebrate that movement:

the Renaissance, the Reformation, the Enlightenment, our own Declaration of Independence and Bill of Rights, the Civil Rights Movement. Though they had other complex effects, all involved the loosening of restraints: religious, legal, and moral. But any progression can at last go too far.

The constraints that made individualism and egalitarianism beneficial included economic necessity, which channeled individualism into productive work, and religion (with its corollaries of morality and law), which tempered self-interest and envy. It is only in this century, and particularly in the years since World War II, that Americans have known an affluence that frees many of us from absorption with making a living, and it is in that same period that the decline in religion, which began centuries ago, reached its low point. Religious belief remains strong but seems to have a diminishing effect on behavior. And only lately have we developed the technologies that not only make work easier but also make the opportunities for sensation almost boundless. We have always known that unfettered human nature does not present an attractive face, but it is that face that is coming into view as modern liberalism progresses. It is difficult to imagine the constraints that could now be put in place to do the work that economic necessity and religion once did.

If the drive of modern liberalism cannot be blunted and then reversed, we are also likely to see an increasingly inefficient economy. The hedonism of radical individualism is not consistent with the habits of work and saving that are essential to a vigorous economy. The quotas and affirmative action that are growing in our educational institutions and in our corporations, the dilution of the achievement principle, coupled with the government's determination to intervene in the economy through manifold regulations, mandates, and taxes, will place additional burdens on productivity. Despite all we have learned from watching other economies, perhaps we are fated to repeat the socialist mistakes and suffer the inevitable consequences.

This is a picture of a bleak landscape, and there are many who disagree. Optimists point out, for example, that American culture is complex and resilient, that it contains much that is good and healthy, that many families continue to raise children with strong moral values. All that is true. I have been describing trends, not the overall condition of the culture, but the trends have been running the wrong way, dramatically so in the past thirty years. It would be difficult to contend that, the end of racial segregation aside, American culture today is superior to, or even on a par with, the culture of the 1950s.

Others might argue that the elections of 1994 are an indication that a cultural swing is taking place, that Americans have rejected huge, regulation-happy government. That may be so, but I remember thinking the same thing in November 1980 when the electorate chose Ronald Reagan and defeated a clutch of the most liberal Senators. But little long-term improvement occurred. Government now regulates more than it did then. It was fifteen years between Reagan's first inauguration and the Republican domination of Congress. We will know that a sea change has happened if, fifteen years from now, government is smaller, less expensive, and less intrusive.

Modern liberalism, moreover, maintains its hold on the institutions that shape values and manipulate symbols. Hollywood and the network evening news will not change their ways because of Republican majorities. Political correctness and multiculturalism will not be ejected from the universities by Newt Gingrich. If the reaction of the left to Reagan's elections is any guide, modern liberalism will become more aggressive and intolerant. In any event, even a persistently conservative government can do little to deal with social deterioration other than stop subsidizing it through welfare, and it remains to be seen whether Republicans have the will to overcome the constituencies that want welfare. Moral decay is evident, moreover, among people who are not on welfare and never will be.

No one can be certain of the future, of course. Cultures in decline have, unpredictably, turned themselves around before. Perhaps ours will too. Perhaps, ultimately, we will become so sick of the moral and aesthetic environment that is growing in America that stricter standards will be imposed democratically or by moral disapproval. Perhaps we will reject a government that is controlling more and more of our lives. A hopeful sign is the degree to which modern liberalism and its works—political correctness, affirmative action, multiculturalism, and the like—is coming under intellectual attack, not merely from conservative but also from liberal intellectuals. If its intellectual and moral bankruptcy is repeatedly exposed, perhaps modern liberalism will die of shame.

But then again, perhaps not. Country singer and social philosopher Merle Haggard, whose perspective is like Irving Kristol's, says that the decade of the 1960s "was just the evening of it all. I think we're into the dead of night now." Chances are, that is too optimistic and the dead of night still lies ahead. For the immediate future, in any event, what we probably face is an increasingly vulgar, violent, chaotic, and politicized culture and, unless the conservative resurgence of 1994 is both long-lasting and effective, an increasingly incompetent, bureaucratic, and despotic government. Kristol refers to himself as a cheerful pessimist. If the argument here is even close to the mark, and if the counterattack falls short, we had all better start working on the cheerful part.

WE SUDDENLY FEEL THAT LAW IS VULNERABLE

The following article, written during the height of the social and cultural turmoil of the Sixties, expresses serious concerns about the stability of law. The turmoil has subsided, at least for the moment, but that is partly, even largely, due to the incorporation of Sixties attitudes and personnel into American mainstream culture and institutions. That is particularly true of the nation's universities and their schools of law. There is little incentive to challenge the legitimacy of institutions you control. The shift from counterculture and rebellion to apparent placidity may therefore be misleading.

———— ———— ————

Law has entered upon troubled times. Along with the other major institutions of Western culture, it is beset by malaise and self-doubt. Seeming strength and sensed weakness combine in an uneasy blend. It is a time when the law lays claim to broad new domains of human life, yet the prestigious Association of the Bar of the City of New York feels impelled to stage a major symposium on the question, "Is Law Dead?" It is a time when young men and women are turning to legal careers in greater numbers than ever before, and when law students are less sure than ever before that their studies have meaning. It is a time when thoughtful men are concerned as rarely before with the need to uphold law against violence, and when scholars can maintain in public that it is wrong to try men for political murder. We look apprehensively toward a future in which the nature of law and its role in our affairs will have altered in ways now almost impossible to discern. We suddenly feel that law is vulnerable.

Law, it is true, has never been as solid and certain an institution as we pretended. The more thoughtful members of the legal profession have always realized that they were not sure what law is or why it has a paramount claim

From *Fortune*, December 1971

upon the citizen's allegiance. To others, however, and certainly to the laity, law was obviously a system of logical and interlocking rules by which life was governed. There were answers to important questions in law libraries. Few troubled to disabuse us. I remember still the shock I felt on being told on the first day in law school that the law is a mystery, that it is, in its deepest essence, unknowable. My classmates and I supposed that the great man (later to become dean of the school and then president of the university) said such things merely to snap us out of our civilian torpor in much the same way as the drill instructor in boot camp speaks some shocking phrases to loosen one's attitudes for the remolding that is to come. It simply could not be the case that the law was unknowable. If that were true, how could Holmes have said that it was possible to live greatly in the law? Why did old lawyers quote approvingly the aphorism that law is a jealous mistress who will brook no other? There must be something that made it worth the devotion of a lifetime.

The attitude was no doubt callow and romantic, as befits young men, but it lured many into the law, and the profession still finds it useful in recruiting new members. My own case was not, I think, untypical. A college instructor, a poet who had taken a law degree himself, confirmed my leaning to the law. He said that law was the most noble of all human studies, for it brought philosophy into the marketplace. That was what my classmates and I knew must be true; it was certainly what we wanted to hear. The law was to be a profession of never ending intellectual endeavor, a study concerned with the ordering of complex human affairs through the application of reason. The law itself seemed almost a tangible thing, accreting like a coral reef over the years through many thousands of arguments and decisions by a procession of lawyers and judges, and yet achieving the form of an unimaginably magnificent cathedral. We could almost discern its structure, vast, adorned with endlessly rich and fascinating detail, containing an infinity of passages and rooms, but with each part in integral relation to the rest and in harmony with the main supports and the foundation. Yet it was a structure, too, that was continuously growing and changing as men labored to see its design and improve small details in the brief light and time given them. A life in the law, we thought, promised battle, demanded devotion, and rewarded learning. And who would not choose to be soldier, priest, and scholar?

The Uncertain Establishment

Some years have passed now, and there are days when that vision seems merely amusing, or perhaps poignant. The magnificent edifice of the law has not become clearer but instead has receded, perhaps finally, into the mists. In middle age we suspect that it was nothing but a product of our imaginations to begin with.

These reflections are not merely personal. There is abroad a feeling of disappointment with and about law, a suspicion that it may be weak and unsure. This feeling is particularly frightening because we turn increasingly to law as other supports seem to fail us. The legal establishment itself is uncertain. The signs are everywhere.

Signs are apparent in our attitudes toward the courts, where we have come to accept major philosophic shifts as inevitable with changes in personnel. Signs are also apparent in the law schools, where the traditional intellectual thrust and self-confidence of the faculties have been damaged. One perceives now, despite rising enrollments, signs of lowered morale and uncertainty about the purposes, content, and even worth of legal education. The major law firms are worriedly attempting to adjust to the altered demands and interests of the new graduates, trying to understand their lessened drive and vague career aspirations, asking the faculties why the top-rated students do not appear to be interviewed. The bar, so sure of itself and its functions just a half dozen years ago, is wondering aloud whether this is a passing phase or the end of the established order and the birth of a new, bewildering, and as yet undefined legal culture.

The Core Is Missing

With the legal establishment itself betraying uncertainty and even timidity, it is not surprising that the public senses trouble in the law. And, since law represents stability and safety, is it surprising that sensed weakness should stir disquiet and even anger?

The trouble springs in large part from our inadequate understanding of law and its uses. The striking, and peculiar, fact about a field of study so old is that it possesses very little theory about itself. There is no body of systematic learning about the law's inherent capabilities and limitations. I have heard an eminent economist who became closely acquainted with a major center of legal scholarship remark with astonishment: "You lawyers have nothing of your own. You borrow from the social sciences, but you have no discipline, no core, of your own." And, a few scattered insights aside, he was right.

Good lawyers, a combative, hard-edged breed, are intellectually imperialistic, priding themselves on their ability to ransack other men's specialties quickly and beat them in argument on their own grounds. But it should cause imperialists some embarrassment to reflect that though they regularly invade and reap the harvest of other men's territories, the home country remains unsubdued. There is a price to be paid for the neglect, and the price appears to be the diminished effectiveness of law and decreasing respect for law. It would be well to begin to talk about the problem. Perhaps parts of it must remain insoluble, but we can do better than we have done, and at the very least we may be able to avoid misidentifying the cause of our troubles, and perhaps head off panicky responses that make matters worse.

One aspect of our unease may derive from our tendency to use law too much, to view it as an infinitely expansible carrier of social policy and norms. Law is not an implement that can be turned to any purpose. It has enormous capabilities, but when we ignore its limitations we damage law and place in peril the benefits it can confer. Law is now in serious danger of overreaching its capabilities, and may in fact already have done so. This is an ominous development, both as a symptom of social decay and as a likely cause of further deterioration in the social fabric. We have also damaged law, and created disrespect for it, through our failure to observe the distinction, essential to a democracy, between judges and legislators. The era of the Warren Court was, in my opinion, deeply harmful to the prestige of law. There are many who insist that, as a direct result of the Warren Court's reformist drive, the prestige of law has never been higher. They point to the greatly increased numbers of young people entering law as evidence. The admirers of the Warren Court, however, are less in love with law than with power, power to produce results they like. Implicit in the idea of judge-made constitutional law are the ideals of adherence to general rules, of consistency, and of intellectual rigor. These were qualities in short supply in the Warren Court's record. If that Court did indeed inspire the young, it taught them to confuse the desirability of ends with the legitimacy of means, perhaps to confuse the idea of law and the fact of power.

Our culture has long stressed the importance of law, and Americans are probably as concerned with law as any people on earth. But there exists a strong counterstrain, a tendency to idealize men or groups who set themselves against law and seek their ends through direct action. The ambivalence toward law that this counterstrain creates appears to be strongest in persons with more education, leisure, and affluence than the average. It is closely related to the tradition—now especially strong in literary and academic circles—according to which the enlightened man must continually be in opposition to society, particularly to bourgeois society. Violence from the political right is abhorred, but not violence from the left. The rhetoric of the left is more appealing to prevailing modes of thought—and after all, the argument runs, society has been slow to undertake necessary reforms. Hence the support and sympathy shown in journalistic and academic quarters for such representative figures of our times as the Berrigans, prison rioters, student militants, Black Panthers, Yippies, *et al.*

The tradition of support for civil disobedience and even violence is deeply disturbing, particularly disturbing because it is so firmly established in the institutions that mold opinion. There is a limit to how much defiance of law a legal system can tolerate. No one knows precisely where the tipping point is, but it is undeniable that our system is beginning to feel the strain. Disrespect for law is contagious. As Hannah Arendt warns, "The practice of violence, like all action, changes the world, but the most probable change is a more violent world." Since violence and defiance of law are often successful in our society, they are not, in the short run, irrational means. But in the slightly longer run, if they become the common mode of political struggle they will be disastrous for everyone.

Those who use or advocate coercion and disruption for political or ideological ends have a ready model in the legally sanctioned struggle between labor unions and management. Our labor law, and the ideology that supports and suffuses it, encourages the organization of employees into fighting groups, and lets the wage bargain depend upon the outcome of the fight. The rhetoric of union organization and struggle is the rhetoric of war. The method of struggle, by both sides, is coercive, each attempting to put intolerable pressures on the other in order to achieve a favorable if temporary treaty of peace.

It becomes increasingly difficult to maintain a consensus that the legal right of private employee unions to strike and disrupt (and of employers to lock out) is somehow different from the desire of other groups to do the same. One element in the inability of some faculties to resist educationally inappropriate student demands, backed by threats of mass disruption, was the frequently advanced analogy of the students' position to that of workers. Sensing the drama and power it created, students eagerly cast themselves in the role of proletarians, and many faculty members accepted the metaphor. Picket lines, strikes, disruptions are now becoming the common coin of political dispute, used by groups ranging from welfare recipients to women's lib. Not law but willingness to inflict inconvenience and discomfort, or sometimes worse, becomes the decisive factor in disputes.

When law is invoked, as in certain strikes by public employees, it is often only partially effective. Frequently it is brought into play with the understanding that sanctions will be modified or lifted entirely if the objectionable behavior ceases. In the course of student disorders the authorities may bring law to bear, but the demand for amnesty is frequently made and frequently granted as part of the bargaining process. Law is then perceived by the immediate participants to the struggle, and by the general public, as merely one weapon usable in combat. Law becomes thought of not as the ultimate command of our society, but as simply one element of power in complex struggle. This view of law denies it any claim to unique respect. It is on a par with any other kind of force.

A Claim of Omnicompetence

In this way, domestic law begins to descend to the status of international law, which means that we begin to recognize the independence, the semi-sovereignty, of various warring groups somewhat as nations, we admit that law has only a limited role to play in governing. Law is successful when there is a consensus that certain behavior cannot be tolerated, when groups with legitimate interests to advance are nevertheless perceived by the society as lacking any legitimate right to disrupt, to wage limited wars. The question, and it is by no means an easy one, is whether we will be able to sustain our denial to nonlabor groups of the tactics we concede to labor organizations.

There may be room for pessimism. William J. McGill, the president of Columbia, argues that the university, in finding forms to cope with the various groups that make demands upon the administration, is providing a model for "pluralism" in society at large. "One of the greatest achievements of American law," he says, "has been construction of the rules of orderly conflict between management and labor, embodied in our now classical concepts of labor law. We need a closely related legal framework for working with social change and with the conflicts engendered by the variety of liberation movements now developing on campus." This is a disturbing view. It should be clear that the management-labor model is a warfare model, and that its acceptance as the general mode of effecting change would be disastrous for law and social peace. The results, indeed, might be so intolerable that law would return in a far more repressive form than any we now know.

Even as we increasingly accept the absence or only partial effectiveness of law in many social controversies, we are simultaneously introducing law into others where it had never before had a role. One of the most striking developments of recent years is the ubiquity that law is attaining. This appears to be an unreflective trend rather than a self-conscious process that anybody has thought out. Law spreads and seeps into ever more aspects of life, claiming an omnicompetence it cannot sustain.

Law is growing from many sources. Floods of regulations are churned out by Congress, state legislatures, municipal governing bodies, courts, executive officers, and administrative agencies. Since the New Deal, we have become accustomed to massive intervention of law in the economic life of the nation, and now we are seeing a similar proliferation in social and cultural spheres. With the substance of much of this law I have no quarrel, but there are costs to the use of law and in some areas of life the costs may exceed any conceivable benefits.

No society can be healthy and effective if all disputes are drawn into legal processes. The spread of law throughout human relations signals not only a decline in individual freedom but also a withering of community, traditional modes of accommodation, and informal authority. A healthy society requires that there be considerable play in human relations, a degree of trust in the good faith of others, confidence that things can be worked out tolerably, a willingness not to insist on every "right" one may think one should ideally possess, and a large amount of individual self-reliance. The attempt to define all the rights of individuals and to enforce them by legal processes signifies the diminution or disappearance of these virtues.

An excessive and oppressive legalism is taking hold even where law in a formal sense has not entered. A prime example is afforded by the universities, where there has been an unprecedented demand (and an astonishingly ready acquiescence to it) that everyone's rights be spelled out in written codes and that special tribunals be created to enforce them. In universities throughout the nation we have seen the adoption of codes, often quite complex, concerning student behavior, faculty and administration powers, the process of decision making within the university, and even such matters as discrimination in hiring by employers who visit the campus. Presidents and deans are stripped of wide areas of discretion, rights and duties are spelled out, special tribunals for indictment, trial, and appeal are created. The analogy to formal legal systems is so powerful that these procedures begin to pick up elements of due process, right to counsel, proof beyond a reasonable doubt, exclusion of hearsay, peer-group representation on tribunals, and so forth.

These developments are further along in universities than elsewhere, but various groups are beginning to make similar demands on other institutions. Demands that corporate boards include representatives of consumers, environmentalists, labor, racial and ethnic groups, and the like, represent a shift toward political decision making as the mode of governance of these organizations. And we keep hearing demands that the internal processes of corporations be judicialized—the theory being that large corporations have as much "power" as state governments.

Reflections of Paranoid Feelings

The increasing legalization of our culture is a sign of the deterioration of the culture, and particularly the breakdown of community. Groups feel themselves set apart and requiring the protection of law from what is perceived as the hostility of strangers—people who not long ago would have been accepted as members of the same community. Such paranoid feelings are reflected, for example, in those student demands for codified rights. It makes little difference that the distrust is usually without objective justification.

Nor is it likely that law will significantly repair the broken sense of community. In an earlier article in this series ("The Angry Young Lawyers," September) my dean, Abraham S. Goldstein, was quoted as saying: "As home, church, and ideology began to lose their cohesive force, law was increasingly seen as a way not only of expressing pre-existing norms but also of creating them." And of course law, though its capacities in that respect are probably quite limited, *can* help generate norms. But a reliance upon law to replace home, church, ideology, and the sense of community seems likely to make matters worse rather than better. The intrusion of law and its coercions is a continuing reminder that trust, community, ease of relationship, have diminished. When even relatively minor disputes are referred to the legal process, they become freighted with emotional and symbolic importance. The divisiveness inherent in adversary procedures begins to operate. Disputes are made more visible and the drama of conflict tends to polarize the participants. Thus law does not always repair broken community; it may, on the contrary, put an additional strain at precisely the wrong time on the waning strength of home, church, and ideology.

The trend toward legalization does more than impair the case and civility of life. It requires the diversion of time and energy from other tasks to those of manning the legal machinery. More than that, the uncritical extension of law to new fields—whether formal law made by legislatures and courts or the informal variety growing within universities and other institutions—brings into adjudicative settings decisions that do not belong there. Adjudication requires standards that are real and susceptible of proof. Law is full of instances in which lack of adequate criteria made the hearing process an empty ritual. Some time ago, as a result of statutory misreading, the Supreme Court demanded that the field prices of natural gas be regulated by the Federal Power Commission. Since the unregulated field price was competitive, regulation, if it was to accomplish anything, had to hold prices below competitive levels. For a variety of reasons, a cost basis made no sense, so the commission and the reviewing courts were left to decide cases without real criteria. At last report they were still floundering in their attempts to find law for the problem.

The Value of Unwritten Standards

Certain forms of discrimination present the problem of criteria that are real but cannot easily be established by evidence. It is easy enough to establish whether a person has been turned away from a restaurant because of race or sex—the variables are few. But employment discrimination presents a different problem. The decision concerning who is to be hired or not hired, who is to be promoted or passed over, does not always, or perhaps even usually, turn upon objective and quantifiable data. Such decisions also rest upon elements of judgment and intuition. On a case-by-case basis, therefore, the employer's decision will usually turn out to be unreviewable. Unless he admits bias, it is almost impossible to prove that he discriminated. This, it appears, is the reason federal programs in this field, including the President's "Philadelphia Plan" for the building trades, have had to impose quotas in order to be effective.

In other cases, law intrudes in decisional processes that are better left to managerial discretion, and so renders institutions less effective and often less humane. Universities, for example, have long had standards of conduct that were customary and unwritten or, if written, so vaguely worded as to be in effect customary. People understood with tolerable certainty where the lines were. Administrators handled most infractions informally and were able to take account of such factors as the character of the student, the likelihood of repetition, and the morale of the student body. These are matters that a formal hearing process cannot deal with. Other difficulties aside, the mere adoption of an adjudicative setting makes such nice judgments about persons seem improper. The trappings of law raise expectations of impersonality and "objectivity." As control over the institution of formal proceeding is itself increasingly formalized, cases are made of situations better left to informal discussion or admonition.

We need more thought and greater sophistication about the kinds of issues and decisions that can profitably be referred to formal legal processes and the kinds that ought to be left to other processes. We are beginning to see that there are areas in which a government of men rather than of laws is to be preferred. Sometimes, as in the case of employment discrimination, we may be willing to pay the costs that the use of law entails, but then we should be skillful enough to frame the criteria in ways that law can handle.

We must remember that law is a blunt instrument, and that we cannot use it effectively if we assign it tasks requiring a scalpel.

A Need for Laissez Faire

Law in our society is overextended in yet another sense. We have pushed too many policies that are too complex into the courts. In judicial institutions as in economic units, there are problems of economies of scale, problems of optimal size and work load. The principle that some specialization is essential to effective work cannot be overlooked. No other nation thrusts as many policy issues upon its courts as do we. In such varied aspects of life as antitrust, labor relations, rules governing elections, entitlement to government benefits, and criminal-law procedures, courts are confronted with major substantive issues left unresolved by other branches of government. As a result, American courts are overloaded with broad and profound questions of economics, sociology, political philosophy, criminology, and so on and on. They do not, it must be said in all candor, handle these questions very well. Very often they do not handle them even passably. That is not surprising. No man or group of men can deal effectively with such a range of subjects. The result is that over the decades there has been a marked decline in judicial performance, and complex social policies are being deformed or rendered simplistic in the very process of their application. The two fields that I know best, antitrust law and constitutional law, are in states of intellectual chaos. My colleagues tell me that their fields of interest are in no better condition.

The lesson may be that a society cannot afford too many complex social policies, that some large admixture of laissez faire is required simply because regulation that might ideally be preferable will in fact, because of our inability to apply it without deforming it, turn out to be worse. Or perhaps the moral is that we must require legislatures to spell out their policies with considerably greater precision and specification than we now expect. In a society where customary modes of doing things are trusted, legislators can leave the detailed working out of policies to administrators, but that is no longer our case. And if we insist upon judicial participation in the application of policies, we must protect the judiciary by also insisting that legislators provide more guidance.

It is sometimes argued that we could devise new institutions to relieve the courts of some of their unmanageable tasks, but that is not a particularly happy thought. Beginning with the establishment of the ICC in 1887, we have spawned any number of administrative tribunals and agencies to frame regulations and decide cases, subject to judicial review. The results, most observers now admit, have been dreadful.

Yet somehow we must make the work of the courts more manageable. The alternative is to lose the benefits that courts can give us: scholarship, a generalist view, wisdom, mature and dispassionate reflection, and—especially important—careful and reasoned explanation of their decisions.

Related to these issues is a development that threatens considerable trouble in the future: the increasing use of litigation as a shortcut to the achievement of desired political and social ends. I do not want to be misunderstood here. Some political and social changes inhere in accepted legal principles, and litigation quite properly both discloses and forwards these changes. All the implications of a principle are not evident on a first enunciation of it. Thus the principle of racial equality before the law, contained in the Fourteenth Amendment, quite properly resulted at length in the Supreme Court's decisions—in *Brown* v. *Board of Education* and the cases that came after—denying government the power to segregate or discriminate on racial grounds. Those litigations wrought an enormous change in our social and political structures and practices, but the result was a correct one for the law to reach.

The problem arises when litigation is used to accomplish results not inherent in any legal principle that the courts may properly rely upon. It is much cheaper and easier to ask a court to order the change you want than to go through the time-consuming, expensive, and messy process of persuading voters or legislators. And there is always the possibility that the voters or legislators will see things differently from you. Naturally, many groups and individuals accepted the invitation to substitute litigation for politics. And the Warren Court too often responded by ordering change based upon no discernible principle other than the majority's personal views.

A Confusion of Roles

It should hardly be necessary to say that this practice is inconsistent with the most fundamental theory of representative democracy. Our Constitution and our political ethos do not call for general government by judges. Many of the results the Warren Court reached were, in my view, politically or socially desirable. I would have voted for them as a legislator or as a citizen in a general referendum. But that does not begin to justify their imposition by a court acting on no existing legal principle.

The confusion of roles encouraged by the Warren Court undermines not only representative government but also the ability of law to govern at all. Though the Warren Court majority pleaded that it was merely applying the Constitution, that pretense fooled fewer and fewer people. Performance of this kind on the part of courts raises several dangers. Many people may decide that the claim of law itself to honesty, integrity, and neutrality is false. If law comes to be seen as something of a trick, political power will be seen as the only reality. In this perception lies the possibility of the destruction of the Supreme Court's constitutional authority. Worse still, those who decide that law is a trick will not easily distinguish between law made by judges and law made by legislators. Cynicism is not so easily confined, and disrespect for the Supreme Court may easily become disdain for what the Court symbolizes, the ideal of government by law rather than by whim, prejudice, or raw power. If the Supreme Court's power comes to be thought illegitimate, where will legitimate authority be seen to lie?

The perception that a Court is willing to be the political ally of certain causes, regardless of law, damages the moral authority of law, and law cannot be effective unless it carries moral weight as well as the threat of sanctions. Should any sizable and cohesive segment of the population come to feel that the only reason to obey law is the possibility of unpleasantness with the police, the costs of maintaining social order with present degrees of freedom will be prohibitive. We live in times when we cannot afford to dissipate any of the law's moral authority.

The present Chief Justice, Warren Burger, appears to be fully aware of the dangers of the misuse of courts. He has publicly worried that efforts to use law to bring about social change have been "creating expectations that are beyond fulfillment." He has warned: "Young people who decide to go into the law primarily on the theory that they can change the world by litigation in the courts I think may be in for some disappointments . . . That is not the route by which basic changes in a country like ours should be made. That is a legislative and policy process, part of the political process. And there is a very limited role for courts in this respect."

A Particular Kind May Die

The Supreme Court, however, may not find it easy to draw back from the activist, legislative pattern of the Warren years. The habit of bringing to the Court claims that belong in the political arena is not the less powerful because it is deeply illegitimate. Various kinds of claims are working their way through the judicial system, and the Supreme Court may ultimately have to face them—suits seeking judicial determination of abortion statutes, the death penalty, environmental issues, the rights of women, the Vietnam war. The Court should refer many of these issues to the political process, even though that will anger groups who have been taught to hope for easier, more authoritarian solutions.

The problem of social order is coming to the forefront in most advanced nations. Law must become more self-conscious if it is to meet the challenges that are being put to it. While it is not, of course, the only institution that creates social order, law is one of society's bulwarks, and it provides an impelling analogy or metaphor for social processes. Law is valuable for itself and because it teaches moral lessons to society. It is important that the lessons be the right ones. The right lessons will be taught only if we learn to use law correctly, to respect it as the ultimate arbiter of disputes where it is applied, to conserve its strengths by employing it only where it has clear benefits to give, and by insisting that the roles of legislators and courts be kept distinct. These tasks are not for lawyers alone, but until they begin to create the body of theory that their profession so desperately requires, there will continue to be unnecessary trouble in the law.

The stakes are far more important than the efficient functioning of law. The answer to the question "Is law dead?" is that law will never die. But a particular kind of law may die. Society will not long tolerate severe social disorder. Should law in its present form fail us, it will ultimately be replaced by other forms of law that will impose order. What is at stake, then, is not law but rather democratically made law allowing wide scope for individual freedom. That is worth preserving.

"Reforming" Foreign Intelligence

Periods of sin and excess are commonly followed by spasms of remorse and moralistic overreaction. That is harmless enough; indeed, the repentance of the hungover reveler is standard comic fare in Washington, however, politicians are apt to rent only the sins of others, and matters become rather less humorous when the moral hangover is written into laws that promise permanent damage to constitutional procedure and institutions.

As expiation for Vietnam, we have the War Powers Resolution, an attempt by Congress to share in detailed decisions about the deployment of U.S. armed forces in the world. It is probably unconstitutional and certainly unworkable. But politically the resolution severely handicaps the President in responding to rapidly developing threats to our national interests abroad. We have, as atonement for illegalities in fund raising for the 1972 campaign, the Federal Election Campaign Act, which limits political expression and deforms the political process. The Supreme Court held that parts of this act violate the First Amendment and probably should have held that all of it does.

Now, in response to past excesses by our intelligence agencies, we have H.R. 7308, the proposed Foreign Intelligence Surveillance Act. (A similar bill is out of committee in the Senate.) Like the other two "reforms" it reflects an unwillingness to recognize that existing processes worked and do not require reform, as well as a certain lightheadedness about the damage the reform will do to indispensable constitutional institutions.

The purpose of H.R. 7308 is to lodge in the federal courts the final power to decide when electronic surveillance of American citizens and lawfully admitted aliens may be done to gather foreign intelligence information important to national security.

Since Franklin Roosevelt at least, every President has claimed the constitutional authority to order such surveillances with out a court order. That

From the *Wall Street Journal*, March 9, 1978.

power has been derived from the President's role under Article II of the Constitution as commander-in-chief and officer primarily responsible for the conduct of foreign affairs. The judicial warrant requirement of the Fourth Amendment, never an absolute in any case, was thought inapplicable because of the fundamental dissimilarity of intelligence gathering and criminal investigation with prosecution in mind.

A Lot of Secrecy

H.R. 7308 provides that the Chief Justice of the United States will publicly designate at least one judge from each of the 11 federal circuits to sit on a special court. Two judges at a time will come to Washington. Warrant applications may be made to either. The Chief Justice will publicly designate six other judges to sit in panels of three to hear government appeals from warrant denials. The government may petition for review by the Supreme Court if turned down by the special court of appeals. All hearings, including presentations to the Supreme Court, will be secret; the rulings will be secret; and the government will be the only party represented.

Each application requires the approval of the Attorney General or his designee and a certification by a high presidential appointee working in the area of national security or defense. Persons to be targeted for surveillance, the means to be used, minimization of the surveillance and close control of the information obtained are provided for.

The most stringent protections are provided for targeting American citizens and aliens lawfully admitted for permanent residence. There must be probable cause to believe they are agents of a foreign power. The bill may also require reason to believe that a crime may be committed.

Much of this tracks existing Executive Branch practice. The political appeal of the bill lies in the introduction of judges and warrants. That is also its major flaw. Procedures appropriate to criminal contexts, where, say, a wiretap is sought to gather evidence to prosecute narcotics smugglers, are not easily transferred to foreign intelligence, where, for example, radio transmissions from hostile powers' establishments in the country are to be monitored with no thought of prosecution.

The difference in context may mean, for one thing, that the law would be unconstitutional. If warrantless surveillance for foreign intelligence is a presidential power under Article II (the only two courts of appeals required to decide the issue held that it is, but the point is unsettled), Congress probably has no authority to require warrants.

Moreover, the attempt to give the Supreme Court an essentially administrative role in intelligence gathering may run afoul of Article III of the Constitution. It is somewhat as if Judge Webster was empowered to run the FBI while remaining on the bench. The job is managerial, not judicial, and the two should not be mixed.

There are and can be no judicial criteria for making decisions about the needs of foreign intelligence, and judges cannot become adequately informed about intelligence to make the sophisticated judgments required. To do an adequate job, they would have to be drawn fully into intelligence work, which is not the point of this enterprise. To suppose that they would defer to the superior expertise of the agencies is either to confess the safeguards will not work or to underestimate the strength of the tendency displayed by the judiciary in recent years to take over both legislative and executive functions.

The requirement that a crime be in the offing would eliminate our ability to learn of foreign intelligence activities vital to our national interests but which violate no federal criminal law.

The law would almost certainly increase unauthorized disclosures of sensitive information simply by greatly widening the circle of people with access to it. In some cases as many as thirteen judges, their clerks, and secretaries would share knowledge. If opinions—required only when warrants are denied—are circulated, or if the judges consult one another, a minimum of 26 judges will have top-secret information. Disclosures are not merely intelligence calamities; they may lead to foreign relations debacles as well. Electronic surveillance is known by everyone to exist, but its public disclosure may be hard to ignore, just as Khrushchev could ignore the U-2, until it was shot down.

The element of judicial secrecy is particularly troubling. Because it reverses our entire tradition, it is difficult to think of secret decisions as "law." The assertion that this bill would ensure that foreign intelligence electronic surveillance was conducted according to "the rule of law" is, therefore, misleading. The bill pretends to create a real set of courts that will bring "law" to an area of discretion. In reality, it would set apart a group of judges who must operate largely in the dark and create rules known only to themselves. Whatever that may be called, it debases an important idea to term it the rule of law, it is more like the uninformed, unknown and uncontrolled exercise of discretion.

The statute would, moreover, present some judges with an impossible dilemma. Suppose that the Supreme Court splits, say five to four, in granting a warrant. If the dissenting Justices felt that the decision and others it presages deny basic constitutional rights of Americans, what are those Justices to do? Must they remain stoically silent about what they believe to be the secret destruction of rights they are sworn to uphold? Should they publish a full opinion and damage national security? Or should they perhaps state publicly that constitutional freedoms are being destroyed but they are not at the moment at liberty to explain how? They appear to have a choice between behavior that is dishonorable or fatuous. That is an intolerable moral and constitutional position in which to place judges.

Diminishing Executive Responsibility

The law seems certain as well to diminish substantially the responsibility and accountability of the Executive Branch. To take the extreme but not improbable case, if even one judge proves excessively lenient, the government can go to him in all doubtful, or even improper cases. Since there is no adverse party to appeal, the "rule of law" will be the temper of one district judge, unknown to the other judges and the Supreme Court.

Whether or not there is such a judge, what can the Congress do if it comes to think the surveillance power granted has been abused? Can a congressional committee summon before it for explanation the judges, perhaps including some members of the Supreme Court, who approved the warrants? I should think certainly not. Can we expect successful criminal or civil actions against the officials who, following statutory procedures, obtained warrants from the judges? That seems hardly likely.

When an attorney general must decide for himself, without the shield of a warrant, whether to authorize surveillance, and must accept the consequences if things go wrong, there is likely to be more care taken. The statute, however, has the effect of immunizing everyone, and sooner or later that fact will be taken advantage of. It would not be the first time a regulatory scheme turned out to benefit the regulated rather than the public.

The intelligence abuses of the past were uncovered through existing processes of investigation. One response was the detailed regulations governing electronic surveillance promulgated by then Attorney General Edward Levi. These are fully as sensitive to Fourth Amendment protections against unreasonable searches and seizures of communications as this bill is, and likely to be as effective. The intelligence officer reckless enough to ignore those regulations and subject himself to criminal liability would be reckless enough to bypass the warrant requirement of the proposed statute as well.

Against the Independent Counsel

For almost fifteen years America has experimented with a second and separate system of criminal-law enforcement. The Ethics in Government Act of 1978 created court-appointed independent counsels, placed outside the control of the President and the Attorney General, to investigate and, where possible, prosecute certain high-ranking executive-branch officials. Members of Congress and the judiciary were exempted. The statutory authorization for the Office of Independent Counsel expired this past December, but as a result of the pardons George Bush extended on Christmas Eve to six former officials involved in the Iran-*contra* affair, the chances that Congress and President Bill Clinton will revive the law seem to have increased. They should first study the record, which has been abominable.

The conventional wisdom, echoed on almost all editorial pages, holds that an independent counsel is essential because the Department of Justice cannot be trusted to prosecute miscreants in the executive branch. The conventional wisdom is wrong. The real effect and, to a large extent, the purpose of a special-prosecutor law has little to do with Department of Justice cover-ups.

"If the institution of the American presidency has grown enfeebled over the past two decades," Suzanne Garment of the American Enterprise Institute writes,

> it is not only because of battles with its opponents over policies or institutional prerogatives. Its adversaries have also waged a crucial and more or less continuous attack on the underlying moral legitimacy of the office, its occupants, and the President's allies in the executive branch.

A spearhead in the assault on the moral legitimacy, and hence the effectiveness, of the presidency has been the independent-counsel statute.

From *Commentary*, February 1993.

The statute has helped tilt the balance between the executive and legislative branches and has, as a result of the prosecutorial incentives it created, produced savage injustices to individuals. All of this to cure a problem that does not exist.

Two instances routinely cited as showing the need for an independent prosecutor are the Department of Justice's handling of the cases of Spiro Agnew and Richard Nixon. If those two examples do not withstand scrutiny, the argument for a new statute collapses, because there could hardly be greater tests of the Department's capacity than its handling of the wrongdoing of a President and a Vice President. As Solicitor General at the time, I participated in both matters and claim some knowledge of what took place.

In the summer of 1973, George Beall, the United States Attorney for Maryland, discovered that Spiro Agnew had taken bribes when Governor of Maryland and had continued to receive payments while Vice President. Beall informed Attorney General Elliot Richardson. There can be few more startling and unhappy messages for an Attorney General to receive, but Richardson informed President Nixon, had a grand jury investigate Agnew, and ultimately indicted him. After Agnew's attorneys and I exchanged briefs on the constitutionality of indicting him before he was removed from office by conviction on impeachment, he plea-bargained, confessed his guilt, and resigned the vice presidency.

Though the Department of Justice thus demonstrated that it could remove an incumbent Vice President, some critics apparently believe that Agnew was treated too leniently, that he should have been sent to prison. That option, however, was not available. The Watergate investigation was closing in on Richard Nixon, and Richardson thought it would be devastating to the nation if the President were defending an impeachment trial while the Vice President was a criminal defendant. Agnew used that as a bargaining chip and the deal was struck to be rid of him so that a new Vice President could be in office if Nixon should be impeached. That seemed to me then, and seems to me now, the only responsible course for Richardson to have taken.

The prime exhibit in the argument of those who want an independent counsel, however, is Watergate and what came to be called the Saturday Night Massacre. In fact, those episodes have been thoroughly misunderstood.

The initial investigation of the break-in at the Watergate complex was conducted by Earl Silbert and his colleagues in the Office of the U. S. Attorney for the District of Columbia. The facts unearthed caused Silbert to order research on the constitutionality of indicting the President before he was removed from office by conviction on impeachment. He also issued a wide-ranging subpoena for White House documents. Silbert and his colleagues were ready to make the case against Nixon and his aides, but Elliot Richardson had just been nominated by Nixon for the post of Attorney General, and the Senate Judiciary Committee conditioned confirmation on Richardson's agreement to appoint a special prosecutor. Richardson chose his old law-school professor, Archibald Cox. Silbert gave Cox about 90 typewritten pages outlining the conspiracy and the evidence. More work remained to be done, but the essential outline of the case was there. Watergate would have played out about the way it did had the U.S. Attorney's Office been allowed to continue.

Though there was no need for a special prosecutor to deal with Watergate, it was politically inevitable that one would be named. But there might not have been a *further* demand for a special prosecutor removed from all executive branch control had it not been for the Saturday Night Massacre (that is, Nixon's firing of Cox, together with the resignations it triggered). For almost 200 years, the public and Congress had been satisfied with what Terry Eastland of the Ethics and Public Policy Center calls the "politics of ethics."[1] The instruments of that politics included investigation and prosecution by the Department of Justice or by special prosecutors brought in for single occasions; congressional investigation; impeachment; clamor in the press; and, most effective, public reaction that determined the political future of those involved in wrongdoing.

The Cox firing changed all that. Although Cox was a man of integrity and ability, Richardson made a mistake in naming him special prosecutor. Nixon was immediately convinced that the investigation would be partisan because Cox was a long-time ally of Nixon's despised and feared political enemy, Senator Edward Kennedy. To compound matters, Cox made the politically maladroit move of taking the oath of office with the Kennedy family in attendance. The newspaper accounts and photographs of that event magnified White House paranoia.

Actually, Cox's behavior as special prosecutor did not warrant distrust. Any prosecutor, on learning of the existence of the tapes Nixon had secretly made, was bound to seek them, by subpoena if necessary. Cox did just that, and panic rolled over the White House. Richardson and the President's top defense lawyers attended a meeting in the office of Alexander Haig, Nixon's

---

1. *Ethics, Politics, and the Independent Counsel: Executive Power, Executive Vice 1789–1989*, National Legal Center for the Public Interest (1989). This is the best scholarly analysis I know of concerning the great deficiencies of the independent-counsel system.

chief of staff, to decide what to do about the subpoena. The answer was in two parts. The first was to offer the "Stennis compromise." Senator John Stennis would listen to the subpoenaed tapes and produce a transcript from which national-security matters were deleted. The second part was to give Cox an order to seek no further tapes.

It is surprising that no one at the meeting realized this was a prescription for disaster. It should have been obvious that Cox could not accept either the compromise or the order. To do so would have been to betray his responsibilities. It should also have been clear that Richardson, given his commitment to the Senate Judiciary Committee, could not fire Cox for refusing the order. Apparently neither of these things was thought through, and once the order was given, the Saturday Night Massacre became inevitable.

Cox predictably refused and explained his decision on national television. Though Cox's decision was correct, Nixon now had to fire him: no President can afford to be faced down in public by a subordinate member of the executive branch. Richardson and the Deputy Attorney General would not carry out the firing and departed. I was the third and last in the line of succession established by Department regulations, and I discharged Cox. Had I not done so, the President would have named an Acting Attorney General from outside the Department who would have discharged Cox and perhaps his entire staff. That would have caused mass resignations in the Department of Justice. As it was, I explained the situation to the top officers of the Department and no one resigned.

Whatever the motivation behind the order to Cox, his firing had nothing to do with any attempt to stop the investigation. No one at the White House suggested that I interfere with the investigation in any way. When I met with Nixon after signing the letter removing Cox from office, the President understood that the investigation would continue and said only that he wanted "a prosecution, not a persecution." Cox's deputies and staff remained in place and, as they noted in their final report, did not miss a day's work.

It is partly my fault that the "firestorm," and hence the demand for a court-appointed prosecutor, followed. When I left the White House that night, I should have held a press conference to explain that only Cox was going and his staff would continue as before. That would have countered the impression that a coup was being attempted. I was new to Washington, however, and a press conference never crossed my mind, nor did anyone suggest the idea. That mistake aside, however, the Department of Justice had nothing to apologize for in its handling of Watergate or the Saturday Night Massacre.

In the Nixon and Agnew cases, no one at the main Department of Justice or in the United States Attorneys' Offices was tempted to ignore the evidence in order to protect the President or the Vice President. It may be objected that the nation cannot rely upon always having persons of integrity in those positions. But anyone familiar with institutions such as the Department of Justice or a U.S. Attorney's Office will realize that there are other safeguards.

Let us suppose that in the Nixon or the Agnew affair either or both the U.S. Attorney and the Attorney General had been men of less exacting ethical standards. They would have found it impossible to suppress the evidence. High-ranking law-enforcement officials do not go about detecting crime on their own. Evidence is brought to them by others. The facts are known to lower level prosecutors, FBI agents, often to a grand jury. These are people of professional integrity who also possess keen instincts of self-preservation. They will not be associated with a cover-up, and cannot afford to be. Nor need they have the courage to go public. They have connections with Congress, the press, and public-interest organizations. If an Attorney General had tried to protect Nixon or Agnew, that fact would have been leaked at once. The more spectacular a case is, the higher it reaches into the executive branch, the less willing is anybody to be connected in any way with a cover-up or even the suspicion of one.

Richard Nixon's presidency was doomed from the moment the investigation started, and it really did not matter whether the U.S. Attorney's Office, Cox, or his successor, Leon Jaworski, was in charge. The Watergate investigation could not have been avoided, and once started, it could not have been stopped. There is simply no danger that any criminal violation by a high-ranking official in the executive branch will be hidden by the Department of Justice. Though the fact has been overwhelmed by the mythology of Watergate and the Saturday Night Massacre, there is no case in our history in which the Department failed in its duty to prosecute executive-branch wrongdoing.[2]

That is one reason I testified to both the Senate and House Judiciary Committees in 1973, very shortly after the firing of Cox, that a mechanism for obtaining court-appointed special prosecutors was unnecessary as well as unconstitutional, and that I would therefore recommend to the President that he veto any bill seeking to establish such an office.

No bill was passed, and we escaped the predictable horrors of the institution, until Jimmy Carter became President and supported such a measure.

2. Charges are being made that an exception to this rule is the BNL case. As yet, however, these charges are unproven.

Carter's Attorney General, Griffin Bell, understood the evil of the scheme but loyally backed his President. Since Carter left office, Bell, freed of his commitment, has consistently argued against the legislation.

The independent-counsel statute went through several versions but all versions displayed the features that make the law a recipe for irresponsibility, injustice, and the deformation of the constitutional balance between the legislative and executive branches.

In the office of the Independent Counsel, Congress created, for the first time in our history, a federal prosecutor who is not really responsible to anyone. Under this statute, when the Attorney General receives allegations of criminal behavior by a high-ranking executive-branch official he must make an inquiry, but he is now deprived of most means of investigation. Unless, thus handicapped by the statute, he can determine that there are *no* reasonable grounds to believe that further investigation is warranted, he must ask the court to appoint an independent counsel. If a designated number of members of the Judiciary Committee of either House requests an independent counsel, the Attorney General must either agree or submit a report to Congress explaining his negative decision. In short, despite the Constitution's commitment of law enforcement to the President, he and his Attorney General are effectively stripped of that function in cases covered by the statute.

To make matters worse, when an independent counsel finishes his assignment, he must file a report with the court "setting forth fully and completely" a description of his work, the disposition of all cases brought, and his reasons for *not* prosecuting any matter. The court may then release the report, or such portions of it as it deems appropriate. No regular prosecutor would make public his reasons for not indicting, but the release of the special counsel's report can result in considerable embarrassment to the persons involved.

It is hardly surprising that such a statute is subject to abuse and that lawyers of great distinction have thought it unconstitutional. Thus, in the case of *Morrison* v. *Olson,* former Attorneys General Edward Levi, Griffin Bell, and William French Smith, who served, respectively, under Presidents Gerald Ford, Jimmy Carter, and Ronald Reagan, submitted a brief *amicus curiae* asking the Supreme Court to invalidate the law. It is a great pity that the Court did not follow their recommendation.

Morrison v. *Olson* was a classic use of the independent-counsel statute to weaken the presidency by punishing an executive-branch official for carrying out his duties. A committee of the House demanded files of cases the Department of Justice and the Environmental Protection Agency were investigating or prosecuting. No law-enforcement officer could properly reveal that information. On the advice of the Department of Justice, President Reagan refused disclosure. The committee, enraged at this display of responsibility, asked the House Judiciary Committee to investigate the role of the Department in advising the President.

The Judiciary Committee subpoenaed all the memoranda prepared by Justice in advising the President and called Theodore Olson, the Assistant Attorney General responsible for giving legal advice to the Attorney General and the President. Some materials had been produced and a file search was continuing. Olson said he did not recall whether certain documents existed. Later they were found and produced to the committee.

Still, the committee was angered by Olson's forthright defense of the President's law-enforcement powers. On one occasion, the committee demanded any handwritten notes the Department's lawyers might have made in preparing their advice. Olson replied that he was sure the committee could arrange an exchange of those notes for the handwritten notes of the committee's staffers. One member rose, slammed the file down, and said that was the most outrageous remark he had ever heard.

The hearings were so inconsequential that they were not even published. But over two years later, the committee delivered a 3,100-page report accusing Olson of making false statements to Congress when—to cite one instance—he said he could not recall documents that were later produced. Alexia Morrison was appointed independent counsel and Olson's travails began.

Within six months, in seeking unsuccessfully to expand her jurisdiction to others, Morrison stated that, standing alone, Olson's testimony probably did not violate any criminal statute. Nevertheless, she took almost three years before she announced that there was no case against him.

In the course of these proceedings, Olson challenged a subpoena on the grounds that the independent-counsel statute was unconstitutional. He lost, but in upholding the constitutionality of the law, the Supreme Court created a number of constitutional anomalies that the Founders certainly never contemplated.

One of the most serious is to involve Congress in law enforcement directed at the executive branch. The Constitution protects members of Congress from executive-branch prosecution through the Speech and Debate Clause which makes them legally immune for anything said or written in the course of their duties. No such constitutional protection was thought necessary for the executive branch because it was given control of prosecutions. But now the Court has allowed prosecutions of the executive branch that are effectively initiated by Congress. That is not quite a bill of attainder, but it is a lot closer than the Constitution, properly interpreted, allows. The unfortunate outcome of *Morrison* v. *Olson* leaves the executive branch largely defenseless against this sort of assault. The power to pardon is one of the few shields the President has left.

Though Chief Justice Rehnquist's *Morrison* opinion was unpersuasive, only Justice Scalia dissented, so it is clear that hopes for the law's permanent demise rest not with the Court but with the wisdom and good will of Congress. Given the use Congress has made of the law in the past, the prospect is bleak.

In addition to everything else that is wrong with it, the institution of the independent counsel damages lives and reputations in ways that few regular prosecutors ever could or would. The human as well as the institutional costs are described rivetingly by Elliott Abrams in *Undue Process: A Story of How Political Differences Are Turned Into Crimes.*[3]

When he left the State Department in 1989 after serving there in a variety of positions since 1981, Abrams intended to write a book, but this is not the one he planned. Abrams's last job at State was Assistant Secretary for Inter-American Affairs. Among his many duties was carrying out RonaldReagan's policy of keeping the Nicaraguan *contras* a viable force against the Sandinistas. That involved him in two wars:

> a guerrilla war in Central America, and an almost equally violent political war about Central America between the Reagan administration and the Democratic-controlled Congress.

In the fall of 1986, the Iran-*contra* affair exploded and Abrams was called to testify before Congress, the Tower Commission, and a grand jury about the nature of U.S. support for the *contras*. An independent counsel, Lawrence Walsh, had also been appointed to investigate Iran-*contra*. He and his staff interviewed Abrams endlessly and took him before the grand jury three times. In early 1988, he was told that the Office of the Independent Counsel believed his statements, and he heard no more about the matter.

Until 1991. Taking into account everything else we now know about that Office, it seems too much of a coincidence that the prosecutors' interest in Abrams should have reawakened right after they lost the case against

---

3. *Free Press*

their most famous target, Oliver North, and when all indications were that they would also lose their other most important case—the one against John Poindexter. After all, they had no information about Abrams they had not had three-and-one-half years earlier.

The supposition that Walsh and his staff went after Abrams because they badly needed trophies to justify their existence is strengthened by the absurdity of the misdemeanor charges they leveled against him. The first was that he knew North had been encouraging a private supply network to support the *contras* when he, Abrams, had testified to the Senate Foreign Relations Committee that the United States government was not involved with that network. But there was never any secret about the fact of encouragement. Abrams thought he was talking about illegal operational involvement.

The second charge was that when asked by a House committee whether any foreign government was helping the *contras,* Abrams had said none was, although he knew that funds not yet delivered had been promised by the Sultan of Brunei (who had asked for, and received, pledges of absolute secrecy from our government). Subsequently he made the same denial to a Senate committee, but ten days later, feeling that the denial, while literally true, might have been a bit too close to the line, he went back and informed the Senate committee. The independent counsel charged him with withholding evidence from the House committee.

The answers Abrams gave were not prepared in advance; they were spontaneous responses to hostile questioning. Five years later, equally hostile prosecutors scrutinized every nuance, like lawyers examining a stock prospectus, to see if something, anything, could be said to have been withheld. They had picked their man and had only to imagine a crime. Indeed, a former member of Walsh's team, Jeffrey Toobin, wrote a book disclosing the team's eagerness to prosecute Abrams and their disappointment that they had not found sufficient evidence. Walsh rejoined: "He [Toobin] missed his target. He was supposed to get Abrams. We hit the target after he left."

If the charges were based on prosecutorial hair-splitting, why did Abrams plead guilty to these two misdemeanor counts? There was the prospect of another two years of agony for himself, his wife, and his children and of an estimated $1 million in legal fees that would have drained his and his relatives' savings and left him in debt. But the greatest pressure was the threat that the independent counsel would file an indictment charging multiple felonies in the expectation that the jury would compromise by acquitting him of most but convicting him of one or two. That would mean time in prison as well as disbarment as an attorney.

Abrams was right to fear that outcome. Judge Learned Hand once said that above almost all things, he would dread having his fate in the hands of a jury. The misdemeanor pleas allowed Abrams and his family to resume their lives. It was an eminently sensible decision. Walsh's office offered Clair George, a high CIA officer, the misdemeanor route, George rejected it, was then indicted on seven felony counts, and ultimately convicted of two of them. Later, Walsh's office offered former Secretary of Defense Caspar Weinberger the chance to plead guilty to a misdemeanor with no jail time, in return, according to Weinberger, for implicating Ronald Reagan. Weinberger rejected the offer and Walsh indicted him on five felony charges.

Of course, it is clear that Walsh and his staff wanted bigger game than Elliott Abrams. They repeatedly tried to get him to implicate an aide to George Bush, "trying [to] start something up that would end in impeaching the President." They were also eager to get former Secretary of State George Shultz. Walsh has now made it clear that his office is still trying to get Bush.

Weinberger's case was awaiting trial when Bush pardoned him, as well as George, Abrams, and three other former officials involved in Iran-*contra*. Angered at the escape of his prey, Walsh accused Bush of a "cover-up" and stated that the lame-duck President was a "subject" of investigation. These are remarks that would be highly inappropriate, and perhaps punishable under the code of professional ethics, if made by a regular prosecutor. They are no less so when flung out by an independent counsel.

Walsh's fury is not hard to understand. For, having set out to uncover a conspiracy, and to prosecute for real crimes, his office has ended up—after spending six years and $35 million—with a record that ranges from poor to disastrous, prosecuting people for not being sufficiently forthcoming. If they could add a former President or Secretary of State to their game bag, they seem to feel, at least something might be retrieved.

In the process, Walsh's prosecutorial team has behaved in ways more morally questionable than did their victims. Walsh's chief deputy, Craig Gillen, in writing to the probation officer who was preparing a recommendation to the judge who would sentence Abrams, both withheld information and made an allegation the prosecutors knew to be false. Not only did the letter give the impression that Abrams had initiated the idea of soliciting third countries for *contra* support—ignoring that President Reagan had made that decision and that Secretary Shultz had authorized every action taken; Gillen also said that Abrams went to London under an assumed name to meet the Sultan of Brunei's representative, when the prosecutors had numerous documents that showed he had traveled under his own name. As meticulous as Gillen and the others had been in analyzing every detail to "get" Abrams, it passes belief that this letter, designed to influence the sentence, could have been the result of an oversight.

The lessons of Elliott Abrams's book are several. Some independent counsels have performed their tasks admirably. But the incentives the statute creates ensure that others will bring prosecutions that no regular prosecutor would bring, and that never should be brought. The independent counsel is set up with an unlimited budget to investigate one person or a small group of persons. The job, moreover, offers the chance to become a national figure, but only if scalps are taken. The independent-counsel statute, therefore, has built into it the certainty of pain and injustice to many innocent people. Abrams and his family are only one example.

The main problem, however, is that the independent counsel is accountable to no one. Four days before the 1992 presidential election, Walsh filed a second indictment of former Secretary of Defense Caspar Weinberger, which included a note suggesting that George Bush knew more about Iran-*contra* than he had admitted. The judge dismissed the new count as barred by the statute of limitations. The point of the charge was that Weinberger had kept notes he did not disclose and so it was wholly unnecessary to include that particular note. Moreover, the prosecutors can count as well as the judge, and their theory of why the new count was timely was implausible, so they must have known when they filed the indictment that the charge would likely be dismissed. Any regular prosecutor, accountable to a superior, would undoubtedly be called on the carpet, and probably discharged, for what looks remarkably like a partisan attempt to influence the outcome of a presidential election. So far as is known, no action is being taken against Walsh.

The independent-counsel law, however, has achieved its main objective: undermining the legitimacy and efficiency of the executive branch. Abrams, for example, advises officials of that branch to take no notes. Years later, you may not remember what certain phrases in your notes meant, but the independent counsel will be able to suggest sinister implications. Caspar Weinberger would probably give the same advice. Officials will undoubtedly be less energetic in asserting the President's interests and powers before Congress, even when they would be absolutely correct to do so. One wonders how resolute the next Theodore Olson will be.

Except for George Bush's pardons, Presidents themselves have been loath to stand up to the independent-counsel system. Abrams felt he was abandoned by Ronald Reagan and his administration. The State Department's lawyers may assist an official in an investigation of his official conduct until it is clear that he is targeted for indictment, but, at Walsh's insistence, those lawyers were ordered not to assist Abrams in connection with the independent counsel's inquiries even while Abrams was an Assistant Secretary and not targeted. It is not surprising that he speaks contemptuously of "Reagan-administration officials who had gone on to their glory and had left me and a few others out there on the beach to take the incoming fire." It has been observed before that the Reagan administration demanded loyalty up but did not practice loyalty down. The question is not merely one of loyalty to subordinates and behaving honorably oneself; by cutting the lifelines to people like Abrams, the Reagan administration made it likely that future Presidents will get less loyalty up and more subordinates whose primary concern is their own skins.

The subtitle of Abrams's book alleges that political differences were turned into crimes. It is difficult to disagree. The charges against him were for statements of a kind that had never before been made criminal. Abrams's real offense was battling for Reagan's policies against a Congress that kept changing its attitudes but often favored the Sandinistas over the *con-tras*. Worse, he was intelligent, tough, and self-confident—qualities which, though they annoy some Congressmen, are not usually regarded as criminal. As the Abrams, Olson, and Weinberger cases show, in operation the independent-counsel statute has criminalized political differences, but the only "criminals" it has turned up have been, as Congress intended, in the executive branch. If the law is reenacted, that will not be because Congress has not understood what it has seen; it will be because Congress likes what it has seen.

The Independent Counsel:
An Exchange

To the editor of *Commentary*,

 The article by Robert H. Bork, "Against the Independent Counsel" [February], is remarkable for its lack of objectivity and its intolerance. According to Judge Bork, the "horrors of the institution could have been predicted," the record under the independent counsel statute has been "abominable," and it has produced "savage injustice" to individuals.

 Not content with arguing his point philosophically or legally, he himself takes savage and unjust swipes at the independent counsel in the Iran-*contra* affair, Judge Lawrence Walsh, and his staff, accusing them of lying to the Court, and characterizing Judge Walsh's record as being from "poor to disastrous." He follows this scurrilous attack by criticizing seven Justices of the Supreme Court of the United States for being so inept as to uphold the constitutionality of the independent-counsel statute, and by condemning the jury system.

 Judge Bork opines, with no basis in fact, that the job of independent counsel "offers the chance to become a national figure, but only if scalps are taken." It is ludicrous for anyone to suggest that Judge Walsh longed to become a "national figure." He already was a national figure. Seventy-four years of age when he accepted this difficult assignment, he was a former United States District Court Judge, a past president of the American Bar Association, Deputy Attorney General during the Eisenhower administration, and later a senior partner in the firm of Davis, Polk & Wardwell.

 None of the other independent counsels has become a "national figure," or ever aspired to become one. There have been thirteen independent counsels appointed since the statute was enacted in 1978. Indictments were brought by only four of them. No scalps were sought or taken by the other

From *Commentary*, June 1993

nine. (Allow me to state my own experience: I was appointed as independent counsel to investigate possible law violations by then-Assistant Attorney General Theodore Olson in 1986, but resigned after a short time because of an apparent conflict of interest. In 1987, I was appointed as independent counsel to investigate possible law violations by Lyn Nofziger, and my mandate was later expanded to include then-Attorney General Edwin Meese 3rd.)

Judge Walsh's investigations were confounded and substantially handicapped by the grants of immunity by Congress and by the refusal of the Department of Justice to cooperate in important respects. Those unprecedented complications added enormously to the expenses of the investigations. Despite those serious obstructions, Judge Walsh obtained convictions of eleven defendants. Two of them (North and Poindexter) were found guilty by juries of multiple felony counts, and final convictions were avoided only because of the immunity grants. The four counts against Joseph F. Fernandez were dismissed because Attorney General Thornburgh, another bitter foe of the independent-counsel statute, blocked the disclosure of classified information relative to the defense.

Judge Bork wallows in sympathy for Elliott Abrams, accusing Judge Walsh and his staff, again with no factual support, of "taking an interest" in Abrams only because of the dismissal of the *North* case and the predicted dismissal of the *Poindexter* case. It is Judge Bork's belief that Judge Walsh and his staff "went after Abrams because they badly needed trophies."

Judge Bork then minimizes the offenses to which Abrams pled guilty, and refers to Jeffrey Toobin's book, which, according to Judge Bork, disclosed "the team's eagerness to prosecute Abrams and their disappointment that they had not found sufficient evidence."

Judge Bork's sympathy for Abrams might have receded, if not disappeared, had he read everything Toobin said about him. Toobin branded Abrams's answers to questions by Senator John Kerry as reeking with falsehood. A later statement by Abrams to Lee Hamilton, chairman of the House Intelligence Committee, is characterized by Toobin as being a "whopper." Still another answer to a question from Senator Bradley was, according to Toobin, "a flatout, bald-faced lie." Abrams, after thinking that one over for ten days, recanted his false testimony.

In justifying Abrams's decision to plead guilty to two misdemeanor charges of withholding evidence from Congress, Judge Bork condemns the jury system by asserting in effect that no jury trying Abrams would decide the charges based on the evidence, and refers to a purported statement by Judge Learned Hand who, according to Judge Bork, "once said that above all things, he would dread having his fate in the hands of a jury." We are not told the context in which Judge Hand is supposed to have made that alleged comment, and the truth is, it pertained to his dread of being involved in litigation, and was not meant to be an attack on the jury system. But, in any event, it is rather amazing that a constitutional expert, a former Federal Circuit Court Judge, and an appointee to a position on the Supreme Court of the United States would subscribe to that strange thesis.

Judge Bork asserts that the statute ensures that independent counsel will bring prosecutions that no regular prosecutor would bring, and that never should be brought. That remarkable statement is a sweeping denigration of all past and future independent counsels, and ignores the hundreds, perhaps thousands, of prosecutions each year that end in dismissals or jury verdicts, and also overlooks that fact that only four of thirteen independent counsels brought prosecutions. And it is pertinent to point out that, whereas, in the second Meese investigation, I declined to prosecute the Attorney General, the Deputy Attorney General and the Assistant Attorney General in charge of the Criminal Division resigned, and angrily denounced my decision, asserting publicly and before Congress that they would have prosecuted their boss, a sitting Attorney General of the United States.

Judge Bork conveniently overlooks the fact that an independent counsel cannot be appointed except upon application by the Attorney General. It is worth noting also that Meese himself requested the appointment of an independent counsel prior to my investigation. And to say that an independent counsel is not accountable to anyone and is free of supervision simply defies reality. No one is any more open to public view than an independent counsel charged with investigating a high-level member of the executive branch. He or she operates in a glass bowl; every move is scrutinized, analyzed, and frequently criticized by Congress and the media. Moreover, an independent counsel can be removed for cause by the Attorney General, is subject to biannual audits by the Government Accounting Office, and is required to follow the guidelines laid down by the Department of Justice.

Judge Bork also asserts that no "regular prosecutor" would make public his or her reasons for not indicting. The fact is that the statute *required* an independent counsel to state the reasons for not prosecuting matters within his or her jurisdiction. However, the independent counsel did not have the power to release the report to the public. Only the Court had that power. And the Court had the additional power to make such orders as were appropriate to protect the rights of any individuals named in the report. If any person named in the report believed that its public release would be inappropriate or prejudicial, he or she had the right to file a motion seeking to have all or any portion withheld from the public.

The most insupportable episode in the history of the independent counsel statute was the Christmas Eve pardons issued by President Bush. Both President Bush and Judge Bork referred to the felonies allegedly perpetrated by Caspar Weinberger and Duane Clarridge, and the crimes of which the other four pardoned defendants were convicted, as expressions of "policy differences." President Bush went even further, and emphasized that the single common denominator for the motivation of those individuals was "patriotism." Since when, one could fairly ask, do perjury before Congress, false statements to Congress, and withholding information from Congress become mere expressions of policy differences? When was it ever considered "patriotic" to defy the laws of Congress, and lie about it in the process?

No court has ever come close to saying that conduct such as that engaged in by those individuals reflected only policy differences. If they had such differences with Congress, they could have loudly proclaimed them, or sought to change the laws with which they disagreed. But they could not lie to, or withhold information from, Congress.

Judge Gerhard A. Gesell answered forcefully the grotesque assertion that a high-level official of the government, or anyone, can be excused from lying to Congress based on the assertion of a difference in policy beliefs:

> It is essential that Congress legislate based on fact, not falsification, in the realm of foreign affairs as well as in domestic legislation. If Congress is increasing its power in a manner that infringes upon the President's prerogatives, the President may assert executive privilege or direct (his subordinates) not to answer. . . . The thought that any one of the hundreds of thousands of persons working for the President can affirmatively and intentionally mislead Congress when it seeks information to perform one of its assigned functions for any reason . . . is unacceptable on its face. Such a disdainful view of our democratic form of government has no constitutional substance.

I believe the independent-counsel statute served a useful purpose, and that the system, which eliminated institutional conflicts of interest, was not abused. Most of the independent-counsel investigations resulted in decisions not to prosecute. The public accepted those decisions because they were made by an independent entity. The refusals to prosecute would not have been so readily accepted had the decisions been made by the Department of Justice.

There is no doubt that the independent-counsel statute could be improved, and it is to be hoped that objective and rational views can be brought to bear on legitimate issues when the legislation is again before Congress. However, so long as the opponents of the statute wear blinders and rely on mean-spirited arguments, there is little chance that those issues will be seriously debated.

—James C. McKay, Washington, D.C.

To the Editor of *Commentary:*

Robert H. Bork continues to be delightfully provocative in his article opposing the independent counsel. However, the article is partisan and slipshod, and does not represent Judge Bork at his best.

With one curt sentence only, characterizing as "unpersuasive" the Supreme Court's seven-to-one decision upholding the enabling statute as constitutional, Judge Bork dismisses the Court's opinion authored by the Chief Justice. Judge Bork declines to discuss the obstacles faced by independent counsel Walsh in the prosecutions of Oliver North and John Poindexter— problems caused by congressionally immunized testimony, which the U.S. Court of Appeals held tainted the trial testimony against both men. Judge Bork makes no reference to the prosecution of Joseph Fernandez, which was effectively blocked in 1989 by Attorney General Thornburgh, who prohibited the use at trial of publicly known information, on the pretext that such information could not be declassified. Finally, Judge Bork brushes aside the convictions after trial of Thomas Clines and Clair George; and the numerous negotiated pleas of guilty by major players, such as Alan Fiers, Richard Secord, Albert Hakim, Robert McFarlane, Carl Channell, and Richard Miller. Little recognition is given to the indictments of Caspar Weinberger (former Secretary of Defense) and Duane Clarridge, whose pending trials were aborted by President Bush's pardons.

In 1978, Congress authorized the appointment of an independent counsel to investigate and prosecute, if warranted, high government officials in the executive branch. The appointment of independent counsel was to be made by the U.S. Court of Appeals, in Washington, on application of the Attorney General. The Supreme Court upheld the constitutionality of the statute and its mechanism for the appointment of the independent counsel. In a strong opinion by Chief Justice Rehnquist, with only Justice Scalia in dissent, the Court discounted the many arguments of invalidity now advanced by Judge Bork, whose article merely tracks the solitary dissent of Justice Scalia. Judge Bork's criticism that the Court "weakened the presidency" is ironic, for Chief Justice Rehnquist is a forceful spokesman for a strong executive. . . .

In cynical fashion, Judge Bork would have us believe that each independent counsel has "a chance to become a national figure." . . . Judge Bork just does not remember that some distinguished attorneys, like himself, respond to the call of public service. It really is in poor taste for him to question the public service of others when he himself rendered significant public service for years (and was prepared, in 1987, to continue public service indefinitely until the Senate denied him confirmation to the Supreme Court).

Citing Teapot Dome and Watergate, the U.S. Court of Appeals (in *In Re Olson*) noted that

> the need for a special counsel who is to some extent independent of the Justice Department and free of the conflicts of interest that exist when an administration investigates the alleged wrongdoing of its own high officials *has been demonstrated* several times this century.

In 1984, Congress enacted the Boland Amendment prohibiting intelligence agencies from providing military support to the rebel *contras* attempting to overthrow the Sandinista government in Nicaragua. In November 1986, after news reports revealed a clandestine shipment of arms to Iran, Attorney General Meese reviewed National Security Council activities with respect to Iran, and learned that monies paid by representatives of Iran for American arms had been illegally deposited into bank accounts controlled by the *contras*. The Attorney General applied for the appointment of an independent counsel, and the Court appointed Judge Lawrence Walsh. During this period, Congress commenced a broad investigation into the Iran-*contra* affair. Congress exercised its power to grant immunity to numerous witnesses, including the soon-to-be-famous Oliver North (National Security Council staff member) and John Poindexter (National Security Adviser). Public interest in the lengthy televised congressional hearings was intense. Oliver North, his counsel Brendan Sullivan, and his secretary Fawn Hall, became instant folk heroes. The cloak-and-dagger operations of the CIA proved fascinating. North—always the colonel—raised the Nuremberg defense. He candidly admitted his involvement, claiming he was "merely following orders." The public received an education in clandestine Middle East diplomacy. Obviously, the crucial question became who in the National Security Council or the White House was issuing the orders Congress never did learn the full picture. The presidential pardons quashed Walsh's efforts just as he was pressing closer to the White House.

North, Poindexter, Secord, and Hakim were jointly indicted. The indictment included charges of conspiring to violate the Boland Amendment and other laws, and also to participate in a cover-up by lying to and withholding information from Congress and other federal investigators. At the separate North and Poindexter trials, Walsh limited his evidentiary presentations to avoid problems caused by the prior congressionally immunized testimony of North and Poindexter. A jury convicted North of altering and destroying documents, and aiding and abetting in the obstruction of Congress. Another jury convicted Poindexter of obstruction of Congress, false statements, and conspiracy to obstruct official inquiries.

The U.S. Court of Appeals reversed the conviction of North, and remanded the proceedings to the trial court to determine whether the immunized congressional testimony had tainted the trial testimony. Subsequently Walsh conceded he could not meet the stringent test of the Court of Appeals, and did not oppose North's application to dismiss the indictment.

A different panel of the U.S. Court of Appeals reversed the conviction of Poindexter on the very same ground and dismissed the indictment.

In chastising Walsh for having lost the North and Poindexter prosecutions, Judge Bork makes no reference to the problems caused by the congressionally immunized testimony. He refers to Walsh's record as "poor to disastrous." He would have us believe that Walsh's prosecution of those who gave perjured testimony to Congress to cover up illegal acts was "criminalizing political differences," even though many of them pleaded guilty. Congress has the right to expect truthful testimony from high government officials as to their compliance with the laws enacted by Congress.

I do not suggest that there cannot be legitimate objections to the Office of Independent Counsel. I do suggest that Judge Bork has not substantially contributed to the debate. He has not been careful or accurate in his recitation of past events.

Legislation extending the Office of Independent Counsel is now pending and is expected to be enacted. Legitimate proposals to limit the office have been voiced, including limitations upon the tenure of the office. There is also concern about the requirement that independent counsel file a written report with Congress on his activities; this concern focuses on the reporting of unsubstantiated allegations of wrongdoing by unindicted persons.

The comments of Judge Bork are so partisan and misleading that they will have little impact. Judge Bork's article did a disservice, not only to the readers of *Commentary,* but also to those who have reasonable doubts as to the wisdom of continuing the office.

—Elliot Wales, New York

Robert H. Bork writes:

Neither James C. McKay nor Elliot Wales chooses to discuss the main theses of my article: (1) that there is no need for an independent-counsel statute because historic procedures have always proved entirely adequate to deal with executive-branch wrongdoing; and (2) that the law has been used by Congress to participate in law enforcement, which the Constitution lodges in the President, in order to assail the moral legitimacy and the effectiveness of the presidency. Instead, they offer a series of misrepresentations of the article and the facts, reinforced by heavy-breathing invective.

What exercises these gentlemen most is my criticism of the Office of the Independent Counsel (OIC) headed by Lawrence Walsh. Such criticism as I offered was mild compared to what might have been said, so it is to be feared that Messrs. McKay and Wales will like this reply even less.

I have always liked Lawrence Walsh. When I was a third-year law student, he made the first job offer I had ever received. Though much impressed by him, I declined because the job involved the regulation of public utilities in New York, not a terribly romantic beginning to a legal career. When one of the judges on the panel that appointed Walsh to the OIC remarked to me that he had the ideal resume and temperament for the job, I agreed completely and even enthusiastically. But the performance of his office, sad to say, decisively refutes that assessment. It is, of course, possible that Walsh is not directly responsible for much of what has been done (he has said he rarely makes a recommendation anymore), but the record of the Iran-*contra* investigations is a decisive reason for not reenacting the independent-counsel law.

Consider the record. Iran-*contra* was supposedly about massive executive-branch criminality. Not one charge of illegal acts in violation of congressional restrictions reached trial. Most of the substantive offenses charged involved trivia—e.g., Oliver North accepting the gift of a security fence for his home—or were derivative offenses allegedly committed in the course of various investigations. From the beginning, Walsh has denounced a massive conspiracy to cover up illegal behavior. Yet he has uncovered no such conspiracy and the evidence indicates that none exists. What the OIC has done instead is indict people for what they said or did not say in congressional hearings or to the OIC's investigators. Lacking any case about Iran-*contra* itself, this pursuit of those who misspoke is said to be justified in order to establish the principle that executive- branch officials must not lie to Congress. But that principle has little or no relation to many of the cases that were brought and certainly does not justify the shabby persecutions of individuals.

First, the matter of Elliott Abrams. Contrary to Mr. McKay, I have read everything Jeffrey Toobin said about Abrams, and a singularly unedifying experience it was. After noting that he was no Republican, Toobin wrote:

> I undertook the investigation of Abrams with an enthusiasm that bordered on the unseemly. The prosecution of Abrams would serve as a warning to all those who thought they could dispense truth like charity favored on a chosen few. Getting the bad guys—this was what being a prosecutor was all about.

Toobin knew that Abrams was a "bad guy" before he had collected and analyzed the evidence, presumably because Abrams had implemented Reagan's policy of supporting the *contras*. (That is one trouble with independent counsels, or indeed any special prosecutors: they attract staff that is politically motivated to "get" people whose politics they detest.) But even Toobin concluded Abrams had broken no law. Discussing the distinction between doing something wrong and committing a crime, Toobin wrote: "Elliott Abrams's dissembling before Congress well earned him derision and contempt. But not jail."

The OIC never charged or could have charged that Elliott Abrams engaged in illegal actions, knew of any, or attempted to conceal illegal actions from Congress. But Walsh and his deputy, Craig Gillen, thought Abrams should have, if not jail time, the blot of a criminal conviction on his record. The charges, of not being sufficiently forthcoming in two unsworn appearances before congressional committees, were the same ones Toobin found insufficient, but by Walsh's own statement, the task was to "get" Abrams. By unremitting pressure, threats of a multi-count indictment and financial ruin, the OIC finally coerced the plea they wanted. As explained in my article, the charges to which Abrams pled involved an arguable overstatement of the truth and a truth that was misleading and which Abrams corrected shortly afterward. This is a remarkable record for a man who testified on these subjects, without counsel, over twenty times before hostile congressional committees, had scores of meetings with individual Congressmen, and was repeatedly questioned by members of the OIC, both in their offices and before a grand jury.

Toobin had two things wrong: there was no "dissembling," and Abrams's performance has earned him "contempt and derision" only from fanatical political enemies; to others, myself included, he remains an example of integrity and courage under great pressure. Few things in his presidency became George Bush as well as the pardons he extended to Abrams and others.

But Elliott Abrams's ordeal is far from the only episode that condemns the Iran-*contra* OIC's performance. Prosecutors are not supposed to try defendants in the press, and the first generation of independent counsels was careful to avoid press contact. Not so this independent counsel. Michael Ledeen, writing in the *American Spectator,* notes that Walsh

> had so much direct contact with the press that one finds, on perusal of his media calendar, that he would often process journalists like so many widgets on an assembly line, bringing in a new one every 45 minutes for hours on end.

Terrence O'Donnell, who participated in the defense of Oliver North, testified to a congressional committee that at the high point, Walsh had three full-time press aides who "helped to shape the story and engaged in 'spin control' in the courthouse halls during trial as if it were some sort of political contest."

The OIC over time employed more than 70 lawyers (a total of 40 lawyers eventually signed pleadings in North's case alone) in 6 offices around the country, and over 50 FBI, IRS, and Customs Agents were sent around the globe to gather evidence. These people were used in a pursuit of prey that was fanatical to the point of absurdity. O'Donnell recounts that in the OIC's unsuccessful effort to find that North profited from his actions in Iran-*contra,* North's wife was called before the grand jury, her sister was questioned about the cost of feeding their daughter's horse, their babysitter and the teenager who mowed their lawn were questioned about how much they were paid, and their minister was asked how much the Norths contributed on Sunday.

And what was the lying that North was charged with? Not, as most people suppose, with lying under oath to Congress, but with lying at a meeting where he was not under oath and of which there was no transcript. (Two of Walsh's other triumphs consisted of getting guilty pleas from two individuals on a tax-law theory that the head of the Department of Justice's Tax Division thought highly dubious and would not have prosecuted under.)

The OIC's second indictment of Caspar Weinberger, filed on the eve of the 1992 election with the wholly gratuitous suggestion that George Bush was covering up knowledge of Iran-*contra,* is only one of the outrages committed in the hounding of Weinberger. Ledeen relates a particularly instructive one. General John Vessey, the former Chairman of the Joint Chiefs of Staff, once told Weinberger that he had heard that the Saudis were giving money to the *contras.* Shortly thereafter, Weinberger mentioned this to John McMahon, the deputy director of Central Intelligence, and McMahon included it in his memorandum of this meeting. Testifying to a congressional committee two years later, Weinberger did not recall having any knowledge of Saudi payments. The congressional committees investigating this matter later showed Weinberger a copy of McMahon's memorandum. Weinberger said the memorandum did not "refresh his memory," he still did not remember having heard about the Saudi funding, but if McMahon said it was so, it must have been so. The independent counsel indicted Weinberger for "making false statements to Congress."

If these are not examples of an office out for scalps, of prosecutors out of control, it is hard to know what evidence would satisfy Messrs. McKay and Wales. McKay finds solace in the fact that only four of thirteen independent counsels have brought indictments. I don't know why. As Theodore Olson's travails show, it is possible to punish by a three-year investigation of baseless charges. As will be discussed, it was possible to punish Edwin Meese in the independent counsel's final report without indicting him. Moreover, the fact that some investigations proved fruitless and many independent counsels proved fair does not remove the fact that the statute creates perverse incentives for prosecutors and allows them to overwhelm their victims.

But not all OICs prove fair or drop baseless charges. Having failed to prove illegal acts, the Iran-*contra* prosecutors have settled for the most dubious, in some cases ridiculous, attempts to get convictions or pleas for things said or not said. Yes, I do call what was done to Weinberger, Abrams, and others "savage injustices." And at what cost in addition to human suffering and the deformation of our criminal-justice system? It is commonly said that Walsh has expended $35 million in these pursuits, but O'Donnell estimates that when other costs are counted, such as those for the investigating agents and of compliance by government agencies with the OIC's massive subpoenas and document requests, the total is probably closer to $100 million.

In defending Walsh, Messrs. McKay and Wales are not loath to suggest illegal acts by others, without any evidence whatever. Both refer to the dismissal of the charges against Joseph F. Fernandez because the government would not disclose classified information. Mr. McKay implies that this was dishonest: it was done by "Attorney General Thornburgh, another bitter foe of the independent-counsel statute"; Mr. Wales says it directly: Thornburgh "prohibited the use at trial of publicly known information, on the pretext that such information could not be declassified." If the information had been publicly known, Thornburgh's refusal to declassify it would have been futile. Richard Thornburgh is an honorable man, and those who suggest otherwise should have at least one fact to support a slur.

In noting that the independent counsel position offers the chance to become a national figure, but only if scalps are taken, I was not speaking of Walsh but of the incentives built into the statute. Nevertheless, both Messrs. McKay and Wales choose to misread the piece and offer a spirited argument that Walsh already was a national figure and so could have had no such incentive to take the job. I have no idea why Walsh accepted the position and will not try to guess. For the benefit of Messrs. McKay and Wales, however, it should be said that Walsh was a national figure only among lawyers, and many other independent counsels were not even that. The insidious effects of the system probably operate most strongly on the deputies and legal staffs of the independent counsel. For them, a high-profile indictment and trial is viewed as a career-making step. There is no satisfaction in leaving a law firm to come to Washington and, after months or years of arduous labor, writing a report explaining why no indictment was brought. This probably explains why the staff often seems more eager to prosecute than the independent counsel.

But perhaps the most damning aspect of the Iran-*contra* investigations, recounted by persons interrogated by the OIC, is that this office investigated the possibility that at least one target and one potential witness had had extramarital affairs. What conceivable relevance could that information have? What could have been the purpose of such inquiries? It would be helpful if Mr. McKay, Mr. Wales, or other defenders of the Walsh operation could think of a reason other than using the threat of scandal to coerce guilty pleas or testimony—tactics that might be regarded in impolite circles as blackmail. Perhaps Walsh did not know of these investigations into sex; it would be good to think so, but his office is responsible for them.

When Bush pardoned Weinberger, Abrams, and four other officials, Walsh went ballistic. He referred to what he called Bush's "own misconduct." He asserted that Weinberger was guilty. When Weinberger said that Walsh had abused his powers, Walsh proved the point by saying on television that Weinberger "lied just as readily to the media as he lied to Congress. He's making it quite clear that his first line of defense when he has a troublesome problem is to lie." So much for Weinberger's long and distinguished career of public service. So much for prosecutorial responsibility.

Mr. McKay accuses me of "a sweeping denigration of all past and future independent counsels." He reads too hastily. The article expressly stated that "[s]ome independent counsels have performed their tasks admirably." One of these was Jacob Stein who, quite correctly, refused to indict Edwin Meese. Had Stein allowed the staff to discuss what they regarded as Meese's administrative deficiencies in the final report, it is quite possible Meese would not have been confirmed as Attorney General. But Stein did not. His task was solely to discover whether the criminal law had been violated. He was aware of the dangers in the almost unlimited powers of the independent counsel and remarked that, given the office's unlimited staff and budget, "you can overpower anyone. . . . Nobody can compete with you, especially an individual."

But an independent counsel has powers other than the power to indict or to coerce pleas. One of them is the power to smear by his final report. Mr. McKay, like Stein, investigated Edwin Meese and declined to prosecute him. (Mr. McKay's memory fails him here. The Deputy Attorney General and Assistant Attorney General to whom he refers resigned before Mr. McKay announced his decision and hence did not "angrily denounce" it. The AAG said later that he would have indicted but that reasonable men could differ.)

When leaks and rumors about the investigation of Meese bade fair to making his continuation as Attorney General untenable, Mr. McKay, admirably, issued a statement that there would be no indictment. But unlike Stein's report of his earlier investigation, Mr. McKay's report stated, quite gratuitously, and far less than admirably, that though Meese would not be prosecuted, Mr. McKay found that he had violated two laws. In fact, Meese had not, and his counsel told Mr. McKay that he had no authority to make such charges when he was not indicting. As Mr. McKay says, the statute requires an independent counsel to state his reasons for not prosecuting; it most certainly does not require him to say that the man is nevertheless guilty. The appointing court, apparently unwilling to be charged with suppression of a politically-charged document, released the report and Meese was damaged without a chance to clear his name. It is unheard of for a regular prosecutor to refuse to indict but announce to the world that the man is guilty.

We may now look forward to the report Walsh and his staff are preparing. If the intemperateness of the past is any guide to the future, we may expect to learn that Walsh regards George Bush, Caspar Weinberger, and a number of others as guilty, and that these accusations and the OIC's one-sided versions of the evidence will be spread on the public record with no opportunity for effective rebuttal. Individuals will be maligned, their reputations tarnished, and two Republican administrations found morally wanting, and probably criminal.

If the independent-counsel statute did not require the criminalization of policy differences, it certainly permitted just that. If, after Congress has started the process out of political motives, an overly zealous independent counsel is not himself motivated by political considerations, the result is the same as if he were. The institution of the court-appointed independent counsel is an abomination in the halls of justice.

POETIC INJUSTICE

William Jefferson Clinton, whose Administration has been marked, among other things, by an extraordinary streak of good luck, may be, much against his will, about to make a major contribution to our national well-being through sheer bad luck. Our President is being immolated on the altar of the ethics he promised. An Aztec priest, dressed in the garb of an independent counsel, hovers over him, obsidian knife in hand, ready to excise one portion or another of Mr. Clinton's anatomy.

Given the evidence and the man's past history, there seems no doubt that Clinton is guilty of something in the Monica Lewinsky affair. He is certainly sexually compulsive and a master of the cover up. Though this pattern began in Arkansas (Gennifer Flowers was telling the truth), the tactics of cover up, a.k.a. obstruction of justice, continued and reached a crescendo in the White House years (the Travel Office, the FBI files, the rummaging through Vincent Foster's office, the flight of those witnesses who did not conveniently forget everything or take the Fifth Amendment, and so on, apparently ad infinitum.)

White House apparatchiks and the First Lady say the President is the victim of "a vast right-wing conspiracy." That the Administration is driven to such preposterous allegations is enough in itself to convict Mr. Clinton. It is to be doubted that a dozen members of the so-called "right wing" could manage to line up in alphabetical order. But the First Lady and the President's henchmen are engaged in the classic strategy of the guilty: if the facts are against you, argue the law; if the law is against you, argue the facts; if the law and the facts are against you, put the prosecutor on trial. Having mortgaged the integrity of her marriage in return for political power, Mrs. Clinton will fight to the last to receive her end of the quid pro quo.

From *National Review,* February 23, 1998

The spectacle now unfolding is so heartening to those who always thought Mr. Clinton lacked character that many, including conservatives, are perceiving previously unsuspected virtues in the independent-counsel statute. They should not. It is a bad statute whatever the outcome of Mr. Clinton's travails. For a moment I rejoiced in the squirmings of the man who had promised us the most ethical Administration in our history. But the most obvious distinction between conservatives and the Bill and Hillary White House is integrity—which means adherence to principle, precisely when it is most tempting to depart from it.

It should matter that the independent counsel statute is patently unconstitutional. The Constitution vests the entire enforcement power in the President. But the Supreme Court in *Morrison* v. *Olson* upheld the law, lopsidedly, in a particularly wretched opinion. The Court said in effect that if the law left the President with much of the power over law enforcement, that was good enough.

In practical effect, however, the independent counsel is what the Democrats intended, an institutionalized wolf on the executive's flank. Past Democratic Congresses, supposing that Republican control of the White House had become the normal state of affairs, used independent counsels to assault the moral legitimacy of the Presidency. Men who carried out the President's policies or defended his constitutional authority were subjected to lengthy investigations, and sometimes trials, by prosecutors with unlimited resources whose sole mission was to convict. The *in terrorem* effect of the law is magnified many times over because the investigatee can recover part of his attorney's fees only if he is not indicted. If he is indicted, he must pay hundreds of thousands of dollars from his own pocket even if the indictment is eventually dismissed or he is acquitted at trial. Some men accepted plea-bargains simply because they could not carry on a one-sided financial war. The statute has become a powerful engine for injustice.

A system with so much politics, ego, and heavily disproportionate resources built into it requires, but does not always get, an independent counsel of moral strength and judicial temperament. Kenneth Starr is just such a prosecutor. He has proceeded with caution, and those who pleaded guilty to his charges (notably Webster Hubbell) or were convicted (Jim Guy Tucker, the then governor of Arkansas) were faced with overwhelming evidence. It is more than a little sickening to hear the charges leveled against Starr by the White House and its sycophants in the press. The main one seems to be that he is, heaven forfend, a *Republican*. That crime, according to James Carville, automatically makes Ken Starr a "bitter partisan." There was no liberal rage, however, when Archibald Cox, a liberal and a very close ally of Ted Kennedy's, was chosen to investigate Richard Nixon. Nor were there any protests when Lawrence Walsh, using his office in a blatantly political manner, went after Reagan and Bush appointees, even announcing indictments, which he knew to be barred by the lapse of time, of major Republican figures on the eve of the 1992 election. Mr. Starr, by contrast, has conducted himself professionally and without a credible hint of partisanship.

The irony is that we owe this abominable statute to the myth of what *New Republic* editor David Grann casually refers to as "the political connections that corrupted the Justice Department during Watergate." The reality is that there was absolutely no corruption of the Department. The local U.S. Attorney's Office began making the case against the Watergate conspirators, including the President, and handed the main outlines of that case to the special prosecutor. No attempt, then or later, was made to interfere with the work of the Office of the Special Prosecutor, and the final report of that Office stated that not a day had been lost.

It is time we abandoned the myth of the need for an independent counsel and faced the reality of what that institution has too often become. We must also face another reality. A culture of irresponsibility has grown up around the independent-counsel law. Congress, the press, and regular prosecutors have found it too easy to wait for the appointment of an independent counsel and then to rely upon him rather then pursue their own constitutional and ethical obligations. The mere existence of the statute acts as a shield both for wrongdoers and for those who should be exposing them. If the statute were allowed to lapse, however, wouldn't some number of official miscreants escape justice? They would. We may doubt that some attorneys general (Janet Reno springs to mind, for some reason) would investigate their own President rigorously. But let us admit where the blame must ultimately rest. The American people elected Bill Clinton twice, knowing that he is a womanizer, a draft dodger, and a liar. The fact is that many Americans appear not to care about morality in government so long as prosperity reigns and the sitcoms continue to roll. If that is our sickness, it will not be cured, it will only be encouraged, by shifting responsibility to the misbegotten device of the independent counsel.

Dubious Counsel

No higher tribute to the independent-counsel stature could he paid than the outpouring of hatred directed at Kenneth Starr by congressional Democrats and the liberal media. Starr is routinely depicted as an out-of-control prosecutor obsessed with sex and a pawn of the "Christian Right." That there is no foundation for these charges matters not in the slightest in view of Starr's real crime: He proved that President Bill Clinton committed repeated perjuries, tampered with witnesses in federal investigations, and obstructed justice. Without an independent counsel—and one as devoted to truth as Starr—we would never have known to the president's crimes.

There can be no doubt that Starr made his case, as did the House managers. Yet Democratic senators and other Clinton sycophants say there is no case and cast Starr as a villain. Now the ever-compliant Janet Reno will investigate—not Clinton or Al Gore or Harold Ickes, for taking money from the Chinese army to finance the Democrats' 1996 election campaign (she has given them a pass without even looking)—but Starr, for "collusion" with Paula Jones's attorneys. If there was communication between the two staffs, the correct response is, So what? There is no reason on God's green earth that a prosecutor should not seek information from attorneys in a parallel case. Clinton's smear-and-destroy police are at it again.

What, then, should we think about reauthorizing the independent-counsel statute when it comes up for renewal in June? That the law has served us well in Clinton's case does not obscure the fact that it has served us ill in many others. Given the intense partisanship that too often infects the independent counsel's office, the law is as likely to produce spectacular injustice as it is to achieve justice.

The statute creates an officer who has it in his power—and has incentives—to work grave injustices. Lawrence Walsh set the all-time record for

From *National Review*, March 8, 1999.

abuse of the office, applying statutes in radical ways never attempted before and vindictively pursuing individuals until, their funds exhausted, they had little alternative to admitting something. As Jacob Stein, one of the fairest of the independent counsel, remarked, "You can overpower anyone. . . . Nobody can compete with you, especially an individual." Starr, by contrast, has done none of this.

In instances like Walsh's, the statute creates an institutionalized wolf to harry the executive's flank. The law was used by Democrats to assault the moral legitimacy of the presidency and weaken the resolve of members of the executive branch. Men who carried out the president's policies or defended his constitutional powers found themselves under lengthy investigation by prosecutors whose sole mission was to convict them. The coercive power of the statute is enormously magnified by the provision that the investiga-tee's legal expenses can be reimbursed only if he is not indicted. Otherwise he must pay hundreds of thousands in legal fees even if the indictment is dropped or he is acquitted. Such provisions were thoughtfully crafted by Democratic Congresses with Republican presidents in mind. They did not anticipate that George Bush would hand them the presidency. Democrats created the statute and now, so far as impeachment is concerned, have defeated it by an unprecedently vicious campaign organized from the White House, a campaign Starr could not with propriety answer.

The law provides an excuse, it is said, for the Justice Department and Congress to shirk their constitutional duties. That is true to an extent, but this department needs no excuse for shirking (and worse), and Congress often shows little or no appetite to call a popular president to account. Paula Jones's lawsuit, Linda Tripp's tapes, and the stained blue dress together initi-ated and then revealed Clinton's cover-up, but the clues would not have been followed up with the necessary determination and resources were it not for the existence of the independent counsel. Neither House of Congress would have pursued the matter with the same expertise and dogged determination. Clinton would once more have slicked by.

A further virtue of the law is that it mitigates somewhat the politiciza-tion of the Justice Department, which has reached unprecedented depths under Clinton and Janet Reno. The reliability of the department had been demonstrated, I once thought, by the indictment of, and plea bargain with, Vice President Spiro Agnew, and the U.S. attorney's investigation and fram-ing of the case against Nixon and his aides, the results of which were handed over to Archibald Cox. Moreover, I thought, any attempt at concealment would surely be defeated by leaks from career prosecutors. But in this case there have been no leaks adverse to Clinton, and Justice under Reno has systematically failed to investigate or seek independent counsel for any matters that come too close to the White House. (How was she to know of the stained blue dress when she let Starr investigate?) The instances of her malfeasance are almost too many to recount.

It is, furthermore, easier to trigger the appointment of an independent counsel, the mechanism being already in place, than it is to obtain a special prosecutor. Archibald Cox would never have been appointed but for a miscalculation by Richard Nixon. Nixon fired Richard Kleindienst and nominated Elliot Richardson, thus playing into the Democrats' hands. The Senate Judiciary Committee conditioned Richardson's confirmation on his appointment of a special prosecutor who could be fired only for cause. Had Nixon not fired Kleindienst, there probably would have been no special prosecutor. If the statute had been in effect then, however, pressure would have forced Kleindienst to seek an independent counsel. Reno may have been kept in place so long because Clinton, learning from Nixon's mistake, realized that a Republican Senate might attach conditions to the confirmation of a new attorney general.

There are a variety of ways in which the independent-counsel law could be amended to make it less unjust, but no amendment that preserves the integrity if the office can overcome one flaw that ought to prove fatal: the law is flatly unconstitutional, despite the Supreme Court's ruling in *Morrison* v. *Olson*.

Article II of the Constitution vests the entire executive power of the United States in the president, including the sole duty that he "shall take Care that the Laws be faithfully executed." The Supreme Court was particularly unpersuasive in *Morrison*, in effect saying that if the law left the president with much of the law-enforcement power, that was good enough. In a fit of pique, I gave a constitutional-law examination in which Congress created an "independent colonel" to take over military operations when Congress was unsatisfied with the leadership of the armed forces. Most of the class thought *Morrison* authorized Congress to share the executive's duties as commander in chief. The independent-counsel law creates a second system of criminal justice, one over which the president has little formal legal control and no politically viable control whatever. That, the Constitution does not permit.

Congressmen take their own oath to support the Constitution and may properly disagree with the Court in this matter without being chargeable with civil disobedience. They may properly take into account the law's unconstitutionality when the law comes up tor reauthorization. It is one thing for Congress to exercise a power the Court has denied it, but quite another for Congress to refuse to exercise a power the Court has allowed it.

This seems to leave a gaping hole in our justice system. There is nothing between a criminal prosecution in the hands of a Justice Department already shown to be subservient to the president and an impeachment process unlikely to be successful against a popular president. If the independent-counsel law cannot save us, what could? Perhaps if the framers and ratifiers of the Constitution had anticipated a president simultaneously as popular and dishonest as Clinton, they might have arranged matters differently. Perhaps. But they did not.

Now that impeachment has failed and no indictment of the president is likely, we must learn to live with an emotionally deformed and dangerous president, a sociopath who is unable to resist immediate gratification, able to charm people for whom he cares not at all, a man who puts himself above all other causes and displays unmistakable totalitarian tendencies. Al Gore in a moment of unintended insight, said: "We can have the future we deserve because we already have the president we deserve!" As unconscious calumnies go, that one may be all too accurate.

Nevertheless, Congress should let the independent-counsel statute lapse. Were they men and women of honor, they would simultaneously adopt a resolution of thanks to Ken Starr for doing his best with a bad law.

——— ——— ———

Although Congress allowed the independent counsel statute to expire in 1999, the topic has continued relevance because attorneys general retain authority to appoint special prosecutors on a case by case basis. Special prosecutors pose many of the same problems as did independent counsel.

THOMAS MORE FOR OUR SEASON

The continuing contemporary interest in Thomas More (1478–1535) is hardly to be accounted for by popular fascination with sixteenth-century English politics or even by admiration for a martyr to a religious cause no longer universally popular. It is more likely that More's memory remains fresh after almost half a millennium because his life casts light on our time. More lived, as we live today, in a time of rapid social and cultural unraveling. The meaning of his life, at least for us, is not so much his worldly success and religious piety, extraordinary as both of these were, but rather the courage and consistency with which he opposed the forces of disintegration.

The culture war of the early sixteenth century was fought over the breaking apart of Christianity, its loss of central authority, and the consequent fragmentation of European civilization. Our war rages about the collapse of traditional virtues across all of the West and the rise of moral indifference and cheerful nihilism. Many parallels between the two eras could be drawn, but a crucial similarity lies in the central role played by law in each. Though More was a profoundly religious man, it should not be forgotten that he was also a preeminent lawyer and judge. The law, quite as much as Catholicism, is crucial to an understanding of the man and the martyr. Law and its institutions were, of course, major forces of cohesion in More's age, and are perhaps the primary symbols in ours of stability and continuity as well as justice. When moral consensus fades, as it did in More's time and does in ours, we turn to law; when law falters, as it must when morality is no longer widely shared, society and culture teeter on the brink of chaos.

That is another way of saying that law cannot be divorced from morality—and, there is reason to think, morality, at least in the long run, cannot be divorced from religion. Law and religion are alike, therefore, as reinforcements of social order. It is a subject for speculation at least, whether

From *First Things*, June/July 1999.

either can long remain healthy and self-confident without the other. Each imposes obligations, but each is subject to the therapeutic heresy, softening those obligations to accommodate individual desires. It is a sign of our distemper that Thomas More is today so often regarded as a hero of civil disobedience, a man who refused to obey law with which he was in profound moral disagreement. That is a considerable distortion of the truth, and it was not More's understanding of his motives. For him, in a very real sense, law *was* morality. It is equally true that for More morality was superior to law and was the standard by which law must be judged. If that seems a paradox, I do not think it truly is one.

More, as his biographers make clear, had the utmost respect for authority, hierarchy, and social discipline. He was born into an age when schooling stressed these virtues. Early education, including the study of musical harmony, as Peter Ackroyd informs us, emphasized the paramount importance of order and hierarchy. Then came the study of rhetoric, memorization of simple syllogisms and verbal formulas, by which young students were "made aware of the presence of external authority while at the same time becoming familiarized with the implicit demands of order and stability. . . . Beyond all this, too, was the image of God." These tendencies were confirmed in More's study of the law. "The central and important point," Ackroyd writes, "is that both [religion and law] were conceived to be visible aspects of the same spiritual reality. . . . The attitude More adopted towards the primacy and authority of law governed all his subsequent actions."

Contrast this with today's anarchic popular music and primary education, embodied at their extremes in rap and the self-esteem movement, which cater to and encourage the natural indiscipline of the young. It should not be surprising that similar manifestations of the disorder appear in adult fields of endeavor, including law and religion. These tendencies were present in More's age as well, as Ackroyd makes clear:

> It is of the greatest significance in understanding his [More's] behavior
> . . . to realize that he wrote about the law in precisely the same way he
> described the Church. There was, for him, no essential or necessary difference. That is why he understood at once the nature of Martin Luther's
> heresy, when the German monk spoke of judgment "according to love . . .
> without any law books." When Luther emphasized the importance of the
> "free mind," as opposed to the tenets of "the law books and jurists," More
> recognized instinctively that he was mounting an attack upon the whole
> medieval polity as constituted by the Catholic Church; when Luther argued that law was written within the heart of man, and that judges should

ignore matters of precedent and tradition, he was assaulting the principles
by which More's life and career were guided.

More saw Luther's advocacy of lawless law to be at the heart of their culture
war. Luther spoke for the individual conscience and so necessarily attacked
the authority of precedent and tradition in the law. More's view of law and
the duty of judges was quite different. R. W. Chambers quotes him as saying:
"If the parties will at my hands call for justice, then, all were it my father
stood on the one side, and the devil on the other, his cause being good, the
devil should have right." Luther and many modern jurists would reinterpret
the law to do the devil down, and the moderns, at least, would reserve to
themselves authority to decide which is the father and which the devil.

Robert Bolt's *A Man for All Seasons* got More remarkably right. In one
scene, More, then the Lord Chancellor, argues with family members who
are urging him to arrest Richard Rich, the man who was later to betray him.
More's daughter, Margaret, says, "Father, that man's bad." More answers,
"There is no law against that." His son-in-law, William Roper: "There is!
God's law!" More: "Then God can arrest him. . . . The law, Roper, the law.
I know what's legal, not what's right. And I'll stick to what's legal. . . . I'm
not God. The currents and eddies of right and wrong, which you find such
plain sailing, I can't navigate. I'm no voyager. But in the thickets of the law,
oh, there I'm a forester."

Bolt, in a familiar passage, has More say when assailed by his son-in-law
with the charge that he would give the devil the benefit of law:

> MORE: Yes. What would you do? Cut a great road through the law to get
> after the devil?
> ROPER: I'd cut down every law in England to do that!
> MORE: Oh? . . . And when the last law was down, and the Devil turned
> round on you—where would you hide, Roper, the laws all being flat? . . .
> This country's planted thick with laws from coast to coast—man's laws,
> not God's—and if you cut them down . . . d'you really think you could
> stand upright in the winds that would blow then? . . . Yes, I'd give the
> Devil benefit of law, for my own safety's sake.

To understand More, then, it is equally important to realize his absolute
commitment to law and his recognition of the fallibility of human moral reasoning. To be ruled by each individual's moral beliefs is to invite, indeed to
guarantee, social tumult and disorder. The law alone is uniform, a composite or compromise of varying moral assessments, to be applied to all alike,
regardless of personal attitudes about the persons involved: father or devil,

it makes no difference. If an acceptable mix of freedom and order are to be maintained, obedience to law must be accepted as a primary moral duty.

The veneration More gave to law, he also gave, and for the same reason, to constituted authority. More served Henry VIII, a sovereign whose policies he often believed to be immoral or profoundly unwise. He was under no illusions about his king, even as we should be under no illusions about our governors or even the democratic will. When Roper rejoiced at how friendly Henry was to More, he replied, "I have no cause to be proud thereof, for if my head could win him a castle in France it should not fail to go." Yet he did not disobey; he might give contrary advice, but, the policy or the law once decided upon, he complied. He disapproved of Henry's ruinous war with France, but, as Speaker, he asked Parliament for extraordinary and unpopular taxes to support that war. Later, when More was Lord Chancellor, and it was proposed to put Parliament in control of the Church, Richard Marius tells us "More was sick at heart at the prospect . . . [but] he could not control events. Worse, he was a respectable figurehead, kept by the government to lend it whatever authority his reputation gave him, serving by his very presence in the post of Lord Chancellor a cause which was to him abominable." He wanted to resign. "Yet he could not resign, for to do so would have been to run the risk of making his opposition to the king public."

Henry commanded More to speak in the House of Lords to say that the king was pursuing his divorce from Catherine as a matter of religious scruple and not for love of any other woman. In doing so, More pointed out that various universities agreed the first marriage had been unlawful. Someone asked More's opinion and he replied that he had given it to the king and said no more. As Chambers put it, "Respect for authority . . . was the foundation of [More's] political thinking." He presented the king's case, but would not go an inch further.

Why, then, this obedience to constituted authority and to law, even when he regarded them as immoral? It may have been partly ambition; it was surely, in large part, fear of the alternative to law. An Elizabethan play, probably written by Shakespeare, has More attempt to quell rioters against aliens in London:

> Grant them removed, and grant that this your noise
> Hath chid down all the majesty of England.
> Imagine . . .
> Authority quite silenced by your brawl. . . .
> What had you got? I'll tell you. You had taught
> How insolence and strong hand should prevail,

How order should be quelled; and by this pattern
Not one of you should live an aged man;
For other ruffians, as their fancies wrought
With self same hand, self reasons and self right
Would shark on you; and men like ravenous fishes
Would feed on one another.

It may be counted unfortunate that More's speech was followed immediately by a riot. He was no more successful than were a few professors in the sixties extolling the virtues of prudence and order to rampaging students.

But there is more than the fear of lawlessness and tumult. There is the thought that he is not sure about morality, that he may be wrong. When Roper says to him, "The law's your god," More replies, "Oh, Roper you're a fool, God's my god. . . . But I find Him rather too subtle. . . . I don't know where He is nor what He wants."

Again he says: "God made the *angels* to show Him splendor—as He made animals for innocence and plants for their simplicity. But man He made to serve Him wittily, in the tangle of his mind." Not in the pride and certainty of the individual conscience, but in the tangle of his mind. It was because More recognized the fallibility of individual minds that he obeyed authority but saw no need or virtue in doing more than authority required when his mind told him that what was ordered was wrong. The recalcitrance that brought More to the headsman was his refusal to take the oath that Henry was the Supreme Head of the Church in England and endorse a series of acts ending the supremacy of the Pope. The source of More's devotion to papal supremacy illuminates the man. The point was not that the Pope's authority had been instituted immediately by God (indeed Christianity was several centuries old before papal authority as it would come to be understood was clearly established), but that the Pope's power rested upon the inherited traditions and beliefs and the general councils of the Church. The councils, of course, and the evolution of the Church were believed to be guided by God. Here again, More's faith and his view of law became almost indistinguishable.

His recalcitrance may be seen, as it often is, as More's one great act of disobedience. Bolt writes that More seemed to him "a man with an adamantine sense of his own self." "He knew where he began and left off, what areas of himself he could yield to the encroachments of his enemies, and what to the encroachments to those he loved. . . . But at length he was asked to retreat from that final area where he located his self. And there this supple, humorous, unassuming, and sophisticated person set like metal, was overtaken by an absolutely primitive rigor, and could no more be budged than a cliff." It is this behavior that causes Bolt to refer to More as a "hero of selfhood." Indeed it was extraordinary behavior: More was the only person not a member of the clergy who died rather than take the oath.

Yet it seems wrong, or at least potentially misleading, to attribute More's behavior to "selfhood." It is a symptom of our disorder that we glorify, practically deify, the individual conscience. It was not always so. It must have been well into this century before "civil disobedience" and "heresy" became terms of praise. To the contrary, More's behavior may be seen as submission to external authority, a conscious and difficult *denial* of self.

The refusal to take the oath should not, of course, be viewed as disobedience at all. There was a law higher than Henry's and Parliament's, and More knew that the oath violated that law. There were few other occasions on which that could be said with certainty. More, an exemplary courtier, servant, and confidante of the king, did not suppose that God's will was clear enough to require refusal to serve the king even when his purposes seemed to More unjust; he even assisted the king in temporal struggles against the Pope, as, given his understanding of his respective duties, he should have. God's law is not often clear to the tangled mind of man, but there was a central fact about which More could have no doubt: Christ did not leave behind a book but a Church, and that Church must not be divided. As to this ultimate thing, he, at last, knew where God was and what He wanted. More was caught between two authorities and the question for him, the commands of both being clear, was which authority was superior. At this extremity, God was no longer too subtle for him, and More obeyed God's law and went to his death. This was not disobedience but obedience, a thought he expressed in his last words as he placed his head on the block: "I die the king's good servant, but God's first."

Individualism in the law, as in matters of faith, produces the substitution of private morality for public law and duty. This is precisely what More thought Luther was encouraging in his own day, and it is even more prominent in ours. That may be seen in the growth of legal nullification, the refusal to be bound by external rules, that is not only widespread among the American people but, more ominously, in the basic institutions of the law. More applied his injunction as much to the judge on the bench as to rioters in the street. We all recognize rioters as civil disobedients but we are less likely to recognize that the judge who ignores law or who creates constitutional law out of his own conscience is equally civilly disobedient. In 1975 Alexander Bickel, in *The Morality of Consent,* recounted the then recent American experience with disrupters in the streets, but added: "The assault upon the legal order by moral imperatives was not only or perhaps even most effectively an assault from the outside." It came as well from a Court that cut through law to do what it considered "right" and "good." Our law schools now construct theoretical justifications for that particularly corrosive form of civil disobedience, explaining that judges should create, and enforce as constitutional law, individual rights that are nowhere to be found in the Constitution.

Against the backdrop of Justices disregarding the law, it is not surprising that jurors are refusing to be bound by either law or evidence if the results do not fit their personal views. Our representatives enact the laws but juries scattered across the country vote on them again, often overturning the democratic choice. This pernicious practice occurs not only *sub silentio* but is coming into the open. There is even a national organization, the "Fully Informed Jury Association," to justify and encourage jury lawlessness. Some nullification occurs because black jurors think the law is arrayed against them or out of racial solidarity (the O. J. Simpson verdict), but other defiances reflect libertarian attitudes and personal disapproval of the law (the Jack Kevorkian acquittals). According to the *Washington Post,* a poll shows that three out of four Americans say they would disregard the judge's instructions if the law contravened their own ideas of right and wrong.

Now we have seen Senate nullification of the law of impeachment. The evidence left no doubt that the President had deliberately and repeatedly committed perjury, tampered with witnesses, and obstructed justice. Felonies, all of them. Nor is there any doubt, based on the Framers' understanding and prior Senate precedent, that these offenses constituted "high crimes and misdemeanors" requiring removal from office. Yet the Senate felt free to prefer partisan interests to law, and refused to convict.

These are manifestations in the law of the absorption with self and the disrespect for inconvenient rules that permeate our culture. This absorption, variously called radical individualism or autonomy, is taken to justify even institutional lawlessness. As Bickel noted, civil disobedience, no matter by whom or in what cause, is always "a decision in favor of self, in favor of the idea of self." That is why, in the law, it encourages moral relativism, which is a leading feature of modern constitutional adjudication as well as jury verdicts and legislatures sitting as courts of impeachment.

To all this Thomas More provides the sharpest contrast. As Chambers notes, "From [his book] *Utopia* to the scaffold, More stands for the common cause, as against the private commodity of the single man." If obedience to constituted authority and to established law was at the center of More's morality in the reign of Henry VIII, how much more would it have been his guiding principle when law and policy owe their legitimacy to being democratically made, when they are, in the most real sense they can be, the will of the community?

For More, morality was superior to both human law and the will of the sovereign in that it could be used to shape or to alter that law and that will, though not to justify disobedience to it. This clearly appears in *Utopia,* where he argued that it was a man's duty to enter public life despite the evil necessarily entailed, saying, "That which you cannot turn to good, so to order it that it be not very bad." In a word, try to make law as moral as you can, More constantly argued, but when it is made, whatever it commands, morality lies in obedience. If disobedience is ever justified, it is only when the issue is of transcendent importance and when you are absolutely sure of the right and wrong of the matter. In a democratic polity there can be such occasions, but they will be extremely rare.

These are issues of law and morality internal to the United States, but they arise internationally as well. What we call international law is, of course, in many respects not yet law in any real sense. It is in a formative stage, the stage at which More would have felt free to infuse morality. This raises the increasingly important question whether we should try to build an international law, or pretend there is one, about the use of armed force between nations. In the present condition of the world—a condition that looks permanent or at least likely to be of indefinite duration—I think More would say no. It must be "no" because such law cannot be moral, since, to be called international, rules about armed force must necessarily express a "morality" acceptable to immoral regimes.

Go back to the debate over the legality of the United States' invasion of Grenada in October 1983. At the time, a number of people denounced the invasion as illegal, while others defended its legality. In a discussion with an international law expert, I pointed to three factors that most people deemed relevant to the American action in Grenada. First, the Grenadan government had been formed by a minority that seized power by violence and maintained it by terror. Second, it was a Marxist-Leninist regime and so represented a further advance in this hemisphere of a power that threatened freedom and democracy throughout the world. Third, the people of Grenada were ecstatic at being relieved of that tyrannical government.

I said then that these three factors seemed to me morally relevant and asked whether they were relevant in international law. The answer was no. That answer was correct because there is no consensus among nations that any of these considerations justifies an invasion. This means that when we act for moral reasons, we cannot give those reasons and must, to the degree we acquiesce in the false notion that there is already a binding international law, cast ourselves in a false position. When the rules we are asked to call "law" must exclude, and indeed condemn, moral action, it would appear better not to call them laws or confer upon them the prestige of that name. Otherwise, we are forced to renounce our morality or else accept the role of disobedients. Thomas More could hardly approve of either course.

A somewhat different problem with international law is posed by the detention in London of General Auguste Pinochet with the possibility of extraditing him to Spain for crimes—namely, the murder of Spaniards—allegedly ordered or condoned by him in Chile. The claim is that there exists an international law that justifies his trial and punishment. I pass by a point that some may consider to have weight: Pinochet saved Chile from a Marxist dictatorship and the despotism, horrors, and bloodshed all such regimes inevitably bring, and, having converted the economy to prosperity through free market reforms, he voluntarily relinquished power to a democratic government. We cannot know what Thomas More would have thought of this episode, but if his attitude toward the heretics of his day is any guide, he might have approved what Pinochet did. The worldwide Communist advance was certainly an assault upon the human soul.

However one comes out on that issue, what is perhaps more worrying is that Pinochet's arrest sets a precedent all free countries may come to regret. By a parity of reasoning, Ronald Reagan might have been subject to arrest and trial abroad for the bombing of Libya, George Bush for the invasion of Iraq, and Bill Clinton for the air strikes on Afghanistan, Sudan, Iraq, and Yugoslavia. These may not be realistic examples, but one wonders about a "law" that will, inevitably, apply only to leaders of small nations who happen to be caught abroad. After all, nothing is said about international law when our government greets with elaborate ceremonies the most murderous Chinese officials. More's warnings to the rioters in London could equally be applied to England and Spain in Pinochet's case: You have taught that insolence and self-righteousness should prevail. Other nations may shark on you and like ravenous fishes feed on one another.

International "law" provides a warning of what domestic law can become if the nullification of law by courts, juries, and legislatures continues on its present course. If some find the obedience More taught too austere for comfort, they ought at least reflect on the question of how much glorification of the individual conscience any legal order can tolerate and remain a legal order. They ought also to ask how much privatization of morality the moral order can withstand and remain a moral order.

In the culture war of the sixteenth century, More was an active combatant for the binding force of law and the uniformity of religion under the Catholic Church. Our culture war is more confusing and diffuse, but at its center it too is a struggle over the uniformity and stability of law. What is true of law is true of other social restraints, not only of morality, ethics, and manners, but also of respect for craftsmanship, which requires, at its highest, the sublimation of self-will to external standards. Hence, as one might expect from the progress of radical autonomy in the law, we observe formless music, meaningless and offensive art, adolescent entertainment, subjective journalism, and an enthusiasm for genetic technology that may soon threaten the essence of what it is to be human. One important segment of a culture does not collapse and leave the adjacent structures intact. Law both reflects the state of our culture and actively alters it. The divisions between areas of culture are only membranes, and permeable ones at that.

More's life reminds us that the struggle between order and disorder, between authority and the urges of self, is a permanent feature of our condition. Liberty of conscience is a concept easily blurred, or indeed born blurry, and, misunderstood, it can be a force for social fragmentation. Liberty of conscience, insofar as it means the freedom of the individual to construct his own norms, moves from religion to morality, from morality to law, and hence to religious, moral, and legal anarchy. As Ackroyd said: "[More] embodied the old order of hierarchy and authority at the very moment when it began to collapse all around him." He died for the sake of that order.

More lost, and so may we, but he has much to teach us nonetheless, about steadfastness as a minority, even perhaps as a permanent and dwindling minority. He may even teach us that sometimes staunch minorities are remembered well.

The Necessary Amendment

Within the next two or three years, the Supreme Court will almost certainly climax a series of state court rulings by creating a national constitutional right to homosexual marriage. The Court's ongoing campaign to normalize homosexuality—creating for homosexuals constitutional rights to special voting status and to engage in sodomy—leaves little doubt that the Court has set its course for a right to marry. This is but one of a series of cultural debacles forced upon us by judges following no law but their own predilections. This one, however, will be nuclear. As an example of judicial incontinence, it will rival *Roe* v. *Wade,* and will deal a severe and quite possibly fatal blow to two already badly damaged but indispensable institutions—marriage and the rule of law in constitutional interpretation.

The wreckage may be subtler but more widespread even than that. Such a decision would ratify, in the most profound way, the anarchical spirit of extreme personal and group autonomy that is the driving force behind much of our cultural degradation. Call it what you will—moral chaos, relativism, postmodernism—extreme notions of autonomy already suffuse our culture, quite aside from any assistance from the courts. But judicial endorsement, which is taken by much of the public to state a moral as well as a legal truth, makes the anything-goes mentality even harder to resist. The principle undergirding radical autonomy is essentially unconfineable. Thus, Justice Byron White, Senator Rick Santorum, and William Bennett have all made the point that the rationale for same-sex marriage would equally support group marriage, incest, or any other imaginable sexual arrangement.

That surely is the meaning, insofar as it has a discernible meaning, of the imperialistic "mystery passage" first articulated by three justices in a case upholding the right to abortion and repeated in the majority opinion creating a right to homosexual sodomy:

From *First Things*, August/September 2004.

> [Our] law affords constitutional protection to . . . the most intimate and personal choices a person may make in a lifetime, choices central to personal dignity and autonomy, [which] are central to the liberty protected by the Fourteenth Amendment. At the heart of liberty [protected by the Constitution] is the right to define one's own concept of existence, of meaning, of the universe, and of the mystery of human life.

Reading these words, it is hard to know what there is left for legislatures to do, since each individual is now a sovereign nation.

The only real hope of heading off the judicial drive to constitutionalize homosexual marriage is in the adoption of an amendment to the Constitution. The language of the amendment now before Congress is this:

> Marriage in the United States shall consist only of the union of a man and a woman. Neither this Constitution nor the constitution of any state shall be construed to require that marital status or the legal incidents thereof be conferred upon unmarried couples or groups.

The amendment is intended primarily to stop activist courts from redefining marriage in any way they see fit, as the Supreme Judicial Court of Massachusetts has recently done. The first sentence, however, also limits legislatures by defining marriage as the people of the United States and of the West have known it.

Given that the stakes riding on the outcome of the effort to adopt the Federal Marriage Amendment (FMA) are so high, it is surprising that so many social conservatives have expressed opposition. Though these are men for whom I have the highest regard, in this instance I think they are mistaken. Their mistake, it seems to me, derives from a conservative constitutionalism which, though laudable in the past, is now, most unfortunately, obsolete. Walter Bagehot, writing of the English constitution in the nineteenth century, said, "[I]n the full activity of an historical constitution, its subjects repeat phrases true in the time of their fathers, and inculcated by those fathers, but now no longer true." So it is with us. Michael Greve correctly places the same-sex marriage issue in a wider context: "[T]he broader, more menacing problem is judicial usurpation. . . . [W]hat truly grates is the notion of having [homosexual marriage] dictated by willful, contemptuous judges." Conservative constitutionalism today requires taking back the original Constitution to restore the constitutional order and representative government. If that requires amending the Constitution to recall the judges to their proper function, so be it. There is no other remedy available to save or, more accurately, to restore a republican form of government.

The conservative columnists George F. Will and Charles Krauthammer, however, seem to me to illustrate Bagehot's maxim. Will has written that "amending the Constitution to define marriage as between a man and a woman would be unwise for two reasons. Constitutionalizing social policy is generally a misuse of fundamental law. And it would be especially imprudent to end state responsibility for marriage law at a moment when we require evidence of the sort that can be generated by allowing the states to be laboratories of social policy." To his point about the unwisdom of putting social policy in the Constitution, it is fair to reply that the entire document can be seen as expressing social policy, and certainly parts of the Bill of Rights, such as the guarantee of the free exercise of religion, do exactly that. The real difficulty with Will's position, however, is his notion that the states will be allowed to be laboratories of social policy. They will not; the Supreme Court, as in the case of *Roe*, will simply replace the social policies of all of the states with its own policy.

The most likely route to that ruling is the following. A homosexual couple will marry in Massachusetts, move to another state (say, Texas), and claim the status and benefits of marriage there. They will cite the Full Faith and Credit Clause of Article IV of the Constitution, which declares that states must accept the public acts of every other state. Texas will refuse recognition, relying on the federal Defense of Marriage Act (DOMA), passed in reliance on Article IV'S further provision that Congress may prescribe the effect of such out-of-state acts. The couple will respond with a challenge to DOMA under the federal Due Process and Equal Protection Clauses. The Supreme Court will then uphold their challenge by finding a federal constitutional right to same-sex marriage that invalidates DOMA. The FMA would prevent this almost-certain outcome. Instead of state-by-state experimentation, we are going to have a uniform rule one way or the other: homosexual marriage everywhere or nowhere. The choice is that stark and judges are forcing us to make it.

Charles Krauthammer agrees that "there is not a chance in hell that the Supreme Court will uphold" DOMA. He concludes, nonetheless, that "I would probably vote against the amendment because for me the sanctity of the Constitution trumps everything, even marriage." His point would be well taken if it were not much too late to worry about the sanctity of a document the Supreme Court has been shredding for fifty years. Surely the Court's diktats, which are themselves profoundly unconstitutional, are not sacred. As matters now stand, the "sanctity of the Constitution" is a smoke screen providing cover for judicial activism. Taking action through authentically constitutional means to prevent yet another constitutional travesty shows greater respect for the document than standing by while five of nine justices chisel into the tablets of the law the caprices of the elite class to which they respond. An amendment preventing one instance of judicial depredation would at least represent a democratic choice—indeed a choice by supermajorities, given the requirement of a two-thirds vote in each house of Congress and then ratification by three-quarters of the states.

There is one other objection expressed by Krauthammer, however: "I would be loath to see some future democratic consensus in favor of gay marriage (were that to come to pass) blocked by such an amendment." That objection could, of course, be made to every provision of the Constitution; each and every one precludes some action by a future democratic consensus. If, for example, a national majority should want to make foreign-born naturalized citizens eligible for the presidency or to abolish jury trials in complex lawsuits, that democratic consensus would be frustrated by the Constitution.

Michael Greve suggests a constitutional amendment that would preserve the value of state experimentation while heading off the Supreme Court creation of homosexual marriage:

> The United States Constitution shall not be construed to require the federal government, or any state or territory, to define marriage as anything except the union of one man and one woman. The United States Constitution shall not be construed to require any state or territory to give effect to any public act, record, or judicial proceeding respecting a relationship between persons of the same sex that is treated as a marriage under the laws of another state or territory.

This amendment would leave states free to give effect to the acts of other states or not, as they see fit. Greve suggests that state legislatures could control the choice through legislation allowing or forbidding their courts to honor out-of-state homosexual marriages.

There seem both legal and sociological problems with this proposal. The language leaves out of account what state courts may do with state constitutions. A state supreme court could very well hold—and a number of them certainly will—that its state constitution contains a right to homosexual marriage or, alternatively, that its constitution mandates recognition of such marriages contracted elsewhere. It is not a sufficient answer that the citizenry could respond by amending the state constitution. In many states the amending process is quite difficult and time-consuming; and a state supreme court's ruling will itself affect the balance in the electorate. The cultural aristocracy—the news media, university faculties, many churches, foundations, television networks, and Hollywood—will continue, as they have already been doing, to propagandize massively and incessantly for the normality of homosexuality and the right to marry. It may be doubted that many states will muster supermajorities overruling their courts in the face of this cultural tsunami. There seems no way to guard against state court activism on this issue, which we have already seen in Hawaii, Vermont, and Massachusetts, except by a federal amendment that binds state as well as federal courts.

As seems inevitable in discussions about reining in runaway courts, some have suggested that instead of amending the Constitution, Congress should deny all federal courts jurisdiction to deal with the marriage issue. Congress has power under Article III of the Constitution to make exceptions to the appellate jurisdiction of the Supreme Court and to remove lower court jurisdiction. This proposal, though endorsed by a commentator as sound as Arnold Beichman, is, as always, a nonstarter, and merely diverts some Congressmen from addressing the problem seriously. If the Supreme Court allowed its jurisdiction over a particular subject to be abolished, which is by no means a certainty, the result would be to leave jurisdiction in the state courts. Article VI provides that "the Judges in every State shall be bound" by the Constitution and laws of the United States, and there is no power in either Congress or the state legislatures to take away that jurisdiction. The result, if Congress acted and the Court acquiesced, would be the same as under the constitutional amendment suggested by Michael Greve, except that state courts could rely upon both the federal and state constitutions to invent, as the courts of Massachusetts and Hawaii have under their state constitutions, a right to same-sex marriage.

Amending the United States Constitution to save it and marriage from freebooting judges would be extremely difficult in the best of circumstances, but it is made immeasurably more difficult because so many people ask: How does homosexual marriage affect me? What concern is it of mine or of anybody else what homosexuals do? The answer is that the consequences of homosexual marriage will affect you, your children, and your grandchildren, as well as the morality and health of the society in which you and they live.

Studies of the effects of same-sex marriage in Scandinavia and the Netherlands by Stanley Kurtz raise at least the inference that when there is a powerful (and ultimately successful) campaign by secular elites for homosexual marriage, traditional marriage is demeaned and comes to be perceived as just one more sexual arrangement among others. The symbolic link between marriage, procreation, and family is broken, and there is a rapid and persistent decline in heterosexual marriages. Families are begun by cohabiting couples, who break up significantly more often than married couples, leaving children in one-parent families. The evidence has long been clear that children raised in such families are much more likely to engage in crime, use drugs, and form unstable relationships of their own. These are pathologies that affect everyone in a community.

Homosexual marriage would prove harmful to individuals in other ways as well. By equating heterosexuality and homosexuality, by removing the last vestiges of moral stigma from same-sex couplings, such marriages will lead to an increase in the number of homosexuals. Particularly vulnerable will be young men and women who, as yet uncertain of and confused by their sexuality, may more easily be led into a homosexual life. Despite their use of the word "gay," for many homosexuals life is anything but gay. Both physical and psychological disorders are far more prevalent among homosexual men than among heterosexual men. Attempted suicide rates, even in countries that are homosexual-friendly, are three to four times as high for homosexuals. Though it is frequently asserted by activists that high levels of internal distress in homosexual populations are caused by social disapproval, psychiatrist Jeffrey Satinover has shown that no studies support this theory. Compassion, if nothing else, should urge us to avoid the consequences of making homosexuality seem a normal and acceptable choice for the young.

There is, finally, very real uncertainty about the forms of sexual arrangements that will follow from homosexual marriage. To quote William Bennett: "Say what they will, there are no principled grounds on which advocates of same-sex marriage can oppose the marriage of two consenting brothers. Nor can they (persuasively) explain why we ought to deny a marriage license to three men who want to marry. Or to a man who wants a consensual polygamous arrangement. Or to a father to his adult daughter." Many consider such hypotheticals ridiculous, claiming that no one would want to be in a group marriage. The fact is that some people do, and they are urging that it be accepted. There is a movement for polyamory—sexual arrangements, including marriage, among three or more persons. The outlandishness of such notions is no guarantee that they will not become serious possibilities or actualities in the not-too-distant future. Ten years ago, the idea of a marriage between two men seemed preposterous, not something we needed to concern ourselves with. With same-sex marriage a line is being crossed, and no other line to separate moral and immoral consensual sex will hold.

We are in a time of deep moral confusion about sex and particularly about homosexuality. Consider: the Catholic Church is berated for putting homosexual men in charge of boys while the Boy Scouts are punished for not putting homosexual men in charge of boys. At the same time, as Mary Eberstadt points out, the rightness or wrongness of pedophilia (involving boys, not girls) is "demonstrably not yet settled within certain parts of the gay rights movement." Eberstadt reports that the taboo against pedophilia is weakening. Some homosexual activists, such as the North American Man/Boy Love Association, are working to that end. Nothing, one is tempted to say, is any longer unimaginable, and what is imaginable is doable.

Is passing the FMA worth the energy and the political risk for politicians, especially when it may well be a losing battle? Social conservatives, Max Boot notes, have been fighting and losing culture wars for decades. That is obvious, but his recommendation that we acknowledge defeat on the issue of homosexual marriage and move on to other issues is bad advice. This issue seems to me so important that a fight against it, whatever the odds, is mandatory. Abandoning resistance here might nevertheless be seen by some as an intelligent strategy, but that would be true only if there were a more defensible line to fall back to. It is difficult to see what line that might be. The cultural left, including homosexual activists, will keep pressing for more. The BBC, as a foretaste of what is to come, has ordered its staff not to use the words "husband" and "wife," since that might seem to indicate that marriage is preferable to other sexual arrangements. In Canada, a pastor has been charged under a hate speech law for publishing instances of the Bible's disapproval of homosexuality. Church leaders who imagine they can negotiate immunities from laws applying to the rest of the population are almost certainly fooling themselves. Liberal autonomists have little or no respect for religion, except to the extent that some clergy can be recruited to advance their causes in the name of religion. The Catholic Church will be a particular target of attack, as it already has been in California, where the state supreme court ruled that Catholic Charities had to provide prescription contraceptive coverage in its health insurance plan for employees.

Boot's advice to cut and run on this issue thus ignores the fact that there are fewer and fewer places to run to. The autonomous drive toward cultural degradation will not leave us in peace, ever. Boot may be right to predict that Republican support for a marriage amendment would make the party "look 'intolerant' to soccer moms whose views on this subject, as on so many others, will soon be as liberal as elite opinion already is." But if that is true, it means that we will lose all the cultural battles of the future, as the soccer moms trail along behind elite opinion. If Republicans refuse to fight cultural battles on that reasoning, they will look cowardly to conservatives, which could be equally disastrous. It would be better to try to convince the soccer moms, who would not be at all happy if their children and grandchildren cohabited instead of marrying, or "married" persons of the same sex.

Finally, it is worth considering that a vigorous campaign for the FMA could have a salutary effect on the American judiciary. The debates, win or lose, might also lead the public to a more realistic view of the courts. As William F. Buckley Jr. has written on another occasion, "The public—under the tutelage of its moral and intellectual leaders—is being trained, as regards the Supreme Court of the United States when it is interpreting the Constitution, to accept its rulings as if rendered ex cathedra, on questions of faith and morals." Thus, a constitutional amendment "done athwart the will of the Court for the first time in modern history . . . would deliver the Republic from a presumptuous ethical-legal tribunal." "The public," Buckley argues, "needs to experience a release from a subtle thralldom to judicial morality." Quite right.

Conservative opinion leaders must recognize that the illegitimacy of the rampant judicial constitution-making that is before their eyes changes all the old rules about the place of amendments in our polity. The comfortable shibboleths about a heavy presumption against amending the Constitution no longer have much relevance to the brute facts of our political life. So profound is the departure from a republican form of government that the presumption must now be in favor of amending the Constitution whenever the Court runs wild. Homosexual marriage presents just such an occasion, but if our politicians wait until the Supreme Court has done the inevitable, it will probably be too late for an effective response. Catastrophes ought not to be faced in a spirit of resignation.

A DARK FUTURE SEEN AT TWILIGHT

Review of *Twilight of Authority* by Robert Nisbet (Oxford, 1975)

N isbet's thesis is that the West is in a state of decline, a "twilight age," characterized by a loss of social authority and hierarchy, and a decline in attachment to political values, coupled, perhaps not paradoxically, with the spread of an oppressive state machinery. As the state, in the name of equality, attempts to ensure not equality of opportunity but equality of result, and is supported in this effort by a "clerisy of power" (including "the greater part of the intellectual, especially academic, class"), it necessarily becomes an engine of leveling. Private power centers and institutions that mediate between the individual and the state are weakened so that ultimately the state will face only a mass of individuals. In that lies the prospect of tyranny.

Indeed, Nisbet predicts that the future lies with military socialisms presiding over masses of persons unsupported by intermediate institutions, barbaric regimes governing in the name of equality. "If our problem were *only* a world scene increasingly dominated by the military socialisms or *only* a domestic setting of combined political centralization and social erosion, there would be reason for doubting that America will, like other Western nations, turn increasingly to a variant of the war state. But the fact is, *both* of those conditions are present, and in mounting intensity, and against them any thought of arresting or reversing the processes of militarization of society seems rather absurd."

This is an impressive book, an erudite book, a necessary book, and none of that is intended to be diluted by the observations that in a few places the chain of logic seems fragile and that one wishes it had been a heavier book. As Nisbet acknowledges, parts of his book have appeared in very different

From *National Review*, November 21, 1975

form in magazines and newspapers and, while there is no doubt this is a book rather than a collection of articles, there remains something of the quickness of style and ellipsis of argument characteristic of the shorter forms.

This would not be worth mentioning were it not also true that Nisbet's style is trenchant, his message important, and his insights often brilliant. Nisbet can be taken at two levels. The first, which is perhaps a dispensable overlay, consists of the concept of a "twilight age," which parallels previous periods of decline, and the prediction of the militarization of society and the rise of a line of Caesars. I do not say this may not be accurate, only that it is not necessary to the argument, that it may be overly dramatic, and that the demonstration of coming militarization seems rather weak.

But all that may be laid aside and the remaining argument is still compelling and disturbing. Despotism is hardly more welcome if the new governors turn out to be not a clutch of colonels but a supposedly benevolent governmental bureaucracy operating in the name of equality of condition and imposing uniformity because of bureaucracy's own dynamic and requirements.

And it is here that Nisbet is at his best: demonstrating the connection between centralization of power and the ideal of equality of condition as contrasted with equality of opportunity; pointing out the affinity of modern left-liberal intellectuals for both central power and egalitarianism; showing the increasing legalization of our culture and our individual relationships, which is a way of replacing social forces with state coercion; delineating the growth of state power in new, softer, and hence less resistible forms; linking the current wave of subjectivism and irrationality, manifested in occultism and the state of the arts, to the decline of the political community; showing the reciprocal relationship between the degradation of language, which is essential to the social bond, and the spread of state power. In these and a dozen other things, Nisbet is insightful, provocative, and, sad to say, probably quite right.

Though pessimistic that the forces of political centralization and social disintegration can be reversed, Nisbet closes with a plea for pluralism and the rescue of the social order from the political order, and he identifies some faint causes for hope. The reader will not be much heartened.

Early reaction to his book appears to confirm part of Nisbet's thesis. A lengthy review recites with approval Nisbet's analysis of the ominous trends in governmental power and abuse but takes offense at his perception that one driving force in these developments is the intellectual's appetite for an equality of condition that can be implemented only through a pervasive and stifling bureaucracy. So long as Nisbet denounces government deception and intrusion, he is a "social analyst and prophet"; when he identifies the particular source of the evil, be descends at once, in the reviewer's estimation, to the status of "ideologue." Yet as long as we do not see the connection, so long academic intellectuals will assist in creating the results they deplore. If they were alone in the boat, it would be first-rate farce.

But there does seem to be an encouraging, though still small, counter-trend against left-liberalism among intellectuals. Nisbet's book is an example, as is the posthumous book *The Morality of Consent,* by Alexander Bickel. Other names come to mind. The counter-trend, which one hesitates to call conservative because of the danger of being misunderstood, tends to cite the tradition of Burke and Tocqueville. Its emphasis is social and historical, as in the case of Nisbet. or constitutional, as with Bickel, and appears not terribly at ease with economics. (The few times Nisbet traverses economic terrain are among the book's weaker passages.) Should this counter-trend incorporate elements of the free market tradition, an intellectual force of really major proportions would appear to challenge the "clerisy of power" now driving us toward centralization and uniformity. The makings are there.

The Living and the Dead

Review of *Post-Liberalism: Studies in Political Thought,* by John Gray (Routledge, 1993)

Political Theory sometimes seems an intellectual parlor game, an arena for academic poseurs, with little or no relevance to political reality. Isaiah Berlin remarked that this century's history was massively shaped by "the great ideological storms that have altered the lives of virtually all mankind: the Russian Revolution and its aftermath—totalitarian tyrannies of both Right and Left and the explosions of nationalism, racism, and, in places, of religious bigotry, which, interestingly enough, not one among the most perceptive social thinkers of the nineteenth century had ever predicted."

Worse still, many twentieth-century philosophers, even in the face of those calamities, go on building airy liberal-egalitarian models for society without apparently noticing that actual societies show no inclination to conform to the models. As the Communist world shatters, so too do many of the nations newly freed from its tyranny. Ethnic and religious hatreds and slaughters abound in Asia, Africa, and Eastern Europe, and the end is nowhere in sight. It seems certain that soon some of the most vicious regimes on earth will have nuclear weapons capable of reaching our allies and, not long afterward, ourselves.

Ethnic and racial hatreds, though not yet slaughters, are rising even in the democracies of the West. The state of public contentment with Western political leadership may be seen in the fact that Bill Clinton's miserable approval ratings are nevertheless among the highest of the leaders of the G-7 countries. In the Western industrialized democracies, government has grown so intrusive and expensive that economic growth, a necessity for so-

From *National Review,* August 9, 1993.

cial peace, falters or declines while national debt due to the welfare state grows uncontrollably, taking us toward bankruptcy. The thirst for equality of results, especially in the United States, steadily diminishes not only productivity but personal freedoms. If any major trends provide reason for cheerfulness about our immediate future, they are quite well disguised.

Much of the blight in our domestic affairs flows directly from the state of contemporary liberalism, and it is said there is cause for hope in the obtrusive fact that that outlook is intellectually bankrupt. So, one supposes, was the animating philosophy of the Mongol Empire. Bankrupt enterprises can survive and do extensive damage for long periods, as the Soviet Union did, and that is probably particularly true when the bankruptcy in question is merely intellectual. I use the word "merely" advisedly. Though the inmates of universities and think tanks keep telling themselves that ideas are ultimately decisive, it is not true that the better ideas invariably win out in the political marketplace. Ideas, or moods posing as ideas, that become dominant are decisive, but their coherence, as a philosopher would define that, may have little to do with their popular acceptance.

The question naturally arises: What, then, is the use of political philosophy? A persuasive answer is given in John Gray's latest book, *Post-Liberalism: Studies in Political Thought*. The title stirs hope. If there is anything I feel ready for it is a post-liberal era. But the book itself dispels any such euphoria.

Mr. Gray, a fellow of Jesus College, Oxford, has collected a number of his recent essays, apparently disparate but connected by an overall theme. In the first section, "Thinkers," he examines the merits of the philosophies of Thomas Hobbes, George Santayana, Friedrich Hayek, Michael Oakeshott, James Buchanan, and Isaiah Berlin. "Critiques," the second section, consists of essays about Marxism, totalitarianism, the post-totalitarian attempt to construct a civil society in the former Soviet Union, the forms of liberalism, and much more. "Questions," the final section, takes up the politics of cultural diversity, conservatism, and the political thought of the New Right, and concludes with a new essay entitled "What Is Dead and What Is Living in Liberalism?" Though all the essays are rich with insights, this last one caps the major theme that holds the book together.

What is dead is liberal political philosophy as practiced by John Stuart Mill and his intellectual heirs. What is living, though in most cases badly damaged and certainly endangered, is liberal institutions and practices. This living liberalism is not the modem, authoritarian variety exemplified by the left wing of the Democratic Party but the classical version, to which much of modem liberalism is hostile and much of modem conservatism is friendly.

The answer, then, to the question, Of what use is political philosophy? is that there is little enough in the attempts to construct overarching systems to be found in the writings of Mill, John Rawls, Robert Nozick, and Ronald Dworkin. Such attempts to establish liberalisms—of whatever variety, classical or modern—as universal prescriptions flounder on any realistic look at the facts of the world in which we live. This project of liberalism is doomed and we would do well to abandon it, for it is worse than useless, it is harmful. The political philosophizing that remains useful relates to the understanding, preservation, and improvement of the liberal civil society which is ours in the West by inheritance, and largely by historical accident. Theory should, therefore, address the actual institutions and practices of the liberal societies of the West. This is not to say that those societies are undergirded by irrefutable philosophy but that the ways of life they allow are ours, we have come to value them, and we would feel impoverished if we lost them.

The liberal philosophical enterprise, by contrast, was and is to demonstrate by abstract theorizing that Western-style liberal societies are superior to all other societies, past, existing, or imaginable, and therefore present the model to which the world must ultimately come. Moreover, these societies themselves must be altered to fit more closely the theoretical model. There is in this, of course, a strong authoritarian impulse, since actual societies are not likely to conform themselves to some philosopher's dream without coercion by government. In its extreme form, this coercion in the pursuit of a dream results in Stalinism. In milder forms, it resembles President Clinton's attempt to remake America according to notions concocted in the bull sessions of 1960s student radicals.

Mr. Gray identifies the four philosophic elements of the "liberal syndrome" as "moral or normative individualism" (the idea that ultimate value lies only in the states of mind, feeling, or lives of individuals), "universalism" (the idea that certain rights inhere in all human beings and that every political institution is to be judged by the degree to which it secures the specified rights), "meliorism" (the idea that human institutions may be improved indefinitely through critical reason), and "egalitarianism" (the idea that, because all humans are morally equal, hierarchy and authority require an ethical defense).

Mr. Gray's argument that philosophy can establish none of these elements as having universal authority borrows from Isaiah Berlin's demonstration that ultimate values often conflict with one another, and that there are bound to be conflicts even within values. The value of liberty, for example, is not monolithic because claimed liberties often, perhaps always, conflict with one another. Nor can such conflicts be resolved by any overarching standard, and so ultimate values are uncombinable in a single society. Thus, according to Berlin, "the ancient ideal, common to many cultures and especially to that of the Enlightenment, of a perfect society in which all true ends are reconciled, is conceptually incoherent." The resultant "objective pluralism" and "value incommensurability" means that there is no single good life and certainly no single conception or model of a good society. There are many varieties of "human flourishing," which seems to be Gray's ultimate value. But if there are many ways for humans to flourish, as no doubt there are, then it is not demonstrable that individual feeling must always trump collective claims, that there can be a specified list of rights against which all societies must be measured, that critical reason can always identify "progress" as between two cultures, or that egalitarianism is a requirement of a good society.

The demonstration that the philosophic, though not the practiced, project of liberalism is impossible in a society of multiple visions of the good life is immensely valuable in itself, and perhaps it will turn some of the academic theorists to socially more useful pursuits, such as becoming tax lawyers, where their metaphysical casuistries would be more appropriate. But the same conclusion might have been reached empirically by the observation that none of the liberal philosophers has ever succeeded in constructing a system with which all men of good faith must agree. If, after a couple of centuries, very powerful minds have not succeeded, there is strong reason to suspect that success is impossible. Of course, that is not entirely satisfactory, just as it was not entirely satisfactory that Fermat's Last Theorem held true for all numbers tried in computer calculations. Mathematicians' excitement and satisfaction were reserved for the apparent theoretical demonstration that FLT must be true for all numbers. So it is with the demonstration that liberal philosophizing of the grand, overarching variety is false in all its manifestations.

Gray's ultimate value, "human flourishing," is a concept not much developed in this book, though most of us probably have a tolerably clear idea of what he means. He is quite clear, however, that for us in the West, human flourishing can occur only within a "civil society." That concept is developed. "A civil society is one which is tolerant of the diversity of views, religious and political, that it contains, and in which the state does not seek to impose on all any comprehensive doctrine." Second, both the government and its subjects are constrained by the rule of law, which implies limited government so that most social and economic activities will be independent of government.

Third, it is essential that the institution of private property be protected and that economic activity proceed through market institutions, though not necessarily through capitalist corporations.

Gray himself, however, gives reasons to think that civil society as so defined may be unlikely to survive. A major reason is the emergence in our time of mass democracy in which political competition thrusts the government into ever more aspects of our economic and social lives. The result is what he calls the "Hobbesian state," an omnipresent government which does not rescue men from the brutal competition of the state of nature but which is itself the arena for such competition as interest groups combat one another for the levers and rewards of state power. This seems to me fairly to describe the situation of the United States today, which suggests that the institutions and practices of civil society are in sharp decline and their existence probably imperiled.

It may seem unlikely that our government will refuse to tolerate the varieties of views prevalent in the United States or attempt to impose any comprehensive view of its own. The major instance in which the state, through the Supreme Court, may be said to be attempting something of the sort is in the banishment of religion and religious symbolism from our public life. As government reaches further and further into our lives, carrying the Court's misinterpretation of the religion clauses of the First Amendment with it, secularization becomes the official view. There may be worse to come. Political correctness is no longer confined to campuses, and some subjects (e.g., homosexual rights, affirmative action) may soon become almost undiscussable. Though government will not command any such result, it is leading the way, the actual coercion being moral and already accepted by many private institutions.

The rule of law, the institutions of private property, and the coordination of economic activities by the market seem less healthy. No one of that trio is highly regarded in the universities, and large segments of the intellectual world are actively hostile. All three are damaged every day by the proliferation of administrative agencies that govern us under broad, often meaningless, delegations of power from Congress and state legislatures. Agency discretion is only minimally constrained by the courts. The rule of law is also threatened by the politicization of judicial decision-making. The Warren Court, for example, is routinely cited by liberal elites as the very epitome of what a court should be. But the Warren Court was notable precisely for its contempt for law and the imposition of its own views not only on the Constitution but on antitrust and patent statutes, labor law, indeed on any body of law where an ideological opportunity presented itself.

That attitude is prevalent among too many Justices and judges today. Ronald Reagan and George Bush sought, with only partial success, to correct it by appointing judges who would respect law as having its own integrity—a view now widely denigrated as producing "conservative ideologues"—but Bill Clinton clearly intends to repoliticize the bench along liberal lines. It turns out that the morality of process, which is what judicial restraint is about, is no match for the morality of results as judicial activists define that morality.

The prospects of limited government are not particularly bright either. In the United States the courts have long since given up enforcement of limits on federal power, and calls for rejuvenating the Tenth Amendment are merely plaintive laments of conservative nostalgia. Edward Banfield has shown that the idea of a national government limited to its enumerated powers was doomed from the outset because Americans do not want such restraints and, sooner or later, the political branches will get the kind of judges they want. The growth of mass democracy and the brutal competition of interest groups within the Hobbesian state ensures that government will never again limit the spheres of its claimed competence. Gray mentions the possibility of a balanced budget amendment, but that, too, is a conservative chimera. There would be no way to enforce such an amendment except by turning the budget over to the federal courts, which would continually be ruling on fiscal years long gone by.

Though Gray's is an urgent plea for the preservation of civil society, he sees that the prospects are gloomy. He thinks that the "likely course of the coming century . . . virtually inevitably will encompass fundamentalist convulsions, near-apocalyptic ecological catastrophes, Malthusian wars, and the spread of technologies of mass destruction in an increasingly anarchic world." Nor does danger exist only abroad. He speaks of "the prospect of a slow decline in our own civil societies, as traditional practices of law and civil association are eroded by the inordinate demands of abstract conceptions of equality and rights."

> [I]f civil society is among us in danger, it is in virtue precisely of the hubris of fundamental liberalism—the liberalism of those (such as Ackerman, the early Nozick and Rawls, or Dworkin) who seek to use the hallucinatory perspectives of uncritical philosophy to distract us from the practice of liberty. We are not far from the point at which the mass availability of hubristic philosophy imposes impossible strains on the institutions and practices from which it illicitly derives ail its genuine content.

The danger is "the corrosion of liberal practices by liberal ideology."

To those unacquainted with the academic world, this may seem an over-blown statement of the danger. But the state of our universities is such that there is "mass availability" of the sort of philosophy Gray attacks. Students may not retain the details of such theorizing, but they do retain the attitudes taught. They come away fixated with vulgar conceptions of "equality" and "rights," and hence vulnerable to rhetoric of that sort. A friend assures me that all is well because the inanities of the academic Left are creating con-servative students. There is such an effect, to be sure, but it seems heavily outweighed by the creation of left liberals. The results may be seen every-where: in the media, in the churches, in the entertainment industry, and in our politics.

But, Gray correctly contends, matters in the United States are worse than that. "The legalist turn in recent American liberal thought has predict-ably deleterious consequences . . . In political contexts, it has generated a se-ries of intractable conflicts, which portend deepening division, growing un-governability, and even a sort of chronic, low-intensity civil war." Standards of argument have been debauched and "[c]omplex questions about restraint of liberty such questions as the control of pornography, and the termination of life in abortion and euthanasia—that in other countries, and other tradi-tions of liberal discourse, are treated as issues in legislative policy, involving a balance of interests and sometimes a compromise of ideals, have come to be treated in the United States, primarily or exclusively, as questions of fun-damental rights."

This is much the same point made by Mary Ann Glendon in *Rights Talk: The Impoverishment of Political Discourse*. Anyone who has heard Kate Michelman's argument for "freedom of choice" knows that the beginning, middle, and end consist of the assertion that abortion is a "woman's funda-mental right." When someone on the other side simply says "murder," politi-cal discourse is not merely debauched but abolished.

Sadly, the phenomenon John Gray and Mary Ann Glendon identify may be an almost inevitable effect of the American Bill of Rights, which, in our time, exerts a constant pressure toward less and less restrained individual-ism and personal autonomy. The guarantees of the Bill of Rights symbolize freedom and there are no counter symbols in the Constitution; or, if the po-litical powers conferred there are taken as (weak) counter symbols, it is clear that they are overridden both in law and in prestige by the idea of freedom from legal restraint.

This is not solely because the Bill of Rights is the primary vehicle the law provides for judicial power and human nature tempts judges constantly to expand that power, which means, of course, constantly expanding the area of individual autonomy at the expense of the legitimate claims of the community. More than that, some judges and their academic acolytes cannot resist seeing the Bill of Rights as flowing from a moral and political philosophy which the written guarantees do not fully express. By a leap of logic, it becomes the judge's duty, or at least his option, to discern that more complete philosophy and to fill out the law by finding and enforcing new rights. This was precisely and explicitly the process by which *Griswold* v. *Connecticut* invented the "right of privacy," which led to *Roe* v. *Wade.,* which led to the new "right of personal dignity and autonomy" announced by three Justices in *Planned Parenthood* v. *Casey,* which will lead to God knows what.

The whole technique is ahistorical, since the Bill of Rights neither derives from nor implies philosophic reasoning about the proper sphere of individual autonomy but is rather an expression of historical experience (the Third Amendment's prohibition of quartering troops in private homes except in time of war) or fear of what the new federal power might do (the First Amendment's prohibition of a congressional establishment of religion). But the legalism of modern liberal thought means that the broader philosophy of ever more extensive autonomy spills over into our intellectual and political arenas.

There is an associated force for decline that Gray does not much deal with: the unrestrained individualism and moral relativism that are rampant in our culture and most visible in popular culture. Indeed, he seems a bit complacent on this subject: "None of the manifestations of contemporary decadence about which conventional conservative opinion is so alarmed are threats to the survival of society." In this, he seems both somewhat inconsistent and wrong. In another book, *Liberalism,* Gray speaks of the "vital truth that the maintenance of moral and cultural traditions is a necessary condition of lasting progress," and in this book he states that the culture of individualism is "threatened, especially in the United States, by a left liberalism which regards the undergirding institutions of liberal civil society—marriage, private property, and so forth—as constraints upon, and not as conditions of, individual freedom."

It may be wondered, moreover, whether a healthy political culture or a viable civil society can be maintained by a people increasingly given to the pursuit of instant and endless titillation, a people who think that only the self matters and that the individual's right to define himself and choose his pleasures without hindrance is virtually absolute. Not only are undergirding institutions, such as marriage, threatened, but the self-discipline essential to productive work, both intellectual and physical, is likely to decline, and the self-restraint essential to healthy political and judicial institutions is likely to be in short supply. This is a decadence that has been growing for a very long time, though it accelerated and became blatant in the 1960s. Individualism lies at the heart of prosperity and freedom in the West, but individualism without limits is antipathetical to both.

Gray may be largely right that there is little government can do directly about this decadence—he cites Wittgenstein's remark that seeking deliberately to shore up an ailing tradition is like trying to repair a broken spider's web with one's bare hands—but that does not mean that nothing should be tried or that government has no role. Elsewhere, Gray notes that both the English and the American varieties of individualism were sustained for so long because they were not merely liberal but were more properly called "authoritarian individualism," dependent on a "nexus of beliefs, practices, and inhibitions which conferred legitimacy and constrained the corrosive tendencies . . . of the anonymity and moral laxity that were latent in individualist life." James Q. Wilson has written, "In the mid nineteenth century England and America reacted to the consequences of industrialization, urbanization, immigration, and affluence by asserting an ethos of self-control, whereas in the late twentieth century they reacted to many of the same forces by asserting an ethos of self-expression."

A primary, though not the only, constraint in both countries in the last century was religious tradition. There is still a strong religious strain in the United States, and modem liberals, recognizing the danger that strain poses to their agenda, try to discredit it by speaking of the "religious Right." Religious conservatives are no particular threat to anything other than the prevailing mood of moral relativism. The problem with relying upon religion today is that there are not enough religious conservatives and that much mainstream religion has been largely secularized, so that it often becomes the ally of left-liberalism.

It remains to be seen, therefore, whether an ethos of self-control can be reinstituted in some other way, by some other means, since betting on the chances of a religious revival does not seem a particularly astute strategy. A revival may come or it may not, but there is a secular language of morality and we must be prepared to use it despite the ridicule, and cries of danger, to be anticipated from the elites of modern liberalism. Moral intimidation is their favorite tactic. Political philosophers like John Gray expose the Left's pretensions and help us put the debate on the grounds most favorable to the preservation of our liberties.

CONSERVATISM AND THE CULTURE

In moments of despair, when I think America is indeed slouching towards an unfashionable address, when I contemplate the apparent indifference of the public to corruption and perjury in high places, I am consoled by one thing. Conservative thought and conservative intellectuals must be gaining ground or the liberals would not be constantly lecturing us on the meaning of "true conservatism." They would admire us, they claim, if we would return to that philosophy. But there is, as one might suspect, a catch.

"True conservatism," it turns out, is that form of conservatism that liberals find congenial. Today's conservatives simply fail to measure up. That is the measure of our success. We know we have arrived when liberal lecturing moves from the pages of liberal opinion magazines of small circulation to the pages of the Sunday *New York Times Magazine.*

It turns out that conservatives should emulate the optimism and good cheer of Ronald Reagan. You may have some difficulty recalling that the liberals admired Reagan all that much when he was in office. Now, however, a heavily revised version of the man is the standard by which liberals judge conservatives, and, not surprisingly, find us wanting. "Reagan's view of America," we are informed by Andrew Sullivan, "was never bleak, and he was careful to stay away from the front lines of the cultural wars. . . . Moralism, for him, was always a vague but essentially positive construct. . . . And it was far more in touch with the center of American culture."

"True conservatism," we are informed, requires that we be at the center of American culture. That would be a liberal panacea. If their opponents are careful to stay in the center while liberals pull from the left, the center will continually move left and "true conservatives" will, by definition, be bound to move with it. This is a liberal ratchet and a recipe for the destruction of

This address was delivered upon acceptance of the ISI Henry Salvatori Prize during the Intercollegiate Studies Institute's 45th anniversary celebration on November 5, 1998.

any effective conservatism. I wonder how Mr. Sullivan, formerly editor of *The New Republic,* would react to the suggestion that "true liberalism" means staying at the center of American culture while conservatives are free to tug the center to the right.

The major themes of 1980s conservatism are said to be economic freedom, smaller government, and personal choice. Opposed to this sunny outlook, today's conservatism is accused of being "inherently pessimistic," returning to older themes of cultural decline, moralism, and the need for greater social control.

But this is not a true opposition. The conservatism of the 1990s is not opposed to the conservative themes of the 1980s. Rather, the new stress on morality complements the stress on freedom to make one whole and complete conservative philosophy. Thus, conservatives favor free markets as by far the best way to create wealth for all Americans. But we also recognize that wealth and individual pleasure are not everything, that society requires moral standards, and that it is not moral to allow everything on the market.

Liberals and libertarians tend to shy away from the subject of traditional morality, but it is obvious that neither the free market nor limited government can perform well without a strong moral base. The free market requires men and women whose word can be trusted and who have formed personal traits of self-discipline, prudence, and self-denial or the deferment of gratifications. Smaller government requires many of the same qualities so that individuals will not constantly turn to a powerful state to offer them complete security and a cornucopia of favors bought with other people's money.

The need for smaller government is obvious and urgent. "It is a commonplace," Pierre Manent writes, "that totalitarianism is defined as the absorption of civil society by the state. . . . One of the sources of the totalitarian project is found in the idea that it is possible for man to model society in accordance with his wishes, once he occupies the seat of power and possesses an exact social science and employs adequate means for this task." Nazism and communism are the obvious examples.

There are, however, slower, less well-marked roads to totalitarianism that are more acceptable to a democratic people. Rather than being actuated by an exact social science or an explicit desire to remake society, the impelling force is a set of quite amorphous, but urgent, ideas about social justice coupled with a sense of moral superiority.

Tocqueville sounded the warning about government that "covers the surface of society with a network of small complicated rules, minute and uniform, through which the most original minds and the most energetic characters cannot penetrate to rise above the crowd. The will of man is not shattered, but softened, bent, and guided. . . . Such a power . . . stupefies a people, till each nation is reduced to nothing better than a flock of timid and industrious animals, of which the government is the shepherd."

As government regulations grow slowly, we become used to the harness. Habit is a powerful force, and we no longer feel as intensely as we once would have constrictions of our liberties that would have been utterly intolerable a mere half century ago.

We are all too familiar with heavy governmental regulation of private property and economic activity, as well as federal, state, and local taxation that takes well over half the earnings of many people. Statutes pour out like the Americans with Disabilities Act, the Occupational Safety and Health Act, and the Endangered Species Act. Agencies with the zealotry of the EPA turn environmentalism into a pantheistic religion, while medical care is made less effective by a web of bureaucratic controls. Our bureaucracies grind out 70,000 pages of new regulations a year. Common law tort actions increasingly control product designs and the delivery of services. Useful and harmless products have been driven from the market altogether by the costs of litigation.

Economic freedoms are not all that is under assault, however. In other areas, the force of government is augmented, and in many ways surpassed, by that of private institutions and communities enforcing new and destructive moralisms. Government, businesses, and universities practice affirmative action or quotas for ethnic groups and for women. Corporations, universities, and even primary and secondary schools police speech and attitudes to prevent expressions that might offend various newly sensitized and favored groups. Multiculturalism, which attacks America's traditions as well as its European heritage, insists that all cultures are equal. A person who offends this new morality, even inadvertently and tangentially, may be sentenced to sensitivity training—America's version of Maoist reeducation camps.

Radical feminism both exercises a virulent form of censorship and thought control and damages indispensable institutions. Organizational discipline may be applied for even referring to a woman's dress or attractiveness. A major corporation for which I have done legal consulting requires all employees to attend training sessions designed to root out sexist attitudes. One of the topics is the vexed question of whether it is insulting for a man to remove his hat when a woman gets on an elevator. A man approaching an office building heard the sounds of high heels behind him. He opened the door and held it to let the woman go first. She kicked him in the kneecap. These are the more amusing manifestations of feminism's power. There are less amusing aspects. Feminism is rife in education where it teaches antagonism toward men and provides debased education by distorting such subjects as literature, history, and law. In the armed forces standards of performance are lowered to allow a pretense of physical equality.

The new liberal morality demands freedom from restraints in ways that produce moral anarchy. The facts are familiar: the sexual revolution, births out of wedlock, drug use, crime, popular entertainment reliant on sex and violence. Softcore pornography is everywhere and the hardcore variety is not far behind. More ominously, what John Paul II calls the "culture of death," the practice of killing for convenience through abortion and now assisted suicide, which rapidly becomes euthanasia, is gaining ground. Quite recently some of these social pathologies, which have had a spectacular rise since the Sixties, have declined, albeit rather modestly. This has led to claims that America has turned a corner. Those claims, to say the least, are premature. The pathologies are still far more common than they were just a few decades ago. There may be a pendulum effect in such matters, but that does not mean the pendulum arm will swing all the way back. It seems more likely that the nadir of the swing will move steadily in the direction of social disorder.

We will be faced shortly with the ability to clone human beings, to design individuals through genetic manipulation, and to grow human bodies for the harvesting of organs. It is at best an open question whether the superficial utility of such actions will not overbear any moral qualms. Science, heretofore regarded as benign, may pose the most serious moral crises of the twenty-first century.

In the meantime, we already have more than enough to worry about in our culture. Roger Kimball wrote of the depth and power and devastation wrought by the cultural revolution that has swept America:

> [T]he radical emancipationist demands of the Sixties [have] triumphed throughout society. They have insinuated themselves, disastrously, into the curricula of our schools and colleges; they have dramatically altered the texture of sexual relations and family life; they have played havoc with the authority of churches and other repositories of moral wisdom; they have undermined the claims of civic virtue and our national self-understanding; they have degraded the media and the entertainment industry, and subverted museums and other institutions entrusted with preserving and transmitting high culture. They have even, most poignantly, addled our hearts and innermost assumptions about what counts as the good life.

We are now two nations. These are not, as Disraeli had it, the rich and the poor, or, as presidential commissions regularly proclaim, whites and blacks. Instead, we are two cultural nations. One embodies the counter-culture of the 1960s, which is today the dominant culture. Their values are propagated from the commanding heights of the culture: university faculties, journalists, television and movie producers, the ACLU, and major segments of the Democratic Party. The other nation, of those who adhere to traditional norms and morality, is now a dissident culture. Its spokesmen cannot hope to match the influence of the dominant nation. The dissident culture may survive by withdrawing, so far as possible, into enclaves of its own. The home-schooling movement is an example of that, an attempt to keep children out of a public educational system that, in the name of freedom, all too often teaches moral relativism and depravity.

Are there any solutions? For the problem of increasing economic regulation, we can recover the classical liberal philosophy, which is the conservatives' birthright: any proposal for government regulation is to be examined under a presumption of error. That is not an absolutist or extreme libertarian position. It merely holds that those who would decrease our freedoms in any area should bear the burden of proof.

The reformation of our culture, or more precisely, the recapture of what has been best in our cultural history, requires a different approach, for here the problem is not too little individual freedom but too much. Law may have a role to play here but it is strictly a secondary role, because without a fairly widespread public consensus laws will not be enacted or enforced. How is such a public consensus to be formed and maintained?

In an era of moral decline, a reversal probably depends on a revival of biblical religion. I have not been religious for most of my life, and I come to this conclusion not out of piety but through observation.

The role of religion—traditional, biblical religion—is crucial to cultural health. I commend to you Gertrude Himmelfarb's article "From Clapham to Bloomsbury." Clapham was a district in London inhabited by intensely religious and moral people. Bloomsbury you know about. When religion faded in England, the next generation insisted upon the strict demands of morality, not realizing that they were living on, and using up, the moral capital left behind by prior religious generations. Gradually, the imperatives of morality faded. We have entered a period in which morality is privatized. We are entering Bloomsbury.

A journalist I know has travelled our country inquiring about public attitudes toward our president's indiscretions. The usual response ran along the lines of "What he has done is wrong, but who am I to judge?" Religion, where it has not been subverted by the culture, is an antidote, perhaps the only antidote, to that variety of moral nihilism. Religion insists that there is right and wrong, and that the difference is knowable and comes with sanctions attached.

Yet the American public is now erroneously taught by the courts that religion is dangerous, that the First Amendment itself establishes a public religion—the religion of secular humanism. Is that serious? There is reason to think so. The late Christopher Lasch, a man of the Left, asked, "What accounts for [our society's] wholesale defection from the standards of personal conduct—civility, industry, self-restraint—that were once considered indispensable to democracy?" He answered that a major reason is the "gradual decay of religion." Our liberal elites, whose "attitude to religion," Lasch said, "ranges from indifference to active hostility," have succeeded in removing religion from public recognition and debate.

According to James Q. Wilson: "In the mid-nineteenth century England and America reacted to the consequences of industrialization, urbanization, immigration, and affluence by asserting an ethos of self-control, whereas in the late twentieth century they reacted to many of the same forces by asserting an ethos of self-expression."

The difference between the two centuries was the presence in the last century of religion and church-related institutions that taught morality. This suggests that a society deadened by a smothering network of laws while finding release in moral chaos is not likely to be either happy or stable.

This is not a counsel of despair. There is no iron law that bad trends must continue in a straight line forever. Perhaps we will stop the seemingly inexorable growth of government control of our lives. There are signs of a religious revival in the recent growth of the evangelical churches as well as in the apparent growth of orthodoxy in all our major religions—among Catholics, Protestants, Jews, and Mormons.

Taking back the culture will not be easy, but religion rejects despair. The four cardinal Christian virtues, paralleled in other religions, are, after all, prudence, justice, fortitude, and temperance. These are quite enough to take back the culture. In our current cultural wars, perhaps the most important of the virtues for conservatives is fortitude—the courage to take stands that are not immediately popular, the courage to ignore the opinion polls. Otherwise, we will never change the polls. That is what true conservatism means, or it means nothing.

Addicted to Health

When moral self-righteousness, greed for money, and political ambition work hand in hand they produce irrational, but almost irresistible, policies. The latest example is the war on cigarettes and cigarette smokers. A proposed settlement has been negotiated among politicians, plaintiffs' lawyers, and the tobacco industry. The only interests left out of the negotiations were smokers,' who will be ordered to pay enormous sums with no return other than the deprivation of their own choices and pleasures.

It is a myth that today's Americans are a sturdy, self-reliant folk who will fight any officious interference with their liberties. That has not been true at least since the New Deal. If you doubt that, walk the streets of any American city and see the forlorn men and women cupping their hands against the wind to light cigarettes so that they can get through a few more smokeless hours in their offices. Twenty-five percent of Americans smoke. Why can't they demand and get a compromise rather than accepting docilely the exile that employers and building managers impose upon them?

The answer is that they have been made to feel guilty by self-righteous non-smokers. A few years back, hardly anyone claimed to be seriously troubled by tobacco smoke. Now, an entire class of the morally superior claim to be able to detect, and be offended by, tobacco smoke several offices away from their own. These people must possess the sense of smell of a deer or an Indian guide. Yet they will happily walk through suffocating exhaust smoke from buses rather than wait a minute or two to cross the street.

No one should assume that peace will be restored when the the last cigarette smoker has been banished to the Alaskan tundra. Other products will be pressed into service as morally reprehensible. If you would know the future, look to California—the national leader in health fanaticism. Af-

From *National Review*, July 28, 1997.

ter a long day in Los Angeles flogging a book I had written, my wife and I sought relaxation with a drink at our hotel's outdoor bar. Our anticipation of pleasure was considerably diminished by a sign: "Warning! Toxic Substances Served Here." They were talking about my martini!

And martinis *are* a toxic substance, taken in any quantity sufficient to induce a sense of well being. Why not, then, ban alcohol or at least require a death's head on every martini glass? Well, we did once outlaw alcohol; it was called Prohibition. The myth is that Prohibition Increased the amount of drinking in this country; the truth is that it reduced it. There were, of course, some unfortunate side effects, like Al Capone and Dutch Schultz. But by and large the mobsters inflicted rigor mortis upon one another.

Why is it, then, that the end of Prohibition was welcomed joyously by the population? Not because alcohol is not dangerous. Not because the consumption of alcohol was not lessened. And not in order to save the lives of people with names like Big Jim and Ice Pick Phil. Prohibition came to an end because most Americans wanted to have a drink when and where they felt like it. If you insist on sounding like a law-and-economics professor, it ended because we thought the benefits of alcohol outweighed the costs.

That is the sort of calculation by which we lead our lives. Automobiles kill tens of thousands of people every year and disable perhaps that many again. We could easily stop the slaughter. Cars could be made with a top speed often miles an hour and with exteriors the consistency of marshmallows. Nobody would die, nobody would be disabled, and nobody would bother with cars very much.

There are, of course, less draconian measures available. On most highways, it is almost impossible to find anyone who observes the speed limits. On the theory of the tobacco precedent, car manufacturers should be liable for deaths caused by speeding; after all, they could build automobiles incapable of exceeding the legal speed limits.

The reason we are willing to offer up lives and limbs to automobiles is, quite simply, that they make life more pleasant (for those who remain intact)—among other things, by speeding commuting to work, by making possible family vacations a thousand miles from home, and by lowering the costs of products shipped from a distance. The case for regulating automobiles far more severely than we do is not essentially different from the case for heavy regulation of cigarettes or, soon, alcohol.

But choices concerning driving, smoking, and drinking are the sort of things that ought to be left to the individual unless there are clear, serious harms to others.

The opening salvo in the drive to make smoking a criminal act is the proposed settlement among the cigarette companies, plaintiffs' lawyers, and the states' attorneys general. We are told that the object is to protect teenagers and children (children being the last refuge of the sanctimonious). But many restrictions will necessarily affect adults, and the tobacco pact contains provisions that can only be explained as punishment for selling to adults.

The terms of the settlement plainly reveal an intense hatred of smoking. Opposition to the pact comes primarily from those who think it is not severe enough. For example, critics say the settlement is defective in not restricting the marketing of cigarettes overseas by American tobacco companies. Connecticut's attorney general, Richard Blumenthal, defended the absence of such a provision: "Given our druthers we would have brought them to their knees all over the world, but there is a limit to our leverage." So much for the sovereignty of nations.

What the settlement does contain is bad enough. The pact would require the companies to pony up $60 billion; $25 billion of this would be used for public-health issues to be identified by a presidential panel and the rest for children's health insurance. Though the purpose of the entire agreement is punitive, this slice is most obviously so.

The industry is also required to pay $308 billion over 25 years, in part to repay states for the cost of treating sick smokers. There are no grounds for this provision. The tobacco companies have regularly won litigation against plaintiffs claiming injury on the grounds that everybody has known for the past forty years that smoking can cause health problems. This $308 billion, which takes from the companies what they have won in litigation, says, in effect, that no one assumed the risk of his own behavior.

The provision is groundless for additional reasons. The notion that the states have lost money because of cigarettes ignores the federal and state taxes smokers have paid, which cover any amount the states could claim to have lost. Furthermore, a percentage of the population dies early from smoking. Had these people lived longer, the drain on Medicare and Medicaid would have been greater. When lowered pension and Social Security costs are figured in, it seems certain that government is better off financially with smoking than without it. If we must reduce the issue to one of dollars, as the attorneys general have done, states have profited financially from smoking. If this seems a gruesome and heartless calculation, it is. But don't blame me.

The state governments advanced the financial argument and ought to live with its consequences, however distasteful.

Other provisions of the settlement fare no better under the application of common sense. The industry is to reduce smoking by teenagers by 30 percent in five years, 50 percent in seven years, and 60 percent in ten years. No one knows how the industry is to perform this trick. But if those goals are not met, the industry will be amerced $80 million a year for each percentage point it falls short.

The settlement assumes teenage smoking can be reduced dramatically by requiring the industry to conduct an expensive anti-smoking advertising campaign, banning the use of people and cartoon characters to promote cigarettes, and similar tactics. It is entirely predictable that this will not work. Other countries have banned cigarette advertising, only to watch smoking increase. Apparently the young, feeling themselves invulnerable, relish the risk of smoking. Studies have shown, moreover, that teenagers are drawn to smoking not because of advertising but because their parents smoke or because of peer pressure. Companies advertise to gain or maintain market share among those who already smoke.

To lessen the heat on politicians, the pact increases the powers of the Food and Drug Administration to regulate tobacco as an addictive drug, with the caveat that it may not prohibit cigarette smoking altogether before the year 2009. The implicit promise is that the complete prohibition of cigarettes will be seriously contemplated at that time. In the meantime, the FDA will subject cigarettes to stricter and stricter controls on the theory that tobacco is a drug.

Another rationale for prohibiting or sharply limiting smoking is the supposed need to protect non-smokers from secondhand smoke. The difficulty is that evidence of causation is weak. What we see is a possible small increase in an already small risk which, as some researchers have pointed out, may well be caused by other variables such as misclassification of former smokers as non-smokers or such lifestyle factors as diet.

But the tobacco companies should take little or no comfort from that. Given today's product-liability craze, scientific support, much less probability, is unnecessary to successful lawsuits against large corporations.

The pact is of dubious constitutionality as well. It outlaws the advertising of a product it is legal to sell, which raises the problem of commercial speech protected by the First Amendment. The settlement also requires the industry to disband its lobbying organization, the Tobacco Institute. Lobbying has traditionally been thought to fall within the First Amendment's guarantee of the right to petition the government for the redress of grievances.

And who is to pay for making smoking more difficult? Smokers will have the price of cigarettes raised by new taxes and by the tobacco companies' costs of complying with the settlement. It is a brilliant strategy: Smokers will pay billions to have their pleasure taken away.

But if the tobacco settlement makes little sense as public policy, what can be driving it to completion? The motivations are diverse. Members of the plaintiffs' bar, who have signally failed in litigation against tobacco to date, are to be guaranteed billions of dollars annually. The states' attorneys general have a different set of incentives. They are members of the National Association of Attorneys General, NAAG, which is commonly, and accurately, rendered as the National Association of Aspiring Governors,

So far they have got what they wanted. There they are on the front pages of newspapers all over the country, looking out at us, jaws firm, conveying images of sobriety, courage, and righteousness. They have, after all, done battle with the forces of evil, and won—at least temporarily.

Tobacco executives and their lawyers are said to be wily folk, however. They may find ways of defeating the strictures laid upon them. It may be too soon to tell, therefore, whether the tobacco settlement is a major defeat or a victory for the industry. In any case, we can live with it. But whenever individual responsibility is denied, government control of our behavior follows. After cigarettes it will be something else, and so on *ad infinitum*. One would think we would have learned that lesson many times over and that we would have had enough of it.

V.

Personal Appreciations

These are appreciations of two men who meant a great deal to my intellectual development and with whom I became very good friends. A third man was Aaron Director, an economist on the University of Chicago law school faculty. Though I never published an article about him, my debt is acknowledged in the Preface to The Antitrust Paradox.

ALEXANDER M. BICKEL 1924–1974

Alex Bickel's gifts were so great and so many that we would have envied him if we had not loved him. For years we knew that he was an extraordinary man. But the warm haze of personal friendship and the diversions of colleagueship obscured at first what gradually became clear—that he can be called, without hesitation or embarrassment, a great man.

It would be enough perhaps that Alex was a magnificent legal scholar, but his talents ranged much farther. He moved with distinction into history, journalism, courtroom argument, legislative drafting, appearances before congressional committees, public debates and speeches, and even into political campaigning.

These were the accomplishments for which we honored and stood in awe of him but they were not the reasons we cherished him. Upon the occasion of Felix Frankfurter's death Alex told his students that there are men who are far more in person than the written legacy they leave. That is certainly true of Alex. He was and, through our memories, he remains much more than his written product, marvelous as it is. The resources of language are not adequate, in my hands at least, to convey the full man. The particular cannot be recaptured—his style, vitality, gaiety, courage, his argumentative drive, the astonishing flow of words, ideas, insights, wit, his rapid sympathy and genuine affections. Sure of himself, he showed his thoughts and feelings freely. He created for us a sense of community, and even in death he does that again, creating a community of those who knew and loved him, who may not know each other but do know a bond of common sorrow and shared memory.

Alex achieved greatness in the law and he achieved it early. It is startling to realize that this man who died at forty-nine, with his powers still developing, had published five books, all of them important, and at least

From *The Alternative: An American Spectator*, April 1975.

two of them—*The Least Dangerous Branch* and *The Warren Court and the Idea of Progress*—major intellectual events in the law. Furthermore, there are two more books coming. One is a volume of the Holmes Devise History of the Supreme Court. The other is a collection of some of his shorter pieces, including some that are as beautifully written, perceptive, and provocative as anything he ever did.

His intellectual legacy consists also of the things he did not write but said to hundreds and hundreds of students and scores of friends and colleagues. He was a teacher and the impact of his spoken thoughts is impossible to measure. But there will always be a difference in the things we choose to do and the way we do them because we knew Alex Bickel.

An obituary spoke of the tension between Alex's judicial conservatism and political liberalism. That tension he resolved in the last several years, though whether the resulting symmetry was liberal or conservative need not trouble us here. He was, as his writings amply attest, quite pessimistic about the judiciary's capacity to manage large social reforms, as well as, to put the point mildly, highly dubious about the legitimacy of much asserted judicial authority.

In an article for *Commentary* this year, he argued that: "The assault upon the legal order by moral imperatives wasn't only or perhaps even the most effectively an assault from the outside. It came as well from within, in the Supreme Court headed for fifteen years by Earl Warren. . . . More than once, and in some of its most important actions, the Warren Court got over doctrinal difficulties or issues of the allocation of competences among various institutions by asking what it viewed as a decisive practical question: If the Court did not take a certain action which was *right* and *good,* would other institutions do so, given political realities?"

That, Alex thought, was deeply, profoundly wrong. Expressing a thought central to his philosophy, he said: "It is the premise of our legal order that its own complicated arrangements, although subject to evolutionary change, are more important than any momentary objective."

Where others saw legal technicalities to be cut through, Alex saw process, order, stability, safety from arbitrary power, a mechanism for change that is gradual and accepted as legitimate by the society. He understood that our form of law is a social creation of enormous value but also complex, delicate, and distinctly vulnerable.

To read his *New Republic* piece on Edmund Burke is to see that his political philosophy had come into alignment with his legal philosophy. "Our problem," Alex wrote, "has been, and is most acutely now, the tyrannical tendency of ideas and the suicidal emptiness of a politics without ideas. . . ." Alex approved both Burke's principles and "Burke's steady sense of their limits," his ability to apply to every question both principle and expediency or prudence, his pragmatism, and his stress upon the importance of place and circumstance.

Alex argued that our problem, like Burke's, is that we cannot govern with abstract theories of rights and values and yet cannot live, let alone govern, without a coherent scheme of values. He concluded that "Burke's conservatism, if that is what it was, which at any rate belongs to the liberal tradition, properly understood and translated to our time, is the way."

It is no mystery that Alex found Burke so congenial, for Alex, too, though deeply and consistently moral, hated the assertion of ultimate and transcendent principles and the apocalyptic rhetoric that so often accompanies them. He thought such principles always pernicious, and their joinder to popular movements frightening. In politics, as in law, he believed in the importance of context, of the particular, in weighing, balancing, judging differences in degree, and most certainly in the importance of organic growth and tradition.

We often taught seminars together. In our last one I was groping for hard, sharp doctrine to control judicial review. Alex insisted that the doctrine could not be constructed and that we must rely instead upon tradition and wisdom. I am afraid I never gave him reason to doubt the soundness of his insight. Finally, in considerable frustration, I told the class, "Mr. Bickel's legal philosophy is a cross between Edmund Burke and Fiddler on the Roof." That was a remark he liked and repeated, perhaps because it fit much more about him than just his legal philosophy.

At the time of his death Alex was moving on to a new range of work in political theory. The Burke article was a first probe. He started from a combined base in law and history that is unmatched. And he possessed the genius to bring his vast erudition into focus, being able to move easily between the most technical legal doctrine and the broadest political speculation, to relate, say, the decline of the Article III case-or-controversy requirement to the discouraging impact of the French Revolution and the Enlightenment upon contemporary American political trends. The years of his accomplishment that we look upon with amazement were in fact only the prelude to work of a range and profundity that we can only begin to imagine, and whose loss is a national loss.

I almost hesitate to speak of Alex as a friend, for that was a relationship so precious that talking may put at risk the full richness of the memory. But

I must because one of the man's great talents was his gift for friendship, and others have had the experience with him that I had. It is rare to have a friend with whom one shares every level of experience, from drinking and joking, to intensely personal concerns, to discussions of law and legal theory, and speculations about the order of things. It is true that, as the activity ascended in the intellectual scale, my share tended to shrink, mostly because of Alex's talents but also, it must be stated candidly, because of his flow of words. I once told him that it was the dream of my life to appear against him in the Supreme Court because that was the only place where, by the law of the forum, I would get half of the time for talking.

It is also rare for friendship to extend to both families so completely. Each of us felt that we were friends with each of the Bickels, except possibly Punch Bickel, their dog, who likes the way I taste. We were friends with them individually and not just derivatively through Alex. Indeed, our children felt that Alex and Joanne and Francesca and Claudia were our extended family and largely made up for the aunts and uncles and cousins they lacked.

At a time of my own personal tragedy I went to Alex and Joanne and cried out my grief. Later, on a night of good fortune, I went to them and celebrated late. As I left, touched by Alex's unmixed joy for me, I said to him, "In good times and bad times, I come to you first." I had not realized until I said it that it was true. Without a pause for thought or choice, I always turned to Alex. And he always helped, with sympathy or advice, often with just the right wisecrack.

And now, at the last, I must speak of the manner of his dying. With many friends, one prefers to remember them in full vigor and wipe from mind the memory of the end. Not so with Alex Bickel. The way in which he went to his death will always remain for me and for the others who witnessed it one of the most profoundly moving experiences of our lives. For eleven months he knew that death was the likely outcome; for several of those months he knew it was the inevitable outcome. As soon as he learned what his illness was, he made a conscious resolve to die well. Joanne knew his wish and helped him to achieve it. They supported each other and found support in Francesca and Claudia. I have never seen such courage in a man or a family.

The doctor warned Joanne to expect periods of rage but they never came. What came instead was an intensification of every quality that made us love the man and stand in awe of him. With increasing difficulty in moving, toward the end almost totally paralyzed and blind, he read while he could, listened to reading when he could not, talked of ideas, of people and, unbelievably, tried to comfort his friends. In our frequent telephone conversations and my less frequent visits, it was the same as before, only more concentrated, because now time did not stretch on before us to be squandered.

He outlined the intellectual work he had intended to do, identified the themes, and the authors that had to be studied. As long as he could speak, he could be brought out of himself by an idea floated in conversation and he would take it on, dissect it, put it back together, and trace its linkages to other ideas. I think that helped him; I know it helped us.

He retained to the last his enjoyment of sardonic wit. When the headaches were very bad and the drugs making him drowsy and think-tongued, I would telephone and, before starting a subject, ask, "How is it today, Alex?" He would say, "Not so good. Not so good. But don't worry, I can still take care of you." And I was always relieved to find out, once again, that he could.

On our last visit to New Haven, we, talked a long, long time and he spoke about the life he had had and he found it good. He was glad to have the little extra time the doctors could give him with cortisone to talk with his family and friends. Often in pain, unable to move much more than his right arm, unable to see much more than shadows, he said, "These are good days, good days." And he meant it.

Because his life had been happy, he said, he did not mind death. He recalled that when Charles James Fox lay dying he told his wife, "It don't signify. It don't signify." For the first and only time in my presence, and then only for a moment, tears ran down Alex's cheek. And for once Alex was wrong. It does signify, and it will signify—to scholarship, to the nation, and to all who knew him for as many years as are left to us.

The Legacy of Alexander M. Bickel

It is four and one-half years since Alex Bickel died and, while a number of his friends are here, it is something of a shock to realize that there are many in this room who did not know him, who cannot summon up the memory of that rather small, carefully-tailored, almost dapper, figure; who cannot recall the flow of words, the expressive face, the wit and gaiety, the passionate engagement with ideas; who never experienced the sense of being more fully aware and alive that the beginning of a conversation with him always brought.

That is sad, because it means that part of Alex Bickel's legacy—the part that required immediate acquaintance and can live only in memory—is already in the course of extinction.

But there is much more to the legacy than that, a part that will be with the law and with us for a long time to come. At his memorial service, within days of his death, I began by saying: "Alex Bickel's gifts were so great and so many that we would have envied him if we had not loved him. For years we knew that he was an extraordinary man. But the warm haze of personal friendship and the diversions of colleagueship obscured at first what gradually became clear—that he can be called, without hesitation or embarrassment, a great man."

That may be thought the natural and forgiveable exaggeration of a friend shaken by a loss greater than he had ever before experienced, but I think not, and the mere fact of this chair in his name should persuade you otherwise. Consider how unusual it is for a university to so memorialize one of its own professors, how rare it is that a number of willing donors should so quickly come forward to endow the chair. But consider how extraordinary it is that all of this should be done, without a doubt as to its rightness, to honor a man whom fate allowed a scholarly career of only half the normal length.

From *Yale Law Report*, Fall 1979.

That alone should suggest something of the admiration and love that Alex commanded, something of his intellectual drive, his scholarly vigor, his concentrated genius.

We have long since talked out our grief over Alex's death. It is time now to begin discussing his legacy. That is a topic that cannot be adequately covered today, much less exhausted, but it is important to begin. In part, it is important because of the difficulty in knowing what greatness in the law consists of. We are a court-centered profession, but we remember the names of very few judges or advocates. The experience of teaching the opinions of the judges conventionally thought of as great often has the unfortunate effect of diminishing their memories. The lasting fame of the advocate may be suggested by the name of the man who had more Supreme Court arguments—317—than any other lawyer in our history: Walter Jones. Such men may have been among the greats of their times but they practice a plastic art and when they die their legacy is little more than a name.

There is, nevertheless, a real sense in which the legacy of Alex in person, the man of memory, will remain when no living person can say he or she knew him. He has altered the intellectual life of the law by his impact upon others in conversation and example. No one could become engaged with him without seeing law and the world differently. Without coming to admire erudition worn lightly and the habit of giving shibboleths and absolutes no quarter, without experiencing a shift in his understanding of what is important and what is not. To cite a personal instance, it is doubtful that I would have returned to the academic world without Alex's example and without our discussions about it. I and others think in certain ways because of things he said that he did not write. Many have had their lives changed by Alex. It is why I said at his memorial service, "there will always be a difference in the things we choose to do and the way we do them because we knew Alex Bickel." Because that impact is unknowable does not make it any the less real or effective in shaping the law.

Alex had two other qualities that may be essential to greatness in a lawyer but are not the thing itself. If Holmes was even partially right in thinking there may be "no true measure of men except the total of human energy which they embody," Alex qualified. He read, pondered, discussed, and wrote continually, In the half a career he was given, he wrote nine books, enough articles for a freelance journalist, taught courses, wrote briefs, testified before congressional committees, argued cases—the list of activities seems endless. Part of his genius was composed of driving energy focused by a powerful self-discipline.

Again, if Holmes was right in saying that "as life is action and passion, it is required of a man that he share the passion and action of his time at peril of being judged not to have lived," Alex lived fully. He wrote and spoke continually of public events and issues, he counseled those involved, he cared greatly about the trends of his time and helped affect them. Though a scholar, he was fully engaged. His scholarship guided his public action, and his public action enriched his scholarship. There was with Alex no sharp break between the life of ideas and the life of affairs, which is why he was a most principled and thoughtful man of ideas. That may be why he liked the tension he found in Edmund Burke. Alex wrote, "Our problem has been, and is most acutely now, the tyrannical tendency of ideas and the suicidal emptiness of politics without ideas . . ." Alex lived in that tension, and made it fruitful.

This brings us closer to his central legacy, which is, of course, intellectual. It took me a long time, many arguments and classes taught together, much reading of his work, to see precisely what the legacy is. Even now I am sure I cannot state it adequately.

Any effort to summarize Alex Bickel's intellectual legacy must fall short, because the effort involves two kinds of distortion. In the first place, his thought was complex, rich, and valuable as much for the prolific and often profound insights he scattered in the course of an argument as for the conclusions he reached and supported. Bickel was not a systematizer. Indeed, his lesson was the danger and the ultimate impossibility of systems. A statement of the major features of his thought thus, more than in the case of most scholars, misses much of his genius.

Secondly, his thought was in continual evolution. He regarded every book, every article, as an experiment, not a final statement. He was always, moreover, open to argument, and his thinking changed in response to it, as well as to his own experience and second thoughts. Positions that he took in his early writings were frequently expanded, modified, or qualified, explicitly or implicitly, in his later work, as well as in his teaching and conversation. This does not mean that his approach was not consistent over time. It was. But because he was not frozen into a system, because he believed in the central importance of circumstance, the limited range of principles, the complexity of reality, he learned and evolved. It is impossible to give a snapshot of his philosophy. It was moving, deepening, to the end of his life.

I have said enough of the difficulties of summing up Bickel's intellectual legacy. Now, having assured you the futility of the attempt, I will undertake it.

I should say at the outset that, though Alex Bickel has no greater admirer, I will occasionally disagree with him. It would be no compliment to the memory of an intellectually honest and alive man to treat his work as a shrine. Alex is not a monument; he is a living intellectual force and he must be dealt with in those terms. That is what he would have demanded.

Political morality and governance were the central subject of all of Alex's thought and writing, and central to that, or at least the beginning point for that, was the role of the federal judiciary, most particularly the role of the Supreme Court of the United States.

The problem, of course, the problem with which all constitutional lawyers must grapple, is the legitimacy of judicial review—the power of the Court to set aside and nullify the choices of elected representatives—and the proper scope of that power. The problem is created by the fact that our political ethos has been, and largely remains, majoritarian, not democratic, not elected, and not representative, yet purporting to have the final say in our governance. The problem becomes acute when the Court undertakes to impose principles that are not fairly to be found in the Constitution. These are currently called trans-textual principles, a concept the least of whose difficulties is that it requires careful pronunciation.

Bickel addressed that problem repeatedly, and, if I do not think he achieved an entirely successful resolution of it, his effort was a triumph in many ways. He stated the problem with a clarity that has not been achieved elsewhere. In the course of his argument he provided a series of dazzling insights that are a major and lasting contribution to our understanding of a variety of legal doctrines. This may be viewed as his technical legacy, and that alone is sufficient to ensure his place in legal thought. But the significant thing is that Alex's scholarship, while it was magnificent about technical law, was never merely technical. He enlarged our understanding by relating what seems to be law only a lawyer could love to much larger themes, the role of courts in a democracy or the egalitarian trend of western political thought. The essence of his genius, or the aspect that most impressed me, was his ability to see connections between ideas that everyone else thought separate and discrete.

It is to be said, moreover, that Alex laid down the lines of the arguments that defenders of a Court that assumes broad extra constitutional powers find it wise to adopt today. But we must not be misled by that. Alex was no friend of what has become known as judicial activism or imperialism. He relied upon a tradition of restraint and modesty to curb the judicial appetite for power. Many of those who adopt his other arguments today leave that element out and thus welcome far more judicial activism than Bickel thought we ought to tolerate.

Consistently with what he later called the Whig political tradition, Bickel placed steady and heavy weight upon the importance of political democracy, and, at the outset, rejected a common line of defense of an activist Court. This defense proceeds by arguing that our majoritarian processes are in reality not very majoritarian, that we are governed by evanescent coalitions of minorities, so that the anti-democratic aspects of judicial rule are not that important.

"[I]t remains true nevertheless," he said, "that only those minorities rule which can command the votes of a majority of individuals in the legislature who can command a vote of a majority of individuals in the electorate . . . [N]othing can finally deprecate the central function that is assigned in democratic theory and practice to the electoral process; nor can it be denied that the policy-making power of representative institutions, born of the electoral process, is the distinguishing characteristic of the system. Judicial review works counter to this characteristic."

He justified judicial review on the ground that courts could introduce into our political processes something of great value that the legislature and the executive could not: the formulation and application of enduring principles. Judges are uniquely fitted for this function, he wrote, because they "have, or should have, the leisure, the training, and the insulation to follow the ways of the scholar in pursuing the ends of government."

(We need not pause to remember what we know of the ways of the scholars when collectively engaged in governance of institutions rather smaller and simpler than the United States.)

The mix of judicial principle and democratic expediency were important, for, as Bickel said, "No society, certainly not a large and heterogeneous one, can fail in time to explode if it is deprived of the arts of compromise, if it knows no ways of muddling through. No good society can be unprincipled; and no viable society can be principle-ridden."

The Court must, therefore, live in a constant tension between the equally legitimate demands of principle and of expediency. And it is here, on this subject, that Bickel's technical work is most subtle, most exciting, and most provocative. The Court can maintain itself in this tension, avoiding both ruinous confrontation with the political branches and abdication in their favor, by techniques he called "the passive virtues." He analogized the Court's position to Lincoln's. Lincoln knew that slavery was wrong, that it must ultimately be ended, but he also wanted the Union preserved, and so, while he refused to attack the institution head on, he also refused to accept principles or compromises that ratified it. So the Court, according to Bickel, can temporize, as Lincoln had, by masterful use of doctrines such as standing, ripeness, political question, and, of course, the power to deny certiorari, until the time came to announce the principle to which it has been helping to lead us.

A problem arises here. If the Court is leading us toward a principle that it honestly believes located in the Constitution, these techniques are entirely legitimate. But if it is leading us toward something else, toward principles that do not in some real sense come out of the Constitution, the problem of legitimate authority has not been solved. I think Alex, at least in his early writing, meant both things. *Brown* v. *Board of Education* could, of course, be said to come out of the Constitution. The Court could legitimately work toward a flat rule of non-discrimination without announcing it until the society could be brought to accept it. Judicial abolition of the death penalty, on the other hand, a penalty whose legitimacy the document explicitly assumes, cannot be recoiled with the Constitution. In 1962, at least, Bickel thought both decisions proper ones for the Court to work toward. And there I disagree.

He tried to tame the anti-democratic thrust of this position with a series of qualifications. The Justices of the Court are not to derive principles from their own sympathies or politics; rather they are to discover and enforce the "fundamental presuppositions of our society" from the "evolving morality of our tradition." Moreover, they must not anticipate that evolution too much, but must declare as supreme law only that which "will—in time, but a rather immediate foreseeable future—gain general assent."

This is a modest, pragmatic role, and the process is further saved from being hopelessly countermajoritarian because the Court is not ultimately all-powerful. "The Supreme Courts law . . . ," Bickel said, "could not in our system prevail—not merely in the very long run, but within the decade—if it ran counter to deeply felt popular needs or convictions, or even if it was opposed by a determined and substantial minority and received with indifference by the rest of the country. This, in the end, is how and why judicial review is consistent with the theory and practice of political democracy. This is why the Supreme Court is a court of last resort presumptively only."

It is a powerful argument delivered with great erudition and persuasiveness, and I am fortified in my conclusion that it does not ultimately persuade by the fact that in later work Bickel seemed to concede its limitations.

The argument leaves it unclear why democratic institutions must accept from the Court, even provisionally, more principle of different kinds of principle than the democratic process generates—including in that the principles that have been placed in the constitution itself by super-majorities.

No reason appears why the Court should lead the society at all, certainly not to the point where it is safe to announce as law that which society will come to accept. We may accept much that we would not freely choose simply because the Court tells us it is, in truth, to be found in the basic document of our nation, or because there are strong political constituencies that support the outcome, though they could not attain it democratically themselves, or because we have few ways to fight back that would not damage the Court in ways we do not wish. Its vulnerability is the Court's protection and hence a source of its power.

One may doubt as well that there are "fundamental presuppositions of our society" that are not already located in the Constitution but must be placed there by the Court. These presuppositions are likely, in practice, to turn out to be the highly debatable political positions of the intellectual classes. What kind of a "fundamental presupposition of our society" is it that cannot command a legislative majority?"

The Court has, in fact, turned out to be final in many more instances than Bickel thought it should. Effective political opposition has not been mustered to its most unjustified assertions of final authority. And the Court has adopted sweeping principles of precisely the kind he warned against. By the time he delivered the Holmes Lectures he knew that no "rigorous general accord between judicial supremacy and democratic theory" had been achieved; he said he had "come to doubt in many instances the Court's capacity to develop 'durable principles,' and to doubt, therefore, that judicial supremacy can work and is tolerable in broad areas of social policy," and to ask that it confine itself, for the most part, to narrow, interstitial lawmaking.

Those today who repeat his arguments for judicial power to enforce principles not located in the Constitution tend to be what he was not, apologist for an activist Court. They forget that he counted on a judicial tradition of modesty, intellectual coherence, the morality of process, to make judicial supremacy tolerable. These traits have often been lacking on the Court and Alex felt they may have been damaged beyond repair by the Warren Court. We have never had a rigorous theory of judicial restraint; for a time we had a tradition; now that is almost gone.

Lest there be any doubt where Alex's sympathies lay, just what he did not mean to justify or encourage, it should be remembered that he, a man not given to rhetorical excess or easy excitement, described the Warren Court as comparable to other defiances of the law in the name of moral righteousness. In an acticle entitled "Watergate and the Legal Order," he said:

"The assault upon the legal order by moral imperatives wasn't only or perhaps even the most effectively an assault from the outside. It came as well from within, in the Supreme Court headed for fifteen years by Earl Warren. When a lawyer stood before him arguing his side of a case on the basis of some legal doctrine or other, or making a procedural point, or contending that the Constitution allocated competence over a given issue to another branch of government than the Supreme Court or to the states rather than the federal government, the chief justice would shake him off by saying, 'Yes, yes, yes, but is it [whatever the case exemplified about law or about the society], is it *right* is it *good?*' More than once, and in some of its most important actions, the Warren Court got over doctrinal difficulties or issues of the allocation of competences among various institutions by asking what it viewed as a decisive practical question: If the Court did not take a certain action which was *right* and *good,* would other institutions do so, given political realities?"

This, or something like it, though the political thrust may vary, is what a Court, encouraged to believe it is more than a court, or perhaps less—a collection of philosophers empowered to find and apply the best in America's moral tradition—this is what such a Court will ultimately come to. Alex recognized it for what it was instantly, and he knew that it was deeply, profoundly wrong. "It is," he wrote, "the premise of our legal order that its own complicated arrangements, although subject to evolutionary change, are more important than any momentary objective." There spoke the Whig conservative and a man, if I may say so, who was deeply and profoundly right.

This sense of values carried over into his political thought. Alex Bickel came to regard himself as a conservative and I will suggest to you that he was always conservative in a very real sense even when his political positions and affiliations were liberal-left. The point is important, for much of what is most distinctive and valuable about his work derives from the cast of mind I describe.

It is necessary to be careful about a word like "conservative" because it stirs associations and connotations, many of which are wholly foreign to Alex's thought. Shortly before his illness he tried to locate himself. He wrote of two diverging traditions, one liberal and the other conservative which compete for control of the democratic process and the direction of our judicial policy.

"One of these, the contractarian tradition . . . long ago captured, and substantially retains possession of, the label liberal . . . The other tradition can, for lack of a better term, be called Whig in the English eighteenth-century sense. "It is," wrote Bickel, "usually called conservative, and I would associate it chiefly with Edmund Burke. This is my own model."

He specified the characteristic of Whig-conservative thought. It assesses human nature as it is seen to be. It begins not with theoretical rights but with a real society, whose values evolve but must, at any given moment, be taken as given. "The task of government [within the limits set by culture, by time- and place-bound conditions] is to make a peaceable, good, and improving society." "The Whig model," he said, "obviously is flexible, pragmatic, slow-moving, highly political. It partakes, in substantial measure, of the relativism that pervades Justice Oliver Wendell Holmes' theory of the First Amendment, although not to its ultimate logical exaggeration. Without carrying matters to a logical extreme, indeed without pretense to intellectual valor, and without sanguine spirit, the Whig model rests on mature skepticism."

This approach, this habit of mind, which Bickel calls conservative, is apparent in him from first to last, from the time when his political views can only be called liberal to the time when they can appropriately be called conservative. There is a distinction between a conservative process of thought and the location of the spectrum of one's substantive views, and the question whether one tends to produce the other is too complex and too far from my subject to be pursued.

But to use Bickel's terminology, he thought, and I agree with him, that the Whig-conservative way of thinking is essential to good politics, hence to good law, hence to good lawyers, hence to good law schools. If one were to look for a model of such thought, it is to be found, for example, in the *The Federalist Papers*. If one were to look for the antithesis of it, it would be in much of the highly abstract, philosophic writing and thinking now enjoying something of a vogue in some major law schools.

Here, I think, we are close to the central legacy of Alex Bickel. He left us an example, in print and in person, of what it is not merely to be a great lawyer, nor again merely to be great constitutional lawyer, but to be a great constitutionalist. He taught us to see the marvelous complexity of our law and our society and their innumerable relations. He taught us how to engage in reform and change, how to decide what to keep and what to discard.

That is one reason he tended to be hostile to structural reform such as one man-one vote, the abolition of the electoral college, and all tinkerings with structural features of government. "The institutions of a secular, democratic government," he wrote, "do not generally advertise themselves as mysteries. But they are. What they do, how they do it,or why it is necessary to do what they do is not always outwardly apparent. Their actual operation must be assessed often in sheer wonder, before they are tinkered with, lest great expectations be not only defeated, but mocked by the achievement of their antithesis."

Before he died he began to worry that revulsion to the complex events summed up in the word "Watergate" would lead to a wave of reform that could do enormous damage to political institutions. He was right to worry. The Federal Election Campaign Act, the spread of presidential primaries, the involvement of the judiciary in foreign intelligence, the diminution of the Presidency, already a week office, and many other "reforms" have been accomplished with a light-headedness that amounts almost to frivolity. They will have and are having totally unanticipated and undesirable results. The same willingness to tinker with structure in order to achieve minor or even symbolic ends accounts for the movements to amend the Constitution. Thus, ERA, the amendment to give the District of Columbia the status of a state in Congress, and the movement to abolish the electoral college all rest on inadequate constitutional thought.

Alex's insight flowed from his organic view of society. The nostrums of ignorant physicians have unintended and potentially disastrous consequences. It is no accident that one of Alex's favorite sayings was, "Unless it is necessary to change, it is necessary not to change." He often spoke for reform but only after thinking long, and thinking a second and a third time. He left us far more sophisticated about, and respectful of, established ways and institutions than he found us.

But he did more than that. He taught us again a style, an angle of attack, a temper and mode of thought which is, I believe, essential to the health of representative government and its institutions.

Alex contrasted his own mode of thought with that of the social contractarians. In truth, the contrast may be more properly with thinkers who love systems and transcendental principles. He had the greatest aversion to them, and not merely because he thought, in my view rightly, that they were impossible to construct logically, but also because he thought them ultimately inhuman and therefore pernicious. The ultimate principles will never be found by the legal philosophers because they do not exist, and the attempt to frame them must necessarily become so abstract that much which is valuable and human is left out.

This might be all right if system-building were only an academic exercise. But it never is, and particularly not when it is engaged in by lawyers. It is meant to guide decisions, which means that real men and women must be bent or trimmed to fit the abstractions, not the other way around. The morality of comprehensive systems tends to be manipulative and destructive because it must reduce life to its own terms or admit intellectual error, which, to a person who has committed everything to a speculative enterprise, is to admit ultimate failure. That is something intellectuals rarely do.

This habit of thought infects the courts and encourages them to think that law is unimportant. Alex was content with what he called "principles in the middle distance," principles that incorporate the values we have now, which are of limited range, which will change over time, which collide with and contradict one another and which must be adjusted, compromised, and refined in their application, and all this must be done in the full knowledge that the result is impermanent and all is to be done again. To know that and nevertheless to devote one's life and full energies to the task is intellectual and moral valor. It is to accept mortality in a way that the seekers of abstract systems do not.

Some of this is what Alex meant when, in speaking on the question "what is happening to morality today?" he answered, "It threatens to engulf us." He meant that abstractions and moral imperatives as guides to action would make life intolerable. The politics of compromise and adjustment makes everything else possible. "Without it," he wrote, "in the stark universe of imperatives, in the politics of ideal promises and inevitable betrayals, justice is not merely imperfect . . . but soon becomes injustice."

The institutions and the secular religion of the American republic are our best chance for happiness and safety. And it is precisely these that are weakened and placed in jeopardy by the habit of abstract philosophizing about the rights of men or just society. Our institutions are built for humans, they incorporate and perpetuate compromise. They slow change, tame it, deflect and modify principles as well as popular simplicities. And in doing that they provide safety and the mechanism for a morality of process. It follows that real institutions can never be as pure as abstract philosophers demand, and their philosophy must always teach the young a lesson in derogation of institutions for that reason. That is a dangerous lesson for a republic.

Alex was appalled by the first manifestations of the abstract, philosophical style in legal scholarship. Had he lived to see its proliferation in the law schools today, he would have attacked it with a ferocity it gives me pleasure to contemplate even hypothetically.

In one of his last articles, "Watergate and the Legal Order," Alex showed us that Watergate was an episode in a rising tradition of anti-institutional imperatives and transcendental moralities. There is danger in the way we are moving. Walter Bagehot wrote:

> The characteristic danger of great nations, like the Romans and the English, which have a long history of continuous creation, is that they may at last fail from not comprehending the great institutions which they have created.

It was Alex's constant attempt to understand and to make us understand the great institutions of constitutional government we have created. Whether or not we will remains to be seen. Alex's death, perhaps, makes it less likely that we will

George F. Will wrote a column shortly after Alex died:

> Hell, Hobbes said, is truth seen too late. Republics—at least fortunate republics—can be saved from damnation by a few constitutionalists like Bickel. But threats to republics are many and constant. Great constitutionalists are few and mortal. Alexander Bickel, the keenest public philosopher of our time, died of cancer late in this, his forty-ninth year.

That is the legacy of Alex Bickel, a tradition of constitutionalism that we badly need to keep alive—in the law schools, in the profession, in the courts, and in the nation. This chair is a means of perpetuating that tradition. No incumbent will ever equal Alex in range, depth, and productivity. Some incumbents, doubtless, will be in active opposition to Alex's philosophy and may disagree with his entire approach. But the chair itself, the mere fact that there will always be someone known as the Alexander M. Bickel Professor of Public Law, will always remind us and those who come after us of the man, his work, and the tradition which he followed and enriched. That is no small thing. It is a gift not only to Yale but to the law and to American political democracy. To the school, and to the donors who made this contribution to a memory and to a tradition, all of us owe a debt of profound gratitude.

EDWARD LEVI

For generations of its graduates, to think of the University of Chicago is inevitably to think of Edward Levi. That is, of course, especially true of the alumni of the Law School but by no means of them alone. Edward Levi is largely a product of the University but it is equally true that much of today's University is the product of Levi. He received his elementary and secondary education at the Laboratory School, his undergraduate training in the College, his legal training in the Law School, and then, after service in the Department of Justice, became, successively, professor of law, dean of the Law School, provost of the University, and, finally, its president. Rarely have a man and Institution been so identified. It must be even more rare that the identification proves so beneficial to both.

Though it would be difficult to prove, it has always seemed to me that those who not only attended but were shaped by the University of Chicago have a special quality, not merely of intellect but of respect for ideas and their, rigorous examination, an absence of sentimentality coupled with profound regard for the virtue of intellectual honesty. Having said that, I must admit that notable exceptions spring to mind, but Edward Levi is not one of them. Though the Levi career extended well beyond the University, he is so rooted there, so integral a part of it as it is of him, that he seemed to take Chicago's strengths with him wherever he went.

So wide-ranging has been Levi's career that the tributes carried in the University of Chicago Law Review in 1985 had to be divided into separate pieces on the man as professor, dean, and attorney general of the United States. (It is difficult to know what to make of the omission of his service as provost and then president of the University. Perhaps the editors thought that if it wasn't law, it didn't count.)

From *Remembering the University of Chicago: Teachers, Scientists, and Scholars* (1991).

I.

Assessments focusing on the man's extraordinary accomplishments necessarily miss much of his distinctive personal style. Let it be said at the outset that Edward Levi is an exceedingly complex man. (One of his few entirely predictable reactions is irritation at tributes paid to him, such as this one.) His mind has, at a minimum, a double aspect. This was apparent in his teaching, it remains so in his writings, and it is today apparent in every conversation with the man. By a "double (or multiple) aspect" I mean that he is keenly aware of the complexities of ideas and of the world, suspicious of overarching systems, and hence very hard to pin down to many certainties. That does not mean he cannot act—or he would never have been the successful administrator he repeatedly proved to be—or that he was not certain about a few fundamental values, including those of the law. But it does mean, in his writing as in his speech, his full meaning is sometimes elusive and his pronouncements are occasionally delphic. On days when he is at the top of his form, all of his pronouncements are delphic. These qualities of mind make for richness of thought, teaching, and writing, and certainly contribute to his irony and wit. That wit is not always gentle but it is always germane and not, I think, employed for its own sake, though Edward himself enjoys it.

Those who have known Edward Levi at various times and in various contexts frequently give different accounts of the man. I think that is the case because to excel in different fields—fields as diverse as teaching in a university and running the Department of Justice—is to adopt the styles appropriate to each. The trial lawyer, the appellate advocate, and the negotiator are likely to display very different demeanors. So, too, the teacher, whose object it is to provoke thought and argument, and the administrator, whose goal is to lead others to desired objectives without provoking opposition, adopt very different personae. Hence it was, I think, that Edward Levi left very different impressions on people in his various roles. I observed him in both his teaching and his administrative capacities. He was my first law professor and my last attorney general. The contrast in styles was marked; the achievement in each was the same: top of the line.

II.

Edward Levi was, quite simply, the greatest classroom teacher I have ever seen. There is no point in pretending to a balance and moderation of view on the subject. It would be artificial. As a student at Chicago and a professor at Yale I saw a great deal of teaching, and it is useless to argue with me on this point. That opinion of his performance was, I believe, universally held by his students. Our first experience of him came on the opening day of the first year of law school in his course on the "Elements of the Law." We were quickly and incisively informed of our current gross intellectual inadequacies and of the dizzying heights we would reach in the next three years at the school. We believed half of that. Those of us who had come from the college of the University of Chicago, whose curriculum was then much influenced by Robert Hutchins, anticipated some relief from the steady diet of Aristotle, Plato, and others now disparagingly known as "dead, white, European males." We had not that objection to them, but there is in such matters, for most people, a point of sufficiency. But there we were, in "Elements," reading Plato and Aquinas once more. Not only that, but in the course materials Levi had put together, seeing Aquinas being played off against transcribed debates of the Illinois legislature, decisions by various state and federal courts, and the wisdom of newspaper columnists such as Westbrook Pegler.

"Elements" was an imperialistic course. It canvassed the major ideas of the law and in the process anticipated the most interesting material in the courses we would take later in our three years. But what made the course a success was not so much its undoubtedly fascinating material as the way Levi juggled, dissected, juxtaposed, reassembled, and displayed the most unexpected connections between the ideas of the law. Ideas seemed to ricochet around the room, leaving a number of wounded in their paths. This was done in rapid-fire questioning of students, a questioning that could be painful but invariably uncovered a point most of us had never considered. The point was then turned upside down and refuted in more rapid-fire questioning. Most of us came to wonder what it was we were supposed to believe.

"Elements" was a mystery course. There were 100 students in that course and one professor, and it was unclear whether the mystery enshrouded 100 persons or 101, There was no way to find out. When pressed as to "the truth," Levi deployed one of his most effective weapons, silence and a Mona Lisa smile. (He was also said to resemble Groucho Marx. He did not, really, and the comparison would have been a calumny but for one of Levi's other devices: his way of waggling, simultaneously, an enormous cigar and his eyebrows to deflate overly passionate bursts of student oratory.) The mystery was actually one of the points of the course, and entirely natural to a man who saw complexity where others sought simplicity. The great questions, including the great questions of the law, do not lend themselves to certain answers. We were led into a discourse that, if we wished, we could pursue to the end of our lives.

I have mentioned that there was a certain amount of pain associated with the class. Levi did not tolerate slow responses, silly answers, or opinions held on sentimental rather than intellectual grounds. Remarks such as "Put pennies on that man's eyes" were not infrequent. He had an extensive repertoire of such encouragements to clear thinking. I do not wish to convey a sense of bluntness, much less brutality, but there was certainly, as there should be, a price to be paid for sloppy thought. Most of the wit was situational, arose out of the particular turn of the argument, and cannot easily be recaptured. Levi had the facility, through questioning, to lead a student to affirm what a moment ago he had fervently denied. Such episodes were so deft that the class often broke into applause and the student himself usually appreciated the lesson. Some of us enjoyed the rigors of the classroom hour, some did not. I did. But that rigor served a valuable purpose, the way the shock of boot camp serves to snap new recruits out of indolent civilian habits. We were to learn to think logically, respond quickly, and turn ideas around. A student would advance an argument, another would be asked to rebut it but would say he could not because he agreed. "For ten thousand dollars, refute the argument." That suggestion had a remarkably stimulating effect on the thinking of lawyers-to-be.

Levi's mind is quicksilver and he greatly admires intellectual speed. I once had the temerity to suggest that a man he admired was a bit of a charlatan. He replied, "Perhaps, but he's so fast." It was the admiration of one intellectual gunslinger for another. Nor is that derogatory. Gunslingers, as we know from the movies, can be virtuous and valuable men.

Having mentioned the mystery and the occasional wounded ego that attended the "Elements" course, I should say that it was far and away the most popular course I have ever known. It is the custom for students to applaud at the conclusion of a course, and law teachers develop very sensitive ears to the decibel level. Sometimes the applause is perfunctory, sometimes enthusiastic, very occasionally absent altogether. I was three years a law student and fifteen years a professor and I have never seen anything like the end of Levi's class in "Elements of the Law." In the Law School building of those days, the professor was in the well of an amphitheater and had to walk up through the middle of the class to leave the room. As Levi closed his book and started up, the entire class rose to its feet in a thunderous standing ovation. They applauded wildly, stamped their feet, threw books and papers in the air. Though Levi had not courted popularity, he had produced a triumph.

Five years after graduation a reunion of that class met in the law school's auditorium. Levi, seated in a chair on the stage, spoke extemporaneously, praising the class in one sentence and taking it all back in the next. The class was delighted. Men were nudging their wives—in those days the class was almost entirely male—whispering, "See what I told you."

III.

Levi wrote in the fields he taught. An Introduction to Legal Reasoning, first published as an article and then as a slim book, was read by scholars and students inside and outside the law. We pored over it as seminarians do Holy Writ. The book explicates the nature of legal reasoning, the role of analogy, the syllogistic quality of legal argument and the logical fallacy that necessarily inheres in it (as I recall, it is the fallacy of the undistributed middle term), and the differences between judicial reasoning relating to common law, statutory law, and constitutional law. Levi destroyed claims of the scientific quality of the theory of precedent in an article entitled "Natural Law, Precedent, and Thurman Arnold."

Levi's other primary field is antitrust. He wrote the definitive intellectual demolition of the Robinson-Patman Act, which purports to control price discrimination in the service of competition. With Aaron Director, in another article, he explored the paradoxes and unsatisfactory quality of antitrust doctrine generally. Later, when I came to write in the field, Levi thought my arguments and conclusions too certain, and I must concede at least an outside chance that he is right, though I have never been sure whether he actively disagrees on fundamental points or is merely uneasy, as he is uneasy with all attempts to construct a complete system.

The relationship with Aaron Director is worth at least an article in itself, for it resulted in what has come to be called the "law and economics movement." There have been a great many "law and . . ." ventures but none remotely approaches the success of the economic analysis of legal doctrine and legal institutions. The Chicago Law School was the first to put an economist on its faculty; Director's predecessor in that capacity was Henry Simon. Levi brought Director into the antitrust course to provide an analysis of the case law. Though the basic antitrust statute, the Sherman Act, was then almost sixty years old, this was, incredibly, the first time a first-class price theorist had looked systematically at what judges had developed and fondly imagined to be economic reasoning. Antitrust, dealing with competition and monopoly, was the natural place for economics to find its initial lodgement in the law. But the success achieved there stimulated the application of economic analysis to other branches of the law, sometimes with more, sometimes with less, success, depending upon the amenability of the area to this form of reasoning.

Levi occasionally seemed a bit ambivalent about the enterprise, perhaps because of his ambivalence about doctrines that seemed to him not sufficiently to allow for ambiguity. Nonetheless, he encouraged the intellectual effort, hired people to engage in it, and supported the establishment of the influential Journal of Law and Economics. His support was strong and critical to the success of the endeavor. What came to be known as the "Chicago school," was in fact merely the application of rigorous economics to the law. That it started at Chicago rather than elsewhere is to be attributed to the combination of Levi and Aaron Director.

IV.

Despite this and other examples of intellectual vitality on its staff, in the late 1940s the Law School of the University of Chicago was in decline. The faculty had areas of great strength but also, it must be said, pockets of considerable weakness. The decline in the school's ability to attract first-rate students was for a time masked by the return of the veterans of the Second World War. Over 100 of us entered in 1948, about the capacity of the school at the time, and, as student bodies go, it was a mature, intellectually vigorous group. I left for the service once more in 1950 and, upon returning in 1952, found a startlingly different class, smaller, less mature, and intellectually more passive. The veterans' pool now being exhausted, the school was learning its real drawing power. But Edward Levi had become dean in 1950 and a thoroughgoing renovation was already under way—of the physical plant, the teaching staff, the student body, and, most important, of the morale of the entire institution. There was, in candor, much room for improvement in all four.

The old Law School had its charms; a building of somewhat grim medieval aspect and a dim, uncomfortable, and inconvenient interior, it fitted my idea at the time of a proper temple of the law. It was seriously inadequate in classroom space, offices, and library facilities. Levi embarked on a fundraising campaign that was enormous for a school of that size, and ultimately built the new Law School on the south side of the Midway. The main building is a striking glass structure designed by Eero Saarinen. It was one of Levi's more remarkable accomplishments that he managed to wring four separate dedication ceremonies, complete with major national figures as speakers, out of a single building.

The teaching body of the Law School already had a solid, even spectacular, core. Aside from Levi and Director, there were men such as Walter Blum, Harry Kalven, and Bernard Meltzer. These were close friends of Levi's and supported the dean, as not all teaching bodies do, in his efforts. Soon such well-known scholars as Karl Llewellyn, Kenneth Culp Davis, and Roscoe Steffen were lured from other schools and gave Chicago added attractiveness. Younger teachers were recruited, and the teaching staff that emerged was among the most lustrous and intellectually productive in the nation.

All of this, of course, began to attract more and better applicants for places in the entering classes. But Levi, not disposed to wait upon gradual progress, began a program of national scholarships that brought in a very high-quality student body in a relatively short time. I had joined a prominent Chicago law firm which had not particularly sought Chicago graduates in the past but now began eagerly to recruit them.

The moral and intellectual excitement of the school was enhanced by a series of programs that brought speakers prominent in the law to the campus. At one such occasion, Levi was described by Thurman Arnold, his old boss at the Antitrust Division of the Department of Justice, as the "tutelary divinity of this great theological seminary." By that time it seemed to us an accurate assessment.

V.

Levi's performance as dean led to his becoming the University's first provost in 1962, under President George Beadle. By this time, my direct observation of Levi's work had ended, but I think I know how he must have operated in the higher reaches of university administration by what I saw of him later as attorney general of the United States during Gerald Ford's presidency.

In 1968, President Beadle left and the trustees of the University made Edward Levi president. It was a fitting culmination to an academic career that had, from first to last, been rooted in the University of Chicago. Levi's particular strength was that he was able to deal effectively, and on their own terms, with groups as diverse as the teachers, the alumni, leaders of bench, bar, and business, and with the city administration. He developed a particular admiration for Mayor Richard J. Daley, who worked effectively with all of the city's diverse constituencies and was particularly helpful to the University of Chicago during a lengthy period of neighborhood transition and rebuilding. Daley was once asked why he was so cooperative with the University, many of whose teachers could not appreciate his virtues, and he said, "Because it is the only great university with Chicago in its name."

Those were troubled times at the University. Not only did the deterioration of the surrounding neighborhood threaten its ability to attract the best teachers and students but in the late 1960s student turmoil broke out as it did at almost all universities. Chicago, under Levi, handled it far better than most. When the main administration building was seized and occupied, the University waited the radicals out and then, unlike other universities that remained supine, instituted disciplinary hearings that resulted in a number of expulsions and suspensions. It was a salutary reaffirmation of the purposes of a university and the limits of acceptable behavior within it. Levi was determined to preserve the intellectual culture that had come into his keeping. If Edward Levi is in large measure a product of the University of Chicago, it is equally true that much of today's University, much more than new buildings and faculty, is attributable to Edward Levi.

VI.

Events elsewhere were to take Levi away from Hyde Park. By 1973, the presidency of Richard Nixon was unraveling, a process that I observed at first hand from the position of solicitor general of the United States, and, for a brief period, as acting attorney general. In the summer of 1974, President Nixon resigned and Vice President Gerald Ford, who succeeded to the presidency, proceeded to restaff the executive branch. The incumbent attorney general, William Bart Saxbe, was reassigned as ambassador to India and President Ford asked Edward Levi to become the new attorney general. I was extremely pleased but a trifle apprehensive on Edward's behalf. Those were turbulent times in Washington and it was not entirely clear that the town's blood lust had dissipated. In just over a year, the Department of Justice had known three attorneys general, not counting my time as acting, and three deputies attorney general. The turnover of assistant attorneys general had also been high. The department was badly in need of stability.

Edward came to the Department of Justice at a time, moreover, when some of its major branches, as well as other institutions in the executive branch with whose performance the department should have been concerned, had been allowed to edge out of control, to develop attitudes and habits worrisome in a country devoted to the rule of law. I do not mean to suggest wholesale lawlessness, a charge made by some congressional and journalistic demagogues. Nor was it true that what was worrisome had developed only during the Nixon years. The problems went back much further than that. Yet these were fundamentally sound institutions whose vigor as well as integrity were essential to the American society.

Reforming entrenched practices in government is not easily done. No headway might have been made with executive branch agencies outside the department, or indeed with some organizations in, if not of, the department, if Levi had not had the president's confidence and complete backing. It is incorrect to suppose that an attorney general has merely to give orders to correct matters in the Department of Justice. Like a major university, the department is a sprawling collection of fiefdoms and baronies: the various divisions, each headed by an assistant attorney general (Criminal, Civil, Civil Rights, Tax, Lands and Natural Resources, and so on), as well as the Federal Bureau of Investigation, the Bureau of Immigration and Naturalization, the Bureau of Prisons, and much more. It is reasonable to suppose that the experience of heading a major university stood Levi in good stead in Washington. Aside from the normal—and high—degree of organizational inertia, the department's baronies have a capacity for deliberate, if often oblique, resistance. Those who disagree with an attorney general's policies possess all the resources of obfuscation, ambiguity, recalcitrance, pretended misunderstanding, professed inability to pinpoint responsibility, and all of the other devices familiar to bureaucrats the world over. Moreover, each of the fiefdoms with its own agenda is likely to have allies on the outside, in the press, in Congress, in the manifold "public interest" organizations, and even elsewhere in the administration. If their agendas are threatened by an attorney general, they will leak word of the fact, or their versions of the fact, and hostile stories will appear, congressmen and their staffs will call and write.

Levi and I once had what was supposed to be a highly confidential conference with the head of a division who disagreed with a course of action we were contemplating. Despite his promise of confidentiality, that assistant attorney general was seen in the halls as soon as the meeting ended giving his version of the meeting to several members of the press. The next day's stories, not surprisingly, portrayed him as the sole defender of truth and justice at the meeting.

The national media were uniformly respectful of Levi's integrity and intelligence but sometimes disagreed sharply with his policies. One morning I found him in his office grumbling about an uncomplimentary, and uninformed, story in the *Washington Post*. I said, "Don't worry about it, Ed. They've said much worse things about me." He said, "Yes, but it didn't feel the same when they said it about you." (One of Edward Levi's few entirely predictable reactions is irritation at tributes paid him, but he demonstrates balance by displaying equal irritation over unfriendly pieces.)

An attorney general's policies are thus frequently compromised, deflected, or even reversed in the process of their transmittal and application. All of this means that an attorney general is held responsible for much more than he actually controls. It also means that reforming institutions which do not believe they need reform requires patience, subtlety, and light but unrelenting pressure.

Though I had known Edward Levi as a teacher and scholar, I had never witnessed firsthand his style of management. That was a revelation. He practiced administration by discussion, often by seminar. In that way he undertook the enormously arduous, politically difficult, and intellectually demanding task of reform. He did this without the fanfare, recriminations, and moral posturing that would have made him enormously popular with the press and that segment of the public which thinks real reform inseparable from confrontation, firings, and the public utterance of pieties.

Though Levi made it plain that reform was coming, the very process of discussion, and the demonstration that he was alert to real problems, gained the confidence of the various organizations. With them he engaged in a process of rethinking their missions, identifying their difficulties, and redefining the appropriate limits to their discretion. The FBI under J. Edgar Hoover, for example, had often failed to distinguish between a subversive organization's illegal underground activities and its legitimate role in open political processes. There were instances in which the legitimate role was subjected to surveillance or even disrupted by covert actions. Levi ended that. (Ironically, one organization sued him personally because a surveillance was continued for a brief time before he reached the matter, studied it, and ordered the surveillance ended.) In particularly delicate areas, written procedures were worked out that closely defined what might or might not be done. Where the problems did not allow for detailed definition, the regulations located responsibility, required periodic reviews, and limited the uses that could be made of information.

Edward Levi thus introduced reforms and reorganizations that brought several institutions of government into conformity with legal principles and did it without destroying their morale or effectiveness. It was a job that the country badly needed, though it was done so quietly that the country remained almost entirely unaware that it was accomplished and what was owed in gratitude to the man who did it.

The attorney general's share of the regular work of the department, at least where major or sensitive decisions were concerned, was carried on in much the same fashion. I saw Levi making decisions about prosecutions, about desegregation remedies, about the drafting of legislation, and about the interaction of the demands of the Constitution with the imperatives of national security. These decisions were not made by the attorney general alone nor even just with the advice of people directly responsible in the area involved.

He brought into the discussion people within the department whose judgment he valued, and even occasionally brought in as discussants persons from outside the department whose discretion and wisdom he trusted and admired. This was not a device for avoiding responsibility, for Levi often went against the advice he was give. It was, rather, a way of ensuring that every aspect of a problem had been uncovered and weighed. These small conferences were like good seminars and the decisions made reflected sensitivity to individuals as well as to competing institutional claims and the basic values of law. Though there was humor even in the gravest discussions, Levi on these occasions displayed no ambiguity and made no delphic pronouncements but explored problems with acute awareness of all their ramifications.

To take a single example, one of the most difficult decisions for any government lawyer is the decision in a close case not to prosecute. For some reason, people generally regard the decision to prosecute as somehow heroic, even though the prosecutor risks little himself. Prosecutors further down in the department wanted to ask a grand jury for an indictment, which they certainly could have gotten, but Levi was troubled. The man in question, a high-ranking government official, had acted in a national security matter in a way that seemed appropriate to most people at the time. But standards of conduct and public morality had undergone a sudden shift. The question was whether to apply the new expectations retroactively. It was not, strictly speaking, a legal question but an issue of justice to the individual. Levi presided over several extended small-group discussions, and in the end the consensus, which was not quite unanimous, was that, though we could get an indictment and had a good chance of obtaining a conviction, the department should not go forward. A decision the other way would have gained favorable publicity for the department and the attorney general, but the decision taken was the correct one, because it was just.

The quality of decision-making determines the integrity and vitality of an institution. In the case of the Department of Justice that quality also determines the degree to which justice is done. The quality of decision-making in Levi's tenure as attorney general was superb. I regret only that, of necessity, it could not be made visible to the public.

Edward and Kate, who greatly assisted his career in all of its phases, are back in Hyde Park, vital members of the university community once more. I like to think of them there—the University would not be itself without them—and look forward to our next meeting, though, given that I have just written a tribute, I do so with some apprehension.

VI.

FRIVOLITIES

The Agatha Christie piece was requested by the editors of The American Enterprise *as part of a series. It is not a topic I would have chosen without prompting. The third article is a response to an essay on the "near perfect martini" (perfect being unobtainable) written by Eric Felton in his popular* Wall Street Journal *column "How's Your Drink?"*

WHAT WOULD THEY THINK OF THE 90S?
AGATHA CHRISTIE

The editors' choice of this topic, if not simply frivolous (a possibility by no means to be discounted), arises from some profound reason not shared with me. To make anything of this wretched assignment, it is necessary to invent a rationale: Perhaps Agatha Christie may serve as a fixed point from which to measure cultural change. Her best-known fictional detectives, the Belgian refugee Hercule Poirot and the English spinster Jane Marple, in somewhat exaggerated form, typify a time within living memory that is probably irretrievably lost. They have much in common aside from their implausibly frequent encounters with rigor mortis: Both would have despised the 1990s.

The primary passions of Poirot, the small, slightly rotund, dapper, gloriously mustachioed, exuberantly egotistical genius, were neatness and order. Confronted at breakfast with two eggs of different sizes, he finds his appetite destroyed by the gaudy asymmetry. As Captain Hastings, Poirot's dim stooge, said, "He has an absolute passion for neatness of any kind. If he sees an ornament set crookedly, or a speck of dust, even a slight disarray in someone's attire, it's absolute torture to him."

Miss Marple lives in the hamlet of St. Mary's Mead, which, contrary to popular belief in the unsophisticated goodness of rusticity, is a sinkhole of depravity, full to the brim with greed, lust, adultery, malice, treachery, and murder. Thus Marple remains unsurprised by the wickedness of the wider world into which she occasionally ventures. A chief inspector says of the demure and dithery Miss Marple that she has "a mind like a sewer"—rather like an eminent woman I know who constantly reminds herself that to understand today's Washington, one must learn to "think low."

The 1990s have been a decade of slaughter, as have most decades in this century, but Christie made a sumptuous living out of ingeniously transform-

From *The American Enterprise*, November/December 1999.

ing warm bodies into corpses. Both Poirot and Marple, accustomed to the odd body turning up here and there, deal with murder at retail while our decade supplies it wholesale, yet the principle is much the same. Christie's sleuths would have been saddened by the massacres of this decade but utterly unastonished. Christie was careful to present her prim sleuths only with corpses decorously slain, "cozy murders." The real slaughters of this decade have been anything but decorous. Poirot and Marple would have found such gross lapses in aesthetic taste almost as horrendous as the deaths themselves.

But Poirot's torture would have been even more excruciating. What would he make of the meetings of the Modern Language Association, the nightly network news, the Republican and Democratic conventions, the President's fluctuating versions of reality, Hillary's '60s-speak, and the screeching of TV's talking heads? What would he have thought of backwards baseball caps, casual Fridays metastasizing into week-long slovenliness at major corporations, tongue studs, navel rings, rap music, and Jerry Springer? His little gray cells completely disarranged, the man would have been a walking nervous breakdown. He might have dyed his moustache orange, pulled on faded blue jeans (with an elasticized waist band), sported a nose ring, and become a candidate for adimission to the local laughing academy. Or he would have been a candidate if he did not then look like much of the rest of the population. Today, he would more likely have been committed for wearing a wing collar, bow tie, and waistcoat.

Which brings us to sex, as everything seems to today. It cannot be an accident that Marple and Poirot are celibates. Marple is a spinster, and it is better not even to try to imagine Poirot, mustache aquiver, advancing to, as he would put it, a "liaison" or, as the '90s would have it, a "hook up." Neither he nor Marple would have owned a television where, at any moment, one may be confronted by writhing, panting, half-naked embraces and ghastly mouth-chewing kisses by couples who have just met five minutes earlier and do not even know each other's last names. In the sexual revolution, Dame Agatha's characters would have prayed for Thermidor.

Those of us of a certain age remember what life was like not too long ago—when men wore suits rather than t-shirts in elegant restaurants and professors offered logic and evidence, rather than ideology and deconstruction. It is comforting to have Poirot and Marple to remind us of vanished virtues, and to offer a trembling hope that some of them will one day reappear.

On the other hand, one cannot be sure of any of renascence of sanity and decorum. As Christie said about overcoming her tendency to faint as a nurse in an operating room, "The truth of it is one gets used to anything." Now there's a requiem for the world of Marple and Poirot and an ominous forecast of the staying power of the 1990s. Try not to think about it.

Ambrosia and Amnesia

It was the worst of the worst of times *and* the worst of times. It was the election from hell. Our long national nightmare turned out to be only halfway over.

How can we forget, how can take the edge off our pain (perhaps the only pain Bill Clinton does not feel?) different strategies will occur, but one of the most promising is the judicious use of alcohol. One cannot, of course, begin the forgetting process at breakfast and continue through the day, since that would have devastating effects on one's career, marriage, and liver. The tactic is definitely recommended, however, for the early evening hours when, as you zap around the TV channels, you are all too likely to come without warning upon the Clinton visage. That can be a nasty shock to your nervous system. If you have not prepared yourself in advance, it will be too late to avoid the damage and you will totter off to bed to lie awake staring into the dark or to toss fitfully dreaming of fallen republics. Just the right amount of alcohol taken at the right time will, however, enable you to see the humor in America's having a Banana Republic government, and to fall asleep congratulating yourself on having risen above the despair.

The choice of drink, however, is crucial. Wine spritzers will not do it. Here we enter upon controversial territory, and what I am about to say will doubtless be resented bitterly by some conservatives. We must face the fact, however, that these things are not mere matters of personal preference. There is no room here for alcoholic relativism. Just as there are spiritual truths, so there are spiritous truths.

Wine having been dismissed, we may also eliminate, though with less certainty, bourbon. It is sweeter than alcohol should be, and it is likely to depress and make one maudlin when confronted with the Clinton countenance. Scotch is a better bet, but it is not a bracing drink and so lacks

From *National Review*, November 25, 1996

the capacity to tone us up in the way that we will need in these dark days. No, there is only one drink that conveys conservative correctness, spreads warmth and courage throughout one's soul, and has the additional merit of being the most delicious cocktail ever invented. I refer, of course, to the dry martini, a distinctively American invention, which Bernard DeVoto called the "supreme American gift to world culture." (Not that the world accepted the gift very eagerly: until recently the only sure way to get a decent martini in England was to go behind the bar and make it yourself. Most of the rest of the world is hopeless.)

The awful truth, however, is that the martini was on the verge of extinction. Just a few years back, no one under the age of forty drank it. Though I can hardly take full credit for the drink's resurgence, I made a contribution. When I was a judge, I used to tell my clerks, who had never tasted one, that martinis are essential to cultural conservatism. Furthermore, I described the ideal recipe. Several of them accepted my argument, with only one unfortunate result: they took to entering bars in Washington and ordering "Judge Bork martinis." This gave a somewhat false picture of life in my chambers.

Well, then, what is the description of the proper, indeed the perfect, martini? There is in this matter, as on every serious subject, a number of heresies. In the first place, a drink made with vodka is not a martini. A martini means gin. Second, olives are to be eschewed, except by people who think a martini is a type of salad.

Finally, the martini must be straight up. I recall once seeing a martini "on the rocks" and murmuring, "Oh the horror, the horror!" Insofar as "on the rocks" indicates a form of bankruptcy, it is a perfectly accurate description of gin and vermouth on ice. There should be some small amount of water in a martini (that is inevitable in the chilling process and makes the drink smoother), but when it is served on the rocks, the amount of water keeps increasing, depriving the martini of its special tang. That is no doubt why Lowell Edmunds writes in *The Silver Bullet* that "the martini on the rocks is an abomination, and must be classed with fast foods, rock n' roll, snowmobiles, acid rain, polyester fabrics, supermarket tomatoes, and books printed on toilet paper as a symptom of anomy."

Well, what is the recipe for the perfect martini? Edmunds says the proportion of gin to vermouth may range from 4:1 to 8:1. The upper end of that range is preferable, and one may even go to 10:1 (the martini that American officers called "the Montgomery" to annoy British officers with a reminder of the Field Marshall's unwillingness to fight except with overwhelming odds). Some years back a despairing producer of vermouth took out ads advocating

3:1 and asserting that "a dry martini is not a hooker of gin." Not quite, but a hooker of icy gin would be infinitely preferable to a 3:1 martini.

The three best gins, in my view, are Bombay, Bombay Sapphire, and Tanqueray, but it is possible to make a fine martini with lesser gins. Domestic vermouths are to be avoided. My favorite French vermouth is Boissière. A piece of lemon rind is to be twisted so that lemon oil comes out of the skin. I am usually unable, however, to get enough oil to drop from the rind to the surface of the martini and so, contrary to the best practice, I place the rind in the drink. The martini should be served in a stemmed glass that has been chilled until it is as cold as possible.

The martini is a very potent cocktail. It is not to be drunk rapidly, but rather sipped and savored. That said, this cocktail is not merely the best means of restoring the tissues, as Bertie Wooster would put it, but also the best means of restoring one's sanity and sense of humor after the carnage of the '96 election. The martini was brought back by Republicans with the '94 elections, it will help us forget '96 as we yearn for 1998 and 2000.

Martini's Founding Fathers:
Original Intent Debatable

Eric Felten's essay on the dry martini is itself near-perfect ("Don't forget the Vermouth," Leisure & Arts, Pursuits, Dec. 10). His allusion to constitutional jurisprudence is faulty, however, since neither in law nor martinis can we know the subjective, "original intent" of the Founding Fathers. As to martinis, the intent may have been to ease man's passage through this vale of tears or, less admirably, to employ the tactic of "candy is dandy, but liquor is quicker."

What counts in mixology is the "original understanding" of the martini's essence by those who first consumed it. The essence remains unaltered but allows proportions to evolve as circumstances change. Mr. Felten's "near-perfect martini" is the same in principle as the "original-understanding martini" and therefore its legitimate descendant. Such latter-day travesties as the chocolate martini and the raspberry martini, on the other hand, are the work of activist bartenders.

Mr. Felten lapses into heresy only once. He prefers the olive to the lemon peel because the former is a "snack." Dropping a snack into a classic drink is like garnishing filet mignon with ketchup. The correct response when offered an olive is, "When I want a salad, I'll ask for it."

From the *Wall Street Journal*, December 13, 2005.

Index

About the Author

R obert H. Bork is the author of two *New York Times* best-sellers, *Slouching Towards Gomorrah: Modern Liberalism and American Decline* and *The Tempting of America: The Political Seduction of the Law*, and several other books, including *Coercing Virtue: The Worldwide Rule of Judges*. A Distinguished Fellow of the Hudson Institute and a professor at the Ave Maria Law School, and formerly was the Tad and Diane Taube Distinguished Visiting Fellow at the Hoover Institution. He was a partner in the law firm of Kirkland & Ellis and later became the Alexander M. Bickel Professor of Public Law at Yale University Law School. Bork served as the United States Solicitor General from 1973 to 1977 and as a Circuit Judge on the U.S. Court of Appeals for the District of Columbia Circuit from 1982 to 1988.